W9-BTI-699

WITHDRAWN
NDSU

VARIATIONAL METHODS IN ECONOMICS

ADVANCED TEXTBOOKS IN ECONOMICS

VOLUME 1

Editor:

C. J. BLISS
University of Essex

1971

NORTH-HOLLAND PUBLISHING COMPANY
AMSTERDAM · LONDON
AMERICAN ELSEVIER PUBLISHING CO., INC.–
NEW YORK.

VARIATIONAL METHODS IN ECONOMICS

G. HADLEY

M. C. KEMP

1971

NORTH-HOLLAND PUBLISHING COMPANY
AMSTERDAM · LONDON
AMERICAN ELSEVIER PUBLISHING CO., INC.–
NEW YORK.

248992

© *North-Holland Publishing Company, 1971*

All rights reserved. No part of this publication may be reproduced, stored in a retrieval system, or transmitted in any form or by any means, electronic, mechanical, photocopying, recording, or otherwise, without the prior permission of the copyright owner.

Library of Congress Catalog Card Number: 79–157027
North-Holland ISBN for this series: 0 7204 3600 1
North-Holland ISBN for this volume: 0 7204 3601 X
Elsevier ISBN: 0 444 10097 0.

HB
74
M3
H29

PUBLISHERS:
NORTH-HOLLAND PUBLISHING COMPANY – AMSTERDAM
NORTH-HOLLAND PUBLISHING COMPANY LTD. – LONDON

SOLE DISTRIBUTORS FOR THE U.S.A. AND CANADA:
AMERICAN ELSEVIER PUBLISHING COMPANY, INC.
52 VANDERBILT AVENUE, NEW YORK, N.Y. 10017

PRINTED IN THE NETHERLANDS

Preface

In this text we have attempted to provide students of economics and related disciplines with a fairly comprehensive treatment of the classical calculus of variations and its modern generalizations. It is hardly necessary to argue the need for such a text. Recent issues of the professional journals, especially in economics and management, are littered with references to the Legendre-Clebsch conditions, the DuBois-Reymond equations and the other paraphernalia of the subject. Nor shall we attempt to justify our selection of topics and illustrations. However we must describe the class of readers we have had in mind. We have tried to cater to the rapidly growing number of students of economics and related disciplines who have a grounding in the multi-variable calculus and linear algebra, together with some acquaintance with the theory of differential equations and with the methods of ordinary linear and non-linear optimization. No knowledge of functional analysis, topology, or other advanced mathematical topics is assumed; nor do we pre-suppose any knowledge of the calculus of variations itself. Perhaps the most distinctive feature of the text is the inclusion of a large number of worked examples. Most of the examples are taken from economics and, more specifically, from the theory of optimal growth. However, while the book does provide an introduction to the theory of optimal growth, we have not attempted to make the exposition comprehensive or systematic; we have set out to write a mathematics text, not an economics text. The reader who, having mastered the mathematics, wishes to further sample the economic applications of the variational calculus is referred to Professor Chakravarty's new book [9] and to the symposia [13] and [34].

The manuscript was begun during the summer of 1969 when both authors were at the Wenner-Gren Center in Stockholm and Kemp was a guest of the Institute for International Economic Studies, University of Stockholm. The manuscript was completed while Kemp was Ford Rotating Professor of Economics at the University of California, Berkeley. Grateful acknowledgement is made to the Wenner-Gren Foundation, to the Institute for International Economic Studies, to the Ford Foundation and to the University of California. We also acknowledge the helpful remarks of Professor Ken-ichi Inada (Osaka University) and Professor Yasuo Uekawa (Kobe University of Commerce) concerning certain problems encountered in writing Chapter 6. Finally, to Claire Gilchrist go our admiration and gratitude for the skill and devotion she brought to the task of typing a very difficult manuscript.

G. H.
M. C. K.

Contents

1

Growth models in economics

1.1. Introduction

This book is a text in the calculus of variations. However, it is addressed to a rather special audience – social scientists, but especially economists and those interested in management science – and this has determined our choice of illustrations. Most of these come from a particular variety of growth theory. Our purpose in this first chapter, therefore, is to provide the necessary background in that area. We emphasize, however, that nothing in this chapter is essential to an understanding of our development of the calculus of variations; the reader who is interested only in the pure mathematics may begin at once with Chapter 2.

1.2. Growth models in economics

There has in the postwar period been a rekindling of interest in the process of economic development. Not since the classical economists has the subject been so far to the fore. In some measure this renewal of interest can be traced to the problems of reconstruction created by a war of unprecedented violence and destructiveness. Of much greater importance, however, is the awakening of a world conscience concerning the plight of the poor countries of the world. Certain new developments in mathematics also have played a part. In particular, those developments in the calculus of variations which are usually referred to as the theory of optimal control have had a considerable influence. It is precisely these developments that we seek to expound in the chapters which follow.

In its first phase theoretical enquiry focused on the task of formulating highly aggregative *descriptive* models of the growth process. Roughly speaking, this phase terminated with the publication in 1956 of the well known papers of Solow [35]* and Swan [38]. The achievement of this phase was the articulation of a self-contained model of the growth process: given only their initial values, the model generates the complete subsequent time path of each variable of interest.

Since 1956 descriptive models of increasing complexity and realism have been constructed. At the same time, however, there has emerged an interest in the *evaluation* of the alternative paths of development available to the economy. In the simple model of Solow and Swan, for example, there appear two constant parameters, the savings ratio s and the rate of population growth γ. Each of these parameters can be influenced, directly or indirectly, as a matter of government policy. To each pair of time dependent functions $[\gamma(t), s(t)]$ there corresponds a different growth path; and the feasible paths are not all equally attractive. There emerges the problem of finding the *optimal* paths of $s(t)$ and $\gamma(t)$. How this problem might be formulated and solved will occupy us, on and off, throughout this book.

In this very rapid scanning of the horizon many things have been left unsaid or unclear. We now go over the ground more slowly, beginning with an exposition of the descriptive model introduced by Solow and Swan. A single commodity is produced with the services of capital and labor. Choosing units so that one unit of labor service is provided by one unit of population in one unit of time, and so that one unit of capital service is provided by one unit of capital in one unit of time, we may write

$$Y(t) = \Psi(K(t), L(t)) \tag{1-1}$$

where $K(t)$ is the stock of capital at time t, $L(t)$ is the labor force at time t, and $Y(t)$ is the output per unit of time at t. In later chapters the production function Ψ will be restricted in various ways. For the time being, however, we need assume only that it is homogeneous of degree one in K and L and that it possesses continuous second derivatives. The population and labor force are supposed to grow at the steady exponential rate γ:

$$L(t) = L(0)e^{\gamma t}, \quad \gamma \gtreqless 0 \tag{1-2}$$

and the accumulation of capital is governed by the constant average savings ratio s:

$$\dot{K}(t) = sY(t), \quad 0 \leq s \leq 1 \tag{1-3}$$

where $\dot{K}(t) \equiv \mathrm{d}K(t)/\mathrm{d}t$.

---

* Numbers in brackets refer to the bibliography at the end of the text.

In view of the homogeneity of Ψ we may rewrite (1-1) as

$$y(t) \equiv Y(t)/L(t) = \Psi(K(t)/L(t), 1) \equiv \psi(k(t)) \tag{1-4}$$

where $y(t)$ is the average product of labor at time t and $k(t)$ is the capital: labor ratio. The first derivative $\psi'(k)$ is then the marginal productivity of capital, and $\psi - k\psi'$ is the marginal productivity of labor. From (1-2) and (1-3)

$$\dot{k}(t) \equiv \frac{\mathrm{d}}{\mathrm{d}t}(K(t)/L(t)) = sy(t) - \gamma k(t). \tag{1-5}$$

Equations (1-4) and (1-5) are the bare bones of the system; (1-4) is the static production relationship, and (1-5) tells us how the system behaves through time. Consolidation of the two equations yields the single differential equation

$$\dot{k}(t) = s\psi(k(t)) - \gamma k(t). \tag{1-6}$$

If this equation can be solved for $k(t)$, the solution can then be substituted into (1-4) to yield the time path of $y(t)$ and, using (1-2), of $Y(t)$.

The equations (1-4) and (1-6) cannot be solved explicitly unless $\psi(k)$ is assigned a particular mathematical form. In the Cobb-Douglas case, for example, the two equations reduce to

$$y(t) = [k(t)]^{\alpha}, \quad 0 < \alpha < 1 \tag{1-4a}$$

and

$$\dot{k}(t) = s[k(t)]^{\alpha} - \gamma k(t) \tag{1-6a}$$

respectively, and are readily soluble. Figure 1.1 illustrates the behavior of

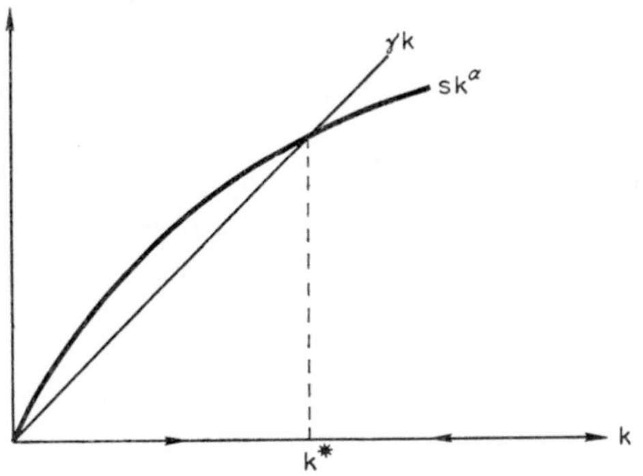

Fig. 1.1.

the system for $\gamma > 0$, $1 > s > 0$. For values of k less than k^*, $\dot{k} > 0$; and for values of k greater than k^*, $\dot{k} < 0$. Clearly $k(t)$ approaches k^* asymptotically, whatever the initial value of k (provided only that it is positive); hence the average product of labor approaches $(k^*)^\alpha$, consumption per capita approaches $(1 - s)(k^*)^\alpha$, and in the limit all quantities undeflated by population grow at the same rate as the population itself.

However we are not at this stage concerned with specific solutions. The important thing to notice is that the solutions, if they exist, depend on the parameters γ and s, that these parameters can be influenced by government, and that there is therefore potentially a problem of choosing the *optimal* γ and s. More generally, there is potentially a problem of choosing the optimal *time paths* $\gamma(t)$ and $s(t)$. But optimal in relation to what criterion? Until the criterion is specified, the problem is not even defined. Collective decisions about the temporal distribution of consumption are of course political decisions, based on compromise. We therefore cannot hope to find a criterion which will carry conviction to everyone. The most that we can hope is that any criterion the implications of which we analyze will be found interesting. It will be assumed, here and later, that it is the stream of consumption $C(t)$ or the stream of consumption per capita $c(t)$ which 'matters'. What we need then is a rule for associating with each function $C(t)$ or $c(t)$ a number $\mathscr{U}[C(t)]$ or $\mathscr{U}[c(t)]$ which provides a numerical evaluation of the entire consumption stream. The number will be referred to as the *utility* of the consumption stream. Even if it is agreed that only consumption matters, however, there is still no single compelling rule of association, that is, definition of $\mathscr{U}$. Among many more-or-less plausible possibilities, economists have been especially interested in the simple or undiscounted sum or integral, over some finite or infinite planning period, of some function U of total or average consumption. The function of consumption is often referred to, not quite appropriately, as an instantaneous utility function. In a special case, the function may be a constant positive multiple of total or average consumption so that, in effect, $\mathscr{U}$ is simply the integral of consumption. Let us, for the sake of illustration, choose as our desideratum the simple or unweighted integral of the instantaneous utility derived from consumption per capita. Now consumption per capita at time t is $c(t) = (1 - s(t))y(t)$. Thus the problem is to find $\gamma(t)$ and $s(t) \leq 1$ such that

$$\int_0^T U((1 - s(t))y(t), t)\mathrm{d}t \quad 0 < T \leq \infty$$

is a maximum subject to (1-4) and (1-6) and to the requirement that $k(t)$

be non-negative, and given $k(0) = k_0$. Notice that we have not at this stage imposed the requirement that $s(t) \geq 0$.

This problem is typical of those we shall consider in later chapters. To pose the problem it was necessary to provide: (i) A description of the welfare criterion. (In the above example the time horizon and the utility function had to be specified.) (ii) A description of the economy. (In the above example the description is conveyed by (1-4) and (1-6).) Once the problem is properly posed there remains the further problem of solving it; and that is a matter of mathematical technique. The relevant techniques are discussed in the following four chapters.

2

Calculus of variations — classical theory

2.1. Introduction

Much of modern economic theory is concerned with the optimal behavior of the economy through time. Mathematically, the problem very often is that of determining one or more functions with the characteristic that they maximize (or minimize) the integral over time of a utility function. Problems of this type cannot be solved by the methods for maximizing a function learned in elementary mathematics. For the types of problem now being considered, it is not a question of finding the values of one or several variables which yield the maximum or minimum of a function; rather it is a question of finding one or more complete functions which maximize or minimize an integral the value of which depends upon these functions. This type of optimization problem must be solved by different methods, and the subject matter dealing with the solution of such problems is referred to as the *calculus of variations.*

In this chapter and the following three chapters, we shall cover those portions of the theory of the calculus of variations which are especially relevant for economists. Work on trajectory problems and on the guidance of space vehicles and missiles has led in recent years to a greatly renewed interest in the calculus of variations; and this has in turn given rise to a number of extensions of the classical theory. These new developments form part of what is usually called *optimal control theory* and are of special interest to mathematical economists.

It is possible to develop the calculus of variations strictly from the point of view of optimal control. However, we have chosen not to proceed in this way; instead, we shall first expound the classical theory and then move on to more modern topics. The latter approach makes the subject somewhat easier to understand, makes it easier for the reader to refer to other literature on the calculus of variations, and provides the background needed to understand that part of the Economics literature in which the classical theory is employed. Finally, our approach makes it possible to emphasize the connections between the classical theory and the newer results in optimal control, and to depict the modern theory as emerging naturally from the classical. In this chapter and the next the classical theory will be developed, then in Chapters 4 and 5 we shall consider the newer optimal control theory.

2.2. Historical foundation and some classical problems

The calculus of variations has formed an important part of applied mathematics for more than two and one half centuries, and the names of some of the greatest mathematicians, including Lagrange, Euler, Legendre, Jacobi and Weierstrass, are associated with its development. Attention was drawn to the subject matter of the calculus of variations when the famous old brachistochrone problem, originally discussed by Galileo in 1630, was solved by the Swiss mathematicians James and John Bernoulli in the 1690's. Consider two points in a vertical plane, one being higher than the other, and some smooth curve passed between these two points. If a particle of mass starting from rest slides down this smooth frictionless curve under the action of gravity alone, what curve will give the minimum time of descent from the higher to the lower point? (The name brachistochrone is derived from two Greek words meaning shortest time.)

Let us formulate the brachistochrone problem mathematically. Without loss in generality we can take the higher point to be $(0, y_0)$, so that it lies on the y-axis, and the lower point to be $(x_1, 0)$, so that it lies on the x-axis. If s is the distance measured along the curve from $(0, y_0)$ to any point (x, y) on the curve, then $v = \mathrm{d}s/\mathrm{d}t$ is the speed of the particle at (x, y). The time required to reach the point (x, y) is then

$$t = \int_0^s \frac{\mathrm{d}s}{v} \tag{2-1}$$

because $\mathrm{d}t = \mathrm{d}s/v$.

Since there is no friction, the law of conservation of energy must hold. This means that as the particle moves from a higher to a lower position potential energy is converted into kinetic energy. The potential energy at an elevation y above the x-axis is mgy, where g is the gravitational constant. Since the particle starts from rest, the kinetic energy $\frac{1}{2}mv^2$ of the particle at any point (x, y) on the curve must be the difference between the initial potential energy mgy_0 and the potential energy mgy at y. Thus, by conservation of energy,

$$\tfrac{1}{2}mv^2 = mg(y_0 - y)$$

or

$$v = (2g)^{\frac{1}{2}}(y_0 - y)^{\frac{1}{2}}. \tag{2-2}$$

Let us denote by Δs the change in length along the curve for two closely spaced points (x, y) and $(x + \Delta x, y + \Delta y)$. Then Δs is given approximately by $(\Delta s)^2 = (\Delta x)^2 + (\Delta y)^2$. Dividing both sides by $(\Delta x)^2$, taking the square root and considering the limit as $\Delta x \to 0$, we see that

$$\frac{ds}{dx} = [1 + (y')^2]^{\frac{1}{2}} \tag{2-3}$$

where $y' \equiv dy/dx$ and is the slope of the curve at x. On applying (2-3) and (2-2) to (2-1), we obtain

$$t = \frac{1}{(2g)^{\frac{1}{2}}} \int_0^{x_1} \frac{[1 + (y')^2]^{\frac{1}{2}}}{[y_0 - y]^{\frac{1}{2}}} dx. \tag{2-4}$$

We seek that function $y(x)$ the graph of which passes through the points $(0, y_0)$ and $(x_1, 0)$ and which minimizes the integral (2-4). Here then we have a situation in which we wish to find a function which minimizes an integral the value of which depends on the function. This is a problem in the calculus of variations. In the above derivation it was necessary to use certain elementary ideas from physics. The reader who is not familiar with these ideas can ignore them, since they will not be needed again.

We now formulate two other problems each of which has played a role in the development of the calculus of variations and which we shall later use as examples.

Consider the problem of finding the equation of the curve which joins the origin in the xy-plane to the point (x_0, y_0), $x_0 \neq 0$, and for which the distance measured along the curve is as small as possible. Everyone knows that a straight line joining the points yields the curve for which the distance is as short as possible. How is this proved, however? The proof will be provided later. At this stage we are content to show that the problem can be formulated in terms of the calculus of variations. Let s be the distance along the curve (the curve must be rectifiable and have a length, of course). Then, from (2-3), the total distance D from $(0, 0)$ to (x_0, y_0) is

$$D = \int_{0}^{x_0} [1 + (y')^2]^{\frac{1}{2}}\, dx. \tag{2-5}$$

We seek the function $y(x)$ which minimizes the integral (2-5); and this is a problem in the calculus of variations. More complicated versions of this problem have played an important role in the development of the calculus of variations. These problems are concerned with the determination of the curve of minimum length which lies on a specified surface and joins two points on the surface. Problems of this sort are called *geodesic problems* and the resulting curves are known as *geodesic curves*.

As a final elementary example, suppose that a curve is passed through the points (x_0, y_0) and (x_1, y_1) in the xy-plane, where $y_0 > 0$, $y_1 > 0$ and $x_1 > x_0$, and that everywhere in the interval $x_0 \leq x \leq x_1$ this curve lies on or above the x-axis. The curve is then rotated above the x-axis to yield a surface of revolution. It is desired to find that curve which will minimize the area of the surface of revolution.

To formulate this problem mathematically, let $y(x)$ be the function the graph of which is rotated to form the surface of revolution. If we consider a plane perpendicular to the x-axis at x and another plane parallel to this which cuts the x-axis at $x + \Delta x$, Δx being small, the area ΔA of the surface contained between these two planes is approximately $\Delta A = 2\pi y \Delta s$, where y is the radius at x and Δs is the length of the curve between x and $x + \Delta x$. Also Δs is approximately $[1 + (y')^2]^{\frac{1}{2}} \Delta x$. Thus we see that

$$A = 2\pi \int_{x_0}^{x_1} y[1 + (y')^2]^{\frac{1}{2}}\, dx. \tag{2-6}$$

The problem is then to determine the function $y(x)$ which satisfies $y(x) \geq 0$, $x_0 \leq x \leq x_1$, and which minimizes the integral in (2-6). This again is a problem in the calculus of variations.

These three problems were an important stimulus to early developments in the calculus of variations. We shall carry them through the present chapter, partly to motivate the theoretical exposition and partly to illustrate how the theory may be applied. After some of the theory is behind us, we shall also introduce examples from economics to illustrate its applicability there. Particular attention will be paid to the well-known model of Ramsey [30] and to some later generalizations of it.

We are now almost ready to begin the formal development of the theory. First, however, we introduce some elementary notions concerning functions and phase spaces. This will be the work of the next two sections.

2.3. Functions

From his earlier study of mathematics, the reader will be familiar with the elementary concept of a function of one or more variables. For our purposes, however, a more general and possibly unfamiliar concept is needed. This concept we now seek to make clear.

Suppose that we wish to associate with each element of some arbitrary non-null set* $\mathscr{D}$ one and only one element in another set $\mathscr{G}$. For example, $\mathscr{D}$ may be all the students in a classroom, and $\mathscr{G}$ a set of family names which includes all the family names of students in $\mathscr{D}$. Then, associated with each student in $\mathscr{D}$ is a unique element in $\mathscr{G}$–his family name. This rule of association is an example of a function. In general a function is defined in the following way.

Function. Let $\mathscr{D}$ be any non-null set. A rule which associates with each element in $\mathscr{D}$ one and only one element in some other set $\mathscr{G}$ is called a function from $\mathscr{D}$ to $\mathscr{G}$.

In the most general terms, then, a function is merely another name for a rule which serves to associate with each element of some given set one and only one element of another set. It is important to note that the elements of the sets $\mathscr{D}$ and $\mathscr{G}$ need not be numbers. They can be any sort of elements whatever. In more advanced mathematics one often finds a function from $\mathscr{D}$ to $\mathscr{G}$ symbolized by $\mathscr{D} \overset{f}{\to} \mathscr{G}$, where the rule is indicated by the letter f. We shall not have need of this notation but will normally use the more familiar notation f or $f(x)$.

The set $\mathscr{D}$ is called the *domain* of the function. $\mathscr{D}$ must be made explicit; otherwise the function is incompletely specified. If $x \in \mathscr{D}$ is an element of the domain and $y \in \mathscr{G}$ is the unique element in $\mathscr{G}$ associated with x under the function, then y is called the *image* of x and we frequently indicate this by writing $y = f(x)$. Note however that, while we have adopted the familiar notation for a function of a single variable, we have not required that x or y be numbers; $y = f(x)$ is simply the notation used to indicate that y is the image of x under the function f. While the definition of a function requires that only one element of $\mathscr{G}$ be associated with any particular element x of $\mathscr{D}$, it may well be true that some element y of $\mathscr{G}$ is the image of more than one element of $\mathscr{D}$ (y may even be the image of an infinite number of different

* Sets are often denoted by upper case Roman letters. However, many upper case letters of this type will be needed later to describe the Ramsey and related economic models. To avoid the possibility of confusion, therefore, sets will be denoted by upper case script letters.

elements of $\mathscr{D}$). Thus if, in terms of our example, exactly two students in the classroom have the family name Smith, then Smith, an element of $\mathscr{G}$, will be the image of two different elements in $\mathscr{D}$. It is not necessarily true that every element in $\mathscr{G}$ will be the image of one or more elements in the domain. There may be elements in $\mathscr{G}$ which are not the image of any element in $\mathscr{D}$. In terms of our example, if the family name Wallis is included in $\mathscr{G}$, but no student in $\mathscr{D}$ has the family name Wallis then this element of $\mathscr{G}$ is not the image of any element in the domain. Thus we see that in defining a function there is a certain arbitrariness in the choice of $\mathscr{G}$. Of $\mathscr{G}$ it is required only that it contains as elements the image of each element in the domain. Let us denote by $\mathscr{F}$ that subset of $\mathscr{G}$ which contains each element of $\mathscr{G}$ that is an image of an element in $\mathscr{D}$ and no other elements of $\mathscr{G}$. The set $\mathscr{F}$ is called the *range* of the function. Thus the image of every element of $\mathscr{D}$ is in $\mathscr{F}$ and every element of $\mathscr{F}$ is the image of at least one element of $\mathscr{D}$. It is the range $\mathscr{F}$ of the function which is of interest; but any set $\mathscr{G}$ which contains $\mathscr{F}$ as a subset can be employed in the definition of the function.

Examples. 1. If $\mathscr{D}$ and $\mathscr{G}$ are both sets of real numbers then the function f, $\mathscr{D} \overset{f}{\rightarrow} \mathscr{G}$ is simply a function of one real variable. Typically, in elementary mathematics, the symbolism $y = f(x)$ is used in two different ways. It is used to indicate that the number y is the image of some specific number x in the domain, and it is also used as a shorthand for the entire function. This can be a little confusing in some applications. Normally, however, no confusion is possible and we shall frequently make use of notations such as $f(x)$, $g(x)$ or $y(x)$ to denote functions of a single variable. They will also be used sometimes to denote the image of a particular element x of the domain.

In representing a function explicitly it is necessary both to describe the domain of the function and to provide a formula or a set of formulas which indicate how to compute the image for each element in the domain. Thus a function of one variable x the domain of which is the set of all real numbers might be defined as

$$f(x) = \begin{cases} 2x - 1, & x < -17 \\ 3x^2 + 4, & -17 \leq x \leq 6 \\ \log x, & x > 6. \end{cases}$$

It is important to note that it need not be true that a single formula suffices to define the function throughout the entire domain. As in the example just given, different formulas may be needed in different parts of the domain.

Often we shall write formulas such as

$$y = \frac{x^2 + 1}{x - 1}$$

without specifying the domain. Then the domain must be understood to include all numbers x for which a number y can be computed. In the example just given, the domain includes all real numbers except 1. The value $x = 1$ is not in the domain. If we wish the domain to include all real numbers, it is necessary to separately specify the image of 1. The image of 1 can be taken to be any number we desire, perhaps $y(1) = 16$. Thus the domain of the following function is the set of all real numbers:

$$y = \begin{cases} \dfrac{x^2 + 1}{x - 1}, & x \neq 1 \\ 16, & x = 1. \end{cases}$$

For a function of one variable, the image y of some specific number x in the domain is called *the value of the function at* x.

2. In elementary mathematics, a function of n variables is often written $y = f(x_1, \ldots, x_n)$. What is the domain in this case? The element of the domain here is an ordered n-tuple $(x_1, \ldots, x_n)$. Such an ordered n-tuple can be thought of as a point in an n-dimensional Euclidean space $\mathscr{E}^n$ or, equivalently, as a vector with n components. Thus the domain of a function of n variables is a subset of $\mathscr{E}^n$ (of course, this subset may be all of $\mathscr{E}^n$). Conversely, a function in which the domain is a subset of $\mathscr{E}^n$ and for which the range is a set of real numbers is called a function of n variables or a real-valued function of n variables.

It will be convenient to use a single symbol to represent both an n-component vector and a point in $\mathscr{E}^n$. We shall use boldface letters such as $\mathbf{x}$ or $\mathbf{y}$, for example, to represent vectors. Thus $\mathbf{x} = (x_1, \ldots, x_n)$. We shall usually think of vectors as column vectors, although on occasion they may be interpreted as row vectors. Vector notation makes it possible to considerably simplify the writing of functions of n variables. The notation $f(\mathbf{x})$ or $F(\mathbf{y})$ can be used for example to represent a function of n variables, that is, a function the domain of which is some subset of $\mathscr{E}^n$.

We shall be especially interested in *real-valued functions*. A function is real-valued if the elements of the range are real numbers. The elements in the domain of a real-valued function can be anything at all. Generally speaking, the domain will be viewed as a subset of some sort of *space* and the elements of the domain will then be called points in the space. The reader should not misinterpret the use here of the words space and point. We are using them in the sense of topology, in which a space is simply a name for a set of elements with some specified properties. Space has nothing necessarily to do with ordinary three-dimensional physical space or the spaces of elementary geometry. Space is merely a convenient word to apply to a set of elements. The elements of a space are called points.

A special case which will be of great interest to us is that in which the elements of $\mathscr{D}$ are functions. It may be difficult for the reader to visualize a function defined on a domain the elements of which are themselves functions, but in fact this type of function is quite important in the calculus of variations. Recall that the basic problem in the calculus of variations is that of determining one or more functions with the property that they maximize or minimize the value of some integral. The integral then serves as a rule which associates with each possible function a number, which is the value of the integral; and this rule defines a real-valued function in which the elements of the domain are themselves functions of some sort. When the elements of the domain are themselves functions, it is not easy to visualize the space of which the domain is a subset. It might, for example, be the collection of all continuous functions. Nonetheless, it is still convenient to refer to it as a space; in this case it can be referred to as a *function space*. Functions in which the elements of the domain are themselves functions are sometimes referred to as *functionals*. A functional is simply a special type of function.

The reader is probably familiar with problems of a type in which a real-valued function f is defined over some subset $\mathscr{D}$ of $\mathscr{E}^n$ and it is of interest to find the point (or points) $\mathbf{x} \in \mathscr{D}$ which yield the largest or smallest value of f. This type of problem includes, for example, linear and nonlinear programming problems. In variational problems, on the other hand, there is given a real-valued functional, say J, defined over some subset $\mathscr{D}$ of a function space, and it is of interest to find that element (or elements), that is, function (or functions) in $\mathscr{D}$ which yield the largest or smallest value of J. When described in these broad terms, problems in the calculus of variations seem no different from problems concerned with ordinary maxima and minima. Behind these generalities, however, there lurk all-important differences in the structure of the spaces which form the domains, and these differences dictate the adoption of quite different procedures for finding a solution.

In ordinary maximization problems, there may not exist any point x in $\mathscr{D}$ at which f reaches its maximum. This can occur, for example, if f can be made arbitrarily large. However, it can also occur even if f is bounded. Let us illustrate such a situation with a trivial example. Suppose that $f(x) = 2x$ and $\mathscr{D} = \{x | 0 \le x < 5\}$, and that we wish to determine the number x in $\mathscr{D}$ which yields the largest value of $f(x)$. Note that $f(x)$ increases as x increases; thus x should be made as large as possible. However, the interval $\mathscr{D}$ is open at the upper end; x can be made as close to 5 as desired, but it cannot be set equal to 5 since $5 \notin \mathscr{D}$. Consequently, $f(x)$ can be made as close as desired to 10, but not equal to 10. Here then we have an example in which there is no x which maximizes f. For all $x \in \mathscr{D}$, $f(x) \le 10$; and f can be made arbitrarily close to 10; but there is no value x for which $f(x) = 10$. If the domain is redefined as $\mathscr{D} = \{x | 0 \le x \le 5\}$ by including $x = 5$, there then exists an x which maximizes f; it is $x = 5$. The same sorts of problems can occur in the calculus of variations. However, they are often more subtle and more complicated than in the case of ordinary maximization and minimization.

Let f be any real-valued function whatever. We need not be concerned with what the elements of the domain happen to be. Consider the range $\mathscr{F}$. If the set of real numbers $\mathscr{F}$ has an upper bound, it has a least upper bound; call it α. The number α is also called the *supremum* of the numbers in $\mathscr{F}$ and we write $\alpha = \sup y$, $y \in \mathscr{F}$; alternatively, it is called the supremum of the function f over the domain $\mathscr{D}$ and we write

$$\alpha = \sup_{x \in \mathscr{D}} f(x). \tag{2-7}$$

Here x is an element of $\mathscr{D}$ and need not be a real number. If there is an element, say $u \in \mathscr{D}$, for which $\alpha = f(u)$, then f actually takes on a maximum over $\mathscr{D}$ and we can write

$$\alpha = \max_{x \in \mathscr{D}} f(x). \tag{2-8}$$

Note that f can have a supremum (least upper bound) without having a maximum.

Similarly, if the numbers in $\mathscr{F}$ have a lower bound they also have a greatest lower bound β. The number β is often referred to as the *infimum* of the numbers in $\mathscr{F}$ and we write $\beta = \inf y$, $y \in \mathscr{F}$; alternatively, it is called the infimum of f over $\mathscr{D}$ and we write

$$\beta = \inf_{x \in \mathscr{D}} f(x). \tag{2-9}$$

If there is an element v in $\mathscr{D}$ for which $\beta = f(v)$, then f actually takes on a minimum over $\mathscr{D}$ and we can write

$$\beta = \min_{x \in \mathscr{D}} f(x). \tag{2-10}$$

As we have already noted, real-valued functions for which the domain is $\mathscr{E}^n$, that is, functions of n variables, will appear frequently (a special case being functions of one variable). We shall assume that the reader is familiar with the concept of continuity for such functions and with the definition of and procedures for computing partial derivatives. We shall usually find it convenient to abbreviate $\partial F/\partial y_j$ to F_{y_j} and $\partial^2 F/\partial y_i \partial y_j$ to $F_{y_i y_j}$. The notation $F_{y_j}(\mathbf{y}_0)$ indicates that $\partial F/\partial y_j$ is evaluated at $\mathbf{y}_0$. The notation $F \in C'$ indicates that F and all of its first partial derivatives are continuous over some specified domain. Similarly, $F \in C''$ means that F and all of its first and second partial derivatives are continuous over some specified domain.

For any function F, the set

$$\mathscr{S} = \{(y, z) \mid z = F(y),\ y \in \mathscr{D}\} \tag{2-11}$$

is called the *graph* of the function. Consider now a function of n variables $F(\mathbf{y})$. Then $\mathscr{S}$ is a set of points in $\mathscr{E}^{n+1}$, since each element (y, z) can be viewed as a point in $\mathscr{E}^{n+1}$. If F is continuous, the graph of F is called a *hypersurface* or *manifold* of dimension n in $\mathscr{E}^{n+1}$. In particular the graph of $z = f(y_1, y_2)$ is a surface in three dimensions. Suppose that we have two functions of n variables F_1 and F_2 with graphs $\mathscr{S}_1$ and $\mathscr{S}_2$. Then the set $\mathscr{S}_1 \cap \mathscr{S}_2$, which is the intersection of the two hypersurfaces, is referred to as a hypersurface or manifold of dimension $n - 1$ in $\mathscr{E}^{n+1}$ when there is indeed an intersection. Surfaces of lower dimension can be formed by the intersection of several hypersurfaces of dimension n. Thus in $\mathscr{E}^3$ the intersection of two surfaces yields a curve which can be thought of as a surface or manifold of dimension 1.

A real-valued function the domain of which is also a set of real numbers will be referred to as a function of one variable. Functions of this type will play a basic role in our analysis because, in economics, all quantities of interest are functions of time, that is, of one variable. We shall confine our attention to two types of functions of one variable, *viz. piecewise smooth* and *piecewise continuous* functions. Let us now define these terms.

Piecewise Continuous Function. The function of one variable $y(x)$ is said to be piecewise continuous over the interval $x_0 \leq x \leq x_1$ if:

(1) *There exists not more than a finite number of points in the interval where $y(x)$ is not continuous.*

(2) *At any point where $y(x)$ is not continuous it has a jump discontinuity.*

The reader may recall that $y(x)$ is continuous at $x = \xi$ if $y(\xi)$ is defined and if

$$\lim_{x \to \xi+} y(x) = \lim_{x \to \xi-} y(x) = y(\xi) \tag{2-12}$$

where, for example, $\lim_{x \to \xi+}$ means the limit as x approaches ξ from the right, i.e. for values of $x > \xi$. Thus both one-sided limits must exist and be equal to ξ. We say that $y(x)$ is continuous at the end point x_0 if $\lim_{x \to x_0+} y(x) = y(x_0)$ and that it is continuous at the end point x_1, if $\lim_{x \to x_1-} y(x) = y(x_1)$. We say that $y(x)$ has a jump discontinuity at ξ if

$$\lim_{x \to \xi+} y(x) = \alpha, \qquad \lim_{x \to \xi-} y(x) = \beta, \quad \alpha \neq \beta. \tag{2-13}$$

Both one-sided limits must exist, but they are not equal. Note that the definition of a piecewise continuous function does not exclude the possibility that it is continuous over the entire interval.

Piecewise Smooth Function. The function $y(x)$ is said to be piecewise smooth over the interval $x_0 \leq x \leq x_1$ if:

(1) *It is continuous at each point in the interval and there are not more than a finite number of values of x in the interval where it does not possess a derivative.*

(2) *The function $y'(x)$ is continuous at each point where the derivative exists. At any point ξ where $y'(\xi)$ does not exist, the right and left side derivatives $y'_+(\xi)$ and $y'_-(\xi)$ do exist but are not equal. Furthermore, $\lim_{x \to \xi+} y'(x) = y'_+(\xi)$ and $\lim_{x \to \xi-} y'(x) = y'_-(\xi)$.*

By the right and left side derivatives at ξ we mean

$$y'_+(\xi) = \lim_{h \to 0+} \frac{y(\xi + h) - y(\xi)}{h}; \qquad y'_-(\xi) = \lim_{h \to 0+} \frac{y(\xi - h) - y(\xi)}{h}. \tag{2-14}$$

If both one-sided derivatives exist and are equal then $y'(\xi)$ exists and is equal to their common value. We now note that alternatively and more simply we might define a piecewise smooth function as a function the derivative function of which is piecewise continuous. Therefore the derivative of a piecewise smooth function is piecewise continuous and the integral of a piecewise continuous function is piecewise smooth.

We have spent considerable time discussing various types of real-valued functions. There is a closely related type of function of which we shall make occasional use. This is a function of which the domain is a set of real numbers and the range a set of points in $\mathscr{E}^n$. Such a function, which can be represented symbolically by $\mathbf{y}(x)$, will be called a *vector-valued function of one (real) variable*. For each x, $\mathbf{y}(x) = (y_1(x), \ldots, y_n(x))$ and the image of x is an n-component vector. Now each component $y_j(x)$ can be thought of merely as a real-valued function of one variable. Conversely, if we have n real-valued functions of one variable, these can be viewed jointly as a single vector-valued function of one variable. Thus a vector-valued function of one variable is equivalent to n real-valued functions $y_1(x), \ldots, y_n(x)$.

2.4. Phase diagrams and phase spaces

Consider some function of a single variable $y(x)$ such as $y = 0.1x^2$. The graph of this function can be easily represented in the xy-plane (it is a parabola). Frequently, one is interested in the behavior not only of the function $y(x)$ but also of the derivative function $y'(x)$. For our example, $y' = 0.2x$ and the graph of this function can easily be represented in the xy'-plane (it is a straight line). Thus by drawing two different graphs we can easily display the variation of y and y' with x. There is, however, another type of graph which is frequently of use. This shows the relationship between y and y' and can be obtained by eliminating x between $y(x)$ and $y'(x)$. Note carefully that the relationship between y and y' need not be representable by a function. Thus from $y' = 0.2x$ we obtain $x = 5y'$ and if this is substituted into $y = 0.1x^2$ we obtain $y = 2.5(y')^2$, the graph of which is the parabola displayed in Figure 2.1. Clearly it is not possible to express y' as a function of y.

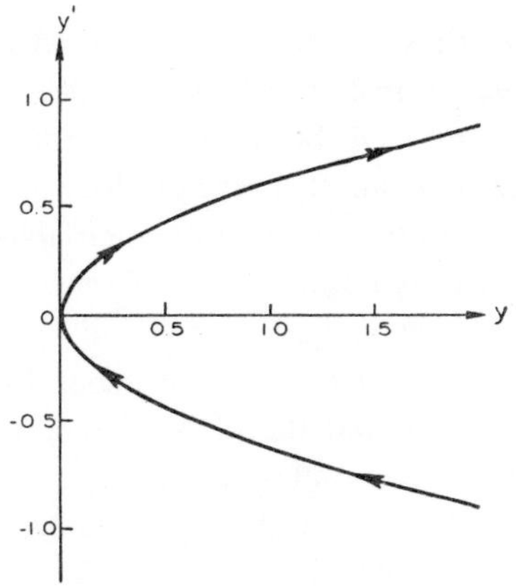

Fig. 2.1.

As another example, consider $y = 2\sin x$. Then $y' = 2\cos x$. On squaring y and y', adding the resulting equations and recalling that $\cos^2 x + \sin^2 x \equiv 1$, we obtain $y^2 + (y')^2 = 4$. The graph of this relation is a circle with center

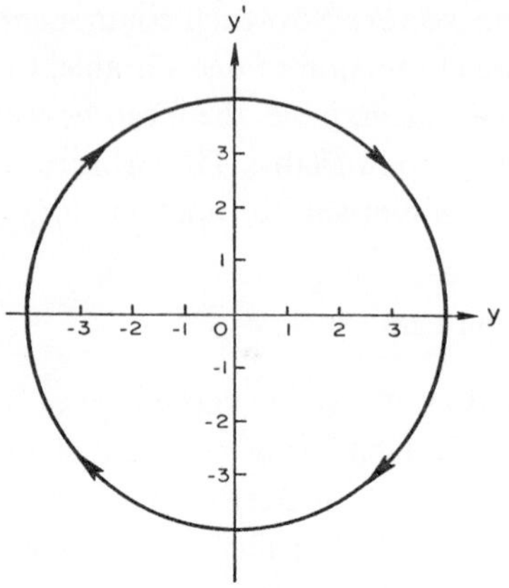

Fig. 2.2.

at the origin and radius 2; it is shown in Figure 2.2. Diagrams which show the graph of the relation between y and y' for a function $y(x)$ are called *phase diagrams* or *phase plane* plots.

Phase diagrams and their generalizations were first used in physics. To describe the state of a particle in motion it is necessary to specify its position and velocity. It is of interest not only to know how these quantities vary with time, but also to know how the velocity varies with position. For one-dimensional motion this information can be conveniently displayed in a phase diagram. Later, phase diagrams were found useful in the study of ordinary differential equations, especially nonlinear differential equations. Recently, phase diagrams have been gaining popularity in economics as well. We shall introduce later another type of phase diagram which shows the relationship between a variable y and another variable λ called its conjugate variable. In physics, there is no essential difference between the two types of diagram; for the variable conjugate to position y is the momentum, which in our terminology is my', where m is the mass. Thus the momentum is proportional to the velocity and the phase diagrams are equivalent. This is not typically the case in economics, however.

In economics x is usually taken to be time, and $(y(x), y'(x))$ describes the motion of the economic system through time. As time elapses, the system moves along a curve in the yy'-phase plane. Accordingly, we often associate with the curve a direction, and indicate the direction by arrow heads attached to the curve. Consider our first example, in which $y = 0.1x^2$, and suppose that we start at some negative value of x. As x (time) increases, y initially decreases and y' increases, until $x = 0$ is reached; then y begins to increase and continues to increase forever, while y' decreases. The direction of motion along the phase plane curve is then that indicated in Figure 2.1. In our second example, $y = 2\sin x$. If we start at $x = 0$, $y = 0$ and y' has its largest value. As x increases, y increases and y' decreases until $x = \pi/2$, when $y = 2$ and $y' = 0$. As x increases further, both y and y' decrease until $x = \pi$. Then y decreases and y' increases until $x = 3\pi/2$. Finally, y and y' increase until $y = 0$ and y' attains its maximum value at $x = 2\pi$. At this point a new cycle is begun and the circle is traversed again. Thus as time elapses the system moves around the circle over and over again, the direction of movement being that shown in Figure 2.2.

The phase plane is an ordinary Euclidean space $\mathscr{E}^2$. It is therefore possible to define real-valued functions the domain of which is some subset of the phase plane, and it is possible to discuss the continuity and differentiability of such functions. The latter might be represented symbolically by the notation $F(y, y')$. As a matter of fact, in the examples of Section 2.2 we have already introduced functions of this type. Thus

$$F(y, y') = y[1 + (y')^2]^{\frac{1}{2}} \tag{2-15}$$

from (2-6) is such a function (a function of two variables y and y'), and we can take the domain of this function to be the entire phase plane. The function is continuous at each point, and it possesses first partial derivatives everywhere:

$$\frac{\partial F}{\partial y} = F_y = [1 + (y')^2]^{\frac{1}{2}}; \qquad \frac{\partial F}{\partial y'} = F_{y'} = yy'[1 + (y')^2]^{-\frac{1}{2}}. \tag{2-16}$$

These partial derivative functions are continuous everywhere. Note that here it is perfectly natural to differentiate with respect to y'; y' is simply the name of some variable—it could have been called ζ, for example. F also possesses second partial derivatives at every point, and the second partial derivative functions are continuous everywhere. These functions are

$$\frac{\partial^2 F}{\partial y' \partial y} = F_{y'y} = y'[1 + (y')^2]^{-\frac{1}{2}}; \qquad \frac{\partial^2 F}{\partial y^2} = F_{yy} = 0; \tag{2-17}$$

$$\frac{\partial^2 F}{\partial y \partial y'} = F_{yy'} = y'[1 + (y')^2]^{-\frac{1}{2}}; \qquad \frac{\partial^2 F}{\partial y'^2} = F_{y'y'} = y[1 + (y')^2]^{-3/2}. \tag{2-18}$$

Notice that $F_{yy'} = F_{y'y}$; this is always the case if F_y and $F_{y'}$ are continuous and one of $F_{yy'}$ or $F_{y'y}$ is known to be continuous. That is, in taking a mixed second partial derivative the same result will be obtained whatever the order in which the differentiation is carried out.

A phase diagram provides one way of illustrating graphically the behavior of a function $y(x)$. A still more complete and vivid description of the behavior of $y(x)$ can be obtained by including the variable x and considering a three-dimensional Euclidean space $\mathscr{E}^3$ of points (x, y, y') which we shall refer to as an *extended phase space*. In this space we can for each x represent both $(y(x), y'(x))$ and x by the point $(x, y(x), y'(x))$. As x ranges over the values of interest it generates a set of such points, and this set is a curve in $\mathscr{E}^3$; indeed, we can think of $(x, y(x), y'(x))$ as the parametric representation of the curve, x itself serving as the parameter. This curve will be called the *graph* of $y(x)$ *in extended phase space*. If $y = 2\sin x$, so that $y' = 2\cos x$, the resulting curve in extended phase space is the spiral curve shown in

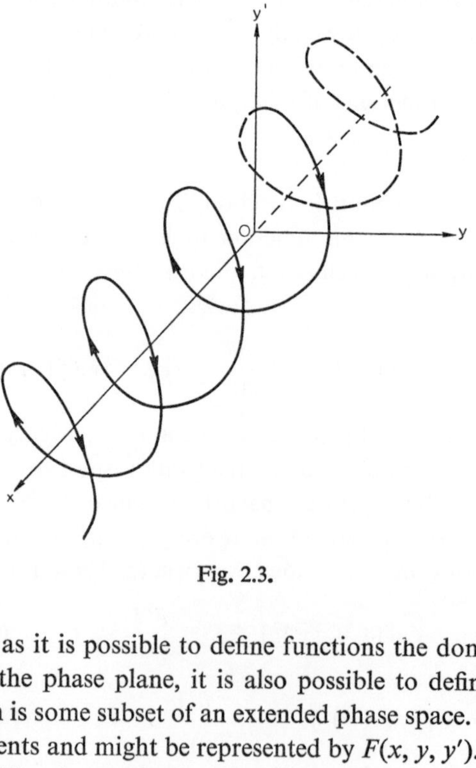

Fig. 2.3.

Figure 2.3. Just as it is possible to define functions the domain of which is some subset of the phase plane, it is also possible to define functions the domain of which is some subset of an extended phase space. Such a function has three arguments and might be represented by $F(x, y, y')$. It is, of course, possible to consider the continuity of such functions and, when they exist, to compute the various partial derivatives.

The ideas introduced above can be generalized to vector-valued functions of one variable $\mathbf{y}(x)$. The graph of $\mathbf{y}(x)$ can normally be thought of as a curve in $\mathscr{E}^{n+1}$; for $n = 1$ and 2 it is a curve. Suppose that each of the real-valued functions $y_1(x), \ldots, y_n(x)$ which make up the components of $\mathbf{y}(x)$ are differentiable over the range of values of x which are of interest. We can then form a new vector-valued function of one variable $\mathbf{y}'(x) = (y_1'(x), \ldots, y_n'(x))$ which we can refer to as the derivative function for $\mathbf{y}(x)$. Consider now the set of points $(\mathbf{y}(x), \mathbf{y}'(x))$ in $\mathscr{E}^{2n}$ generated as x varies over the domain. In analogy with the case $n = 1$, we can think of this set of points as constituting a curve in $\mathscr{E}^{2n}$. The Euclidean space $\mathscr{E}^{2n}$ of points $(\mathbf{y}, \mathbf{y}')$ will be called a *phase space*.

Just as it is possible to define an extended phase space in the case $n = 1$, so it is possible in the general case. For $n = 1$ the *extended phase space* is the set of all points (x, y, y'). The extended phase space is a $(2n + 1)$-dimensional Euclidean space $\mathscr{E}^{2n+1}$. The set of points $(x, \mathbf{y}(x), \mathbf{y}'(x))$ generated as x varies over $\mathscr{D}$ will be referred to as a curve, since it is normally represented by a curve in the case $n = 1$ (which is the only case in which a geometric representation is possible).

As might have been expected, it is possible to define functions the domain of which is a subset of the phase space $\mathscr{E}^{2n}$ and such a function might be represented by $F(\mathbf{y}, \mathbf{y}')$. Similarly, it is possible to define functions the domain of which is a subset of the extended phase space $\mathscr{E}^{2n+1}$, and such a function might be represented by $F(x, \mathbf{y}, \mathbf{y}')$. In either case it is possible to consider the continuity of such functions and their partial derivatives.

We conclude this section with some additional remarks concerning the notation we shall use for vectors and matrices. These will *always* be indicated by boldface type. Lower case letters in boldface type will always indicate vectors. Thus $\mathbf{f}$ and $\mathbf{y}$ stand for vectors, the number of components being determined from the context. Upper case boldface letters may stand for vectors or matrices; again it will be clear from the context which is implied. Consider a real-valued function $F(x, \mathbf{y}, \mathbf{y}')$, $\mathbf{y} \in \mathscr{E}^n$. We shall denote by $\mathbf{F}_\mathbf{y}(x_0, \mathbf{y}_0, \mathbf{y}_0')$ the n-component vector containing the partial derivatives of F with respect to the variables in $\mathbf{y}$ evaluated at a particular point $(x_0, \mathbf{y}_0, \mathbf{y}_0')$. The jth component of the vector is F_{y_j}. Similary, $\mathbf{F}_{\mathbf{y}'}(x_0, \mathbf{y}_0, \mathbf{y}_0')$ is the n-component vector containing the partial derivatives of F with respect to the variables in $\mathbf{y}'$ evaluated at $(x_0, \mathbf{y}_0, \mathbf{y}_0')$.

By $\mathbf{F}_{\mathbf{y}'\mathbf{y}'}(x_0, \mathbf{y}_0, \mathbf{y}_0')$ we shall mean the nth order matrix, the ijth element of which is $F_{y_i'y_j'}$ evaluated at $(x_0, \mathbf{y}_0, \mathbf{y}_0')$. A boldface character with a double boldface subscript is then a matrix. Occasionally, we shall encounter situations in which we have n functions $R^u(x, \mathbf{y}, \mathbf{y}')$ which can be represented by the vector-valued function $\mathbf{R}(x, \mathbf{y}, \mathbf{y}')$. In such situations we may be interested in forming, for example, the nth order matrix $||R^u_{y_j}||$. We cannot represent this matrix by $\mathbf{R}_\mathbf{y}$, for this denotes a vector containing the partial derivatives of a real-valued function R with respect to the variables in $\mathbf{y}$. Thus we shall simply use $||R^u_{y_j}||$ to denote the matrix. The uth column of this matrix is the vector $\mathbf{R}^u_{\mathbf{y}}$. To avoid confusion with the notation for partial derivatives, we shall often use superscripts rather than subscripts to distinguish the individual members (such as R^u) of a set of functions. By $\mathrm{d}\mathbf{f}/\mathrm{d}x$ we shall mean the vector the jth component of which is the derivative with respect to x of the jth component of $\mathbf{f}$. Similarly, by

$$\int_{x_0}^{x_1} \mathbf{f}\mathrm{d}x,$$

we shall mean the vector the jth component of which is

$$\int_{x_0}^{x_1} f^j \,\mathrm{d}x.$$

A scalar product of two column vectors $\mathbf{a}$ and $\mathbf{b}$ will be written $\mathbf{a} \cdot \mathbf{b}$. If $\mathbf{A}$ is a matrix and $\mathbf{b}$ a column vector, $\mathbf{Ab}$ is the column vector which is the matrix product of $\mathbf{A}$ and $\mathbf{b}$. Then $\mathbf{a} \cdot \mathbf{Ab}$ is a scalar which is the scalar product of the vectors $\mathbf{a}$ and $\mathbf{Ab}$.

2.5. The simplest problem in the calculus of variations

We now have enough background to make it possible to begin a study of the calculus of variations. The classical theory developed as a result of studying 'simple' problems of the type formulated in Section 2.2. In each of the three problems formulated there it is of interest to determine a function $y(x)$ which passes through two specified points and which minimizes the value of an integral of the form

$$\int_{x_0}^{x_1} F(y, y')\mathrm{d}x.$$

In the brachistochrone problem, for example,

$$F(y, y') = \frac{[1 + (y')^2]^{\frac{1}{2}}}{[y_0 - y]^{\frac{1}{2}}}.$$

This is essentially the type of problem we shall study first. We shall be slightly more general, however, and add x to the arguments of F, so that F will be of the form $F(x, y, y')$. The value of the integral of F depends on the particular function $y(x)$ used in F. Thus the integral will be a functional defined on some subset of an appropriate function space. We shall denote the integral by $J[y]$. Our problem then is to determine that function or functions $y(x)$ which satisfies $y(x_0) = y_0$ and $y(x_1) = y_1$ and which maximizes or minimizes

$$J[y] = \int_{x_0}^{x_1} F(x, y, y')\,dx. \tag{2-19}$$

In analyzing any problem in the calculus of variations, one must be absolutely clear about the domain of J, that is, about the type of functions to be considered and about the restrictions, if any, to be placed on the functions. *We shall assume that the functions $y(x)$ which are to be considered are piecewise smooth*; that is, y must be continuous and it must have a piecewise continuous derivative function. We shall not consider problems in which y can have jump discontinuities. In particular cases additional restrictions may be imposed on $y(x)$ or $y'(x)$ or both. Thus in the example involving the minimum area of the surface of revolution, formulated in Section 2.2, there was imposed the requirement that $y \geq 0$ at each point in the interval $x_0 \leq x \leq x_1$. The general form of all such restrictions is easy to see. Recall that the curve representing $y(x)$ in extended phase space simultaneously describes the behavior of $y'(x)$ as well. Thus we need only require that the curve representing $y(x)$ in extended phase space lie in some specified set $\mathscr{R}$, open or closed or neither. The set $\mathscr{R}$ takes care of all constraints on y and y'. We shall impose no restrictions on the higher derivatives of $y(x)$. Any piecewise smooth function such that $y(x_0) = y_0$ and $y(x_1) = y_1$ and of which the graph in extended phase space lies in $\mathscr{R}$ will be called an *admissible function*. The requirements that $y(x_0) = y_0$ and $y(x_1) = y_1$ are called *boundary conditions*. When it is required that the graph of $y(x)$ begin at a specified point (x_0, y_0) and terminate at a specified point (x_1, y_1), the problem is said to have *fixed end points*. The domain of J is then the collection of all admissible functions. If we think of a function as being represented by a curve in extended phase space, the domain of J is the set of all piecewise smooth curves lying in $\mathscr{R}$ and with the characteristic that $y(x_0) = y_0$ and $y(x_1) = y_1$.

Yet other restrictions relate to the function F. The domain of F is some subset of extended phase space. It is not possible to consider an arbitrary function F since in later proofs we shall require various of its derivatives. Specifically, we shall assume that $F \in C''$ over some open set which contains $\mathscr{R}$. Thus the first and second partial derivative functions of F must exist and be continuous over $\mathscr{R}$. This is not a serious limitation, however, since the conditions are satisfied in most practical problems. It will be observed that, when $F \in C''$, F is a continuous function of the variables x, y and y'. Now if $y(x)$ is piecewise smooth, and therefore continuous, $y'(x)$ will be piecewise continuous. Hence if a specific $y(x)$ and its derivative function $y'(x)$ are substituted in F then the latter, considered as a function of a single variable x, must be piecewise continuous. F need not be continuous since $y'(x)$ may not be continuous. However, the integral of a piecewise continuous function over a finite interval always exists; hence, for any particular function y in the domain of J, the integral $J[y]$ does indeed exist. Finally, we note that F need not be defined at every point in the interval x_0 to x_1. However, the integral (2-19) is still well defined even if there is a finite number of points at which F itself is not defined.

There is one more generalization of the problem which we may allow for at the outset. Problems encountered in economics often involve an infinite time horizon, so that the upper limit on the integral in (2-19) is ∞. There is in this case no point (x_1, y_1) through which the graph of $y(x)$ must pass, although there may be some restrictions placed on the behavior of $y(x)$ as $x \to \infty$. Moreover, when the upper limit on the integral is ∞ we can no longer be sure that the integral exists. In such cases we must restrict the domain of J to include only those $y(x)$, if any, for which the integral converges. Then the domain of J consists of all piecewise smooth functions $y(x)$ for which $y(x_0) = y_0$, which satisfy any specified condition on their behavior as $x \to \infty$, the graphs of which in extended phase space lie in $\mathscr{R}$, and such that $J[y]$ exists (that is, the integral converges). When the interval of integration is infinite, we shall assume in addition that each function $y(x)$ has only a finite number of corners; then all corners must lie to the left of some x sufficiently large. For most of our analysis it makes absolutely no difference whether the integral is proper, with a finite upper limit, or improper, with an infinite upper limit. However, there are certain features of the case in which the interval of integration is infinite that will require special attention.

Sometimes, when we do not wish to specify whether the problem involves a maximum or a minimum, it is convenient to refer to it simply as an optimization problem. Similarly, we can refer to an optimizing function and to the optimal value of $J[y]$. Adopting this terminology then, our task is to develop a technique for finding that function or functions in the domain of J which yields the optimal value of J.

In this task we encounter roughly the same sorts of difficulties as in the search for ordinary maxima and minima. The analytical methods for solving ordinary maximization problems do not directly determine the point or points in $\mathscr{D}$ at which the function takes on its absolute or global maximum. In general, these methods are only a criterion for locating the stationary points of the function. Suppose, for example, that $f(x)$ is a differentiable function of one variable. The stationary points of $f(x)$ are the solutions to the equation $f'(x) = 0$. This equation may have no solutions, as we have pointed out earlier; or it may have more than one solution. At most solution points f attains a relative maximum or minimum; but this is not necessarily the case, for it is possible also that $f'(x) = 0$ defines a point of inflection. On the other hand, if x must lie in a specified interval, there is no guarantee that the maximizing point will satisfy $f'(x) = 0$. The maximizing point may lie on one of the boundaries, where $f' \neq 0$.

In ordinary maximization problems it is usually clear that a maximum does exist; the job is to find it. A straightforward, though possibly inefficient, procedure consists in searching out all roots of $f'(x) = 0$ and then evaluating f both at each of these points and at the boundaries. The largest of all these numbers is the absolute maximum of f over the interval. If a value of x which maximizes f does not lie on the boundary it must be a solution to $f'(x) = 0$ (provided f is differentiable). Thus the condition $f'(x) = 0$ is often referred to as a necessary condition which the desired point must satisfy if the maximum is not a boundary maximum.

If certain regularity conditions are satisfied, it is possible to generalize the necessary conditions to include boundary maxima. These more general necessary conditions are often referred to as the Kuhn-Tucker conditions and are discussed in Hadley [18]. The problem is then reduced to that of finding all points which satisfy the necessary conditions. If there is only one, and if a maximum exists, then the maximizing point has been found. If there are more than one, additional investigations must be made to determine which one or ones actually yields the maximum.

As we have indicated above, the situation is roughly the same for problems in the calculus of variations as for problems of ordinary maxima and minima. In the calculus of variations also, the methods on the whole are for locating relative maxima or minima or, more precisely, stationary values of the integral rather than the absolute or global maximum or minimum. Again a set of necessary conditions is obtained, this time for locating the optimizing functions. The conditions we will first develop have something in common with the condition $f'(x) = 0$; thus if the optimizing function lies partly on the boundary of $\mathscr{R}$ it may not be true that the optimizing function satisfies the conditions. Later, the conditions will be generalized to encompass boundary points. Then we will have true necessary conditions comparable to the Kuhn-Tucker conditions. Provided certain regularity requirements are met, every optimizing function must satisfy these conditions. In any particular case, there may be several functions which satisfy the necessary conditions. Then, as with ordinary maxima and minima, additional investigations will be needed to determine which function or functions does indeed yield the optimum. As we have already noted, in ordinary optimization problems it is usually clear either that an optimum does indeed exist or that it does not exist. In problems involving the calculus of variations the situation is considerably more complicated and more subtle. It is by no means always obvious that a maximum or a minimum does in fact exist, and considerable thought and analysis may be needed to settle the matter. The methods we shall develop for solving variational problems, like the methods for solving ordinary optimization problems, are especially useful in theoretical work but do not necessarily constitute the most efficient procedures for solving problems numerically. We shall not attempt to develop in detail efficient procedures for obtaining numerical solutions; from time to time, however, we shall make some remarks concerning this aspect of the subject.

We have indicated above that, both for ordinary maximization problems and for problems in the calculus of variations, there may exist more than one solution to the necessary conditions and that it may be difficult to determine whether in any particular case the true maximum has been found. In ordinary maximization problems, this particular difficulty is substantially reduced, or even eliminated, if the functions involved have certain concavity or convexity properties; for then any solution to the necessary conditions yields an absolute maximum, and in certain cases of strict concavity and convexity it is certain that there is only one solution. Concavity and convexity play a similar role in the calculus of variations and are especially important in economic applications.

2.6. The Euler equation and corner conditions

Suppose now that there exists an admissible function $z(x)$ which yields the maximum of (2-19) over the domain of $J[y]$. We here wish to determine a set of necessary conditions which the function $z(x)$ must satisfy. *For the time being, we shall make the important assumption that the curve representing $z(x)$ lies everywhere in the interior of the set $\mathscr{R}$ in extended phase space.* We shall then say that the maximum is an interior maximum.

Since $z(x)$ does indeed yield the maximum, for *any* other admissible function $y(x)$ it must be true that $J[y] - J[z] \leq 0$. We shall proceed as with ordinary maxima and minima by introducing the notion of a relative maximum. In the calculus of variations, however, it has been found convenient to introduce two different concepts. Recall that a function $f(\mathbf{x})$ has a relative maximum at $\mathbf{x}^*$ if there exists an $\varepsilon > 0$ such that for every $\mathbf{x}$ in an ε-neighborhood of $\mathbf{x}^*$, $f(\mathbf{x}) - f(\mathbf{x}^*) \leq 0$. Essentially the same sort of definition is used in the calculus of variations. First it is necessary to define an ε-neighborhood of a function. This will be done in two different and alternative ways.

N_ε Neighborhood: An N_ε neighborhood of a piecewise smooth function $z(x)$ is the set

$$\mathcal{N}(\varepsilon) = \left\{ (x, y) \,\middle|\, |y - z(x)| < \varepsilon, \quad x \in \mathscr{D} \right\} \tag{2-21}$$

in $\mathscr{E}^2$, where $\mathscr{D}$ is the domain of $z(x)$.

P_ε Neighborhood: A P_ε neighborhood of a piecewise smooth function $z(x)$ is the set

$$\mathscr{P}(\varepsilon) = \left\{ (x, y, y') \,\middle|\, |(y, y') - (z(x), z'(x))| < \varepsilon, \quad x \in \mathscr{D}' \right\} \tag{2-22}$$

in $\mathscr{E}^3$, where $\mathscr{D}'$ is the domain of $z'(x)$.

An N_ε neighborhood of $z(x)$ can be thought of as a band of width 2ε surrounding the curve representing $z(x)$ in the xy-plane. Geometrically, this band might be represented by the shaded region shown in Figure 2.4. A P_ε

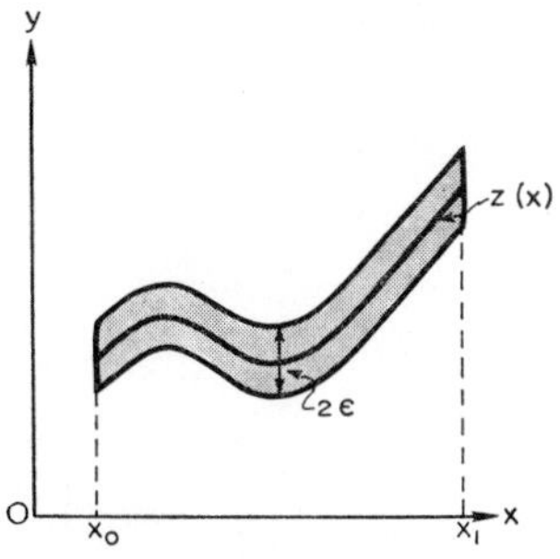

Fig. 2.4.

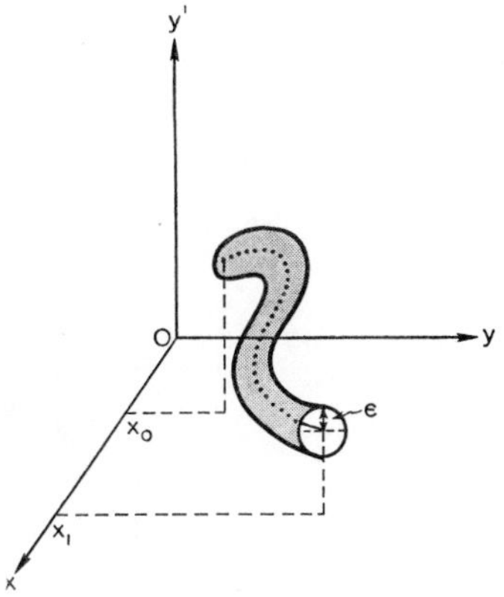

Fig. 2.5.

neighborhood of $z(x)$ can be thought of as a tube of radius ε surrounding the graph of $z(x)$ in extended phase space, such as that shown in Figure 2.5. In the event that $z(x)$ has one or more corners, the graph of $z(x)$ in the extended phase space will have one or more jump discontinuities and the tube $\mathscr{P}(\varepsilon)$ may consist of several disconnected pieces. This fact will not be of any concern to us. We can now introduce the following definitions:

Strong Relative Maximum. The admissible function $z(x)$ yields a strong relative maximum of $J[y]$ or a relative maximum for strong variations if there exists an N_ε neighborhood of $z(x)$ such that for every admissible function $y(x)$ the graph of which lies in $\mathscr{N}(\varepsilon)$, $J[y] - J[z] \leq 0$.

Weak Relative Maximum. The admissible function $z(x)$ yields a weak relative maximum or a relative maximum for weak variations of $J[y]$ if there exists a P_ε neighborhood of $z(x)$ such that for every admissible function $y(x)$ the graph of which in extended phase space lies in $\mathscr{P}(\varepsilon)$, $J[y] - J[z] \leq 0$.

It is obvious that strong and weak relative minima can be defined in a precisely analogous manner.

The difference between a strong and a weak relative maximum turns on the behavior of the derivative function for any specified function $y(x)$. For a weak relative maximum, with ε small, not only must the value of $y(x)$ be close to the value of $z(x)$ but also the value $y'(x)$ must be close to $z'(x)$. For a strong relative maximum, $y(x)$ must be close to $z(x)$ if ε is small; but it is not required that $y'(x)$ be close to $z'(x)$. Suppose, for example, that $z(x)$ and $y(x)$ have graphs like those shown in Figure 2.6. In this case it is possible that $y(x)$ lies within an N_ε neighborhood of $z(x)$ but, since

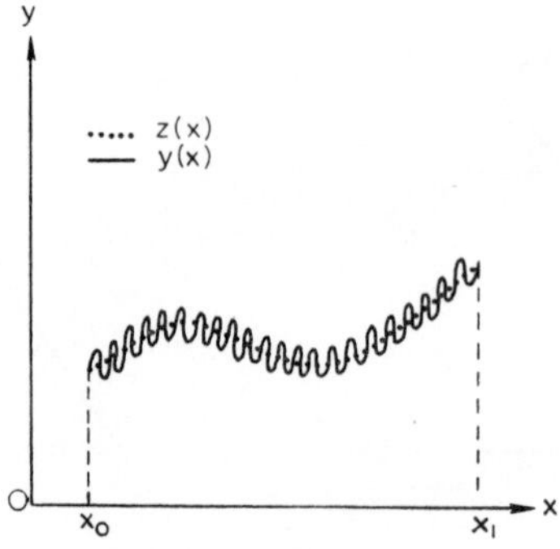

Fig. 2.6.

$y'(x)$ is so different from $z'(x)$, not within a P_ε neighborhood of $z(x)$. Thus in considering whether $z(x)$ yields a strong relative maximum one must consider a larger class of functions than in considering whether $z(x)$ yields a weak relative maximum. Clearly, if $z(x)$ yields a strong relative maximum it also yields a weak relative maximum. It is not necessarily true, however, that a function which yields a weak relative maximum also yields a strong one. It is also important to notice that if $z(x)$ yields the absolute maximum of $J[y]$ then it also yields a strong and a weak relative maximum.

We are now ready to return to the problem of determining a useful set of necessary conditions. We have assumed that $z(x)$ yields the absolute maximum of $J[y]$ and that this is an interior maximum. To derive a useful set of necessary conditions it is not essential that we consider all functions in the domain of $J[y]$. It suffices to consider a very restricted collection of functions–those which lie in a P_ε neighborhood of $z(x)$ and therefore define weak variations. An analogous situation arises in the theory of ordinary maxima and minima; to obtain the condition $\partial f/\partial x_j = 0$ for an interior maximum of a function of n variables it is not necessary to consider all points lying in an ε-neighborhood of the optimizing point $\mathbf{x}^*$ but only variations in the directions of the coordinate axes. Since $z(x)$ is everywhere in the interior of $\mathscr{R}$ there exists a P_ε neighborhood of $z(x)$ which lies entirely in $\mathscr{R}$; and *every* piecewise smooth function $y(x)$ for which $y(x_0) = y_0$ and $y(x_1) = y_1$ (or for which appropriate conditions are satisfied as $x \to \infty$) and the graph of which in extended phase space lies in $\mathscr{P}(\varepsilon)$ has the property that $J[y] - J[z] \leq 0$.

It is not even necessary to consider all of these functions; however it requires insight to see just what is the most convenient collection of admissible functions to consider. Lagrange was the first to suggest the procedure we shall use. Consider any two values of x, say a and b, such that $x_0 \leq a < b \leq x_1$ and such that $z(x)$ does not have a corner in the open interval $a < x < b$. Next let $\eta(x)$ be a function such that $\eta \in C'$, $x_0 \leq x \leq x_1$, and of the following form

$$\eta(x) = \begin{cases} 0, x \leq a \text{ and } x \geq b \\ \\ \text{arbitrary subject to } \eta \in C', a < x < b. \end{cases} \tag{2-23}$$

Thus $\eta(x)$ is continuous and differentiable at each point in the interval $x_0 \leq x \leq x_1$. It can differ from 0, however, only between a and b. Between a and b we can use any continuous differentiable function such that $\eta(a) = \eta(b) = 0$, $\eta_+'(a) = \eta_-'(b) = 0$. Let us imagine that a specific function $\eta(x)$ has been chosen, and consider the collection of functions

$$y(x;\xi) = z(x) + \xi\eta(x) \tag{2-24}$$

where ξ is a specified real number. For each ξ we obtain a different function $y(x)$, and to indicate that we have a one parameter family of functions y we have written $y(x;\ \xi)$ rather than simply $y(x)$. Note that, regardless of the value of ξ, $y(x)$ can differ from $z(x)$ only in the interval $a < x < b$. Note also that each $y(x;\ \xi)$ is piecewise smooth, with the same corners as $z(x)$; furthermore $y(x_0;\ \xi) = y_0$ and $y(x_1;\ \xi) = y_1$ (alternatively, the behavior as $x \to \infty$ of $y(x;\ \xi)$ is the same as that of $z(x)$). In addition, if ξ is chosen sufficiently small, $y(x;\ \xi)$ lies in a P_ε neighborhood of $z(x)$, so that not only will y be close to z but y' will be close to z' at all points where z' exists. Hence, for small enough ξ, say $|\xi| < \xi_0$, every function $y(x;\ \xi)$ that can be constructed in this way from the given $\eta(x)$ is admissible. Furthermore, an $\xi_0 > 0$ can be found for every $\eta(x)$ of the type specified. The graphs of $z(x)$ and $y(x;\ \xi)$ might then look like those shown in Figure 2.7.

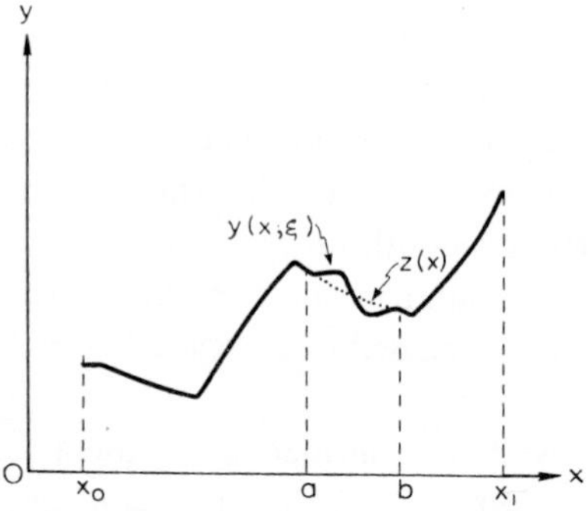

Fig. 2.7.

Notice that $y_\xi(x;\ 0) = \eta(x)$ and $y'(x;\ 0) = \eta'(x)$. We shall find it convenient to refer to $\eta(x)$ as the *variation* of $z(x)$, although some authors apply that label to $\xi\eta(x)$.

Now since $y(x;\ \xi)$ is admissible for every ξ, $|\xi| < \xi_0$, and since $z(x)$ yields the absolute maximum of $J[y]$, we must have $J[y] - J[z] \le 0$ for $|\xi| < \xi_0$. However, if we fix $\eta(x)$ and vary only ξ, $J[y]$ becomes a function of a single variable ξ, which we can write $\Phi(\xi)$. Thus

$$\Phi(\xi) = J[y(x;\ \xi)] = \int_{x_0}^{x_1} F(x,\ y(x;\ \xi),\ y'(x;\ \xi))dx. \tag{2-25}$$

Next observe that when $\xi = 0$, $y(x;\ 0) = z(x)$, so that $\Phi(0) = J[z]$. Thus

$\Phi(\xi) - \Phi(0) \leq 0$ for all ξ, $|\xi| < \xi_0$, and the function of one real variable $\Phi(\xi)$ has a relative maximum at $\xi = 0$. Consequently, if $\Phi(\xi)$ is differentiable at 0, it must be true that $\Phi'(0) = 0$. We shall see that $\Phi'(0)$ exists and then deduce from the necessary condition $\Phi'(0) = 0$ a useful necessary condition which must be satisfied by $z(x)$.

Since $y(x; \xi) = z(x)$ when x is not in the interval $a < x < b$,

$$\Phi(\xi) = \gamma + \int_a^b F(x, y(x; \xi), y'(x; \xi))dx \tag{2-26}$$

where γ is independent of ξ and

$$\gamma = \int_{x_0}^{a} F(x, z, z')dx + \int_{b}^{x_1} F(x, z, z')dx. \tag{2-27}$$

Now $\Phi'(\xi)$ exists and can be computed by differentiating under the integral sign, since

$$\frac{\partial F}{\partial \xi} = F_y y_\xi + F_{y'} y'_\xi = F_y \eta + F_{y'} \eta' \tag{2-28}$$

is continuous over the interval $a < x < b$. (See Apostol [1], pp. 219–220 for a proof of the relevant theorem.) Hence, on differentiating $\Phi(\xi)$ and setting $\xi = 0$ we obtain

$$\Phi'(0) = \int_a^b [F_y(x, z, z')\eta + F_{y'}(x, z, z')\eta']dx = 0. \tag{2-29}$$

Notice that, when $\xi = 0$, the arguments of F_y and $F_{y'}$ become z and z'.

In the foregoing development we have supposed that $\eta(x)$ is fixed. However, (2-29) holds for all η functions of the form (2-23), and we shall now make use of this fact to obtain the desired necessary conditions. After proving a lemma, which is a little more general than we need at the moment but which will be needed in its general form later, we shall be able to obtain immediately the desired conditions.

Fundamental Lemma. If $g(x)$ and $h(x)$ are piecewise continuous functions in the interval $a \leq x \leq b$, with discontinuities at the same values of x, and if

$$\int_a^b [g(x)\eta(x) + h(x)\eta'(x)]dx = 0 \tag{2-30}$$

for every function $\eta(x)$ which is piecewise smooth over the interval $a \leq x \leq b$ and for which $\eta(a) = \eta(b) = 0$, then if

$$G(x) = \int_a^x g(\zeta)d\zeta$$

there exists a constant λ such that $h(x) = G(x) + \lambda$ for every x in the interval $a \leq x \leq b$. Furthermore, $h'(x)$ exists for each x which is not a point of discontinuity of $g(x)$ and $h'(x) = g(x)$.

To prove the lemma, consider

$$G(x) = \int_a^x g(\zeta)d\zeta.$$

$G(x)$ is differentiable at each x which is not a point of discontinuity of $g(x)$, and $G'(x) = g(x)$; thus $G(x)$ is a primitive function for $g(x)$. On integration by parts, we see that

$$\int_a^b g(x)\eta(x)dx = G(x)\eta(x)\Big|_a^b - \int_a^b G(x)\eta'(x)dx = -\int_a^b G(x)\eta'(x)dx.$$

Thus (2-30) can be written as

$$\int_a^b [h(x) - G(x)]\eta'(x)dx = 0. \tag{2-31}$$

We now show that

$$h(x) - G(x) = \lambda, \quad a \leq x \leq b \tag{2-32}$$

where λ is a constant, independent of x. Let us write $\alpha(x) = h(x) - G(x)$, and define λ to be the number

$$\lambda = (b - a)^{-1} \int_a^b \alpha(x)dx$$

so that

$$\int_a^b [\alpha(x) - \lambda]dx = 0. \tag{2-33}$$

We next introduce a particular η function defined as

$$\eta(x) = \int_a^x [\alpha(\zeta) - \lambda]d\zeta. \tag{2-34}$$

Then $\eta(a) = \eta(b) = 0$ and η is piecewise smooth in the interval of interest; thus $\eta(x)$ is an allowable η function. For any $\eta(x)$, and hence for the one defined by (2-34), we have

$$\int_a^b [\alpha(x) - \lambda]\eta'(x)dx = \int_a^b \alpha(x)\eta'(x)dx - \lambda[\eta(b) - \eta(a)] = 0 \tag{2-35}$$

since both terms of the second expression are zero. On the other hand, in view of (2-34),

$$\int_a^b [\alpha(x) - \lambda]\eta'(x)dx = \int_a^b [\alpha(x) - \lambda]^2dx. \tag{2-36}$$

On combining (2-35) and (2-36) we find that

$$\int_a^b [\alpha(x) - \lambda]^2dx = 0. \tag{2-37}$$

Now $[\alpha(x) - \lambda]^2$ is piecewise continuous and non-negative; hence, if (2-37) holds, $\alpha(x) - \lambda = 0$ or $\alpha(x) = \lambda$ at each x where $\alpha(x)$ is defined. Let us define $\alpha(x)$ to be equal to λ at those points, finite in number, at which it is not yet defined. Then $\alpha(x)$ is continuous and a constant everywhere. Thus if we define $h(x)$ to be equal to $G(x) + \lambda$ at those points where it is not yet defined then for *all* x, $a \leq x \leq b$, $h(x) - G(x) = \lambda$ or $h(x) = G(x) + \lambda$, which is what we wished to show. Note that we have shown that $h(x)$ must be continuous–it has no jump discontinuities; only $g(x)$ can have jump discontinuities.

Now at each x which is not a point of discontinuity of $g(x)$, $G(x) + \lambda$ is a differentiable function with a derivative function $g(x)$; thus $h(x)$ must be differentiable at all such points and its derivative function must be $g(x)$. Hence

$$h'(x) = g(x) \tag{2-38}$$

at all points which are not points of discontinuity of $g(x)$; and we can interpret (2-38) as holding at a point of discontinuity of $g(x)$ if for $h(x)$ we use a left or right hand derivative as required, i.e. $h'_+(x^*) = g(x^*_+), h'_-(x^*) = g(x^*_-)$ at a point x^* of discontinuity of $g(x)$. That concludes the proof of the lemma.

We can now apply the lemma to (2-29), with $g(x) = F_y(x, z(x), z'(x))$ and $h(x) = F_{y'}(x, z(x), z'(x))$. F_y and $F_{y'}$ are continuous between a and b since by assumption there are no corners of $z(x)$ inside this interval. It is permissible, however, for a and/or b to be a corner of $z(x)$. F_y and $F_{y'}$ can be made continuous at a and/or b in this case merely by defining their values to be the right or left side limit as appropriate. If that is done, $g(x)$ and $h(x)$ are continuous over $a \leq x \leq b$ and we may conclude that in the interval $a \leq x \leq b$, $F_{y'}(x, z(x), z'(x))$ is differentiable and

$$\frac{\mathrm{d}}{\mathrm{d}x} F_{y'}(x, z(x), z'(x)) = F_y(x, z(x), z'(x)). \tag{2-39}$$

Thus we have proved the important result that if $z(x)$ maximizes $J[y]$, and the maximum is an interior maximum, then in any interval which does not contain a corner of $z(x)$ in its interior, $z(x)$ must be a solution to the differential equation

$$\frac{\mathrm{d}}{\mathrm{d}x} F_{y'} - F_y = 0. \tag{2-40}$$

This differential equation is called *Euler's differential equation*. It was discovered by Euler in 1744. Clearly, it is also true that if $z(x)$ minimizes $J[y]$, then in any interval which does not contain a corner of $z(x)$, $z(x)$ must satisfy (2-40) if the minimum is an interior minimum. In particular, what we have shown is that between corners of $z(x)$, $z(x)$ must be a solution to Euler's equation. If it has no corners, $z(x)$ must be a single solution to (2-40). If it has one or more corners, $z(x)$ is constructed by joining together two or more pieces of specific solutions to (2-40). It should be kept in mind, however, that the various segments of $z(x)$ need be solutions to (2-40) only if the solution is an interior solution. Not until later shall we concern ourselves in detail with problems created by boundaries.

In general, (2-40) is a nonlinear second order ordinary differential equation. Written out in detail, it is

$$F_{y'y'}y'' + F_{yy'}y' + F_{xy'} - F_y = 0. \tag{2-41}$$

Note that $\mathrm{d}F_{y'}/\mathrm{d}x$ is not the same as $\partial F_{y'}/\partial x = F_{xy'}$. In evaluating $\mathrm{d}F_{y'}/\mathrm{d}x$ we must recognize that y and y' are functions of x and use the chain rule. In applying the chain rule to obtain (2-41) we had to assume the existence and continuity of y''. We have not actually proved that y'' has these properties.

Normally this is the case, however; and, in the problems, we ask the reader to prove that if $F_{y'y'}$ (the coefficient of y'' in (2-41)) is never 0 along $z(x)$ then $z''(x)$ exists and is continuous between corners of $z(x)$. The optimizing function $z(x)$ is called *regular* if $F_{y'y'} \neq 0$ along $z(x)$.

Let us next turn our attention to the conditions which must be satisfied at a corner of $z(x)$. Suppose that $z(x)$ has a corner at x^*. Let a and b be values of x such that $a < x^* < b$ and x^* is the only value of x in the interval at which $z(x)$ has a corner. Now let $\eta(x)$ be a function such that $\eta \in C'$ for $x_0 \leq x \leq x_1$ and of the following form:

$$\eta(x) = \begin{cases} 0, x \leq a, x \geq b \\ \text{arbitrary subject to } \eta \in C', a < x < b. \end{cases} \tag{2-42}$$

Next write $y(x; \xi) = z(x) + \xi\eta(x)$. For ξ sufficiently small, $y(x; \xi)$ lies in a P_ε neighborhood of $z(x)$. (Notice that each $y(x; \xi)$ has a corner at x^*). In fact, $y(x; \xi)$ differs from $z(x)$ only over the interval $a < x < b$; the graphs of $y(x; \xi)$ and $z(x)$ might look like the curves shown in Figure 2.8. Notice

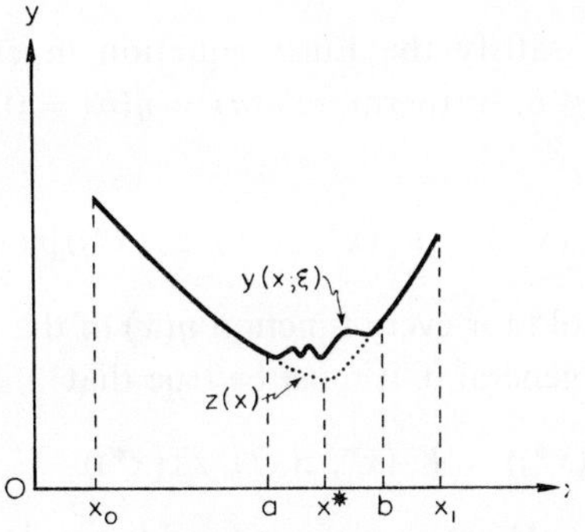

Fig. 2.8.

that $y(x; \xi)$ has a derivative at every point in the interval $a < x < b$ except x^*. Let $\Phi(\xi) = J[y(x; \xi)]$. Then we can write

$$\Phi(\xi) = \gamma + \int_a^{x^*} F(x, y(x; \xi), y'(x; \xi))dx + \int_{x^*}^{b} F(x; y(x; \xi), y'(x; \xi))dx \tag{2-43}$$

where γ is a number independent of ξ and of the form (2-27). Once again $\Phi(0) = J[z]$ and $\Phi(\xi)$ has a relative maximum at 0. Now $\partial F/\partial \xi$ is continuous over the intervals $a \leq x \leq x^*$ and $x^* \leq x \leq b$ provided the appropriate one-sided limits are applied at x^*. Thus each integral on the right in (2-43) is a differentiable function of ξ; hence $\Phi'(0)$ exists and

$$\Phi'(0) = \int_a^{x^*} [F_y(x, z, z')\eta(x) + F_{y'}(x, z, z')\eta'(x)]\mathrm{d}x + \int_{x^*}^{b} [F_y(x, z, z')\eta(x) + F_{y'}(x, z, z')\eta'(x)]\mathrm{d}x = 0.$$

Since $F_{y'}$ is differentiable over each interval, we can integrate by parts to obtain

$$\Phi'(0) = \int_a^{x^*} \left[F_y - \frac{\mathrm{d}}{\mathrm{d}x} F_{y'}\right] \eta \mathrm{d}x + \int_{x^*}^{b} \left[F_y - \frac{\mathrm{d}}{\mathrm{d}x} F_{y'}\right] \eta \mathrm{d}x + F_{y'}\eta \Big|_a^{x^*} + F_{y'}\eta \Big|_{x^*}^{b} = 0. \tag{2-44}$$

However, $z(x)$ must satisfy the Euler equation in each of the intervals $a \leq x \leq x^*$, $x^* \leq x \leq b$; furthermore $\eta(a) = \eta(b) = 0$. Thus (2-44) reduces to

$$[F_{y'}(x^*, z(x^*), z'_-(x^*)) - F_{y'}(x^*, z(x^*), z'_+(x^*))]\eta(x^*) = 0. \tag{2-45}$$

This equation must hold for every function $\eta(x)$ of the type specified above. Since $\eta(x^*)$ is not in general 0, it must be true that

$$F_{y'}(x^*, z(x^*), z'_-(x^*)) = F_{y'}(x^*, z(x^*), z'_+(x^*)) \tag{2-46}$$

where $z'_-(x^*)$ and $z'_+(x^*)$ are the left and right side derivatives respectively of $z(x)$ at x^*. At each corner the condition (2-46) must be satisfied. The condition is often referred to as *the Weierstrass-Erdmann corner condition.* It says that the function $F_{y'}$ is continuous across a corner of the optimizing function $z(x)$, that is, $\lim_{x \to x_+^*} F_{y'} = \lim_{x \to x_-^*} F_{y'}$. Of course, (2-46) must also be satisfied at a corner of a minimizing function. As we shall ask the reader to show in the problems, the corner condition could have been obtained much more simply by a different argument. However, the present method was used here, as well as in deriving the Euler equations, to make quite clear that the corner condition in no way depends on the boundary conditions.

Thus we have proved the following important theorem.

Theorem 2.6.1. Necessary Conditions: Euler Equation and Corner Condition. Suppose that $z(x)$ is an admissible function which yields an interior maximum or minimum of $J[y]$. Then it is necessary that

(1) *In any interval $a \leq x \leq b$ which does not contain a corner of $z(x)$ in its interior, $z(x)$ satisfies the Euler equation*

$$\frac{d}{dx} F_{y'} - F_y = 0 \tag{2-47}$$

at each point in the interval.

(2) *$F_{y'}$ is continuous across any corner of $z(x)$ (the Weierstrass-Erdmann corner condition).*

The above development has been totally independent of whether the integral has a finite or infinite upper limit. If it has a finite upper limit, we have required that $y(x_1) = y_1$ in order that $y(x)$ be an admissible function. When the upper limit is infinite there is no such condition. However, there may sometimes be imposed an analogous condition, *viz.*

$$\lim_{x \to \infty} y(x) = y_1 \tag{2-48}$$

or, more generally,

$$\lim_{x \to \infty} [y(x) - f(x)] = 0 \tag{2-49}$$

where $f(x)$ is a specified function; and to be admissible any function must possess this property. In other cases, however, no restriction is imposed on $y(x)$ as $x \to \infty$.

We now develop a general condition which must be satisfied as $x \to \infty$. Consider any function $y(x; \xi) = z(x) + \xi\eta(x)$. When the condition (2-49) is imposed, it is necessary that $\lim_{x \to \infty} \eta(x) = 0$ if $y(x; \xi)$ is to be admissible. If (2-49) is not imposed, $\eta(x)$ can differ from 0 for arbitrarily large x. However, we do not want $\eta(x)$ to grow arbitrarily large or small, for then we cannot guarantee that, for all x, $y(x; \xi)$ lies in a P_ε neighborhood of $z(x)$. Thus we must require that $|\eta(x)|$ is bounded; however, the bound can be made as large as desired.

Suppose now that a is a value of x sufficiently large to ensure that all corners of $z(x)$ lie to the left of a. And let us define $\eta(x)$ so that $\eta(x) \in C'$ for $x \geq x_0$, $\eta(x) = 0$ for $x \leq a$, and $|\eta(x)|$ is bounded for $x \geq x_0$. If (2-49) must hold, we also require that $\lim_{x \to \infty} \eta(x) = 0$. Otherwise $\eta(x)$ is arbitrary.

Next consider the functions $y(x; \xi) = z(x) + \xi\eta(x)$. For ξ sufficiently small, each of these lies in a P_ε neighborhood of $z(x)$; $y(x; \xi)$ and $z(x)$ might

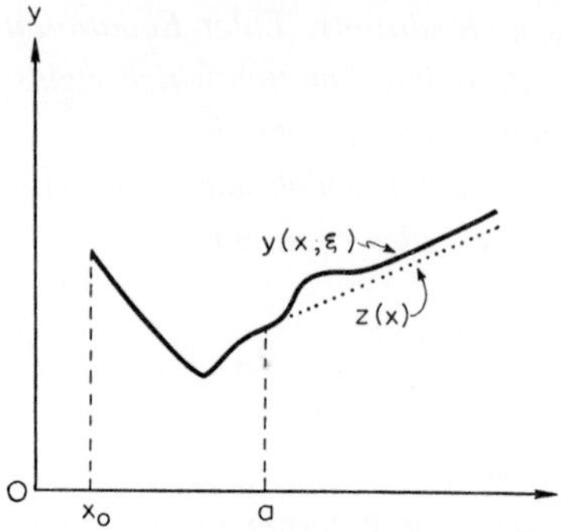

Fig. 2.9.

then have graphs like those displayed in Figure 2.9. We shall assume that $J[y]$ exists for all ξ sufficiently close to 0. Then

$$\Phi(\xi) = J[y(x;\xi)] = \gamma + \int_a^\infty F(x, y(x;\xi), y'(x;\xi))dx \tag{2-50}$$

and $\Phi(0) = J[z]$ so that $\Phi(\xi)$ must have a relative maximum at 0. To be sure in this case that $\Phi'(\xi)$ exists, we must require that the integral obtained by differentiating under the integral sign converges uniformly. (See Apostol [1], pp. 437–443, for a definition of uniform convergence and a proof that the derivative exists in this case.) We shall assume that these conditions are satisfied. Then $\Phi'(0)$ exists and is obtained in the usual way. Thus

$$\Phi'(0) = \int_a^\infty [F_y(x, z, z')\eta + F_{y'}(x, z, z')\eta']dx = 0. \tag{2-51}$$

On integration by parts we obtain

$$\begin{aligned}\Phi'(0) &= \int_a^\infty \left[F_y(x, z, z') - \frac{d}{dx} F_{y'}(x, z, z')\right] \eta(x)dx \\ &\quad + \lim_{x\to\infty} F_{y'}(x, z, z')\eta(x) - F_{y'}(x, z, z')\eta(a) \\ &= \lim_{x\to\infty} F_{y'}(x, z, z')\eta(x) = 0 \end{aligned} \tag{2-52}$$

since $z(x)$ satisfies the Euler equation for all $x \geq a$ and $\eta(a) = 0$. Equation (2-52) is basic; it must be satisfied in all cases. Suppose however that no condition (2-49) is imposed, so that $\eta(x)$ is arbitrary and, in particular, it need not be true that $\lim_{x\to\infty} \eta(x) = 0$. Since $\eta(x)$ is arbitrary we may simply take $\eta(x) = \lambda$, a constant, for large x; then we see that $z(x)$ must be such that

$$\lim_{x\to\infty} F_{y'}(x, z, z') = 0. \tag{2-53}$$

Thus we have proved the following theorem.

Theorem 2.6.2. Additional Necessary Condition when the Upper Limit on the Integral is Infinite. If the upper limit on the integral (2-19) is ∞ *and if* $z(x)$ *is an admissible function which maximizes or minimizes* $J[y]$, *then* $z(x)$ *must satisfy the necessary condition of Theorem 2.6.1 and, in addition,* $\lim_{x\to\infty} F_{y'}\eta' = 0$. *Consequently, if it is not required that* $\lim_{x\to\infty} (z(x) - f(x)) = 0$, *then it must be true that* $\lim_{x\to\infty} F_{y'}(x, z(x), z'(x)) = 0$.

The results developed in this section provide a basis for solving variational problems of the form (2-19). The set of all solutions to the Euler equation is obtained; then that particular solution (or combination of two or more solutions joined together at corners) which satisfies the boundary conditions is determined. Normally, this will be the desired solution, although in certain cases additional analysis may be needed to verify that this is so. A solution to the Euler equation without corners will be called an *extremal*. Since the Euler equation is normally a second order differential equation, the general solution will involve two arbitrary constants, that is, the extremals are represented by a two-parameter family of curves. To define a particular extremal the value of each of the two parameters must be specified. This implies that two independent restrictions on the extremal be given. The boundary conditions $y(x_0) = y_0$ and $y(x_1) = y_1$ (or, alternatively, (2-49) or (2-53)) provide two conditions which can often serve to determine a unique extremal. If two extremals are to be joined together at a corner to form $z(x)$, four constants must be determined. The above two conditions, together with the requirement that $z(x)$ and $F_{y'}$ be continuous at the corner provide four conditions that can be used for this purpose. Thus it appears that in all cases we have the right number of conditions to determine the unknown constants.

The possibility of corners no doubt puzzles the reader. How does one know whether or not the solution contains corners? It is difficult to give a complete answer to this question, especially at this stage; however, the following remarks may be helpful. Normally, if one can find at least one extremal which satisfies the boundary conditions then it is not necessary to look for other solutions involving corners. Corners are usually caused by restrictions on the values of y and/or y' which force the optimizing curve to lie on the boundary of $\mathscr{R}$ over some interval of x, a case we shall not consider in detail until later. Thus if it be required that $y' \geq 5$ for $x \leq 6$ and $y' \leq 2$ for $x > 6$, it is clear that any solution must have a corner at $x = 6$. However, corners may arise even when the optimizing curve does not lie on the boundary of $\mathscr{R}$; an example will be provided later (see Example 4 of Section 2.8). In certain cases it can be easily verified from the corner condition (that $F_{y'}$ be continuous) that there are no corners; for satisfaction of this condition may imply that $y'(x)$ be continuous. This is all we shall attempt to say about corners for the present. After discussing some special cases of (2-19), we shall consider some specific examples which should help considerably in making clear how the Euler equation may be applied.

2.7. The Euler equation in special cases

The task of solving the Euler equation can be greatly simplified if y, y' or x does not appear explicitly in F. We now consider these cases.

(1) If y' does not appear explicitly in F then F has the form $F(x, y)$, so $F_{y'} \equiv 0$ and the Euler equation becomes

$$F_y(y, x) = 0. \tag{2-54}$$

The analogy with the first order condition for ordinary maxima and minima is obvious; in this case, indeed, the variational problem reduces to a series (ordered by x) of ordinary optimization problems. (2-54) is not a differential equation but a relation between y and x which serves to define one or more functions $y(x)$. Notice that in this uninteresting case it is in general not possible to specify both $y(x_0)$ and $y(x_1)$; if $y(x)$ is specified at both end points it may be necessary to look beyond the class of piecewise smooth functions. Moreover, when F is of the form $F(x, y)$ the integral often does not possess a maximum or a minimum, as we shall later illustrate.

(2) If y does not appear explicitly in F then F has the form $F(x, y')$, so $F_y \equiv 0$ and the Euler equation is $dF_{y'}/dx = 0$. This can be immediately integrated to yield

$$F_{y'} = \lambda, \quad \lambda \text{ a constant} \tag{2-55}$$

which is a first order differential equation. Thus in this case $z(x)$ must satisfy (2-55) in any interval which does not contain a corner of $z(x)$ in its interior.

(3) When x does not appear explicitly in F, the latter has the form $F(y, y')$. In this case, $z(x)$ must satisfy the first order differential equation

$$F(y, y') - y'F_{y'}(y, y') = \lambda, \quad \lambda \text{ a constant} \tag{2-56}$$

over any interval which does not contain a corner of x in its interior. We shall prove this under the restriction that $z(x)$ is regular in the interval, so that $z''(x)$ exists and is continuous. Later, we shall employ an alternative method of proof to show that (2-56) must hold even if $z''(x)$ does not exist. Under our present assumptions, we have from (2-41) and the fact that $F_{xy'} = F_{y'x} \equiv 0$

$$F_{y'y'}z'' + F_{yy'}z' - F_y = 0. \tag{2-57}$$

On multiplying this equation by z' we obtain

$$F_{y'y'}z'z'' + F_{yy'}(z')^2 - F_yz' = \frac{d}{dx}[z'F_{y'} - F] = 0.$$

Thus $F - z'F_{y'}$ is a constant and $z(x)$ satisfies (2-56).

2.8. Examples

In this section we return to the three problems formulated in Section 2.2 and solve them by finding in each case an appropriate solution to the Euler equation. Very often it is not easy to find a general solution to the Euler equation. One reason is that the solution cannot be expressed in terms of known functions. However, even when the solutions can be expressed in terms of known functions it may not be a simple matter to do so. Each problem requires a special analysis, and often special mathematical tricks must be employed to effect a solution.

1. Let us begin by finding the curve of shortest length joining two points. From (2-5), F in this case is $[1 + (y')^2]^{\frac{1}{2}}$. From the corner condition that $F_{y'}$ must be continuous across a corner, we can immediately infer that the optimizing function cannot have any corners, for the continuity of $F_{y'}$ implies that y' must be continuous. Thus the solution must consist of a single extremal the graph of which passes through the points (0, 0) and (x_0, y_0). Since x does not appear explicitly in F, we know from the previous section that the optimizing function must satisfy the differential equation (2-56). In the case under consideration that equation reduces to

$$[1 + (y')^2]^{\frac{1}{2}} - (y')^2[1 + (y')^2]^{-\frac{1}{2}} = [1 + (y')^2]^{-\frac{1}{2}} = \lambda \tag{2-58}$$

which implies that y' is a constant, independent of x.

Thus the general solution to the Euler equation is the two-parameter family of lines $y = ax + b$. Precisely one of these lines passes through the points (0, 0) and (x_0, y_0). It is $y = y_0 x/x_0$. The solution must be an interior solution since there are no restrictions on y and y'. Thus the minimizing function from the set of admissible functions must be a solution to the Euler equation, and it must be represented by just a single extremal since there are no corners. There is only one extremal which satisfies the boundary conditions; it therefore must yield the absolute minimum distance and not merely a local minimum. The only thing missing from the argument just given is a proof that a minimum does in fact exist. It is clear intuitively that there is a minimum, but we shall not attempt to provide a proof now. More will be said about this later.

2. Consider next the problem of finding the curve which yields the surface of revolution with minimum area. From (2-6), $F = 2\pi y[1 + (y')^2]^{\frac{1}{2}}$. Here $F_{y'} = 2\pi yy'[1 + (y')^2]^{-\frac{1}{2}}$ and from the corner condition (that $F_{y'}$ be continuous at a corner) we infer that z' also must be continuous at a corner unless $z = 0$ at the corner. We recall that in the formulation of the problem it was required that $y \geq 0$. Thus, if $z = 0$ at a corner, the optimizing curve touches the boundary of $\mathscr{R}$ there and is not an interior optimum. It follows that, if the minimizing function represents an interior minimum, it cannot have any corners and must be represented by a single extremal.

F does not contain x explicitly; hence, from (2-56), $z(x)$ must be a solution to the differential equation

$$y[1 + (y')^2]^{\frac{1}{2}} - y(y')^2[1 + (y')^2]^{-\frac{1}{2}} = \lambda, \quad \lambda \text{ a constant} \tag{2-59}$$

(the factor 2π has been included in λ). We now proceed to solve this equation, which can be written as

$$y = \lambda[1 + (y')^2]^{\frac{1}{2}} \quad \text{or} \quad y^2 = \lambda^2[1 + (y')^2]. \tag{2-60}$$

If $\lambda = 0$, we obtain the solution $y(x) \equiv 0$. If $\lambda \neq 0$, we can solve for y' to obtain

$$y' = \left[\left(\frac{y}{\lambda}\right)^2 - 1\right]^{\frac{1}{2}} \quad \text{or} \quad y' = -\left[\left(\frac{y}{\lambda}\right)^2 - 1\right]^{\frac{1}{2}} \tag{2-61}$$

or

$$\pm\left[\left(\frac{y}{\lambda}\right)^2 - 1\right]^{-\frac{1}{2}} y' = 1, \quad y \neq \lambda. \tag{2-62}$$

Here we have a case of separable variables. A primitive function for $[(y/\lambda)^2 - 1]^{-\frac{1}{2}}$ is $\lambda \cosh^{-1}(y/\lambda)$, where the function $\cosh^{-1}$ is the inverse of cosh x, the hyperbolic cosine, for $x \geq 0$. We recall that cosh $x = (e^x + e^{-x})/2$. Thus the solutions to (2-62) are

$$\lambda\cosh^{-1}\left(\frac{y}{\lambda}\right) = x + \rho, \qquad -\lambda\cosh^{-1}\left(\frac{y}{\lambda}\right) = x + \rho, \quad \rho \text{ a constant.} \tag{2-63}$$

Now the two functions $\cosh^{-1}$ and $-\cosh^{-1}$ taken together form the inverse representation of cosh. Thus the two equations (2-63) are equivalent to

$$y = \lambda\cosh\left(\frac{x + \rho}{\lambda}\right), \quad \lambda \neq 0 \tag{2-64}$$

and the set of all solutions to (2-59) consists of the two parameter family (2-64) plus the function $y \equiv 0$.

The graph of (2-64) is called a *catenary*. It looks something like a parabola. It has $x = -\rho$ as an axis of symmetry and opens upwards if $\lambda > 0$ and downwards if $\lambda < 0$. If $\lambda > 0$, the smallest value of y is λ; and, if $\lambda < 0$, the largest value of y is λ. A catenary can never cross or touch the x-axis.

Let us now take the next step and find that catenary which passes through the points (x_0, y_0) and (x_1, y_1). We shall confine our attention to the case in which $y_1 = y_0$, for this case displays all the possibilities, and when $y_1 \neq y_0$ the analysis becomes quite tedious. It is clear that it makes no difference where on the x-axis we begin the interval of length $x_1 - x_0$. It will be convenient to take the midpoint of the interval to be the origin, so that $x_0 = -x_1$. Then

$$y_1 = \lambda\cosh\left(\frac{x_1 + \rho}{\lambda}\right) = \lambda\cosh\left(\frac{-x_1 + \rho}{\lambda}\right) \tag{2-65}$$

so that $\rho = 0$; that is, $x = 0$ is the axis of symmetry.

Consequently λ must satisfy the equation

$$y_1 = \lambda\cosh(x_1/\lambda).$$

If we write $u = x_1/\lambda$, the problem reduces to that of finding the solution or solutions to

$$\frac{y_1}{x_1}u = \cosh u \quad \text{or} \quad \alpha u = \cosh u, \quad \alpha = \frac{y_1}{x_1}. \tag{2-66}$$

Graphically, the solutions are the first coordinates of the points of intersection of the graphs of $v = \alpha u$ and $v = \cosh u$. The situation is illustrated in Figure 2.10. It will be noted that there does not always exist a unique solution to (2-66). There may be 0, 1 or 2 solutions, depending on the value

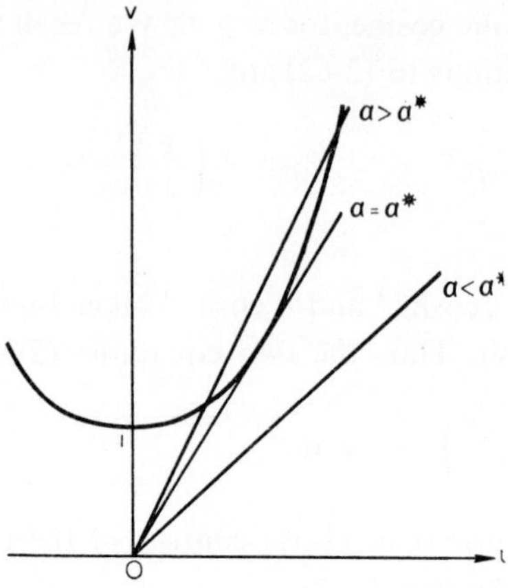

Fig. 2.10.

of $\alpha = y_1/x_1$. There is a unique solution when the line through the origin is tangent to $\cosh u$. Let us denote the slope of this line by α^*; α^* is approximately 1.5089. When $\alpha > \alpha^*$ there are two solutions, and when $\alpha < \alpha^*$ there is no solution.

We have run into some unexpected problems. There is only one razor's edge case in which there is a unique catenary passing through the specified points. This catenary does not touch the boundary $y = 0$ of $\mathscr{R}$; thus, if the minimum does exist and is an interior minimum, this curve must yield the surface with minimum area. Interestingly enough, the curve does *not* yield a minimum.

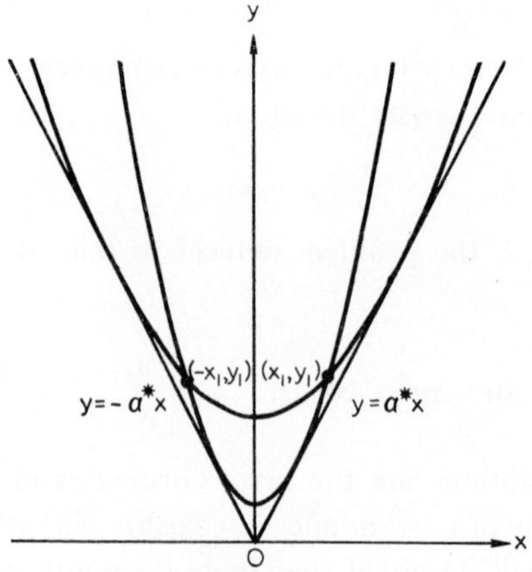

Fig. 2.11.

Let us next examine in a little more detail the case in which there are precisely two extremals which satisfy the given boundary conditions. Notice that as λ is increased the catenary $y = \lambda\cosh(x/\lambda)$ is moved up the y-axis and is spread out. In fact, this one parameter family of catenaries has the lines $y = \alpha^* x$ and $y = -\alpha^* x$ as envelope curves. This is illustrated by Figure 2.11. To prove that these lines are envelopes, one need only recall that the envelope curves for a one parameter family $y = f(x;\ \lambda)$ are found by eliminating λ between $y = f(x;\ \lambda)$ and $\partial y/\partial\lambda = 0$. Now

$$\frac{\partial y}{\partial \lambda} = \cosh\frac{x}{\lambda} - \frac{x}{\lambda^2}\sinh\frac{x}{\lambda} = 0. \tag{2-67}$$

When $y = \lambda\cosh(x/\lambda)$, (2-67) is equivalent to the differential equation $dy/dx = y/x$, which has the solution $y = \gamma x$. The values of γ must be chosen so that the graph of this equation is tangent to each catenary at some point. We have already noted that, for it to be tangent to the catenary $y = \cosh x$ when $x > 0$, we must choose $\gamma = \alpha^*$; $\gamma = -\alpha^*$ yields a tangent for $x < 0$. Thus the envelope curves are the graphs of $y = \alpha^* x$ and $y = -\alpha^* x$.

Figure 2.11 depicts a case in which two catenaries pass through the points $(-x_1, y_1)$ and (x_1, y_1). In this case, of course, $\alpha > \alpha^*$, for (x_1, y_1) lies to the left of $y = \alpha^* x$ and $(-x_1, y_1)$ to the right of $y = -\alpha^* x$. Should we conclude that the solution is not unique, with both extremals yielding the minimum, or that only one yields the minimum? We shall see later that the upper extremal, with the larger value of λ, yields the minimum while the other yields neither the absolute minimum nor a relative maximum or minimum.

Let us consider finally the case in which $\alpha < \alpha^*$ so that no extremal can be passed through the points. If y_1 is too small compared to x_1, a catenary would have to be quite spread out to pass through the points. However, a catenary which is spread out is associated with a large value of λ and crosses the y-axis at a large value of y; hence such a catenary cannot pass through

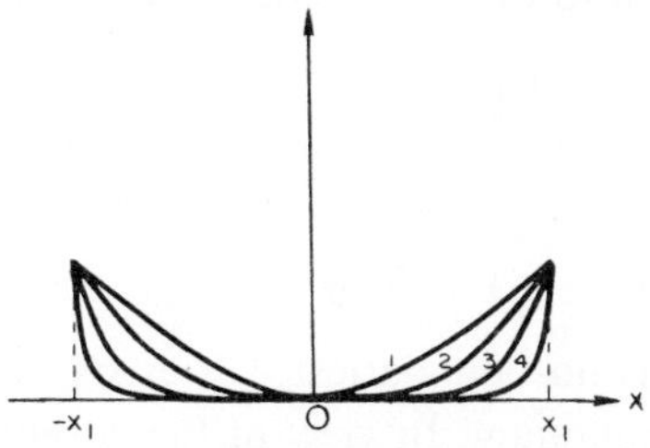

Fig. 2.12.

the given points. What then is one to make of this case? In Figure 2.12 we have shown several different curves which lie more and more on the x-axis. It happens to be true that the surface area decreases as we move from curve 1 to 2 to 3 to 4. In this case the minimum surface area is given by a broken curve, of the type shown in Figure 2.13, which consists of a segment of $y = 0$

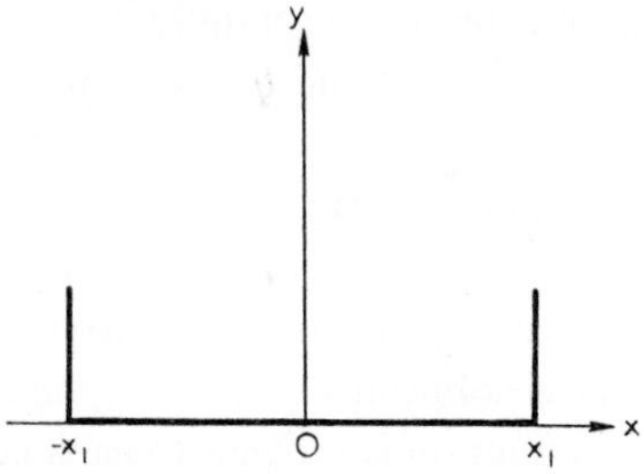

Fig. 2.13.

and segments of $x = -x_1$ and $x = x_1$; the surface consists of two circular disks and the area is $2\pi y_1^2$. Because of the vertical segments, this broken curve is not represented by a function $z(x)$; on the basis of our present formulation, therefore, it is not admissible. However, we shall later introduce an alternative parametric formulation in which the broken curve is admissible and hence yields the minimum area. In fact, the broken curve will be made up of extremals pieced together. We have already noted that $y = 0$ is a solution to the Euler equation. We now further note that if in this case the constraint $y \geq 0$ is replaced by $y > 0$, so that the x-axis is excluded, there is no minimizing solution; $\inf F[y]$ exists but there is no function (even in the parametric formulation) which yields a minimum.

This example has played an important role in the development of the calculus of variations. It shows that the solution of apparently very simple problems may involve many complications and require a considerable analysis.

3. Let us now return to the brachistochrone problem. From (2-4),

$$F = (2g)^{-\frac{1}{2}}[1 + (y')^2]^{\frac{1}{2}}[y_0 - y]^{-\frac{1}{2}}$$

and

$$F_{y'} = (2g)^{-\frac{1}{2}}y'[(1 + (y')^2]^{-\frac{1}{2}}[y_0 - y]^{-\frac{1}{2}}. \tag{2-68}$$

In this problem $\mathscr{R}$ has no boundaries; if it exists, therefore, the minimum must be an interior minimum. In view of the corner condition that $F_{y'}$ be continuous, and of the continuity of $z(x)$, we may infer from (2-68) that

$z(x)$ cannot have any corners and must be represented by a single extremal.

Since x does not appear explicitly in F, $z(x)$ must be a solution to the differential equation (2-56), that is,

$$[1 + (y')^2]^{\frac{1}{2}}[y_0 - y]^{-\frac{1}{2}} - (y')^2[1 + (y')^2]^{-\frac{1}{2}}[y_0 - y]^{-\frac{1}{2}} = \lambda \quad (2\text{-}69)$$

or

$$[y_0 - y]^{-\frac{1}{2}} = \lambda[1 + (y')^2]^{\frac{1}{2}}$$

with $y \leq y_0$ to avoid the square root of a negative number. On squaring,

$$[y_0 - y]^{-1} = \lambda^2[1 + (y')^2]. \quad (2\text{-}70)$$

There is no solution corresponding to $\lambda = 0$. For $\lambda \neq 0$, we have

$$y' = [\gamma(y_0 - y)^{-1} - 1]^{\frac{1}{2}} \quad \text{or} \quad y' = -[\gamma(y_0 - y)^{-1} - 1]^{\frac{1}{2}} \quad (2\text{-}71)$$

where $\gamma = 1/\lambda^2 > 0$ and, to avoid the square root of a negative number, $(y_0 - y)/\gamma \leq 1$. Thus the slope of an extremal will always be non-negative or nonpositive. Since it must go through the points $(0, y_0)$, $y_0 > 0$, and $(x_1, 0)$, the extremal must have a nonpositive slope. The equations (2-71) have separable variables, and the curve must pass through $(0, y_0)$; hence

$$x = -\int_{y_0}^{y} [\gamma(y_0 - y)^{-1} - 1]^{-\frac{1}{2}} dy. \quad (2\text{-}72)$$

At this point it is helpful to introduce a change of variable which yields a special form of parametric representation. Let

$$\frac{y_0 - y}{\gamma} = \sin^2 \frac{\theta}{2}. \quad (2\text{-}73)$$

This can be done since $(y_0 - y)/\gamma \leq 1$. When $y = y_0$, $\theta = 0$. Also, for some value of θ, $0 < \theta \leq \pi/2$, $y = 0$. (Ultimately γ is selected so that $x = x_1$ for this value of θ.) On applying (2-73), we see that, for $0 \leq \theta \leq \pi/2$, (2-72) becomes

$$x = \gamma \int_0^{\theta} \frac{\sin^2 \frac{\theta}{2} \cos \frac{\theta}{2}}{\left[1 - \sin^2 \frac{\theta}{2}\right]^{\frac{1}{2}}} d\theta = \gamma \int_0^{\theta} \sin^2 \frac{\theta}{2} d\theta = \frac{\gamma}{2} \int_0^{\theta} (1 - \cos \theta) d\theta.$$

Thus

$$x = \frac{\gamma}{2}(\theta - \sin \theta) \quad (2\text{-}74)$$

and, from (2-73),

$$y = y_0 - \frac{\gamma}{2}(1 - \cos\theta). \tag{2-75}$$

The curve described parametrically by (2-74) and (2-75) is known as a cycloid. It is the curve generated by a point on the circumference of a wheel moving along a horizontal surface without slipping. This result was quite surprising to the Bernoullis' contemporaries. We leave to Problem 6 the evaluation of γ and the verification that there is only one extremal which satisfies the boundary conditions.

4. We now consider an example in which $\mathscr{R}$ has no boundaries and yet the minimizing curve has a corner. Typically, this possibility is illustrated by the problem of minimizing

$$J[y] = \int_{-1}^{1} y^2(1 - y')^2 dx \tag{2-76}$$

where $y(-1) = 0$ and $y(1) = 1$. It is clear that $J[y] \geq 0$. Thus if there can be found an admissible function for which $J[z] = 0$ then there does indeed exist a minimum.

Here $F = y^2(1 - y')^2$ and $F_{y'} = -2y^2(1 - y')$; thus if a corner exists it must lie on the x-axis. Since F does not involve x explicitly, between corners $z(x)$ must satisfy

$$y^2(1 - y')^2 + 2y^2(y' - y'^2) = \lambda \tag{2-77}$$

or

$$y^2 - y^2(y')^2 = \lambda. \tag{2-78}$$

If $\lambda = 0$ then $y \equiv 0$ is a solution to (2-78); moreover, $y' = 1$ or -1 satisfies (2-78) so that $y = x + \gamma$ and $y = -x + \gamma$ are also solutions. If $\lambda \neq 0$ then y cannot be 0; hence we can divide by y to obtain

$$y' = \left(1 - \frac{\lambda}{y^2}\right)^{\frac{1}{2}} \quad \text{or} \quad y' = -\left(1 - \frac{\lambda}{y^2}\right)^{\frac{1}{2}}. \tag{2-79}$$

In the problems we ask the reader to find the solutions to these equations and to illustrate them graphically.

Of all the various solutions obtained none passes through the points $(-1, 0)$ and $(1, 1)$. However, it is possible to join two solutions together so that both the boundary and corner conditions are satisfied and so that, in addition, $J[z] = 0$. Such a solution does indeed yield the minimum.

It is $z(x) = 0, -1 \leq x \leq 0, z(x) = x, 0 \leq x \leq 1$, with a corner at $x = 0$. The reader should verify the above statements.

5. Consider the problem of determining the function which passes through the points (0, 1) and (1, 2) and which minimizes

$$J[y] = \int_0^1 y^2 dx. \tag{2-80}$$

It is clear that for any admissible function $J[y] \geq 0$. The Euler equation is in this case $F_y = 0$ or $2y = 0$, so that the only solution is $y(x) \equiv 0$. However, this solution does not pass through the points (0, 1) and (1, 2). If the specified points were (0, 0) and (1, 0) then the graph of $y(x) \equiv 0$ would pass through them and would indeed yield the absolute minimum. When the points do not lie on the x-axis, however, one is faced with a situation similar to that depicted in Figures 2.12 and 2.13. One can find functions $z(x)$ which yield a value of $J[y]$ arbitrarily close to zero but not zero. The limiting case shown in Figure 2.13 yields $J[y] = 0$, but this is not a function and is not admissible. Thus the problem does not have a solution when the boundary points do not fall on the x-axis.

The problem of minimizing

$$J[y] = \int_0^1 y^3 dx \tag{2-81}$$

where $y(0) = y_0$ and $y(1) = y_1$ leads to the same Euler equation $y \equiv 0$. In this case, however, $y \equiv 0$ does not yield the absolute minimum (or a relative maximum or minimum) for any values of y_0 and y_1. In this case $J[y]$ has no minimum and no infimum; $J[y]$ can be made arbitrarily small (that is, an arbitrarily large negative number).

6. Care must be exercised in specifying the boundary conditions; otherwise, there may not exist a maximum or a minimum. For example, suppose that we attempt to determine the curve of minimum length joining the origin to the point (x_0, y_0) such that the slope of the curve is 0 at the origin and a number $\beta \neq y_0/x_0$ at (x_0, y_0). No solution to the Euler equation can be found with these characteristics; the only solution to the Euler equation passing through the given points is the straight line joining them, and it has neither slope 0 at the origin nor slope β at (x_0, y_0). The difficulty, here also, is that although $\inf J[y]$ exists there is no minimum. It is possible to find curves which pass through the specified points with the specified slopes and which come arbitrarily close to yielding a distance which is the same as that

along the straight line joining the points; but equality of the two distances is unattainable. Thus a problem which at first glance seems perfectly well formulated turns out on closer inspection to be insoluble.

2.9. Ramsey's problem

We now turn to an example which illustrates very well how the material developed thus far can assist in the analysis of economic growth. It will also further illustrate the unpleasant fact that the solution of apparently simple problems may prove to be exceedingly complicated. The model we shall study was introduced by F. P. Ramsey of Cambridge in 1928 [30]. A considerable literature has developed concerning various aspects of this model and even at the present time it is the subject of a lively interest. Ramsey was perhaps the first to apply the calculus of variations to a problem in economic growth and his paper remains a classic in the field.

Ramsey's is a one sector model in which the rate of investment, that is, the time rate of change of the stock of capital, is viewed as a variable which the society can control as it sees fit. How should the stock of capital change with time? Briefly, Ramsey sought that time path of the stock of capital which maximizes a particular utility functional and which at the same time satisfies certain technical constraints on output. We now describe Ramsey's model in detail.

In Ramsey's world there is just a single homogeneous good which is produced with the aid of the stock of capital K and labor force L. However the labor force is assumed to be constant, so that production Y may be written as a function of a single variable $Y = \Psi(K)$. It will be assumed that Ψ, $\Psi \in C''$, is a concave function. It will be assumed also that there is no deterioration or depreciation of the stock of capital. Production is divided between consumption C and investment $\dot{K}$ ($\equiv \mathrm{d}K/\mathrm{d}t$). Thus

$$C + \dot{K} = Y = \Psi(K)$$

so that

$$C = \Psi(K) - \dot{K}. \tag{2-82}$$

We shall require that $C \geq 0$ (a negative consumption rate is not possible) and that $\Psi(K) \geq 0$ (a negative output rate is not possible). However, we shall allow $\dot{K}$ to be negative; since depreciation is assumed away, this implies that capital may be consumed.

That completes our description of the technological aspects of the economy.

The economy just described will be imagined to operate over all future time, that is, the 'planning horizon' is infinitely distant.

It remains to consider the utility functional the maximization of which determines the development of the economy through time. If there is specified an investment program $\dot{K}(t)$, the consumption rate C is determined as a function of t. As explained in Chapter 1, in developing a utility measure we are seeking to associate with each function $C(t)$ a number $\mathcal{U}[C(t)]$ which provides a numerical evaluation of the entire consumption program. The number is referred to as the utility of the function $C(t)$, that is, of the consumption program. This association defines a functional $\mathcal{U}$ on the function space consisting of all possible consumption programs.

There is no single, compelling way of defining $\mathcal{U}$. Ramsey defined $\mathcal{U}$ to be

$$\mathcal{U}[C] = \int_0^\infty U(C(t))\mathrm{d}t \tag{2-83}$$

where U is a real-valued, continuous, concave and non-decreasing function of the consumption rate. U may be viewed as measuring the 'instantaneous utility' or the rate of utility at any particular time t. We shall follow the common practice of referring to $U(C)$ as the utility function. Thus the numerical evaluation placed on a program $C(t)$ is the integral over all future time of the utility function $U(C)$. No discounting or weighting of utilities is admitted. This measure has a number of convenient properties, including that of time additivity (the rates of consumption of different periods make an additive contribution). It has the disadvantage, however, that in general, that is, in the absence of as yet unspecified restrictions on U and Ψ, the integral may diverge, implying that the domain of $\mathcal{U}$ cannot include all programs $C(t)$. Possible restrictions on U and Ψ will be considered shortly.

The reader may wonder how much freedom there is in the choice of U (and therefore $\mathcal{U}$) and how sensitive the optimal path is to the choice of U. The requirement that the contribution of consumption at different points of time make an additive contribution severely limits the choice of the $\mathcal{U}$. We shall prove in Appendix I that if $\mathcal{U}_1$ is one specific utility functional then every other utility functional $\mathcal{U}$ with the same additivity properties is related to $\mathcal{U}_1$ by a positive affine transformation, so that $\mathcal{U} = a\mathcal{U}_1 + b$, $a > 0$. This in turn restricts all possible utility functions U to the form $U = aU_1$, $a > 0$. Now the Euler equations and corner conditions are unchanged if F is replaced by aF. Thus for Ramsey's problem the optimal policy is invariant under the choice of utility function from the class of functions that can be used in place of U_1.

Our problem then is to determine the path $K(t)$ of capital accumulation which maximizes $\mathscr{U}[C]$, that is, maximizes the undiscounted integral of utility over all future time, with the initial capital stock given. In the notation of earlier sections, and after applying (2-82) to (2-83), our problem is that of finding the piecewise smooth function $K(t)$ which maximizes

$$J[K] = \int_{0}^{\infty} U(\Psi(K) - \dot{K})\mathrm{d}t \tag{2-84}$$

subject to $K(0) = K_0$. Thus the problem is of a type we have already discussed. we note that K and $\dot{K}$ are subject to the requirement that $C \geq 0$ and hence $\dot{K} \leq \Psi(K)$.

When the interval of integration is unbounded, the problem is properly formulated and our theory applicable only when the integral converges for the set of permissible functions $K(t)$. As we have noted already, this will not be true of (2-84) for an arbitrary choice of utility function and production function. For convergence of the integral it is necessary that U as a function of time goes to zero as t goes to infinity. And for the satisfaction of this condition it is necessary that either (a) there exists some finite value of K, say K^*, which is such that $0 = U[\Psi(K^*)] \geq U[\Psi(K)]$ for all K, or (b) $U[\Psi(K)]$ is an increasing function of K and $\lim_{K\to\infty} U[\Psi(K)] = 0$. Condition (a) is satisfied if U has the form depicted in Figure 2.15 and if, for some K, $\Psi(K) = C^*$; it is satisfied also if U is of the form depicted in Figure 2.16 and if Ψ has the form shown in Figure 2.15 (with Ψ substituted for U, K for C and K^* for C^* and with the origin of the vertical axis moved down) and reaches a maximum of C^* at K^*. Condition (b) is satisfied if U has the form displayed in Figure 2.14 and if Ψ is unbounded; it is satisfied also if U has the form of Figure 2.15 or of Figure 2.16 and if $\lim_{K\to\infty} \Psi(K) = C^*$.

Thus we may allow the utility curves to take any of the forms shown in

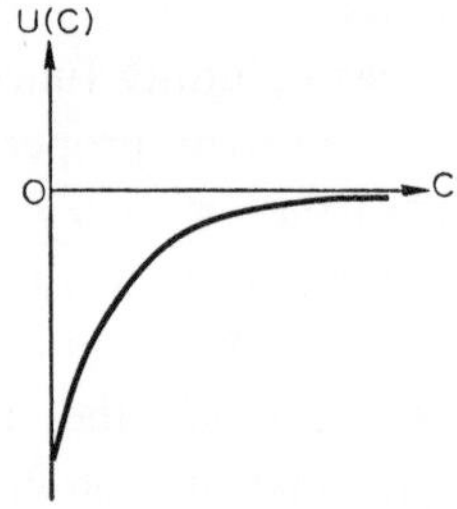

Fig. 2.14.

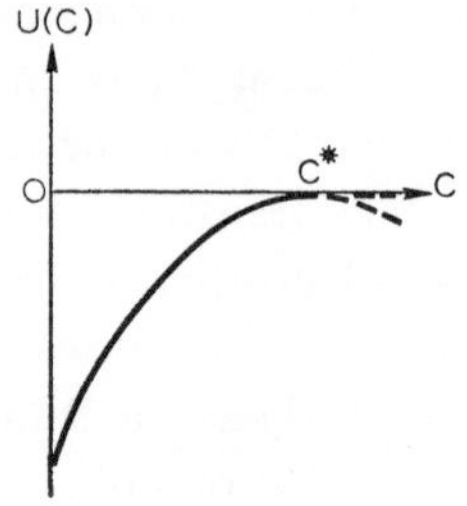

Fig. 2.15.

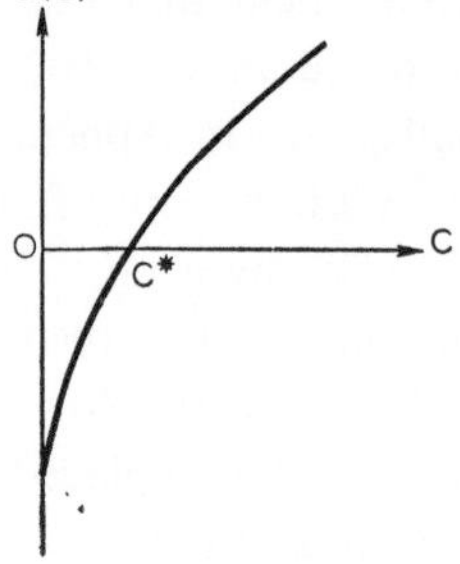

Fig. 2.16.

Figures 2.14 to 2.16. In Figure 2.14, $\sup U(C)$ exists but $U(C)$ does not possess a maximum; $\sup U(C)$ is approached asymptotically as C approaches infinity. In Figure 2.15, $\sup U(C)$ exists and there is at least one value of C for which $U(C) = \sup U(C)$. In Figure 2.16, $\sup U(C)$ does not exist. If $\sup U(C)$ exists it is customary to say that the utility function *saturates*. In Figure 2.15 the utility function saturates at a finite value of C; in Figure 2.14 it saturates as C approaches infinity. In Figures 2.14 to 2.16 the curves have been so drawn that $U(0)$ is defined. This is not something we insist on, however; it is permissible for $U(C)$ to have a vertical asymptote at $C = 0$ or for $U(C)$ to be defined only for values of C greater than some minimum positive value.

Similarly, we may allow the production function to have any of the forms illustrated by Figures 2.14 to 2.16. (Of course, the axes must be suitably relabelled and the origin of the vertical axis moved down.) The production function is said to saturate of $\sup \Psi(K)$ exists. It may saturate in either of the ways depicted in Figures 2.14 and 2.15.

Of the nine utility-production function pairs suggested by Figures 2.14 to 2.16, that containing unbounded utility and production functions must be omitted; for then the integral cannot be made convergent. On the other hand, for pairs containing utility and production functions both of which are bounded, it may be necessary to treat separately the case in which the upper bound on utility is the result of utility function saturation and the case in which, in the long run, utility is bounded because of production function saturation. Thus suppose that $U(C)$ is of the form represented in Figure 2.15 and that the graph of $\Psi(K)$ has one of the forms displayed in Figures 2.14 and 2.15. Whenever $C^* \leq \sup \Psi(K)$ we may say that the utility function determines the largest attainable utility; and whenever $C^* > \sup \Psi(K)$ we may say that the long-run upper bound on utility is determined by technological considerations. The behavior of the system may differ considerably from one case to the other; hence the two cases must be treated separately.

Thus we shall confine our attention to cases in which at least one of the functions $U(C)$ and $\Psi(K)$ has a supremum. We now define U^* as the supremum of levels of utility which can be maintained indefinitely. If the utility function has a supremum, we set $U^* = \sup U(C)$. If only the production possesses a supremum, we set $U^* = U[\sup \Psi(K)]$. Thus in every case U^* is defined; and in every case $U^* = 0$. Following Ramsey, U^* will be called the *bliss* level of utility.

We have placed severe restrictions on the set of admissible utility-production function pairs. Nevertheless, they do not by themselves ensure that the integral (2-84) converges or that we have a meaningful problem in the calculus of variations. We shall see later that in cases in which bliss cannot be attained with a finite stock of capital it is still possible for the integral to diverge (to minus infinity) for all feasible $K(t)$. However, if bliss can be attained with finite capital, there always exist admissible paths for which the integral is finite. (The proof is left to the reader as a problem.) Then it is possible, but still not certain, that $J[y]$ has a maximum.

That concludes our formal statement of Ramsey's problem. Before turning to the solution of the problem we note one slightly disturbing feature of it. Suppose that C^* is defined by the saturation of the production function at $K = K^*$: $C^* = \Psi(K^*)$. We then require that U be such that $U(C^*) = 0$. This means that any shift in the technical conditions of production which changes the value of K^* requires an offsetting change in U; otherwise, the problem ceases to be well posed. Of course, this precise dependence of preferences on technical conditions makes little economic sense. As mathematicians, however, we can perhaps swallow it.

2.10. Ramsey's problem–finite planning horizons

Ramsey assumed that the economy will operate for all future time and sought to maximize the integral of $U(C)$ over an infinite planning period. Before turning to Ramsey's problem we shall study the case in which the planning horizon is of finite length T and it is specified that K must have the value K_1 at time T. We then have $K(0) = K_0$, $K(T) = K_1$ and our problem is to determine the function $K(t)$ which maximizes

$$J[y] = \int_0^T U[\Psi(K) - \dot{K}]\mathrm{d}t. \tag{2-85}$$

If we write

$$F(K, \dot{K}) = U[\Psi(K) - \dot{K}] \tag{2-86}$$

this can be recognized as an example of the kind of problem we have already studied. The mathematics required for the analysis of a finite horizon is no easier than that required for the analysis of an infinite horizon; but a finite horizon is easier to visualize, and the possibility of non-convergence is avoided altogether. Moreover, problems involving a finite horizon have interesting properties of their own.

Economists usually are more interested in the general properties of a model than in explicit numerical solutions to special cases. However, it is sometimes very helpful to examine specific numerical examples; they provide insights into the behavior of the system and suggest general results which it may be possible to prove. Thus we shall begin with a specific example, that is, one in which specific forms are assumed for $U(C)$ and $\Psi(K)$. It is surprisingly difficult to construct examples for which the Euler equation can be solved readily, but in the example we have chosen this can be done.

Before considering the example, we offer a couple of general observations concerning Ramsey's problem. We note first that

$$F_{\dot{K}} = -U'[\Psi(K) - \dot{K}]. \tag{2-87}$$

Since U' is assumed to be continuous, the corner condition which requires the continuity of $F_{\dot{K}}$ also requires the continuity of $\dot{K}$; thus there can be no corners if the maximum is interior. Next, we note that t does not appear explicitly in F. (A system of this sort, in which the independent variable is time, is called *autonomous.*) It follows that if the maximum is an interior maximum, that is, if $\dot{K} < \Psi(K)$ always, then, at each point, $K(t)$ must satisfy the differential equation

$$U[\Psi(K) - \dot{K}] + U'[\Psi(K) - \dot{K}]\dot{K} = \lambda. \tag{2-88}$$

Let us now consider the specific example in which

$$U(C) = -\alpha(C - C^*)^2, \quad \alpha > 0; \qquad \Psi(K) = \beta K, \quad \beta > 0 \tag{2-89}$$

so that

$$U'(C) = -2\alpha(C - C^*). \tag{2-90}$$

The utility and production functions are graphed in Figures 2.17 and 2.18.

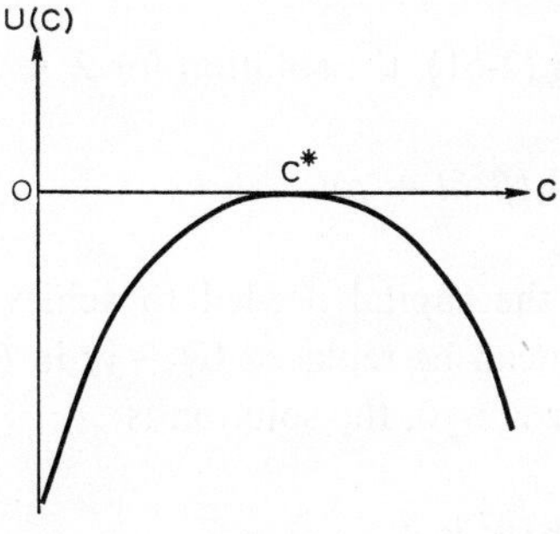

Fig. 2.17.

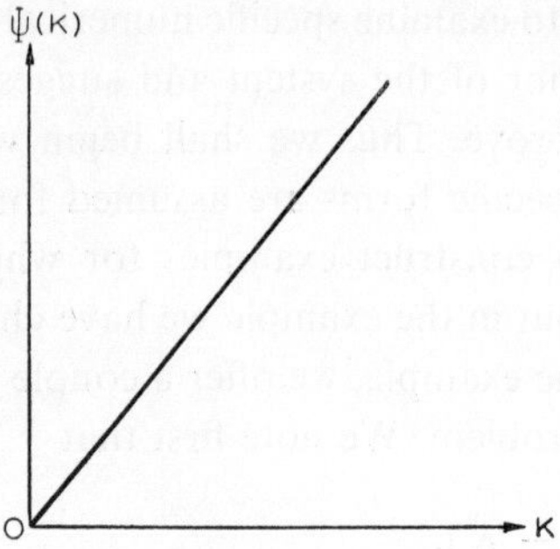

Fig. 2.18.

Under these assumptions (2-88) reduces to

$$-\alpha(C - C^*)^2 - 2\alpha(C - C^*)\dot{K} = \lambda \tag{2-91}$$

or, on completing the square,

$$-(C - C^* + \dot{K})^2 + \dot{K}^2 = \lambda/\alpha. \tag{2-92}$$

Since in this example

$$C = \beta K - \dot{K} \tag{2-93}$$

(2-92) reduces to

$$\dot{K}^2 - (\beta K - C^*)^2 = \lambda/\alpha = \gamma. \tag{2-94}$$

If we write $y = \beta K - C^*$ then

$$\dot{y}^2 = \beta^2|\gamma|\left[\left(\frac{y}{\delta}\right)^2 + 1\right], \quad \lambda > 0; \qquad \dot{y}^2 = \beta^2|\gamma|\left[\left(\frac{y}{\delta}\right)^2 - 1\right], \quad \lambda < 0;$$

$$\dot{y}^2 = \beta^2 y^2, \quad \lambda = 0 \tag{2-95}$$

where $\delta = \sqrt{|\gamma|}$. From (2-61), the solution for $\lambda < 0$ is

$$K = K^* \pm \frac{\delta}{\beta}\cosh(\beta^2\delta t + \rho) \tag{2-96}$$

where $K^* = C^*/\gamma$ is the capital needed to achieve bliss if all output is consumed. In (2-95), y can be replaced by $-y$; in (2-96), therefore, either sign may be taken. For $\lambda > 0$, the solution is

$$K = K^* \pm \frac{\delta}{\beta}\sinh(\beta^2\delta t + \rho) \tag{2-97}$$

where $\sinh u = (e^u - e^{-u})/2$ is the hyperbolic sine function. Finally, when $\lambda = 0$

$$y = \rho e^{\beta t} \quad \text{or} \quad y = \rho e^{-\beta t}$$

that is,

$$K = K^* + \zeta e^{\beta t} \quad \text{or} \quad K = K^* + \zeta e^{-\beta t} \tag{2-98}$$

the first expression holding on the line $\dot{K} = \beta K - C^*$ and the second on the line $\dot{K} = -(\beta K - C^*)$. Thus the solutions to the Euler equation are segments either of the hyperbolic sine or cosine functions or of exponential functions. The two constants of integration are λ (or, equivalently, γ or δ) and ρ; λ can have either sign, but $\delta > 0$.

Eventually we shall draw curves which show explicitly how K varies with time. We find it helpful, however, to first construct a phase diagram in the $K\dot{K}$-plane. A phase diagram, it will be recalled, shows the relationship between $\dot{K}$ and K and is merely a graphical representation of the relation (2-94). (Notice that for a first order differential equation the phase diagram can be constructed without first solving the equation. It is therefore an especially useful device whenever it is difficult to solve the equation.) There will be a different curve for each value of γ. When $\gamma = 0$, (2-94) is equivalent to $\dot{K} = \beta K - C^*$ and $\dot{K} = C^* - \beta K$, so that the graph in this case consists of two straight lines which intersect at the point $(K^*, 0)$ as shown in Figure 2.19. For $\gamma > 0$, the curves are hyperbolas which open upwards and downwards and have as asymptotes the lines corresponding to $\gamma = 0$. For $\gamma < 0$, the curves are hyperbolas which open to the right and to the left and again have the lines corresponding to $\gamma = 0$ as asymptotes. These also are shown in Figure 2.19. The direction of movement of the system along each of the curves is indicated. The direction is determined by the sign of $\dot{K}$; if $\dot{K} > 0$ then the system is moving in the direction of increasing K.

We can obtain a very good intuitive understanding of the behavior of the system by studying the phase diagram in detail. Let us consider the specific values of K_0 and K_1 shown in Figure 2.19. For an interior maximum, the economy will move along one of the curves, starting at $K = K_0$ and ending at $K = K_1$. There is, of course, an infinity of different curves along which the economy could move from K_0 to K_1. These differ one from the other, however, in the time required to go from K_0 to K_1. The higher curves have larger values of $\dot{K}$ all the way and hence reach K_1 in a shorter time than the lower curves. We can imagine therefore that each curve is labelled with a value of T, the time required to move from K_0 to K_1 (of course the labelling

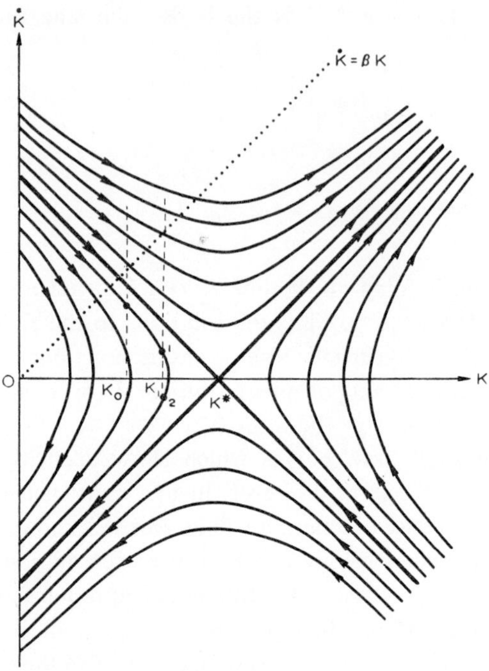

Fig. 2.19.

depends on K_0 and K_1). We thus see that the specification of T determines the value of γ. A small T corresponds to a large positive value of γ; as T is reduced γ decreases and finally becomes negative. An interesting type of behavior occurs when T is large, so that a long time is allowed for the economy to increase its capital from K_0 to K_1. Consider the curve marked 1, 2. The interesting thing about this curve is that the capital level K_1 is reached at two distinct points. It is reached first at point 1. However, if we continue along the curve, $\dot{K}$ continues to fall and eventually becomes negative; K at first rises above K_1 then, when $\dot{K}$ becomes negative, begins to fall, eventually returning to K_1 at point 2. This curve should therefore be labelled with two times, T_1 and T_2, with T_1 associated with point 1 and T_2 associated with point 2. This suggests that when T is sufficiently large it may be optimal to let K first rise above K_1 then later drop back to K_1 at time T. Of course, for this outcome it is necessary that capital consumption be possible. Notice that in general $\dot{K} \neq 0$ at T; that is, at the terminal point the economy is not consuming all it produces.

Since $\dot{K}$ can be negative, it is possible to specify that $K_1 < K_0$, that is, that the terminal capital stock be smaller than the initial stock. The smaller is T the lower on the diagram will we find the curve along which the economy must move. When T is sufficiently small, $\dot{K}$ will be negative from beginning to end. However, if T is sufficiently large, $\dot{K}$ will at first be positive, with K increasing before decreasing.

Bliss can be achieved with capital K^*; hence there is no good economic reason to set $K_1 > K^*$. On the other hand, there is nothing in the mathematics to prevent us requiring that $K_1 > K^*$ if we should perversely desire to do so. If that requirement is imposed, the system moves along one of the lines defined by $\gamma > 0$ until K_1 is reached. Notice that, at the point where $K = K^*$, $\dot{K} \neq 0$ and $\mathrm{d}\dot{K}/\mathrm{d}K = (\mathrm{d}\dot{K}/\mathrm{d}t)(\mathrm{d}t/\mathrm{d}K) = \ddot{K}/\dot{K} = 0$, so that $\ddot{K} = 0$. Thus the curve representing $K(t)$ has a point of inflection at $K = K^*$.

From the above discussion we can see that, for relatively small T, the curves representing $K(t)$ would look like those shown in Figure 2.20; each curve corresponds to a different value of K_1. Note that the curve for $K_1 > K^*$ has an inflection point where it crosses the line $K = K^*$. In Figure 2.21 we have drawn curves for the same values of K_1 but a larger T. Finally, in Figure 2.22 there are shown curves for the same values of K_1 but an even larger value of T. (In this figure the unit of time has been increased to compress the scale.)

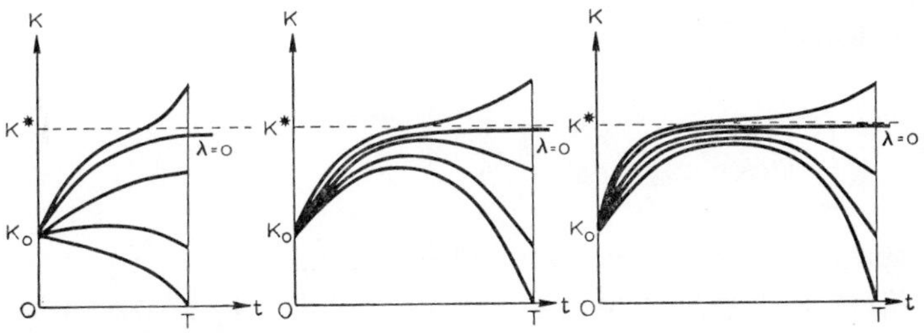

Fig. 2.20. Fig. 2.21. Fig. 2.22.

We have not considered cases in which $K_0 > K^*$, since this means that there is available initially more than enough capital to produce bliss. However, this case is allowable within the framework of the model, and the reader can easily follow through the various possibilities for himself. We note only that in the present case there is never more than one extremal which satisfies the boundary conditions. Thus never more than one curve will be labelled with any particular value of T. The present problem differs therefore from the earlier problem concerning the minimum surface of revolution, which involved the same sorts of solutions. The reason for the difference is that the constant of integration δ in (2-96) and (2-97) and the constant λ in (2-64) appear in different ways.

Utility U is a function of K and $\dot{K}$, since $U(C) = U[\Psi(K) - \dot{K}]$. The graph of U as a function of K and $\dot{K}$ is then a surface with a ridge running along the line $\dot{K} = \beta K - C^*$. At any point on the line $U = U^*$; that is, every point is a bliss point. On either side of the line utility falls off and has a value less than U^*. Notice that $(K^*, 0)$ is not the only point at which bliss can be maintained indefinitely. It is also possible to maintain $U = U^*$ indefinitely by moving upwards from $(K^*, 0)$ along $\dot{K} = \beta K - C^*$. In this case $C = C^*$ always and the remaining output is used to build up the capital stock unendingly. It is also possible to maintain bliss while moving from $(K^*, 0)$ in the other direction along $\dot{K} = \beta K - C^*$ with $\dot{K} < 0$; in this case, however, the capital stock is being eaten into and bliss can be maintained only for a finite length of time. When $K = 0$ is reached, there is a sudden fall from bliss and U changes discontinuously from U^* to $U(0)$.

Can we be sure that it is always possible to find an extremal which lies in the interior of $\mathscr{R}$? The answer is no. It is clear that if K_1 is sufficiently large, then for given T there will be no solution at all; the technology of the economy does not permit a sufficiently rapid accumulation of capital. At most the economy can devote all output to capital accumulation, so that $\dot{K} = \beta \dot{K}$ or $K = K_0 e^{\beta t}$. The minimum time T required to move from K_0 to K_1 is therefore

$$T_m = \int_{K_0}^{K_1} \frac{dK}{\Psi(K)} = \int_{K_0}^{K_1} \frac{dK}{\beta K} = \frac{1}{\beta} \log \frac{K_1}{K_0}.$$

This expression can also be obtained by setting $K = K_1$ and $t = T_m$ in $K = K_0 e^{\beta t}$, and solving for T_m. For the problem to possess a solution, therefore, it is necessary that $T \geq T_m$. The line representing $\dot{K} = \beta K$ is the dotted one in Figure 2.19. The economy moves along this line when growing at the fastest possible rate.

It will be recalled that we have imposed the additional constraint that $\dot{K} \leq \beta K$ at each point of time. In terms of Figure 2.19 this means that the point $(\dot{K}, K)$ must always lie on or to the right of the dotted line. That $T \geq T_m$ does not by itself guarantee that $\dot{K} \leq \beta K$ always. As may be seen from Figure 2.19, however, if $\dot{K} \leq \beta K$ initially then this condition will always be satisfied as the system moves along the extremal curve. What happens if there is no extremal with $\dot{K}(0) \leq \beta K_0$? Then there does not exist an interior maximum, and the problem lies beyond the scope of the theory we have considered so far. We might expect intuitively that in this case the economy at first moves along the boundary, with $\dot{K} = \beta K$ until K is sufficiently large, and then switches to an extremal curve. However, we shall have to postpone a detailed analysis of such behavior until we have examined the modern theory of optimal control. At this stage we merely note that analysis of even the simplest economic model points up the need for a theory more comprehensive than the classical calculus of variations.

We have not required that the consumption rate C be positive or that it not fall below some minimal value. C will certainly be 0 if the system ever moves along the dotted line representing $\dot{K} = \beta K$. Furthermore C can be arbitrarily close to zero initially along the extremals. To ensure that the consumption rate is always positive economists sometimes require that $U(C)$ approach $-\infty$ or that $U'(C)$ approach ∞ as $C \to 0$. An alternative and perhaps more natural procedure is to require that $C \geq C_m > 0$, that is, that at all times the consumption rate must have at least the subsistence value C_m. This merely generalizes the constraint from $\dot{K} \leq \beta K$ to $\dot{K} \leq \beta K - C_m$ and shifts to the right the dotted line in Figure 2.19. It affects our analysis only to the extent that it changes the points at which the boundary becomes active. A more complicated consumption constraint has the form $C \geq C_m(t)$ where perhaps $C_m(t)$ increases with t. This type of constraint cannot be conveniently represented in Figure 2.19, for in that diagram time does not appear explicitly; however it can be handled by the methods to be developed in later chapters.

Even in those cases in which it is possible to find an interior extremal which satisfies the boundary conditions, there still remains the question whether the extremal does indeed yield a maximum. We cannot answer this question now; however we shall be able to give a complete answer in a later section of this chapter.

To conclude this section we briefly consider a second example. Suppose that

$$U(C) = -U_0 e^{-\alpha C} + \mu, \quad \mu = U_0 e^{-\alpha C^*}; \qquad \Psi(K) = C^* - \beta(K - K^*)^2 \quad \text{for } \Psi \geq 0. \tag{2-99}$$

Then if $\gamma = \log|\rho|/U_0$, $\rho = \mu - \lambda$,

$$K = K^* \pm \beta^{-\frac{1}{2}}[\gamma + \alpha C^* - \dot{K} - \log(\alpha\dot{K} - 1)]^{\frac{1}{2}}, \quad \rho > 0 \tag{2-100}$$

$$K = K^* \pm \beta^{-\frac{1}{2}}[\gamma + \alpha C^* - \alpha\dot{K} - \log(1 - \alpha\dot{K})]^{\frac{1}{2}}, \quad \rho < 0 \tag{2-101}$$

$$\dot{K} = 1/\alpha, \quad \rho = 0 \tag{2-102}$$

and the phase diagram looks something like that shown in Figure 2.23.

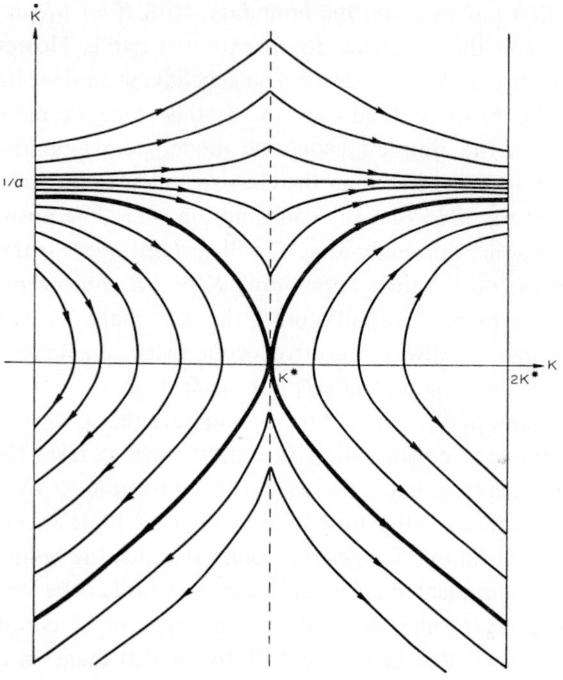

Fig. 2.23.

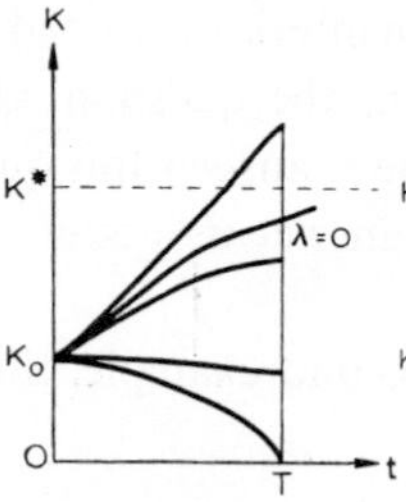

Fig. 2.24.

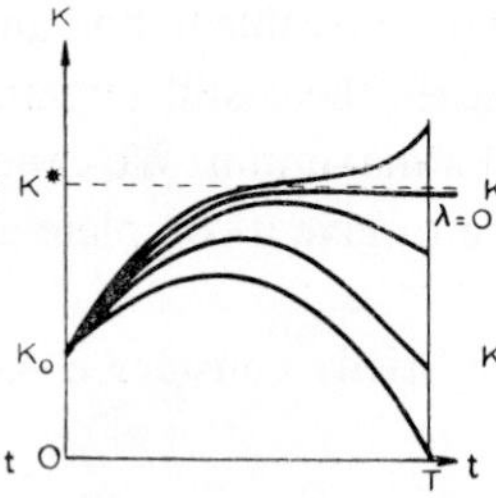

Fig. 2.25.

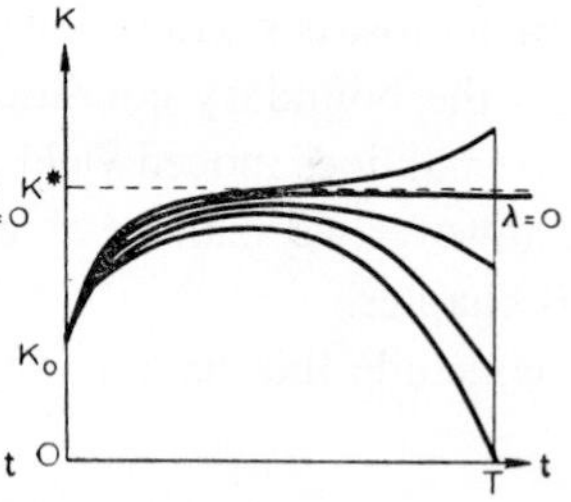

Fig. 2.26.

The curves for this case are displayed in Figures 2.24, 2.25 and 2.26; they are quite similar to the curves of Figures 2.20, 2.21 and 2.22, respectively.

2.11. Ramsey's problem–infinite planning horizons

We now turn our attention to the class of problems in which the planning horizon is taken to be infinite and it is imagined that the economy will continue to function for all future time. This, it will be recalled, is the class of problems considered by Ramsey. Our task is to determine the admissible function $K(t)$ which maximizes (2-84); in particular, we seek a function which satisfies $K(0) = K_0$ and $\dot{K} \leq \Psi(K)$. The case of special interest to us is that in which $C = \Psi(K_0)$ is too small to produce bliss, so that it is optimal to accumulate capital over time.

If there exists an interior maximum, we can be sure that $K(t)$ must satisfy the differential equation

$$U[\Psi(K) - \dot{K}] + U'[\Psi(K) - \dot{K}]\dot{K} = \lambda \tag{2-103}$$

over the entire interval, for in that case there cannot be any corners. A most important question concerns the value of λ. To this question we devote the present paragraph and the two following it. We note first that U must approach 0 as $t \to \infty$, for otherwise the integral cannot converge. What can be said about $U'\dot{K}$, the other term on the left of (2-103)? Suppose first that there is a finite capital stock K^* such that if $C^* = \Psi(K^*)$, then bliss $U^* = U(C^*) = 0$. Such a stock could exist because either the utility function or the production function saturates at a finite value. Then since it must be true that $U \to 0$, $C \to C^*$ as $t \to \infty$. In this case there is no need to build up the stock of capital above K^*; hence we may impose the condition that $\lim_{t\to\infty} K(t) = K^*$. Thus $\lim_{t\to\infty} \Psi(K) = \Psi(K^*) = C^*$. Since both Ψ and C approach C^*, and since $\dot{K} = \Psi(K) - C$, $\lim_{t\to\infty} \dot{K} = 0$. On the other hand, U' is bounded near 0. Hence we may conclude that $\lim_{t\to\infty} U'\dot{K} = 0$.

Consider next the case in which $\Psi(K)$ saturates but approaches the saturation value C^* asymptotically. Again $U^* = 0$ and $C \to C^*$ as $U \to 0$. Moreover, $t \to \infty$ it must also be true that $\Psi(K) \to C^*$; otherwise C cannot approach C^*. Hence $\dot{K} = \Psi(K) - C$ must approach 0. Since U' is bounded near 0, it then follows that $\lim_{t\to\infty} U'\dot{K} = 0$.

Consider finally the case in which $U(C)$ approaches 0 asymptotically as $C \to \infty$. Then $U'(C) \to 0$ as $C \to \infty$ and hence as $t \to \infty$. In this case $\Psi(K)$ cannot saturate for, to approach bliss, it is necessary that capital increase unendingly. Hence there is no requirement that $K(t)$ must satisfy as $t \to \infty$. We recall from Section 2.6 that in this case it is necessary that $F_{y'} \to 0$ as $t \to \infty$. This condition reduces simply to $U' \to 0$ as $t \to \infty$, a requirement we have already noted. What can be said about $U'\dot{K}$ in this case? If $\dot{K}$ is bounded or increases sufficiently slowly, then $U'\dot{K} \to 0$ as $t \to \infty$. In general, however, $\dot{K}$ may become arbitrarily large, as we shall see. It is therefore not at all obvious what happens to $U'\dot{K}$. It is in fact true, here also, that $U'\dot{K} \to 0$ as $t \to \infty$. However we shall prove this only later, with the aid of an alternative approach based on a parametric representation which handles all cases simultaneously. (See Section 2.14, Example 3.) Thus in every case $U \to 0$

and $U'\dot{K} \to 0$ as $t \to \infty$, that is, $U + U'\dot{K} \to 0$ as $t \to \infty$. However, $U + U'\dot{K} = \lambda$, a constant. In every case, therefore,

$$U + U'\dot{K} = 0 \tag{2-104}$$

along an optimal path. This is the basic result for the Ramsey model with an infinite planning horizon. The solution of (2-104) contains only one constant of integration, and this is determined by the requirement that $K(0) = K_0$. The paths corresponding to $\lambda = 0$ in the phase diagrams of the previous section are then the paths along which the system moves when the planning horizon is infinite.

Might it be possible and optimal to reach bliss in finite time? If so, is the possibility consistent with the analysis provided so far? It will be obvious that if bliss cannot be attained with finite capital then it cannot be reached in finite time. When bliss can be attained with finite capital, however, conditions can be imagined in which it would be optimal to reach bliss in finite time. (See Section 4.9 for an example.) Suppose then that it is possible and optimal to reach bliss at some time T. For $t > T$, $U = 0$ and $\dot{K} = 0$; and it will be noted that $U = 0 = \dot{K}$ is a solution to (2-104). Moreover, the corner condition requires that, at T, $\dot{K}$ be continuous; thus $K(t)$ must approach K^* from the left with zero slope. Thus the above analysis is valid whether or not bliss is reached in finite time; there is no need to know before solving the problem which case is relevant.

As with finite T, it is possible that the solution to (2-104) will imply that $\dot{K}(0) > \Psi(K_0)$, in violation of the constraint that consumption be non-negative. Again we must defer consideration of this possibility. We can show, however, that if $\dot{K}(0) \leq \Psi(K_0)$, then at no later time will the constraint ever be violated. Indeed if $U(C)$ is strictly concave, so that $U'' < 0$, then the rate of consumption must be strictly increasing whenever $\dot{K} \neq 0$. The following proof is valid both for finite and infinite planning horizons. Let $K(t)$ yield an optimal path for the given boundary conditions and let $C(t)$ describe the corresponding path of optimal consumption. Then in every case $U(C) + U'(C)\dot{K} = \lambda$. Also, $C + \dot{K} = \Psi(K)$. Differentiating both of these equations with respect to time, we obtain

$$U'\dot{C} + U''\dot{C}\dot{K} + U'\ddot{K} = 0 \tag{2-105}$$

$$\dot{C} = \Psi'\dot{K} - \ddot{K}. \tag{2-106}$$

Solving (2-106) for $\ddot{K}$ and substituting into (2-105), we obtain

$$U''\dot{C}\dot{K} + U'\Psi'\dot{K} = 0. \tag{2-107}$$

It follows immediately that if $U'' = 0$, so that U is merely weakly concave, then $\dot{K} = 0$ and $C = \Psi(K) > 0$; and that if U is strictly concave, so that $U'' < 0$, then

$$\dot{C} = -\frac{U'\Psi'}{U''} \tag{2-108}$$

whenever $\dot{K} \neq 0$ and the system is not at bliss; and that is what we wished to prove.

We now provide some examples to illustrate the sort of behavior which can occur when the planning horizon is at infinity. For some of these examples the integral is finite, so that a maximum actually exists, while for others it turns out that the integral does not converge and there is no maximum.

Examples. 1. Suppose that

$$U(C) = -U_0 e^{-\alpha C}; \qquad \Psi(K) = \beta K. \tag{2-109}$$

Then $U' = \alpha U_0 e^{-\alpha C}$, so that (2-104) becomes

$$U_0 e^{-\alpha C}(-1 + \alpha \dot{K}) = 0 \quad \text{or} \quad \dot{K} = 1/\alpha. \tag{2-110}$$

Here we have an interesting case, with $\dot{K}$ a constant. The reader might check that the only utility function for which $\dot{K}$ is a constant is the one given and that this is so whatever the form of $\Psi(K)$. Thus

$$K = \frac{t}{\alpha} + K_0, \qquad Y = \frac{\beta}{\alpha} t + \beta K_0, \tag{2-111}$$

$$C = \frac{\beta}{\alpha} t + \beta K_0 - \frac{1}{\alpha} = \gamma t + \delta. \tag{2-112}$$

If $U(t)$ denotes utility as a function of time then

$$U(t) = -U_0 e^{-\alpha\delta} e^{-\beta t} \tag{2-113}$$

and the integral has the value

$$J[K] = -U_0 e^{-\alpha\delta} \int_0^\infty e^{-\beta t} dt = -U_0 \beta^{-1} e^{-(\alpha\beta K_0 - 1)/\alpha}. \tag{2-114}$$

Thus the integral does indeed converge.

Figure 2.27 is the phase diagram representing the equation $U + U'\dot{K} = \lambda$ in this case. The horizontal straight line indicates the path followed by the economy when the planning horizon is infinite. The other curves correspond to finite values of T.

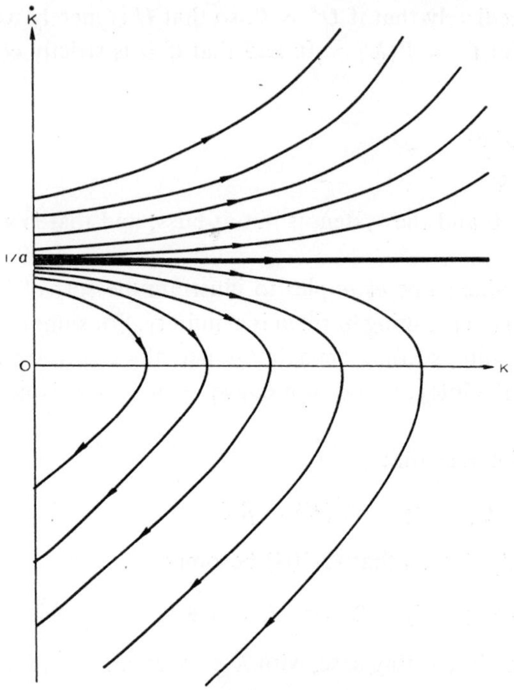

Fig. 2.27.

2. Suppose that

$$U(C) = -\alpha(C - C^*)^2; \qquad \Psi(K) = \beta K. \tag{2-115}$$

Then $U'(C) = -2\alpha(C - C^*)$ and (2-104) becomes

$$(C - C^*)^2 + 2\dot{K}(C - C^*) = 0 \tag{2-116}$$

or, on completing the square,

$$(C - C^* + \dot{K})^2 - \dot{K}^2 = 0 \quad \text{or} \quad (\beta K - C^*)^2 - \dot{K}^2 = 0.$$

Hence

$$\dot{K} = \beta K - C^* \quad \text{or} \quad \dot{K} = -\beta K + C^*.$$

The second equation is appropriate when $K_0 < C^*/\beta$, as we shall assume. Thus,

$$K = K^* - (K^* - K_0)e^{-\beta t}, \quad K^* = C^*/\beta \tag{2-117}$$

and

$$C = \beta K - \dot{K} = 2\beta K - C^* = C^* - 2\beta(K^* - K_0)e^{-\beta t}. \tag{2-118}$$

Utility at time t is then

$$U(t) = -4\alpha\beta^2(K^* - K_0)^2 e^{-2\beta t}. \tag{2-119}$$

The integral therefore converges and

$$J[K] = -2\alpha\beta(K^* - K_0)^2. \tag{2-120}$$

Notice that $\dot{K}(0) = \beta(K^* - K_0)$; if this is to satisfy the constraint then $\beta K^* - \beta K_0 \leq \beta K_0$ or $K^* \leq 2K_0$.

3. Let us next consider the case in which

$$U(C) = -U_0 e^{-\alpha C}; \qquad \Psi(K) = \beta \log(K + 1). \tag{2-121}$$

Then, as in Example 1, $\dot{K} = 1/\alpha$ and $K = (t/\alpha) + K_0$, so that

$$C = \beta \log\left(\frac{t}{\alpha} + K_0 + 1\right) - \frac{1}{\alpha} \tag{2-122}$$

and utility at time t is

$$\begin{aligned} U(t) &= -U_0 e^{-1} \exp\left[-\alpha\beta \log\left(\frac{t}{\alpha} + K_0 + 1\right)\right] \\ &= -U_0 e^{-1}\left(\frac{t}{\alpha} + K_0 + 1\right)^{-\alpha\beta}. \end{aligned} \tag{2-123}$$

Here we have a case in which the integral converges if $\alpha\beta > 1$ and diverges when $0 < \alpha\beta \leq 1$. We can also see that when $0 < \alpha\beta \leq 1$ the integral must diverge for every admissible function. For if there exists an admissible function for which the integral converges then there must exist a maximizing path; and if the boundary conditions are suitable it will be an interior maximum with $K(t)$ satisfying (2-104), implying that the integral converges for the solution to (2-104). This is a contradiction.

4. We now provide an example in which it is quite clear that the integral diverges for every admissible path. Suppose that

$$U(C) = -U_0 e^{-\alpha C}; \qquad \Psi(K) = \beta \log\log(K + e) \tag{2-124}$$

where e is the base of the natural logarithms. If K could increase as rapidly as $K = K_0 e^{\gamma t} - e$ (which it cannot) and if all output could be used for consumption, then

$$C = \log(\varepsilon + \gamma t), \quad \varepsilon = \log K_0$$

and utility at time t would be

$$U(t) = -U_0(\varepsilon + \gamma t)^{-\alpha\beta}. \tag{2-125}$$

The integral of utility would then diverge for $0 < \alpha\beta \leq 1$. Since for every admissible path $U(t)$ must be less than or equal to the value given by (2-125), it is clear that the integral in this case must diverge for every admissible path.

Throughout our discussion so far we have used K as the fundamental variable. We now note that it is also possible to use output $Y = \Psi(K)$ as the fundamental variable. Since $\dot{Y} = \Psi'\dot{K}$, Y is piecewise smooth and has no jump discontinuities. Thus Y has the required properties and can be used in place of K. If this substitution is made, the problem becomes one of determining how output Y should vary through time to maximize the integral of utility. In certain cases the computations are simplified somewhat by the use of Y. We now give a simple example in which Y plays the role of fundamental variable.

Suppose that

$$U(C) = -\alpha(C - C^*)^2; \qquad \Psi(K) = C^*(1 - e^{-\beta K}). \tag{2-126}$$

For simplicity we have arranged things so that $\Psi(K)$ saturates at just the output which yields $U(C) = U^* = 0$. Here $Y = C^*(1 - e^{-\beta K})$ and, inverting,

$$K = -\frac{1}{\beta}\log\left(\frac{C^* - Y}{C^*}\right). \tag{2-127}$$

It follows that

$$\dot{K} = \frac{1}{\beta}\left(\frac{C^*}{C^* - Y}\right)\left(\frac{\dot{Y}}{C^*}\right) = \frac{\dot{Y}}{\beta(C^* - Y)}. \tag{2-128}$$

In this case, equation (2-104) can be written as

$$(C - C^* + \dot{K})^2 - \dot{K}^2 = 0$$

or

$$(Y - C^*)^2 - \frac{\dot{Y}^2}{\beta^2(C^* - Y)^2} = 0. \tag{2-129}$$

Hence, on taking the positive square root (which is the appropriate one when Y must increase),

$$\dot{Y} = \beta(C^* - Y)^2 \tag{2-130}$$

so that

$$(C^* - Y)^{-1} = \beta t + \rho$$

or

$$Y = C^* - \frac{1}{\beta t + \rho}. \tag{2-131}$$

Thus, from (2-127),

$$K = -\frac{1}{\beta}\log\frac{1}{C^*(\beta t + \rho)} = \beta^{-1}\log C^*(\beta t + \rho) \tag{2-132}$$

so that

$$\dot{K} = \frac{1}{\beta t + \rho}$$

and

$$C = C^* - \frac{1}{\beta t + \rho} - \frac{1}{\beta t + \rho} = C^* - \frac{2}{\beta t + \rho}. \tag{2-133}$$

Utility at time t is therefore

$$U(t) = -\frac{4\alpha}{(\beta t + \rho)^2}. \tag{2-134}$$

Hence the integral converges and

$$J[Y] = -4\alpha\int_0^\infty \frac{dt}{(\beta t + \rho)^2} = -\frac{4\alpha}{\beta\rho}. \tag{2-135}$$

5. As still another example, let us suppose that

$$U(C) = -\frac{\alpha}{C + \delta}, \qquad \Psi(K) = \beta K. \tag{2-136}$$

Then $U'(C) = \alpha/(C + \delta)^2$ so that (2-104) becomes

$$-\frac{\alpha}{C + \delta} + \frac{\alpha}{(C + \delta)^2}\dot{K} = 0 \quad \text{or} \quad -(C + \delta) + \dot{K} = 0. \tag{2-137}$$

Hence

$$-(C + \dot{K} + \delta) + 2\dot{K} = 0$$

and

$$2\dot{K} = \beta K + \delta. \tag{2-138}$$

Therefore

$$\frac{2}{\beta}\log(\beta K + \delta) = t + \varepsilon$$

so that

$$K = \frac{1}{\beta} e^{\beta(t+\varepsilon)/2} - \frac{\delta}{\beta} \tag{2-139}$$

and

$$\dot{K} = \frac{1}{2} e^{\beta(t+\varepsilon)/2}. \tag{2-140}$$

It will be noted that in this case $\dot{K}$ increases exponentially with time.

Now

$$C = \beta K - \dot{K} = \frac{1}{2} e^{\beta(t+\varepsilon)/2} - \delta \tag{2-141}$$

and utility at time t is

$$U(t) = -2\alpha e^{-\beta(t+\varepsilon)/2}. \tag{2-142}$$

Thus the integral converges and

$$J[K] = -\frac{4\alpha}{\beta}. \tag{2-143}$$

Here we have an example in which bliss is approached asymptotically and $\dot{K} \to \infty$ as $t \to \infty$. At the beginning of this section we claimed, but did not prove, that $U'\dot{K} \to 0$ as $t \to \infty$. Let us check that this is indeed the case here. Substituting for C in $U'(C)$ we see that U' as a function of time is

$$U'(t) = 4\alpha e^{-\beta(t+\varepsilon)}.$$

This has been obtained by substituting $C(t)$ into $U'(C)$, not by differentiating (2-142) with respect to t. Thus

$$U'\dot{K} = 2\alpha e^{-\beta(t+\varepsilon)/2}$$

and it is indeed true that $U'\dot{K} \to 0$ as $t \to \infty$.

7. In this our final example the production function saturates asymptotically. Suppose first that the utility function saturates also and that C^*, the value of C which saturates $U(C)$, just happens to be $\sup \Psi(K)$. Thus we consider the razor's edge case in which the limiting output rate, if devoted entirely to consumption, just saturates $U(C)$. More specifically, we assume that $U(C) = -\alpha(C - C^*)^2$, $\Psi(K) = C^*(1 - e^{-\beta K})$ so that $U'(C) = -2\alpha(C - C^*)$ and the basic differential equation is

$$-\alpha(C - C^*)^2 - 2\alpha(C - C^*)\dot{K} = 0$$

or, on completing the square,

$$\dot{K} = C^* e^{-\beta K} \quad \text{or} \quad \dot{K} = -C^* e^{-\beta K} \tag{2-144}$$

Only the positive sign is relevant. Thus

$$K = \frac{1}{\beta}\log(\beta C^*t + \gamma) = \frac{1}{\beta}\log(\omega t + \gamma)$$

$$\dot{K} = \frac{\omega}{\beta}(\omega t + \gamma)^{-1}$$

and, from (2-144),

$$C(t) = C^* - \frac{2\omega}{\beta}(\omega t + \gamma)^{-1}.$$

Hence

$$U(C) = -\frac{4\alpha\omega^2}{\beta^2}(\omega t + \gamma)^{-2}$$

and

$$J[K] = -\frac{4\alpha\omega^2}{\beta^2}\int_0^\infty (\omega t + \gamma)^{-2}\mathrm{d}t = -\frac{4\alpha\omega}{(\beta\gamma)^2}.$$

Suppose alternatively that $\Psi(K)$ saturates asymptotically as $K \to \infty$ but the limiting output is not sufficient to saturate $U(C)$; thus, if $\sup \Psi(K) = C^*$, $U(C^*)$ is not the maximum attainable value of $U(C)$ and $U'(C^*) > 0$. Here we have a case in which $K \to \infty$ as $t \to \infty$ and it is not required that $K(t)$ approach a specified function as $t \to \infty$. Hence, from Theorem (2-62), it is necessary that $F_{y'} = -U' \to 0$ as $t \to \infty$. However, U' does not approach 0 as $t \to \infty$; instead it approaches $U'(C^*) \neq 0$. We conclude that in this case the necessary condition cannot be satisfied and there is no interior optimizing function. It follows that there is no function $K(t)$ which yields a finite value of $J[K]$; the integral must diverge in every case. On the other hand, in the razor's edge case considered in the preceding paragraph, $U'(C^*) = 0$ and the necessary condition is satisfied. The case in which $\Psi(K)$ saturates asymptotically is therefore a rather unusual one.

2.12. Samuelson's catenary turnpike theorem

An examination of Figures 2.22 and 2.26 suggests that, for large T, the optimal $K(t)$ lies close to K^* for a large part of the time. Of course the two figures correspond to two very special examples. However, this property happens to be common to all systems in which only a finite amount of capital is needed to reach bliss. That this must be true is fairly clear intuitively, for otherwise it would be possible to construct an admissible function which is close to K^* for most of the time and therefore gives a larger value of the integral. This observation provides the basis of a precise proof of what Samuelson [32] has called the *catenary turnpike theorem*. The theorem can be stated as follows.

Theorem 2.12.1. Suppose that bliss can be achieved with a finite capital K^* and that, given the initial condition $K(0) = K_0$, $K_0 < K^*$, there exists for every $T \geq T_m$ an admissible function $K(t)$ which maximizes

$$\int_0^T U\mathrm{d}t \text{ with } K(T) = K_1.$$

Suppose also that U and Ψ are concave functions and that the derivative of U or Ψ, whichever defines bliss, vanishes only once. Then given any $\varepsilon > 0$ and $\rho > 0$, however small, there exists a T^* such that, for all $T > T^*$, $|K(t) - K^*| < \varepsilon$ for an interval of time of duration at least $(1 - \rho)T$.

In other words, it is possible to choose T sufficiently large so that K does not deviate by more than ε from K^* for a fraction $1 - \rho$ of the total time, this fraction being as close to 1 as desired. The justification for calling the proposition the catenary turnpike theorem will be given below.

The proof is in principle very simple, but the details are quite space-consuming. We therefore provide a detailed proof only for the case in which bliss is defined by the saturation of the production function. For the time being we suppose that $K_0 < K^*$. We begin by constructing an admissible function $K_c(t)$ such that $K_c(t) = K^*$ and $\dot{K}_c(t) = 0$ for all t in the planning period with the exception of an initial interval of length T_a and a final interval of length T_b. In the initial interval we simply set $\dot{K} = \Psi(K)$ until K^* is reached; K^* will be reached in time

$$T_a = \int_{K_0}^{K^*} \frac{\mathrm{d}K}{\Psi(K)}. \tag{2-145a}$$

The value of

$$\int_0^{T_a} U\mathrm{d}t = U(0)T_a$$

along this path. If $U(0)$ is not defined, as when $U \to -\infty$ as $C \to 0$, we merely select some small consumption rate ξ, a constant, and use $\dot{K} = \Psi(K) - \xi$. Thus we have defined T_a and noted that the integral has some finite value Δ_1 over this interval.

Next, we observe that it is possible to move from K^* to K_1 in a finite interval of time T_b. If $K_1 > K^*$ we can set $\dot{K} = \Psi(K)$ and T_b is given by an expression like (2-145a). If $K_1 < K^*$, we can assign $\dot{K}$ an arbitrary negative value, say $-\omega$, so that $K = K^* - \omega t$ and $T_b = (K^* - K_1)/\omega$. The integral $\int U dt$ will have a specific value Δ_2 over this time period.

Consider now a time interval of length $T \geq T_a + T_b$, and let $K_c(t)$ have the characteristics that, for $0 \leq t \leq T_a$, K_c is determined by $\dot{K} = \Psi(K)$ (or $\Psi(K) - \xi$); for $T_a < t < T - T_b$, $K_c = K^*$ and $\dot{K}_c = 0$; for $T - T_b \leq t \leq T$, $\dot{K} = \Psi(K)$ or $-\omega$ according as $K_1 > K^*$ or $K_1 < K^*$. Then $K_c(T) = K_1$ and $K_c(t)$ is an admissible function. From $t = T_a$ to $t = T - T_b$ the system is in a state of bliss; hence

$$\int_{T_a}^{T-T_b} U dt = 0.$$

Regardless of the value of T, therefore,

$$J[K_c] = \Delta_1 + \Delta_2 = \Delta.$$

The optimizing function $K(t)$ must then have the property that for every $T > T_a + T_b$, $J[K] \geq \Delta$.

Given this observation, it is now relatively easy to prove the theorem. Suppose that ε and ρ have been selected. We wish to determine a T^* such that, for all $T \geq T^*$, $|K - K^*| < \varepsilon$ over an interval of length at least $(1 - \rho)T$.

Imagine that we have an optimal path. Consider first the interval or intervals during which $\dot{K} \geq 0$ and $|K - K^*| \geq \varepsilon$. If $K \leq K^* - \varepsilon$ then $U \leq U[\Psi(K^* - \varepsilon)] < 0$; and if $K \geq K^* + \varepsilon$ then $U \leq U[\Psi(K^* + \varepsilon)] < 0$. Thus $U(t) \leq \Lambda$, where Λ is the larger of $U[\Psi(K^* - \varepsilon)]$ and $U[\Psi(K^* + \varepsilon)]$. Let T_+ be the total length of the intervals during which $\dot{K} \geq 0$ and $|K - K^*| \geq \varepsilon$. Then the integral of U over these intervals is not greater than ΛT_+, $\Lambda < 0$.

It might be observed that the condition stated in the theorem, that U' or Ψ' vanishes only once, is needed here to guarantee that $U[\Psi(K^* + \varepsilon)] < 0$. For if U reaches its maximum at some finite value of C, say C^*, and thereafter maintains that level, and if $\Psi' > 0$ always, then $U[\Psi(K^* + \varepsilon)] = 0$ if $\dot{K}$ is sufficiently small that $C > C^*$.

Consider next the total period during which $\dot{K} < 0$ and $|K - K^*| \geq 0$. We offer four preliminary observations. First, $\dot{K}$ cannot be negative if $K_1 \geq K^*$. For if $\dot{K}$ were negative the path of K would not be optimal (as we ask the reader to prove as a problem). Second, if $K_1 < K^*$ then $K \leq K^*$ always. For suppose that $K = K^*$. Then $U + U'\dot{K} = \lambda$ reduces to $U'\dot{K} = \lambda$ and $\dot{K}$ is uniquely determined. Together with the assumption that both K_0 and K_1 are less than K^*, this rules out $K > K^*$. Next we note that when $\dot{K} < 0$, $\Psi(K) - \dot{K} > \Psi(K)$ so that, with bliss determined by production saturation, it is possible that $U > 0$. Finally, we calculate an upper bound for $\int U\mathrm{d}t$ over the interval during which $\dot{K} < 0$. Since $U(C)$ is concave and $U(C^*) = 0$ we have, for all C, $U(C) \leq U'(C^*)(C - C^*)$. Thus

$$\int U\mathrm{d}t \leq U'(C^*) \int (C - C^*)\mathrm{d}t. \tag{2-145b}$$

However,

$$C = |\dot{K}| + \Psi(K) \leq |\dot{K}| + \Psi(K^*) = |\dot{K}| + C^*. \tag{2-146}$$

Hence

$$\int U\mathrm{d}t \leq U'(C^*) \int |\dot{K}|\mathrm{d}t.$$

Now $\int |\dot{K}|\mathrm{d}t \leq K^* - K_1$, the upper bound to the decline in K. Hence

$$\int U\mathrm{d}t \leq U'(C^*)\,(K^* - K_1) \equiv \Delta_+ \geq 0 \tag{2-147}$$

say, where the integral is taken over the intervals during which $\dot{K} < 0$.

Let us now restrict the integral in (2-147) to the interval or intervals during which $|K - K^*| \geq \varepsilon$ and $U \geq U[\Psi(K^* - \frac{1}{2}\varepsilon)]$. By an argument similar to that just given, the value of this integral is not greater than Δ_+. An upper bound for the total period over which the integration is performed may be calculated in the following way. By assumption,

$$|\dot{K}| + \Psi(K) \geq \Psi\left(K^* - \frac{\varepsilon}{2}\right)$$

or

$$|\dot{K}| \geq \Psi\left(K^* - \frac{\varepsilon}{2}\right) - \Psi(K)$$

Hence

$$\begin{aligned}|\dot{K}| &\geq \Psi\left(K^* - \frac{\varepsilon}{2}\right) - \Psi(K^* - \varepsilon)\\ &\equiv m\end{aligned}$$

say. On the other hand, the total change in capital during the period when

$\dot{K} < 0$ is not greater than $K^* - K_1$. Hence the required upper bound is $T_0 = (K^* - K_1)/m$. Thus the total period during which $U \geq U[\Psi(K^* - \frac{1}{2}\varepsilon)]$ and $|K - K^*| \geq \varepsilon$ is not greater than T_0; and the value of $\int U dt$ during that period is not greater than Δ_+.

For the remainder of the interval during which $\dot{K} < 0$ and $|K - K^*| \geq \varepsilon$, $C \leq \Psi(K^* - \frac{1}{2}\varepsilon)$ and $U \leq U[\Psi(K^* - \frac{1}{2}\varepsilon)] = \Upsilon < 0$. If T_- is the total period of time during which $|K - K^*| \geq \varepsilon$ and $\dot{K} < 0$ then $\int U dt$ over this period is not greater than $\Delta_+ + \Upsilon(T_- - T_0)$.

Thus the integral of $U(t)$ over those intervals for which $|K - K^*| \geq \varepsilon$ is not greater than

$$\Delta^* \equiv \Lambda T_+ + \Upsilon(T_- - T_0) + \Delta_+.$$

It remains to consider the integral over the remaining time intervals, when $|K - K^*| < \varepsilon$. For the interval during which $\dot{K} < 0$ we have, by reasoning similar to that which yielded (2-147),

$$\int U dt \leq U'(C^*)\varepsilon \equiv \Gamma$$

say. This bound is independent of T. For the interval or intervals during which $\dot{K} \geq 0$, the integral is non-positive.

Thus the integral of U over the entire interval of length T must be not greater than $\Delta^* + \Gamma$; that is, $J[K] \leq \Delta^* + \Gamma$. However, if $K(t)$ is optimal, $J[K] \geq \Delta$, where Δ is the value of the integral over our original path and is independent of T. Thus

$$\Lambda T_+ + \Upsilon(T_- - T_0) \geq \Delta - \Delta_+ - \Gamma.$$

If Θ is the larger of Λ and Υ then

$$\Theta(T_+ + T_- - T_0) \geq \Delta - \Delta_+ - \Gamma$$

or

$$T_+ + T_- \leq \frac{\Delta - \Delta_+ - \Gamma}{\Theta} + T_0 \equiv \nabla \tag{2-148}$$

where ∇ is independent of T. Thus the length of time for which $|K - K^*| \geq \varepsilon$ is not greater than ∇. Let us now choose $T^* = \nabla/\rho$. Then for all $T > T^*$ the proportion of the time for which $|K - K^*| < \varepsilon$ is not satisfied is less than ∇/T, which is less than ρ. Thus, when $T > T^*$, $|K - K^*| < \varepsilon$ for at least a proportion $1 - \rho$ of the total time T, which is what we wished to prove.

We have carried out the proof only for the normal case in which $K_0 < K^*$. The theorem also holds if $K_0 \geq K^*$ and we ask the reader to modify the proof to cover this case. (See Problem 1.)

It is worth emphasizing that the theorem is valid only if $\dot{K}$ can be negative. If it is assumed that output once invested is 'bolted down' and ceases to be available for consumption, then $\dot{K} \geq 0$ and the theorem is no longer true. It is also worthy of note that the proof holds in all cases provided only that the maximizing functions exist; it is not necessary that the maxima be interior maxima. At one point we made use of the integrated Euler equation, but that part of the argument can be replaced by alternative reasoning which does not rely on the Euler equation.

Samuelson called his proposition the catenary turnpike theorem. The reason may be found in the shape, in one important case, of the solution curves in the tK-plane. That case is characterized by solution curves which lie always below the horizontal line $K = K^*$–the 'turnpike'. In a neighborhood of the turnpike the curves are approximately catenaries. In other cases, however, the solution curves do not have this catenary property. Thus solution curves which cross $K = K^*$ are essentially of the form $K = \delta + a \sinh bt$ when K is close to K^*. Close to $K = K^*$, indeed, all solutions are essentially cosh and sinh functions. (Earlier we provided an example in which the solutions are of the form $\delta - a \cosh bt$ or $\delta + a \sinh bt$ in the large; but that was an exceptional case.) The proof consists in showing that when K is close to K^* the Euler equation becomes essentially $\ddot{y} - ay = 0, a > 0$, with characteristic costs which are real and opposite in sign. We leave it for the reader to demonstrate that the Euler equation is essentially of the form stated when K is close to K^*. (See Problem 4.)

Ramsey assumed that the sizes of the population and labor force are fixed. However, it is a simple matter to modify the model to allow for the possibility that the population and labor force grow exponentially at the rate γ, so that $\dot{L} = \gamma L$, $L(t)$ being the size of the labor force at time t. This can be done by introducing per capita quantities, as in our discussion of Solow's model in Section 1.2. Although there is a slight change in economic interpretation, the resulting model is mathematically equivalent to the original Ramsey model.

We now set down the model with exponential growth of labor and note how the catenary turnpike theorem should be interpreted in this case. Reverting to the notation of Section 1.2, and denoting by i the rate of saving or investment per capita, we have

$$c + i = \psi(k); \qquad \psi(k) \equiv \Psi(K/L, 1) \tag{2-149}$$

$$\dot{k} = i - \gamma k \tag{2-150}$$

so that

$$c + \dot{k} = \psi(k) - \gamma k \tag{2-151}$$

where

$$i \leq \psi(k) \quad \text{or} \quad \dot{k} + \gamma k \leq \psi(k). \tag{2-152}$$

Introducing the new function

$$\phi(k) = \psi(k) - \gamma k \tag{2-153}$$

equations (2-151 and (2-152) become

$$c + \dot{k} = \phi(k), \quad \dot{k} \leq \phi(k). \tag{2-154}$$

If we now seek to maximize the integral of the utility of *per capita* consumption, our mathematical problem is the same as Ramsey's. Note, however, that $\phi(k)$ is not the production function but $\psi(k) - \gamma k$. It is this fact which makes for the difference in economic interpretation.

Once again, if the integral is to be finite it is necessary that either $\phi(k)$ or the utility function $U(c)$ saturate. The same cases emerge as under Ramsey's assumptions. However, saturation of $\phi(k)$ in the present case does not imply saturation of the production function but rather the existence of a maximum of $\psi(k) - \gamma k$. Economists usually assume that $\phi(k)$ saturates at some finite value k^* (as in Figures 2.28 and 2.29) and that $U^* \equiv U(\phi(k^*)) =$

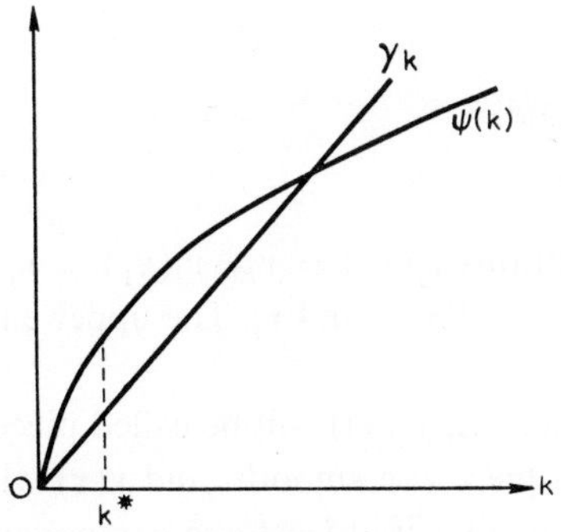

Fig. 2.28.

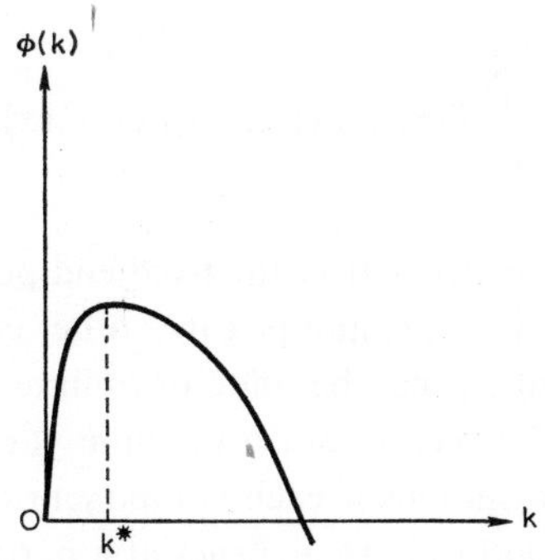

Fig. 2.29.

0, with $U(\phi)$ an increasing function; and we shall do the same. As with Ramsey's model, it is not possible to achieve a constant higher utility for more than a finite time (and then only at the expense of decreasing k). The turnpike is the line $k = k^*$, along which consumption per capita is at its maximum maintainable level. Here also the catenary turnpike theorem holds, with no modification in the proof: for T sufficiently large, the optimizing function $k(t)$ will satisfy $|k - k^*| < \varepsilon$ for at least a fraction $1 - \eta$ of the total time T. Notice that in the present case $\dot{k}$ can be negative without $\dot{K}$ being negative; if we set $\dot{K} = 0$, so that K remains constant, k will decrease as the result of population growth.

Ramsey's model can be modified in many other ways. The integral might be generalized to accommodate the possibility of utility discounting; capital might be allowed to depreciate; technical improvements might be allowed for; and so on. Some of these possibilities will be considered in the problems.

After a long digression to illustrate how a simple economic growth model can be handled by variational methods, we can now return to our exposition of the calculus of variations. For illustrative purposes we shall continue to rely on Ramsey's model or simple extensions of it.

2.13. Generalization to n functions

The variational problem to which we have devoted most attention so far is that of determining a single real-valued function which optimizes a specified integral and the value of which is specified at the end points of the interval of integration. We now seek to generalize by studying the problem of determining n real-valued functions $y_1(x), \ldots, y_n(x)$ which maximize or minimize the integral

$$\int_{x_0}^{x_1} F(x, y_1(x), \ldots, y_n(x), y_1'(x), \ldots, y_n'(x))\mathrm{d}x$$

and which satisfy the fixed end point conditions $y_j(x_0) = y_{j0}, y_j(x_1) = y_{j1}$, $j = 1, \ldots, n$, and possibly other constraints on the y_j and y_j'. The upper end point x_1 may be finite or infinite.

The vector-valued function $\mathbf{y}(x) = (y_1(x), \ldots, y_n(x))$ will be called piecewise smooth if each component of $\mathbf{y}(x)$ is piecewise smooth; and $\mathbf{y}(x)$ will be said to have a corner at a particular value of x if at least one component of $\mathbf{y}(x)$ has a corner at that value of x. A function $\mathbf{y}(x)$ will be called an *admissible function* if it is piecewise smooth, has a finite number of corners, satisfies the boundary conditions $\mathbf{y}(x_0) = \mathbf{y}_0$ and $\mathbf{y}(x_1) = \mathbf{y}_1$, and has the property that for each x, $x_0 \leq x \leq x_1$, the point $(x, \mathbf{y}(x), \mathbf{y}'(x))$ lies in some subset $\mathscr{R}$ of the extended phase space $\mathscr{E}^{2n+1}$ of points $(x, \mathbf{y}, \mathbf{y}')$. Now let us suppose that F is a real-valued function defined on the extended phase space $\mathscr{E}^{2n+1}$ of points $(x, \mathbf{y}, \mathbf{y}')$, with $F \in C''$ over an open set which includes

$\mathscr{R}$. Then the problem may be reformulated as that of finding the admissible function $\mathbf{z}(x)$ which maximizes or minimizes

$$J[\mathbf{y}] = \int_{x_0}^{x_1} F(x, \mathbf{y}(x), \mathbf{y}'(x))dx \tag{2-155}$$

or showing that no such function exists.

The optimum is an interior optimum if there exists a P_ε neighborhood of $\mathbf{z}(x)$ which lies in $\mathscr{R}$ (the notion of a P_ε neighborhood generalizes easily from the case $n = 1$). Suppose then that $\mathbf{z}(x)$ is an admissible function which optimizes $J[\mathbf{y}]$ and which everywhere lies in the interior of $\mathscr{R}$. Then we can derive a generalized set of necessary conditions which $\mathbf{z}(x)$ must satisfy.

Generalization from $n = 1$ poses similar problems in the calculus of variations as in the theory of ordinary maxima and minima. It will be recalled that in the theory of ordinary maxima and minima the necessary conditions are obtained by changing just one variable at a time, so that the n-variable case is reduced to the one-variable case; in the latter case the necessary condition for an interior maximum or minimum is $f'(x) = 0$, in the n-variable case it is $f_{x_j} = 0, j = 1, \ldots, n$. In the calculus of variations we compare $J[\mathbf{z}]$ with $J[\mathbf{y}]$ for functions $\mathbf{y}(x)$ only one component of which differs from $\mathbf{z}(x)$. Let a and b be two values of x such that $\mathbf{z}(x)$ has no corner in the interval $a < x < b$ and let $\eta(x)$ be defined as on page 29. Consider now the functions $\mathbf{y}(x; \xi) = \mathbf{z}(x) + \xi\eta(x)\mathbf{e}_u$, where $\mathbf{e}_u$ is the uth unit vector. Thus only for $j = u$ does $y_j(x)$ differ from $z_j(x)$. When ξ is sufficiently close to 0, each such function is admissible. For these functions $J[\mathbf{y}]$ becomes a function $\Phi(\xi)$ which has a relative maximum at $\xi = 0$. The arguments of Section 2.6 show that $\Phi'(0)$ exists and that

$$\Phi'(0) = \int_a^b [F_{y_u}\eta + F_{y_u'}\eta']dx = 0. \tag{2-156}$$

Applying the fundamental lemma of Section 2.6, we then conclude that $\mathbf{z}(x)$ must satisfy the differential equation

$$\frac{d}{dx} F_{y_u'} - F_{y_u} = 0.$$

This must be true for each u. Thus, for any interval which does not contain a corner of $\mathbf{z}(x)$ in its interior, $\mathbf{z}(x)$ must satisfy the n differential equations

$$\frac{d}{dx} F_{y_j'} - F_{y_j} = 0, \quad j = 1, \ldots, n. \tag{2-157a}$$

These are referred to as the Euler equations. Each of the equations is normally of the second order and nonlinear. In principle, each equation can involve all n functions $y_j(x)$; thus the equations are linked together and it is not possible to solve one independently of the others. Generally speaking, solution is difficult; indeed one cannot be sure that the general solution will be expressible in terms of familiar functions. Even approximate solution, with the aid of numerical methods, presents many difficulties.

It is often convenient to write the Euler equations in vector form. If $\mathbf{F}_{\mathbf{y}'}$ is the vector the jth component of which is $F_{y_j'}$ and if $\mathbf{F}_{\mathbf{y}}$ is the vector the jth component of which is F_{y_j} then (2-157a) can be written

$$\frac{d}{dx}\mathbf{F}_{\mathbf{y}'} - \mathbf{F}_{\mathbf{y}} = \mathbf{0}. \tag{2-157b}$$

When we have in mind the individual equations we shall refer to the Euler equation*s*, i.e. (2-157a), and when we have in mind the whole set of equations we shall refer to the Euler equation, i.e. (2-157b). This terminology will be applied to all equations which can be represented in vector form.

Suppose that $\mathbf{z}(x)$ has a corner at x^*. We can obtain the conditions which must be satisfied at x^* by means of exactly the same reasoning as was employed in Section 2.6. An interval with end points a and b is chosen so that $a < x^* < b$ and so that the corner at x^* is the only one in the interior of the interval. Then, defining $\eta(x)$ as on page 35 and considering the functions $\mathbf{y}(x) = \mathbf{z}(x) + \xi\eta(x)\mathbf{e}_u$, in which only the uth component of $\mathbf{y}(x)$ differs from $\mathbf{z}(x)$, we find, by the reasoning of Section 2.6, that at x^*

$$F_{y_u'}(x^*, \mathbf{z}(x^*), \mathbf{z}'_-(x^*)) = F_{y_u'}(x^*, \mathbf{z}(x^*), \mathbf{z}'_+(x^*)) \tag{2-158a}$$

so that $F_{y_u'}$ is continuous across the corner. (2-158a) must hold for $u = 1, \ldots, n$. Thus each of the n functions $F_{y_j'}$ must be continuous across any corner. The corner conditions can be written in vector form as

$$\mathbf{F}_{\mathbf{y}'}(x^*, \mathbf{z}(x^*), \mathbf{z}'_-(x^*)) = \mathbf{F}_{\mathbf{y}'}(x^*, \mathbf{z}(x^*), \mathbf{z}'_+(x^*)). \tag{2-158b}$$

Thus we have proved the following basic theorem, which is the equivalent for vector-valued functions of Theorem 2.6.1.

Theorem 2.13.1. Necessary Conditions: Euler Equations, and Corner Conditions. Suppose that $\mathbf{z}(x)$ *is an admissible function which yields an interior maximum or minimum of* $J[\mathbf{y}]$. *Then:*

(1) *In any interval* $a \le x \le b$ *which does not contain a corner of* $\mathbf{z}(x)$ *in its interior,* $\mathbf{z}(x)$ *satisfies the system of n Euler equations*

$$\frac{d}{dx}F_{y_j'} - F_{y_j} = 0, \quad j = 1, \ldots, n \tag{2-159}$$

at each point in the interval.

(2) *Each of the n functions* $F_{y_j'}$ *is continuous across any corner of* $\mathbf{z}(x)$ *(the Weierstrass-Erdman corner conditions).*

The above theorem applies whether or not the interval of integration is of finite length. Let us now consider the case in which the interval is infinite. In this case there are no conditions of the form $\mathbf{y}(x_1) = \mathbf{y}_1$. If we are to determine the $2n$ constants appearing in the solutions to (2-159), we must find n new conditions to replace them. For some or all components of $\mathbf{y}(x)$ there may be imposed the condition that

$$\lim_{x\to\infty} y_j(x) = f_j(x). \tag{2-160}$$

If there is no condition of this sort then, from the reasoning of Section 2.6, we have

$$\lim_{x\to\infty} F_{y_j'}(x, \mathbf{y}(x), \mathbf{y}'(x)) = 0 \tag{2-161}$$

for each j such that, for arbitrarily large x, $y_j(x)$ can differ from $z_j(x)$. The following theorem must then hold.

Theorem 2.13.2. Additional Necessary Conditions when the Upper Limit on the Integral is Infinity. Suppose that the upper limit on the integral (2-155) *is* ∞. *Then if* $\mathbf{z}(x)$ *is an admissible function which maximizes or minimizes* $J[\mathbf{y}]$ *it must satisfy the necessary conditions of Theorem 2.13.1 and, in addition,* $\lim_{x\to\infty} F_{y_j'}\,\eta_j = 0$. *Consequently, if it is not required that* $\lim_{x\to\infty} (z_j(x) - f_j(x)) = 0$ *then it must be true that* $\lim_{x\to\infty} F_{y_j'}(x, \mathbf{z}(x), \mathbf{z}'(x)) = 0$.

Example. Consider the problem of finding the piecewise smooth curve of minimum length joining the origin to the point $(x_0, \mathbf{y}_0)$ in $\mathscr{E}^3$. This is a generalization of the example for the plane considered previously. If we suppose that the curve is described by the functions $y_1(x)$ and $y_2(x)$, and hence is the set of points $(x, y_1(x), y_2(x))$, then our problem is to determine the functions $y_1(x)$ and $y_2(x)$ which minimize

$$J[\mathbf{y}] = \int_0^{x_0} [1 + (y_1')^2 + (y_2')^2]^{\frac{1}{2}} dx.$$

This is a problem of the type we have just been considering. Here $F_{y_1} \equiv 0$ and $F_{y_2} \equiv 0$. Also

$$F_{y_1'} = [1 + (y_1')^2 + (y_2')^2]^{-\frac{1}{2}} y_1'; \qquad F_{y_2'} = [1 + (y_1')^2 + (y_2')^2]^{-\frac{1}{2}} y_2'.$$

Thus the Euler equations reduce to

$$\frac{\mathrm{d}}{\mathrm{d}x} F_{y_1'} = 0; \qquad \frac{\mathrm{d}}{\mathrm{d}x} F_{y_2'} = 0$$

so that $F_{y_1'} = \lambda_1$ and $F_{y_2'} = \lambda_2$. From these latter equations one obtains

$$(y_2')^2 = \frac{\lambda_2(1 - \lambda_1)}{\lambda_1 \lambda_2 - (\lambda_2 - 1)(\lambda_1 - 1)}$$

so that y_2' is a constant. Similarly, y_1' is a constant and the solutions to the Euler equations are straight lines in $\mathscr{E}^3$, as expected.

2.14. Parametric representation

We normally think of the set of points $\mathscr{G} = \{(x, y) \mid y = y(x)\}$ in $\mathscr{E}^2$ as a curve and, similarly, the set of points $\mathscr{G} = \{(x, \mathbf{y}) \mid \mathbf{y} = \mathbf{y}(x)\}$ as a 'curve' in $\mathscr{E}^{n+1}$. In each case the curve is a graph of a function. Sometimes it is convenient to represent the graph $\mathscr{G}$ of a function in an alternative way, referred to as a parametric representation. To achieve a parametric representation, we introduce a new variable called the parameter and denoted by τ. Both x and $\mathbf{y}$ are made functions of τ, so that the set of points $(x(\tau), \mathbf{y}(\tau))$ generated as τ ranges over its possible values is precisely $\mathscr{G}$. For example, the function $y = ax^2 + b$, $x > 0$ can be represented parametrically by $x = \log \tau$ and $y = a(\log \tau)^2 + b$, $\tau > 0$. This is just one of many possible parametric representations of the function. In the simplest imaginable parametric representation, $x = \tau$, so that τ is merely another name for x. A parametric representation $(x(\tau), \mathbf{y}(\tau))$ can be converted into a function $\mathbf{y}(x)$ if $\mathring{x}(\tau) > 0$ always (open dots will be used to denote differentiation with respect to the parameter τ); for in this case $x(\tau)$ has an inverse. Let us call the inverse $f(x)$. Then $\mathbf{y}(\tau)$ is simply the compound function $\mathbf{y}[f(x)]$.

Not only the graphs of functions (or, equivalently, functions) can be given a parametric representation; complicated closed curves, which otherwise would have to be represented as the union of the graphs of two or more functions can be conveniently represented parametrically. This is one of the great advantages of the parametric representation, at least in certain types of problems. Thus the circle with center at the origin and radius r can be represented parametrically by $x = r \cos \tau$, $y = r \sin \tau$, $0 \leq \tau \leq 2\pi$.

When a curve is represented parametrically, we usually associate a direction with the curve; this is the direction in which a point moves along the curve as τ is increased. In practice parametric representations often arise very naturally. Consider, for example, a curve in the $K\dot{K}$-phase plane of the type encountered in our study of the Ramsey model. Such a curve can be represented parametrically by specifying the functions $K(t)$ and $K'(t)$; the natural parameter here is t and the direction associated with the curve is the direction in which the system moves as time elapses.

In handling certain types of variational problems it is essential that a parametric representation be used. There are other types of problems in which a parametric representation makes it possible to prove rather easily propositions which otherwise could be proved only with difficulty. In this section we shall provide a general parametric formulation of the basic n-function problem (2-155) and then discuss some applications of the parametric method. Consider the problem (2-155) and suppose that we introduce a parametric representation $x(\tau)$ and $\mathbf{y}(\tau)$. For this representation to be admissible we shall require that $x(\tau)$ be a monotonic increasing function of τ, so that $x(\tau)$ has an inverse. Then $\mathring{x}(\tau) > 0$ at all points where the derivative exists. The functions $x(\tau)$, $\mathbf{y}(\tau)$ will be assumed to be piecewise smooth, with a finite number of corners. If $f(x)$ is the inverse of $x(\tau)$, then $f'(x) = 1/\mathring{x}(\tau)$, $x = x(\tau)$; and if $\mathbf{y}(x) = \mathbf{y}[f(x)]$ then $\mathbf{y}'(x) = \mathring{\mathbf{y}}(\tau)f'(x) = \mathring{\mathbf{y}}(\tau)/\mathring{x}(\tau)$. If now we replace x by $x(\tau)$ in (2-155), we obtain

$$J[x, \mathbf{y}] = \int_{\tau_0}^{\tau_1} F(x(\tau), \mathbf{y}(\tau), \mathring{\mathbf{y}}(\tau)/\mathring{x}(\tau))\mathring{x}(\tau)d\tau \tag{2-162}$$

where $\tau_0 = f(x_0)$ and $\tau_1 = f(x_1)$. Note carefully the term $\mathring{x}(\tau)$ which appears after the F and which is introduced by the change in the variable of integration from x to τ. Finally, for the functions $x(\tau)$, $\mathbf{y}(\tau)$ to be admissible it is necessary that $\mathbf{y}(\tau_0) = \mathbf{y}_0$ and $\mathbf{y}(\tau_1) = \mathbf{y}_1$, and that $(x(\tau), \mathbf{y}(\tau), \mathring{\mathbf{y}}(\tau)/\mathring{x}(\tau)) \in \mathscr{R}$ for each τ, $\tau_0 \leq \tau \leq \tau_1$.

Thus every admissible function of the type $x(\tau)$, $\mathbf{y}(\tau)$ can be converted into an admissible function $\mathbf{y}(x)$, and for every admissible function $\mathbf{y}(x)$ there is an admissible parametric representation $x(\tau)$, $\mathbf{y}(\tau)$. Furthermore, the values of the integrals will be the same for the corresponding admissible functions. The parametric and non-parametric formulations of the optimum problem are therefore equivalent.

We now see, however, that (2-162) is merely another problem of the type (2-155), except that it involves $n + 1$ functions. If we write $y_0(\tau) = x(\tau)$, $\mathbf{y}_p = (y_0, \mathbf{y})$ and

$$\mathscr{F}(\mathbf{y}_p(\tau), \mathring{\mathbf{y}}_p(\tau)) = F(x(\tau), \mathbf{y}(\tau), \mathring{\mathbf{y}}(\tau)/\mathring{x}(\tau))\mathring{x}(\tau) \tag{2-163}$$

(2-162) becomes

$$J[\mathbf{y}_p] = \int_{\tau_0}^{\tau_1} \mathscr{F}(\mathbf{y}_p, \mathring{\mathbf{y}}_p)\mathrm{d}\tau. \tag{2-164}$$

The conditions which must be satisfied if the admissible function $\mathbf{y}_p(\tau)$ optimizes $J[\mathbf{y}_p]$ are just those set out in the previous section, but applied to $\mathscr{F}$. The usefulness of the parametric representation can now be illustrated by means of examples.

Examples. 1. Suppose that the function $\mathbf{z}(x)$ optimizes (2-155). Then the function $\mathbf{z}_p(\tau) = (\tau, \mathbf{z}(\tau))$, with $x = \tau$, is a parametric representation of $\mathbf{z}(x)$ and must optimize (2-164). Let us write down the Euler equation just for $y_0(\tau) = x$, using (2-162). Then

$$\frac{\mathrm{d}}{\mathrm{d}\tau}\mathscr{F}_{\mathring{y}_0} - \mathscr{F}_{y_0} = \frac{\mathrm{d}}{\mathrm{d}\tau}\left[F - \sum_{j=1}^{n} \frac{\mathring{y}_j}{\mathring{x}} F_{y_j'}\right] - F_x = 0$$

or

$$\frac{\mathrm{d}}{\mathrm{d}\tau}\left[F - \sum_{j=1}^{n} \frac{\mathring{y}_j}{\mathring{x}} F_{y_j'}\right] = F_x. \tag{2-165}$$

Thus $\mathbf{z}_p(x)$ must satisfy (2-165) over any interval not containing a corner in its interior. However, $x = \tau$ and $\mathbf{z}(\tau) = \mathbf{z}(x)$, so that $\mathring{x} = 1$ and $\mathring{y}_j = y_j'$; hence in any interval not containing a corner of $\mathbf{z}(x)$ ($x = \tau$ has no corners) $\mathbf{z}(x)$ must satisfy the differential equation

$$\frac{\mathrm{d}}{\mathrm{d}x}\left[F - \sum_{j=1}^{n} y_j' F_{y_j'}\right] = F_x. \tag{2-166}$$

Suppose now that x does not appear explicitly in F so that $F_x \equiv 0$. Then (2-166) implies that between corners $\mathbf{z}(x)$ must satisfy the differential equation

$$F - \sum_{j=1}^{n} y_j' F_{y_j'} = \lambda, \quad \lambda \text{ a constant.} \tag{2-167}$$

Notice that the present derivation does not depend on the existence of z_j'' for any j. If we set $n = 1$, we see that $z(x)$ must satisfy (2-56) between corners in all cases. Whereas our earlier proof required the existence and continuity of z'', we now see that the existence of z'' is not essential.

2. We next set out a parametric formulation of the problem involving the minimum area of the surface of revolution. We shall no longer assume that the curve is the graph of a function $y(x)$. Rather we shall suppose that it is represented parametrically as $x(\tau)$, $y(\tau)$. If then s is the distance along the curve measured from (x_0, y_0), $2\pi \int y ds$ is the area of the surface of revolution in all cases, even when the curve is a vertical line. In terms of the parametric representation, $\mathring{s} = [\mathring{x}^2 + \mathring{y}^2]^{\frac{1}{2}}$. Hence

$$A = 2\pi \int_{\tau_0}^{\tau_1} y[\mathring{x}^2 + \mathring{y}^2]^{\frac{1}{2}} d\tau$$

and $\mathscr{F} = y[\mathring{x}^2 + \mathring{y}^2]^{\frac{1}{2}}$. Thus

$$\mathscr{F}_y = [\mathring{x}^2 + \mathring{y}^2]^{\frac{1}{2}}; \qquad \mathscr{F}_x \equiv 0$$

$$\mathscr{F}_{\mathring{y}} = y\mathring{y}[\mathring{x}^2 + \mathring{y}^2]^{-\frac{1}{2}}; \quad \mathscr{F}_{\mathring{x}} = y\mathring{x}[\mathring{x}^2 + \mathring{y}^2]^{-\frac{1}{2}}.$$

The Euler equations are then

$$\frac{d}{d\tau} \mathscr{F}_{\mathring{x}} - \mathscr{F}_x = 0 \quad \text{or} \quad y\mathring{x}[\mathring{x}^2 + \mathring{y}^2]^{-\frac{1}{2}} = \rho, \quad \rho \text{ a constant}$$

$$\frac{d}{d\tau} \mathscr{F}_{\mathring{y}} - \mathscr{F}_y = 0 \quad \text{or} \quad \frac{d}{d\tau} [y\mathring{y}(\mathring{x}^2 + \mathring{y}^2)^{-\frac{1}{2}}] - [\mathring{x}^2 + \mathring{y}^2]^{\frac{1}{2}} = 0.$$

We shall not concern ourselves in detail with the solutions to these equations; however we can see that, for $\rho = 0$, both $\mathring{x} \equiv 0$ (x = constant) and $y \equiv 0$ can be made solutions to the system of equations. Thus, given the parametric formulation of the problem, the curve consisting of the lines $x = x_0$, $y = 0$, $x = x_1$ shown in Figure 2.13 can be constructed from solutions to the Euler equations. With the earlier, non-parametric formulation of the problem, this was not possible. It will be remembered that in certain cases the curve shown is optimal.

3. Working with a parametric formulation, it is easy to derive the basic result for the Ramsey model. We adopt a representation of the form (2-162). Thus $\mathring{t} > 0$, so that the time variation of capital still is represented by a function. (There cannot be two or more stocks of capital at the same point in time.) It will be assumed that $\tau \to \infty$ as $t \to \infty$ and that, for $t = 0$, $\tau = 0$. The integral then becomes

$$J[K, t] = \int_0^\infty U\left[\Psi(K) - \frac{\mathring{K}}{\mathring{t}}\right] \mathring{t} d\tau. \tag{2-168}$$

There is no requirement that $t(\tau)$ approach a given function as $\tau \to \infty$. From the results of Section 2.13, therefore, along the optimizing path

$$\lim_{\tau \to \infty} \mathscr{F}_{\dot{x}} = 0.$$

However,

$$\mathscr{F}_{\dot{x}} = U + U' \frac{\mathring{K}}{\mathring{t}}.$$

Furthermore, since $\mathscr{F}_x = 0$ we may infer from the Euler equation that, for all τ, $\mathscr{F}_{\dot{x}} = \lambda$, a constant. Therefore $\lim_{\tau \to \infty} \lambda = 0$, which can only be true if $\lambda = 0$ and

$$U + U' \frac{\mathring{K}}{\mathring{t}} = 0$$

along the optimizing path, except possibly at corners. If we now switch over to the normal $K(t)$ representation we see that in all cases $U + U'\dot{K} = 0$. This is the basic equation for the Ramsey model. By resort to a parametric representation, we have been able to show without difficulty that the equation must hold in all cases. Our earlier method of analysis (in Section 2.11) ran into difficulty in one case; that case is now included. From this result and our previous analysis we may conclude that in every case $U'\dot{K} \to 0$ as $t \to \infty$.

2.15. The Weierstrass and Legendre necessary conditions

Let us return to the n-function problem studied in Section 2.13. We now introduce a function called the *Weierstrass E function* which is associated with this problem and which will play an important role in our later exposition. The Weierstrass E function is defined, on some subset of Euclidean space $\mathscr{E}^{3n+1}$ of points $(x, \mathbf{y}, \mathbf{y}', \mathbf{p}')$, to be

$$E(x, \mathbf{y}, \mathbf{y}', \mathbf{p}') = F(x, \mathbf{y}, \mathbf{p}') - F(x, \mathbf{y}, \mathbf{y}') - \mathbf{F}_{\mathbf{y}'}(x, \mathbf{y}, \mathbf{y}') \cdot (\mathbf{p}' - \mathbf{y}'). \quad (2\text{-}169)$$

The domain of E consists of all points $(x, \mathbf{y}, \mathbf{y}', \mathbf{p}')$ for which $(x, \mathbf{y}, \mathbf{y}') \in \mathscr{R}$ and $(x, \mathbf{y}, \mathbf{p}') \in \mathscr{R}$. Notice that E is the difference between $F(x, \mathbf{y}, \mathbf{p}')$ and what is obtained by retaining the first two terms of Taylor's expansion in the variables $\mathbf{p}'$ about the point $\mathbf{y}'$. (See Appendix I for a discussion of Taylor's expansion.)

We now prove the following theorem.

Theorem 2.15.1. Weierstrass' Necessary Condition. If $\mathbf{z}(x)$ *yields an interior maximum of* $J[\mathbf{y}]$ *then for each value of* x, $x_0 \leq x \leq x_1$,

$$E(x, \mathbf{z}, \mathbf{z}', \mathbf{p}') \leq 0 \tag{2-170}$$

for all $\mathbf{p}'$ *such that* $(x, \mathbf{z}, \mathbf{p}') \in \mathscr{R}$. *If* $\mathbf{z}(x)$ *yields an interior minimum of* $J[\mathbf{y}]$, *the inequality sign in* (2-170) *is reversed.*

As with the derivation of other necessary conditions, we proceed by constructing a special set of functions $\mathbf{y}(x)$ and noting that for a maximum $J[\mathbf{y}] - J[\mathbf{z}] \leq 0$. This will yield the desired result. Let x^* be any value of x, $x_0 \leq x^* < x_1$, which is not a corner of $\mathbf{z}(x)$, and let a, $a > x^*$, be another value of x such that there is no corner of $\mathbf{z}(x)$ in the interval $x^* < x < a$. Next let θ be a number satisfying $0 \leq \theta < a - x^*$. Then $x^* + \theta$ lies in the interval $x^* \leq x < a$. Consider now the functions

$$\mathbf{y}(x; \theta) = \begin{cases} \mathbf{z}(x), & x \text{ not in the interval } x^* \leq x \leq a \\ \mathbf{z}(x) + [\mathbf{p}' - \mathbf{z}'(x^*)]\,(x - x^*), & x^* \leq x \leq x^* + \theta \\ \mathbf{z}(x) + \left(\dfrac{\theta}{a - x^* - \theta}\right)[\mathbf{p}' - \mathbf{z}'(x^*)]\,(a - x), & x^* + \theta \leq x \leq a \end{cases} \tag{2-171}$$

where it will be supposed that $(x^*, \mathbf{z}(x^*), \mathbf{p}')$ is an interior point of $\mathscr{R}$. Note that $\mathbf{y}'(x; \theta) = \mathbf{z}'(x) + \mathbf{p}' - \mathbf{z}'(x^*)$, $x^* < x < x^* + \theta$, and $\mathbf{y}'(x; \theta) = \mathbf{z}'(x) - \theta(a - x^* - \theta)^{-1}\,[\mathbf{p}' - \mathbf{z}'(x^*)]$, $x^* + \theta < x < a$. When a and θ are sufficiently small $\mathbf{y}(x; \theta)$ is admissible; moreover, $\mathbf{y}(x; 0) = \mathbf{z}(x)$. Then if $\Phi(\theta) = J[\mathbf{y}(x; \theta)]$ we have $\Phi(\theta) - \Phi(0) \leq 0$. (Recall that $\theta \geq 0$.) Thus $\Phi'_+(0) \leq 0$, that is, the right side derivative of Φ at 0 is not positive. Now we can write $\Phi(\theta) = \Lambda(\theta) + \Upsilon(\theta)$, where

$$\Lambda(\theta) = \int_{x^*}^{x^*+\theta} F(x, \mathbf{y}, \mathbf{y}')dx \tag{2-172}$$

and

$$\Upsilon(\theta) = \int_{x^*+\theta}^{a} F(x, \mathbf{y}, \mathbf{y}')dx. \tag{2-173}$$

Note carefully that because of (2-171) the integrand in (2-172) is independent of θ, whereas the integrand in (2-173) depends on θ. Now

$$\Lambda'_+(0) = F(x^*, \mathbf{z}(x^*), \mathbf{p}'). \tag{2-174}$$

To compute $\Upsilon'_+(0)$ we use the fact that if

$$f(\theta) = G(h_1(\theta), F(\theta)) = \int_{h_1(\theta)}^{a} F(\theta, x)\mathrm{d}x$$

then

$$f'(\theta) = -F(\theta, h_1(\theta)) + \int_{h_1(\theta)}^{a} \frac{\partial}{\partial\theta} F(\theta, x)\mathrm{d}x. \tag{2-175}$$

Thus

$$\begin{aligned} \Upsilon'_+(0) &= -F(x^*, \mathbf{z}(x^*), \mathbf{z}'(x^*)) + \int_{x^*}^{a} \Big\{ \mathbf{F}_{\mathbf{y}'}(x^*, \mathbf{z}(x^*), \mathbf{z}'(x^*)) \\ &\quad \cdot [\mathbf{p}' - \mathbf{z}'(x^*)]\left(\frac{a - x}{a - x^*}\right) - \mathbf{F}_{\mathbf{y}'}(x^*, \mathbf{z}(x^*), \mathbf{z}'(x^*)) \\ &\quad \cdot [\mathbf{p}' - \mathbf{z}'(x^*)]\left(\frac{1}{a - x^*}\right)\Big\} \mathrm{d}x \\ &= -F(x^*, \mathbf{z}(x^*), \mathbf{z}'(x^*)) + \tfrac{1}{2}\mathbf{F}_{\mathbf{y}}(x^*, \mathbf{z}(x^*), \mathbf{z}'(x^*)) \\ &\quad \cdot [\mathbf{p}' - \mathbf{z}'(x^*)]\,(a - x^*) - \mathbf{F}_{\mathbf{y}'}(x, \mathbf{z}(x^*), \mathbf{z}'(x^*)) \cdot [\mathbf{p}' - \mathbf{z}\,(x^*)]. \end{aligned} \tag{2-176}$$

Since $\Phi'_+(0) \leq 0$, $\Lambda'_+(0) + T'_+(0) \leq 0$; and, on applying (2-175) and (2-176), we see that

$$E(x^*, \mathbf{z}(x^*), \mathbf{z}'(x^*), \mathbf{p}') + \tfrac{1}{2}\mathbf{F}_{\mathbf{y}}(x, \mathbf{z}, \mathbf{z}') \cdot [\mathbf{p}' - \mathbf{z}'(x^*)]\,(a - x^*) \leq 0.$$

On taking the limit as $a \to x^*$, we obtain $E(x^*, \mathbf{z}(x^*), \mathbf{z}'(x^*), \mathbf{p}') \leq 0$, which is what we wished to show. We have proved the theorem for all $x \neq x_1$ which are not corners of $\mathbf{z}(x)$. By continuity, using either right or left side limits, the theorem holds at those points too.

We now apply the Weierstrass necessary condition $E \leq 0$ to derive another necessary condition which is sometimes useful. The new necessary condition is referred to either as the Legendre condition or as the Clebsch condition. Since $F \in C''$, we have by Taylor's theorem

$$\begin{aligned} F(x, \mathbf{z}, \mathbf{p}') &= F(x, \mathbf{z}, \mathbf{z}') + \mathbf{F}_{\mathbf{y}'}(x, \mathbf{z}, \mathbf{z}') \cdot (\mathbf{p}' - \mathbf{z}') \\ &\quad + \tfrac{1}{2}(\mathbf{p}' - \mathbf{z}') \cdot \mathbf{F}_{\mathbf{y}'\mathbf{y}'}(x, \mathbf{z}, \mathbf{z}' + \theta(\mathbf{p}' - \mathbf{z}'))\,(\mathbf{p}' - \mathbf{z}'), \\ &\quad 0 \leq \theta \leq 1. \end{aligned} \tag{2-177}$$

Here

$$\mathbf{F}_{\mathbf{y}'\mathbf{y}'} = ||F_{y_i'y_j'}|| \tag{2-178}$$

is the nth order symmetric matrix the ijth element of which is $F_{y_i'y_j'}$. Note that we can think of $\mathbf{F}_{\mathbf{y}'\mathbf{y}'}$ as a function defined on extended phase space. Observe that in (2-177) the argument of $\mathbf{F}_{\mathbf{y}'\mathbf{y}'}$ contains not $\mathbf{z}'$ but in general a point lying on the line segment joining $\mathbf{z}'$ and $\mathbf{p}'$. From (2-177) we see that

$$2E(x, \mathbf{z}, \mathbf{z}', \mathbf{p}') = (\mathbf{p}' - \mathbf{z}') \cdot \mathbf{F}_{\mathbf{y}'\mathbf{y}'}(x, \mathbf{z}, \mathbf{z}' + \theta(\mathbf{p}' - \mathbf{z}'))\,(\mathbf{p}' - \mathbf{z}') \tag{2-179}$$

where the right hand side can be recognized as the quadratic form

$$\mathbf{h} \cdot \mathbf{F}_{\mathbf{y}'\mathbf{y}'}\mathbf{h} = \sum_{i=1}^{n} \sum_{j=1}^{n} h_i F_{y_i'y_j'} h_j. \tag{2-180}$$

If the Weierstrass necessary condition is satisfied, the expression on the right in (2-179) is non-positive for all allowable $\mathbf{p}'$. Suppose that we write $\mathbf{p}' = \mathbf{z}' + \varepsilon\mathbf{h}$, where $\mathbf{h}$ is any specified vector. For ε small enough, $\mathbf{p}'$ is admissible. Then for $\varepsilon \neq 0$

$$\varepsilon^2 \mathbf{h} \cdot \mathbf{F}_{\mathbf{y}'\mathbf{y}'}(x, \mathbf{z}, \mathbf{z}' + \theta\varepsilon\mathbf{h})\mathbf{h} \leq 0$$

or

$$\mathbf{h} \cdot \mathbf{F}_{\mathbf{y}'\mathbf{y}'}(x, \mathbf{z}, \mathbf{z}' + \theta\varepsilon\mathbf{h})\mathbf{h} \leq 0. \tag{2-181}$$

On taking the limit as $\varepsilon \to 0$ we obtain

$$\mathbf{h} \cdot \mathbf{F}_{\mathbf{y}'\mathbf{y}'}(x, \mathbf{z}, \mathbf{z}')\mathbf{h} \leq 0 \tag{2-182}$$

for all $\mathbf{h}$. We have then proved the following theorem.

Theorem 2.15.2. Legendre or Clebsch Necessary Condition. If $\mathbf{z}(x)$ *yields an interior maximum of* $J[\mathbf{y}]$ *then for each* x, $x_0 \leq x \leq x_1$, *it is necessary that*

$$\mathbf{h} \cdot \mathbf{F}_{\mathbf{y}'\mathbf{y}'}(x, \mathbf{z}, \mathbf{z}')\mathbf{h} \leq 0, \quad \textit{all} \quad \mathbf{h}$$

that is, the quadratic form is negative semidefinite and the matrix $\mathbf{F}_{\mathbf{y}'\mathbf{y}'}(x, \mathbf{z}, \mathbf{z}')$ *is negative semidefinite. Similarly, if* $\mathbf{z}(x)$ *yields an interior minimum, the above quadratic form must be positive semidefinite at each* x.

2.16. An n-sector generalization of Ramsey's model

In their 1956 paper [33] Samuelson and Solow set out a model which can be viewed as a multi-sectoral generalization of Ramsey's. Consider an economy which produces n goods, and denote by C_j the consumption rate of commodity j and by K_j the stock of commodity j. Each commodity is assumed to be of a type which can be consumed and which can also serve as a capital good. No goods are specialized, strictly for consumption or strictly for investment.

As in Ramsey's model, it is assumed that the population is of fixed size and that capital does not deteriorate with time or use. Then $\dot{K}_j = I_j$, the investment rate for good j. We allow $\dot{K}_j$ to be negative; that is, the stock of the jth good can be run down by consumption. Finally, we have the basic identity $C_j + \dot{K}_j = Y_j$, the rate of output of the jth commodity.

Consider now the problem of relating the rates of output to the capital stocks. Samuelson and Solow chose to represent the relation by an equation of the form $\Omega(Y_1, \ldots, Y_n, K_1, \ldots, K_n) = 0$. Given $K_1, \ldots, K_n$, any production vector $\{Y_1, \ldots, Y_n\}$ which satisfies $\Omega = 0$ is feasible. (For the derivation of $\Omega = 0$ from industrial production functions and for some of the properties of Ω, see Herberg and Kemp [19].) It will be assumed that $\Omega = 0$ can be solved uniquely for any rate of output in terms of the other $2n - 1$ variables so that, for example, we may write

$$Y_1 = \Psi(\mathbf{Y}, \mathbf{K}) \tag{2-183}$$

where $\mathbf{Y} = (Y_2, \ldots, Y_n)$ and $\mathbf{K} = (K_1, \ldots, K_n)$. Notice that $\mathbf{Y}$ and $\mathbf{K}$ do not here have the same number of components. We will find it more convenient to work with the asymmetrical (2-183) than with $\Omega = 0$. After applying $Y_j = C_j + \dot{K}_j$, (2-183) can be written as

$$C_1 + \dot{K}_1 = \Psi(\mathbf{C} + \dot{\mathbf{K}}, \mathbf{K}) \tag{2-184}$$

where $\mathbf{C}$ and $\dot{\mathbf{K}}$ have the same number of components as $\mathbf{Y}$. For any set of n consumption functions $(C_1(t), \mathbf{C}(t))$, the utility measure $\mathscr{U}[C_1, \mathbf{C}]$ will be taken to be the undiscounted integral of an instantaneous utility or utility rate $U(C_1, \mathbf{C})$. Thus

$$\mathscr{U}[C_1, \mathbf{C}] = \int_0^\infty U(C_1(t), \mathbf{C}(t))\mathrm{d}t. \tag{2-185}$$

We can now apply (2-184) to eliminate $C_1(t)$ from (2-185), obtaining

$$J[\mathbf{K}, \mathbf{C}] = \int_0^\infty U[\Psi(\mathbf{C} + \dot{\mathbf{K}}, \mathbf{K}) - \dot{K}_1, \mathbf{C}]\mathrm{d}t. \tag{2-186}$$

We seek those functions $\mathbf{K}(t)$ and $\mathbf{C}(t)$ which maximize (2-186) subject to the initial condition that $\mathbf{K}(0) = \mathbf{K}_0$ and whatever conditions are appropriate as $t \to \infty$. In carrying out the maximization, certain boundary conditions must be considered. We have already decided to follow Ramsey in allowing each $\dot{K}_j$ to be negative. However, consumption rates cannot be negative; nor can output rates be negative. Thus $C_j \geq 0, j = 1, \ldots, n$, and $Y_j \geq 0$, $j = 1, \ldots, n$. Now the requirement that $Y_j \geq 0$ is equivalent to the requirement that $C_j + \dot{K}_j \geq 0$. Hence the set of solutions to the inequalities $C_j \geq 0$, $C_j + \dot{K}_j \geq 0, j = 1, \ldots, n$ describes the set $\mathscr{R}$.

In the model of Samuelson and Solow it is not possible to eliminate all the consumption rates from the integrand. This is an important point of departure from the original model of Ramsey, and it creates a type of problem which must be handled with care. We have decided to rule out functions $y_j(x)$ with jump discontinuities; all $y_j(x)$ must be piecewise smooth. However, the C_j can in principle undergo jump changes. How can this difficulty be handled? There is a very simple way of rephrasing the Samuelson-Solow problem so that it falls into the class of problems we have considered. We merely introduce $n - 1$ functions $M(t)$ defined by $\dot{M}_j = C_j, j = 2, \ldots, n$. Then the M_j are piecewise smooth and take their place in the statement of the variational problem. Once the M_j are determined, the C_j can be computed immediately by differentiation. Since only the derivatives of the M_j are of interest, we can arbitrarily specify the initial value, say $\mathbf{M}(0) = 0$. Then the problem becomes that of finding piecewise smooth functions $\mathbf{K}(t)$ and $\mathbf{M}(t)$ which satisfy $\mathbf{M}(0) = \mathbf{0}$, $\mathbf{K}(0) = \mathbf{K}_0$ and $\dot{K}_1 \leq \Psi(\dot{\mathbf{K}}, \mathbf{K})$ and which maximize

$$J[\mathbf{K}, \mathbf{M}] = \int_0^\infty U[\Psi(\dot{\mathbf{M}} + \dot{\mathbf{K}}, \mathbf{K}) - \dot{K}_1, \dot{\mathbf{M}}]dt. \tag{2-187}$$

This is a problem of the type we have considered. The device we have used to convert piecewise continuous into piecewise smooth functions is one that we shall use again. Samuelson and Solow avoided the present problem by assuming that the functions $C_j(t)$ are smooth and possess a second derivative.

For the present model, as for the Ramsey model, either the production function or the utility function must saturate if the integral is to converge; and, as before, there are several cases which might be considered. Samuelson and Solow confined their attention to cases in which saturation occurs at finite levels of capital. In this section, we consider just one of these cases, that in which the production function saturates and it is this saturation which defines bliss. In a later section we shall consider the alternative case in which $U(C_1, \mathbf{C})$ saturates at a unique point $(C_1^*, \mathbf{C}^*)$ while the production function need not saturate.

Saturation of the production function is a slightly more complicated concept here than in the one-good case. The reason is that we can no longer speak of a largest output rate, for there are n different rates. We shall say that the production function saturates at $\mathbf{K}^*$, with outputs $(Y_1^*, \mathbf{Y}^*)$ where $Y_1^* = \Psi(\mathbf{K}^*, \mathbf{Y}^*)$, if, for any other $\mathbf{K} \neq \mathbf{K}^*$ and any associated $(Y_1, \mathbf{Y})$ where $Y_1 = \Psi(\mathbf{K}, \mathbf{Y})$, $Y_j > Y_j^*$ for some j implies $Y_l < Y_l^*$ for some l. More specifically, if $\mathbf{Y}^*$ is held constant then $Y_1 = \Psi(\mathbf{K}, \mathbf{Y}^*)$ must be not greater than Y_1^*.

The largest utility achievable from $\mathbf{K}^*$ can be determined in the following way. Set $(\dot{K}_1, \dot{K}) = \mathbf{0}$, so that $(C_1, \mathbf{C}) = (Y_1, \mathbf{Y})$. Consider the equation $C_1 = \Psi(\mathbf{K}^*, \mathbf{C})$. In general, the solution to this equation is not unique. Determine that solution (or solutions) which yield the largest value of $U(C_1, \mathbf{C})$. Any such solution $(C_1^*, \mathbf{C}^*)$ yields bliss, and $U^* \equiv U(C_1^*, \mathbf{C}^*)$ is the bliss level of utility. We must assume that $U^* = 0$ if the integral is to converge. It will be assumed that the utility function does have this property. That completes the formulation of the problem.

As we ask the reader to show in the problems, it is always possible to find paths along which bliss is reached in a finite time. The integral converges for all such paths; thus we expect that there always exists an optimal path for which the integral converges.

In the present case $\mathbf{K}(t) \to \mathbf{K}^*$ and $(C_1(t), \mathbf{C}(t)) \to (C_1^*, \mathbf{C}^*)$ as $t \to \infty$; or, since there is no restriction on the M_j's, $F_{\dot{M}_j} \to 0$. The reader can easily write down the $2n - 1$ Euler equations for this case. We shall not write them out, but shall instead consider a specific example.

Example. We consider a two sector model in which

$$U(C_1, C_2) = -\alpha_1(C_1 - C_1^*)^2 - \alpha_2(C_2 - C_2^*)^2 + \beta \tag{2-188}$$

and

$$C_1 + \dot{K}_1 = \gamma - \beta_1(K_1 - K_1^*)^2 - \beta_2(K_2 - K_2^*)^2 - C_2 - \dot{K}_2. \tag{2-189}$$

The production function saturates at (K_1^*, K_2^*) and the set of solutions to $C_1 = \Psi(\mathbf{K}^*, \mathbf{C})$ is the set of solutions to $C_1 + C_2 = \gamma_1$. For the problem to fall within the scope of the methods we are considering, β must be such that $\max U(C_1, C_2)$ subject to $C_1 + C_2 = \gamma_1$ is 0. Now the utility function saturates at (C_1^*, C_2^*). To simplify the mathematics a little, we shall assume that $C_1^* + C_2^* = \gamma$, so that it is possible to achieve the maximum utility at the point where the production function saturates. Then if $\beta = 0$, $U(C_1^*, C_2^*) = 0 = U^*$. We shall assume that this is the case.

To keep the example as simple as possible, we shall not introduce the M_j variables. Instead we shall work with the C_j, treating $C_j(t)$ as piecewise smooth; this is permissible because there are no corners. Then

$$F(K_1, K_2, C_2, \dot{K}_1, \dot{K}_2) = U[\Psi(K_1, K_2, \dot{K}_2 + C_2) - \dot{K}_1, C_2]. \quad (2\text{-}190)$$

The Euler equations are

$$F_{C_2} = U_{C_1}\Psi_{C_2} + U_{C_2} = 0 \quad (2\text{-}191)$$

$$\frac{d}{dt} F_{\dot{K}_1} - F_{K_1} = -\frac{d}{dt} U_{C_1} - U_{C_1}\Psi_{K_1} = 0 \quad (2\text{-}192)$$

$$\frac{d}{dt} F_{\dot{K}_2} - F_{K_2} = \frac{d}{dt}(U_{C_1}\Psi_{\dot{K}_2}) - U_{C_1}\Psi_{K_2} = 0. \quad (2\text{-}193)$$

Now

$$\begin{aligned} U_{C_1} &= -2\alpha_1(C_1 - C_1^*); & U_{C_2} &= -2\alpha_2(C_2 - C_2^*) \\ \Psi_{K_1} &= -2\beta_1(K_1 - K_1^*); & \Psi_{K_2} &= -2\beta_2(K_2 - K_2^*) \\ \Psi_{\dot{K}_2} &= -1; & \Psi_{C_2} &= -1. \end{aligned} \quad (2\text{-}194)$$

Thus the first Euler equation (2-191) reduces to

$$-2\alpha_1(C_1 - C_1^*)(-1) - 2\alpha_2(C_2 - C_2^*) = 0. \quad (2\text{-}195)$$

This merely serves to relate C_1 and C_2, and tells us that

$$C_1 - C_1^* = \frac{\alpha_2}{\alpha_1}(C_2 - C_2^*). \quad (2\text{-}196)$$

If we solve (2-189) for C_1 and substitute in (2-196), then solve for C_2, we obtain

$$C_2 = C_2^* - \delta_1(K_1 - K_1^*)^2 - \delta_2(K_2 - K_2^*)^2 - \rho\dot{K}_1 - \rho\dot{K}_2 \quad (2\text{-}197)$$

where $\rho = \alpha_1(\alpha_1 + \alpha_2)^{-1}$ and $\delta_j = \beta_j\rho$. In view of (2-196),

$$C_1 = C_1^* - \delta_1\theta(K_1 - K_1^*)^2 - \delta_2\theta(K_2 - K_2^*)^2 - \rho\theta\dot{K}_1 - \rho\theta\dot{K}_2 \quad (2\text{-}198)$$

where $\theta = \alpha_2/\alpha_1$.

Since $\Psi_{\dot{K}_2} = -1$, the remaining Euler equations, (2-192) and (2-193), reduce to $\Psi_{K_1} = \Psi_{K_2}$ or $U_{C_1} = 0$. Thus for the Euler equations to be soluble it is necessary that one or the other of these conditions be satisfied. The condition $U_{C_1} = 0$ implies that $C_1 = C_1^*$ so that, from (2-196), $C_2 = C_2^*$ and the system is always at bliss. If the system is not at bliss, the only solution to the Euler equations is $\Psi_{K_1} = \Psi_{K_2}$ or

$$K_2 - K_2^* = \frac{\beta_1}{\beta_2}(K_1 - K_1^*). \tag{2-199}$$

Thus, if the system is not always at bliss the Euler equations have a solution only if (K_1^0, K_2^0) falls on the line defined by (2-199); this is a surprising and interesting result. Let us suppose that the system is not initially at bliss and that the above condition is satisfied; we shall have to postpone until later a study of other cases.

From (2-199)

$$\dot{K}_2 = \frac{\beta_1}{\beta_2}\dot{K}_1. \tag{2-200}$$

If (2-199) and (2-200) are applied to (2-197), we find that

$$C_2 - C_2^* = -\Delta(K_1 - K_1^*)^2 - \omega\dot{K}_1 \tag{2-201}$$

where $\Delta = \delta_1 + \delta_2(\beta_1/\beta_2)^2$ and $\omega = \rho[1 + (\beta_1/\beta_2)]$.

At this point we note that, since t does not appear explicitly in the integrand, (2-167) must hold. Furthermore, by reasoning similar to that applied earlier to Ramsey's model, $\lambda = 0$. Hence

$$F - \dot{K}_1 F_{\dot{K}_1} - \dot{K}_2 F_{\dot{K}_2} - C_2 F_{\dot{C}_2} = 0 \tag{2-202}$$

or

$$U + \dot{K}_1 U_{C_1} + \dot{K}_2 U_{C_2} = 0. \tag{2-203}$$

Applying (2-196) and the fact that $\dot{K}_2 = \beta_1\dot{K}_1/\beta_2$, (2-203) becomes

$$(C_2 - C_2^*)^2 + 2\omega(C_2 - C_2^*)\dot{K}_1 = 0.$$

On completing the square we have

$$(C_2 - C_2^* + \omega\dot{K}_1)^2 - \omega^2\dot{K}_1^2 = 0$$

or

$$\beta_1^2\omega^2(K_1 - K_1^*)^4 = \omega^2\dot{K}_1. \tag{2-204}$$

Hence

$$\dot{K}_1 = \beta_1(K_1 - K_1^*)^2 \quad \text{or} \quad \dot{K}_1 = -\beta_1(K_1 - K_1^*)^2.$$

Thus we can write

$$\dot{K}_1 = a(K_1^* - K_1)^2, \quad a = \pm\beta_1. \tag{2-205}$$

Hence

$$K_1(t) = K_1^* - (at + \lambda)^{-1} \tag{2-206}$$

and, therefore,

$$K_2(t) = K_2^* - \frac{\beta_1}{\beta_2}(at + \lambda)^{-1}. \tag{2-207}$$

From (2-201)

$$C_2(t) = C_2^* - (\Delta + a\omega)(at + \lambda)^{-2} \tag{2-208}$$

and

$$C_1(t) = C_1^* - \theta(\Delta + a\omega)(at + \lambda)^{-2}. \tag{2-209}$$

Consequently

$$U(t) = -(\Delta + a\omega)^2(\alpha_1\theta^2 + \alpha_2)(at + \lambda)^{-4} = -b(at + \lambda)^{-4}.$$

Hence

$$J[K_1, K_2, C_2] = -b\int_0^\infty (at + \lambda)^{-4} = -\frac{b\lambda^3}{3a}. \tag{2-210}$$

For the solution obtained to lie in $\mathscr{R}$, it is necessary that

$$\dot{K}_1(0) + \dot{K}_2(0) \leq \gamma - \beta_1(K_1^0 - K_1^*)^2 - \beta_2(K_2^0 - K_2^*)^2.$$

We have then obtained the complete solution to the problem for the case in which (K_1^0, K_2^0) lies on the line (2-199).

As an alternative solution to the Euler equations we have $U_{C_1} = 0$, i.e., $C_1 = C_1^*$ and, by (2-196), $C_2 = C_2^*$. Thus when $U_{C_1} = 0$ the system is at bliss. Then (2-192) and (2-193) reduce to $0 = 0$. The only remaining equation is (2-189) which now reduces to

$$\dot{K}_1 + \dot{K}_2 = -\beta_1(K_1 - K_1^*)^2 - \beta_2(K_2 - K_2^*)^2. \tag{2-211}$$

The system will be at bliss if $K_1 = K_1^*$, $K_2 = K_2^*$, $\dot{K}_1 = 0$ and $\dot{K}_2 = 0$. However, this is not the only possible solution to (2-211). If $K_1^0 > K_1^*$ and $K_2^0 > K_2^*$, the system can remain at bliss with (2-211) satisfied but with $\dot{K}_1 < 0$, $\dot{K}_2 < 0$ in such a way that $K_1 \to K_1^*$, $K_2 \to K_2^*$. However, for such initial conditions, if (K_1^0, K_2^0) is not on the line discussed above, the path along which $K_1 \to K_1^*$ and $K_2 \to K_2^*$ is not unique.

Thus we could set

$$\dot{K}_1 = -\beta_1(K_1 - K_1^*)^2, \qquad \dot{K}_2 = -\beta_2(K_2 - K_2^*)^2$$

yielding solutions

$$K_1 = K_1^* + \left(\beta_1 t + \frac{1}{K_1^0 - K_1^*}\right)^{-1}$$

$$K_2 = K_2^* + \left(\beta_2 t + \frac{1}{K_0^0 - K_2^*}\right)^{-1}$$

or, if we express K_2 in terms of K_1,

$$K_2 - K_2^* = \frac{\beta_1}{\beta_2}\left[\frac{K_1 - K_1^*}{1 + \varepsilon(K_1 - K_1^*)}\right] \tag{2-212}$$

$$\varepsilon = \frac{1}{K_1^0 - K_1^*} - \frac{1}{K_2^0 - K_2^*}.$$

There are, however, many other paths along which the system can move from (K_1^0, K_2^0) to (K_1^*, K_2^*) while maintaining bliss.

We have been able to solve the problem only for cases in which (K_1^0, K_2^0) lies on the special line or in which $K_1^0 > K_1^*$ and $K_2^0 > K_2^*$. We shall examine the remaining cases in Chapter 4, where the modern theory of the calculus of variations is treated.

2.17. Sufficient conditions based on the concavity of F

Thus far we have been concerned with the derivation of conditions which must be satisfied by an admissible function $\mathbf{z}(x)$ which yields an interior maximum or minimum of $J[\mathbf{y}]$, and in determining functions which satisfy these necessary conditions. We have not yet paused to consider whether a function $\mathbf{z}(x)$ which satisfies the necessary conditions actually yields the absolute (or even a relative) maximum or minimum of $J[\mathbf{y}]$. If there is only one solution to the necessary conditions, and if it is known that an optimal solution exists and lies everywhere in the interior of $\mathscr{R}$, then it is clear that the optimal solution has been found. In many cases physical or economic reasoning shows that an optimal solution must exist and lie in the interior of $\mathscr{R}$. In other cases, however, the very existence of an optimal solution may be in doubt. Moreover, if there exist several solutions to the necessary conditions, it may be quite difficult to determine which one or ones actually yields an optimum. In the face of these uncertainties it is desirable to have at hand conditions which, if satisfied, guarantee that a solution to the necessary conditions does indeed yield an optimum. Such conditions are studied both in the present section and in several later sections.

We could begin with the classical theory of sufficiency; but that theory is rather complicated and deals only with relative maxima and minima. Instead, we begin with a condition which, if satisfied, guarantees that the optimum is global, not just local. This condition has been found especially useful in dealing with economic problems.

It will be recalled that in economic models it is typically assumed that the functions are concave or convex. These concavity or convexity properties provide a basis for a convenient sufficiency condition.

Before proceeding to the statement of the condition, we review some of the basic properties of concave and convex functions of m variables. To begin, the line segment joining two points $\mathbf{v}_1$ and $\mathbf{v}_2$ in $\mathscr{E}^m$ is defined to be the set of points $\{\mathbf{v} \mid \mathbf{v} = \lambda \mathbf{v}_2 + (1 - \lambda)\mathbf{v}_1, 0 \leq \lambda \leq 1\}$. Consider now a function $z = f(\mathbf{u})$, $\mathbf{u} \in \mathscr{E}^m$, the graph of which can be viewed as a surface in $\mathscr{E}^{m+1}$. Let $(\mathbf{u}_1, f(\mathbf{u}_1))$ and $(\mathbf{u}_2, f(\mathbf{u}_2))$ be two points on this graph. The line segment joining them is the set of points

$$\{(\mathbf{u}, z) \mid (\mathbf{u}, z) = \lambda(\mathbf{u}_2, f(\mathbf{u}_2)) + (1 - \lambda)(\mathbf{u}_1, f(\mathbf{u}_1))\}, \quad 0 \leq \lambda \leq 1.$$

We can think of the line segment as being the graph of a function $h(\mathbf{u})$ the domain of which is the set $\mathbf{u} = \lambda \mathbf{u}_2 + (1 - \lambda)\mathbf{u}_1$ and for which $h(\mathbf{u}) = \lambda f(\mathbf{u}_2) + (1 - \lambda) f(\mathbf{u}_1)$. Now the value of f at $\mathbf{u}$ is $f(\lambda \mathbf{u}_2 + (1 - \lambda)\mathbf{u}_1)$. If $f(\mathbf{u}) \geq h(\mathbf{u})$ for each $\mathbf{u} = \lambda \mathbf{u}_2 + (1 - \lambda)\mathbf{u}_1$, $0 \leq \lambda \leq 1$, and for every $\mathbf{u}_1$ and $\mathbf{u}_2$, then the function $f(\mathbf{u})$ is said to be concave; for any two points on the graph of the function, the line segment joining these two points lies on or below the surface. More precisely, a concave function is defined as follows.

Concave Function. Let $f(\mathbf{u})$ be defined over an open convex set X which is a subset of $\mathscr{E}^m$. The $f(\mathbf{u})$ is said to be a concave function over X if given any two points $\mathbf{u}_1$ and $\mathbf{u}_2$ in X and any number λ, $0 \leq \lambda \leq 1$,

$$f(\lambda \mathbf{u}_2 + (1 - \lambda)\mathbf{u}_1) \geq \lambda f(\mathbf{u}_2) + (1 - \lambda) f(\mathbf{u}_1). \tag{2-213}$$

Also $f(\mathbf{u})$ is said to be strictly concave if the strict inequality holds in (2-213) when $0 < \lambda < 1$ and $\mathbf{u}_1 \neq \mathbf{u}_2$. We have required X to be convex because we want every point on the line segment joining $\mathbf{u}_1$ and $\mathbf{u}_2$ to be in X. (Recall that X is convex if and only if the line segment joining any two points in X is also in X.) A function is said to be *convex* under the above conditions if the inequality in (2-213) is reversed. In $\mathscr{E}^3$ the graph of a concave function might look like an inverted bowl, the graph of a convex function like a bowl.

To be convex or concave it is not necessary that a function possess derivatives everywhere. Suppose. however, that $f \in C'$ over an open set containing X. By Taylor's theorem

$$\begin{aligned} f(\lambda \mathbf{u}_2 + (1 - \lambda)\mathbf{u}_1) &= f(\mathbf{u}_1 + \lambda(\mathbf{u}_2 - \mathbf{u}_1)) = f(\mathbf{u}_1) \\ &\quad + \lambda \nabla f(\mathbf{u}_1 + \theta\lambda(\mathbf{u}_2 - \mathbf{u}_1)) \cdot (\mathbf{u}_2 - \mathbf{u}_1) \end{aligned} \tag{2-214}$$

where $0 \leq \theta \leq 1$. Suppose now that $f(\mathbf{u})$ is a concave function over $\mathbf{u}$ and that $\lambda > 0$. Then from (2-213) and (2-214)

$$f(\mathbf{u}_2) \leq f(\mathbf{u}_1) + \nabla f(\mathbf{u}_1 + \theta\lambda(\mathbf{u}_2 - \mathbf{u}_1)) \cdot (\mathbf{u}_2 - \mathbf{u}_1).$$

Taking the limit as $\lambda \to 0$ and bearing in mind the continuity of the derivatives, we obtain

$$f(\mathbf{u}_2) \leq f(\mathbf{u}_1) + \nabla f(\mathbf{u}_1) \cdot (\mathbf{u}_2 - \mathbf{u}_1) \tag{2-215}$$

for *any* $\mathbf{u}_1$ and $\mathbf{u}_2$ in X. That is, the surface lies below everywhere on or below any tangent plane to the surface. If $f(\mathbf{u})$ is a convex function the inequality in (2-215) is reversed. We have then proved the following theorem.

Theorem 2.17.1. Suppose that f is a concave function and $f \in C'$ over the open convex set X. Then for any two points $\mathbf{u}_1$ and $\mathbf{u}_2$ in X, (2-215) holds. If f is a convex function under the same conditions, (2-215) holds with the inequality reversed.

Now imagine that $f(\mathbf{u})$ is a concave function over X and that $f \in C''$. By Taylor's theorem

$$f(\mathbf{u}_2) = f(\mathbf{u}_1) + \nabla f(\mathbf{u}_1) \cdot (\mathbf{u}_2 - \mathbf{u}_1) + \tfrac{1}{2}(\mathbf{u}_2 - \mathbf{u}_1) \cdot \mathbf{H}(\mathbf{u}_1 + \theta(\mathbf{u}_2 - \mathbf{u}_1))(\mathbf{u}_2 - \mathbf{u}_1) \tag{2-216}$$

where $\mathbf{H} = ||f_{u_i u_j}||$ is the Hessian matrix for f. On combining (2-216) with (2-215), we see that

$$(\mathbf{u}_2 - \mathbf{u}_1) \cdot \mathbf{H}(\mathbf{u}_1 + \theta(\mathbf{u}_2 - \mathbf{u}_1))(\mathbf{u}_2 - \mathbf{u}_1) \leq 0 \tag{2-217}$$

for every $\mathbf{u}_1$ and $\mathbf{u}_2$ in X. Now fix $\mathbf{u}_1$ and let $\mathbf{u}_2 = \mathbf{u}_1 + \varepsilon\mathbf{r}$, where $\mathbf{r}$ is specified but arbitrary. Since X is open, for ε small enough $\mathbf{u}_2 \in X$. Thus

$$\mathbf{r} \cdot \mathbf{H}(\mathbf{u}_1 + \theta\varepsilon\mathbf{r})\mathbf{r} \leq 0.$$

Taking the limit as $\varepsilon \to 0$ and noting the continuity of the derivatives, we may conclude that the quadratic form

$$\mathbf{r} \cdot \mathbf{H}(\mathbf{u}_1)\mathbf{r} \leq 0 \tag{2-218}$$

for every $\mathbf{u}_1$ in X. *In other words, if $f(\mathbf{u}) \in C''$ is a concave function over X, the Hessian matrix is negative semidefinite at each point in X. Similarly, if $f(\mathbf{u}) \in C''$ is a convex function over X, the Hessian matrix is positive semidefinite.*

Suppose that $f \in C''$ over a convex set X and that the Hessian matrix for

f is negative semidefinite over X. We can now show that $f(\mathbf{u})$ is a concave function over X. Let $\mathbf{u}_1$ and $\mathbf{u}_2$ be any two points in X, and λ a number satisfying $0 \le \lambda \le 1$. Then by Taylor's theorem, writing $\mathbf{u}_1 = [\mathbf{u}_1 + \lambda(\mathbf{u}_2 - \mathbf{u}_1)] - \lambda(\mathbf{u}_2 - \mathbf{u}_1)$ or $\mathbf{u}_1 = \mathbf{u} - \lambda\mathbf{r}$,

$$f(\mathbf{u}_1) = f(\mathbf{u}) - \lambda\nabla f(\mathbf{u}) \cdot \mathbf{r} + \tfrac{1}{2}\lambda^2\mathbf{r} \cdot \mathbf{H}(\mathbf{u} - \theta_1\lambda\mathbf{r})\mathbf{r}. \tag{2-219}$$

Also, writing $\mathbf{u}_2 = \mathbf{u} + (1 - \lambda)\mathbf{r}$,

$$f(\mathbf{u}_2) = f(\mathbf{u}) + (1 - \lambda)\nabla f(\mathbf{u}) \cdot \mathbf{r} + \tfrac{1}{2}(1 - \lambda)^2\mathbf{r} \cdot \mathbf{H}(\mathbf{u} + \theta_2(1 - \lambda)\mathbf{r})\mathbf{r}. \tag{2-220}$$

Multiplying (2-219) by $1 - \lambda$ and (2-220) by λ then adding, and noting that $\mathbf{H}$ is negative semidefinite for every point in X and that $\mathbf{u} - \theta_1\lambda\mathbf{r}$ and $\mathbf{u} + (1 - \lambda)\mathbf{r}$ are in X and on the line segment joining $\mathbf{u}_1$ and $\mathbf{u}_2$, we see that

$$\lambda f(\mathbf{u}_2) + (1 - \lambda)f(\mathbf{u}_1) \le f(\mathbf{u}) = f(\lambda\mathbf{u}_2 + (1 - \lambda)\mathbf{u}_1) \tag{2-221}$$

which is what we wished to prove.

Thus we have proved the following theorem.

Theorem 2.17.2. Suppose that $f \in C''$ over the open convex set X. Then f is a concave function over X if and only if the Hessian matrix $\mathbf{H}$ *for f is negative semidefinite at each point in X. Under the same conditions f is a convex function if and only if* $\mathbf{H}$ *is positive semidefinite at each point in X.*

Corollary. Under the conditions of Theorem 2.17.2, if $\mathbf{H}$ *is negative definite at each point in X, f is strictly concave; and if* $\mathbf{H}$ *is positive definite, f is strictly convex.*

We ask the reader to prove the corollary as a problem.

Suppose now that $z = f(\mathbf{u})$ is a concave function over X and that the real-valued function of one variable $h(z)$ is concave over an interval which includes the range of $f(\mathbf{u})$. It is *not* in general true that the composite function $h[f(\mathbf{u})]$ is a concave function over X. However, the following related propositions are valid.

Theorem 2.17.3. Suppose that the real-valued function $f(\mathbf{u})$ is concave over an open convex set X and that $h(z)$ is concave over an interval which includes the range of $f(\mathbf{u})$. Then if $h(z)$ is monotone nondecreasing $h[f(\mathbf{u})]$ is a concave function over X. Suppose further that $h(z)$ is both strictly concave and monotone increasing and that for all $\mathbf{u}_1$ and $\mathbf{u}_2$, $\mathbf{u}_1 \neq \mathbf{u}_2$, such that

$$f(\lambda \mathbf{u}_2 + (1 - \lambda)\mathbf{u}_1) = \lambda f(\mathbf{u}_2) + (1 - \lambda) f(\mathbf{u}_1)$$

it is true that $f(\mathbf{u}_1) \neq f(\mathbf{u}_2)$. *Then* $h[f(\mathbf{u})]$ *is strictly concave over* X.

We now prove the theorem. Suppose that $\mathbf{u}_1$ and $\mathbf{u}_2$ are any two points in X and λ is any number satisfying $0 \leq \lambda \leq 1$. Since $f(\mathbf{u})$ is a concave function

$$z_1 = f(\lambda \mathbf{u}_2 + (1 - \lambda)\mathbf{u}_1) \geq \lambda f(\mathbf{u}_2) + (1 - \lambda) f(\mathbf{u}_1) = z_2.$$

Since $z_1 \geq z_2$, and because $h(z)$ is nondecreasing, $h(z_1) \geq h(z_2)$. Furthermore, when $h(z)$ is monotone increasing and $z_1 > z_2$ then $h(z_1) > h(z_2)$. Since $h(z)$ is a concave function, however,

$$h(z_2) = h[\lambda f(\mathbf{u}_2) + (1 - \lambda) f(\mathbf{u}_1)] \geq \lambda h[f(\mathbf{u}_2)] + (1 - \lambda) h[f(\mathbf{u}_1)]$$

with the strict inequality holding if $h(z)$ is strictly concave, $0 < \lambda < 1$, and $f(\mathbf{u}_1) \neq f(\mathbf{u}_2)$. Thus

$$h(z_1) = h[f(\lambda \mathbf{u}_2 + (1 - \lambda)\mathbf{u}_1)] \geq h(z_2) \geq \lambda h[f(\mathbf{u}_2)] + (1 - \lambda) h[f(\mathbf{u}_1)].$$

Therefore $h[f(\mathbf{u})]$ is concave. If $h(z)$ is monotone increasing, the first inequality in the above equation is strict except when $f(\lambda \mathbf{u}_2 + (1 - \lambda)\mathbf{u}_1) = \lambda f(\mathbf{u}_2) + (1 - \lambda) f(\mathbf{u}_1)$. If $f(\mathbf{u}_1) \neq f(\mathbf{u}_2)$ under these conditions then the second inequality is strict if $0 < \lambda < 1$. This establishes the strict concavity of $h[f(\mathbf{u})]$ under the conditions stated in the theorem. That completes the proof.

There is a slightly more general version of the theorem which is sometimes useful and which we ask the reader to prove as a problem. The proof follows the same lines as that just given.

Theorem 2.17.4. Suppose that $f(\mathbf{u}, \mathbf{z})$ *is a concave function of the variables* $(\mathbf{u}, \mathbf{z})$ *over the open convex set* X *and that* $h(z_1, \mathbf{z})$ *is a concave function over a convex set* Z *such that* $(z_1, \mathbf{z}) \in Z$ *whenever* $(\mathbf{u}, \mathbf{z}) \in X$. *Then if* h *has the property that* $h(z_2, \mathbf{z}) \geq h(z_1, \mathbf{z})$ *whenever* $z_2 > z_1$ *and if* $(z_1, \mathbf{z})$ *and* $(z_2, \mathbf{z})$ *are in* Z, *the function* $h[f(\mathbf{u}, \mathbf{z}), \mathbf{z}]$ *is a concave function of* $(\mathbf{u}, \mathbf{z})$ *over* X. *Suppose further that* $h(z_1, \mathbf{z})$ *is strictly concave and* $h(z_2, \mathbf{z}) > h(z_1, \mathbf{z})$ *when* $z_2 > z_1$, *and that, for all* $\mathbf{u}_1$ *and* $\mathbf{u}_2$, $\mathbf{u}_1 \neq \mathbf{u}_2$, *such that* $f(\lambda \mathbf{u}_2 + (1 - \lambda)\mathbf{u}_1, \mathbf{z}) = \lambda f(\mathbf{u}_2) + (1 - \lambda) f(\mathbf{u}_1)$, $f(\mathbf{u}_1) \neq f(\mathbf{u}_2)$. *Then* $h[f(\mathbf{u}, \mathbf{z}), \mathbf{z}]$ *is strictly concave over* X.

We are now ready to consider sufficiency conditions. Suppose that $F(x, \mathbf{y}, \mathbf{y}')$ is, for each x, $x_0 \leq x \leq x_1$, a concave function of the variables

y and **y**′ over an open convex set which includes every point (**y**, **y**′) for which $(x, \mathbf{y}, \mathbf{y}') \in \mathscr{R}$. We shall then show that if the upper limit on the integral is finite and if we have found an admissible function $\mathbf{z}(x)$ which satisfies both the Euler equations and the corner conditions, then $\mathbf{z}(x)$ yields the absolute maximum of $J[\mathbf{y}]$ over the space of admissible functions. The proof is quite easy.

Consider any other admissible function $\mathbf{y}(x)$. We shall prove that $J[\mathbf{y}] \leq J[\mathbf{z}]$. Let $\boldsymbol{\eta}(x) = \mathbf{y}(x) - \mathbf{z}(x)$ and $\boldsymbol{\eta}'(x) = \mathbf{y}'(x) - \mathbf{z}'(x)$. There may exist a finite number of values of x for which $\mathbf{y}(x)$ or $\mathbf{z}(x)$ has a corner. At such points we can specify $\mathbf{y}'(x)$ or $\mathbf{z}'(x)$ arbitrarily, subject only to the requirement that (**y**, **y**′) and (**z**, **z**′) are in the convex set. With this convention $\boldsymbol{\eta}'(x)$ is defined for all x of interest. Then, from Theorem 2.17.1,

$$F(x, \mathbf{y}, \mathbf{y}') \leq F(x, \mathbf{z}, \mathbf{z}') + \mathbf{F}_{\mathbf{y}}(x, \mathbf{z}, \mathbf{z}') \cdot \boldsymbol{\eta} + \mathbf{F}_{\mathbf{y}'}(x, \mathbf{z}, \mathbf{z}') \cdot \boldsymbol{\eta}'. \tag{2-222}$$

Integrating (2-222) from x_0 to x_1, we find that

$$J[\mathbf{y}] \leq J[\mathbf{z}] + \int_{x_0}^{x_1} [\mathbf{F}_{\mathbf{y}} \cdot \boldsymbol{\eta} + \mathbf{F}_{\mathbf{y}'} \cdot \boldsymbol{\eta}']dx. \tag{2-223}$$

Now between corners of $\mathbf{z}(x)$, $d\mathbf{F}_{\mathbf{y}'}(x, \mathbf{z}, \mathbf{z}')/dx$ exists; hence between corners (2-223) may be integrated by parts. Let us denote by $a_1, \ldots, a_{m-1}$ the values of x at which $\mathbf{z}(x)$ has a corner, and write $x_0 = a_0$ and $x_1 = a_m$. Then, integrating by parts and noting that $\boldsymbol{\eta}(x_0) = \boldsymbol{\eta}(x_1) = \mathbf{0}$, (2-223) becomes

$$J[\mathbf{y}] \leq J[\mathbf{z}] + \sum_{i=1}^{m} \int_{a_{i-1}}^{a_i} \left[\mathbf{F}_{\mathbf{y}}(x, \mathbf{z}, \mathbf{z}') - \frac{d}{dx} \mathbf{F}_{\mathbf{y}'}(x, \mathbf{z}, \mathbf{z}')\right] \cdot \boldsymbol{\eta}(x)dx$$

$$+ \sum_{i=1}^{m-1} [\mathbf{F}_{\mathbf{y}'}(a_i, \mathbf{z}(a_i), \mathbf{z}'_-(a_i)) - \mathbf{F}_{\mathbf{y}'}(a_i, \mathbf{z}(a_i), \mathbf{z}'_+(a_i))] \cdot \boldsymbol{\eta}(a_i). \tag{2-224}$$

Because $\mathbf{z}(x)$ satisfies the Euler equations between corners as well as the corner conditions, both sums in (2-224) vanish and (2-224) reduces to $J[\mathbf{y}] \leq J[\mathbf{z}]$. This is true for any admissible $\mathbf{y}(x)$; hence $\mathbf{z}(x)$ does yield the absolute or global maximum of $J[\mathbf{y}]$ over the space of admissible functions. For the case in which the integral is taken over an interval of finite length, our proof is complete.

The situation is more complicated when the upper limit of the integral is ∞. For the above analysis to be meaningful then, we must know that $J[\mathbf{z}]$ does in fact exist, that is, that the integral converges for $\mathbf{z}(x)$. Furthermore, in this case another term

$$\lim_{x\to\infty} \mathbf{F}_{\mathbf{y}'}(x, \mathbf{z}, \mathbf{z}') \cdot \boldsymbol{\eta}(x) \tag{2-225}$$

appears. If $\mathbf{z}(x)$ satisfies the necessary conditions then either $F_{y_j'} \to 0$ or $\eta_j \to 0$ as $x \to \infty$. However, satisfaction of these conditions does not guarantee that the limit in (2-225) is 0. It is possible, for example, that $F_{y_j'} \to 0$ but $\eta_j \to \infty$ in such a way that $F_{y_j'}\eta_j$ approaches a constant or $-\infty$. Suppose, on the other hand, that we can show that for every admissible function $\mathbf{y}(x)$ the limit in (2-225) is not positive. Then, when $J[\mathbf{z}]$ exists we can be sure that $J[\mathbf{y}] \leq J[\mathbf{z}]$, where $\mathbf{y}(x)$ is any other admissible function. Thus we have proved the following theorem.

Theorem 2.17.5. Sufficiency Conditions. Suppose that for each x in the interval of integration $F(x, \mathbf{y}, \mathbf{y}')$ is a concave function with respect to $(\mathbf{y}, \mathbf{y}')$ over an open convex set which includes all $(\mathbf{y}, \mathbf{y}')$ such that $(x, \mathbf{y}, \mathbf{y}') \in \mathcal{R}$. Then if the interval of integration is finite and if $\mathbf{z}(x)$ is an admissible function which satisfies both the Euler equations and the corner conditions, $J[\mathbf{z}]$ is the absolute maximum of $J[\mathbf{y}]$ over the space of admissible functions. If the interval of integration is infinite and if the same conditions are satisfied then, provided it can be shown that, for **every** *admissible function $\mathbf{y}(x)$, $\mathbf{F}_{\mathbf{y}'}(x, \mathbf{z}, \mathbf{z}') \cdot \boldsymbol{\eta}(x)$ is non-positive for all x sufficiently large, $\mathbf{z}(x)$ again yields the absolute maximum of $J[\mathbf{y}]$ over the space of admissible functions. Note that in this case the requirement that $\mathbf{z}(x)$ is admissible implies that $J[\mathbf{z}]$ exists.*

We can now easily prove the following corollary.

Corollary. If the conditions of Theorem 2.17.5 are satisfied and if in addition $\mathcal{R}$ is a convex set and $F(x, \mathbf{y}, \mathbf{y}')$ is strictly concave over a set including $\mathcal{R}$, then the admissible function $\mathbf{z}(x)$ which maximizes $J[\mathbf{y}]$ is unique.

To prove the corollary we suppose that there are two different functions $\mathbf{z}_1(x)$ and $\mathbf{z}_2(x)$ each of which maximizes $J[\mathbf{y}]$, and establish a contradiction. Consider then the function $\mathbf{z}_3(x) = [\mathbf{z}_1(x) + \mathbf{z}_2(x)]/2$. For the case in which the interval of integration is finite, $\mathbf{z}_3(x)$ lies in $\mathcal{R}$ and satisfies the boundary conditions. However, since F is strictly concave,

$$F(x, \mathbf{z}_3, \mathbf{z}_3') > \tfrac{1}{2}F(x, \mathbf{z}_1, \mathbf{z}_1') + \tfrac{1}{2}F(x, \mathbf{z}_2, \mathbf{z}_2') \tag{2-226}$$

for any x such that $(\mathbf{z}_1, \mathbf{z}_1') \neq (\mathbf{z}_2, \mathbf{z}_2')$. The components of $\mathbf{z}_j(x)$ are continuous functions of x; thus if at a particular value of x two components are not equal there exists an interval over which they are not equal. It follows that there exists at least one interval for which (2-226) holds. Hence, bearing in mind that $J[\mathbf{z}_1] = J[\mathbf{z}_2] = J[\mathbf{z}]$, the maximum of $J[\mathbf{y}]$,

$$J[\mathbf{z}_3] > \tfrac{1}{2}J[\mathbf{z}_1] + \tfrac{1}{2}J[\mathbf{z}_2] = J[\mathbf{z}].$$

This is a contradiction. The same conclusion is reached when the interval of integration is unbounded.

A precisely analogous theorem and corollary are available when F is a convex function with respect to $(\mathbf{y}, \mathbf{y}')$ and it is of interest to minimize $J[\mathbf{y}]$.

Although Theorem 2.17.5 is quite useful in economic theory one must be careful in applying it. In many problems F is concave in some regions but not in others. It is necessary to verify that F is concave in the region of interest.

Examples. 1. Consider the problem of finding the curve which yields the shortest distance between two points in the plane. Here $F = [1 + (y')^2]^{\frac{1}{2}}$, and F is a strictly convex function of y' since

$$F_{y'y'} = [1 + (y')^2]^{-3/2} > 0$$

and as can easily be checked by plotting F. F is also a convex, but not strictly convex function of y and y' (the surface is a cylinder). Thus by Theorem 2.17.5 we know that an admissible function which satisfies the Euler equation does indeed yield the absolute minimum distance over the space of admissible functions. Thus the straight line passing through the given points does yield the minimum distance.

2. Let us now consider the Ramsey model. We have assumed that $U(C)$ is a concave function of C over its domain and that $\Psi(K)$ is a concave function of K over its domain. Consider now the function

$$\Omega(K, \dot{K}) = \Psi(K) - \dot{K}.$$

This is a concave function of the two variables K and $\dot{K}$ since

$$\begin{aligned}\Omega(\lambda K_2 + (1 - \lambda)K_1, \lambda\dot{K}_2 + (1 - \lambda)\dot{K}_1) &= \Psi(\lambda K_2 + (1 - \lambda)K_1) \\ &\quad - \lambda\dot{K}_2 - (1 - \lambda)\dot{K}_1 \\ &\geq \lambda\Psi(K_2) + (1 - \lambda)\Psi(K_1) - \lambda\dot{K}_2 - (1 - \lambda)\dot{K}_1 \\ &= \lambda\Omega(K_2, \dot{K}_2) + (1 - \lambda)\Omega(K_1, \dot{K}_1).\end{aligned}$$

Consider next the function

$$F(K, \dot{K}) = U[\Omega(K, \dot{K})] = U[\Psi(K) - \dot{K}].$$

Not only is $U(C)$ concave, it is monotone nondecreasing whenever C is less than or equal to the possibly infinite value at which $U(C)$ saturates. Thus, from Theorem 2.17.5, $F(K, \dot{K})$ is a concave function of K and $\dot{K}$ whenever C is less than or equal to its critical saturating value. If the planning horizon is finite, therefore, any admissible function which satisfies the Euler equations and which implies that C never exceeds its saturating value must yield the absolute maximum utility for all admissible functions.

Whether or nor $F(K, \dot{K})$ is strictly concave for C not greater than its saturating value depends on U and Ψ. If both U and Ψ are strictly concave, F also will be strictly concave. For then

$$\Omega[\lambda(K_2, \dot{K}_2) + (1 - \lambda)(K_1, \dot{K}_1)] = \lambda\Omega(K_2, \dot{K}_2) + (1 - \lambda)\Omega(K_1, \dot{K}_1)$$

only when $K_1 = K_2$. However, for points $(K, \dot{K}_1)$ and $(K, \dot{K}_2)$, $\dot{K}_1 = \dot{K}_2$, $\Omega(K, \dot{K}_1) \neq \Omega(K, \dot{K}_2)$; hence, by Theorem 2.17.3, F is strictly concave.

Suppose now that the planning horizon is infinite. The worked examples of Section 2.11 will be used to illustrate the situations which can arise.

Example 3 illustrates a case in which F is concave and there exists a solution to the Euler equation which satisfies the boundary conditions but in which nevertheless the solution does not maximize $J[K]$ because the integral diverges for the $K(t)$ obtained (and all other $K(t)$). It must be shown that the integral converges before any conclusions can be drawn concerning the maximizing properties of the solution.

To apply our sufficiency theorem (Theorem 2.17.5) we must be able to show that, for all t sufficiently large and for *all* other admissible functions, $F_{y'}\eta = -U'\eta$ is non-positive. When bliss is producible with a finite stock of capital K^*, as in Example 2, we may be sure that $K(t) \to K^*$ or $\eta \to 0$. Since U' is bounded for large t, we can immediately conclude that $U'\eta \to 0$ in every case, so that the conditions of the sufficiency theorem are satisfied. In such cases, therefore, an admissible solution to the Euler equation does indeed maximize utility.

When $\Psi(K)$ does not saturate but $U(C)$ saturates asymptotically as $C \to \infty$, one cannot be sure that $U'\eta \to 0$. It must be true that $U' \to 0$, but it is not clear what η may do for an arbitrarily chosen admissible comparison function. In specific cases, however, it is possible to show that the conditions of the sufficiency theorem are satisfied. Thus, in Example 1, along the path satisfying the Euler equation, $K = (t/\alpha) + K_0$ and $U'(t) = U^*\alpha e^{-\alpha\delta}e^{-\beta t}$. If, for any comparison function $y(t)$, $U'\eta$ is to approach a negative constant, η must behave like $-ae^{\beta t} + f(t)$ as $t \to \infty$, where $\lim_{t\to\infty} f(t)e^{-\beta t} = 0$. However, this implies that $y(t)$ would behave as $-ae^{\beta t} + f(t) - (t/\alpha) - K_0$, so that on this path capital would approach $-\infty$ as

$t \to \infty$. This is impossible. Thus, for all sufficiently large t and for every admissible $K(t)$, $U'\eta \geq 0$. Hence the conditions of the sufficiency theorem are satisfied and the solution obtained does indeed yield the maximum.

For example 4, $K = (t/\alpha) + K_0$ and $U'(t) = U^*\alpha e^{-1}[(t/\alpha) + K_0 + 1]^{-\alpha\beta-1}$. If $U'\eta$ approaches a negative constant, η must behave like $-a[(t/\alpha) + K_0 + 1]^{\alpha\beta+1} + f(t)$ as $t \to \infty$, where $\lim_{t\to\infty} U'(t)f(t) = 0$; and this implies that $y(t)$ behaves as $-[(t/\alpha) + K_0 + 1]^{\alpha\beta+1} + f(t) - (t/\alpha) - K_0$. Thus when $\alpha\beta > 1$, as is required for the convergence of the integral, the stock of capital must approach $-\infty$ as $t \to \infty$. This is impossible. Hence $U'\eta \geq 0$ for all t sufficiently large and we may be sure that the solution determined does indeed yield the maximum.

In Example 5, $U'(t) = 8\alpha(\beta t + \rho)^{-3}$ and $K = \beta^{-1} \log C^*(\beta t + \rho)$. If $U'\eta$ is to approach a negative number, $U'\eta$ must approach $-a(\beta t + \rho)^3 + f(t)$ and $y(t)$ must approach $-a(\beta t + \rho)^3 - \beta^{-1}\log C^*(\beta t + \rho) + f(t)$. However, along this path the stock of capital would approach $-\infty$. This is impossible. Hence the solution obtained must yield the maximum.

Similarly for Example 6; for $U'\eta$ to approach a negative constant $y(t)$ would have to approach $-ae^{\beta(t+\varepsilon)} - \beta^{-1}e^{\beta(t+\varepsilon)/2} + \delta\beta^{-1} + f(t)$, which requires that along this path the stock of capital approach $-\infty$. This is impossible. Hence the solution obtained does indeed yield the maximum.

Thus in every example in which the planning horizon is infinite we have been able to apply Theorem 2.17.5 to show that the solution obtained does indeed yield the maximum.

2.18.° Classical sufficiency conditions*

The sufficiency conditions developed in the preceding section are to economists more useful than the elaborate classical conditions. In the literature of economics, however, one occasionally finds reference to the classical theory. For that reason we now provide a survey of the classical theory, with special attention to the work of Legendre and Jacobi. We shall not attempt to enter into full detail; nevertheless the analysis will be sufficiently intricate for most tastes.

Throughout this section (and the next) we shall find it necessary to place slightly more severe restrictions on F. Specifically, it will be assumed that $F \in C'''$. In practical problems, however, this condition is nearly always satisfied.

We introduce the approach to be taken in the present section by re-

---

* Sections marked ° may be omitted without loss of continuity.

proving Theorem 2.17.5. Suppose that we have an admissible function $\mathbf{z}(x)$ which satisfies the Euler equations between corners as well as the corner conditions. We let $\mathbf{y}(x)$ be any other admissible function and write $\boldsymbol{\eta}(x) = \mathbf{y}(x) - \mathbf{z}(x)$. Then, by Taylor's theorem,

$$F(x, \mathbf{y}(x), \mathbf{y}'(x)) = F(x, \mathbf{z}(x), \mathbf{z}'(x)) + \mathbf{F_y}(x, \mathbf{z}(x), \mathbf{z}'(x)) \cdot \boldsymbol{\eta}$$

$$+ \mathbf{F_{y'}}(x, \mathbf{z}(x), \mathbf{z}'(x)) \cdot \boldsymbol{\eta}'$$

$$+ \tfrac{1}{2}[\boldsymbol{\eta} \cdot \mathbf{F_{yy}}(x, \mathbf{z} + \theta\boldsymbol{\eta}, \mathbf{z}' + \theta\boldsymbol{\eta}')\boldsymbol{\eta}$$

$$+ 2\boldsymbol{\eta}' \cdot \mathbf{F_{y'y}}(x, \mathbf{z} + \theta\boldsymbol{\eta}, \mathbf{z} + \theta\boldsymbol{\eta}')\boldsymbol{\eta}$$

$$+ \boldsymbol{\eta}' \cdot \mathbf{F_{y'y'}}(x, \mathbf{z} + \theta\boldsymbol{\eta}, \mathbf{z}' + \theta\boldsymbol{\eta}')\boldsymbol{\eta}'] \tag{2-227}$$

at all except a finite number of values of x where the derivatives may not exist. (In obtaining (2-227) we relied on the fact that $F_{y_j' y_i'} = F_{y_i' y_j'}$.) Let us now define the matrix of order $2n$

$$\mathbf{H} = \begin{bmatrix} \mathbf{F_{yy}} & \mathbf{F_{y'y}} \\ \mathbf{F_{y'y}} & \mathbf{F_{y'y'}} \end{bmatrix} \tag{2-228}$$

and the vector $\boldsymbol{\eta}_a = (\boldsymbol{\eta}, \boldsymbol{\eta}')$. Then, on integrating (2-227) and recalling that $\mathbf{z}(x)$ satisfies both the Euler equations and the corner conditions, we obtain, when the interval of integration is finite,

$$J[\mathbf{y}] = J[\mathbf{z}] + \tfrac{1}{2}\int_{x_0}^{x_1} \boldsymbol{\eta}_a(x) \cdot \mathbf{H}(x, \mathbf{z} + \theta\boldsymbol{\eta}, \mathbf{z}' + \theta\boldsymbol{\eta}')\boldsymbol{\eta}_a(x)\mathrm{d}x. \tag{2-229}$$

The integrand is a quadratic form; thus we see immediately that if the matrix $\mathbf{H}$ is negative semidefinite everywhere then $J[\mathbf{y}] \leq J[\mathbf{z}]$ and $\mathbf{z}(x)$ does maximize $J[\mathbf{y}]$. When the interval of integration is infinite, the term $\lim_{x\to\infty} F_{\mathbf{y}'}(x, \mathbf{z}(x), \mathbf{z}'(x)) \cdot \boldsymbol{\eta}(x)$ also appears in (2-229). We can conclude that $J[\mathbf{y}] \leq J[\mathbf{z}]$ in this case if we are able to show that this limit is non-positive for *every* $\mathbf{y}(x)$. Thus we have proved in a different way Theorem 2.17.5; for, given our earlier assumptions concerning the derivatives of F, the condition that $\mathbf{H}$ be negative semidefinite everywhere (that is, over an open convex set containing $\mathscr{R}$) is exactly equivalent to the condition that F be a concave function of $(\mathbf{y}, \mathbf{y}')$.

Probably this theorem was known to those who developed the classical theory; but it was disregarded. One possible explanation is that in several of the problems which motivated classical developments F is not concave.

We now modify the approach slightly to derive one of the more frequently used classical sufficiency conditions. Unfortunately we shall have to make a substantial sacrifice of generality, for the condition to be developed guarantees only a weak relative maximum, not a global maximum. It is usually referred to as the *Legendre sufficient condition.*

Suppose that $\mathbf{z}(x)$ is an admissible function which satisfies the necessary conditions and lies in the interior of $\mathscr{R}$. *Suppose furthermore that* $\mathbf{z}(x)$ *has no corners and that the interval of integration is finite.* Now consider functions $\mathbf{y}(x) = \mathbf{z}(x) + \xi\boldsymbol{\eta}(x)$, where $\boldsymbol{\eta}(x_0) = \mathbf{0}$, $\boldsymbol{\eta}(x_1) = \mathbf{0}$ and $\boldsymbol{\eta}(x) \in C'$, so that $\boldsymbol{\eta}$ is an admissible variation; for ξ sufficiently close to 0, $\mathbf{y}(x)$ is admissible for every $\boldsymbol{\eta}(x)$ of the type considered. Then $\mathbf{z}(x)$ yields a weak relative maximum of $J[\mathbf{y}]$ if $J[\mathbf{y}] \le J[\mathbf{z}]$ for every such $\mathbf{y}(x)$ and for all ξ, $|\xi| \le \xi_0$. To see this, we note first that any $\mathbf{y}(x)$, $\mathbf{y} \in C'$, which lies in a P_ε-neighborhood of $\mathbf{z}(x)$ can be expressed as $\mathbf{y}(x) = \mathbf{z}(x) + \xi\boldsymbol{\eta}(x)$, where ξ and $\boldsymbol{\eta}$ are of the type just described. Thus all $\mathbf{y}(x)$ without corners are included in the set of the form $\mathbf{y}(x) = \mathbf{z}(x) + \xi\boldsymbol{\eta}(x)$. Furthermore, no function $\mathbf{y}(x)$ with corners which lies in a P_ε-neighborhood of $\mathbf{z}(x)$ can yield $J[\mathbf{y}] > J[\mathbf{z}]$, since such a function could be approximated so closely by a function $\mathbf{y}^*(x) \in C'$ that $J[\mathbf{y}^*] > J[\mathbf{z}]$, which is a contradiction. (See Problem 14 for Section 2.6.)

We seek now a sufficient condition for $J[\mathbf{y}] \le J[\mathbf{z}]$, where $\mathbf{y}(x) = \mathbf{z}(x) + \xi\boldsymbol{\eta}(x)$. When $\boldsymbol{\eta}(x)$ is fixed, $J[\mathbf{y}] = \Phi(\xi)$; hence, by Taylor's theorem and the fact that $\Phi'(0) = 0$ when $\mathbf{z}(x)$ satisfies the necessary conditions,

$$\Phi(\xi) = J[\mathbf{y}] = J[\mathbf{z}] + \Phi''(\theta\xi). \tag{2-230}$$

Now $\Phi''(\xi)$ is a continuous function of ξ. Hence if $\Phi''(0) < 0$ then $\Phi''(\xi) < 0$ for all ξ, $|\xi| < \xi_1$. Thus if it can be shown that $\Phi''(0) < 0$ for *every* admissible $\boldsymbol{\eta}(x)$ then $\Phi''(\theta\xi) < 0$, $|\xi| < \xi_1$, and we may conclude that $\mathbf{z}(x)$ yields a weak relative maximum of $J[\mathbf{y}]$.

From (2-227) we note that

$$\Phi''(0) = \tfrac{1}{2}\int_{x_0}^{x_1} [\boldsymbol{\eta} \cdot \mathbf{F}_{\mathbf{yy}}(x, \mathbf{z}, \mathbf{z}')\boldsymbol{\eta} + 2\boldsymbol{\eta}' \cdot \mathbf{F}_{\mathbf{y}'\mathbf{y}}(x, \mathbf{z}, \mathbf{z}')\boldsymbol{\eta}$$

$$+ \boldsymbol{\eta}' \cdot \mathbf{F}_{\mathbf{y}'\mathbf{y}'}(x, \mathbf{z}, \mathbf{z}')\boldsymbol{\eta}']dx. \tag{2-231}$$

If we write $2\boldsymbol{\eta}' \cdot \mathbf{F}_{\mathbf{y}'\mathbf{y}'}\boldsymbol{\eta}$ as $\boldsymbol{\eta}' \cdot \mathbf{F}_{\mathbf{y}'\mathbf{y}'}\boldsymbol{\eta} + \boldsymbol{\eta}'\mathbf{F}_{\mathbf{y}'\mathbf{y}'}\boldsymbol{\eta}$ and integrate by parts the first of the two components of the sum, we obtain as one term $-\boldsymbol{\eta} \cdot \mathbf{F}_{\mathbf{y}'\mathbf{y}'}\boldsymbol{\eta}'$, which cancels against the second component. Thus (2-231) reduces to

$$2\Phi''(0) = \int_{x_0}^{x_1} [\boldsymbol{\eta} \cdot \mathbf{A}(x)\boldsymbol{\eta} + \boldsymbol{\eta}' \cdot \mathbf{B}(x)\boldsymbol{\eta}']\mathrm{d}x \tag{2-232}$$

where

$$\mathbf{A}(x) = \mathbf{F}_{\mathbf{yy}}(x, \mathbf{z}, \mathbf{z}') - \frac{\mathrm{d}}{\mathrm{d}x}\mathbf{F}_{\mathbf{y}'\mathbf{y}}(x, \mathbf{z}, \mathbf{z}') \tag{2-233}$$

$$\mathbf{B}(x) = \mathbf{F}_{\mathbf{y}'\mathbf{y}'}(x, \mathbf{z}, \mathbf{z}') \tag{2-234}$$

and where by $\mathrm{d}\mathbf{F}_{\mathbf{y}'\mathbf{y}}/\mathrm{d}x$ we mean the matrix the (i, j)th term of which is the derivative with respect to x of the (i, j)th term of $\mathbf{F}_{\mathbf{y}'\mathbf{y}}$. Note that $\mathbf{A}(x)$ and $\mathbf{B}(x)$ are evaluated along $\mathbf{z}(x)$.

The value of $\Phi''(0)$ in (2-232) depends on the particular $\boldsymbol{\eta}(x)$ chosen. To make this quite clear, we write the right-hand side of (2-232) as $M[\boldsymbol{\eta}] = 2\Phi''(0)$. Then $\Phi''(0)$, considered as a functional in $\boldsymbol{\eta}(x)$, has a maximum if and only if $M[\boldsymbol{\eta}]$ has a maximum. Note that if $\boldsymbol{\eta} \equiv \mathbf{0}$ then $M[\boldsymbol{\eta}] = 0$. Thus the maximum cannot be negative. If, however, there exists an $\boldsymbol{\eta}_1$ such that $M[\boldsymbol{\eta}_1] > 0$ then $M[\boldsymbol{\eta}]$ has no maximum but can be made arbitrarily large. To see this we need only replace $\boldsymbol{\eta}_1$ by $\rho\boldsymbol{\eta}_1$ and note that $M[\rho\boldsymbol{\eta}_1] = \rho^2 M[\boldsymbol{\eta}_1]$ where ρ can be made arbitrarily large. Thus either $M[\boldsymbol{\eta}]$ has a maximum of 0 or it has no maximum. If $M[\boldsymbol{\eta}]$ has a maximum, we must next ask whether there exists an $\boldsymbol{\eta}(x) \not\equiv \mathbf{0}$ which satisfies $\boldsymbol{\eta}(x_0) = \mathbf{0} = \boldsymbol{\eta}(x_1)$ and which yields $M[\boldsymbol{\eta}] = 0$. If there exists such an admissible $\boldsymbol{\eta}$, it must be a solution to the Euler equations associated with the problem of maximizing $M[\boldsymbol{\eta}]$. These equations are

$$\frac{\mathrm{d}}{\mathrm{d}x}[\mathbf{B}(x)\boldsymbol{\eta}'] - \mathbf{A}(x)\boldsymbol{\eta} = \mathbf{0}. \tag{2-235}$$

The problem of maximizing $M[\boldsymbol{\eta}]$ is often referred to as the *accessory maximum problem* and the Euler equation (2-235) for this problem is referred to as the *Jacobi equation* or Jacobi accessory equation. Notice that in writing the Jacobi equation (2-235) we must always have in mind a specific $\mathbf{z}(x)$ which has no corners and which satisfies the Euler equations for the original problem; $\mathbf{z}(x)$ determines $\mathbf{A}(x)$ and $\mathbf{B}(x)$.

The Jacobi equations make up a system of n linear homogeneous differential equations of second order. In general, however, they do not have constant coefficients. The matrix of the coefficients of the second derivatives is $\mathbf{B}(x) = \mathbf{F}_{\mathbf{y}'\mathbf{y}'}$. If $\mathbf{F}_{\mathbf{y}'\mathbf{y}'}$ is nonsingular along $\mathbf{z}(x)$ then $\mathbf{B}(x)$ possesses an inverse for each x and the Jacobi equations can be written*

* If $\mathbf{F}_{\mathbf{y}'\mathbf{y}'}$ is nonsingular along $\mathbf{z}(x)$ it follows that $\mathbf{z}''(x)$ exists and is continuous everywhere and that therefore $\mathrm{d}\mathbf{B}(x)/\mathrm{d}x$ exists. Note that third partial derivatives of F appear in $\mathrm{d}\mathbf{B}/\mathrm{d}x$.

$$\boldsymbol{\eta}'' + \mathbf{B}^{-1}(x)\left[\frac{\mathrm{d}}{\mathrm{d}x}\mathbf{B}(x)\right]\boldsymbol{\eta}' - \mathbf{B}^{-1}(x)\mathbf{A}(x)\boldsymbol{\eta} = \mathbf{0}. \tag{2-236}$$

Every solution $\boldsymbol{\eta}(x)$ to this system of equations can be written as a linear combination

$$\sum_{j=1}^{2n} \delta_j \boldsymbol{\eta}_j(x)$$

of $2n$ linearly independent solutions $\boldsymbol{\eta}_1(x), \ldots, \boldsymbol{\eta}_{2n}(x)$. (A set of functions $\boldsymbol{\eta}_1(x), \ldots, \boldsymbol{\eta}_r(x)$ is said to be linearly dependent over some interval if there exists a set of numbers $\lambda_1, \ldots, \lambda_r$ independent of x and not all 0 such that $\boldsymbol{\lambda} \cdot \boldsymbol{\eta}(x) = 0$ for each x in the interval. Otherwise the functions are said to be linearly independent.) *Let $\boldsymbol{\Delta}(x)$ be an $n \times 2n$ matrix the columns of which are the $2n$ linearly independent solutions $\boldsymbol{\eta}_j(x)$, and let $\boldsymbol{\delta}$ be a vector with the $2n$ components δ_j.* Then for every solution $\boldsymbol{\eta}(x)$ to (2-236) there exists a $\boldsymbol{\delta}$ independent of x such that $\boldsymbol{\eta}(x)$ can be written

$$\boldsymbol{\eta}(x) = \boldsymbol{\Delta}(x)\boldsymbol{\delta}. \tag{2-237}$$

(For a discussion of systems of linear differential equations see, for example, Pontryagin [28], Chapter 3.) We are looking for a solution to (2-236) for which $\boldsymbol{\eta}(x_0) = \boldsymbol{\eta}(x_1) = \mathbf{0}$ with $\boldsymbol{\eta}(x) \not\equiv \mathbf{0}$. It is helpful to now introduce the following definition.

Conjugate Point. The value x^* of x is said to be conjugate to x_0 if there exists a solution $\boldsymbol{\eta}(x)$ to the Jacobi equation which is not identically zero, which satisfies $\boldsymbol{\eta}(x_0) = \mathbf{0}$ and vanishes also at x^*.

If x_1 is conjugate to x_0 there exists an admissible solution to the Jacobi equation; hence there may exist (and, as we shall see later, do exist) functions other than $\boldsymbol{\eta} \equiv \mathbf{0}$ for which $\Phi''(0) = 0$.

We shall not need to consider in much more detail the problem of maximizing $\Phi''(0)$. However, it is worth examining the concept of conjugate points in greater depth since they will play an important role in the sufficiency theory to be developed below.

We now prove the following theorem about conjugate points.

Theorem 2.18.2. The point (number) x^* is conjugate to x_0 along $\mathbf{z}(x)$ if and only if

$$\begin{vmatrix} \boldsymbol{\Delta}(x_0) \\ \\ \boldsymbol{\Delta}(x^*) \end{vmatrix} = 0. \tag{2-238}$$

The determinant on the left in (2-238) is the determinant of the matrix

$$\mathbf{V}(x) = \begin{bmatrix} \boldsymbol{\Delta}(x_0) \\ \\ \boldsymbol{\Delta}(x) \end{bmatrix} \tag{2-239}$$

of order $2n$ evaluated at x^*. Thus x^* is conjugate to x_0 if and only if $\mathbf{V}(x)$ is singular at x^*.

To prove the theorem, suppose that x^* is a point conjugate to x_0. Then there exists an $\boldsymbol{\eta}(x)$, $\boldsymbol{\eta} \not\equiv \mathbf{0}$, which is a solution to the Jacobi equation and such that $\boldsymbol{\eta}(x_0) = \boldsymbol{\eta}(x^*) = \mathbf{0}$. From (2-237), however, there must exist a $\boldsymbol{\delta}$ such that $\boldsymbol{\eta}(x) = \boldsymbol{\Delta}(x)\boldsymbol{\delta}$. Since $\boldsymbol{\eta}(x_0) = \boldsymbol{\eta}(x^*) = \mathbf{0}$, $\boldsymbol{\delta}$ must satisfy the system of $2n$ linear homogeneous equations

$$\boldsymbol{\Delta}(x_0)\boldsymbol{\delta} = \mathbf{0}$$

$$\boldsymbol{\Delta}(x^*)\boldsymbol{\delta} = \mathbf{0}. \tag{2-240}$$

In order that there exist a nontrivial solution ($\boldsymbol{\delta} = \mathbf{0}$ yields $\boldsymbol{\eta} \not\equiv \mathbf{0}$, which we do not want), the matrix of the coefficients must be singular, that is, (2-238) must hold.

Suppose now that (2-238) holds. This implies the existence of a nontrivial solution, $\boldsymbol{\delta}_1$ say, to (2-240). Let us write $\boldsymbol{\eta}(x) = \boldsymbol{\Delta}(x)\boldsymbol{\delta}_1$. Then $\boldsymbol{\eta}(x_0) = \boldsymbol{\eta}(x^*) = \mathbf{0}$ and $\boldsymbol{\eta} \not\equiv \mathbf{0}$, since the solutions in $\boldsymbol{\Delta}(x)$ are linearly independent. This then proves the theorem.

Not all of the $2n$ linearly independent solutions $\boldsymbol{\eta}_j(x)$ to the Jacobi equations need vanish at x_0. Suppose that we now form from these $2n$ solutions a set of n linearly independent solutions $\mathbf{h}_1(x), \ldots, \mathbf{h}_n(x)$ which do vanish at x_0. Such a set can be constructed in the following way. We wish to determine n vectors $\mathbf{a}_u$ such that if $\mathbf{h}_u(x) = \boldsymbol{\Delta}(x)\mathbf{a}_u$ then $\mathbf{h}_u(x_0) = \mathbf{0}$, i.e. $\boldsymbol{\Delta}(x_0)\mathbf{a}_u = \mathbf{0}$. Now the nullity of $\boldsymbol{\Delta}(x_0)$ is at least n since $\boldsymbol{\Delta}(x_0)$ has only n rows; hence the set of solutions to $\boldsymbol{\Delta}(x_0)\boldsymbol{\lambda} = \mathbf{0}$ spans a subspace of dimension at least n. Let us select as the $\mathbf{a}_u$ any n linearly independent vectors in this subspace. Then the $\mathbf{h}_u(x)$ are indeed linearly independent, since $\Sigma_u \lambda_u \mathbf{h}_u(x) = \mathbf{0}$ implies $\boldsymbol{\Delta}(x)[\boldsymbol{\lambda}\mathbf{A}] = \mathbf{0}$, where $\mathbf{A}$ is a matrix the rows of which are the $\mathbf{a}_u$. Now the $2n$ solutions $\boldsymbol{\eta}_j$ are linearly independent, hence $\boldsymbol{\lambda}\mathbf{A} = \mathbf{0}$. In view of the method of selecting the $\mathbf{a}_u$, however, the rank of $\mathbf{A}$ is n. Thus $\boldsymbol{\lambda} = \mathbf{0}$ is the only solution and the $\mathbf{h}_u(x)$ are indeed linearly independent.

Consider now the matrix $\mathbf{T}(x) = (\mathbf{h}_1(x), \ldots, \mathbf{h}_n(x))$ the columns of which are the $\mathbf{h}_u(x)$. We shall now prove the following theorem.

Theorem 2.18.3. The matrix $\mathbf{T}(x)$ *is singular at* x_0*, at the points conjugate to* x_0 *along* $\mathbf{z}(x)$*, and nowhere else.*

Clearly $\mathbf{T}(x_0) = \mathbf{0}$ is singular. It remains to establish that the only other points at which $\mathbf{T}(x)$ is singular are the points conjugate to x_0.

We begin by proving that *every* solution to the Jacobi equation which vanishes at x_0 is a linear combination of the $\mathbf{h}_u(x)$, i.e., that $\boldsymbol{\eta}(x) = \mathbf{T}(x)\boldsymbol{\rho}$ for some $\boldsymbol{\rho}$ independent of x. As a first step we show that the determinant $|\mathrm{d}\mathbf{T}(x_0)/\mathrm{d}x| \neq 0$. Suppose that the determinant does vanish. Then there exists a $\boldsymbol{\rho} \neq \mathbf{0}$, say $\boldsymbol{\rho}_1$, such that if $\boldsymbol{\eta}_1(x) = \mathbf{T}\boldsymbol{\rho}_1$, $\boldsymbol{\eta}_1'(x) = \mathbf{0}$. However, $\mathbf{T}(x_0) = \mathbf{0}$; hence $\boldsymbol{\eta}_1(x_0) = \mathbf{0}$ also. Now the function $\boldsymbol{\eta}(x) \equiv \mathbf{0}$ is a solution to the Jacobi equation with $\boldsymbol{\eta}(x_0) = \mathbf{0}$ and $\boldsymbol{\eta}'(x_0) = \mathbf{0}$ and, from the uniqueness theorem for linear differential equations, this is the only solution with these properties. Hence $\boldsymbol{\eta}_1(x) \equiv \mathbf{0}$. From the assumption that the $\mathbf{h}_u$ are linearly independent, however, $|\mathbf{T}(x)|$ does not vanish everywhere; for some x, say x_c, $|\mathbf{T}(x_c)| \neq 0$. Thus we have $\boldsymbol{\eta}_1(x_c) = \mathbf{0} = \mathbf{T}(x_c)\boldsymbol{\rho}_1$. This implies that $\boldsymbol{\rho}_1 = \mathbf{0}$, a contradiction. Hence $|\mathrm{d}\mathbf{T}(x_0)/\mathrm{d}x| \neq 0$.

Suppose now that $\boldsymbol{\eta}(x)$ is an arbitrary solution to the Jacobi equation, with $\boldsymbol{\eta}(x_0) = \mathbf{0}$. We next show that there exists a $\boldsymbol{\rho}$ such that $\boldsymbol{\eta}(x) = \mathbf{T}(x)\boldsymbol{\rho}$. Observe that for any $\boldsymbol{\rho}$, $\boldsymbol{\eta}_*(x) = \boldsymbol{\eta}(x) - \mathbf{T}(x)\boldsymbol{\rho}$ is a solution with $\boldsymbol{\eta}_*(x_0) = \mathbf{0}$. Furthermore, since $\mathrm{d}\mathbf{T}(x_0)/\mathrm{d}x$ is nonsingular, it is possible to determine a $\boldsymbol{\rho}$ for which $\boldsymbol{\eta}_*'(x_0) = \mathbf{0}$. In fact, $\boldsymbol{\rho} = [\mathrm{d}\mathbf{T}(x_0)/\mathrm{d}x]^{-1}\, \boldsymbol{\eta}'(x_0)$. From $\boldsymbol{\eta}_*(x_0) = \mathbf{0}$ and $\boldsymbol{\eta}_*'(x_0) = \mathbf{0}$ it follows that $\boldsymbol{\eta}_*(x) \equiv \mathbf{0}$ and $\boldsymbol{\eta}(x) = \mathbf{T}(x)\boldsymbol{\rho}$, which is what we wished to show.

Finally, it can be shown, by reasoning much the same as that used in proving Theorem 2.18.2 that if x^* is a point conjugate to x_0 then $|\mathbf{T}(x^*)| = 0$ and if $|\mathbf{T}(x^*)| = 0$ then x^* is a point conjugate to x_0. That completes the proof of Theorem 2.18.3.

We offer one further observation concerning the Jacobi equations, but leave the proof to the reader (Problem 9). Suppose that we have the general solution to the Euler equations for the *primary* problem involving the maximization of $J[\mathbf{y}]$. This solution may be written $\mathbf{y}(x; \lambda_1, \ldots, \lambda_{2n})$, where the λ_j are the $2n$ constants of integration. Then $2n$ solutions to the Jacobi equations can be found by taking the partial derivative of $\mathbf{y}$ with respect to each parameter λ_j and then equating the λ_j to the values for which $\mathbf{y}(x_0) = \mathbf{y}_0$ and $\mathbf{y}(x_1) = \mathbf{y}_1$. Thus $\boldsymbol{\eta}_j(x) = \mathbf{y}_{\lambda_j}(x; \lambda_1, \ldots, \lambda_{2n})$ with the λ_j taking values such that $\mathbf{y}(x_0) = \mathbf{y}_0$ and $\mathbf{y}(x_1) = \mathbf{y}_1$. These $2n$ solutions are linearly independent and can be used to construct the general solution in the manner discussed above.

We are at last ready to state and prove the Legendre sufficient condition.

Theorem 2.18.4. Legendre Sufficient Condition. Suppose that $\mathbf{z}(x)$ *is an admissible function without corners which satisfies the Euler equations for the problem of maximizing* $J[\mathbf{y}]$ *when the interval of integration is finite. Suppose also that the matrix* $\mathbf{F}_{\mathbf{y}'\mathbf{y}'}(x, \mathbf{z}(x), \mathbf{z}'(x))$ *is negative definite at each point in the interval* $x_0 \le x \le x_1$ *(note that* $\mathbf{F}_{\mathbf{y}'\mathbf{y}'}$ *is evaluated along* $\mathbf{z}(x)$*). Suppose finally that there is no point conjugate to* x_0 *in the interval* $x_0 < x \le x_1$*. Then* $\mathbf{z}(x)$ *yields a weak relative maximum of* $J[\mathbf{y}]$*. Under the same conditions, if* $\mathbf{F}_{\mathbf{y}'\mathbf{y}'}$ *is positive definite,* $\mathbf{z}(x)$ *yields a weak relative minimum of* $J[\mathbf{y}]$.

To prove this theorem we shall show that under the stated conditions $M[\boldsymbol{\eta}]$ can be written in the form

$$-\int_{x_0}^{x_1} \mathbf{u} \cdot \mathbf{u} dx,$$

so that it is always nonpositive; and that if $\boldsymbol{\eta} \not\equiv \mathbf{0}$ then $\mathbf{u}(x) \not\equiv \mathbf{0}$, so that the integral is actually negative. This is all that is needed. Note first of all that if $\mathbf{D}(x)$ is an arbitrary symmetric matrix the elements of which possess derivatives, then

$$\frac{d}{dx} \boldsymbol{\eta}(x) \cdot \mathbf{D}(x)\boldsymbol{\eta}(x) = 2\boldsymbol{\eta}'(x) \cdot \mathbf{D}(x)\boldsymbol{\eta}(x) + \boldsymbol{\eta}(x) \cdot \left[\frac{d}{dx} \mathbf{D}(x)\right] \boldsymbol{\eta}(x). \tag{2-241}$$

Also, if $\boldsymbol{\eta}(x_0) = \boldsymbol{\eta}(x_1) = \mathbf{0}$ then

$$\int_{x_0}^{x_1} \frac{d}{dx} \boldsymbol{\eta} \cdot \mathbf{D}\boldsymbol{\eta} dx = \boldsymbol{\eta}(x_1) \cdot \mathbf{D}(x_1)\boldsymbol{\eta}(x_1) - \boldsymbol{\eta}(x_0) \cdot \mathbf{D}(x_0)\boldsymbol{\eta}(x_0) = 0. \tag{2-242}$$

On combining (2-241) and (2-242) we see that, for any admissible function $\boldsymbol{\eta}(x)$ and an arbitrary differentiable symmetric matrix $\mathbf{D}(x)$,

$$0 = 2\int_{x_0}^{x_1} \boldsymbol{\eta}' \cdot \mathbf{D}\boldsymbol{\eta} dx + \int_{x_0}^{x_1} \boldsymbol{\eta} \cdot \frac{d\mathbf{D}}{dx} \boldsymbol{\eta} dx. \tag{2-243}$$

Thus we can add the right hand side of (2-243) to (2-234) without changing the value of the expression. Consequently,

$$M[\boldsymbol{\eta}] = -\int_{x_0}^{x_1} \left[-\boldsymbol{\eta} \cdot \mathbf{A}\boldsymbol{\eta} + \boldsymbol{\eta}' \cdot (-\mathbf{B})\boldsymbol{\eta}' + 2\boldsymbol{\eta}' \cdot \mathbf{D}\boldsymbol{\eta} + \boldsymbol{\eta} \cdot \frac{d\mathbf{D}}{dx} \boldsymbol{\eta}\right] dx. \tag{2-244}$$

We wish to show that the integrand can be written in the form $\mathbf{u} \cdot \mathbf{u}$ or, more precisely, in the form $(\mathbf{R}\boldsymbol{\eta}' + \mathbf{S}\boldsymbol{\eta}) \cdot (\mathbf{R}\boldsymbol{\eta}' + \mathbf{S}\boldsymbol{\eta})$. Note that

$$(\mathbf{R}\boldsymbol{\eta}' + \mathbf{S}\boldsymbol{\eta}) \cdot (\mathbf{R}\boldsymbol{\eta}' + \mathbf{S}\boldsymbol{\eta}) = \boldsymbol{\eta}' \cdot \mathbf{R}^{\mathrm{T}}\mathbf{R}\boldsymbol{\eta}' + 2\boldsymbol{\eta}' \cdot \mathbf{R}^{\mathrm{T}}\mathbf{S}\boldsymbol{\eta} + \boldsymbol{\eta} \cdot \mathbf{S}^{\mathrm{T}}\mathbf{S}\boldsymbol{\eta} \quad (2\text{-}245)$$

where the superscript T on matrices denotes the transpose. If this is to be the integrand of (2-244) we must have $-\mathbf{B} = \mathbf{R}^{\mathrm{T}}\mathbf{R}$, $\mathbf{A} + \mathrm{d}\mathbf{D}/\mathrm{d}x = \mathbf{S}^{\mathrm{T}}\mathbf{S}$ and $\mathbf{R}^{\mathrm{T}}\mathbf{S} = \mathbf{D}$. We shall look for square matrices $\mathbf{R}$ and $\mathbf{S}$ with these properties. In this connection we recall that $\mathbf{B}$ is a negative definite, and therefore nonsingular, symmetric matrix and that $-\mathbf{B}$ is a positive definite matrix. As we ask the reader to show in the problems, there exists a nonsingular symmetric matrix $\mathbf{Q}$ such that $\mathbf{Q}^2 = -\mathbf{B}$. Thus we can set $\mathbf{R} = \mathbf{Q}$. On taking the transpose of $\mathbf{R}^{\mathrm{T}}\mathbf{S} = \mathbf{D}$ we have $\mathbf{S}^{\mathrm{T}}\mathbf{Q} = \mathbf{D}^{\mathrm{T}} = \mathbf{D}$. We next multiply on the right by $-\mathbf{B}^{-1} = \mathbf{Q}^{-1}\mathbf{Q}^{-1}$ to obtain $\mathbf{S}^{\mathrm{T}}\mathbf{Q}^{-1} = -\mathbf{D}\mathbf{B}^{-1}$, then multiply on the right by $\mathbf{Q}\mathbf{S} = \mathbf{D}$ to obtain $\mathbf{S}^{\mathrm{T}}\mathbf{S} = -\mathbf{D}\mathbf{B}^{-1}\mathbf{D}$. Thus the integrand of (2-244) can be written in the form $\mathbf{u} \cdot \mathbf{u}$ if there can be found a matrix $\mathbf{D}$ for which

$$\mathbf{A} + \frac{\mathrm{d}\mathbf{D}}{\mathrm{d}x} = -\mathbf{D}\mathbf{B}^{-1}\mathbf{D}. \quad (2\text{-}246)$$

Then $\mathbf{R} = \mathbf{Q}$ and $\mathbf{S} = \mathbf{Q}^{-1}\mathbf{D}$.

To show that a matrix $\mathbf{D}$ satisfying this equation can indeed be found, we first transform (2-246) by multiplying on the right by a square matrix $\mathbf{T}$, thus obtaining

$$\mathbf{A}\mathbf{T} + \frac{\mathrm{d}\mathbf{D}}{\mathrm{d}x}\mathbf{T} = -\mathbf{D}\mathbf{B}^{-1}\mathbf{D}\mathbf{T}. \quad (2\text{-}247)$$

Suppose now that $\mathbf{T}$ is nonsingular for each x and that $\mathbf{D}\mathbf{T} = \mathbf{B}(\mathrm{d}\mathbf{T}/\mathrm{d}x)$. Then since

$$\frac{\mathrm{d}}{\mathrm{d}x}\left[\mathbf{B}\frac{\mathrm{d}\mathbf{T}}{\mathrm{d}x}\right] = \frac{\mathrm{d}}{\mathrm{d}x}\mathbf{D}\mathbf{T} = \frac{\mathrm{d}\mathbf{T}}{\mathrm{d}x}\mathbf{T} + \mathbf{D}\frac{\mathrm{d}\mathbf{T}}{\mathrm{d}x}$$

(2-247) reduces to

$$\frac{\mathrm{d}}{\mathrm{d}x}\left[\mathbf{B}\frac{\mathrm{d}\mathbf{T}}{\mathrm{d}x}\right] - \mathbf{A}\mathbf{T} = \mathbf{0}. \quad (2\text{-}248)$$

If there can be found a $\mathbf{T}(x)$ which is a solution to (2-248) for each x and which is also nonsingular then there can be found a $\mathbf{D} = -\mathbf{B}(\mathrm{d}\mathbf{T}/\mathrm{d}x)\mathbf{T}^{-1}$ which satisfies (2-246), hence also an $\mathbf{R} = \mathbf{Q}$ ($\mathbf{Q}^2 = -\mathbf{B}$) and an $\mathbf{S} = \mathbf{Q}^{-1}\mathbf{D}$ which reduce the integrand of (2-244) to the form $\mathbf{u} \cdot \mathbf{u}$, $\mathbf{u} = \mathbf{Q}\boldsymbol{\eta}' + \mathbf{Q}^{-1}\mathbf{D}\boldsymbol{\eta}$.

We now note that (2-248) and the Jacobi equation (2-235) are of precisely the same form, with the vector $\boldsymbol{\eta}$ in (2-235) replaced by the matrix $\mathbf{T}$ in (2-248). Moreover $\mathbf{B}$ is nonsingular at each point in the interval. Hence the conversion of (2-248) into the form (2-236) is valid. Thus there are $2n$ linearly independent solutions to the Jacobi equation and from these can be formed n linearly independent solutions which vanish at x_0. Let $\mathbf{T}$ be the matrix with these n linearly independent solutions as its columns. From Theorem 2.18.3 we know that $\mathbf{T}$ is singular only at points which are conjugate to x_0. Thus we have constructed a matrix $\mathbf{T}$ which is nonsingular in the interval $x_0 < x \leq x_1$ and which satisfies (2-248). This in turn guarantees the existence of the matrix $\mathbf{D}(x)$, which allows us to write the integrand in (2-234) as $\mathbf{u} \cdot \mathbf{u}$, where $\mathbf{u} = \mathbf{Q}\boldsymbol{\eta}' + \mathbf{Q}^{-1}\mathbf{D}\boldsymbol{\eta}$. Thus

$$2\Phi''(0) = -\int_{x_0}^{x_1} \mathbf{u}(x) \cdot \mathbf{u}(x) dx$$

for every admissible $\boldsymbol{\eta}(x)$. The integrand is always non-negative. Furthermore, if there exists an x, say x^*, such that $\mathbf{u}(x^*) \cdot \mathbf{u}(x^*) > 0$ then, by continuity, the scalar product is positive over an interval of x and $\Phi''(0)$ is negative.

However, we have not ruled out the possibility that there exists an admissible $\boldsymbol{\eta}(x)$ other than $\boldsymbol{\eta} \equiv \mathbf{0}$ for which $\mathbf{u}(x) \equiv \mathbf{0}$. If $\mathbf{u} \equiv \mathbf{0}$ then

$$\mathbf{Q}\boldsymbol{\eta}' + \mathbf{Q}^{-1}\mathbf{D}\boldsymbol{\eta} \equiv \mathbf{0} \quad \text{or} \quad \boldsymbol{\eta}' - \mathbf{B}^{-1}\mathbf{D}\boldsymbol{\eta} \equiv \mathbf{0} \tag{2-249}$$

since $-\mathbf{B}^{-1} = \mathbf{Q}^{-1}\mathbf{Q}^{-1}$. If $\boldsymbol{\eta}(x)$ is admissible, $\boldsymbol{\eta}(x_0) = \mathbf{0}$. But then (2-249) implies that $\boldsymbol{\eta}'(x_0) = \mathbf{0}$ also, and this in turn requires that $\boldsymbol{\eta} \equiv \mathbf{0}$. Thus $\boldsymbol{\eta} \equiv \mathbf{0}$ is the only admissible function for which $\mathbf{u} \equiv \mathbf{0}$. Consequently, for every admissible $\boldsymbol{\eta}(x)$, $\boldsymbol{\eta} \not\equiv \mathbf{0}$, $\Phi''(0) < 0$ and, for sufficiently small ξ, $J[\mathbf{y}] < J[\mathbf{z}]$. That completes the proof of the sufficiency theorem.

The above theorem does not indicate what happens when $\mathbf{F}_{\mathbf{y}'\mathbf{y}'}$ is negative definite along a function $\mathbf{z}(x)$ which satisfies the necessary conditions but there is at least one point conjugate to x_0 in the interval $x_0 < x \leq x_1$. We now prove that $\mathbf{z}(x)$ cannot yield a relative maximum or minimum of $J[\mathbf{y}]$ if there is a conjugate point in the interval $x_0 < x < x_1$. This result is sometimes known as the Jacobi necessary condition. Before stating the condition and proving its necessity, we shall prove a theorem which will be needed along the way.

Theorem 2.18.5. If x^*, $x_0 < x^* \leq x_1$, is a point conjugate to x_0, if $\boldsymbol{\eta}(x)$ is a solution to the Jacobi equation over the interval $x_0 \leq x \leq x^*$, and if $\boldsymbol{\eta}(x)$ is not identically $\mathbf{0}$ over this interval but satisfies $\boldsymbol{\eta}(x_0) = \boldsymbol{\eta}(x^*) = \mathbf{0}$ then

$$\int_{x_0}^{x^*} [\boldsymbol{\eta} \cdot \mathbf{A}(x)\boldsymbol{\eta} + \boldsymbol{\eta}' \cdot \mathbf{B}(x)\boldsymbol{\eta}']\mathrm{d}x = 0 \tag{2-250}$$

for this $\boldsymbol{\eta}(x)$.

The proof is not difficult. $\boldsymbol{\eta}(x)$ satisfies (2-235); hence, if we multiply on the right by $\boldsymbol{\eta}$ we obtain, for each x in the interval,

$$\boldsymbol{\eta} \cdot \frac{\mathrm{d}}{\mathrm{d}x}[\mathbf{B}(x)\boldsymbol{\eta}'] = \boldsymbol{\eta} \cdot \mathbf{A}(x)\boldsymbol{\eta}. \tag{2-251}$$

If in (2-250) we now replace $\boldsymbol{\eta} \cdot \mathbf{A}\boldsymbol{\eta}$ by the left hand side of (2-251), we arrive at

$$\begin{aligned}\int_{x_0}^{x^*} [\boldsymbol{\eta} \cdot \mathbf{A}\boldsymbol{\eta} + \boldsymbol{\eta}' \cdot \mathbf{B}\boldsymbol{\eta}']\mathrm{d}x &= \int_{x_0}^{x^*} \left[\boldsymbol{\eta} \cdot \frac{\mathrm{d}}{\mathrm{d}x}(\mathbf{B}\boldsymbol{\eta}') + \boldsymbol{\eta}' \cdot \mathbf{B}\boldsymbol{\eta}'\right] \mathrm{d}x \\ &= \int_{x_0}^{x^*} \frac{\mathrm{d}}{\mathrm{d}x}(\boldsymbol{\eta} \cdot \mathbf{B}\boldsymbol{\eta}')\mathrm{d}x \\ &= \boldsymbol{\eta} \cdot \mathbf{B}\boldsymbol{\eta}' \Big|_{x_0}^{x^*} = 0\end{aligned}$$

as desired.

Theorem 2.18.6. Jacobi Necessary Condition. Suppose that $\mathbf{z}(x)$ *is an admissible function without corners such that* $F_{\mathbf{y}'\mathbf{y}'}$ *is nonsingular along* $\mathbf{z}(x)$ *and which yields the global (or a weak or strong relative) maximum or minimum of* $J[\mathbf{y}]$. *Then there exists no point conjugate to* x_0 *in the interval* $x_0 < x < x_1$.

This can be readily proved with the aid of Theorem 2.18.5. Let $\boldsymbol{\eta}(x)$ be a solution to the Jacobi accessory equation which is not identically $\mathbf{0}$ but for which $\boldsymbol{\eta}(x_0) = \boldsymbol{\eta}(x^*) = \mathbf{0}$; and define $\boldsymbol{\eta}(x) \equiv \mathbf{0}$ for $x^* \leq x \leq x_1$. Now the expression (2-232) for $\Phi''(0)$ can be split into two integrals, one from x_0 to x^* and another from x^* to x_1. From Theorem 2.18.5, the first integral vanishes; and, since $\boldsymbol{\eta} \equiv \mathbf{0}$, the second vanishes also. Thus, for this function $\boldsymbol{\eta}$, $\Phi''(0)$ vanishes, and $\boldsymbol{\eta}$ yields the absolute maximum of $M[\boldsymbol{\eta}]$ if $\mathbf{z}(x)$ yields a maximum of $J[\mathbf{y}]$, which we have assumed to be the case. Hence $\boldsymbol{\eta}$ does indeed yield the maximum. Consequently, $\boldsymbol{\eta}$ must satisfy the necessary conditions for this problem. We know that $\boldsymbol{\eta}$ satisfies the Euler equation (Jacobi equation), but it must also satisfy the corner condition at x^*.

If the integrand of $M[\boldsymbol{\eta}]$ is denoted by Q, the term $\mathbf{F}_{\mathbf{y}'}$ becomes $\mathbf{Q}_{\boldsymbol{\eta}'}$ and this must be continuous across x^*. Now

$$\mathbf{Q}_{\boldsymbol{\eta}'} = 2\mathbf{B}(x)\boldsymbol{\eta}'$$

and $\mathbf{Q}_{\boldsymbol{\eta}'}(x_+^*) = \mathbf{0}$ since $\boldsymbol{\eta}'(x_+^*) = \mathbf{0}$. Consequently, $\mathbf{B}(x_-^*)\boldsymbol{\eta}'(x_-^*) = \mathbf{0}$. Since $\mathbf{B}(x_-^*)$ is nonsingular, this implies that $\boldsymbol{\eta}'(x_-^*) = \mathbf{0}$. However, $\boldsymbol{\eta}(x^*) = \mathbf{0}$ also. Therefore, from the theory of differential equations, $\boldsymbol{\eta}(x)$ must be identically $\mathbf{0}$ to the left of x^*. This is a contradiction. Hence there cannot be a conjugate point in the interval $x_0 < x < x_1$.

The Jacobi necessary condition does not apply to the case in which x_1 is conjugate to x_0. Usually $\mathbf{z}(x)$ yields neither a maximum nor a minimum in that case; but this is not certain. To discover whether $\mathbf{z}(x)$ yields a maximum or minimum it is necessary to investigate higher order terms in the expansion of $\Phi(\xi)$.

We conclude this section with another theorem on conjugate points which is sometimes useful.

Theorem 2.18.7. Suppose that F is a strictly concave function of $(\mathbf{y}, \mathbf{y}')$ for each x over an open convex set which includes all $(\mathbf{y}, \mathbf{y}')$ such that $(x, \mathbf{y}, \mathbf{y}') \in \mathscr{R}$, and let $\mathbf{y}(x)$ be any solution to the Euler equations (without corners) such that $\mathbf{y}(x_0) = \mathbf{y}_0$ and $\mathbf{y}(x_1) = \mathbf{y}_1$. Then along $\mathbf{y}(x)$ in the interval $x_0 < x \leq x_1$ there are no points conjugate to x_0.

The proof is by contradiction. Suppose that there exists a conjugate point x^* satisfying $x_0 < x^* \leq x_1$. Then there exists a solution to the Jacobi equation not identically $\mathbf{0}$ but satisfying $\boldsymbol{\eta}(x_0) = \boldsymbol{\eta}(x^*) = \mathbf{0}$. Furthermore, from Theorem 2.18.5, equation (2-250) holds for this integral. However, the integral (2-250) is also given by (2-231) with x_1 replaced by x^*. Now, since F is concave, the integrand in (2-231) is never positive and is always negative except when $\boldsymbol{\eta} = \boldsymbol{\eta}' = \mathbf{0}$. Since $\boldsymbol{\eta} \not\equiv \mathbf{0}$, there is an x and, by continuity, an interval of x, for which $\boldsymbol{\eta} \neq \mathbf{0}$ and the integrand in (2-231) negative. Thus the integral must be negative, and this contradicts the fact that it is 0.

Example. In specific examples it is usually quite difficult to apply Theorem 2.18.4, even when it is clear that $\mathbf{F}_{\mathbf{y}'\mathbf{y}'}$ is negative definite. The reason is that in each case it is necessary to check for conjugate points. Consider again the problem of finding the curve which yields the surface of revolution of minimum area. In the nonparametric formulation,

$$F_{y'y'} = y[1 + (y')^2]^{-3/2}$$

which is positive along any curve which lies above the x-axis. Now in the razor's edge case in which there is just one catenary through the points it turns out that x_1 is conjugate to $-x_1$, and additional analysis shows that the catenary yields neither a minimum nor a maximum. However we shall not provide a detailed demonstration. Consider next the case in which there are two catenaries. It happens to be true that for each catenary there is only one point conjugate to $-x_1$; this is the point of tangency between the curve and the line $y = \alpha^* x$ (see Figure 2.11). For the higher curve this point lies outside the range of integration, while for the lower curve it lies inside. (We ask the reader to show this in the problems.) In view of Theorem 2.18.4, therefore, the upper curve yields a weak relative minimum. According to the Jacobi necessary condition, the lower curve can yield neither a maximum nor a minimum.

In this section we have discussed a sufficient condition for weak relative maxima or minima. There is a more general theory of sufficiency, known as the Weierstrass theory, which applies to strong variations. We shall consider this theory later, in Section 2.20.

2.19. Sensitivity analysis–end point changes

Consider a $2n + 2$ parameter family of vector-valued functions $\mathbf{y}(x; \alpha, \mathbf{a}, \beta, \mathbf{b})$ with the following characteristics. First,

$$\mathbf{y}(\alpha; \alpha, \mathbf{a}, \beta, \mathbf{b}) = \mathbf{a}; \qquad \mathbf{y}(\beta; \alpha, \mathbf{a}, \beta, \mathbf{b}) = \mathbf{b} \tag{2-252}$$

so that the graph of $\mathbf{y}(x; \alpha, \mathbf{a}, \beta, \mathbf{b})$ passes through the points $(\alpha, \mathbf{a})$ and $(\beta, \mathbf{b})$. Second, $\mathbf{y}(x; \alpha, \mathbf{a}, \beta, \mathbf{b})$ possesses continuous partial derivatives of the first order with respect to α, $\mathbf{a}$, β, $\mathbf{b}$ and continuous mixed partial derivatives of second order with respect to x and any one of the parameters from $\mathbf{a}$ or $\mathbf{b}$ over some neighborhood of a particular set of values of the parameters, say $(x_0, \mathbf{y}_0, x_1, \mathbf{y}_1)$. Third, $\mathbf{z}(x) = \mathbf{y}(x; x_0, \mathbf{y}_0, x_1, \mathbf{y}_1)$ satisfies the necessary conditions of Theorem 2.13.1 for the problem

$$J[\mathbf{y}] = \int_{x_0}^{x_1} F dx$$

with $\mathbf{y}(x_0) = \mathbf{y}_0$ and $\mathbf{y}(x_1) = \mathbf{y}_1$. It may or may not be true that, for other values of the parameters $(\alpha, \mathbf{a}, \beta, \mathbf{b})$, $\mathbf{y}(x; \alpha, \mathbf{a}, \beta, \mathbf{b})$ satisfies the necessary conditions for the problem

$$\int_\alpha^\beta F\mathrm{d}x$$

with $\mathbf{y}(\alpha) = \mathbf{a}$ and $\mathbf{y}(\beta) = \mathbf{b}$. In some cases this will be true while for others it will not. We do require, however, that the necessary conditions be satisfied when $\alpha = x_0$, $\mathbf{a} = \mathbf{y}_0$, $\beta = x_1$ and $\mathbf{b} = \mathbf{y}_1$. Often we shall specialize the analysis and confine our attention to an $n + 1$ parameter family $\mathbf{y}(x; \beta, \mathbf{b})$ or $\mathbf{y}(x; \alpha, \mathbf{a})$ with the characteristic that $\mathbf{y}(x_0) = \mathbf{y}_0$ or $\mathbf{y}(x_1) = \mathbf{y}_1$ as the case may be.

Consider now the function

$$J^*(\alpha, \mathbf{a}, \beta, \mathbf{b}) = \int_\alpha^\beta F(x, \mathbf{y}(x; \alpha, \mathbf{a}, \beta, \mathbf{b}), \mathbf{y}'(x; \alpha, \mathbf{a}, \beta, \mathbf{b}))\mathrm{d}x. \tag{2-253}$$

This function is the integral of F along $\mathbf{y}(x, \alpha, \mathbf{a}, \beta, \mathbf{b})$ between $(\alpha, \mathbf{a})$ and $(\beta, \mathbf{b})$. In view of our assumptions concerning $\mathbf{y}(x; \alpha, \mathbf{a}, \beta, \mathbf{b})$, $J^*(\alpha, \mathbf{a}, \beta, \mathbf{b})$ possesses continuous first partial derivatives in a neighborhood of $(x_0, \mathbf{y}_0, x_1, \mathbf{y}_1)$. We now seek to evaluate those derivatives at $(x_0, \mathbf{y}_0, x_1, \mathbf{y}_1)$.

To simplify the notation, we denote the partial derivatives with respect to the parameters by means of the usual partial derivative signs rather than by subscripts. Thus

$$\frac{\partial}{\partial b_j} J^*(x_0, \mathbf{y}_0, x_1, \mathbf{y}_1) = \int_{x_0}^{x_1} \left[\mathbf{F}_{\mathbf{y}}(x, \mathbf{z}, \mathbf{z}') \cdot \frac{\partial \mathbf{y}}{\partial b_j} + \mathbf{F}_{\mathbf{y}'}(x, \mathbf{z}, \mathbf{z}') \cdot \frac{\partial \mathbf{y}'}{\partial b_j}\right] \mathrm{d}x.$$

If we integrate by parts and make use of the fact that $\mathbf{z}(x)$ satisfies the necessary conditions, we obtain

$$\frac{\partial J^*}{\partial b_j} = \mathbf{F}_{\mathbf{y}'} \cdot \frac{\partial \mathbf{y}}{\partial b_j}\bigg|_{x_0}^{x_1}. \tag{2-254}$$

Now, at x_0, $\mathbf{y} = \mathbf{y}_0$; hence $\partial\mathbf{y}/\partial b_j = \mathbf{0}$ at x_0. And at β, $\mathbf{y} = \mathbf{b}$; hence $y_u = b_u$. Thus $\partial y_u/\partial b_j = 0$ if $u \neq j$ and $\partial y_j/\partial b_j = 1$. Hence $\partial\mathbf{y}/\partial b_j = \mathbf{e}_j$, the jth unit vector, and, from (2-254),

$$\frac{\partial}{\partial b_j} J^*(x_0, \mathbf{y}_0, x_1, \mathbf{y}_1) = F_{y_j'}(x_1, \mathbf{y}_1, \mathbf{z}'(x_1)). \tag{2-255}$$

Consider next $\partial J^*/\partial\beta$. Here we may apply (2-175) bearing in mind, however, that the upper limit of integration is variable. Thus

$$\frac{\partial}{\partial\beta} J^*(x_0, \mathbf{y}_0, x_1, \mathbf{y}_1) = F(x_1, \mathbf{y}_1, \mathbf{z}'(x_1)) + \int_{x_0}^{x_1} \left[\mathbf{F}_{\mathbf{y}} \cdot \frac{\partial \mathbf{y}}{\partial\beta} + \mathbf{F}_{\mathbf{y}'} \cdot \frac{\partial \mathbf{y}'}{\partial\beta}\right] \mathrm{d}x. \tag{2-256}$$

Next we integrate by parts and recall that $\mathbf{z}(x)$ satisfies the necessary conditions. This yields

$$\frac{\partial J^*}{\partial\beta} = F + \mathbf{F}_{\mathbf{y}'} \cdot \frac{\partial \mathbf{y}}{\partial\beta}\bigg|_{x_0}^{x_1}.$$

It remains to evaluate $\partial\mathbf{y}/\partial\beta$ at x_0 and x_1. At x_0, $\mathbf{y} = \mathbf{y}_0$ so that $\partial\mathbf{y}/\partial\beta = \mathbf{0}$. At x_1 the situation is a little more tricky. Note first that $\partial\mathbf{y}/\partial\beta$ evaluated at $(x_1, \mathbf{y}_1)$ means the partial derivative of $\mathbf{y}(x;\, x_0, \mathbf{y}_0, \beta, \mathbf{b})$ evaluated at $(x_1, \mathbf{y}_1)$. Now at β, $\mathbf{y} = \mathbf{b}$, i.e. $\mathbf{y}(\beta;\, x_0, \mathbf{y}_0, \beta, \mathbf{b}) = \mathbf{b}$; hence $\mathrm{d}\mathbf{y}/\mathrm{d}\beta = \mathbf{0}$. However,

$$\frac{\mathrm{d}}{\mathrm{d}\beta} \mathbf{y}(\beta;\, x_0, \mathbf{y}_0, \beta, \mathbf{b}) = \mathbf{y}'(x;\, x_0, \mathbf{y}_0, \beta, \mathbf{b})\bigg|_{(x_1,\, \mathbf{y}_1)} + \frac{\partial}{\partial\beta} \mathbf{y}(x;\, x_0, \mathbf{y}_0, \beta, \mathbf{b})\bigg|_{(x_1,\, \mathbf{y}_1)} = \mathbf{0}.$$

Consequently

$$\frac{\partial \mathbf{y}}{\partial\beta} = -\,\mathbf{y}'(x_1, x_0, \mathbf{y}_0, x_1, \mathbf{y}_1) = -\,\mathbf{z}'(x_1). \tag{2-257}$$

Hence

$$\frac{\partial}{\partial\beta} J^*(x_0, \mathbf{y}_0, x_1, \mathbf{y}_1) = F(x_1, \mathbf{y}_1, \mathbf{z}'(x_1)) - \mathbf{F}_{\mathbf{y}'}(x_1, \mathbf{y}_1, \mathbf{z}'(x_1)) \cdot \mathbf{z}'(x_1). \tag{2-258}$$

Precisely the same procedure can be followed in evaluating $\partial J^*/\partial a_j$ and $\partial J^*/\partial\alpha$. Thus

$$\frac{\partial}{\partial a_j} J^*(x_0, \mathbf{y}_0, x_1, \mathbf{y}_1) = -\,F_{y_j'}(x_0, \mathbf{y}_0, \mathbf{z}'(x_0)) \tag{2-259}$$

and

$$\frac{\partial}{\partial\alpha} J^*(x_0, \mathbf{y}_0, x_1, \mathbf{y}_1) = -\,F(x_0, \mathbf{y}_0, \mathbf{z}'(x_0)) + \mathbf{F}_{\mathbf{y}'}(x_0, \mathbf{y}_0, \mathbf{z}'(x_0)) \cdot \mathbf{z}'(x_0). \tag{2-260}$$

It is worthy of note that all of the partial derivatives depend only on $\mathbf{z}(x)$.

Example. The above results are often used in a more or less heuristic way in sensitivity analyses and in studying how the optimal value of $J[\mathbf{y}]$ varies with changes in the end points. In some cases, as the theory of the next section illustrates, the analysis can be made completely rigorous. As an example of the usefulness of the results, consider the Ramsey model with a finite planning horizon of length T. For a fixed K_0, the maximum of $J[K]$ is a function of K_1, the value K must have at T, and of the length of the planning horizon T. Denote this function by $J^*(K_1, T)$. Then from (2-255)

$$\frac{\partial J^*}{\partial K_1} = F_{\dot{K}} = - U'[\Psi(K_1) - \dot{K}_1] \tag{2-261}$$

so that, as we might have expected, for $K_1 < K^*$ the function J^* is decreasing in K_1. Consumption must be foregone to provide the additional terminal capital.

Next, from (2-258),

$$\frac{\partial J^*}{\partial T} = F - F_{\dot{K}}\dot{K} = U + U'\dot{K} = \lambda \tag{2-262}$$

where λ is the constant of integration. Thus $\partial J^*/\partial T$ is independent of K_1 and T. It is positive if $\lambda > 0$, zero if $\lambda = 0$, and negative if $\lambda < 0$.

2.20.° Weierstrass' sufficient conditions

We now consider the more general theory of sufficiency developed by Weierstrass. These conditions relate to a strong relative maximum or minimum and in certain cases can be used to test for a global maximum or minimum. Consider once again the problem of maximizing

$$\int_{x_0}^{x_1} F dx$$

for a finite interval of integration. Suppose that $\mathbf{z}(x)$ is an admissible function *without corners* which satisfies the Euler equations and that $\mathbf{F}_{\mathbf{y}'\mathbf{y}'}$ is non-singular along $\mathbf{z}(x)$. Suppose also that there is no point conjugate to x_0 in the interval $x_0 < x \leq x_1$. Since $\mathbf{z}(x)$ satisfies the boundary conditions, $\mathbf{z}(x_0) = \mathbf{y}_0$ and $z(x_1) = \mathbf{y}_1$.

For the case $n = 1$, $\mathbf{z}(x)$ might be represented graphically by a curve like that shown in Figure 2.30. Note that $\mathbf{z}(x)$ does not terminate at $(x_0, \mathbf{y}_0)$ or $(x_1, \mathbf{y}_1)$ but is imagined to pass on through these points. We choose a value of x, say x_-, such that $x_- < x_0$; and suppose that $\mathbf{z}(x)$ satisfies the Euler

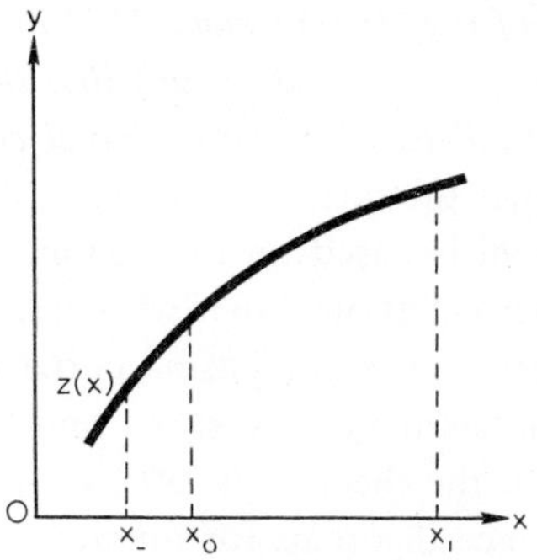

Fig. 2.30.

equations in the interval $x_- \leq x \leq x_1$. We denote by $\mathbf{y}_-$ the value of $\mathbf{z}$ at x_-. Now the general solution to the Euler equations can be imagined to involve $2n$ arbitrary parameters or constants of integration and can be denoted by $\mathbf{y}(x; \lambda_1, \ldots, \lambda_{2n})$. Suppose that we have this general solution. We now seek to determine the collection of solutions which pass through the point $(x_-, \mathbf{y}_-)$. The requirement that $\mathbf{y}_- = \mathbf{y}(x_-; \lambda_1, \ldots, \lambda_{2n})$ reduces the number of arbitrary parameters to n; thus the set of all solutions passing through the point $(x_-, \mathbf{y}_-)$ is an n-parameter family, say $\mathbf{y}(x; \lambda_1, \ldots, \lambda_n)$, and $\mathbf{z}(x)$ is one of these solutions. The n-parameter family is shown in part in Figure 2.31. This collection of solutions we shall refer to as a *field of extremals.*

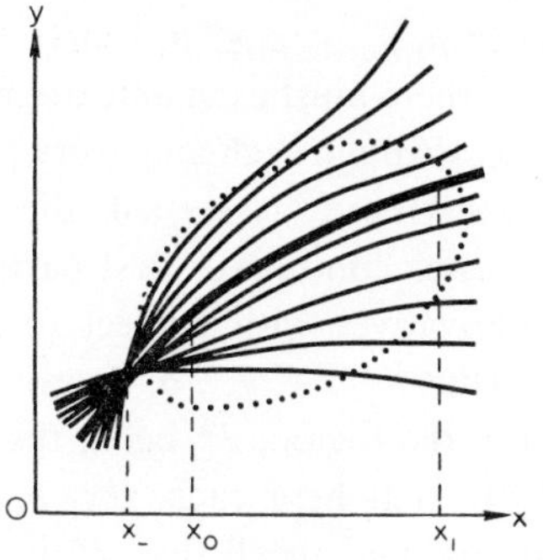

Fig. 2.31.

Consider now any other point $(x, \mathbf{y})$. It might seem possible to determine values of $\lambda_1, \ldots, \lambda_n$ such that there is a solution which passes through $(x, \mathbf{y})$. This need not be true if the point $(x, \mathbf{y})$ is too far removed from $(x, \mathbf{z}(x))$. *However, on assumptions to be listed in a moment, there does exist an* x_-

and an N_ε neighborhood of $\mathbf{z}(x)$ (in the space $\mathscr{E}^{n+1}$ of points $(x, \mathbf{y})$) extending over the interval $x_0 - \varepsilon \leq x \leq x_1 + \varepsilon$ such that through each point $(x, \mathbf{y})$ there does pass one and indeed only one extremal curve which starts at the point $(x_-, \mathbf{y}_-)$. (Note that the interval extends to the left of x_0 and to the right of x_1.) The theorem is based on the assumptions that $F \in C''$, that a solution $\mathbf{z}(x)$ to the Euler equations exists with $\mathbf{z}(x_0) = \mathbf{y}_0$ and $\mathbf{z}(x_1) = \mathbf{y}_1$, that $\mathbf{z}(x)$ lies in the interior of $\mathscr{R}$ and has no corners, that there is no point conjugate to x_0 in the interval $x_0 < x \leq x_1$, and that $\mathbf{F}_{\mathbf{y}'\mathbf{y}'}$ is nonsingular along $\mathbf{z}(x)$. The proof of the theorem is left as a problem (Problem 1). It rests on the basic existence theorems for differential equations and on the implicit function theorems. Statements of these theorems may be found in the appendices.

A field of extremals is said to simply cover a region if through each point in the region there passes one and only one extremal. The above theorem guarantees that when $\mathbf{z}(x)$ is an admissible nonsingular extremal without corners and there are no conjugate points in the interval $x_0 < x \leq x_1$ then there exists an $x_- < x_0$ and an $\varepsilon > 0$ such that there is a field of extremals emanating from $(x_-, \mathbf{y}_-)$ which simply covers an N_ε neighborhood of $\mathbf{z}(x)$, $x_0 - \varepsilon \leq x \leq x_1 + \varepsilon$.

Suppose now that we have a field of extremals of the type discussed above, simply covering some region $\mathscr{W}$ of $\mathscr{E}^{n+1}$. Suppose further that there exist two curves, I and II, in $\mathscr{E}^{n+1}$ which possess continuous derivatives and are represented parametrically by $x = \alpha(\tau)$, $\mathbf{y} = \mathbf{a}(\tau)$ and $x = \beta(\rho)$, $\mathbf{y} = \mathbf{b}(\rho)$, respectively. Suppose also that for each τ in an interval $\tau_0 \leq \tau \leq \tau_1$, curve I lies in $\mathscr{W}$ and that for each ρ, $\rho_0 \leq \rho \leq \rho_1$, curve II lies in $\mathscr{W}$.

From the field property, there must exist an extremal $\mathbf{y}(x, \delta, \mathbf{d})$ emanating from $(x_-, \mathbf{y}_-)$ which passes through each and every point $(\delta, \mathbf{d})$ in the region under consideration. Furthermore, as we ask the reader to show in the problems, $\mathbf{y}(x; \delta, \mathbf{d})$ possesses continuous first partial derivatives and continuous mixed second derivatives with respect to x and any one of the parameters from $(\delta, \mathbf{d})$. Thus $J^*(x_-, \mathbf{y}_-, \delta, \mathbf{d})$ exists and possesses partial derivatives for all $(\delta, \mathbf{d})$ in the region, J^* being the function introduced in the previous section. Note that here each $\mathbf{y}(x, \delta, \mathbf{d})$ is an extremal and satisfies the Euler equations; and recall that J^* is the integral of F along $\mathbf{y}(x)$ from $(x_-, \mathbf{y}_-)$ to $(\delta, \mathbf{d})$.

Consider now the points $(\alpha(\tau), \mathbf{a}(\tau))$ on curve I. For each τ there is an extremal emanating from $(x_-, \mathbf{y}_-)$ which passes through $(\alpha(\tau), \mathbf{a}(\tau))$. Let us write

$$\Omega(\tau) = J^*(x_-, \mathbf{y}_-, \alpha(\tau), \mathbf{a}(\tau)). \tag{2-263}$$

Then, from the observations of the preceding paragraph, $\Omega(\tau)$ is differentiable; and, from (2-255) and (2-258),

$$\Omega'(\tau) = \mathbf{F}_{\mathbf{y}'} \cdot \dot{\mathbf{a}} + (F - \mathbf{F}_{\mathbf{y}'} \cdot \mathbf{y}')\dot{\alpha}. \tag{2-264}$$

Similarly, through each point $(\beta(\rho), \mathbf{b}(\rho))$ on curve II passes an extremal emanating from $(x_-, \mathbf{y}_-)$. If we write for curve II

$$\Lambda(\rho) = J^*(x_-, \mathbf{y}_-, \beta(\rho), \mathbf{b}(\rho)) \tag{2-265}$$

then

$$\Lambda'(\rho) = \mathbf{F}_{\mathbf{y}'} \cdot \dot{\mathbf{b}} + (F - \mathbf{F}_{\mathbf{y}'} \cdot \mathbf{y}')\dot{\beta}. \tag{2-266}$$

Let us now select two values of τ, say τ_0 and τ_1. These determine two points on curve I which in Figure 2.34 we have labeled A and C. The integral of F along $\mathbf{y}$ from $(x_-, \mathbf{y}_-)$ to A is then simply $\Omega(\tau_0)$, and the integral of F from $(x_-, \mathbf{y}_-)$ to C is $\Omega(\tau_1)$. Let us write $J_{QA} = \Omega(\tau_0)$ and $J_{QC} = \Omega(\tau_1)$. Now (2-264) gives an expression for $\Omega'(\tau)$, and if we integrate this from τ_0 to τ_1 we obtain $\Omega(\tau_1) - \Omega(\tau_0)$. Thus we have

$$J_{QC} - J_{QA} = \int_{\tau_0}^{\tau_1} [(F - \mathbf{F}_{\mathbf{y}'} \cdot \mathbf{y}')\dot{\alpha} + \mathbf{F}_{\mathbf{y}'} \cdot \dot{\mathbf{a}}]d\tau. \tag{2-267}$$

The expression on the right in (2-267) is called the Hilbert integral evaluated along curve I and will be denoted by J^{H}_{AC}. We note the interesting fact that $J_{QC} - J_{QA}$ depends only on points A and C and not on the particular curve I used to join them. In other words, the Hilbert integral is independent of the path. (Of course it must lie in the region under consideration.) If curve I can be represented by a function $\mathbf{p}(x)$, then $\mathbf{p}'(x) = \dot{\mathbf{a}}/\dot{\alpha}$ and (2-267) can be written

$$J_{QC} - J_{QA} = \int_{x_A}^{x_C} [F - \mathbf{F}_{\mathbf{y}'} \cdot (\mathbf{y}' - \mathbf{p}')]dx = J^{\mathrm{H}}_{AC} \tag{2-268}$$

where $x_A = \alpha(\tau_0)$ and $x_C = \alpha(\tau_1)$.

Let us suppose now that the extremal which passes through point A of curve I continues on to intersect curve II at a point B in $\mathscr{W}$, as shown in Figure 2.32. Figure 2.32 may give the impression that this intersection must occur. In spaces of arbitrary dimension, however, and even in $\mathscr{E}^2$, the two curves may fail to intersect. We shall assume that the intersection does indeed occur. We shall suppose also that the extremal which passes through the point C of curve I continues on and intersects curve II at a point D.

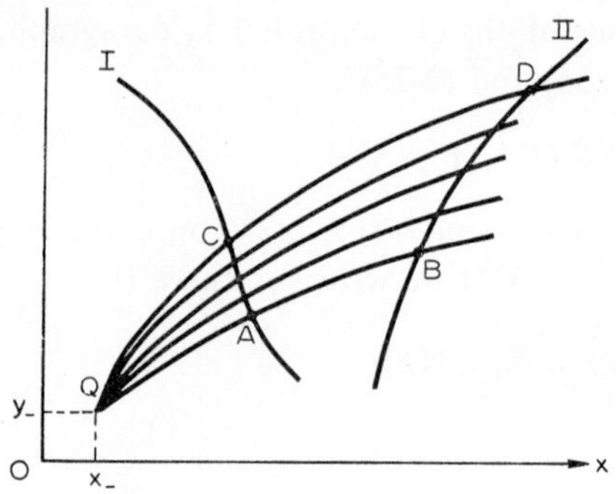

Fig. 2.32.

Let ρ_0 be the value of ρ corresponding to point B and ρ_1 the value of ρ corresponding to point D. Then we can write, analogously to (2-267),

$$J_{QD} - J_{QB} = \int_{\rho_0}^{\rho_1} [(F - \mathbf{F}_{\mathbf{y}'} \cdot \mathbf{y}')\dot{\beta} + \mathbf{F}_{\mathbf{y}'} \cdot \dot{\mathbf{b}}]\mathrm{d}\rho = J^{\mathrm{H}}_{BD} \tag{2-269}$$

or

$$J_{QD} - J_{QB} = \int_{x_B}^{x_D} [F - \mathbf{F}_{\mathbf{y}'} \cdot (\mathbf{y}' - \mathbf{u}')]\mathrm{d}x = J^{\mathrm{H}}_{BD}. \tag{2-270}$$

Let us denote by J_{AB} the value of $J[\mathbf{y}]$ on the extremal starting at A and terminating at B, and by J_{CD} the value of $J[\mathbf{y}]$ on the extremal starting at C and terminating at D. Then by definition

$$J_{AB} = J_{QB} - J_{QA}; \qquad J_{CD} = J_{QD} - J_{QC}. \tag{2-271}$$

Consider next

$$J_{CD} - J_{AB} = J_{QD} - J_{QB} - (J_{QC} - J_{QA}).$$

On applying (2-267) and (2-269), however, we see that

$$J_{CD} - J_{AB} = J^{\mathrm{H}}_{BD} - J^{\mathrm{H}}_{AC}. \tag{2-272}$$

Thus the difference between $J[\mathbf{y}]$ along AB and $J[\mathbf{y}]$ along CD can be computed as the difference between the Hilbert integrals along curve I from A to C and along curve II from B to D. In other words, if we have two extremal curves lying inside a region $\mathscr{W}$ which is simply covered by a field of extremals, and if we select two points A and B on the first, denoting by J_{AB} the value of $J[\mathbf{y}]$ along this extremal from A to B, and two points C

and D on the second, denoting by J_{CD} the value of $J[\mathbf{y}]$ along this extremal, then $J_{CD} - J_{AB}$ can be computed as the difference between two Hilbert integrals, one taken along a curve lying in $\mathscr{W}$ and joining B to D and the other taken along a curve lying in $\mathscr{W}$ and joining A to C. This result is independent of the curves used to join A to C and B to D; it is necessary only that they lie in $\mathscr{W}$ and have the proper continuity and differentiability properties.

We are now prepared to state and prove the Weierstrass sufficiency conditions.

Theorem 2.20.1. Weierstrass' Sufficiency Conditions. Suppose that $\mathbf{z}(x)$ *is an admissible interior solution to the Euler equations without corners, that* $\mathbf{F}_{\mathbf{y}'\mathbf{y}'}$ *is nonsingular along* $\mathbf{z}(x)$ *and that there is no point conjugate to* x_0 *in the interval* $x_0 < x \leq x_1$. *Suppose further that the Weierstrass E function satisfies* $E(x, \mathbf{y}, \mathbf{y}', \mathbf{p}') < 0$ *for all* $(x, \mathbf{y})$ *in an* N_ε *neighborhood of* $\mathbf{z}(x)$ *for which* $(x, \mathbf{y}, \mathbf{y}') \in \mathscr{R}$ *and* $(x, \mathbf{y}, \mathbf{p}') \in \mathscr{R}$, $\mathbf{y}' \neq \mathbf{p}'$. *Then* $\mathbf{z}(x)$ *yields a strong relative maximum of* $J[\mathbf{y}]$. *If* $E > 0$, *with all other conditions satisfied,* $\mathbf{z}(x)$ *yields a strong relative minimum of* $J[\mathbf{y}]$.

We begin the proof by observing that, from our assumptions about $\mathbf{z}(x)$, there exists a point $(x_-, \mathbf{y}_-)$, $x_- < x_0$, lying on the extension of $\mathbf{z}(x)$ and also an N_ε neighborhood of $\mathbf{z}(x)$ such that there is a field of extremals emanating from $(x_-, \mathbf{y}_-)$ which simply cover the N_ε neighborhood. Furthermore, from the hypothesis of the theorem it is possible to choose ε so small that when $(x, \mathbf{y}, \mathbf{y}')$ and $(x, \mathbf{y}, \mathbf{p}')$ are in $\mathscr{R}$ and $(x, \mathbf{y})$ is in the neighborhood then $E < 0$ at each point in the neighborhood.

Consider now *any* admissible function $\mathbf{p}(x)$ lying in the N_ε neighborhood. The graph of this function might look like the curve shown in Figure 2.33.

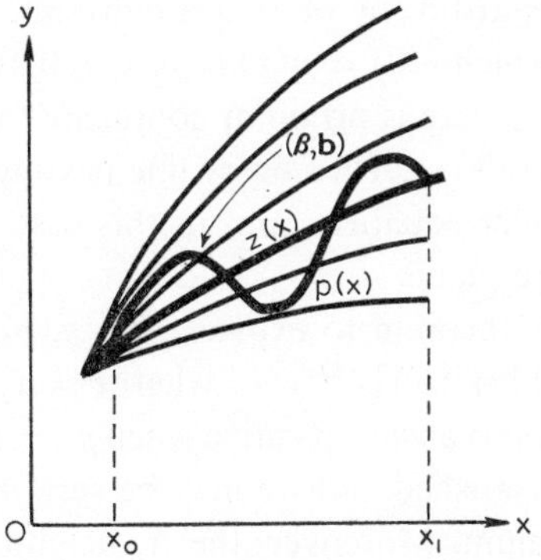

Fig. 2.33.

To prove the theorem we need only make appropriate use of (2-272). Denote by J_0 the value of J along $\mathbf{z}(x)$ from x_- to x_0 and by J_1 the value of J along $\mathbf{z}(x)$ from x_- to x_1. Now $J_1 - J_0 = J[\mathbf{z}]$, where $J[\mathbf{z}]$ is the value of the integral along $\mathbf{z}(x)$ over the actual interval of integration. However, this difference can also be computed as the Hilbert integral along $\mathbf{p}(x)$ from $(x_0, \mathbf{y}_0)$ to $(x_1, \mathbf{y}_1)$. We denote its value simply by J^{H}. Thus $J[\mathbf{z}] = J^{\mathrm{H}}$. If we denote by $J[\mathbf{p}]$ the value of J along $\mathbf{p}(x)$ then

$$J[\mathbf{p}] - J[\mathbf{z}] = J[\mathbf{p}] - J^{\mathrm{H}}$$

$$= \int_{x_0}^{x_1} F(x, \mathbf{p}, \mathbf{p}')\mathrm{d}x - \int_{x_0}^{x_1} [F(x, \mathbf{y}, \mathbf{y}') - \mathbf{F}_{\mathbf{y}'} \cdot (\mathbf{y}' - \mathbf{p}')]\mathrm{d}x. \tag{2-273}$$

Now, at any x, $(x, \mathbf{y}(x))$ is a point on the curve representing $\mathbf{p}(x)$, as is the point $(x, \mathbf{p})$. Thus $\mathbf{p} = \mathbf{y}$ for each x. In general, however, $\mathbf{p}' \neq \mathbf{y}'$; for $\mathbf{y}'$ is the slope vector for the extremal cutting $\mathbf{p}(x)$ at x and $\mathbf{p}'$ is the slope vector for $\mathbf{p}(x)$ itself.

If we now combine the integrals on the right hand side of (2-273), we see that the integrand is precisely the Weierstrass E function, which is negative whenever $\mathbf{p}' \neq \mathbf{y}'$. It is not possible that $\mathbf{p}' = \mathbf{y}'$ for all x unless $\mathbf{p}(x) \equiv \mathbf{z}(x)$. Thus when $\mathbf{p}(x) \not\equiv \mathbf{z}(x)$ the right hand side of (2-273) must be negative and $J[\mathbf{p}] < J[\mathbf{z}]$. This is true for every admissible function lying in the N_ε neighborhood. That completes the proof.

Example. Consider the problem of finding the curve of shortest length joining the origin to the point (x_0, y_0). Here $F = [1 + (y')^2]^{\frac{1}{2}}$ and $F_{y'y'} = [1 + (y')^2]^{-3/2}$. There is a unique admissible solution to the Euler equation, viz. the line $y = y_0(x/x_0)$. Along this line there are no corners, and $F_{y'y'} > 0$. The Jacobi equation is $\alpha(\mathrm{d}/\mathrm{d}x)\eta' = 0$, α a constant, so that $\eta = ax + b$. The only solution for which $\eta(0) = \eta(x) = 0$, $x \neq 0$, is $\eta \equiv 0$. In the interval $0 < x \leq x_0$, therefore, there is no point conjugate to 0. Let us choose any point to the left of 0, say $-x_0$. Then every line passing through $(-x_0, -y_0)$ is a solution to the Euler equation, and in this case the field of extremals simply covers the entire plane.

If we apply Taylor's theorem to expand $F(x, y, p')$ in p' to the squared term, we see that $E = [1 + (v')]^{-3/2} r^2/2$, where $r = p' - z'$ and v lies between p' and z'. This expression is always positive when $p' \neq z'$. Thus the conditions of Theorem 2.20.1 are satisfied and we may be sure that the solution yields a strong relative minimum. Moreover, the N_ε neighborhood is in this case the entire plane; hence the solution also yields a global minimum.

There is an interesting feature of Ramsey's model which has nothing to do with sufficiency conditions but which can be demonstrated by means of the theory of fields introduced in this section. It is clear that if an infinite amount of capital is needed to approach bliss then bliss cannot be achieved in a finite time but must be approached asymptotically as $t \to \infty$. When only a finite capital K^* is needed to achieve bliss, however, there exists the possibility that, even when the planning horizon is infinite, it may be optimal to reach bliss in a finite time and then remain there. We can now easily prove that, even when bliss can be achieved with finite capital, provided $U[\Psi(K) - \dot{K}]$ is strictly concave, and $K_0 < K^*$ it is never optimal to achieve bliss in finite time when the planning horizon is infinite; instead, it is optimal to approach K^* asymptotically as $t \to \infty$. The proof will be by contradiction.

Suppose that it is optimal to reach bliss in a finite time T_b, and let $K(t)$ be the function that describes the growth of capital from K_0 to K^*. Let us assume also that we have an interior solution, so that $C > 0$ everywhere. Then $K(t)$ has no corners up to T_b, and the strict concavity of F rules out any points conjugate to 0 in the interval $0 < t \leq T_b$. For $t > T_b$ the optimal solution is simply $K = K^*$ and $\dot{K} = 0$. Furthermore, the corner condition at T_b requires that $\dot{K}_-(T_b) = 0$.

Now if this is the form of the optimal solution when the planning horizon is infinite, the same path of capital accumulation must be optimal in transferring the economy from K_0 to K^* (bliss capital) in any finite time $T \geq T_b$. However, the nature of $K(t)$ guarantees that there exists a field of extremals emanating from the point $(0, K_0)$ which simply cover a neighborhood of (T_b, K^*). In particular, there is an extremal $K_1(t)$ connecting $(0, K_0)$ to $(T_b + \varepsilon, K^*)$, $\varepsilon < 0$; and $C > 0$ along this extremal. Since $K_1(t)$ satisfies the Euler equation and since F is strictly concave in the region, $K_1(t)$ provides the unique optimal path for transferring the system from $(0, K_0)$ to $(T_b + \varepsilon, K^*)$. But this involves us in a contradiction, for we have claimed that, for all $T \geq T_b$, $K(t)$ describes the optimal path for transferring the system from $(0, K_0)$ to (T, K^*). Thus it can never be optimal to reach bliss in finite time when the planning horizon is infinite and F is strictly concave.

The above proof does not indicate what the situation is when F is merely concave. Interestingly enough, if F is not strictly concave then it can be optimal to reach bliss in finite time. We shall give an example in Chapter 4.

2.21. Variable end points–free boundaries

We have been studying the problem of finding a function which optimizes the functional

$$J[\mathbf{y}] = \int_{x_0}^{x_1} F(x, \mathbf{y}, \mathbf{y}')dx. \tag{2-274}$$

So far, we have restricted our attention to cases in which the end points are fixed, so that only functions the values of which are specified at x_0 and x_1 are considered to be admissible. In this section, and in those which follow it, we shall seek to modify these boundary conditions in two different ways.

First, we shall study the case in which it is still required that $\mathbf{y}(x_0) = \mathbf{y}_0$ but in which no restriction whatever is placed on the value of $\mathbf{y}(x)$ at x_1, except of course that $(x_1, \mathbf{y}(x_1), \mathbf{y}'(x_1)) \in \mathscr{R}$. This value will be determined, as part of the solution to the problem, in such a way as to maximize $J[\mathbf{y}]$. The value x_1, however, will remain prespecified.

As the set of admissible functions we now consider all piecewise smooth functions $\mathbf{y}(x)$ with the property that in extended phase space their graphs lie in the set $\mathscr{R}$, begin at the point $(x_0, \mathbf{y}_0)$ and terminate on the hyperplane $x = x_1$.

Suppose that the admissible function $\mathbf{z}(x)$ yields an interior maximum of $J[\mathbf{y}]$ and that $\mathbf{z}(x_1) = \mathbf{y}_1$. We seek the necessary conditions which must be satisfied by $\mathbf{z}(x)$. If $\mathbf{z}(x)$ yields the maximum value of $J[\mathbf{y}]$ when there is no restriction on its value at x_1, then it must also maximize $J[\mathbf{y}]$ when it is required that $\mathbf{y}(x_1) = \mathbf{y}_1$ (the value of $\mathbf{z}(x)$ at x_1). Thus $\mathbf{z}(x)$ must satisfy the necessary conditions of Theorem 2.13.1. There is an additional condition which must be satisfied at x_1, however.

Let us define

$$\boldsymbol{\eta}(x) = \frac{\mathbf{b} - \mathbf{y}_1}{x_1 - x_0}(x - x_0) \tag{2-275}$$

so that $\boldsymbol{\eta} \in C'$, and let us write $\mathbf{y}(x; \mathbf{b}) = \mathbf{z}(x) + \boldsymbol{\eta}(x)$. Then $\mathbf{y}(x_1; \mathbf{b}) = \mathbf{b}$; and, for all $\mathbf{b}$, $|\mathbf{b} - \mathbf{y}_1| < \varepsilon$, $\mathbf{y}(x; \mathbf{b})$ is admissible, with $\mathbf{y}(x; \mathbf{y}_1) = \mathbf{z}(x)$ since $\mathbf{z}(x)$ yields an interior maximum. Furthermore $\mathbf{y}(x; \mathbf{b})$ possesses continuous first derivatives with respect to $\mathbf{b}$ and continuous mixed derivatives with respect to x and $\mathbf{b}$. Thus $\mathbf{y}(x; \mathbf{b})$ is a special case of the type of functions studied in Section 2.19; hence $J^*(x_0, \mathbf{y}_0, x_1, \mathbf{b})$ exists and is differentiable with respect to $\mathbf{b}$. Furthermore, J^* is the value of $J[\mathbf{y}]$ along $\mathbf{y}$. Since $\mathbf{z}(x)$ maximizes $J[\mathbf{y}]$, J^* must have a relative maximum at $\mathbf{b} = \mathbf{y}_1$. Hence, from (2-255),

$$\frac{\partial}{\partial b_j} J^*(x_0, \mathbf{y}_0, x_1, \mathbf{y}_1) = F_{y_j'}(x_1, \mathbf{y}_1, \mathbf{z}'(x_1)) = 0$$

or, in vector form, it is necessary that

$$\mathbf{F}_{\mathbf{y}'}(x_1, \mathbf{y}_1, \mathbf{z}'(x_1)) = \mathbf{0}. \tag{2-276}$$

Note that (2-276) provides the n additional conditions which are needed to replace $\mathbf{y}(x_1) = \mathbf{y}_1$; it is now possible to determine all constants of integration in the general solution. Equation (2-276) contains what is called the *free boundary condition.* In general, we say that there is a free boundary at an end point if the value of x is specified at the end point but the value of $\mathbf{y}$ can be chosen freely (with the limitation that $\mathbf{y}(x)$ lies in $\mathscr{R}$). Thus we have proved the following theorem.

Theorem 2.21.1. Free Boundary Condition. Suppose that the admissible function $\mathbf{z}(x)$ yields an interior optimum of $J[\mathbf{y}]$ when the left hand end point is fixed and there is a free boundary at the right hand end point. Then $\mathbf{z}(x)$ must satisfy the necessary conditions of Theorem 2.13.1 (the Euler equations and corner conditions). In addition, at x_1, $\mathbf{z}(x)$ must satisfy the free boundary condition

$$\mathbf{F}_{\mathbf{y}'}(x_1, \mathbf{z}(x_1), \mathbf{z}'(x_1)) = \mathbf{0}. \tag{2-277}$$

The following two corollaries are fairly obvious; in the problems we ask the reader to provide the proofs.

Corollary 1. If the right hand end point is fixed and there is a free boundary at the left hand end point then $\mathbf{z}(x)$ must satisfy the necessary conditions of Theorem 2.13.1 and the free boundary condition at the left hand end point.

Corollary 2. If there is a free boundary at each end point, then $\mathbf{z}(x)$ must satisfy the necessary conditions of Theorem 2.13.1 and the free boundary condition at each end point.

We note finally that it is possible to obtain the free boundary condition by means of an alternative analysis similar to that employed in earlier sections of this chapter and based on the equation $\mathbf{y} = \mathbf{z} + \xi\boldsymbol{\eta}$. The details are left to the reader. (See Problem 1.)

Examples. 1. We have already considered the problem of finding the curve of shortest length joining the origin to the point (x_0, y_0) and have shown that it is a straight line. Let us now seek the curve of shortest length joining the origin to the vertical line $x = x_0$. The point at which the curve crosses this vertical line can be freely chosen. Since the curve must be the graph of a solution to the Euler equation, it must be a straight line passing through the origin. To select a particular straight line, we rely on the free boundary condition $F_{y'} = 0$. Here $F_{y'} = y'[1 + (y')^2]^{-\frac{1}{2}}$. Hence $y' = 0$, and the desired line is the horizontal straight line $y = 0$. Of all straight lines linking the origin with $x = x_0$, the shortest is the horizontal line (which is perpendicular to $x = x_0$).

2. Consider again the Ramsey model and suppose that we seek the path of capital accumulation which starts at K_0 and maximizes utility over a time period of length T. The value $K(T)$ is not specified but may be chosen freely. In this case, for an interior maximum $K(t)$ must satisfy the Euler equation $U + U'\dot{K} = \lambda$ and the free boundary condition $F_{\dot{K}} = -U' = 0$ at T. Now in general it is not possible that $U' = 0$ at T, for this would imply that the economy is at bliss. It seems therefore that the necessary conditions cannot be satisfied.

A little thought reveals what has gone wrong. Notice first that if utility is to be maximized over the period T then K must be 0 at T; otherwise, utility could be increased by consuming the terminal capital. Thus the optimal solution must transfer the system from $(0, K_0)$ to $(T, 0)$. Now the free boundary condition was derived under the assumption of an interior maximum, so that the components of $\boldsymbol{\eta}(x_1)$ could take either sign. However, $K = 0$ is on the boundary of $\mathscr{R}$ since we have required that $K \geq 0$. This means that only variations with $\eta(x_1)$ positive are allowed. In the present case, therefore, we cannot insist that $F_{y'} = 0$.

This simple illustration shows how careful one must be in applying the necessary conditions. The path which transfers the system from $(0, K_0)$ to $(T, 0)$ is optimal, but since it ends on the boundary of $\mathscr{R}$ it is not necessary that the free boundary condition be satisfied.

If F is a concave function of $\mathbf{y}$ and $\mathbf{y}'$, if the boundary is free at x_1 (or at x_0 or at both points) and if $\mathbf{z}(x)$ is an admissible function which satisfies the necessary conditions, including the free boundary conditions, then the proof of Section 2.17 immediately shows that $\mathbf{z}(x)$ does indeed yield the global maximum of $J[\mathbf{y}]$. Hence the sufficiency theorem of Section 2.17 can be applied in the case of free boundaries when the free boundary conditions are satisfied. Thus we have

Theorem 2.21.2. Sufficiency. If $F(x, \mathbf{y}, \mathbf{y}')$ is a concave function of $(\mathbf{y}, \mathbf{y}')$ over an open convex set containing $\mathscr{R}$, if one or both end points have free boundaries, and if $\mathbf{z}(x)$ satisfies the necessary conditions of Theorem 2.21.1 (or its corollaries) then $\mathbf{z}(x)$ yields the absolute maximum of $J[\mathbf{y}]$ over $\mathscr{R}$. If F is convex *and the remaining conditions are satisfied then* $\mathbf{z}(x)$ *yields the absolute minimum of* $J[\mathbf{y}]$ *over* $\mathscr{R}$.

2.22. Variable end points–transversality

We now turn our attention to a second type of problem involving variable end points. The problem can be given the following geometric formulation. Suppose we seek the curve $\mathbf{y}(x)$ in $\mathscr{E}^{n+1}$ which begins at the point $(x_0, \mathbf{y}_0)$ and ends on a given manifold $\mathscr{M}$, and which yields the largest value of $J[\mathbf{y}]$, $J[\mathbf{y}]$ being the integral of F along the curve. The problem is illustrated by Figure 2.34. Except in special cases, neither the value of $\mathbf{y}(x)$ nor the

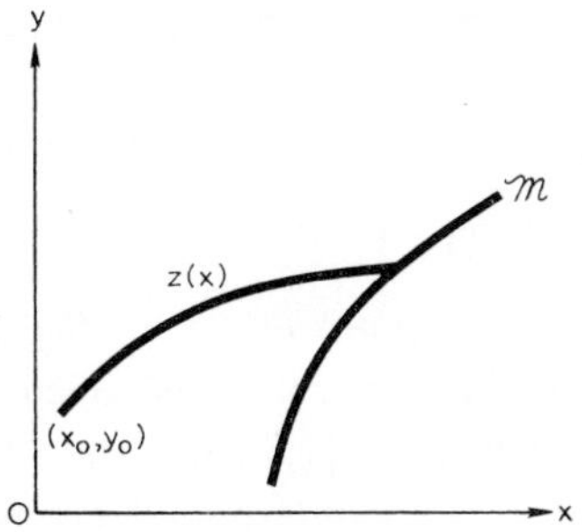

Fig. 2.34.

value of x is specified for the upper boundary. The problem now becomes one of finding the piecewise smooth function $\mathbf{y}(x)$ the graph of which lies in $\mathscr{R}$, which maximizes

$$J[\mathbf{y}] = \int_{x_0}^{\beta} F(x, \mathbf{y}, \mathbf{y}')\mathrm{d}x \qquad \text{(2-278a)}$$

and which satisfies $\mathbf{y}(x_0) = \mathbf{y}_0$ and $(\beta, \mathbf{y}(\beta)) \in \mathscr{M}$. We wish to determine the necessary conditions for an interior maximum in this case. Clearly if $\mathbf{z}(x)$ maximizes (2-278a) it must satisfy the necessary conditions of Theorem 2.13.1. We no longer have the end point conditions $\mathbf{z}(x_1) = \mathbf{y}_1$. Instead we have the *transversality conditions*, n conditions which must be satisfied at the point at which the graph of $\mathbf{z}(x)$ intersects the manifold and which specify the manner in which the intersection takes place.

Before attempting to derive these conditions we shall describe some of the properties of manifolds. The set of points $\mathscr{S}$ satisfying the equation $S(x, \mathbf{y}) = 0$, $(x, \mathbf{y}) \in \mathscr{E}^{n+1}$, will be called a *hypersurface of dimension n in*

$\mathscr{E}^{n+1}$ when $\mathscr{S}$ is not empty. Just as the set of solutions to $f(x_1, x_2) = 0$ can be viewed as the level curve corresponding to $z = 0$ for the surface $z = f(x_1, x_2)$, so we can think of $\mathscr{S}$ as being a level hypersurface in $\mathscr{E}^{n+1}$ for the hypersurface $z = S(x, \mathbf{y})$ in $\mathscr{E}^{n+2}$. Suppose that $S \in C'$ over the set of $\mathbf{y}$ of interest. The vector

$$\nabla S(x_1, \mathbf{y}_1) = (S_x(x_1, \mathbf{y}_1), S_{y_1}(x_1, \mathbf{y}_1), \ldots, S_{y_n}(x_1, \mathbf{y}_1))$$

$$= (S_x(x_1, \mathbf{y}_1), \mathbf{S}_y(x_1, \mathbf{y}_1))$$

is called the *gradient vector* at $(x_1, \mathbf{y}_1)$. It is a vector containing the first partial derivatives of S. A point $(x^*, \mathbf{y}^*)$ for which $\nabla S(x^*, \mathbf{y}^*) = \mathbf{0}$ is called a *singular point* of the hypersurface. A hypersurface for which $S \in C'$ and which possesses no singular points in the region of interest is called a *smooth hypersurface.*

Consider the hyperplane $\mathscr{L}$, which is the set of points satisfying the equation

$$\nabla S(x_1, \mathbf{y}_1) \cdot (x, \mathbf{y}) = \nabla S(x_1, \mathbf{y}_1) \cdot (x_1, \mathbf{y}_1) \tag{2-278b}$$

and which passes through the point $(x_1, \mathbf{y}_1)$. (See Hadley [16] for a discussion of hyperplanes.) This hyperplane is called the *tangent hyperplane* to $\mathscr{S}$ at $(x_1, \mathbf{y}_1)$. The vector $\nabla S(x_1, \mathbf{y}_1)$ is said to be *normal* to the hyperplane because for $n = 1$ and 2, when interpreted geometrically, the vector is normal to the hyperplane (a line for $n = 1$, a plane for $n = 2$). The vector $\nabla S(x_1, \mathbf{y}_1)$ is also said to be *normal* to the hypersurface $\mathscr{S}$ at $(x_1, \mathbf{y}_1)$.

Suppose now that we have s, $s \le n$, smooth hypersurfaces $\mathscr{S}_u$ each of dimension n. Suppose that $\mathscr{S}_u$ is the set of solutions to $S^u(x, \mathbf{y}) = 0$, $u = 1, \ldots, s$, or in vector form $\mathbf{S}(x, \mathbf{y}) = \mathbf{0}$. Then the set of points $\mathscr{M} = \bigcap_{u=1}^{s} \mathscr{S}_u$ is a manifold of dimension $n - s + 1$. Suppose that $(x_1, \mathbf{y}_1)$ is in $\mathscr{M}$, and let $\mathscr{L}_u$ be the hyperplane tangent to $\mathscr{S}_u$ at $(x_1, \mathbf{y}_1)$. The set of points $\mathscr{L}_m = \bigcap_{u=1}^{s} \mathscr{L}_u$ is called the tangent hyperplane to $\mathscr{M}$ at $(x_1, \mathbf{y}_1)$. Note that $\mathscr{L}_m$ is also a manifold of dimension $n - s + 1$. It is a linear manifold or subspace (generally affine) of $\mathscr{E}^{n+1}$. For example, if $s = 2$ and $\mathscr{S}_1$ and $\mathscr{S}_2$ are surfaces in $\mathscr{E}^3$, $\mathscr{M}$ is a curve in $\mathscr{E}^3$ and $\mathscr{L}_m$ is a line tangent to the curve at $(x_1, \mathbf{y}_1)$. If the s vectors $\nabla S^u(x_1, \mathbf{y}_1)$ are linearly dependent at $(x_1, \mathbf{y}_1)$, then $(x_1, \mathbf{y}_1)$ is said to be a singular point of the manifold. *The manifold $\mathscr{M}$ formed by the intersection of s smooth hypersurfaces is said to be smooth if it contains no singular points in the region of interest.* This means that the vectors $\nabla S^u(x_1, \mathbf{y}_1)$ are linearly independent at each point and that the matrix with the vectors $\nabla S^u(x_1, \mathbf{y}_1)$ as columns has rank s.

Consider the hyperplane $\mathscr{L}_u$ tangent to $\mathscr{S}_u$ at $(x_1, \mathbf{y}_1)$. Let $(x, \mathbf{y})$ be any other point in $\mathscr{L}_u$. Then the vector $\mathbf{w} = (x, \mathbf{y}) - (x_1, \mathbf{y}_1)$ is said to *lie in*

$\mathscr{L}_u$ (because, for $n = 2$ and 3, if $\mathbf{w}$ is drawn from $(x_1, \mathbf{y}_1)$ it lies on the line or plane). Furthermore, from (2-278b), $\nabla S^u(x_1, \mathbf{y}_1) \cdot \mathbf{w} = 0$, that is, the vectors $\nabla S^u(x_1, \mathbf{y}_1)$ and $\mathbf{w}$ are orthogonal. This is true of every vector $\mathbf{w}$ in $\mathscr{L}_u$. Intuitively, this is what we mean by $\nabla S^u(x_1, \mathbf{y}_1)$ being a normal to the hyperplane–it is orthogonal to every vector lying in $\mathscr{L}_u$. Now $\mathscr{L}_u$ is a linear space of dimension n. The orthogonal complement of $\mathscr{L}_u$ has dimension 1; hence every vector normal to $\mathscr{L}_u$ must be a scalar multiple of $\nabla S^u(x_1, \mathbf{y}_1)$.

Consider next the linear manifold $\mathscr{L}_m$ of dimension $n - s + 1$ and the point $(x_1, \mathbf{y}_1)$ in $\mathscr{L}_m$. Let $(x, \mathbf{y})$ be any other point in $\mathscr{L}_m$ and let $\mathbf{w} = (x, \mathbf{y}) - (x_1, \mathbf{y}_1)$. Then $\mathbf{w}$ is said to lie in $\mathscr{L}_m$. Since $\mathbf{w}$ lies in $\mathscr{L}_m$ it lies in $\mathscr{L}_u$, $u = 1, \ldots, s$; thus $\nabla S^u(x_1, \mathbf{y}_1) \cdot \mathbf{w} = 0$, $u = 1, \ldots, s$, and $\mathbf{w}$ is orthogonal to each of the normal vectors $\nabla S^u(x_1, \mathbf{y}_1)$. Now since $\mathbf{w}$ is orthogonal to each normal vector, it is orthogonal to any linear combination $\mathbf{v}$ of the $\nabla S^u(x_1, \mathbf{y}_1)$. Thus any such vector $\mathbf{v}$ can be called a normal to the hyperplane $\mathscr{L}_m$ and to $\mathscr{M}$ at $(x_1, \mathbf{y}_1)$. Since $\mathscr{L}_m$ has dimension $n - s + 1$ the orthogonal complement of $\mathscr{L}_m$ has dimension s. Any vector in the orthogonal complement can be considered to be a normal to $\mathscr{L}_m$, and this is true of no other vector. We have assumed that the $\nabla S^u(x_1, \mathbf{y}_1)$ are linearly independent; hence the space spanned by these vectors is of dimension s. Consequently, the orthogonal complement of $\mathscr{L}_m$ is the space spanned by the $\nabla S^u(x_1, \mathbf{y}_1)$ and any vector $\mathbf{v}$ which is a linear combination of these vectors satisfies $\mathbf{v} \cdot \mathbf{w} = 0$ for *every* $\mathbf{w}$ lying in $\mathscr{L}_m$, that is, $\mathbf{v}$ is orthogonal to every $\mathbf{w}$ lying in $\mathscr{L}_m$. Furthermore, each vector which is orthogonal to every vector lying in $\mathscr{L}_m$, that is, is orthogonal to $\mathscr{M}$ at $(x_1, \mathbf{y}_1)$, must be a linear combination of the $\nabla S^u(x_1, \mathbf{y}_1)$, $u = 1, \ldots, s$.

After a long digression on manifolds we are now ready to consider the transversality conditions. Suppose that $\mathbf{z}(x)$ is an admissible function which yields an interior maximum of (2-274) and intersects the manifold $\mathscr{M}$ of dimension $n + 1 - s$, which we shall assume to be smooth, at the point $(x_1, \mathbf{y}_1)$. To determine the conditions which must be satisfied by $\mathbf{z}(x)$ at $(x_1, \mathbf{y}_1)$, let us first extend $\mathbf{z}(x)$ a short distance to the right of x_1 so that $\mathbf{z}(x) \in C'$ in the interval. Normally the solution to the Euler equations will automatically provide the extension desired, but in any event this can always be managed. Next, let $(\beta, \mathbf{b})$ be any point in $\mathscr{M}$ and let us consider the functions

$$\boldsymbol{\eta}(x; \beta, \mathbf{b}) = \frac{\mathbf{b} - \mathbf{z}(\beta)}{\beta - x_0}(x - x_0). \qquad (2\text{-}279)$$

For $(\beta, \mathbf{b})$ in a sufficiently small neighborhood of $(x_1, \mathbf{y}_1)$ the functions

$$\mathbf{y}(x; \beta, \mathbf{b}) = \mathbf{z}(x) + \boldsymbol{\eta}(x; \beta, \mathbf{b}) \tag{2-280}$$

are admissible and possess continuous partial derivatives of the second order with respect to β and $\mathbf{b}$. Furthermore, $\mathbf{z}(x) = \mathbf{y}(x; x_1, \mathbf{y}_1)$. Hence $J^*(x_0, \mathbf{y}_0, \beta, \mathbf{b})$, the value of $J[\mathbf{y}]$ for $\mathbf{y}(x; \beta, \mathbf{b})$, must attain a relative maximum at $(x_1, \mathbf{y}_1)$ for all $(\beta, \mathbf{b}) \in \mathcal{M}$ which are sufficiently close to $(x_1, \mathbf{y}_1)$. Now $\mathcal{M}$ will be imagined to be the intersection of s hypersurfaces $\mathcal{S}_u$ of dimension n in $\mathscr{E}^{n+1}$. Thus if $(\beta, \mathbf{b}) \in \mathcal{M}$, $(\beta, \mathbf{b})$ must satisfy the s equations

$$S^u(\beta, \mathbf{b}) = 0, \qquad u = 1, \ldots, s. \tag{2-281}$$

We now seek to determine the condition that $J^*(x_0, \mathbf{y}_0, \beta, \mathbf{b})$ must satisfy if it attains a relative maximum at $(x_1, \mathbf{y}_1)$ subject to the constraints (2-281). The method of Lagrange multipliers can be used for this purpose (see Hadley [18] for a detailed treatment of the theory of Lagrange multipliers). The Lagrangian function is

$$L(\beta, \mathbf{b}) = J^*(x_0, \beta, \mathbf{y}_0, \mathbf{b}) - \sum_{u=1}^{s} \rho_u S^u(\beta, \mathbf{b}) \tag{2-282}$$

the ρ_u being the Lagrange multipliers. The necessary condition becomes $\nabla L(x_1, \mathbf{y}_1) = \mathbf{0}$ or

$$\nabla J^*(x_0, \mathbf{y}_0, x_1, \mathbf{y}_1) = \sum_{u=1}^{s} \rho_u \nabla S^u(x_1, \mathbf{y}_1) \tag{2-283}$$

where, from Section 2.19,

$$\nabla J^* = (F - \mathbf{F}_{\mathbf{y}'} \cdot \mathbf{z}'(x_1), \mathbf{F}_{\mathbf{y}'}), \tag{2-284}$$

∇J^* being evaluated at $(x_0, \mathbf{y}_1, x_1, \mathbf{y}_1)$. Equation (2-283) is the basic transversality condition. From it we learn that the vector (2-284) must be a linear combination of the $\nabla S^u(x_1, \mathbf{y}_1)$. Equivalently, it tells us that (2-284) must be a normal vector for $\mathscr{L}_m$ (and $\mathcal{M}$) at $(x_1, \mathbf{y}_1)$ or that (2-284) must be orthogonal to every vector lying in $\mathscr{L}_m$. Thus we have proved the following theorem.

Theorem 2.22.1. Transversality Condition. Let $\mathbf{z}(x)$ be an admissible function which yields an interior maximum or minimum of $J[\mathbf{y}]$ when $\mathbf{z}(x_0) = \mathbf{y}_0$ and the terminal point of $\mathbf{z}(x)$ lies in the smooth manifold $\mathcal{M}$ of dimension $n - s + 1$ formed by the intersection of s smooth hypersurfaces $\mathcal{S}_u$. Then $\mathbf{z}(x)$ must satisfy the necessary conditions of Theorem 2.13.1 and, at the point $(x_1, \mathbf{y}_1)$ at which $\mathbf{z}(x)$ intersects $\mathcal{M}$, the $(n + 1)$-component vector $(F - \mathbf{F}_{\mathbf{y}'} \cdot \mathbf{z}'(x_1), \mathbf{F}_{\mathbf{y}'})$ must be a normal vector for $\mathcal{M}$, that is, must be orthogonal to *every vector lying in the tangent hyperplane* $\mathscr{L}_m$ *to* $\mathscr{M}$ *at* $(\mathbf{x}_1, \mathbf{y}_1)$. *Equivalently, (2-283) must hold.*

The following corollary is very easy to prove. (We ask the reader to prove it in the problems.)

Corollary. If the left hand end point is not fixed, it being required only that an admissible curve begin on some smooth manifold, then an interior optimizing function $\mathbf{z}(x)$ *must satisfy the transversality condition at the left hand end point, as well as the condition of Theorem 2.13.1. If both end points must lie in smooth manifolds then* $\mathbf{z}(x)$ *must satisfy the transversality condition at both end points as well as the conditions of Theorem 2.13.1.*

No attempt will be made to discuss sufficiency conditions when a transversality condition must be satisfied at one or both end points. It does not seem easy to obtain a generally useful sufficient condition. The classical theory of sufficiency is quite complicated, applies only to relative maxima and minima, and cannot be easily brought to bear on practical problems.

We note finally that problems involving fixed end points and free boundaries are covered as special cases by the theory just developed. The conditions for those cases can be obtained without difficulty from the transversality condition, as we ask the reader to show as a problem.

Examples. 1. Consider the problem of finding the curve of shortest length joining the origin to the line $y = ax + b$, $b \neq 0$. From Theorem 2.21.3, the function representing the curve must satisfy the Euler equation; hence the curve must be a straight line. To determine which straight line should be used of all those which intersect $y = ax + b$, we apply the transversality condition. Here the smooth manifold is the set of solutions to $y - ax - b =$

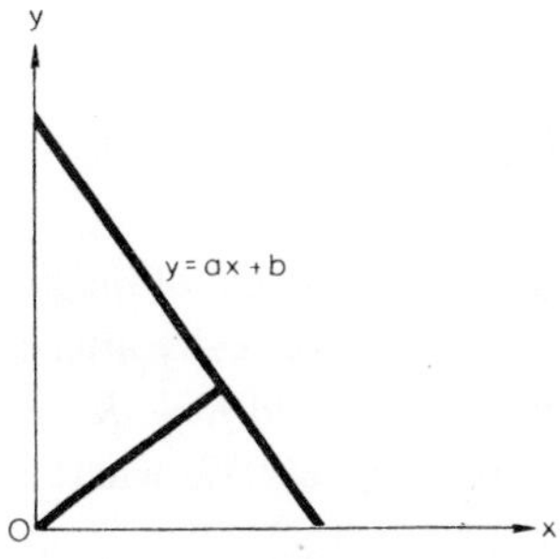

Fig. 2.35.

0 and $\nabla S = (-a, 1)$. Recall that $F_{y'} = y'[1 + (y')^2]^{-\frac{1}{2}}$ and $F - F_{y'}y' = [1 + (y')^2]^{-\frac{1}{2}}$. Thus, since $(F - F_{y'}y', F_{y'}) = \rho \nabla S$, $[1 + (y')^2]^{-\frac{1}{2}} = -\rho a$ and $y'[1 + (y')^2]^{-\frac{1}{2}} = \rho$. Hence $y' = -1/a$ and the line of shortest length is orthogonal to the given line $y = ax + b$. This is illustrated by Figure 2.35.

It is worth noting that when the optimizing curve must end on a specified manifold there can exist local optima different from the global optimum even though this may not be possible when the end points are fixed. For the minimum distance problem, this possibility is illustrated by Figure 2.36. The manifold shown there is smooth, and there are several solutions to the transversality condition not all of which yield the global minimum.

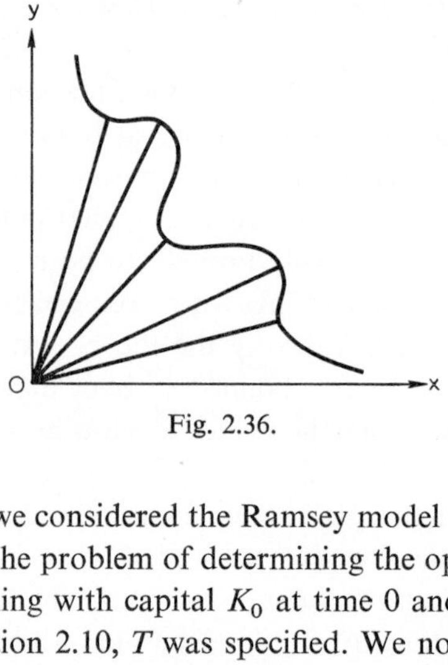

Fig. 2.36.

2. In Section 2.10 we considered the Ramsey model with a finite planning horizon and studied the problem of determining the optimal path of capital accumulation, beginning with capital K_0 at time 0 and ending with capital K_1 at time T. In Section 2.10, T was specified. We now consider a slightly different question. Suppose that an initial stock of capital K_0, $K_0 < K^*$, is required to grow to a final level of K_1, $K_0 < K_1 < K^*$. What is the optimal time to take in effecting the transfer? In others words, if

$$\Omega(T) = \max_K \int_0^T U dt,$$

what T maximizes $\Omega(T)$? This is a problem of the type we have been studying in the present section; for what we are really after is the curve which begins at $(0, K_0)$, ends on the smooth manifold $K - K_1 = 0$ and maximizes $J[K]$. The situation is illustrated by Figure 2.37, where several possible paths of capital accumulation are depicted.

The maximizing path must satisfy the transversality condition. Here

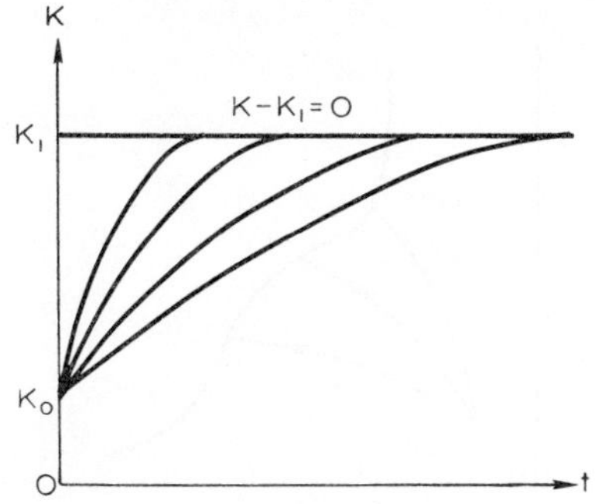

Fig. 2.37.

$\nabla S = (0, 1)$. Also $F - F_{\dot{K}}\dot{K} = \lambda$ and $F_{\dot{K}} = -U'$. Since one vector is a scalar multiple of the other, $(\lambda, -U') = \rho(0, 1)$; hence $\lambda = 0$ and $\rho = 0$. Thus we have reached the interesting conclusion that the optimal path from K_0 to K_1 is the solution to the differential equation $U + U'\dot{K} = 0$; it is therefore the path that would be followed in maximizing $J[K]$ over an infinite planning horizon. It follows that the optimal time to take in effecting the transfer is the time required to effect the transfer on the path which is optimal when the planning horizon is infinite.

2.23. Transversality at infinity

When the planning horizon extends to infinity, the problem of optimization differs only slightly from that considered in Section 2.22; but the differences are sufficient to require a separate analysis. Suppose that it is specified that $\lim_{x\to\infty}\mathbf{y}(x) = \mathbf{b}$. However, $\mathbf{b}$ is not specified explicitly but instead can be any solution to the equation $T(\mathbf{b}) = 0$. What condition must now be satisfied as $x \to \infty$? To see more clearly that this is a transversality problem, note that the graphical representation of $\mathbf{y}(x)$ in the space $\mathscr{E}^n$ of points $\mathbf{y}$ is a curve (x is the parameter here). As $x \to \infty$, this curve approaches the surface which is the graph of $T(\mathbf{y}) = 0$. We wish to know how the curve should approach the surface. For $n = 2$ the problem is represented graphically by Figure 2.38. Thus we can apply the same methods as in Section 2.22, with $\boldsymbol{\eta}(x; \mathbf{b})$ now equal to $(\mathbf{b} - \mathbf{y})(1 - e^{-x})$. We conclude that if $\mathbf{z}(x)$ yields an interior optimum of $J[\mathbf{y}]$ and $\lim_{x\to\infty}\mathbf{z}(x) = \mathbf{y}_1$, and if the integral has the proper convergence properties to allow differentiation under the integral sign, then

$$\lim_{x\to\infty} \mathbf{F}_{\mathbf{y}'}(x, \mathbf{z}(x), \mathbf{z}'(x)) = \rho\nabla T(\mathbf{y}_1). \tag{2-285}$$

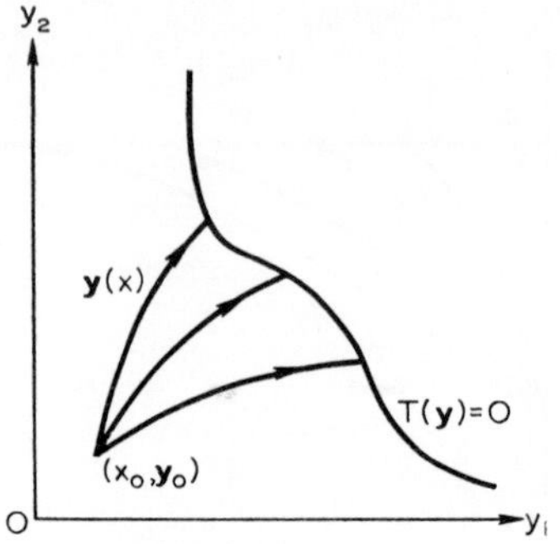

Fig. 2.38.

Equation (2-285) replaces the condition $\lim_{x\to\infty}\mathbf{F}_{\mathbf{y}'} = \mathbf{0}$, which applies when $\mathbf{y}(x)$ is unrestricted as $x \to \infty$, and the condition $\mathbf{y} \to \mathbf{b}$ which applies when it is required that $\lim_{x\to\infty}\mathbf{y}(x) = \mathbf{b}$ with $\mathbf{b}$ specified in advance. Equation (2-285) applies when $\mathbf{b}$ is neither prespecified nor completely arbitrary but is merely constrained to satisfy $T(\mathbf{b}) = 0$. Normally, equations (2-285) and $T(\mathbf{b}) = 0$ between them will determine the value of $\mathbf{b}$. However there is one case which requires special attention. Notice first that when $\lim_{x\to\infty} \mathbf{z}(x) = \mathbf{b}$ then in general $\lim_{x\to\infty}\mathbf{z}'(x) = \mathbf{0}$. The particular case arises when F does not depend on x explicitly and $\mathbf{F}_{\mathbf{y}'}(\mathbf{b}, \mathbf{0}) = \mathbf{0}$ for every $\mathbf{b}$ satisfying $T(\mathbf{b}) = 0$. Condition (2-285) is satisfied by $\rho = 0$; but then we merely obtain $\mathbf{0} = \mathbf{0}$, which does not help to determine the limit of $\mathbf{z}(x)$.

In this case, in spite of the fact that $F_{y_j'} \to 0$ for each j, there will typically be at least one j, say $j = 1$, such that $F_{y_1'} \neq 0$ for all x sufficiently large and $T_{b_1} \neq 0$ at $\mathbf{y}_1$, and such that, in addition, the ratios $F_{y_j'}/F_{y_1'}$ approach definite limits as $x \to \infty$. If something similar to (2-285) could be obtained for the limits of these ratios then a set of relations would be available to determine the limiting value of $\mathbf{z}(x)$. We now show how the ratios may be determined in certain cases. To this end we direct our attention not just to $T(\mathbf{b}) = 0$ but to the one parameter family of hypersurfaces $T(\mathbf{b}, \tau) = 0$ such that $T(\mathbf{b}, \tau)$ and its first partial derivatives are continuous functions of τ and such that when $\tau = 0$ we have the particular hypersurface $T(\mathbf{b}) = 0$ of interest. We assume furthermore that for $\tau > 0$ any admissible function in a neighborhood of $\mathbf{z}(x)$ reaches $T(\mathbf{b}, \tau) = 0$ at finite x, and that if $x^*(\tau)$ is the value of x at which $T(\mathbf{b}, \tau) = 0$ is reached by $\mathbf{z}(x)$ then as $\tau \to 0$, $x^*(\tau) \to \infty$.

Suppose now that the solution to the necessary conditions and the transversality condition has been determined for each $\tau > 0$ in a neighborhood of 0. Denote by $\mathbf{y}(x; \tau)$ the solution when the curve ends on $T(\mathbf{b}, \tau) = 0$.

(See Figure 2.39.) Then for each τ the transversality conditions become

$$\mathbf{F}_{\mathbf{y}'}(\mathbf{b}(\tau), \mathbf{y}'(x; \tau)) = \rho \nabla T(\mathbf{b}, \tau). \tag{2-286}$$

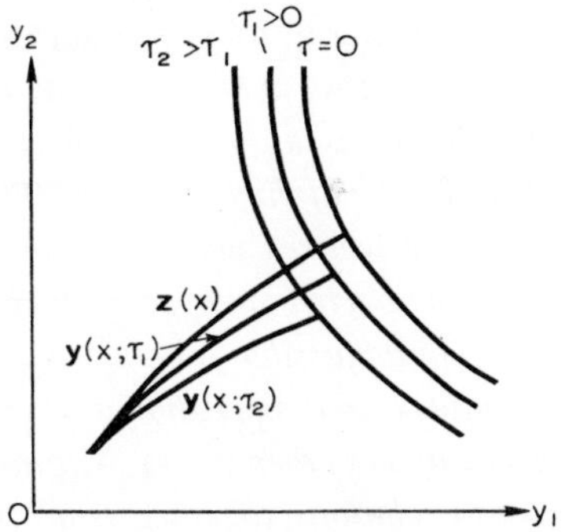

Fig. 2.39.

For large enough x, i.e. for τ sufficiently close to 0, $F_{y_1'} > 0$. Moreover, if $T_{b_1}(\mathbf{y}_1) \neq 0$ then by continuity it does not vanish for a range of τ and $\mathbf{b}$ close to $\mathbf{y}_1$. Hence, for $\tau > 0$, we can write $\rho = F_{y_1'}/T_{b_1}$ and (2-286) reduces to

$$\frac{F_{y_j'}}{F_{y_1'}} - \frac{T_{b_j}(\mathbf{b}, \tau)}{T_{b_1}(\mathbf{b}, \tau)} = 0, \qquad j = 2, \ldots, n. \tag{2-287}$$

Now (2-287) holds for all $\tau > 0$ sufficiently close to 0, and the limits exist; hence, on taking the limit as $\tau \to 0$,

$$\frac{F_{y_j'}(\mathbf{y}_1, 0)}{F_{y_1'}(\mathbf{y}_1, 0)} = \frac{T_{b_j}(\mathbf{y}_1)}{T_{b_1}(\mathbf{y}_1)}, \qquad j = 2, \ldots, n. \tag{2-288}$$

Thus, when the above parameterization can be carried out, the transversality relations take the form of (2-288). These $n - 1$ relations, together with $T(\mathbf{y}_1) = 0$, determine $\mathbf{y}_1$. The interesting thing about the transversality relations (2-288) is that they in no way depend on the initial point $(x_0, \mathbf{y}_0)$. If (2-288) possesses a unique solution then, no matter what the initial point happens to be, $\mathbf{z}(x)$ always approaches the same point $\mathbf{y}_1$ on $T(\mathbf{b}) = 0$. Of course, (2-288) may not possess a unique solution; in that case, there may not be just one point $\mathbf{y}_1$ which serves for all initial points.

Thus we have established.

Theorem 2.23.1. Transversality Condition at Infinity. Let $\mathbf{z}(x)$ be an admissible function which yields an interior maximum or minimum of $J[\mathbf{y}]$ when $\mathbf{z}(x_0) =$

$\mathbf{y}_0$ and $\mathbf{z}(x)$ approaches the surface $T(\mathbf{b}) = 0$ as $x \to \infty$. Then $\mathbf{z}(x)$ must satisfy the necessary conditions of Theorem 2.13.1 and, in addition, (2-285). Normally, (2-285) and $T(\mathbf{b}) = 0$ between them determine $\mathbf{b}$. However, this is not so when F does not depend on x explicitly and $\mathbf{F}_{\mathbf{y}'}(\mathbf{b}, 0) = \mathbf{0}$. Suppose that in this case there is at least one j, say $j = 1$, such that $F_{y_1'} \neq 0$ for all x sufficiently large and $T_{b_1} \neq 0$ at $\mathbf{y}_1$ and such that, in addition, the ratios $F_{y_j'}/F_{y_1'}$ approach definite limits as $x \to \infty$. Suppose that it is possible to construct a one-parameter family of hypersurfaces $T(\mathbf{b}, \tau) = 0$ such that $T(\mathbf{b}, \tau)$ and its first partial derivatives are continuous functions of τ, such that when $\tau = 0$ we obtain the particular hypersurface $T(\mathbf{b}) = 0$ of interest, such that for every $\tau > 0$ any admissible function in a neighborhood of $\mathbf{z}(x)$ reaches $T(\mathbf{b}, \tau) = 0$ at finite x, and such that if $x^*(\tau)$ is the value of x at which $T(\mathbf{b}, \tau) = 0$ is reached by $\mathbf{z}(x)$ then $x^*(\tau) \to \infty$ as $\tau \to 0$. Then (2-288) must be satisfied. These $n - 1$ relations, together with $T(\mathbf{y}_1) = 0$, determine $\mathbf{y}_1$.

2.24. Transversality in the model of Samuelson and Solow

The n sector model of Samuelson and Solow was introduced in Section 2.16. We now revert to that model, for the case in which utility saturates illustrates very well the application of the transversality conditions just discussed. Suppose that utility saturates at the unique point $(C_1^*, \mathbf{C}^*)$ and that this determines bliss. Any vector of capital stocks satisfying $C_1^* = \Psi(\mathbf{K}, \mathbf{C}^*)$ will yield bliss. In the present case, we want $\mathbf{K}$ to approach some vector $\mathbf{b}$ which will produce bliss. However, the vector $\mathbf{b}$ is not unique; any $\mathbf{b}$ satisfying $T(\mathbf{b}) = \Psi(\mathbf{b}, \mathbf{C}^*) - C_1^* = 0$ will do. To determine the specific value (or values) of $\mathbf{b}$ which maximize the time integral of the utility function, the transversality condition must be applied.

Here

$$F_{\dot{K}_1} = -U_{C_1}; \qquad F_{\dot{K}_j} = U_{C_1}\Psi_{C_j}, \quad j = 2, \ldots, n.$$

Now $U_{C_1} = 0$ at bliss; thus, for all j, $F_{\dot{K}_j} = 0$ at every point on the hypersurface $T(\mathbf{b}) = 0$. However, when the system is not at bliss, $U_{C_1} \neq 0$ and the ratios $F_{\dot{K}_j}/F_{\dot{K}_1} = -\Psi_{C_j}$ approach definite limits on any path which approaches a particular point on $T(\mathbf{b}) = 0$. We now show that it is possible to parameterize the constraint $T(\mathbf{b}) = 0$ in the manner described in Section 2.23, thus allowing us to conclude that (2-288) holds.

Consider a smooth curve, in the space $\mathscr{E}^n$ of points $(C_1, \mathbf{C})$, which starts at the point $(C_1^*, \mathbf{C}^*)$ and is represented parametrically by $(C_1(\tau), \mathbf{C}(\tau))$, with $C_1(0) = C_1^*$ and $\mathbf{C}(0) = \mathbf{C}^*$. We shall suppose that this curve is identical with the curve representing the $(C_1(t), \mathbf{C}(t))$ associated with the optimal solution $\mathbf{K}(t)$. Suppose that τ increases as we move from $(C_1^*, \mathbf{C}^*)$ along the curve in the direction opposite to that in which the system moves with the passage of time. For any $\tau > 0$, consider the set of points $\mathbf{K}$ satisfying $\Psi(\mathbf{K}, \mathbf{C}(\tau)) - C_1(\tau) = 0$ (the form taken by $T(\mathbf{b}, \tau) = 0$ in this case); this set is reached at a finite value of t. Here then we have the type of parameterization desired; hence we may conclude that the transversality conditions (2-288) apply on paths where $U_{C_1} \neq 0$. These become

$$-\Psi_{C_j}(\mathbf{b}, \mathbf{C}^*) = \frac{\Psi_{K_j}(\mathbf{b}, \mathbf{C}^*)}{\Psi_{K_1}(\mathbf{b}, \mathbf{C}^*)}, \qquad j = 2, \ldots, n. \tag{2-289}$$

Together with $T(\mathbf{b}, 0)$, (2-289) should determine $\mathbf{b}$.

Let us consider the case in which there is a unique solution to (2-289). Starting from any point $\mathbf{K}_0$ not on $\Psi(\mathbf{K}, \mathbf{C}^*) - C_1^* = 0$, an optimal path then always leads to one specific point $\mathbf{K}^*$ on this hypersurface. Figure 2.40

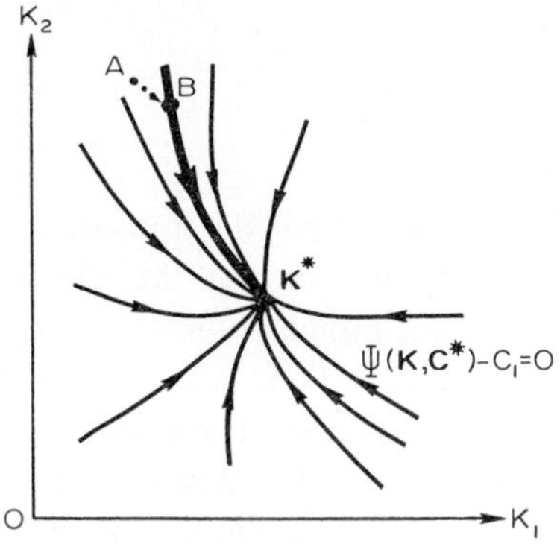

Fig. 2.40.

provides an illustration for the case $n = 2$. Consider an initial point like A, which is close to $T(\mathbf{b}) = 0$ but far from $\mathbf{K}^*$. We might have expected that it would be optimal to follow something like the dotted path, with the system attaining bliss not at K^* but at B. As Figure 2.40 makes clear, however, this is not so. On the other hand, any point on $T(\mathbf{b}) = 0$ yields bliss; if the system starts out at any point on this hypersurface, bliss can be maintained either by simply staying at that point or by moving towards K^* on a curve lying in the hypersurface (as shown in Figure 2.40). The results stated in this paragraph are the essential contribution of the paper by Samuelson and Solow.

Let us now reconsider the specific example introduced in Section 2.16. We there studied the case in which the maximum output is just sufficient to saturate the utility function. However, the same example can be used to illustrate the case in which the utility function saturates first, for in that case, Euler's equations are precisely the same as in Section 2.16. Thus (2-199) must still apply; only when the initial point (K_1^0, K_2^0) lies on this line will there be a solution to the Euler equations (unless the system is always at bliss). We shall call this line the critical line. Let us suppose then that (K_1^0, K_2^0) does lie on (2-199).

Utility saturates at (C_1^*, C_2^*) and any set of values (K_1, K_2) satisfying

$$\beta_1(K_1 - K_1^*)^2 + \beta_2(K_2 - K_2^*)^2 = \delta \tag{2-290}$$

with $\delta = \gamma - C_1^* - C_2^*$ will yield bliss. When $\beta_1 \neq \beta_2$ and neither coefficient is 0, (2-290) is represented graphically by an ellipse. We now show that the transversality conditions (2-289) are satisfied at those points where the line $K_2 - K_2^* = \beta_1(K_1 - K_1^*)/\beta_2$ crosses the ellipse.

For the example under consideration there is just one equation (2-289), viz.

$$-(-1) = \frac{-2\beta_2(K_2 - K_2^*)}{-2\beta_1(K_1 - K_1^*)} \tag{2-291}$$

or $\beta_1(K_1 - K_1^*) = \beta_2(K_2 - K_2^*)$. Thus the transversality condition is indeed satisfied at points where the line crosses the ellipse (and nowhere else). However we have a situation rather different from that contemplated by Samuelson and Solow. For here there are two different solutions to the transversality condition and (2-289). These are the two points of intersection of the line with the ellipse, shown in Figure 2.41.

We now seek to relate the movement of the system along the critical

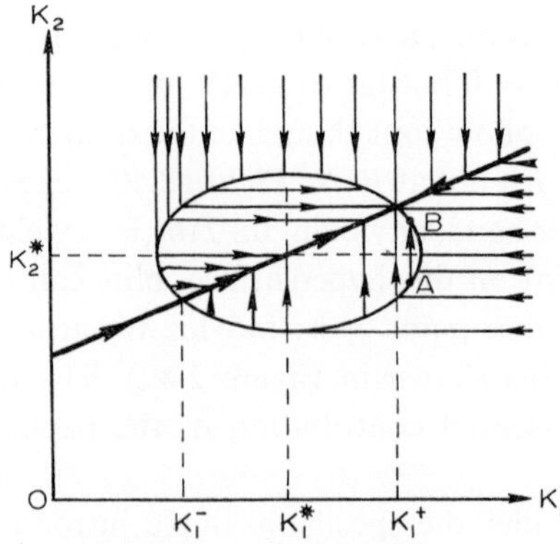

Fig. 2.41.

line to the position on that line of the initial point (K_1^0, K_2^0). The situation is not quite the same as in Section 2.16 because now $\gamma \neq C_1^* + C_2^*$. In place of (2-201), we now have

$$C_2 - C_2^* = \varepsilon - \Delta(K_1 - K_1^*)^2 - \omega \dot{K}_1 \tag{2-292}$$

where $\varepsilon = \rho(\gamma - C_1^* - C_2^*) > 0$. Then on completing the square, $U + \dot{K}_1 U_{C_1} + \dot{K}_2 U_{C_2} = 0$ becomes

$$[\varepsilon - \Delta(K_1 - K_1^*)^2]^2 = \omega^2 \dot{K}_1^2 \tag{2-293}$$

so that

$$\dot{K}_1 = \zeta - \beta_1(K_1 - K_1^*)^2 \quad \text{or} \quad \dot{K}_1 = -\zeta + \beta_1(K_1 - K_1^*)^2 \tag{2-294}$$

where $\zeta = \beta_2(\beta_1 + \beta_2)^{-1}(\gamma - C_1^* - C_2^*)$. Each of the equations in (2-294) is represented by a parabola in the $K_1\dot{K}_1$-phase plane, as shown in Figure 2.42. The first opens downwards, the second upwards. They cross on the K_1-axis at the points K_1^- and K_1^+, the very values of K_1 at which the critical line crosses the ellipse in Figure 2.41.

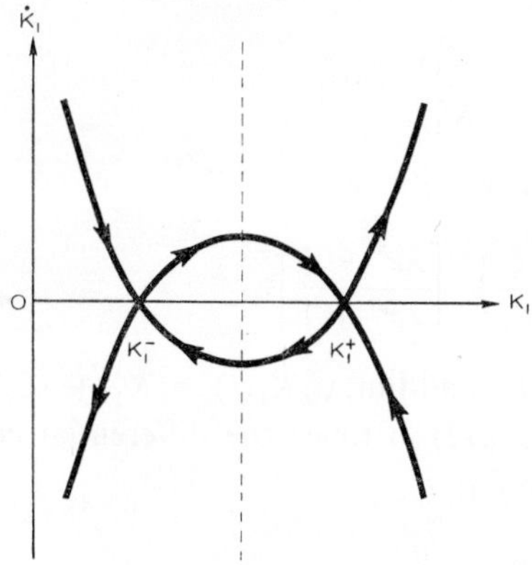

Fig. 2.42.

We next solve each of the equations in (2-294). It is useful to distinguish the three regions $K_1^0 < K_1^-$, $K_1^0 > K_1^+$ and $K_1^- < K_1^0 < K_1^+$. In each of the first two regions, however, the path followed by the system is unmistakable. (See Figure 2.41.) It is only in the third region that the behavior of the system requires elucidation. Figure 2.42 suggests that the economy could move either towards K_1^- or towards K_1^+ and it remains to determine which motion prevails in any particular case. Consider first $\dot{K}_1 = \zeta - \beta_1(K_1 - K_1^*)^2$. On introducing a partial fractions expansion, we see that, when $\zeta > \beta_1(K_1 - K_1^*)^2$, i.e. $K_1^- < K_1 < K_1^+$,

$$\frac{1}{\zeta - \beta_1(K_1 - K_1^*)^2} \equiv \frac{1}{2\zeta^{\frac{1}{2}}}\left[\frac{1}{\zeta^{\frac{1}{2}} - \beta_1^{\frac{1}{2}}(K_1 - K_1^*)} + \frac{1}{\zeta^{\frac{1}{2}} + \beta_1^{\frac{1}{2}}(K_1 - K_1^*)}\right]. \tag{2-295}$$

Hence

$$\int [\zeta - \beta_1(K_1 - K_1^*)^2]^{-1}\mathrm{d}K = -\frac{1}{2(\beta_1\zeta)^{\frac{1}{2}}}\log[\zeta^{\frac{1}{2}} - \beta_1^{\frac{1}{2}}(K_1 - K_1^*)]$$

$$+ \frac{1}{2(\beta_1\zeta)^{\frac{1}{2}}}\log[\zeta^{\frac{1}{2}} + \beta_1^{\frac{1}{2}}(K_1 - K_1^*)]. \tag{2-296}$$

Thus when $K_1^- < K_1 < K_1^+$ the solution to the differential equation is

$$\frac{\zeta^{\frac{1}{2}} + \beta_1^{\frac{1}{2}}(K_1 - K_1^*)}{\zeta^{\frac{1}{2}} - \beta_1^{\frac{1}{2}}(K_1 - K_1^*)} = \lambda e^{\mu t}, \qquad \mu = 2(\beta_1\zeta)^{\frac{1}{2}} \tag{2-297}$$

and

$$\lambda = \frac{\zeta^{\frac{1}{2}} + \beta_1^{\frac{1}{2}}(K_1^0 - K_1^*)}{\zeta^{\frac{1}{2}} - \beta_1^{\frac{1}{2}}(K_1^0 - K_1^*)} > 0. \tag{2-298}$$

Solving (2-297) for K_1, we obtain

$$K_1(t) = K_1^* + \left(\frac{\zeta}{\beta_1}\right)^{\frac{1}{2}}\left[\frac{\lambda e^{\mu t} - 1}{\lambda e^{\mu t} + 1}\right]. \tag{2-299}$$

Notice that $K_1(0) = K_0$ and $\lim_{t\to\infty} K_1(t) = K_1^* + (\zeta/\beta_1)^{\frac{1}{2}} = K_1^+$.

Subtracting from (2-292) ω times the differential equation $\dot{K}_1 = \zeta - \beta_1(K_1 - K_1^*)^2$, we obtain

$$C_2 - C_2^* = \varepsilon - \omega\zeta = 0. \tag{2-300}$$

Thus *everywhere* (not merely in the region for which the differential equation was solved) on the downwards opening parabola of Figure 2.42, $C_2 = C_2^*$ and $C_1 = C_1^*$, that is, the economy is at bliss. For any K_1^0 to the left of K_1^- the economy remains at bliss by using up capital; in finite time it moves along this part of the parabola to $K_1 = 0$. For any K_1^0 between K_1^- and K_1^+ the economy remains at bliss while increasing K_1 (and K_2) and approaching K_1^+ asymptotically. In this case the initial stock of capital is so large that it is possible to set $C_1 = C_1^*$ and $C_2 = C_2^*$ and still have output left over for investment. At K_1^* the production function saturates; then, as K_1 continues to increase, both the rate of output and $\dot{K}_1$ begin to fall. If $K_1^0 > K_1^+$, it is necessary to use up capital in order to maintain bliss. However, since the initial stock of capital exceeds the amount at which the production function saturates, the consumption of capital actually increases the rate of output. Thus K_1^+ is again approached.

Consider now the other differential equation $\dot{K}_1 = -[\zeta - \beta_1(K_1 - K_1^*)^2]$. The same procedure yields the solution

$$K_1(t) = K_1^* + \left(\frac{\zeta}{\beta_1}\right)^{\frac{1}{2}} \left[\frac{\lambda e^{-\mu t} - 1}{\lambda e^{-\mu t} + 1}\right] \tag{2-301}$$

when $K_1^- < K_1^0 < K_1^+$, where λ is given by (2-298). Then $K(0) = K_0$ and $\lim_{t\to\infty} K_1(t) = K_1^-$ as expected.

For this case it is not true that $C_2 = C_2^*$, since the signs in the differential equation are changed. Now

$$C_2(t) = C_2^* + \varepsilon + \omega\zeta - 2\Delta(K_1 - K_1^*)^2.$$

When $K_1^- < K_1 < K_1^+$, $C_2 > C_2^*$ and $C_1 > C_1^*$; hence $U < 0$ and $J[K] < 0$, that is, the value of the integral along this path is negative. Consequently, this path is less desirable than that along which movement is towards K_1^+; hence the latter path is optimal. This explains why Figure 2.41 is drawn as it is. The trouble with the path along which movement is to the left is that $\dot{K}_1$ and $\dot{K}_2$ must be negative; however the output rates are so high that when capital is being used up it is necessary that $C_2 > C_2^*$ and $C_1 > C_1^*$, implying that the system is not at bliss.

We note in passing that the path which moves to the left is an example of a nonoptimal path for which the integral converges and for which $\mathbf{F}_{\mathbf{y}'} \cdot \boldsymbol{\eta} \to 0$ along every other admissible path. Thus we appear to have a counter-example to Theorem 2.17.5. In the region where $K_1^- < K_1 < K_1^+$, however, F is not concave, in spite of the fact that U and Ψ are concave functions everywhere. Hence Theorem 2.17.5 does not apply.

We now know what happens when the point (K_1^0, K_2^0) lies on the line (2-199). With the other possible solution to the Euler equation, the system always remains at bliss and $C_1 = C_1^*$, $C_2 = C_2^*$. The situation is a little different from that of Section 2.16, since the utility function now saturates first. When the system is at bliss

$$\dot{K}_1 + \dot{K}_2 = \delta - \beta_1(K_1 - K_1^*)^2 - \beta_2(K_2 - K_2^*)^2 \tag{2-302}$$

and any pair of functions $K_1(t)$ and $K_2(t)$ which satisfies this equation will keep the system at bliss.

If $K_1^0 > K_1^+$ and $K_2^0 > K_2^+$ it is possible to maintain bliss while $K_1 \to K_1^+$ and $K_2 \to K_2^+$. The path is not unique unless (K_1^0, K_2^0) is on the critical line. For example, if (K_1^0, K_2^0) lies above the critical line we could set $K_1 = K_1^0$ and $\dot{K}_1 = 0$ with

$$\dot{K}_2 = \delta - \beta_1(K_1^0 - K_1^*)^2 - \beta_2(K_2 - K_2^*)^2.$$

Note that $\dot{K}_2 < 0$ at K_2^0 and will remain negative. Thus we move downwards from (K_1^0, K_2^0) on a vertical line. After some finite time, the moving point will meet the critical line. Thereafter, the system moves down the critical line to (K_1^+, K_2^+), always remaining at bliss. If on the other hand (K_1^0, K_2^0) lies below the critical line we set $K_2 = K_2^0$ and $\dot{K}_2 = 0$. Then the system moves leftwards along a horizontal line. When the critical line is reached, a changeover is made. Such paths are illustrated by Figure 2.41. It should be remembered, however, that the curves are not unique, that there exists a variety of paths which might be followed.

It is not only when $K_1^0 > K_1^+$ and $K_2^0 > K_2^+$ that bliss can be maintained indefinitely. Consider points inside the ellipse. For such points, $\beta_1(K_1 - K_1^*)^2 + \beta_2(K_2 - K_2^*)^2 < \delta$. Bliss can then be maintained with $\dot{K}_1 + \dot{K}_2$ positive and satisfying (2-302). Thus for points with $K_1^0 < K_1^+$ and $K_2^0 < K_2^+$ lying inside the ellipse we can again set either $\dot{K}_1 = 0$ or $\dot{K}_2 = 0$, the other variable now increasing until the critical line is reached. Then a change of regime occurs so that thereafter movement takes place along this line towards (K_1^+, K_2^+).

Let us now consider a point like A. Suppose that we keep $\dot{K}_1 = 0$ and let K_2 increase according to (2-302). Bliss will be maintained. In this case, however, the vertical path does not reach the critical line; instead, the ellipse itself is reached. When the ellipse is reached, $\dot{K}_1 = \dot{K}_2 = 0$; hence the economy will remain at this point thereafter. Everywhere on the path AB the economy is in a state of bliss; for the initial point A, therefore, that path is optimal. However, the terminal point B coincides neither with (K_1^+, K_2^+) nor with (K_1^-, K_2^-); hence the transversality conditions (2-289) are not satisfied. The apparent contradiction is immediately resolved by noting that, along the path AB, $U_{C_1} = 0$, a case which was ruled out in the derivation of (2-289). In this case it is not possible to convert to the ratio form of the conditions. On the other hand, it will be observed that in their original form (2-285) the transversality conditions are automatically satisfied at B $(\mathbf{0} = \mathbf{0})$.

We can now easily determine additional initial points (K_1^0, K_2^0) with properties similar to those of A. Consider any point lying above the ellipse such that a vertical line through the point intersects the ellipse. For such a point, set $\dot{K}_1 = 0$ and $K_1 = K_1^0$. Then $\dot{K}_2$, determined from (2-302), is negative initially and remains negative; the system moves down the vertical line to the ellipse, with bliss maintained at each point. Several such lines are shown in Figure 2.41.

In similar fashion, we can consider any point lying to the right of the ellipse such that a horizontal line through the point intersects the ellipse. For such a point, set $\dot{K}_2 = 0$, $K_2 = K_2^0$. Then $\dot{K}_1$, determined from (2-302), is negative and the system moves along the horizontal line to the ellipse, with bliss maintained at each point. Several such lines are shown in Figure 2.41. It is emphasized again that the optimal paths are not unique.

We have concluded that if (K_1^0, K_2^0) lies in the set of solutions to

$$K_1 \geq K_1^* - \sqrt{\frac{\delta}{\beta_1}}$$

$$K_2 \geq K_2^* - \sqrt{\frac{\delta}{\beta_2}}$$

$$(K_1 - K_1^*)^2 + (K_2 - K_2^*)^2 \leq \delta$$

the system can always remain at bliss and there is a path (not unique) leading from the initial point to the ellipse. We have displayed one possible choice of path for each case. For all other initial points the system will not always remain at bliss. The only points in the complement with respect to the set $K_1 \geq 0$, $K_2 \geq 0$ for which we have solved the problem are those lying on the critical line. The nature of the solution for the other initial points will be clarified in Chapter 4.

2.25.° The connection with dynamic programming

The methods of the classical calculus of variations do not in general form the basis of efficient numerical procedures. Even in the simplest case, in which there is only one function $y(x)$ to be determined, it often is difficult to numerically solve the Euler equation. Dynamic programming, on the other hand, is a procedure which makes it possible in principle to numerically solve any of the problems we have considered (though the procedure provides an efficient numerical technique only for $n = 1$ or 2). We now seek to explain the connection between dynamic programming and the methods we have outlined in earlier sections.

Suppose that we wish to determine the function $\mathbf{y}(x)$ which extends from the point $(\alpha, \mathbf{a})$ to the point $(\beta, \mathbf{b})$ and which maximizes $J[\mathbf{y}]$. Suppose further that the interval of integration is finite. This is a variational problem;

but it can be rephrased as a dynamic programming problem if we approximate the integral by a suitable finite sum. Let us then subdivide the interval α to β into r subintervals by the points

$$x_u = \alpha + (\beta - \alpha)\frac{u}{r} \qquad u = 0, 1, \ldots, r.$$

Consider any admissible function $\mathbf{y}(x)$ and denote by $\mathbf{y}_u$ the vector $\mathbf{y}(x_u)$. In subinterval u, $\mathbf{y}(x)$ may be approximated by the line segment joining the two points $\mathbf{y}_{u-1}$ and $\mathbf{y}_u$. Over the entire interval α to β, then, $\mathbf{y}(x)$ is approximated by a polygonal function $\hat{\mathbf{y}}(x)$. For $n = 1$ the functions $\mathbf{y}(x)$ and $\hat{\mathbf{y}}(x)$ might be like those depicted in Figure 2.43. Notice that, in the interval u, $\hat{\mathbf{y}}'(x) = (\mathbf{y}_u - \mathbf{y}_{u-1})/\Delta x$, $\Delta x = (\beta - \alpha)/r$.

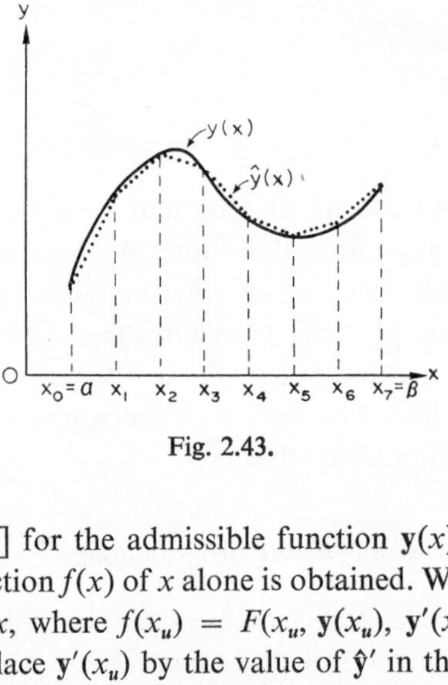

Fig. 2.43.

Now consider $J[\mathbf{y}]$ for the admissible function $\mathbf{y}(x)$. When $\mathbf{y}(x)$ is substituted into F, a function $f(x)$ of x alone is obtained. We might approximate $J[\mathbf{y}]$ by $\Sigma_{u=1}^{r} f(x_u)\Delta x$, where $f(x_u) = F(x_u, \mathbf{y}(x_u), \mathbf{y}'(x_u))$. However it will be convenient to replace $\mathbf{y}'(x_u)$ by the value of $\hat{\mathbf{y}}'$ in the interval $u + 1$, i.e. by $(\mathbf{y}_{u+1} - \mathbf{y}_u)/\Delta x$; for later we shall want to determine the optimal function and, for that purpose, our formulation must contain only values of the function, not of its derivatives. Thus for any admissible function $\mathbf{y}(x)$ we have the approximation

$$J[\mathbf{y}] = \sum_{u=0}^{r-1} F\left(x_u, \mathbf{y}_u, \frac{\mathbf{y}_{u+1} - \mathbf{y}_u}{\Delta x}\right) \Delta x. \tag{2-303}$$

Suppose that we have $r + 1$ points $\mathbf{z}_0, \mathbf{z}_1, \ldots, \mathbf{z}_r$ which maximize (or minimize) the right hand side of (2-303). These points determine a polygonal function $\hat{\mathbf{z}}(x)$ which we can view as an approximation to the optimal solution $\mathbf{z}(x)$. Moreover, the problem of finding those points is an ordinary maximum (or minimum) problem, not a problem in the calculus of variations; and it can be solved as an r-stage dynamic programming problem, as we proceed to demonstrate.

Let us define the sequence of functions

$$\Lambda_v(\xi) = \max_{\mathbf{y}_{v+1},\ldots,\mathbf{y}_{r-1}} \sum_{u=v}^{r-1} F\left(x_u, \mathbf{y}_u, \frac{\mathbf{y}_{u+1} - \mathbf{y}_u}{\Delta x}\right) \Delta x,$$

$$\mathbf{y}_v = \xi, \quad v = 0, \ldots, r-2 \qquad \text{(2-304)}$$

so that $\Lambda_v(\xi)$ is the maximum value of $\Sigma_{u=v}^{r-1} F\Delta x$ when $\mathbf{y}_v = \xi$. For each u, there is a contribution $F\Delta x$ to the sum (2-304); we shall refer to this as the contribution from stage u. Then $\Lambda_v(\xi)$ is the maximum contribution from the last $r - v$ stages when $\mathbf{y}_v = \xi$. For the last stage there is no maximization involved since $\mathbf{y}_r = \mathbf{b}$. Hence

$$\Lambda_{r-1}(\xi) = F\left(x_{r-1}, \xi, \frac{\mathbf{b} - \xi}{\Delta x}\right) \Delta x. \qquad \text{(2-305)}$$

The important thing about the $\Lambda_v(\xi)$ is that they can be determined recursively. Note that

$$\Lambda_v(\xi) = \max_{\mathbf{y}_{v+1}} \left[F\left(x_v, \xi, \frac{\mathbf{y}_{v+1} - \xi}{\Delta x}\right) \Delta x \right.$$

$$\left. + \max_{\mathbf{y}_{v+2},\ldots,\mathbf{y}_{r-1}} \sum_{n=v+1}^{r-1} F\left(x_u, \mathbf{y}_u, \frac{\mathbf{y}_{u+1} - \mathbf{y}_u}{\Delta x}\right) \Delta x \right]. \qquad \text{(2-306)}$$

However,

$$\Lambda_{v+1}(\mathbf{y}_{v+1}) = \max_{\mathbf{y}_{v+2},\ldots,\mathbf{y}_{r-1}} \sum_{u=v+1}^{r-1} F\left(x_u, \mathbf{y}_u, \frac{\mathbf{y}_{u+1} - \mathbf{y}_u}{\Delta x}\right) \Delta x.$$

Hence

$$\Lambda_v(\xi) = \max_{\mathbf{y}_{v+1}} \left[F\left(x_v, \xi, \frac{\mathbf{y}_{v+1} - \xi}{\Delta x}\right) \Delta x + \Lambda_{v+1}(\mathbf{y}_{v+1}) \right], \quad v = 0, \ldots, r-2.$$

$$\text{(2-307)}$$

Finally, note that $\Lambda_0(\mathbf{a})$ is the approximation to the maximum value of $J[\mathbf{y}]$ which we are seeking.

We can now see how, in principle, the problem can be solved numerically. Let us restrict our attention to the case in which $n = 1$, since this case can be most efficiently handled on a computer. We have obtained an approximation by considering not all points in the interval $\alpha \leq x \leq \beta$ but only a finite number x_u. We now do precisely the same thing with y. Instead of allowing y to take all possible values for each x_u, we permit it to take one of a finite number of values $\xi_1, \ldots, \xi_m$, the same set of values for each x_u.

As a first step we compute $\Lambda_{r-1}(\xi_u)$, $u = 1, \ldots, m$, using (2-305), and list these values in a table. Next, for each ξ_u we compute $\Lambda_{r-2}(\xi_u)$, using

$$\Lambda_{r-2}(\xi_u) = \max_{y_{r-1}} \Omega_{r-2}(\xi_u, y_{r-1}) \tag{2-308}$$

$$\Omega_{r-2}(\xi_u, y_{r-1}) = F\left(x_{r-2}, \xi_u, \frac{y_{r-1} - \xi_u}{\Delta x}\right) \Delta x + \Lambda_{r-1}(y_{r-1}). \tag{2-309}$$

To compute $\Lambda_{r-2}(\xi_u)$ we must maximize with respect to a single variable y_{r-1}. This is done merely by evaluating $\Omega_{r-2}(\xi_u, y_{r-1})$ for $y_{r-1} = \xi_1, \xi_2, \ldots, \xi_m$; the largest of these numbers is $\Lambda_{r-2}(\xi_u)$. In addition to $\Lambda_{r-2}(\xi_u)$ we also record that value of y_{r-1}, say $y_{r-1}(\xi_u)$, which yields the maximum. Note that, to compute $\Lambda_{r-2}(\xi_u)$, in general we must know $\Lambda_{r-1}(\xi)$ for all values of $\xi = \xi_1, \ldots, \xi_m$. Suppose then that we compute $\Lambda_{r-2}(\xi_u)$ and $y_{r-1}(\xi_u)$ for each $u = 1, \ldots, m$ and list these in a table. Observe that, in order to do this, it is necessary to solve m problems each involving the maximization of a function of a single variable.

Having obtained a table of $\Lambda_{r-2}(\xi)$, we can appeal to the recurrence relation (2-307) and repeat the procedure to obtain a table of $\Lambda_{r-3}(\xi)$ and a table of $y_{r-2}(\xi)$, the value of y_{r-2} which yields the maximum for each ξ. This procedure can be repeated until $\Lambda_0(\xi)$ and $y_1(\xi)$ are obtained. In reality, at the last step only $\Lambda_0(b)$ and $y_1(b)$ need be determined. $\Lambda_0(b)$ is the approximation to the maximum value of the integral.

To determine $\hat{\mathbf{z}}(x)$, the approximation to the admissible function which yields the maximum, we must next work our way backwards through the tables of the $y_u(\xi)$. Now $z_0 = b$ and $z_1 = y_1(b)$. To determine z_2 we must evaluate $y_2(\xi)$ at $\xi = z_1$. Thus $y_2 = y_2(z_1)$. Similarly, $z_u = y_u(z_{u-1})$, and in this way the sequence of values z_u is determined. By connecting (x_{u-1}, z_{u-1}) to (x_u, z_u) by a straight line segment for each u, the polygonal approximation $\hat{\mathbf{z}}(x)$ to the optimizing curve is determined.

It is possible to give a very clear graphical interpretation of the sequential dynamic programming method. Essentially, we construct approximately a field of extremals emanating from the point (β, b). At each step the field is extended backwards (towards smaller values of x) by one subinterval. The maximization process (2-308) determines the extremal to which the point (x_r, ξ) should be joined. The situation is illustrated graphically by Figure 2.44.

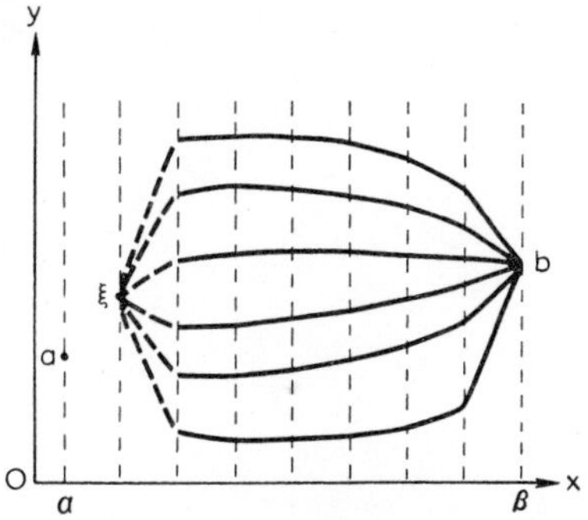

Fig. 2.44.

At the final step, the extremal passing through (α, a) is determined and the problem is solved.

The dynamic programming approach has several useful features. Not only can the variational problem be solved for a specified value of α and a, but with very little additional effort optimal solutions for a variety of alternative values of α and a can be determined. Furthermore, many types of constraints raise no difficulties for the solution procedure. They can easily be taken into account in carrying out the various maximizations.

It will be observed that the dynamic programming approach requires a great deal of numerical computation; usually indeed a large digital computer would be needed to obtain the solution. Even when a digital computer is available, however, n must be quite small if a problem is to be solved numerically by dynamic programming. For in general $\Lambda_v(\xi)$ is a function of n variables, and to compute Λ_v for each ξ requires a maximization over n variables. If m values are used for each component of $\mathbf{y}$, there are m^n possible values of ξ and m^n values in the table of $\Lambda_v(\xi)$. Thus if $m = 100$, there are 100 values for $n = 1$, 10000 for $n = 2$, 10^6 for $n = 3$, and so on. Each entry requires a maximization which becomes increasingly complex as n increases. For the present case, then, the time required to solve a problem for $n = 2$ would be more than 100 times that required for $n = 1$, and for $n = 3$ more than 10000 times that for $n = 1$. Consequently, if 20 seconds of the computer's time are required to solve a problem for $n = 1$, more than 33 minutes would be needed for $n = 2$ and more than 50 hours for $n = 3$. Clearly the time (and the memory requirements) quickly become prohibitive as n increases.

Problems

Section 2.2

1. According to Fermat's principle in optics light moves through a nonhomogeneous medium along a path which minimizes the time required to move from one point to another. A light source is located at the origin in the xy-plane. Let $v(x, y)$ be the velocity of light at the point (x, y). Set up the problem of determining the path followed by a photon in moving from the origin to the point (x_0, y_0).

Section 2.3

1. Let $\mathscr{D}$ be a set of authors and $\mathscr{G}$ the set of books they have written. Does the rule which associates with each author the books he has written define a function? Does your answer depend on precisely how the elements of $\mathscr{G}$ are defined?

2. Let $\mathscr{D}$ be a set of books and $\mathscr{G}$ the set of authors of the books. Does the rule which associates with each element in $\mathscr{D}$ its authors in $\mathscr{G}$ define a function? Does your answer depend on precisely how the elements of $\mathscr{G}$ are defined?

3. Give an example of a function for which the domain contains at least three elements and for which each element in the range is the image of exactly three elements in the domain.

4. Let f be a function with domain $\mathscr{D}$ and let $\mathscr{A}$ be a subset of $\mathscr{D}$. By $f(\mathscr{A})$ we mean the subset of the range having the property that $f(\mathscr{A})$ is the collection of all images of all elements of $\mathscr{A}$. Let $\mathscr{B}$ be another subset of $\mathscr{D}$. Either prove that

(a) $f(\mathscr{A} \cap \mathscr{B}) = f(\mathscr{A}) \cap f(\mathscr{B})$

(b) $f(\mathscr{A} \cup \mathscr{B}) = f(\mathscr{A}) \cup f(\mathscr{B})$

or provide a counterexample to show that the result does not hold in general.

5. Let $\mathscr{F}$ be a subset of the range $\mathscr{R}$ of a function f. By $f^{-1}(\mathscr{F})$ is meant the subset of all elements in the domain the images of which are in $\mathscr{F}$; $f^{-1}(\mathscr{F})$ is called the inverse image of $\mathscr{F}$. Let $\mathscr{H}$ be another subset of $\mathscr{R}$. Either prove that

(a) $f^{-1}(\mathscr{F} \cap \mathscr{H}) = f^{-1}(\mathscr{F}) \cap f^{-1}(\mathscr{H})$

(b) $f^{-1}(\mathscr{F} \cup \mathscr{H}) = f^{-1}(\mathscr{F}) \cup f^{-1}(\mathscr{H})$

or provide a counterexample to show that the result does not hold in general.

6. In each of the following cases determine $\sup f$ if it exists. If there are points in the space for which $\sup f = f(x)$ determine such points and hence determine $\max f$.

(a) $f = 2x - 1, \quad 0 < x < 1$

(b) $f = 3 - x^2$

(c) $f = \sin x$

(d) $f = x\sin x$

(e) $f = 1/x$

(f) $f = \begin{cases} x, 0 < x < 1 \\ 1 - x, 1 < x < 2 \end{cases}$

(g) $f = 3x^2 - 2x - 6, \quad 0 \leq x \leq 4.$

7. Define continuity for a function of one variable and discuss the various types of discontinuities which can occur. Illustrate each type geometrically.

8. Let $f(\mathbf{x})$ be a real-valued function the domain $\mathscr{D}$ of which is a subset of $\mathscr{E}^n$. Then f is said to be continuous at an interior point $\mathbf{x}_0$ of $\mathscr{D}$ if for any $\varepsilon > 0$, there exists a $\delta > 0$ such that for all $\mathbf{x}$, $|\mathbf{x} - \mathbf{x}_0| < \delta$ it is true that $|f(\mathbf{x}) - f(\mathbf{x}_0)| < \varepsilon$. Prove that if $f(\mathbf{x})$ and $g(\mathbf{x})$ are continuous at $\mathbf{x}_0$ then so are $f(\mathbf{x}) + g(\mathbf{x})$, $f(\mathbf{x})g(\mathbf{x})$ and, if $g(\mathbf{x}_0) \neq 0$, $f(\mathbf{x})/g(\mathbf{x})$. (The definition of continuity given here is the familiar one, but it applies only to interior points. In Problem 19 below we shall provide a more general definition which covers the possibility that $\mathbf{x}_0$ is not an interior point.) Hint: $|f(\mathbf{x})g(\mathbf{x}) - f(\mathbf{x}_0)g(\mathbf{x}_0)| = |f(\mathbf{x})g(\mathbf{x}) - f(\mathbf{x}_0)g(\mathbf{x}) + f(\mathbf{x}_0)g(\mathbf{x}) - f(\mathbf{x}_0)g(\mathbf{x}_0)|$. Is there a number γ such that $|g(\mathbf{x})| < \gamma$ for all $\mathbf{x}$ close to $\mathbf{x}_0$?

9. Let $\mathscr{A}$ be a set the elements of which are points in $\mathscr{E}^n$. Define an interior

point and a boundary point. Also define an open and a closed set. How might continuity be defined at a boundary point of the domain of f?

10. Is the function

$$f(\mathbf{x}) = \frac{x_1 x_2}{x_1^2 + x_2^2}, \qquad f(0) = 0$$

continuous for all $\mathbf{x}$? Hint: Consider a neighborhood of the origin and the line $x_1 = x_2$.

11. Let $f(\mathbf{x})$ be defined over some subset of $\mathscr{E}^n$. Give the definition of the partial derivative of f with respect to x_j at $\mathbf{x}_0$. Use vector notation. Let $\nabla f(\mathbf{x}_0) = (f_{x_1}(\mathbf{x}_0), \ldots, f_{x_n}(\mathbf{x}_0))$; ∇f is called the gradient vector for f. Let $\mathbf{r}$ be an arbitrary vector in $\mathscr{E}^n$ of length 1. The rate of change of f at $\mathbf{x}_0$ in the direction $\mathbf{r}$ is called the directional derivative of f in the direction $\mathbf{r}$ and is denoted $D_\mathbf{r} f(\mathbf{x}_0)$. Show that under suitable conditions $D_\mathbf{r} f(\mathbf{x}_0) = \nabla f(\mathbf{x}_0) \cdot \mathbf{r}$. (Here a dot $\cdot$ is used to denote the scalar product of two vectors.) What are the conditions which must be satisfied if this is to be true?

12. Suppose $z = f(\mathbf{u})$ and $\mathbf{u} = \mathbf{g}(\mathbf{y})$. By use of the chain rule for partial differentiation, show that

$$\frac{\partial^2 z}{\partial y_i \partial y_j} = \frac{\partial \mathbf{g}}{\partial x_i} \cdot \mathbf{H} \frac{\partial \mathbf{g}}{\partial x_j}$$

where $\mathbf{H}$ is the Hessian matrix for f with respect to $\mathbf{u}$. Here a dot denotes the scalar product of two vectors and $\partial \mathbf{g}/\partial x_i$ is the vector the jth component of which is $\partial g^j/\partial x_i$.

13. Suppose that $F = y^{-\frac{1}{2}}[1 + (y')^2]^{\frac{1}{2}}$ where y and y' are two different variables. Determine $F_{y'}$, F_y, $F_{yy'}$, F_{yy} and $F_{y'y'}$.

14. The following are to be interpreted as functions the domain of which is a subset of $\mathscr{E}^2$. Sketch the graph of each of these functions in $\mathscr{E}^3$.

(a) $z = 4 - (x_1 - 2)^2 - (x_2 - 3)^2$

(b) $z = x_1^2$

(c) $z = 3x_1^2 - x_2$

(d) $z = |x_1^2 + x_2^2|$.

15. Let $f(x)$ be a piecewise continuous function over the interval $x_0 \le x \le x_1$. Let

$$y(x) = \int_{x_0}^{x} f(\xi) d\xi.$$

Use the properties of integrals to prove that $y(x)$ is piecewise smooth. Thus show the equivalence of the definition of piecewise smooth given in the text and that according to which a piecewise smooth function is one the derivative function of which is piecewise continuous.

16. Sketch the graphs of the following vector-valued functions of one real variable.

(a) $y_1 = 2x$

$y_2 = 3x^2$

(b) $y_1 = \sin x$

$y_2 = \cos x.$

17. Consider the function space which consists of all functions of a single variable of the form $f(x) = ax + b$, $0 \leq x \leq 1$. Consider a real-valued functional $J[f]$ defined by

$$J[f] = \int_0^1 f dx.$$

Evaluate $J[f]$. Does sup J exist? Does inf J exist?

18. Consider the function space which consists of all functions of a single variable of the form $f(x) = ax$, $0 \leq a \leq 1$. Consider a real-valued functional $J[f]$ defined by

$$J[f] = \int_0^a ax dx - a.$$

Does sup J exist? Does max J exist?

19. Let $\mathscr{D}$ be an arbitrary set in $\mathscr{E}^n$ and suppose that the real-valued function $f(\mathbf{x})$ is defined over $\mathscr{D}$. Then, by definition, $\lim_{\mathbf{x} \to \mathbf{x}_0} f(\mathbf{x}) = \alpha$ if, given any $\varepsilon > 0$, there exists a $\delta > 0$ such that, for all $\mathbf{x}$ in $\mathscr{D}$ the distance of which from $\mathbf{x}_0$ is less than δ, $|f(\mathbf{x}) - \alpha| < \varepsilon$. Also, $f(\mathbf{x})$ is said to be continuous at $\mathbf{x}_0$ if $\lim_{\mathbf{x} \to \mathbf{x}_0} f(\mathbf{x}) = f(\mathbf{x}_0)$. Note that this definition applies to any point of $\mathscr{D}$ even if $\mathscr{D}$ contains no interior points. Show that this definition is equivalent to that given in Problem 8 if x_0 is an interior point of $\mathscr{D}$. Consider now the case where $f(x) = x^2 + y^2$ and $\mathscr{D} = \{(x, y) \mid y = 2x + 3\}$. Prove that $f(x)$ is continuous over $\mathscr{D}$. Note that here $\mathscr{D}$ is represented graphically by a straight line. Illustrate the situation graphically in $\mathscr{E}^3$.

Section 2.4

1. Give a phase diagram representation of each of the following functions.

(a) $y = ax$

(b) $y = 3x^3$

(c) $y = 3\sin 2x$

(d) $y = \sqrt{x}$.

2. Sketch the graph in extended phase space of each of the functions presented in Problem 1.

3. Let

$$y(x) = \begin{cases} x^2, & 0 \leq x \leq 1 \\ e^{-(x-1)}, & x \geq 1. \end{cases}$$

Sketch the graph of $y(x)$ in the xy-plane and in extended phase space.

4. Consider the vector-valued function of a real variable $\mathbf{y}(x)$ where the components of $\mathbf{y}(x)$ are $y_1(x) = e^{-x}$ and $y_2(x) = e^{-x}\sin x$. Sketch the graph of $\mathbf{y}(x)$ in $\mathscr{E}^3$.

Section 2.5

1. Assume that $F = [1 + (y')^2]^{\frac{1}{2}}$ and $y(x) = 0, 0 \leq x \leq 1$ and $y(x) = (x - 1), x > 1$. Sketch the graph of F as a function of x.

2. For the minimum surface of revolution problem, what is $\mathscr{R}$? What is $\mathscr{R}$ for the minimum length and brachistochrone problems?

Section 2.6

1. Suppose that $y(x) = x^2$. Represent graphically an N_ε and a P_ε neighborhood of $y(x)$.

2. Suppose that $y(x) = 0, 0 \leq x \leq 2$ and $y(x) = x - 2$ for $x \geq 2$. Represent graphically an N_ε and a P_ε neighborhood of $y(x)$.

3. Suppose that $z(x) = 2x + 3, 0 \leq x \leq 4$. Sketch the graphs of the one parameter family $y(x; \xi) = z(x) + \xi\eta(x), \eta(x) = 4 - (x - 2)^2$.

4. Re-solve Problem 3 with $\eta(x) = \sin \pi x/2$.

5. Show that there exists a constant γ such that

$$F_{y'}(x, z, z') = \int_{x_0}^{x} F_y(\tau, z, z')d\tau + \gamma$$

holds for each x in the interval $x_0 \leq x \leq x_1$ (no values of x are omitted). This can be looked upon as an integrated form of the Euler equation (although this is not the way in which the proof is made) and is often referred to as the DuBois-Reymond relation. Hint: Use an $\eta(x)$ which may differ from 0 everywhere except at the end points and apply a suitable form of the fundamental lemma to the entire interval.

6. Use the results of Problem 5 to obtain very simply the corner conditions.

7. Determine the Euler equation for each of the following integrands:

(a) $F = xy(y')^2 + \exp y^2$

(b) $F = y' + x^3 y$

(c) $F = \log(yy') + \sin xy^2$

(d) $F = xy' + y^{\frac{1}{2}}x^2$.

8. Consider the problem of optimizing

$$J[y] = \int_1^2 x^{-1}[1 + (y')^2]^{\frac{1}{2}} dx$$

with $y(1) = 0$ and $y(2) = 1$. Determine the Euler equation and show that it has the unique solutions $(y - 2)^2 + x^2 = 5$. What are the functions satisfying the Euler equation?

9. Suppose that $F = f(x, y)[1 + (y')^2]^{\frac{1}{2}}$. Show that if y'' exists, then $f_y - f_x y' - f y''[1 + (y')^2]^{-1} = 0$.

10. Suppose that

$$J[y] = \int_{x_0}^{x_1} (x - y)^2.$$

Does there exist a solution passing through arbitrarily specified points (x_0, y_0) and (x_1, y_1)?

11. We have assumed that $F \in C''$ over the region of interest. Suppose now that $F = F_1$ for $x_0 \leq x \leq a$ and $F = F_2$ for $a < x \leq x_1$. $F_1 \in C''$ and $F_2 \in C''$ over some suitable region, but for any piecewise smooth function $y(x)$, there may be a discontinuity in F at a. Develop a set of necessary conditions which must be satisfied by the piecewise smooth function $y(x)$ which maximizes

$$J[y] = \int_{x_0}^{x_1} F dx, \; y(x_0) = y_0 \text{ and } y(x_1) = y_1.$$

Assume as usual that the maximum is an interior maximum.

12. Determine the set of all solutions to the Euler equation when $F = xy' + (y')^2$.

13. Re-solve Problem 12 for $F = y^{-1}[1 + (y')^2]$.

14. Suppose that $z(x)$ is a smooth function which yields a weak interior relative maximum of $J[y]$ for the class of all smooth admissible functions. Then prove that it also yields a weak relative maximum if the class of functions is extended to include piecewise smooth functions. Hint: Prove by contradiction. Assume that there exists a piecewise smooth function $y_*(x)$ in a P_ε neighborhood of $z(x)$ for which $J[y_*] > J[z]$, i.e. $J[y_*] = J[z] + h$, $h > 0$. Show that there then exists a smooth function $y_+(x)$ in the P_ε neighborhood such that $J[y_+] \geq J[z] + (h/2)$, which is a contradiction. The function $y_+(x)$ can be constructed using a process of rounding corners; y_* must have at least one corner – assume x^* is a corner. Consider the graphs of $z'(x)$ and $y_*'(x)$; $z'(x)$ is continuous at x^* but $y_*'(x^*)$ has a jump discontinuity. However, the graph of $y_*'(x)$ always lies close to $z'(x)$, say within ε of $z'(x)$. Now for any small $\delta > 0$ it is possible to introduce a function $y_+'(x)$ which is continuous, has $y_+'(x^* - \delta) = y_*'(x^* - \delta)$, $y_+'(x^* + \delta) = y_*'(x^* + \delta)$ and

$$\int_{x^*-\delta}^{x^*+\delta} y_+' \mathrm{d}x = \int_{x^*-\delta}^{x^*+\delta} y_*' \mathrm{d}x.$$

Describe one precise way of doing this. Let us now write $y_+'(x) = y_*'(x)$ for x not in the interval $x^* - \delta$ to $x^* + \delta$. Then $y_+'(x)$ is continuous and, if

$$y_+(x) = y_0 + \int_{x_0}^{x} y_+' \mathrm{d}x,$$

$y_+(x)$ is smooth and lies within a P_ε neighborhood of $z(x)$. Also δ can be chosen so that $|J[y_*] - J[y_+]| < h/2$. Show this. Then the proof is complete.

15. Suppose that $z(x)$ yields an interior maximum of $J[y]$ for all piecewise smooth functions of the form $y(x; \xi) = z(x) + \xi\eta(x)$, ξ sufficiently small. Show that $z(x)$ yields a weak relative maximum. Hint: Let $y(x)$ be an arbitrary piecewise smooth function in a P_ε neighborhood of $z(x)$. Can this function be written as $y(x; \xi)$?

16. Suppose that $z(x)$ yields an interior maximum of $J[y]$. Prove that if $F_{y'y'}(x, z, z') \neq 0$ along $z(x)$, then $z''(x)$ exists and is continuous for each x^*, $x_0 \leq x^* \leq x_1$, not a corner of $z(x)$. This is referred to as Hilbert's differentiability condition. Hint: $z(x)$ must satisfy the DuBois-Reymond relation of Problem 5. Now consider the equation in u,

$$F_{y'}(x, z(x), u) - \int_{x_0}^{x} F_y(x, z(x), z'(x)) - \gamma = 0.$$

Use the appropriate implicit function theorem to show that there exists a continuous differentiable $u(x)$ in a neighborhood of x^* such that $u(x) = z'(x)$. Why must corners be excluded?

17. Show that a problem involving an integrand F and one involving an integrand $F + f(x)$ will have the same set of optimal solutions. Why is this so?

18. Let $z(x)$ maximize

$$J[y] = \int_{x_0}^{x_1} F dx$$

where $y(x_0) = y_0$ and $y(x_1) = y_1$. Suppose we now select a point ζ, $x_0 < \xi < x_1$ and let $y^* = z(\zeta)$. Prove that $z(x)$ maximizes

$$J[y] = \int_{x_0}^{\zeta} F dx$$

where $y(x_0) = y_0$ and $y(\zeta) = y^*$.

19. Consider the problem of maximizing

$$J[y] = \int_{x_0}^{x_1} F(x, y, y') dx$$

subject to $y(x_0) = y_0$ and $y(x_1) = y_1$, where F is linear in y', so that $F = g(x, y) + y'h(x, y)$. Show successively that the Euler equation reduces to $g_y - h_x = 0$, that F is an exact differential form of the first degree, that J is independent of the choice of $y(t)$, and that the Euler equation does not help you to solve the problem.

Section 2.8

1. Show that $y(x) \equiv \lambda$ is a solution to (2-60) for every λ. Also show that the condition $y \neq \lambda$ is satisfied everywhere by the solution to (2-62).

2. For the solution (2-64) show that the area of the surface of revolution is

$$J[y] = \frac{\lambda^2}{4}\left[\frac{e^{2x} - e^{-2x}}{2} + 2x\right]_{x_0}^{x_1}.$$

For the case in which there are two solutions, try to determine the area for each and select the one which yields the minimum area.

3. Define an envelope for a one parameter family $y = f(x; \lambda)$ and explain why the equation of the envelope can be obtained by eliminating λ between $y = f(x; \lambda)$ and $\partial y/\partial\lambda = 0$. Consider the family $y = [4 - (x - \lambda)^2]^{\frac{1}{2}}$. What is the envelope curve? Illustrate the situation graphically.

4. Consider the integral (2-4) for the brachistochrone problem. Show that the integral is improper at $x_0 = 0$. Actually plot F with $y = ax + b$ and a and b chosen so that the line passes through the appropriate points. Does the integral converge? Must the integral converge for every admissible $y(x)$?

5. Show that the solutions to both equations in (2-71) are represented parametrically by (2-74) and (2-75).

6. Determine the precise equation for the cycloid (2-74) and (2-75) which passes through the specified end points. Sketch the graph of this cycloid.

7. For the situation discussed in Problem 6, find the cycloid passing through the points (2, 0) and (0, 1) and sketch its graph. Also find the cycloid passing through the points (1, 0) and (0, 1) and sketch its graph.

8. Calculate the time required for a particle starting from rest at the point $(0, y_0)$ on the cycloid of Problem 6 to move to another point (x, y_0) on the cycloid. What is the time required to reach the lowest point on the cycloid (consider here the whole cycloid, not merely that part of it joining $(0, y_0)$ to $(x_0, 0)$. Prove the interesting result that it takes the same time for a particle starting from rest to reach the lowest point of the cycloid regardless of the point on the cycloid at which the particle begins its fall. Thus the cycloid is a tautochrone (same time) curve also.

9. Consider the problem of moving a particle from the origin to (1, 0). Can the particle reach x_1 by moving along some curve under the action of gravity alone? Discuss. Does the cycloid give the least time? Compare the time taken on a cycloid with the time taken on a parabola through the same points.

10. Determine the solutions to (2-79) and illustrate them graphically.

11. Is it possible in Example 4 to piece together other extremals to obtain a curve with one or more corners which satisfies the necessary conditions? For example, might one use $y = x + 1$ for $-1 \leq x \leq -\frac{1}{2}$, $y = -x$ for $-\frac{1}{2} \leq x \leq 0$, and $y = x$ for $0 \leq x \leq 1$?

12. We have considered the problem of finding the curve of shortest length joining two points in the xy-plane. Consider the problem of finding the curve of greatest length joining the two points. What is the solution in this case?

13. Weierstrass has given an interesting example of a functional which does not have a minimum in the class of piecewise smooth functions. Show that

$$J[y] = \int_{-1}^{1} x^2 (y')^2 dx$$

with $y(-1) = -1$, $y(1) = 1$ has the property that $\inf J[y] = 0$. Show that there is no piecewise smooth function for which $J[y] = 0$. Hint: To show that $\inf J[y] = 0$, consider the family of admissible functions

$$y(x;\xi) = \frac{\arctan \dfrac{x}{\xi}}{\arctan \dfrac{1}{\xi}}, \qquad \xi > 0.$$

Then

$$J[y(x;\xi)] = \frac{\xi^2}{\left(\arctan \dfrac{1}{\xi}\right)^2} \int_{-1}^{1} \frac{x^2 dx}{(x^2 + \xi^2)^2}$$

$$< \frac{\xi^2}{\left(\arctan \dfrac{1}{\xi}\right)^2} \int_{-1}^{1} \frac{dx}{x^2 + \xi^2} = \frac{2\xi}{\arctan \dfrac{1}{\xi}}.$$

Section 2.9

1. Explain in detail why the integral (2-84) cannot converge if neither the utility function nor the production function saturates.

Section 2.10

1. Consider the Ramsey problem with a finite planning horizon. Compare the solutions with the two alternative boundary conditions $K(T) \geq K_1$ and $K(T) = K_1$.

2. For the Ramsey model with a given finite planning horizon T, does there exist a solution if it is specified that $K(T) = K_1$ and $\dot{K}(T) = 0$?

3. Consider the example discussed in the text and defined by (2-90). Explain in detail why in this example, but not in the example involving the

minimum area of the surface of revolution, there is just one solution which passes through two given points.

4. For the example of the text, calculate the length of time for which bliss can be maintained when moving along $\dot{K} = \beta K - C_0$ with $\dot{K} < 0$.

5. Consider again the example of the text defined by (2-90). Analyze in detail the case in which $K_0 > K^*$. Provide a phase plane analysis and determine the actual solutions.

6. Consider the example described by (2-99). Go through the detailed analysis needed to obtain Figure 2.23, including the curve representing the constraint boundary, and discuss any features of this example which differ from the one studied in detail in the text. Do the curves in Figures 2.24 to 2.26 have a point of inflection where crossing the line $K = K^*$? Can you obtain the solutions $K(t)$ to the differential equations (2-100) and (2-101)?

7. Construct a phase diagram for the Ramsey problem with

$$U(C) = \alpha(C - \gamma); \qquad \Psi(K) = \gamma - \beta(K - K^*)^2; \quad \alpha, \beta, \gamma > 0$$

and discuss the behavior of the system.

8. Construct a phase diagram for the Ramsey problem with

$$U(C) = \alpha(C^{\frac{1}{2}} - \gamma^{\frac{1}{2}}); \qquad \Psi(K) = \gamma - \beta(K - K^*)^2; \quad \alpha, \beta, \gamma > 0$$

and discuss the behavior of the system.

9. Construct a phase diagram for the Ramsey problem with

$$U(C) = -\alpha(C - C_0)^2; \qquad \Psi(K) = \beta K^{\frac{1}{2}}$$

and discuss the behavior of the system.

Section 2.11

1. Derive an expression similar to (2-108) for $\dot{K}$.

2. Go through the detailed construction of Figure 2.27.

3. Solve Example 2 for the case in which $K_0 > K^*$.

4. Solve Example 5 for the case in which $K_0 > K^*$.

5. Solve Example 7 for the case in which $K_0 > K^*$.

6. For cases in which bliss can be achieved with finite capital, show that there always exist paths for which bliss can be reached in finite time and hence paths for which the integral has a finite value.

7. Show that when $U(C) = -C^{1-\alpha}/(\alpha - 1)$, $\alpha > 1$, it is optimal to save a fixed proportion $1/\alpha$ of output, whatever the production function. Is this the only utility function with this property?

8. Determine the integrated Euler equation for the case in which $U(C) =$

$U^* - \alpha(C - C_0)^2$ and $\Psi(K) = \beta K^{\frac{1}{2}}$. If possible, determine the optimal path of capital accumulation.

9. Suppose that discounting is introduced into the Ramsey model. What changes does this bring about? Attempt to solve Example 1 of this section with discounting introduced.

10. Suppose that the planning horizon is infinite, and that bliss can be achieved with a finite stock of capital. Prove that, if $K_0 < K^*$, it is never optimal to first build up K to a level above K^* and then finally cut back K to K^* again.

11. Following a suggestion of Chakravarty and Manne [10], let us introduce a measure of intertemporal complementarity by supposing that the 'instantaneous utility function' U depends not on consumption C but on the time rate of change of C and that U takes the specific form

$$U(\dot{C}) = \frac{\dot{C}^{1-\alpha}}{1-\alpha}, \quad \alpha > 1.$$

Suppose further that the production function is linear, so that

$$Y = \Psi(K) \equiv \beta K, \quad \beta > 0.$$

Since $\beta K = Y = \dot{K} + C$, we have

$$\dot{C} = \beta \dot{K} - \ddot{K}$$

and the utility functional

$$\int_0^\infty U \mathrm{d}t$$

can be written

$$\frac{1}{1-\alpha} \int_0^\infty (\beta \dot{K} - \ddot{K})^{1-\alpha} \mathrm{d}t$$

or, substituting $Z = \dot{K}$, as

$$\frac{1}{1-\alpha} \int_0^\infty (\beta Z - \dot{Z})^{1-\alpha} \mathrm{d}t.$$

Derive the Euler equation and show that the optimal $Z(t)$ can be written as a linear combination of two exponential paths,

$$Z(t) = Ae^{\beta t} + Be^{\beta t/\alpha} = \dot{K}(t).$$

Deduce that

$$K(t) = \frac{A}{\beta} e^{\beta t} + \frac{B}{\beta} e^{\beta t/\alpha} + D$$

$$C(t) = B(\alpha - 1)e^{\beta t/\alpha} + D\beta.$$

Show that $A \neq 0$ is incompatible with an optimum and that B and C can be determined from any *two* of the initial values $C(0)$, $K(0)$ and $\dot{K}(0)$. (The three initial values are not independent since $\beta K = \dot{K} + C$.)

Attempt to generalize the Chakravarty-Manne conclusions by writing an appropriate specialization of $U(C, \dot{C})$.

Section 2.12

1. Prove the catenary turnpike theorem for the case in which $K_0 \geq K^*$.
2. Prove that with a finite planning horizon it is never optimal for $\dot{K}$ to change sign more than once.
3. For the case in which the planning horizon is finite, prove that if $K_1 > K^*$ then it is never optimal to have $\dot{K} < 0$.
4. Prove that in a neighborhood of K^* the linearized Euler equations are as given in the text. Then show that for K close to K^* the solutions are of the cosh, sinh or exp form.
5. Re-solve Examples 1, 2, 5 and 6 of Section 2.11 for the case in which the population is growing exponentially, and for each example discuss the behavior of the system in this case.

Section 2.13

1. Give all of the details of the derivation of Theorem 2.13.1.
2. Write out in detail the equations (2-157) under the assumption that $\mathbf{y}''$ exists.
3. Prove that if the matrix $\mathbf{F}_{\mathbf{y}'\mathbf{y}'} = ||F_{y_i'y_j'}||$ is nonsingular along $\mathbf{z}(x)$ then $\mathbf{z}''(x)$ exists and is continuous between corners of $\mathbf{z}(x)$.
4. Find the Euler equations for integrals with the following integrands. Do not attempt to solve the Euler equations.

(a) $F = y_1 y_2 + y_2^2 y_1'^2 x$

(b) $F = (y_1' y_2')^{\frac{1}{2}} y_1 + y_2 y_1'^3 x$

(c) $F = y_1^2 y_2'(y_3')^2 + y_1' \sin y_2 + y_1 y_2 y_3.$

5. Use the fundamental lemma to show that for the problem studied in this section there exists a γ such that for each x in the interval

$$\mathbf{F}_{\mathbf{y}'}(x, \mathbf{z}, \mathbf{z}') = \int_{x_0}^{x} \mathbf{F}_{\mathbf{y}}(x, \mathbf{z}, \mathbf{z}')\mathrm{d}x + \boldsymbol{\gamma}.$$

These equations are to be interpreted componentwise and are called the DuBois-Reymond equations. (Cf. Problem 5 for Section 2.6.) Use these equations to obtain the results of Theorem 2.13.1.

6. Consider the problem studied in this section and let us define the new set of variables $\mathbf{w} = \mathbf{F}_{\mathbf{y}'}(x, \mathbf{y}, \mathbf{y}')$. These variables are referred to as conjugate variables. Suppose that the above equation can be solved for $\mathbf{y}'$ to yield $\mathbf{y}' = \mathbf{Q}(x, \mathbf{y}, \mathbf{w})$. Consider now the function

$$\begin{aligned} H(x, \mathbf{y}, \mathbf{w}) &= \mathbf{F}_{\mathbf{y}'} \cdot \mathbf{y}' - F \\ &= \mathbf{Q}(x, \mathbf{y}, \mathbf{w}) \cdot \mathbf{w} - F(x, \mathbf{y}; \mathbf{Q}(x, \mathbf{y}, \mathbf{w})). \end{aligned}$$

H is called the Hamiltonian (a term which later will be assigned a rather different meaning). Determine H_{y_j} and H_{w_j}. Show that between corners of $\mathbf{z}(x)$, the following equations

$$\mathbf{y}' = \mathbf{H}_{\mathbf{q}}; \qquad \mathbf{q}' = -\mathbf{H}_{\mathbf{y}}$$

must be satisfied. These are called Hamilton's canonical equations. Prove that along an extremal

$$\frac{\mathrm{d}H}{\mathrm{d}t} = \frac{\partial H}{\partial t}$$

and hence that, if t does not appear explicitly in H, H is a constant along $\mathbf{z}(x)$.

7. Using Hamilton's equations introduced in Problem 6, formulate the problem of finding the curve of shortest length joining two points in the plane. Solve Hamilton's equations to obtain the solution to the problem.

8. Determine the extremals for

$$F = (x^2 + y^2)^{\frac{1}{2}} [1 + (y')^2]^{\frac{1}{2}}$$

using Hamilton's equations.

9. Suppose that it is desired to find a function $\mathbf{y}(x)$, $\mathbf{y}(x) \in C^{\mathrm{iv}}$, which optimizes

$$J[\mathbf{y}] = \int_{x_0}^{x_1} F(x, \mathbf{y}, \mathbf{y}', \mathbf{y}'')\mathrm{d}x$$

with $\mathbf{y}(x_0) = \mathbf{y}_0$, $\mathbf{y}(x_1) = \mathbf{y}_1$, $\mathbf{y}'(x_0) = \mathbf{y}_0'$ and $\mathbf{y}'(x_1) = \mathbf{y}_1'$. Suppose further that $F \in C''$. Determine the differential equations satisfied by $\mathbf{y}(x)$. Do not attempt to give a rigorous justification of every step.

10. Generalize Problem 9 to the case where F involves the rth derivative of $\mathbf{y}$.

Section 2.14

1. Prove that, in changing over to a parametric representation of the type discussed in the text, the value of the integral is unchanged.

2. In the text we converted a problem from the standard formulation to a parametric representation. In certain types of problems (when dealing with closed curves, for example) it is necessary to begin with a parametric representation, since there is no alternative. In such cases one is attempting to determine a parametric representation of some curve in $\mathscr{E}^{n+1}$ which optimizes an integral involving an integrand $\mathscr{F}$. Now the curve, that is, the set of points $(x, \mathbf{y})$, should be independent of the particular parametric representation used. Also the integral should be independent of the parametric representation and this requirement places restrictions on $\mathscr{F}$. Show that $\mathscr{F}$ cannot depend explicitly on the parameter τ. Also show that $\mathscr{F}$ must be homogeneous of the first degree in $(\dot{x}, \dot{\mathbf{y}})$. This means that

$$\mathscr{F}(x, \rho\dot{x}, \mathbf{y}, \rho\dot{\mathbf{y}}) = \rho\mathscr{F}(x, \dot{x}, \mathbf{y}, \dot{\mathbf{y}})$$

for any number ρ. Prove that the $\mathscr{F}$ obtained in the text by converting F does indeed have these properties. Hint: Introduce a new parameter τ_1, using $\tau = \rho\tau_1$ to prove homogeneity.

3. Prove that if $\mathbf{z}(x)$ is an optimal solution to the fixed end points problem, then there exists a constant γ_0 such that for all x, $x_0 \leq x \leq x_1$,

$$F(x, \mathbf{z}, \mathbf{z}') - \mathbf{F}_{\mathbf{y}'}(x, \mathbf{z}, \mathbf{z}') \cdot \mathbf{y}' = \int_{x_0}^{x} \frac{\partial F}{\partial x}\, dx \geq \gamma_0.$$

4. From the homogeneity property of Problem 2, show that in the case $n = 1$

$$\mathscr{F}_{\dot{x}}\dot{x} + \mathscr{F}_{\dot{y}}\dot{y} \equiv \mathscr{F}; \qquad \mathscr{F}_{x\dot{x}}\dot{x} + \mathscr{F}_{x\dot{y}}\dot{y} \equiv \mathscr{F}_x$$

is an identity in all the variables. Also show that

$$\dot{x}\mathscr{F}_{\dot{x}\dot{x}} + \dot{y}\mathscr{F}_{\dot{x}\dot{y}} \equiv 0; \qquad \dot{x}\mathscr{F}_{\dot{x}\dot{y}} + \dot{y}\mathscr{F}_{\dot{y}\dot{y}} \equiv 0$$

are identities in all the variables. Thus

$$\frac{\mathscr{F}_{\dot{x}\dot{x}}}{\dot{y}^2} = \frac{\mathscr{F}_{\dot{x}\dot{y}}}{-\dot{x}\dot{y}} = \frac{\mathscr{F}_{\dot{y}\dot{y}}}{\dot{x}^2}.$$

Denote the common ratio by $\mathscr{F}^*$. Show that $\mathscr{F}^*$ is homogeneous of degree -3 in $(\dot{x}, \dot{y})$. Then

$$\mathscr{F}_{\dot{x}\dot{x}} = \dot{y}^2\mathscr{F}^*; \qquad \mathscr{F}_{\dot{x}\dot{y}} = -\dot{x}\dot{y}\mathscr{F}^*; \qquad \mathscr{F}_{\dot{y}\dot{y}} = \dot{x}\ \mathscr{F}^*.$$

Hint: Differentiate with respect to ρ and then with respect to $\dot{x}$ and $\dot{y}$.

5. Write down the two Euler equations for the parametric form of a problem when $n = 1$. Differentiate them completely so as to display the second derivatives. Use the results of Problem 4 to show that they can be written

$$\dot{y}[\mathscr{F}_{\dot{x}y} - \mathscr{F}_{x\dot{y}} + \mathscr{F}^*(\ddot{x}\dot{y} - \ddot{y}\dot{x})] = 0$$

$$\dot{x}[\mathscr{F}_{\dot{x}y} - \mathscr{F}_{x\dot{y}} + \mathscr{F}^*(\ddot{x}\dot{y} - \ddot{y}\dot{x})] = 0.$$

Since $\dot{x}$ and $\dot{y}$ do not vanish simultaneously, this shows that the Euler equations are not independent but are equivalent to the single equation

$$\mathscr{F}_{\dot{x}y} - \mathscr{F}_{x\dot{y}} + \mathscr{F}^*(\ddot{x}\dot{y} - \ddot{y}\dot{x}) = 0$$

which is called the Weierstrass form of the Euler equations. Show that this equation is invariant under a change in parameterization. Note that if the Euler equations were independent then a particular parameterization would be determined; and that is not possible.

6. Generalize the results of Problems 4 and 5 to the case $n > 1$.

Section 2.15

1. Consider the problem of finding the curve of shortest length joining any two points in the plane. Determine the Weierstrass E function for this problem and show that $E \geq 0$. Show that the Legendre condition also is satisfied. Are these necessary conditions satisfied for any admissible function, not merely the optimizing one?

2. Determine whether the Weierstrass and Legendre necessary conditions are satisfied by the solutions in the example involving the minimum area of the surface of revolution.

3. Show that the Weierstrass and Legendre necessary conditions are satisfied for the brachistochrone problem.

4. Use the Weierstrass necessary condition to prove that if $\mathbf{z}(x)$ satisfies the Euler equations and corner conditions then

$$F(x, \mathbf{z}, \mathbf{z}') - \mathbf{F}_{\mathbf{y}'}(x, \mathbf{z}, \mathbf{z}') - \mathbf{z}'$$

is continuous along $\mathbf{z}(x)$ and hence across corners. Hint: $E(x^*, \mathbf{z}, \mathbf{z}'_-, \mathbf{z}'_+) \leq 0$; $E(x^*, \mathbf{z}, \mathbf{z}'_+, \mathbf{z}'_-) \leq 0$ at a corner x^*.

5. Use the results of Problem 4 to prove that, at a corner of $\mathbf{z}(x)$, $E(x^*, \mathbf{z}, \mathbf{z}'_-, \mathbf{z}'_+) = 0 = E(x^*, \mathbf{z}, \mathbf{z}'_+, \mathbf{z}'_-)$.

Section 2.16

1. What could occur in the Samuelson-Solow model if the constraints $C_j + \dot{K}_j \geq 0$ were not imposed?

2. Write down the Euler equations for the Samuelson-Solow model.

3. Write down the Euler equations for the Samuelson-Solow model using the $\mathbf{M}$ formulation. How do these differ from the equations obtained in solving Problem 2?

4. Show that for the Samuelson-Solow model there always exist paths which reach bliss in a finite time and for which the utility integral therefore has a finite value.

5. Attempt to work out the details of the Samuelson-Solow model when

$$U = -\alpha_1(C_1 - C_1^*)^2 - \alpha_2(C_2 - C_2^*)^2$$

$$C_1 + \dot{K}_1 = \beta_1 K_1 + \beta_2 K_2 - C_2 - \dot{K}_2.$$

Section 2.17

1. Show that $f(\mathbf{u}) = \mathbf{d} \cdot \mathbf{u}$ is both a concave and a convex function over $\mathscr{E}^n$ but is neither strictly convex nor strictly concave.

2. Prove that the quadratic form $\mathbf{u} \cdot \mathbf{A}\mathbf{u}$ is a concave function of $\mathbf{u}$ over $\mathscr{E}^n$ if $\mathbf{A}$ is negative semidefinite and is convex if $\mathbf{A}$ is positive semidefinite. Prove also that it is strictly concave if $\mathbf{A}$ is negative definite and strictly convex if $\mathbf{A}$ is positive definite.

3. Prove that if $f_j(\mathbf{u})$ is concave over the convex set X, $j = 1, \ldots, r$, then $\Sigma_{j=1}^r \alpha_j f_j(\mathbf{u})$ is also concave over X if each $\alpha_j \geq 0$.

4. Prove that if $f(\mathbf{u})$ is concave over the convex set X then f_1 given by $f_1(\mathbf{u}, \mathbf{v}) = f(\mathbf{u})$ is a concave function over the convex set $X \times \mathscr{E}^m$, $\mathbf{v} \in \mathscr{E}^m$; $X \times \mathscr{E}^m$ is the set of points in $\mathscr{E}^{m+n}$ such that $\mathbf{u} \in X$. Note that $z = 4 - x^2$ is a concave function. Represent this function in the zx-plane. Also $z = f(x, y) = 4 - x^2$ is a concave function of x and y. Represent this function in $\mathscr{E}^3$.

5. Prove that if $f(\mathbf{u})$ is a concave function over the convex set X, then f is also a concave function with respect to any subset of the variables in $\mathbf{u}$.

6. Prove that $-e^{-x}$ is a concave function, as is $-e^x$.

7. Prove that if $f(\mathbf{u})$ is a concave function over X, $-f(\mathbf{u})$ is a convex function over X.

8. Prove the converse of Theorem 2.17.1.

9. Prove the corollary to Theorem 2.17.2.

10. State and prove the equivalents of Theorems 2.17.3 and 2.17.4 for convex functions.

11. Prove that if $F(x, \mathbf{y}, \mathbf{y}')$ is a concave function of $\mathbf{y}'$ over $\mathscr{R}$ then the Weierstrass and Legendre necessary conditions are satisfied for any admissible function, nor merely the optimizing function $\mathbf{z}(x)$.

Section 2.18

1. Write down the Jacobi equation for the problem of finding the curve of shortest length joining two points in the plane; and discuss the nature of the solutions to the Jacobi equation.

2. For the situation considered in Problem 1, show how to obtain the linearly independent solutions to the Jacobi equation from the solutions to the Euler equation for the original problem.

3. Go through the details of the proof of Theorem 2.18.4 for the special case in which $n = 1$.

4. Prove that if $\mathbf{B}$ is positive definite, there is a matrix $\mathbf{R}$ such that $\mathbf{R}^2 = \mathbf{B}$. Hint: Diagonalize $\mathbf{B}$, take the square root, and then return to the original representation.

5. Consider the example involving the minimum area of the surface of revolution. Show that if there are two solutions then

$$\eta_1 = \sinh\frac{x}{\lambda}; \qquad \eta_2 = \cosh\frac{x}{\lambda} - \frac{x}{\lambda}\sinh\frac{x}{\lambda}$$

are two linearly independent solutions of the Jacobi equation. Consider then the determination of the points conjugate to x_0. Take $x_0 = -1$. Determine $|\mathbf{V}(x)|$ and show that it does not vanish at 0. Thus the zeros of $|\mathbf{V}(x)|$ are the same as the zeros of

$$\phi(x) = \frac{|\mathbf{V}(x)|}{\left(\sinh\frac{1}{\lambda}\right)\left(\sinh\frac{x}{\lambda}\right)} = \left(\coth\frac{x}{\lambda} - \frac{x}{\lambda}\right) + \left(\coth\frac{1}{\lambda} - \frac{1}{\lambda}\right).$$

Prove that this formula is correct. Show that $\phi'(x) < 0$ for $-1 \leq x < 0$ and $0 < x \leq 1$. Show that $\phi(1) < 0$ for the lower catenary and $\phi(1) > 0$ for the upper catenary, also that $\phi(-1) = 0$ in both cases. Thus conclude that for the lower catenary there is a conjugate point between -1 and 1 while for the upper catenary there is none. Thus conclude further that the upper catenary yields a relative minimum while the lower catenary yields neither a maximum nor a minimum.

6. Consider again the problem involving the minimum area of the surface of revolution. Using a parametric representation, we showed that the curve consisting of the vertical lines $x = -x_0$, $x = x_0$ and $y = 0$ satisfies the necessary conditions. Prove that the curve always yields a strong relative minimum (even when two catenaries can be passed through the points). Can you make use of this observation to determine the absolute minimum in every case? Consider the case in which no catenary can be passed through the points. Show that it is not possible to construct a solution which satisfies the necessary conditions and which consists of two different catenaries joined together at a corner. Thus show that the curve referred to above is the only one which satisfies the necessary conditions in this case. Hint: To prove that there exists a strong relative minimum, consider any curve $\mathscr{A}$ with $y \geq 0$ lying in an N_ε neighborhood of the curve being considered. The length of this curve is greater than $2y_0$. Consider the points on $\mathscr{A}$ which lie a distance y_0 from either end point. Now every point on $\mathscr{A}$ at a distance d from the end point is higher than the corresponding point on the vertical line $x = -x_0$ (or $x = x_0$) at a distance d from the end point. Hence

$$\pi y_0^2 < \int_0^{y_0} y ds,$$

this integral being taken along $\mathscr{A}$ from the end point to an arc length of y_0.

7. Find a weak relative minimum for the functional

$$J[y] = \int_0^{x_1} (y + 1)^{\frac{1}{2}}[1 + (y')^2]^{\frac{1}{2}} dx$$

with $y(0) = 0$ and $y(x_1) = y_1 > -1$. Hint: The set of solutions to the Euler equation which pass through the origin can be written $y = \alpha x + 4^{-1}(1 + \alpha^2)x^2$. The envelope to this family is $y = -1 + 4^{-1}x^2$. If (x_1, y_1) lies outside this parabola there is no solution. If the point (x_1, y_1) lies inside the parabola there are two solutions. The upper one yields the minimum.

8. Determine the conditions under which the extremal solution for

$$J[y] = \int_0^1 (y')^2(1 + y')^2 dx$$

with $y(0) = 0$, $y(1) = \alpha$ yields a weak relative minimum or maximum of $J[y]$.

9. Show that if $\mathbf{y}(x; \boldsymbol{\lambda})$ is a solution to the Euler equations for some problem then $\boldsymbol{\eta}_j = \mathbf{y}_{\lambda_j}(x; \boldsymbol{\lambda})$ is a solution to the Jacobi accessory equation when $\boldsymbol{\lambda}$ is chosen so that the end point conditions are satisfied for the original problem.

10. Investigate in more detail the situation in which x_1 is conjugate to x_0. Apply the analysis to the problem involving the surface of minimum area. Hint: For those $\boldsymbol{\eta}$ for which $\Phi''(0) = 0$, consider $\Phi'''(0)$.

11. Consider a system of first order homogeneous linear differential equations $\boldsymbol{\zeta}' = \mathbf{A}(x)\boldsymbol{\zeta}$, where $\mathbf{A}(x)$ is a given matrix whose elements are functions of x. Suppose that $\boldsymbol{\zeta}_1, \ldots, \boldsymbol{\zeta}_r$ are r different solutions to the system. Show that if there is any value of x, say x^*, such that the vectors $\boldsymbol{\zeta}_1(x^*), \ldots, \boldsymbol{\zeta}_r(x^*)$ are linearly dependent then the functions $\boldsymbol{\zeta}_1(x), \ldots, \boldsymbol{\zeta}_r(x)$ are linearly dependent and cannot form a linearly independent set of solutions to the system of differential equations.

Section 2.20

1. Prove the theorem stated on page 122. Hint: The proof is not too easy and involves a number of steps. The reader may find it helpful to refer to Bliss [5] for assistance. Prove also that the n-parameter family involved possesses continuous first partial derivatives with respect to the parameters and continuous second partial derivatives involving x and one of the parameters.

2. Prove that $y = x$ provides a weak but not a strong relative minimum for the functional

$$J[y] = \int_0^1 (y')^3 dx$$

where $y(0) = 0$ and $y(1) = 1$.

3. Determine the conditions under which the extremal solution for

$$J[y] = \int_0^1 (y')^2(1 + y')^2 dx$$

$y(0) = 0$, $y(1) = b$ yields a strong relative minimum. Ans. $b \geq 0$, $b \leq -1$.

4. Determine whether the extremal solution for

$$J[y] = \int_1^2 y'(1 + x^2 y') dx$$

with $y(1) = 3$ and $y(2) = 5$ yields a strong relative minimum.

5. Determine whether the extremal solution for

$$J[y] = \int_1^2 [x(y')^4 - 2y(y')^3]dx$$

with $y(1) = 0$ and $y(2) = 1$ yields a strong relative maximum or minimum of $J[y]$.

Section 2.21

1. Give an alternative derivation of the free boundary condition.

2. Determine the curve of shortest length joining the vertical lines $x = x_0$ and $x = x_1$. Is there a unique solution in this case?

3. Prove Corollaries 1 and 2 for the theorem of this section.

4. Formulate the Samuelson-Solow model using the **M** variables, $\dot{\mathbf{M}} = \mathbf{C}$, and obtain the necessary conditions, bearing in mind that **M** can be treated as having a free boundary at both end points.

Section 2.22

1. Show that the fixed end points problem can be considered to be a special case of the problem in which the curve begins and ends on a smooth manifold.

2. Show that free boundaries are a special case of the requirement that the curve begin and end on a smooth manifold. Then obtain the free boundary conditions from the transversality conditions.

3. Prove Corollary 1 for this section.

4. Determine the curve of minimum length joining the origin to the ellipse

$$2(x - 8)^2 + 4(y - 5)^2 = 6.$$

Illustrate the situation geometrically.

5. Determine the curve of minimum length joining the ellipse given in Problem 4 to the straight line $x + y = -5$. Illustrate the situation geometrically.

6. Determine the curve of minimum length joining the ellipse given in Problem 4 to the ellipse

$$8(x + 7)^2 + 2(y + 6)^2 = 4.$$

Illustrate the situation geometrically.

7. Determine the functions which satisfy the necessary conditions for

$$J[y] = \int_{0}^{x_1} y^{-1}[1 + (y')^2]^{\frac{1}{2}} dx$$

when $y(0) = 0$ and

(a) The right hand end point lies on the line $x - y = 6$;

(b) The right hand end point lies on the circle $(x - 8)^2 + y^2 = 9$.

8. Consider a particular extremal $\mathbf{y}(x)$ for the function F. Let $G(x, \mathbf{y}) = \mu$, μ a parameter, represent a family of hypersurfaces, each of which is cut by $\mathbf{y}(x)$. Let $x^*(\mu)$ be the value of x at which $\mathbf{y}(x)$ intersects $G = \mu$. Show that

$$\frac{dx^*}{d\mu} = [G_x + \mathbf{G}_{\mathbf{y}'} \cdot \mathbf{y}']^{-1}$$

the right hand side being evaluated at $(x^*, \mathbf{y}(x^*))$. Now consider

$$J^*(\mu) = \int_{x_0}^{x^*(\mu)} F(x, \mathbf{y}, \mathbf{y}')dx.$$

Show that

$$\frac{dJ^*}{d\mu} = F[G_x + \mathbf{G}_{\mathbf{y}'} \cdot \mathbf{y}']^{-1}$$

the right hand side being evaluated at $(x^*, \mathbf{y}(x^*))$. $dJ^*/d\mu$ tells approximately what the change in J^* is from the point where the extremal intersects $G = \mu$ to the point where it intersects $G = \mu + \Delta\mu$. Show that $dJ^*/d\mu$ is greatest when the extremal cuts the hypersurface transversally.

Section 2.23

1. Derive (2-285) in detail.

Section 2.24

1. Solve (2-294) for the cases in which $K_1^0 < K_1^-$ and $K_1^0 > K_1^-$.

2. For the case in which $K_1^0 > K_1^+$ and $K_2^0 > K_2^+$, determine the time behavior of K_1 and K_2 along the horizontal and vertical lines shown in Figure 2.41. Determine the time required to reach the critical line.

3. Determine the time behavior of K_1 and K_2 along the horizontal and

vertical lines which intersect the ellipse in Figure 2.41. Is the ellipse reached in finite time?

Section 2.25

1. Show how dynamic programming could be used to solve the Ramsey model with a finite planning horizon.
2. Develop a discrete analog of the Ramsey model for a finite planning horizon and indicate how it could be solved by dynamic programming.
3. Formulate the calculus of variations problem studied in the text as a dynamic programming problem which works forward in time rather than backwards.
4. Suppose that instead of being fixed, as in the text, the left hand end point must lie on a curve. The right hand end point remains fixed. Explain how this problem can be solved by dynamic programming.

3

Classical theory — constraints

3.1. Introduction

In the theory of ordinary maxima and minima, the most interesting and realistic and also the most difficult problems are those in which constraints are present. Constraints also appear in many applications of the calculus of variations. Not unexpectedly, constraints add to the complexity both of the mathematical theory and of the associated computational methods.

In ordinary optimization problems the domain of the function $z = f(\mathbf{y})$ to be optimized is a subset of $\mathscr{E}^n$ and the constraints are either equations of the form $g(\mathbf{y}) = 0$ or inequalities such as $g(\mathbf{y}) \leq 0$. In the calculus of variations, however, the possible constraints are much more varied in form. We now describe the several types of constraint which may be encountered.

The constraint most like those encountered in ordinary optimization problems is of the form

$$T(x, \mathbf{y}) = 0 \quad \text{or} \quad T(x, \mathbf{y}) \leq 0. \tag{3-1}$$

Equation (3-1) places restrictions on $\mathbf{y}$ for each x. The constraint $y \geq 0$, encountered in the minimum area problem, is of this form. Geometrically, $T(x, \mathbf{y}) = 0$ is represented by a surface in $\mathscr{E}^{n+1}$; if the constraint must be satisfied, the curve representing any admissible function must lie on this surface. If the constraint is of the form $T(x, \mathbf{y}) \leq 0$, the curve representing any admissible function must lie either on the surface or on that side of the surface corresponding to $T(x, \mathbf{y}) < 0$.

Consider next a constraint of the form

$$G(x, \mathbf{y}, \mathbf{y}') = 0. \tag{3-2}$$

This can be thought of as a differential equation which must be satisfied by any admissible function at each value of x where $\mathbf{y}'$ exists. Constraints of this type play an especially important role in modern control theory.

The constraint (3-2) can also be viewed geometrically as a hypersurface in extended phase space; if $\mathbf{y}(x)$ is admissible then the curve representing $\mathbf{y}(x)$ must lie on this surface in $\mathscr{E}^{2n+1}$. Only a limited number of curves on this surface can be admissible, however, for $\mathbf{y}$ and $\mathbf{y}'$ are not independently variable. Like (3-1), the constraint (3-2) places restrictions on $\mathbf{y}(x)$ at each x on the path.

We note that (3-2) is sufficiently general to cover all constraints in the form of ordinary differential equations. It is unnecessary to separately consider constraints such as $G(x, \mathbf{y}, \mathbf{y}', \mathbf{y}'') = 0$, in which there appear derivatives of higher order. For if we write $\mathbf{y}' = \mathbf{w}$ then $\mathbf{y}'' = \mathbf{w}'$ and the above constraint can be replaced by a set of $n + 1$ constraints

$$G(x, \mathbf{y}, \mathbf{w}, \mathbf{w}') = 0$$

$$\mathbf{y}' - \mathbf{w} = \mathbf{0}$$

each of the form (3-2).

One may encounter constraints in the form of differential inequalities $G(x, \mathbf{y}, \mathbf{y}') \leq 0$. This type of constraint also plays an important note in modern control theory.

Finally, constraints may take the form

$$\int_{x_0}^{x_1} G(x, \mathbf{y}, \mathbf{y}')dx = \gamma, \quad \gamma \text{ constant.} \tag{3-3}$$

(3-3) does not place restrictions on $\mathbf{y}(x)$ at each x but on the integral of some function of $(x, \mathbf{y}, \mathbf{y}')$. Constraints of this form are often referred to as *integral* or *isoperimetric constraints*. The way in which they arise will be illustrated in the next section.

In the theoretical developments of Chapter 2 our attention was restricted to functions $\mathbf{y}(x)$ the graphs of which lie in some set $\mathscr{R}$ in extended phase space. $\mathscr{R}$ was never specified, nor was there given any indication of how $\mathscr{R}$ might be determined. We now see that $\mathscr{R}$ may be defined by constraints of the form (3-1) or (3-2). One might think that constraints of the form (3-1) are easiest to handle. This is not so. Such constraints are often the most difficult to treat. In the present chapter we shall consider them only very briefly, and then just in the form of equalities. We shall be concerned mainly with problems in which the constraints are differential equations. First, however, we provide a brief discussion of isoperimetric constraints. Thereafter these will not be of much interest to us.

3.2. Isoperimetric constraints

To see how isoperimetric constraints can arise, consider the problem of finding the piecewise smooth curve of length γ which passes through the points x_0 and x_1 on the x-axis and which, with the x-axis, encloses the greatest possible area. (Of course γ must exceed the distance between x_0 and x_1.) If $y(x)$ is the function the graph of which is the required curve, the area is

$$A = \int_{x_0}^{x_1} y\mathrm{d}x \tag{3-4}$$

and the length of the curve is

$$L = \int_{x_0}^{x_1} [1 + (y')^2]^{\frac{1}{2}}\mathrm{d}x. \tag{3-5}$$

The length is required to be γ. Thus we wish to maximize (3-4) subject to the constraint that $L = \gamma$. The constraint is precisely of the form (3-3); hence we here have a problem involving an isoperimetric constraint.

The name isoperimetric arose in the historical development of the calculus of variations as a result of interest in the problem of finding the closed curve of given length (constant perimeter) which encloses the greatest area. The answer is a circle, as may be shown by first solving the problem of the preceding paragraph and then doing a little further analysis. It is of some interest that this result seems to have been known since earliest times, long before the development of the calculus of variations.

Let us now turn to a study of a general problem involving isoperimetric constraints. Any piecewise smooth vector-valued function $\mathbf{y}(x)$ with n components will be called admissible if it satisfies $\mathbf{y}(x_0) = \mathbf{y}_0$ and $\mathbf{y}(x_1) = \mathbf{y}_1$ and the r, $r \leq n$, isoperimetric constraints

$$\int_{x_0}^{x_1} G^u(x, \mathbf{y}(x), \mathbf{y}'(x))\mathrm{d}x = \gamma_u, \quad u = 1, \ldots, r, \tag{3-6}$$

where n is the number of components in $\mathbf{y}$, and if it lies in some specified set $\mathscr{R}$ in extended phase space. Suppose then that it is desired to determine the admissible function $\mathbf{y}(x)$ which maximizes or minimizes

$$J[\mathbf{y}] = \int_{x_0}^{x_1} F(x, \mathbf{y}(x), \mathbf{y}'(x))\mathrm{d}x. \tag{3-7}$$

We wish to determine a set of necessary conditions, similar to the Euler equations and corner conditions, which must be satisfied by any admissible function which yields an interior global optimum for the problem. We shall show that, in essence, the Lagrange multiplier technique which serves so well in ordinary optimization problems can be applied here too. More precisely, we shall prove the following theorem.

Theorem 3.2.1. Suppose that the admissible function $\mathbf{z}(x)$ *yields an interior maximum or minimum of* $J[\mathbf{y}]$ *subject to the constraints (3-6). Then there exists a set of numbers* $\lambda_0, \lambda_1, \ldots, \lambda_n$ *not all* 0 *(and not unique) such that if*

$$H(x, \mathbf{y}, \mathbf{y}') = \lambda_0 F(x, \mathbf{y}, \mathbf{y}') + \sum_{u=1}^{r} \lambda_u G^u(x, \mathbf{y}, \mathbf{y}') \tag{3-8}$$

then it is necessary that between corners $\mathbf{z}(x)$ *satisfy the Euler equation*

$$\frac{\mathrm{d}}{\mathrm{d}x} \mathbf{H}_{\mathbf{y}'} - \mathbf{H}_{\mathbf{y}} = \mathbf{0} \tag{3-9}$$

and that, in addition, $\mathbf{H}_{\mathbf{y}'}$ *be continuous across corners of* $\mathbf{z}(x)$.

In other words, $\mathbf{z}(x)$ must satisfy the necessary conditions for an unconstrained optimum when the integrand is H not F. Notice that the $2n$ conditions $\mathbf{y}(x_0) = \mathbf{y}_0$ and $\mathbf{y}(x_1) = \mathbf{y}_1$ together with the r conditions (3-6) should serve to determine the $2n$ constants of integration and the multipliers up to a scalar multiple. We now prove the theorem.

The following definitions will be useful. First, a set of q vector-valued piecewise continuous functions $\mathbf{Q}_1(x), \ldots, \mathbf{Q}_q(x)$ defined over some interval $\alpha \leq x \leq \beta$ are said to be linearly dependent if there exists a set of numbers $\lambda_1, \ldots, \lambda_q$ not all 0 (and independent of x) such that $\Sigma_{u=1}^{q} \lambda_u \mathbf{Q}_u(x) = \mathbf{0}$ for *every* x in the interval where $\Sigma \lambda_u \mathbf{Q}_u$ is defined. Let

$$< \mathbf{Q}_u, \mathbf{Q}_v > = \int_{\alpha}^{\beta} \mathbf{Q}_u(x) \cdot \mathbf{Q}_v(x) \mathrm{d}x \tag{3-10}$$

and consider the matrix $\mathscr{G} = ||\langle \mathbf{Q}_u, \mathbf{Q}_v \rangle||$. This matrix is independent of x and will be called the Gram matrix for the functions.

As a further preliminary we show that a necessary and sufficient condition for linear dependence of the functions is that the Gram matrix is singular. To prove the necessity, suppose that the functions are linearly dependent so that there exists a $\boldsymbol{\lambda} \neq \mathbf{0}$ such that $\Sigma_{u=1}^{q} \lambda_u \mathbf{Q}_u(x) \equiv \mathbf{0}$. Take the scalar product of this equation and $\mathbf{Q}_v(x)$, and integrate from α to β, obtaining

$\Sigma_{u=1}^{q}\lambda_u\langle \mathbf{Q}_v, \mathbf{Q}_u\rangle = 0$. This can be done for each v, yielding the system of homogeneous linear equations $\mathscr{G}\boldsymbol{\lambda} = \mathbf{0}$. Since this system has a nontrivial solution $\mathscr{G}$ must be singular.

Suppose next that $\mathscr{G}$ is singular, and let $\boldsymbol{\lambda}$ be any nontrivial solution to $\mathscr{G}\boldsymbol{\lambda} = \mathbf{0}$. Then $\boldsymbol{\lambda}\cdot\mathscr{G}\boldsymbol{\lambda} = 0$. To continue, note that

$$\int_{\alpha}^{\beta}\left[\sum_{u=1}^{q}\lambda_u\mathbf{Q}_u(x)\right]^2 dx = \boldsymbol{\lambda}\cdot\mathscr{G}\boldsymbol{\lambda} = 0.$$

However, since the integrand is piecewise continuous and non-negative everywhere, $\Sigma_{u=1}^{q}\lambda_u\mathbf{Q}_u(x) = \mathbf{0}$ for all x where the integrand is defined and the functions are linearly dependent.

We are now prepared to prove Theorem 3.2.1. Consider the functions

$$\mathbf{Q}_u(x) = \mathbf{G}_{\mathbf{y}'}^u(x, \mathbf{z}(x), \mathbf{z}'(x)) - \int_{x_0}^{x}\mathbf{G}_{\mathbf{y}}^u(\tau, \mathbf{z}(\tau), \mathbf{z}'(\tau))d\tau - \boldsymbol{\delta}_u, \quad u = 0, 1, \ldots, r \tag{3-11}$$

where $G^0 = F$ and $\boldsymbol{\delta}_u$ is chosen so that

$$\int_{x_0}^{x_1}\mathbf{Q}_u(x)dx = \mathbf{0},$$

and where by the integral of a vector is meant the vector of the integrals of the individual components. We now prove that the $\mathbf{Q}_u(x)$ are linearly dependent by showing that the Gram matrix for the functions is singular. To accomplish this we shall rely on a rather subtle argument. Let

$$\boldsymbol{\eta}_u(x) = \int_{x_0}^{x}\mathbf{Q}_u(\tau)d\tau, \quad u = 0, 1, \ldots, r. \tag{3-12}$$

Then $\boldsymbol{\eta}_u(x)$ is piecewise smooth and, from the definition of $\mathbf{Q}_u$, $\boldsymbol{\eta}_u(x_0) = \boldsymbol{\eta}_u(x_1) = \mathbf{0}$. Let us consider next the set of functions

$$\mathbf{y}(x;\boldsymbol{\xi}) = \mathbf{z}(x) + \sum_{u=0}^{r}\xi_u\boldsymbol{\eta}_u(x). \tag{3-13}$$

Clearly $\mathbf{y}(x;\mathbf{0}) = \mathbf{z}(x)$ and for all $\boldsymbol{\xi}$ lying in a sufficiently small neighborhood of $\mathbf{0}$, say $|\boldsymbol{\xi}| < \varepsilon$, the graphs of the $\mathbf{y}(x;\boldsymbol{\xi})$ functions lie in $\mathscr{R}$. Let us write

$$\Omega^u(\boldsymbol{\xi}) = \int_{x_0}^{x_1}G^u(x, \mathbf{y}(x;\boldsymbol{\xi}), \mathbf{y}'(x;\boldsymbol{\xi}))dx. \tag{3-14}$$

Then $\Omega^0(\mathbf{0}) = \Phi(0) = J[\mathbf{z}]$ so that, if $J[\mathbf{z}]$ is maximized, $\Omega^0(\boldsymbol{\xi}) \leq \Omega^0(\mathbf{0})$ for all $\boldsymbol{\xi}$ satisfying $\Omega^u(\boldsymbol{\xi}) = \gamma_u$, $u = 1, \ldots, r$. Any $\mathbf{y}(x; \boldsymbol{\xi})$ for which these r equations hold is admissible if $|\boldsymbol{\xi}| < \varepsilon$. Thus $\Omega^0(\boldsymbol{\xi})$ must have a relative maximum at $\mathbf{0}$ subject to the constraints $\Omega^u(\boldsymbol{\xi}) = \gamma_u$, $u = 1, \ldots, r$. Now all the $\Omega^u(\boldsymbol{\xi})$ are differentiable and we know from the theory of ordinary constrained optimization that the matrix $||\partial\Omega^u(\mathbf{0})/\partial\xi_v||$ of order $r + 1$ must be singular at $\mathbf{0}$ if $\Omega^0(\boldsymbol{\xi})$ does indeed reach a constrained relative maximum there (see Hadley [18], pp. 66–67 and Problem 6 for this section).

We now evaluate this matrix explicitly and show that it is simply the Gram matrix for the functions $\mathbf{Q}_u(x)$. We begin by observing that

$$\Omega^u_{\xi_j}(\mathbf{0}) = \int_{x_0}^{x_1} [\mathbf{G}^u_{\mathbf{y}} \cdot \boldsymbol{\eta}_j(x) + \mathbf{G}^u_{\mathbf{y}'} \cdot \boldsymbol{\eta}'_j(x)]\mathrm{d}x$$

$$= \int_{x_0}^{x_1} \left[\mathbf{G}^u_{\mathbf{y}} \cdot \int_{x_0}^{x} \mathbf{Q}_j(\tau)\mathrm{d}\tau + \mathbf{G}^u_{\mathbf{y}'} \cdot \mathbf{Q}_j(x)\right] \mathrm{d}x. \tag{3-15}$$

If now we write

$$\boldsymbol{\Lambda}_j(x) = \int_{x_0}^{x} \mathbf{Q}_j(\tau)\mathrm{d}\tau; \qquad \boldsymbol{\Upsilon}_u(x) = \int_{x_0}^{x} \mathbf{G}^u_{\mathbf{y}}\mathrm{d}x \tag{3-16}$$

we may recall that $\boldsymbol{\Lambda}_j(x_1) = \mathbf{0}$ and $\boldsymbol{\Lambda}_j(x_0) = \mathbf{0}$. Furthermore, at all points where $\mathbf{Q}_u(x)$ is continuous, $\boldsymbol{\Lambda}'_j(x) = \mathbf{Q}_j(x)$. Also, $\boldsymbol{\Lambda}_j(x)\boldsymbol{\Upsilon}_u(x)$ is continuous across the corners of $\mathbf{z}(x)$. Thus we can integrate by parts the first term of (3-15), obtaining

$$\Omega^u_{\xi_j}(\mathbf{0}) = \int_{x_0}^{x_1} \left[\mathbf{G}^u_{\mathbf{y}'} - \int_{x_0}^{x} \mathbf{G}^u_{\mathbf{y}}\mathrm{d}\tau\right] \cdot \mathbf{Q}_j(x)\mathrm{d}x$$

$$= \int_{x_0}^{x_1} \mathbf{Q}_u(x) \cdot \mathbf{Q}_j(x)\mathrm{d}x = \langle \mathbf{Q}_u, \mathbf{Q}_j \rangle. \tag{3-17}$$

Hence

$$\mathscr{G} = ||\Omega^u_{\xi_j}(\mathbf{0})|| \tag{3-18}$$

as claimed. Since the matrix on the right in (3-18) is singular so is the Gram matrix $\mathscr{G}$. Consequently, the $\mathbf{Q}_u(x)$ are linearly dependent. Hence these exist numbers $\lambda_0, \lambda_1, \ldots, \lambda_r$ not all 0 such that $\Sigma^r_{u=0}\lambda_u\mathbf{Q}_u(x) = \mathbf{0}$ for all x where the $\mathbf{Q}_u(x)$ are defined. However, from (3-11) and the definition of H in (3-8), there exists a $\boldsymbol{\lambda} \neq \mathbf{0}$ such that

$$\mathbf{H}_{\mathbf{y}'}(x, \mathbf{z}(x), \mathbf{z}'(x)) = \int_{x_0}^{x} \mathbf{H}_{\mathbf{y}}(x, \mathbf{z}(x), \mathbf{z}'(x))\mathrm{d}x + \boldsymbol{\rho} \tag{3-19}$$

where $\boldsymbol{\rho} = \boldsymbol{\Delta\lambda}$ and $\boldsymbol{\Delta}$ is the matrix whose columns are the $\boldsymbol{\delta}_u$. Now the right hand side of (3-19), and therefore the left hand side also, is differentiable for all x which are not corners of $\mathbf{z}(x)$. Between corners, therefore, $\mathbf{z}(x)$ must satisfy the differential equation

$$\frac{\mathrm{d}}{\mathrm{d}x}\mathbf{H}_{\mathbf{y}'} - \mathbf{H}_{\mathbf{y}} = \mathbf{0} \tag{3-20}$$

Moreover, the right hand side of (3-19), and therefore the left hand side $\mathbf{H}_{\mathbf{y}'}$, is continuous across any corners of $\mathbf{z}(x)$. That completes the proof of Theorem 3.2.1.

It is also possible to prove that under certain additional restrictions $\mathbf{z}(x)$ must satisfy the Weierstrass and Legendre necessary conditions based on the function H (not F). In the problems we ask the reader to prove this; we also ask him to examine some additional properties of isoperimetric problems.

The similarity between the Lagrange multiplier approach to problems of ordinary maxima and minima and the procedure introduced here is obvious. The same technique – of introducing new variables $\boldsymbol{\lambda}$ and a new function $H = \Sigma_{u=0}^{r}\lambda_u G^u$ – will be applied repeatedly in the derivation of necessary conditions when constraints are present. The same general approach is employed whatever the form of the constraints.

The function H introduced in this section will be referred to always as the *Hamiltonian function*. It is similar to the Lagrangean function of ordinary maxima and minima. However, G^0 will always be the integrand of $J[\mathbf{y}]$ and not the functional $J[\mathbf{y}]$ itself; similarly, the G^u do not always have the same interpretation as in the Lagrangean. For this reason we distinguish the Hamiltonian function by a letter other than L. The quantities $\lambda_0, \ldots, \lambda_r$ will be referred to as *multipliers* or *conjugate variables*.

Example. Consider the problem posed at the beginning of this section. For this problem $F = y$ and $G = [1 + (y')^2]^{\frac{1}{2}}$ (there is just one constraint). Thus

$$H = \lambda_0 y + \lambda_1[1 + (y')^2]^{\frac{1}{2}}$$

and

$$H_y = 0; \qquad H_{y'} = \lambda_1 y'[1 + (y')^2]^{-\frac{1}{2}}.$$

Hence the Euler equation reduces to

$$\frac{d}{dx}\{y'[1 + (y')^2]^{-\frac{1}{2}}\} = \lambda_0/\lambda_1. \tag{3-21}$$

($\lambda_1 \neq 0$, for if $\lambda_1 = 0$ then $\lambda_0 = 0$ also, in contradiction of the fact that not both multipliers are 0; also, $\lambda_0 \neq 0$, for if $\lambda_0 = 0$ the influence of F disappears and the only solution is $y = 0$.) Hence

$$\frac{1}{\gamma} y'[1 + (y')^2]^{-\frac{1}{2}} = x - \rho$$

or

$$y' = \pm \frac{x - \rho}{[\gamma^{-2} - (x - \rho)^2]^{\frac{1}{2}}}$$

so that

$$(y - \delta)^2 = \gamma^{-2} - (x - \rho)^2 \tag{3-22}$$

which is the equation of a circle with its center at (ρ, δ).

When $L \geq x_1 - x_0$ it is indeed possible to pass an arc of a circle through the two points. However, when $L \geq \pi(x_1 - x_0)/2$ the arc does not remain between x_0 and x_1 but extends into the region $x < x_0$ and $x > x_1$, as shown in Figure 3.1. In this case, there is an upper bound but no maximum.

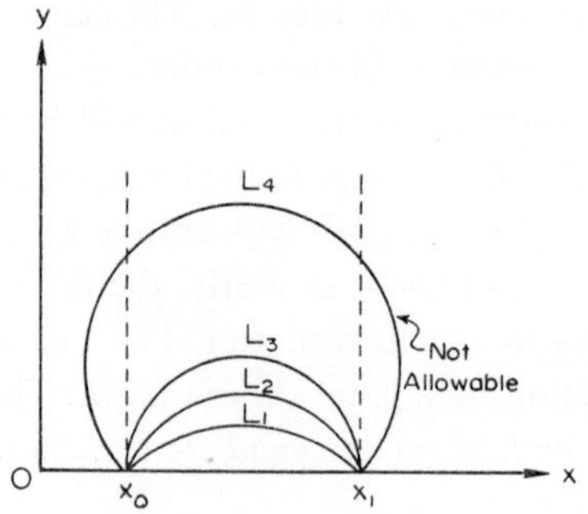

Fig. 3.1.

It is now a short step to the solution to the isoperimetric problem. Suppose that, among the closed curves with perimeter L, $\mathscr{K}$ is the curve which encloses the largest area. Select any point A on the curve, then move a distance $L/2$ along the curve (in either direction) to obtain a point B. Now draw the line segment connecting A to B. The area bounded by the curve on one side of the line segment must be the same as on the other; otherwise, one part of the curve could be replaced by the other part and the total area increased. Thus the curve can be treated as symmetric. If now we select any two points on the x-axis the distance between which is not greater than $L/2$, we can pass an arc of a circle with length $L/2$ through these points. This yields the largest area for the given points. The area is a function of $d = x_1 - x_0$. Maximizing the area with respect to d (in the problems, the reader is asked to obtain an explicit expression for the area), we find that $d = L/\pi$. Thus the arc is a semicircle, implying that the desired curve is a circle of diameter L/π. Alternatively, the isoperimetric problem can be solved directly by representing the closed curve parametrically by $x(\tau)$, $y(\tau)$ and treating the problem as one in which these two functions are to be determined. However, the solution procedure becomes more complicated; in the problems we ask the reader to investigate the nature of the complications.

3.3. The problem of Lagrange

We now turn our attention to the problem that will occupy us for the remainder of the chapter. This is the problem of optimizing $J[\mathbf{y}]$ subject to a set of differential equation constraints of the form (3-2). More specifically, the problem is to determine that piecewise smooth function $\mathbf{y}(x)$ the range of which is a subset of $\mathscr{E}^n$, which satisfies $\mathbf{y}(x_0) = \mathbf{y}_0$ and $\mathbf{y}(x_1) = \mathbf{y}_1$, which maximizes or minimizes

$$J[\mathbf{y}] = \int_{x_0}^{x_1} F(x, \mathbf{y}, \mathbf{y}')dx \tag{3-23}$$

and the graph of which lies in a set $\mathscr{R}$ in extended phase space which we shall specify below. We shall allow for the possibility that $x_1 = \infty$. Thus far, the problem looks exactly like that studied in Section 2.13. The difference hinges on the nature of $\mathscr{R}$. In Section 2.13 we were concerned with interior optima; thus it was implicitly assumed that $\mathscr{R}$ had an interior. In the present case, $\mathscr{R}$ has no interior; thus the curve representing $\mathbf{y}(x)$ must lie on the boundary of $\mathscr{R}$. For this reason, the theory developed in Section 2.13 is not applicable to the problem now being studied.

We shall assume that $\mathscr{R}$ is the manifold formed by the intersection of r hypersurfaces $\mathscr{D}_i$, $i = 1, \ldots, r$, $r < n$,

$$\mathscr{D}_i = \{(x, \mathbf{y}, \mathbf{y}') | G^i(x, \mathbf{y}, \mathbf{y}') = 0\}. \tag{3-24}$$

Equivalently, $\mathbf{y}(x)$ must satisfy the system of first order differential equations

$$G^i(x, \mathbf{y}, \mathbf{y}') = 0, \quad i = 1, \ldots, r, \quad r < n. \tag{3-25}$$

Of all piecewise smooth solutions to these differential equations which satisfy the boundary conditions (that is, of all admissible functions), we wish to determine that which maximizes or minimizes $J[\mathbf{y}]$.

Just as we have found it necessary to place restrictions on F, we shall also have to place restrictions on the G^i. We shall assume that there exists an open set $\mathscr{R}^*$ which contains $\mathscr{R}$ and over which $F \in C''$ and $G^i \in C''$, $i = 1, \ldots, r$. It will be assumed also that the $n \times r$ matrix $\mathbf{M}(x, \mathbf{y}, \mathbf{y}') = ||\partial G^i / \partial y_j'||$ has rank r at each point in $\mathscr{R}$. The columns of this matrix are the vectors $\mathbf{G}^i_{y'}$. This condition guarantees that (3-25) does yield a set of independent differential equations. In particular, it rules out the possibility that some of the G^i do not involve $\mathbf{y}'$ and are simply constraints of the form $G^i(x, \mathbf{y}) = 0$.

The problem of optimizing $J[\mathbf{y}]$ subject to the differential equation constraints (3-25) and the boundary conditions $\mathbf{y}(x_0) = \mathbf{y}_0$ and $\mathbf{y}(x_1) = \mathbf{y}_1$ is usually referred to as *the problem of Lagrange for fixed end points*. If instead of fixed end points it is required that $(x_0, \mathbf{y}(x_0))$ be in a specified smooth manifold $\mathscr{M}_1$ and/or that $(x_1, \mathbf{y}(x_1))$ be in a specified smooth manifold $\mathscr{M}_2$, we have then the *problem of Lagrange with variable end points*.

As usual, our first objective is to provide a useful set of necessary conditions which an optimizing function $\mathbf{z}(x)$ must satisfy. We shall show that there exists a set of multipliers $\boldsymbol{\lambda}$ not all 0 such that if

$$H = \lambda_0 F + \sum_{i=1}^{r} \lambda_i G^i = \lambda_0 F + \boldsymbol{\lambda} \cdot \mathbf{G} \tag{3-26}$$

then $\mathbf{z}(x)$ satisfies the necessary conditions of Theorem 2.13.1 when the integrand is H. For the purpose of stating the necessary conditions, therefore, the introduction of H effectively converts the problem into one without constraints. However we must be prepared for a complication which is absent both from problems involving ordinary maxima and minima and from isoperimetric problems. For the problem of Lagrange the multipliers $\lambda_1, \ldots, \lambda_r$ are not in general constants (λ_0, however, is still a constant); rather they are functions of x.

The basic necessary conditions are given in the following theorem.

Theorem 3.3.1. Necessary Conditions for the Problem of Lagrange – Multiplier Rule. Suppose that $\mathbf{z}(x)$ *is an admissible function which yields the global optimum of* $J[\mathbf{y}]$ *subject to the constraints (3-25) and that* $||G^i_{y_j'}||$ *has rank* r *at each point of* $\mathscr{R}$. *Then there exists a constant* $\lambda_0 \geq 0$ *(which without loss of generality may be taken to be 0 or 1) and piecewise continuous functions* $\lambda_1(x), \ldots, \lambda_r(x)$ *the only possible points of discontinuity of which are the corners of* $\mathbf{z}(x)$ *and such that if*

$$H(x, \mathbf{y}, \mathbf{y}', \boldsymbol{\lambda}) = \lambda_0 F(x, \mathbf{y}, \mathbf{y}') + \sum_{u=1}^{r} \lambda_u(x) G^u(x, \mathbf{y}, \mathbf{y}') \tag{3-27}$$

then between corners of $\mathbf{z}(x)$

$$\frac{\mathrm{d}}{\mathrm{d}x} \mathbf{H}_{\mathbf{y}'}(x, \mathbf{z}, \mathbf{z}') = \mathbf{H}_{\mathbf{y}}(x, \mathbf{z}, \mathbf{z}') \tag{3-28}$$

and $\mathbf{H}_{\mathbf{y}'}$ *is continuous across any corners of* $\mathbf{z}(x)$. *Furthermore, if the problem is of the variable end points type then, as a transversality condition, at any variable end point the vector* $(H - \mathbf{H}_{\mathbf{y}'} \cdot \mathbf{y}', \mathbf{H}_{\mathbf{y}'})$ *must be normal to the manifold in which the end point must lie; that is, the vector* $(H - \mathbf{H}_{\mathbf{y}'} \cdot \mathbf{y}', \mathbf{H}_{\mathbf{y}'})$ *must be a linear combination of the r normal vectors at the point under consideration, one for each of the hypersurfaces the intersection of which generates the manifold. Finally, the multipliers* $\lambda_0, \lambda_1(x), \ldots, \lambda_r(x)$ *do not all vanish for any value of x.*

Theorem 3.3.1. tells us that if $\mathbf{z}(x)$ provides the global optimal solution then there exists a Hamiltonian function H such that $\mathbf{z}(x)$ satisfies the necessary conditions for an unconstrained optimum of the problem

$$\int_{x_0}^{x_1} H \mathrm{d}x.$$

(It is not claimed, however, that $\mathbf{z}(x)$ actually optimizes

$$\int_{x_0}^{x_1} H \mathrm{d}x.)$$

We shall call (3-27) the Euler equation, as usual. The n Euler differential equations (normally of second order) plus the r first order differential equations $G^i = 0$ serve to generate $n + r$ functions $y_j(x)$ and $\lambda_i(x)$ involving $2n + r$ parameters. Intuitively, the conditions $\mathbf{y}(x_0) = \mathbf{y}_0$ and $\mathbf{y}(x_1) = \mathbf{y}_1$ (or the transversality conditions) provide $2n$ restrictions. The remaining r conditions needed to determine the parameters can be provided by specifying the values of $\lambda_1(x), \ldots, \lambda_r(x)$ at some point. Whether $\boldsymbol{\lambda}(x)$ is uniquely determined will be examined in more detail as we proceed.

In Sections 3.8 to 3.14 we shall provide a rigorous proof of Theorem 3.3.1.

The proof will reveal as a byproduct that the Weierstrass and Legendre conditions for an unconstrained optimum of

$$\int_{x_0}^{x_1} H \mathrm{d}x$$

will be satisfied by $\mathbf{z}(x)$ for at least one set of multipliers. Unfortunately, the proof is rather long and complicated. For this reason, before giving the complete proof, we shall provide a much simpler proof which is, however, based on more restrictive assumptions. Even this simpler proof will be approached indirectly. For we shall begin with (a generalized version of) what, in some texts, is presented as a proof for the case of fixed end points. We shall see that this 'proof' contains a flaw. The error will be corrected in the course of our discussion of the more general variable end points case and a rigorous proof will then be obtained under the restrictive assumptions made. These elementary proofs will introduce a number of ideas needed in the complete proof and thus make the latter a little easier to understand. If the reader desires, he may omit the complete proof. However, the necessary conditions for the problem of Lagrange are important, for they form the basis of the rigorous proofs of the theorems in control theory to be developed later.

For the present we shall assume that the interval of integration is finite. This assumption will be relaxed later.

3.4. A simplified 'proof' of the multiplier rule for fixed end points

Let us consider the problem of Lagrange with fixed end points and a finite interval of integration. Suppose that the piecewise smooth admissible function $\mathbf{z}(x)$ maximizes $J[\mathbf{y}]$. We have assumed already that the rank of $\mathbf{M} = ||\partial G^i/\partial y_j'||$ is r over $\mathscr{R}$. We now assume further that the submatrix consisting of the first r rows of $\mathbf{M}$ has rank r along $\mathbf{z}(x)$ (both for $\mathbf{z}_-'$ and for $\mathbf{z}_+'$ at corners of $\mathbf{z}(x)$). In addition we shall assume that $\mathbf{z}''(x)$ exists and is continuous between corners of $\mathbf{z}(x)$.

Consider now the set of functions $\mathbf{y}(x; \xi) = \mathbf{z}(x) + \xi\boldsymbol{\eta}(x)$, where $\boldsymbol{\eta}$ is piecewise smooth and satisfies the conditions $\boldsymbol{\eta}(x_0) = \boldsymbol{\eta}(x_1) = \mathbf{0}$ but otherwise is arbitrary. If $\mathbf{y}(x; \xi)$ is to be admissible for all ξ in a neighborhood of 0 then it is necessary that for each x

$$\Omega_i(\xi) = G^i(x, \mathbf{z} + \xi\boldsymbol{\eta}, \mathbf{z}' + \xi\boldsymbol{\eta}') = 0 \tag{3-29}$$

for all ξ; hence it must be true that $\Omega_i'(0) = 0$, i.e. that

$$\mathbf{G}^i_{\mathbf{y}}(x, \mathbf{z}, \mathbf{z}') \cdot \boldsymbol{\eta} + \mathbf{G}^i_{\mathbf{y}'}(x, \mathbf{z}, \mathbf{z}') \cdot \boldsymbol{\eta}' = 0, \quad i = 1, \ldots, r. \tag{3-30}$$

Here we have a set of r linear differential equations relating the components of $\boldsymbol{\eta}(x)$. Hence $\boldsymbol{\eta}(x)$ must be so restricted that the equations (3-30) are satisfied. In general, this means that only $n - r$ of the components of $\boldsymbol{\eta}$ can be selected arbitrarily. If $\mathbf{y}(x; \xi)$ is to be admissible and satisfy (3-29) it is necessary that $\boldsymbol{\eta}$ satisfy (3-30); notice however that the converse is not necessarily true: from the fact that $\boldsymbol{\eta}$ satisfies (3-30) one cannot infer that the $\mathbf{y}(x; \xi)$ so generated must satisfy (3-29).

Let us next consider the set of r linear differential equations of first order

$$\left[F_{y_j} + \sum_{i=1}^{r} \lambda_i G^i_{y_j}\right] - \frac{\mathrm{d}}{\mathrm{d}x}\left[F_{y_j'} + \sum_{i=1}^{m} \lambda_i G^i_{y_j'}\right] = 0, \quad j = 1, \ldots, r \tag{3-31}$$

in the variable λ_i, where the derivatives of F and the G^i are evaluated along $\mathbf{z}(x)$. Since by assumption $||G^i_{y_j'}||, j = 1, \ldots, r$ is nonsingular for each x along $\mathbf{z}(x)$, the equations (3-31) can be solved explicitly for the λ_j' to yield a set of linear first order differential equations in standard form. Let us restrict our attention to an interval $x_1^* \leq x \leq x_2^*$ between two adjacent corners x_1^* and x_2^* of $\mathbf{z}(x)$ (or the interval from x_0 to the first corner, or the interval from the last corner to x_1, or the entire interval if there are no corners). Over this interval all the functions in (3-31) are continuous in x. From the general theory of linear differential equations (see Pontryagin [28], p. 22, or Appendix III) we know that there then exists a unique solution $\boldsymbol{\lambda}(x)$ which is, of course, continuous and differentiable, defined on the interval $x_1^* \leq x \leq x_2^*$ and with the characteristic that $\boldsymbol{\lambda}(x_1^*) = \boldsymbol{\lambda}_0$, where $\boldsymbol{\lambda}_0$ can be specified arbitrarily. Let us suppose that we have obtained such a solution $\boldsymbol{\lambda}(x)$ for each of the intervals referred to above. These solutions then jointly define a solution to (3-31) for all x; this solution is continuous everywhere except possibly at the corners of $\mathbf{z}(x)$.

We now explain how the constants of integration may be determined. Equation (3-31) can be written as

$$F_{y_j'} + \sum_{i=1}^{r} \lambda_i G^i_{y_j'} = \int_{x_1}^{x} \left(F_{y_j} + \sum_{i=1}^{r} \lambda_i G^i_{y_j}\right) \mathrm{d}\zeta + \left(F_{y_j'} + \sum_{i=1}^{r} \lambda_i G^i_{y_j'}\right)_{x_{1+}} . \tag{3-32}$$

Suppose now that we select a set of arbitrary constants $\gamma_1, \ldots, \gamma_r$ and for the first interval, beginning at x_0, choose $\boldsymbol{\lambda}(x_0)$ so that

$$\left(F_{y_j'} + \sum_{i=1}^{r} \lambda_i G^i_{y_j'}\right)_{x_0} = \gamma_i, \quad i = 1, \ldots, r. \tag{3-33}$$

There is a unique solution to this set of equations. Then for each succeeding interval we chose $\boldsymbol{\lambda}(x_1^*)$ so that $F_{y_j'} + \Sigma_{i=1}^r \lambda_i G_{y_j'}^i$ is continuous across the corner. In this way $\boldsymbol{\lambda}(x)$ is determined uniquely throughout the entire interval $x_0 \leq x \leq x_1$. Furthermore, throughout the entire interval

$$F_{y_j'} + \sum_{i=1}^{r} \lambda_i G_{y_j'}^i = \int_{x_0}^{x} \left(F_{y_j} + \sum_{i=1}^{r} \lambda_i G_{y_j}^i \right) d\zeta + \gamma_j, \quad j = 1, \ldots, r \tag{3-34}$$

where the γ_j are arbitrarily chosen constants.

Returning to (3-30), we multiply each equation by $\lambda_i(x)$ and sum the results, then integrate from x_0 to x_1, obtaining

$$\int_{x_0}^{x_1} \sum_{i=1}^{r} [\lambda_i(x) \mathbf{G}_{\mathbf{y}}^i(x, \mathbf{z}, \mathbf{z}') \cdot \boldsymbol{\eta} + \lambda_i(x) \mathbf{G}_{\mathbf{y}'}^i(x, \mathbf{z}, \mathbf{z}') \cdot \boldsymbol{\eta}'] dx = 0 \tag{3-35}$$

Now for the set of admissible $\mathbf{y}(x; \xi)$ it is possible to write $\Phi(\xi) = J[\mathbf{y}(x; \xi)]$; and if $\mathbf{y}(x; 0) = \mathbf{z}(x)$ maximizes $J[\mathbf{y}]$ then $\Phi(\xi) \leq \Phi(0)$, implying that

$$\Phi'(0) = \int_{x_0}^{x_1} [\mathbf{F}_{\mathbf{y}}(x, \mathbf{z}, \mathbf{z}') \cdot \boldsymbol{\eta} + \mathbf{F}_{\mathbf{y}'}(x, \mathbf{z}, \mathbf{z}') \cdot \boldsymbol{\eta}'] dx = 0. \tag{3-36}$$

On the other hand, if $\boldsymbol{\eta}$ is such that $\mathbf{y}(x; \xi)$ is admissible then (3-30) and hence (3-35) must hold. Adding (3-35) to (3-36), we obtain

$$\int_{x_0}^{x_1} \left[\left(\mathbf{F}_{\mathbf{y}} + \sum_{i=1}^{r} \lambda_i \mathbf{G}_{\mathbf{y}}^i \right) \cdot \boldsymbol{\eta} + \left(\mathbf{F}_{\mathbf{y}'} + \sum_{i=1}^{r} \lambda_i \mathbf{G}_{\mathbf{y}'}^i \right) \cdot \boldsymbol{\eta}' \right] dx = 0. \tag{3-37}$$

This must hold for all $\boldsymbol{\eta}$ for which $\mathbf{y}(x; \xi)$ can be made admissible. To simplify later notation, let us write $H = F + \boldsymbol{\lambda} \cdot \mathbf{G}$. If we now integrate (3-37) by parts and apply (3-34), we obtain

$$\int_{x_0}^{x_1} \sum_{j=1}^{r} \left[H_{y_j'} - \int_{x_0}^{x} H_{y_j} d\zeta - \gamma_j \right] \eta_j' dx + \int_{x_0}^{x_1} \sum_{j=r+1}^{n} \left[H_{y_j'} - \int_{x_0}^{x} H_{y_j} d\zeta \right] \eta_j' dx = 0 \tag{3-38}$$

Here we have introduced

$$\int_{x_0}^{x} H_{y_j} d\zeta + \gamma_j$$

as a primitive function for H_{y_j}, $j = 1, \ldots, r$ and

$$\int_{x_0}^{x} H_{y_j} d\zeta$$

as the primitive function for $j = r + 1, \ldots, n$. Because of (3-34), the first integral vanishes and (3-38) reduces to

$$\int_{x_0}^{x_1} \sum_{j=r+1}^{n} \left[H_{y_j'} - \int_{x_0}^{x} H_{y_j} d\zeta \right] \eta_j' dx = 0. \tag{3-39}$$

Let us next select an arbitrary set of η_j, $j = r + 1, \ldots, n$ with the characteristics that $\eta_j \in C'$ and $\eta_j(x_0) = \eta_j(x_1) = 0$. When these η_j are substituted into the system of equations (3-30), there emerges a system of differential equations in $\eta_1, \ldots, \eta_r$ with continuous coefficients between corners of $\mathbf{z}(x)$. Furthermore, because $||G^i_{y_j'}||$, $j = 1, \ldots, r$ is nonsingular, it is possible to solve explicitly for $\eta_1', \ldots, \eta_r'$. In each interval then there exist continuous solutions $\eta_1, \ldots, \eta_r$ to this system of equations. It is possible to choose the constants of integration so that $\eta_j(x_0) = 0$, $j = 1, \ldots, r$; and the solutions are continuous throughout the entire interval $x_0 \leq x \leq x_1$. Thus for any choice of $\eta_{r+1}, \ldots, \eta_n$ of the type described it is possible to determine $\eta_1, \ldots, \eta_r$ such that $\boldsymbol{\eta}(x)$ satisfies (3-30); hence we might expect that $\mathbf{y}(x; \xi) = \mathbf{z}(x) + \xi\boldsymbol{\eta}(x)$ will be admissible if ξ is sufficiently close to 0. On this argument we should be able to freely select $\eta_{r+1}, \ldots, \eta_n$. Consequently, if we were to apply the fundamental lemma to (3-39) with only one η_j different from zero, we should conclude that there exist constants γ_j such that

$$H_{y_j'} = \int_{x_0}^{x} H_{y_j} dx + \gamma_j, \quad j = r + 1, \ldots, n \tag{3-40}$$

along $\mathbf{z}(x)$, $x_0 \leq x \leq x_1$.

If we now combine (3-40) with (3-34), we are tempted to conclude that $\mathbf{z}(x)$ must satisfy

$$\mathbf{H}_{\mathbf{y}'} = \int_{x_0}^{x} \mathbf{H}_{\mathbf{y}} d\zeta + \boldsymbol{\gamma}. \tag{3-41}$$

Equation (3-41) can be differentiated between corners to yield (3-27); and the right hand side of (3-41), and therefore the left hand side, is continuous across corners. It would seem therefore that for the case of fixed end points the necessary conditions of Theorem 3.3.1. must be satisfied, with $\lambda_0 = 1$.

Putting aside for the moment any reservations one may have concerning the special assumptions made, what is wrong with the above proof? One gap in the proof may be mentioned at once: we did not demonstrate that if $\boldsymbol{\eta}(x)$ satisfies (3-30) then, for ξ close enough to 0, $\mathbf{y}(x; \xi) = \mathbf{z}(x) + \xi\boldsymbol{\eta}(x)$ satisfies (3-29). However, this proposition does happen to be essentially correct, as we shall prove later. The real flaw in the argument lies in a slightly different direction. When arbitrary η_j, $j = r+1, \ldots, n$, $\eta_j \in C'$, $\eta_j(x_0) = \eta_j(x_1) = 0$ are selected, it is indeed possible to find η_j, $j = 1, \ldots, r$ with $\eta_j(x_0) = 0$ such that $\boldsymbol{\eta}(x)$ satisfies (3-30). In general, however, we cannot guarantee that $\eta_j(x_1) = 0$, $j = 1, \ldots, r$. For example, if $\mathbf{z}(x)$ has no corners then the coefficients in (3-30) are continuous throughout the whole interval and $\eta_1, \ldots, \eta_r$ have no corners. However, the constants of integration are determined by requiring that $\eta_j(x_0) = 0$ and no freedom exists to require also that $\eta_j(x_1) = 0$. In some elementary textbooks one finds a simplified version of the above analysis of the problem of Lagrange with fixed end points. The analysis shows clearly how the multiplier rule can emerge; but it is not rigorous and, because of the defect just referred to, cannot easily be made rigorous. Indeed, it is in general impossible to arbitrarily select $\eta_{r+1}, \ldots, \eta_n$ and then generate an $\boldsymbol{\eta}(x)$ which satisfies the constraints and $\boldsymbol{\eta}(x_0) = \boldsymbol{\eta}(x_1) = \mathbf{0}$. It is possible that no such $\boldsymbol{\eta}$ exists. In fact, there may not be any admissible function other than $\mathbf{z}(x)$. Thus the above 'proof' is not really a proof at all. From it, however, we have learned something of importance: To obtain a rigorous proof we cannot proceed, as we have done in the past and as we have attempted to do here, by constructing a set of admissible functions of the form $\mathbf{y}(x; \xi) = \mathbf{z}(x) + \xi\boldsymbol{\eta}(x)$; it is possible that no such functions exist. Using this observation as a point of departure, we shall in the following sections provide a rigorous derivation of the necessary conditions. In Sections 3.5 and 3.6 we shall continue to work with the special assumptions introduced in the present section. However, we shall study the problem in which $\mathbf{z}(x)$ must end on a manifold $\mathscr{M}$ and of which the problem with fixed end points emerges as a special case.

We note in passing that, when the constraints are not differential equations but are of the form (3-2), it is possible by the arguments used above to deduce a multiplier rule very similar to that already derived. Thus suppose that there are r constraints of the form

$$G^i(x, \mathbf{y}) = 0 \quad i = 1, \ldots, r \tag{3-42}$$

where $G^i \in C''$, $\|G^i_{y_j}\|$ has rank r over $\mathscr{R}$, and $\|G^i_{y_j}\|$, $j = 1, \ldots, r$, has rank r along the function $\mathbf{z}(x)$ which optimizes (3-23) subject to (3-42). Now consider functions $\mathbf{y}(x;\,\xi) = \mathbf{z}(x) + \xi\boldsymbol{\eta}(x)$. If $\mathbf{y}(x;\,\xi)$ is admissible, it is necessary that

$$\mathbf{G}^i_{\mathbf{y}} \cdot \boldsymbol{\eta} = 0, \quad i = 1, \ldots, r. \tag{3-43}$$

Suppose next that arbitrary numbers $\gamma_1, \ldots, \gamma_r$ are selected and let $\lambda_1(x), \ldots, \lambda_r(x)$ be the unique solution to the system of linear equations

$$\sum_{i=1}^{r} G^i_{y_j}\lambda_i = -F_{y_j} + \int_{x_0}^{x} F_{y_j'}\mathrm{d}x + \gamma_j, \quad j = 1, \ldots, r. \tag{3-44}$$

The $\lambda_i(x)$ are then continuous except perhaps at the corners of $\mathbf{z}(x)$. If we now introduce $H = F + \boldsymbol{\lambda} \cdot \mathbf{G}$, (3-44) can be written

$$H_{y_j} = \int_{x_0}^{x} H_{y_j}\mathrm{d}\zeta + \gamma_j, \quad j = 1, \ldots, r. \tag{3-45}$$

Next, we multiply equation i of (3-43) by $\lambda_i(x)$, sum over i, and integrate from x_0 to x_1, obtaining

$$\int_{x_0}^{x_1} \sum_{i=1}^{r} \lambda_i \mathbf{G}^i_{\mathbf{y}} \cdot \boldsymbol{\eta}\mathrm{d}x = 0. \tag{3-46}$$

Now if $\mathbf{z}(x)$ optimizes $J[\mathbf{y}]$, (3-36) must hold. Adding (3-46) to (3-36), and recalling the definition of H, we obtain

$$\int_{x_0}^{x_1} [\mathbf{H}_{\mathbf{y}} \cdot \boldsymbol{\eta} + \mathbf{H}_{\mathbf{y}'} \cdot \boldsymbol{\eta}']\mathrm{d}x = 0. \tag{3-47}$$

Integrating by parts and applying (3-45), we conclude that

$$\int_{x_0}^{x_1} \sum_{j=r+1}^{n} \left(H_{y_j'} - \int_{x_0}^{x} H_{y_j}\mathrm{d}\zeta \right)\eta_j\mathrm{d}x = 0. \tag{3-48}$$

Let us now select arbitrary η_j, $j = r + 1, \ldots, n$, with the property that $\eta_j \in C'$ and $\eta_j(x_0) = \eta_j(x_1) = 0$. If these functions are substituted into (3-43) we can determine unique continuous η_j, $j = 1, \ldots, r$ such that $\boldsymbol{\eta}$ satisfies (3-43). Furthermore, in this case, by continuity, $\eta_j(x_0) = \eta_j(x_1) = 0$, $j = 1, \ldots, r$. For each such $\boldsymbol{\eta}$ we should expect that, for ξ sufficiently close to 0, $\mathbf{y}(x;\,\xi)$ is admissible. Thus η_j, $j = r + 1, \ldots, n$, can be selected arbitrarily and, by the fundamental lemma, (3-45) also holds for $j = r + 1, \ldots, n$. It then immediately follows that Theorem 3.3.1. holds for fixed end points, with $\lambda_0 = 1$.

Notice that this proof is completely rigorous except for the omitted verification that a solution to (3-43) leads to a set of admissible functions $\mathbf{y}(x; \xi)$. (The verification can be carried out, though we leave it to the reader as a problem.) The difficulty encountered when the constraints were assumed to take the form of differential equations does not arise.

Constraints of the form $G^i(x, \mathbf{y}) = 0$, with a strict equality in (3-1), are called *holonomic* constraints. All other constraints, including those of the form $G^i(x, \mathbf{y}) \leq 0$, are called *nonholonomic*. We have just shown that, if the special assumptions imposed in this section are met, the same multiplier rule can be applied to holonomic constraints as to constraints in the form of differential equations.

Finally, we note that any problem with isoperimetric constraints can be reduced to a problem of Lagrange with fixed end points. (The demonstration is left to the reader as Problem 10.) Thus a separate treatment of isoperimetric constraints was not strictly necessary. However it is instructive to see how they can be handled directly; and Section 3.2 has served as a useful introduction to later developments.

3.5. Transversality

Consider now the problem of Lagrange with variable end points. We seek to derive the transversality conditions referred to in Theorem 3.3.1 and also to provide a more rigorous treatment of the case of fixed end points than that given in the preceding section. It will be assumed that only the right hand end point is variable and that the smooth manifold $\mathcal{M}$ is the intersection of s smooth hypersurfaces $S^u(x, \mathbf{y}) = 0$, $u = 1, \ldots, s$, $s \leq n + 1$.

We recall at the outset an observation made in the preceding section and which is crucial to the developments of the present section: In general, when $\mathbf{z}(x)$ optimizes $J[\mathbf{y}]$, it may not be possible to find an $\boldsymbol{\eta}(x)$ such that if $\mathbf{y}(x; \xi) = \mathbf{z}(x) + \xi\boldsymbol{\eta}(x)$ then, for all $|\xi| < \varepsilon$, $\mathbf{y}(x; \xi)$ is admissible, that is, satisfies both the constraining differential equations and the boundary conditions. Accordingly we now abandon the search for such functions and introduce a new definition of admissibility for variations $\boldsymbol{\eta}(x)$. *We shall say that the variation $\boldsymbol{\eta}(x)$ is admissible if it is piecewise continuous, satisfies (3-30) and has* $\boldsymbol{\eta}(x_0) = \mathbf{0}$. No restrictions will be placed on $\boldsymbol{\eta}$ at the right hand boundary. Thus an admissible variation $\boldsymbol{\eta}$ may not yield a $\mathbf{y}(x; \xi)$ which is admissible. However, we shall prove in Section 3.8 that if $\boldsymbol{\eta}(x)$ is an admissible variation then, for all ξ sufficiently close to 0, there exists a one-parameter family of functions $\mathbf{y}(x; \xi)$ such that $\mathbf{y}(x; 0) = \mathbf{z}(x)$, $\mathbf{y}(0; \xi) = \mathbf{y}_0$ and $\mathbf{y}_\xi(x; 0) = \boldsymbol{\eta}(x)$, and which satisfy $G^i = 0$, $i = 1, \ldots, r$, over the interval $x_0 \le x \le \beta = x_1 + \xi \Delta$, where Δ is arbitrary. (Notice that the right hand end point of the interval varies with ξ and that, while $\mathbf{y}(0; \xi) = \mathbf{y}_0$, we cannot guarantee that $\mathbf{y}(x; \xi)$ ends on $\mathscr{M}$.) Then from the fundamental lemma for derivatives it follows that

$$\mathbf{y}(x; \xi) = \mathbf{z}(x) + \xi\boldsymbol{\eta}(x) + \mathbf{o}(x; \xi)$$

where $\mathbf{o}(x; \xi)$ has the property that $\lim_{\xi \to 0} \mathbf{o}(x; \xi) = \mathbf{0}$ and $\lim_{\xi \to 0} \mathbf{o}(x; \xi)/\xi = \mathbf{0}$. Note that we do not quite claim that $\mathbf{z}(x) + \xi\boldsymbol{\eta}(x)$ will satisfy $G^i = 0$. There is an extra term $\mathbf{o}(x; \xi)$. This is not something to be concerned about, however, since all we really require is the fact that $\mathbf{y}_\xi(x; 0) = \boldsymbol{\eta}(x)$ (the reader might check back to note that we never used $\mathbf{y} = \mathbf{z} + \xi\boldsymbol{\eta}$ directly, only $\mathbf{y}_\xi(x; 0) = \boldsymbol{\eta}(x)$).

We shall in fact prove a more general result: If $\boldsymbol{\eta}_1, \ldots, \boldsymbol{\eta}_\sigma$ are admissible variations then there exists a σ parameter family of functions $\mathbf{y}(x; \boldsymbol{\xi})$ such that $\mathbf{y}(x; \mathbf{0}) = \mathbf{z}(x)$, $\mathbf{y}(0; \boldsymbol{\xi}) = \mathbf{y}_0$ and $\mathbf{y}_{\xi_k}(x; \mathbf{0}) = \boldsymbol{\eta}_k(x)$, and which satisfy $G^i = 0$, $i = 1, \ldots, r$, for all $\boldsymbol{\xi}$, $|\boldsymbol{\xi}| < \varepsilon$, over the interval $x_0 \le x \le \beta$, $\beta = x_1 + \boldsymbol{\Delta} \cdot \boldsymbol{\xi}$, where $\boldsymbol{\Delta}$ can be chosen arbitrarily. (However, we cannot guarantee that $\mathbf{y}(x; \boldsymbol{\xi})$ ends on $\mathscr{M}$.) In this more general case

$$\mathbf{y}(x; \boldsymbol{\xi}) = \mathbf{z}(x) + \sum_{k=1}^{\sigma} \xi_k \boldsymbol{\eta}_k(x) + \mathbf{o}(x; \boldsymbol{\xi})$$

where $\lim_{\boldsymbol{\xi} \to \mathbf{0}} \mathbf{o}(x; \boldsymbol{\xi}) = \mathbf{0}$. For the moment, we shall make use of this theorem without having given the proof.

Suppose now that $\mathbf{z}(x)$ optimizes $J[\mathbf{y}]$, that we have $s + 1$ admissible variations $\boldsymbol{\eta}_k(x)$, and that $s + 1$ arbitrary values $\mathbf{V}_k$ have been selected. Then we know that for every $\boldsymbol{\xi}$, $|\boldsymbol{\xi}| < \varepsilon$, there exists a function $\mathbf{y}(x; \boldsymbol{\xi}) = \mathbf{z}(x) + \Sigma_{k=1}^{s+1} \xi_k \boldsymbol{\eta}_k(x) + \mathbf{o}(x; \boldsymbol{\xi})$ which satisfies the constraints over the interval $x_0 \le x \le \beta$, $\beta = x_1 + \boldsymbol{\xi} \cdot \boldsymbol{\Delta}$, $\boldsymbol{\Delta}$ arbitrary, and for which $\mathbf{y}(x_0; \boldsymbol{\xi}) = \mathbf{y}_0$. Furthermore $\mathbf{y}(x; \mathbf{0}) = \mathbf{z}(x)$. However, it may not be true that $(\beta, \mathbf{y}(\beta; \boldsymbol{\xi})) \in \mathscr{M}$ when $\boldsymbol{\xi} \ne \mathbf{0}$.

Consider

$$\Phi(\boldsymbol{\xi}) = \int_{x_0}^{\beta} F(x, \mathbf{y}(x; \boldsymbol{\xi}), \mathbf{y}'(x; \boldsymbol{\xi}))dx \tag{3-49}$$

Let

$$\Phi(\boldsymbol{\xi}) = \Phi(0) + \zeta \tag{3-50a}$$

and

$$\Omega^u(\boldsymbol{\xi}) = S^u(\beta, \mathbf{y}(\beta; \boldsymbol{\xi})), \quad u = 1, \ldots, s. \tag{3-50b}$$

Then the Jacobian matrix for the $s + 1$ functions $\Phi(\boldsymbol{\xi})$ and $\Omega^u(\boldsymbol{\xi})$, $u = 1, \ldots, s$ cannot have rank $s + 1$ at $\boldsymbol{\xi} = \mathbf{0}$. In proof of this important proposition, we note first that for $\boldsymbol{\xi} = \mathbf{0}$, $\zeta = 0$ and $\Phi(0)$ is the optimal value of $J[\mathbf{y}]$. Furthermore $\Omega^u(\mathbf{0}) = 0$, since $(x_1, \mathbf{z}(x_1)) \in \mathscr{M}$. If the Jacobian matrix of Φ and the Ω^u is nonsingular at $\mathbf{0}$ then, since all the functions have continuous first derivatives, the implicit function theorem guarantees that for *all* ζ sufficiently close to 0 the equations $\Phi(\boldsymbol{\xi}) = \Phi(\mathbf{0}) + \zeta$, $\Omega^u(\boldsymbol{\xi}) = 0$, $u = 1, \ldots, s$ have a solution $\boldsymbol{\xi}(\zeta)$. This implies, first, that for each such ζ there is an $\boldsymbol{\xi}$ such that $(\beta, \mathbf{y}(\beta; \boldsymbol{\xi})) \in \mathscr{M}$, so that $\mathbf{y}(x; \boldsymbol{\xi})$ is admissible; second, that if $\zeta > 0$ then $\Phi(\boldsymbol{\xi}) > \Phi(\mathbf{0})$. Consequently, there exist admissible functions for which $J[\mathbf{y}] > J[\mathbf{z}]$, in contradiction of the assumption that $\mathbf{z}(x)$ maximizes $J[\mathbf{y}]$. Therefore the rank of the Jacobian matrix must be less than $s + 1$ at $\boldsymbol{\xi} = \mathbf{0}$.

Given that the Jacobian matrix is of rank less than $s + 1$ at $\mathbf{0}$, its columns are linearly dependent; hence there exist numbers λ_0, ρ_u, not all zero, such that

$$\lambda_0 \boldsymbol{\Phi}_{\boldsymbol{\xi}}(\mathbf{0}) + \sum_{u=1}^{s} \rho_u \boldsymbol{\Omega}^u_{\boldsymbol{\xi}}(\mathbf{0}) = \mathbf{0}. \tag{3-51}$$

In general, we might expect λ_0 and the ρ_u to depend on the particular $\boldsymbol{\eta}_k(x)$ used. We now show, however, that it is possible to select a single set of numbers λ_0, ρ_u, $u = 1, \ldots, s$, such that (3-51) holds for all $\boldsymbol{\eta}_k(x)$. To this end, we suppose that at $\mathbf{0}_1$ the maximum rank of the Jacobian matrix for the set of all admissible $\boldsymbol{\eta}_1(x), \ldots, \boldsymbol{\eta}_{s+1}(x)$ is q. Let $\boldsymbol{\eta}_1^*(x), \ldots, \boldsymbol{\eta}_{s+1}^*(x)$ be a set of admissible variations for which the Jacobian matrix has rank q at $\boldsymbol{\xi} = \mathbf{0}$, and suppose that we have a nontrivial solution to the system of equations (3-51) based on the $\boldsymbol{\eta}_j^*$. We now show that (3-51) must hold for every set of admissible $\boldsymbol{\eta}_k$ using this particular solution. Notice first that equation v in (3-51) depends only on $\boldsymbol{\eta}_v$ and not on the other $\boldsymbol{\eta}_k$. Notice also that instead of using just $s + 1$ functions $\boldsymbol{\eta}_k$ in the definition of $\mathbf{y}$ we could use more, and that each additional $\boldsymbol{\eta}_k$ and ξ_k would add one more row to the Jacobian matrix and one more equation. Suppose now that there is an admissible $\boldsymbol{\eta}$, say $\boldsymbol{\eta}_-(x)$, such that if we add it as $\boldsymbol{\eta}_{s+2}$ then equation $s + 2$ in (3-51) is not satisfied. If the rank of the new Jacobian is q, there must exist a submatrix which contains q rows different from the last and the rank of which is q (for the original Jacobian had rank q). These q rows yield equations which satisfy (3-51); and since each other row is a linear combination of these rows it too must satisfy (3-51). This cannot be so;

hence the rank must be greater than q. However, this leads to a contradiction also. For if the rank of the original Jacobian matrix were s, the rank of the new Jacobian must be $s + 1$, which we have proved to be impossible; and if the rank of the original Jacobian were less than s, we could select $s + 1$ of the $\boldsymbol{\eta}$'s, including $\boldsymbol{\eta}_-(x)$, to obtain a matrix of rank $q + 1$, which contradicts the fact that we started with a matrix of maximal rank. Hence there is a set of numbers λ_0, ρ_u such that (3-51) holds for all $\boldsymbol{\eta}_k$.

We can imagine that for every admissible $\boldsymbol{\eta}_j$ there is a corresponding equation in (3-51). All of these equations can be satisfied by one set of numbers λ_0, ρ_u. The equation in (3-51) corresponding to $\boldsymbol{\eta}_j$ is exactly what would be obtained if we were to write $\mathbf{y}(x; \xi) = \mathbf{z}(x) + \xi\boldsymbol{\eta}_j(x)$, using just one $\boldsymbol{\eta}$-function $\boldsymbol{\eta}_j$. Consequently, if $\boldsymbol{\eta}$ is *any* admissible $\boldsymbol{\eta}$-function and we write $\mathbf{y}(x; \xi) = \mathbf{z}(x) + \xi\boldsymbol{\eta}(x)$ then there exist numbers λ_0, ρ_u which are independent of $\boldsymbol{\eta}$ and such that

$$\lambda_0\Phi_\xi(0) + \sum_{u=1}^{s} \rho_u\Omega_\xi^u(0) = 0. \tag{3-52}$$

Let us now evaluate $\Phi_\xi(0)$ and $\Omega_\xi^u(0)$ explicitly. From (3-49), using an $\boldsymbol{\xi}$ with only one component, we see that

$$\Phi_\xi(0) = F(x_1, \mathbf{z}(x_1), \mathbf{z}'(x_1))\Delta + \int_{x_0}^{x_1} [\mathbf{F}_\mathbf{y} \cdot \boldsymbol{\eta} + \mathbf{F}_{\mathbf{y}'} \cdot \boldsymbol{\eta}']dx \tag{3-53}$$

where Δ is the derivative of $\beta = x_1 + \xi\Delta$ with respect to ξ, evaluated at 0. Similarly, from (3-50) we obtain

$$\Omega_\xi^u(0) = (S_x^u + \mathbf{S}_\mathbf{y}^u \cdot \mathbf{y}')\Delta + \mathbf{S}_\mathbf{y}^u \cdot \boldsymbol{\eta},$$

the right side being evaluated at x_1. Let us now add (3-35) to λ_0 times (3-53), integrate by parts and apply (3-41). We shall assume that, in the equations (3-31) which define $\boldsymbol{\lambda}(x)$, $\lambda_0 F$ appears instead of F. Notice also that when $\mathbf{z}(x)$ satisfies the constraints, $\lambda_0 F(x_1, \mathbf{z}(x_1), \mathbf{z}'(x_1)) = H(x_1, \mathbf{z}(x_1), \mathbf{z}'(x_1))$. Thus (3-53) reduces to

$$\Phi_\xi(0) = H\Delta + \mathbf{H}_{\mathbf{y}'} \cdot \boldsymbol{\eta}, \tag{3-54}$$

the right side of (3-54) being evaluated at x_1. Next we multiply $\Omega_\xi^u(0)$ by ρ_u, sum over u and subtract from (3-54), obtaining

$$\left[H - \sum_{u=1}^{s} \rho_u(S_x^u + \mathbf{S}_\mathbf{y}^u \cdot \mathbf{y}')\right]\Delta + \left[\mathbf{H}_{\mathbf{y}'} - \sum_{u=1}^{s} \rho_u \mathbf{S}_\mathbf{y}^u\right] \cdot \boldsymbol{\eta} = 0. \tag{3-55}$$

From (3-52), this equation holds for every admissible $\boldsymbol{\eta}$.

To continue the argument, we now go back some distance and recall that in the determination of the multipliers $\lambda_i(x)$ we introduced arbitrary constants γ_j, $j = 1, \ldots, r$. Let us now select these so that the coefficients of $\eta_1, \ldots, \eta_r$ are 0. Since $\eta_{r+1}, \ldots, \eta_n$ are arbitrary, the coefficients of these functions must be 0 also if (3-55) is to hold. Finally, since Δ may be selected arbitrarily, its coefficient must vanish as well. Thus at x_1

$$H - \sum_{u=1}^{s} \rho_u(S_x^u + \mathbf{S}_\mathbf{y}^u \cdot \mathbf{y}') = 0 \tag{3-56}$$

$$\mathbf{H}_{\mathbf{y}'} - \sum_{u=1}^{s} \rho_u \mathbf{S}_\mathbf{y}^u = \mathbf{0}. \tag{3-57}$$

If (3-57) is now substituted in (3-56), we obtain

$$H - \mathbf{H}_{\mathbf{y}'} \cdot \mathbf{y}' - \sum_{u=1}^{s} \rho_u S_x^u = 0. \tag{3-58}$$

On combining (3-57) and (3-58), we see that the vector

$$(H - \mathbf{H}_{\mathbf{y}'} \cdot \mathbf{y}', \mathbf{H}_{\mathbf{y}'}) \tag{3-59}$$

must be a linear combination of the normal vectors ∇S^u for the hypersurfaces $S^u = 0$ at $(x_1, \mathbf{y}_1)$. This establishes the transversality condition.

Given the simplifying assumptions introduced in Section 3.4, the proof is completely rigorous. The same procedure can be used to derive an analogous transversality condition for holonomic constraints; we ask the reader to provide the details as a problem.

We now have a rigorous development of the necessary conditions for the fixed end points problem studied in the previous section–under the assumptions introduced there. For the requirement that $\mathbf{y}(x_1) = \mathbf{y}_1$ is merely a special case of the requirement that the right hand end point of $\mathbf{y}(x)$ lie in a smooth manifold $\mathscr{M}$. To see this, we need only define $\mathscr{M}$ by $x - x_1 = 0$, $\mathbf{y} = \mathbf{y}_1 = \mathbf{0}$. There is only one point in this manifold, and the matrix of the gradient vectors is an identity matrix of order $n + 1$. Any vector of order $n + 1$ can then be represented as a linear combination of the gradient vectors, hence the transversality conditions at x_1 impose no restrictions other than $\mathbf{y}(x_1) = \mathbf{y}_1$. Notice the importance of the multiplier λ_0. By introducing a multiplier of F, our earlier analysis can be made rigorous. In particular, we need not worry whether or not $\boldsymbol{\eta}(x_1) = \mathbf{0}$. Roughly speaking, λ_0 is needed so that things can be fixed up at x_1 in cases in which $\mathbf{y}(x_1; \xi) \neq \mathbf{y}_1$ for $\xi \neq 0$.

3.6. Free boundary conditions

From the transversality conditions derived in the previous section we may determine the conditions to be satisfied when there is a *free boundary* at x_1, that is, when the upper limit on the integral is given as x_1 but $\mathbf{y}(x_1)$ is not specified. For then the right hand end point of $\mathbf{y}(x)$ must lie in a particularly simple smooth manifold $\mathscr{M}$, viz. the hyperplane $x - x_1 = 0$, which is perpendicular to the x-axis at x_1. The situation is illustrated for $n = 2$ in Figure 3.2.

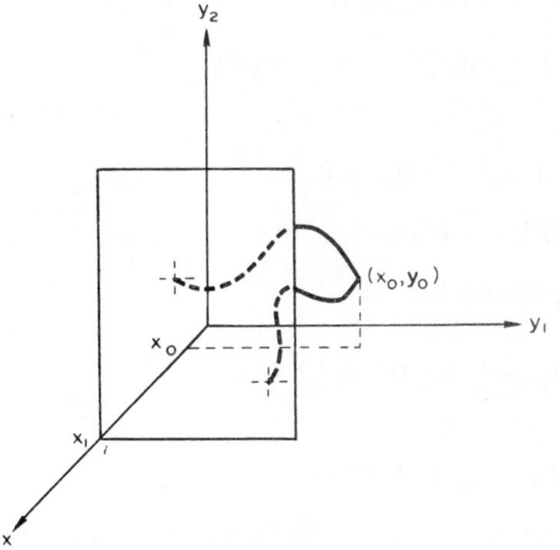

Fig. 3.2.

In the present case there is only one hypersurface and $\nabla S = \mathbf{e}_1$, where $\mathbf{e}_1 = (1, 0, 0, \ldots, 0)$. Thus, from the transversality conditions, there exists a number ρ such that (3-59) is equal to $\rho\mathbf{e}_1$. In other words,

$$H - \mathbf{H}_{\mathbf{y}'} \cdot \mathbf{y}' = \rho; \quad \mathbf{H}_{\mathbf{y}'} = \mathbf{0}. \tag{3-60}$$

These are the free boundary conditions which must be satisfied by a minimizing arc.

3.7. Examples

We now provide some simple examples which illustrate how differential equation constraints can arise.

1. Consider again the Ramsey model with a finite planning horizon T. In Chapter 2 we used the relationship

$$C + \dot{K} - \Psi(K) = 0 \tag{3-61}$$

to eliminate C from $U(C)$. Alternatively, we might retain the two unknown functions C and K and treat (3-61) as a differential equation constraint of the type we have been considering. Note that in principle C can have jump discontinuities. Thus one must be cautious about treating it as a piecewise smooth variable (the only type of variable allowed in our development of the calculus of variations). We have noted earlier, however, that for an interior maximum C can have no jumps. Provided we confine our attention to interior maxima, therefore, it is permissible to treat C as piecewise smooth.

The Hamiltonian in this case is

$$H = \lambda_0 U(C) + \lambda_1(t)[C + \dot{K} - \Psi(K)] \tag{3-62}$$

so that

$$H_C = \lambda_0 U' + \lambda_1; \qquad H_{\dot{C}} = 0 \tag{3-63}$$

$$H_K = -\lambda_1 \Psi'; \qquad H_{\dot{K}} = \lambda_1 \tag{3-64}$$

and the Euler equations become

$$\frac{\mathrm{d}}{\mathrm{d}t} H_{\dot{C}} - H_C = -(\lambda_0 U' + \lambda_1) = 0 \tag{3-65}$$

$$\frac{\mathrm{d}}{\mathrm{d}t} H_{\dot{K}} - H_K = \dot{\lambda}_1 + \lambda_1 \Psi' = 0. \tag{3-66}$$

On inserting the value of λ_1 provided by (3-65) into (3-66), we obtain

$$\frac{\mathrm{d}}{\mathrm{d}t} U' + U'\Psi' = 0 \quad \text{or} \quad \lambda_0 = 0. \tag{3-67}$$

However, if $\lambda_0 = 0$ then, by (3-65), $\lambda_1 = 0$. This is not possible since both multipliers cannot be 0 at any point. Consequently, the differential equation given in (3-67) must hold. This is precisely the Euler equation for

$$F = U[\Psi(K) - \dot{K}]. \tag{3-68}$$

Thus, as expected, the current and earlier approaches produce the same conclusions.

We can easily obtain the familiar integrated form of the Euler equation by reverting to a parametric representation, as in Section 2.14, this time with $t = \tau$. There are now three variables C, K and t. The Euler equation for t is

$$\frac{\mathrm{d}}{\mathrm{d}\tau} \mathscr{H}_{t^\circ} - \mathscr{H}_t = 0 \tag{3-69}$$

where $\mathscr{H} = H\mathring{t}$ and where we now use the symbol $^\circ$ to indicate differentiation with respect to the parameter τ. Since $\mathscr{H}$ does not depend explicitly on t, (3-69) reduces to $\mathscr{H}_{\mathring{t}} = \lambda$, a constant; that is,

$$\mathscr{H}_{\mathring{t}} = H - H_{\dot{C}}\dot{C} - H_{\dot{K}}\dot{K} = \lambda. \tag{3-70}$$

Since $\lambda_0 \neq 0$, so that without loss of generality we may choose $\lambda_0 = 1$, and since the constraint is satisfied, (3-70) emerges as the familiar

$$U + U'\dot{K} = \lambda.$$

As $\tau \to \infty$, it should be necessary that $\mathscr{H}_{\mathring{t}} \to 0$, $\mathscr{H}_{\mathring{K}} \to 0$ and $\mathscr{H}_{\mathring{C}} \to 0$, i.e. $U + U'K \to 0$ so that $\lambda = 0$ and $\lambda_1 \to 0$ or, since $\lambda_1 = U'$, $U' \to 0$. These are familiar results.

2. Suppose that an airplane is flying in a closed curve in a horizontal plane, that its speed with respect to the air is v_0, and that the wind velocity is a constant vector $\mathbf{a}$ (fixed in magnitude and direction). The problem is to find that closed curve which can be traversed in a fixed time T and which encloses the greatest possible area.

This problem can be formulated and solved in terms of the calculus of variations with differential equation constraints. Let $\mathbf{v}_e$ be the velocity of the airplane with respect to a coordinate system fixed to the earth and let $\mathbf{v}_a$ be the velocity with respect to the air. Then $\mathbf{v}_e = \mathbf{v}_a + \mathbf{a}$. Suppose that we now select an xy-coordinate system in a horizontal plane fixed to the earth such that the wind direction is along the positive x-axis; then $\mathbf{a} = a\mathbf{e}_1$. The choice of origin is irrelevant; we shall make a special choice later. Now at any point in time $\mathbf{v}_a$ forms an angle $\theta(t)$ with the positive x-axis, so that

$$v_{ax} = v_0 \cos\theta(t), \qquad v_{ay} = v_0 \sin\theta(t). \tag{3-71}$$

Let us denote by $\dot{x}$ and $\dot{y}$ the components of $\mathbf{v}_e$. Then at each t

$$\begin{aligned} &\dot{x} - v_0 \cos\theta(t) + a = 0 \\ &\dot{y} - v_0 \sin\theta(t) = 0. \end{aligned} \tag{3-72}$$

The area enclosed by the curve traced by the airplane is

$$A = \tfrac{1}{2} \int_0^T (x\dot{y} - y\dot{x})dt. \tag{3-73}$$

(See Problem 3 of Section 3.2 for the parametric representation of areas.) It is desired to maximize (3-73) subject to the differential equation constraints (3-72).

The Hamiltonian in this case is

$$H = \frac{\lambda_0}{2}(x\dot{y} - y\dot{x}) + \lambda_1(t)(\dot{x} - v_0\cos\theta(t)) + \lambda_2(t)(\dot{y} - v_0\sin\theta(t)) \qquad (3\text{-}74)$$

There are three variables, x, y and θ. None can be changed discontinuously; that is, all must be piecewise smooth. The Euler equations are

$$\frac{\mathrm{d}}{\mathrm{d}t}H_{\dot{x}} - H_x = \frac{\mathrm{d}}{\mathrm{d}t}[-\tfrac{1}{2}\lambda_0 y + \lambda_1] - \tfrac{1}{2}\lambda_0\dot{y} = 0 \qquad (3\text{-}75)$$

$$\frac{\mathrm{d}}{\mathrm{d}t}H_{\dot{y}} - H_y = \frac{\mathrm{d}}{\mathrm{d}t}[\tfrac{1}{2}\lambda_0 x + \lambda_2] + \tfrac{1}{2}\lambda_0\dot{x} = 0 \qquad (3\text{-}76)$$

$$\frac{\mathrm{d}}{\mathrm{d}t}H_{\dot{\theta}} - H_\theta = \lambda_1 v_0\sin\theta - \lambda_2 v_0\cos\theta = 0. \qquad (3\text{-}77)$$

Now if $\lambda_0 = 0$, (3-75) and (3-76) imply that λ_1 and λ_2 are constants; not both can be 0. Hence, from (3-77), θ is a constant. However, it would be impossible to describe a closed curve with θ a constant. Thus $\lambda_0 \neq 0$ and without loss in generality we can choose $\lambda_0 = 1$.

Equations (3-75) and (3-76) can be immediately integrated to yield

$$-y + \lambda_1 = \rho_1; \qquad x + \lambda_2 = \rho_2. \qquad (3\text{-}78)$$

As we have indicated earlier, the choice of origin is arbitrary. Let us now choose the origin so that $\rho_1 = \rho_2 = 0$ and $\lambda_1 = y$, $\lambda_2 = x$. If these results are applied to (3-77) we obtain

$$y\sin\theta + x\cos\theta = 0.$$

This equation says that the vector (x, y) is orthogonal to $(\cos\theta, \sin\theta)$, that is, to $\mathbf{v}_a$. Every vector orthogonal to $\mathbf{v}_a$ can be written

$$x = r\sin\theta; \qquad y = -r\cos\theta \qquad (3\text{-}79)$$

where r is an arbitrary positive number for each t.

When (3-79) is applied to (3-71) and (3-72) we obtain

$$\begin{aligned} &\dot{r}\sin\theta + r\dot{\theta}\cos\theta - v_0\cos\theta + a = 0 \\ &-\dot{r}\cos\theta + r\dot{\theta}\sin\theta - v_0\sin\theta = 0. \end{aligned} \qquad (3\text{-}80)$$

Next we multiply (3-77) by $\sin\theta$, (3-78) by $-\cos\theta$, and add, obtaining

$$\dot{r} = a\sin\theta.$$

However, from (3-72), $\sin\theta = \dot{y}/v_0$; hence

$$\dot{r} = \frac{a}{v_0}\dot{y}$$

or, since $r^2 = x^2 + y^2$,

$$(x^2 + y^2)^{\frac{1}{2}} = \frac{a}{v_0} y + \delta. \tag{3-81}$$

This is the equation of an ellipse with one focus at the origin, its major axis perpendicular to the direction of the wind and an eccentricity of a/v_0.

3. Problems of the Lagrange type have a number of special and complicated features. For example, there may exist only one piecewise smooth function which satisfies the differential equation constraints and the boundary conditions. This function then yields the optimal solution. However, the problem is trivial in the sense that there is no other solution (just as a linear programming problem is trivial when there is only one feasible solution).

We now give an example with $n = 2$ which involves fixed end points and in which there is just a single solution. Suppose that there is one differential equation constraint

$$y_1' - [(y_2')^2 - y_1^2]^2 = 0. \tag{3-82}$$

It will be noted that $y_1' \geq 0$ always. Suppose now that the interval of integration extends from 0 to 1 and that the end points are $y_1(0) = 1$, $y_2(0) = 0$; $y_1(1) = 1$, $y_2(1) = 1$. Since $y_1(0) = y_1(1) = 1$, it must be true that $y_1' \equiv 0$ and $y_1(x) \equiv 1$. Hence $y_2' = 1$ or -1. Since $y_2(1) = 1 > y_2(0) = 0$, $y_2' = 1$ and $y_2 = x$. Moreover, $\mathbf{y} = (1, x)$ is the only solution with these end points. Notice that if we had specified that $y_2(1) = b$, with $b > 0$ but $b \neq 1$, there would have been no solution at all. Notice also that the necessary conditions of Theorem 3.3.1 apply even in odd cases in which there is only one solution. (In cases like this, one needs not only λ_0 but the possibility of setting $\lambda_0 = 0$.)

3.8. Preliminary results

We are now ready to begin a rigorous development of the multiplier rule for the problem of Lagrange in the more general case, and to prove that the Weierstrass and Legendre necessary conditions are also satisfied.

We shall begin by proving a proposition introduced without proof in Section 3.5, *viz.* that for any σ admissible variations $\boldsymbol{\eta}_k(x)$ there exists a σ parameter family of functions $\mathbf{y}(x; \boldsymbol{\xi})$ which satisfy the constraints $G^i = 0$

for all $|\boldsymbol{\xi}| < \varepsilon$ over the interval $x_0 \leq x \leq \beta = x_1 + \boldsymbol{\xi} \cdot \boldsymbol{\Delta}$ and such that $\mathbf{y}_{\xi_k}(x; \mathbf{0}) = \boldsymbol{\eta}_k$ and $\mathbf{y}(x; \mathbf{0}) = \mathbf{z}(x)$. Recall that we have called $\boldsymbol{\eta}_k$ admissible if it is piecewise smooth and satisfies (3-30) and $\boldsymbol{\eta}_k(x_0) = \mathbf{0}$. We now seek additional generality by allowing each end point to lie on a smooth manifold; thus the most general case will be covered by the proofs. For this case we need not require that $\boldsymbol{\eta}_k(x_0) = \mathbf{0}$, and any piecewise smooth solution to (3-30) will be referred to as an admissible variation. We shall prove that given any σ admissible variations there exists a σ parameter family of solutions to the constraints $G^i = 0$ over the interval $x_0(\boldsymbol{\xi}) \leq x \leq x_1(\boldsymbol{\xi})$, where $x_0(\boldsymbol{\xi}) = x_0 + \boldsymbol{\xi} \cdot \boldsymbol{\Delta}_0$ and $x_1(\boldsymbol{\xi}) = x_1 + \boldsymbol{\xi} \cdot \boldsymbol{\Delta}_1$, $\boldsymbol{\Delta}_0$ and $\boldsymbol{\Delta}_1$ being arbitrary. Also $\mathbf{y}_{\xi_k}(x; \mathbf{0}) = \boldsymbol{\eta}_k$ and $\mathbf{y}(x; \mathbf{0}) = \mathbf{z}(x)$. Notice that now the interval over which the $G^i = 0$ are satisfied can be varied at both end points. For the case in

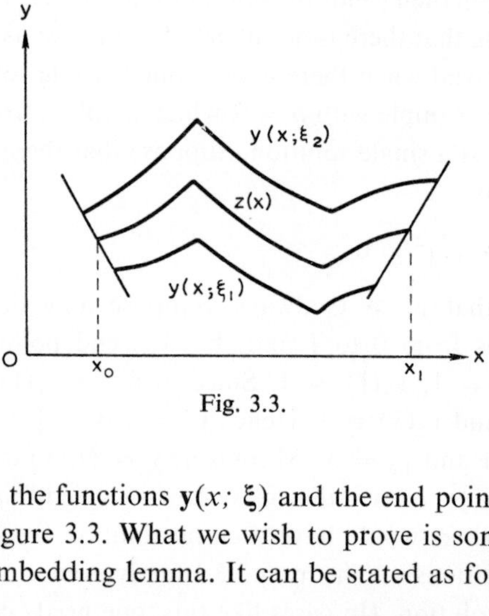

Fig. 3.3.

which $r = n = 1$, the functions $\mathbf{y}(x; \boldsymbol{\xi})$ and the end points might look like those shown in Figure 3.3. What we wish to prove is sometimes known as the fundamental imbedding lemma. It can be stated as follows:

Lemma. Fundamental Imbedding Property. Suppose that $\mathbf{z}(x)$ *is an admissible function which maximizes* $J[\mathbf{y}]$ *subject to the differential equation constraints* $G^i = 0$, $i = 1, \ldots, r$, *and that* $\boldsymbol{\eta}_k(x)$, $k = 1, \ldots, \sigma$ *are* σ *admissible variations and* $\boldsymbol{\Delta}_0$ *and* $\boldsymbol{\Delta}_1$ *arbitrarily specified* σ*-component vectors. Then there exists a* σ*-parameter family of solutions* $\mathbf{y}(x; \boldsymbol{\xi})$ *to* $G^i = 0$, $i = 1, \ldots, r$ *such that* $\mathbf{y}(x; \mathbf{0}) = \mathbf{z}(x)$ *and with the characteristic that for each* $\boldsymbol{\xi}$, $|\boldsymbol{\xi}| < \varepsilon$, $\varepsilon > 0$, $\mathbf{y}(x; \boldsymbol{\xi})$ *satisfies* $G^i = 0$, $i = 1, \ldots, r$ *over the interval* $x_0(\boldsymbol{\xi}) = x_0 + \boldsymbol{\xi} \cdot \boldsymbol{\Delta}_0 \leq x \leq x_1(\boldsymbol{\xi}) = x_1 + \boldsymbol{\xi} \cdot \boldsymbol{\Delta}_1$. *Also* $\mathbf{y}_{\xi_k}(x; \mathbf{0}) = \boldsymbol{\eta}_k(x)$, $\mathbf{y}'_{\xi_k}(x; \mathbf{0}) = \boldsymbol{\eta}'_k(\mathbf{0})$ *and both* $\mathbf{y}$ *and* $\mathbf{y}'$ *have continuous first partial derivatives with respect to* $\boldsymbol{\xi}$ *except possibly at corners of* $\mathbf{z}(x)$ *or the* $\boldsymbol{\eta}_k(x)$.

It is important to note that the lemma says nothing about $\mathbf{y}(x; \boldsymbol{\xi})$ satisfying the end point conditions. We need not worry whether or not $\mathbf{y}(x; \boldsymbol{\xi})$ does satisfy the end point conditions and is admissible. From the properties of derivatives we know that

$$\mathbf{y}(x; \boldsymbol{\xi}) = \mathbf{z}(x) + \sum_{k=1}^{\sigma} \boldsymbol{\eta}_k(x)\xi_k + \mathbf{o}(x; \boldsymbol{\xi}).$$

Let us now prove the lemma. We begin by annexing to the r differential equation constraints $n - r$ (n being the number of components in $\mathbf{z}(x)$) additional differential equation constraints of the form $G^i(x, \mathbf{y}, \mathbf{y}') = \phi_i(x)$, $i = r + 1, \dots, n$, where $\phi_i(x)$ is a specified function of x and it is required that $G^i \in C''$ over $\mathscr{R}$, $i = r + 1, \dots, n$. The only other requirement we shall place on the new G^i is that the nth order matrix $\|G^i_{y_j'}\|$ be non-singular along $\mathbf{z}(x)$. There is no unique set of additional functions G^i with this property. (It has been shown by Bliss [4] that it is possible to select G^i which are linear in $\mathbf{y}'$, with the coefficients functions of x only. However we shall not need this fact.) Having chosen G^i, $i = r + 1, \dots, n$, the functions $\phi_i(x)$ are then selected so that $\mathbf{z}(x)$ satisfies the new equations also, that is

$$\phi_i(x) = G^i(x, \mathbf{z}(x), \mathbf{z}'(x)), \quad i = r + 1, \dots, n. \tag{3-83}$$

The ϕ_i are continuous except possibly at corners of $\mathbf{z}(x)$.

Consider now the equivalent of (3-30) for the new differential equations. If we substitute $\boldsymbol{\eta}_k(x)$ for $\boldsymbol{\eta}$ in $\mathbf{G}^i_{\mathbf{y}'} \cdot \boldsymbol{\eta}' + \mathbf{G}^i_{\mathbf{y}} \cdot \boldsymbol{\eta}$, $i = r + 1, \dots, n$, we obtain some function of x, say $\zeta_{ik}(x)$. (Notice that this depends on k; a different function $\zeta_{ik}(x)$ will be obtained for each $\boldsymbol{\eta}_k$.) Thus $\boldsymbol{\eta}_k(x)$ satisfies the system of differential equations

$$\begin{aligned} &\mathbf{G}^i_{\mathbf{y}'} \cdot \boldsymbol{\eta}_k' + \mathbf{G}^i_{\mathbf{y}} \cdot \boldsymbol{\eta}_k = 0, \quad i = 1, \dots, r \\ &\mathbf{G}^i_{\mathbf{y}'} \cdot \boldsymbol{\eta}_k' + \mathbf{G}^i_{\mathbf{y}} \cdot \boldsymbol{\eta}_k - \zeta_{ik}(x) = 0, \quad i = r + 1, \dots, n \end{aligned} \tag{3-84}$$

where the derivatives of G^i are evaluated along $\mathbf{z}(x)$. The functions $\zeta_{ik}(x)$ are continuous except possibly at corners of $\mathbf{z}(x)$ or $\boldsymbol{\eta}_k(x)$.

We next study the system of equations

$$\begin{aligned} &G^i(x, \mathbf{y}, \mathbf{y}') = 0, \quad i = 1, \dots, r \\ &G^i(x, \mathbf{y}, \mathbf{y}') - \theta_i(x) = 0, \quad i = r + 1, \dots, n \end{aligned} \tag{3-85}$$

where for the moment the $\theta_i(x)$ are unspecified. We know that $\mathbf{z}(x)$ satisfies these equations when $\theta_i(x) = \phi_i(x)$ and that $\|\partial G^i/\partial y_j'\|$ has rank n along $\mathbf{z}(x)$. Let us consider then the curve in $\mathscr{E}^{2n-r+1}$ consisting of the points $(x, \mathbf{z}(x), \boldsymbol{\phi}(x))$, $x_0 \leq x \leq x_1$, and let us denote by $\mathscr{F}$ any segment of the curve not containing a corner of $\mathbf{z}(x)$. For each point on $\mathscr{F}$ there exists a number $\mathbf{z}'(x)$ such that (3-85) holds, that is, there exists a function $\mathbf{z}' = \mathbf{\Lambda}(x, \mathbf{z}, \boldsymbol{\phi})$ defined on $\mathscr{F}$ and this function is continuous in the sense of the second implicit function theorem of Appendix II. Hence, by that theorem, there is an N_ε neighborhood $\mathscr{N}_\varepsilon$ of $\mathscr{F}$ (in $\mathscr{E}^{2n-r+1}$) such that there exists a vector-valued function

$$\mathbf{y}' = \mathbf{\Upsilon}(x, \mathbf{y}, \boldsymbol{\theta}) \tag{3-86}$$

with domain $\mathscr{N}_\varepsilon$ (not $\mathscr{F}$) and such that, when $(x, \mathbf{y}, \boldsymbol{\theta}) \in \mathscr{N}_\varepsilon$ and $\mathbf{y}'$ is computed from (3-86), $(x, \mathbf{y}, \boldsymbol{\theta}, \mathbf{y}')$ satisfies the equations (3-85). Furthermore, each component of $\mathbf{\Upsilon}$ is continuous and possesses continuous partial derivatives with respect to each of its arguments. It should be observed that if $\mathbf{\Lambda}$ is defined for x satisfying $a \leq x \leq b$, then $\mathbf{\Upsilon}$ is defined over a somewhat longer interval $a - \varepsilon \leq x \leq b + \varepsilon$. This also follows from the second implicit function theorem.

Now let x^* be the first value of x following x_0 at which either $\mathbf{z}(x)$ or one of the $\boldsymbol{\eta}_k(x)$ has a corner. If there are no corners, x^* can be taken to be equal to x_1. Let us consider the interval $x_0 \leq x \leq x^*$. We know that the function (3-86) exists over the interval $x_0 - \varepsilon \leq x \leq x^* + \varepsilon$. The functions $\phi_i(x)$ and $\zeta_{ik}(x)$ are continuous over the interval $x_0 \leq x \leq x^*$. Let us extend their domain of definition so that they too are continuous over the interval $x_0 - \varepsilon \leq x \leq x^* + \varepsilon$. (This can always be done.)

We now define $\boldsymbol{\theta}$ as

$$\boldsymbol{\theta}(x; \boldsymbol{\xi}) = \boldsymbol{\phi}(x) + \sum_{k=1}^{\sigma} \xi_k \boldsymbol{\zeta}_k(x). \tag{3-87}$$

Evidently $\boldsymbol{\theta}(x; \boldsymbol{\xi})$ is continuous and has continuous partial derivatives with respect to the ξ_k over $x_0 - \varepsilon \leq x \leq x^* + \varepsilon$. Suppose that (3-87) is substituted into (3-86) to yield

$$\begin{aligned} \mathbf{y}' &= \mathbf{\Upsilon}\left(x, \mathbf{y}, \boldsymbol{\phi}(x) + \sum_{k=1}^{\sigma} \xi_k \boldsymbol{\zeta}_k(x)\right) \\ &= \mathbf{\Omega}(x, \mathbf{y}, \boldsymbol{\xi}). \end{aligned} \tag{3-88}$$

Then $\mathbf{\Omega}$ is a continuous function of its arguments when $\mathbf{y}$ is sufficiently close to $\mathbf{z}(x)$ and $|\boldsymbol{\xi}|$ is sufficiently close to 0; and its components possess continuous partial derivatives with respect to $(\mathbf{y}, \boldsymbol{\xi})$. (We do not know and do not need to know whether the components of $\mathbf{\Omega}$ possess continuous partial derivatives with respect to x.)

We next observe that

$$\mathbf{y}' = \mathbf{\Omega}(x, \mathbf{y}, \boldsymbol{\xi}) \tag{3-89}$$

can be viewed as a system of first order differential equations involving parameters $\boldsymbol{\xi}$. We know that this system has a solution $\mathbf{z}(x)$ for $x_0 \leq x \leq x^*$ when $\boldsymbol{\xi} = \mathbf{0}$. From the relevant existence theorem for differential equations (Theorem AIII-3 of Appendix III), we know then that, for any point $(x_-, \mathbf{y}_-)$ with $\mathbf{y}_-$ sufficiently close to $\mathbf{z}(x_-)$, there exists a unique solution to (3-89) for every $\boldsymbol{\xi}$, $|\boldsymbol{\xi}|$ sufficiently close to 0, over an interval $x_0 - \varepsilon_1 \leq x \leq x^* + \varepsilon_1$, $\varepsilon_1 > 0$. The σ-parameter set of solutions through $(x_-, \mathbf{y}_-)$ will be denoted by

$$\mathbf{y} = \mathbf{Y}(x, x_-, \mathbf{y}_-, \boldsymbol{\xi}). \tag{3-90}$$

Furthermore, the components of $\mathbf{Y}$ and $\mathbf{Y}'$ are continuous and have continuous partial derivatives with respect to $(\mathbf{y}_-, \boldsymbol{\xi})$.

In particular, if $|\boldsymbol{\xi}|$ is sufficiently close to 0, we can take $x_- = x_0$ and $\mathbf{y}_- = \mathbf{y}_0 + \Sigma_{k=1}^{\sigma}\xi_k\boldsymbol{\eta}_k(x_0)$. Let us denote the solution so obtained $\mathbf{y}^{(1)}(x; \boldsymbol{\xi})$, i.e.

$$\mathbf{y} = \mathbf{Y}\left(x; x_0, \mathbf{y}_0 + \sum_{k=1}^{\sigma} \xi_k\boldsymbol{\eta}_k(x_0), \boldsymbol{\xi}\right) = \mathbf{y}^{(1)}(x; \boldsymbol{\xi}). \tag{3-91}$$

Not only does $\mathbf{y}^{(1)}(x; \boldsymbol{\xi})$ satisfy (3-89); from the manner in which (3-89) was obtained, $\mathbf{y}^{(1)}(x; \boldsymbol{\xi})$ also satisfies (3-85), with $\boldsymbol{\theta}$ given by (3-87), and thus in particular satisfies the constraint $G^i = 0$, $i = 1, \ldots, r$ for $x_0 - \varepsilon_1 \leq x \leq x^* + \varepsilon_1$. Furthermore $\mathbf{y}^{(1)}(x_0; \boldsymbol{\xi}) = \mathbf{y}_0 + \Sigma_{k=1}^{\sigma}\xi_k\boldsymbol{\eta}_k(x_0)$. Since $\mathbf{y}_1(x; \boldsymbol{\xi})$ satisfies both $G^i = 0$, $i = 1, \ldots, r$ and $G^i = \phi_i + \Sigma_{k=1}^{\sigma}\xi_k\zeta_{ik}$, $i = r + 1, \ldots, n$ for all $\boldsymbol{\xi}$ with $|\boldsymbol{\xi}|$ sufficiently small, it must be true that at $\boldsymbol{\xi} = \mathbf{0}$

$$\begin{aligned} \frac{\partial G^i}{\partial \xi_k} &= \mathbf{G}_{\mathbf{y}'} \cdot \mathbf{y}'_{\xi_k} + \mathbf{G}_{\mathbf{y}} \cdot \mathbf{y}_{\xi_k} = 0, \quad i = 1, \ldots, r \\ \frac{\partial G^i}{\partial \xi_k} &= \mathbf{G}_{\mathbf{y}'} \cdot \mathbf{y}'_{\xi_k} + \mathbf{G}_{\mathbf{y}} \cdot \mathbf{y}_{\xi_k} = \zeta_{ik}(x), \quad i = r + 1, \ldots, n \end{aligned} \tag{3-92}$$

where the partial derivatives of the G^i are evaluated along $\mathbf{z}(x)$, since $\mathbf{y}^{(1)}(x; \mathbf{0}) = \mathbf{z}(x)$. Now at x_0, $\mathbf{y}_{\xi_k}^{(1)}(x_0) = \boldsymbol{\eta}_k(x_0)$, from the way in which the initial point was chosen. Let us next compare (3-92) and (3-84). We see that $\boldsymbol{\eta}_k(x)$ is a solution to (3-92). There exists only one solution to (3-84) or (3-92) the initial value of which at x_0 is $\boldsymbol{\eta}_k(x_0)$. Thus $\mathbf{y}_{\xi_k}^{(1)}(x; \mathbf{0}) = \boldsymbol{\eta}_k(x)$. Furthermore, $\mathbf{y}^{(1)}(x; \boldsymbol{\xi})$ has continuous first partial derivatives with respect to $\boldsymbol{\xi}$, for (3-90) has continuous partial derivatives with respect to $(\mathbf{y}_-, \boldsymbol{\xi})$. On substituting $\mathbf{y}^{(1)}$ into (3-89) we see that $(\mathbf{y}^{(1)})'$ also has continuous partial derivatives with respect to $\boldsymbol{\xi}$. Thus a family of the type required by the lemma has been constructed for the interval $x_0 - \varepsilon_1 \leq x \leq x^* + \varepsilon_1$.

The same argument may be applied to x^{**}, the next corner (after x^*) of $\mathbf{z}(x)$ or of one of the $\boldsymbol{\eta}_k(x)$. If $x_- = x^*$ and $\mathbf{y}_- = \mathbf{y}^{(1)}(x^*; \boldsymbol{\xi})$ then, from (3-90), $\mathbf{y} = \mathbf{Y}(x, x^*, \mathbf{y}^{(1)}(x^*; \boldsymbol{\xi}), \boldsymbol{\xi})$ is a solution to (3-85), with $\boldsymbol{\theta}$ given by (3-87) over the interval $x^* - \varepsilon_2 \leq x \leq x^{**} + \varepsilon_2$. Let us call this solution $y^{(2)}(x; \boldsymbol{\xi})$. Furthermore, at x^*, $\mathbf{y}^{(2)}(x^*; \boldsymbol{\xi}) = \mathbf{y}^{(1)}(x^*; \boldsymbol{\xi})$ and $\mathbf{y}^{(2)}_{\xi_k}(x^*; \mathbf{0})$ is equal to $\mathbf{y}^{(2)}_{\xi_k}(x^*; \mathbf{0}) = \boldsymbol{\eta}_k(x^*)$. Finally, $\mathbf{y}^{(2)}_{\xi_k}(x; \mathbf{0}) = \boldsymbol{\eta}_k(x)$ over this interval. And so on, for the remaining intervals.

In this way we generate a sequence of solutions $\mathbf{y}^{(v)}(x; \boldsymbol{\xi})$ with the property that the end point of the last solution interval is $x_1 + \varepsilon_\rho$. If we write

$$\mathbf{y}(x; \boldsymbol{\xi}) = \begin{cases} \mathbf{y}^{(1)}(x; \boldsymbol{\xi}), & x_0 - \boldsymbol{\xi} \cdot \boldsymbol{\Delta}_0 \leq x \leq x^* \\ \mathbf{y}^{(2)}(x; \boldsymbol{\xi}), & x^* \leq x \leq x^{**} \\ \vdots & \\ \mathbf{y}^{(\rho)}(x; \boldsymbol{\xi}), & x^{**} \cdots \leq x \leq x_1 + \boldsymbol{\xi} \cdot \boldsymbol{\Delta}_1 \end{cases} \tag{3-93}$$

then, for all $\boldsymbol{\xi}$ with $|\boldsymbol{\xi}|$ sufficiently small, each of the functions satisfies $G^i = 0$, $i = 1, \ldots, r$ over the interval $x_0 - \boldsymbol{\xi} \cdot \boldsymbol{\Delta}_0 \leq x \leq x_1 + \boldsymbol{\xi} \cdot \boldsymbol{\Delta}_1$ and $\mathbf{y}_{\xi_k}(x; \mathbf{0}) = \boldsymbol{\eta}_k(x)$. Also, $\mathbf{y}$ and $\mathbf{y}'$ have continuous first partial derivatives with respect to $\boldsymbol{\xi}$, except possibly at corners of $\mathbf{z}(x)$ and the $\boldsymbol{\eta}_k(x)$. This is what we wished to prove.

In our earlier simplified treatment of the multiplier rule we required that the square matrix $||\partial G^i/\partial y_j'||$, $j = 1, \ldots, r$ have rank r along $\mathbf{z}(x)$. The assumption is unnecessarily restrictive. We now introduce a slightly modified approach to the multipliers. We shall prove the following lemma:

Lemma. Determination of Multipliers. For any arbitrarily selected constants λ_0 and γ_j, $j = 1, \ldots, n$, the equation

$$\mathbf{H}^*_{\mathbf{y}'}(x, \mathbf{z}(x), \mathbf{z}'(x)) = \int_{x_0}^{x} \mathbf{H}^*_{\mathbf{y}}(x, \mathbf{z}(\tau), \mathbf{z}'(\tau))d\tau + \boldsymbol{\gamma} \tag{3-94}$$

uniquely determines a set of multipliers $\lambda_i(x)$, $i = 1, \ldots, n$ which are continuous except possibly at corners of $\mathbf{z}(x)$, where they possess right and left hand limits, when H^* is defined as

$$H^* = \lambda_0 F + \sum_{i=1}^{n} \lambda_i(x) G^i.$$

Notice that H^* is not what we have previously called the Hamiltonian since there are included the $n - r$ new differential equation constraints $G^i = \phi^i$ which we added at the beginning of the section.

To prove the lemma, let us first introduce new variables

$$\mathbf{s}(x) = \mathbf{H}^*_{\mathbf{y}'}(x, \mathbf{z}(x), \mathbf{z}'(x)) = \lambda_0 \mathbf{F}_{\mathbf{y}'}(x, \mathbf{z}(x), \mathbf{z}'(x)) + \sum_{i=1}^{n} \lambda_i(x) \mathbf{G}^i_{\mathbf{y}'}(x, \mathbf{z}(x), \mathbf{z}'(x)). \tag{3-95}$$

We next recall that the nth order matrix $||G^i_{y_j'}||$ has rank n for each x along $\mathbf{z}(x)$. Thus if we think of (3-95) as a system of linear equations in the variables $\lambda_i(x)$, we can solve them uniquely for $\boldsymbol{\lambda}$ at each x, obtaining

$$\boldsymbol{\lambda}(x) = \mathbf{Q}(x)\mathbf{s}(x) + \mathbf{r}(x)\lambda_0. \tag{3-96}$$

Now $\mathbf{H}^*_{\mathbf{y}}$ can be written

$$\mathbf{H}^*_{\mathbf{y}} = \lambda_0 \mathbf{F}_{\mathbf{y}} + \mathbf{D}(x)\boldsymbol{\lambda}(x) \tag{3-97}$$

where $\mathbf{D}(x)$ is a matrix the ith column of which is $\mathbf{G}^i_{\mathbf{y}}$. On applying (3-96) to (3-97), we obtain

$$\begin{aligned} \mathbf{H}^*_{\mathbf{y}} &= [\mathbf{F}_{\mathbf{y}} + \mathbf{D}(x)\mathbf{r}(x)]\lambda_0 + \mathbf{D}(x)\mathbf{Q}(x)\mathbf{s}(x) \\ &= \mathbf{g}(x)\lambda_0 + \mathbf{A}(x)\mathbf{s}(x). \end{aligned} \tag{3-98}$$

The vector $\mathbf{g}$ and the nth order matrix $\mathbf{A}$ have elements which are continuous except possibly at corners of $\mathbf{z}(x)$.

We can now see that the equivalent of (3-94) in terms of the new variables is

$$\mathbf{s}(x) = \int_{x_0}^{x} [\mathbf{g}(x)\lambda_0 + \mathbf{A}(x)\mathbf{s}(x)]dx + \boldsymbol{\gamma}. \tag{3-99}$$

If it can be shown that there is a unique $\mathbf{s}(x)$ satisfying (3-99), then (3-96) must determine a unique $\boldsymbol{\lambda}(x)$ satisfying (3-94). Equation (3-99) shows that the components of $\mathbf{s}(x)$ must be continuous. Notice next that if we can determine a continuous function $\mathbf{s}(x)$ which satisfies the set of linear differential equations

$$\frac{d\mathbf{s}}{dx} = \mathbf{A}(x)\mathbf{s}(x) + \mathbf{g}(x)\lambda_0 \tag{3-100}$$

and such that $\mathbf{s}(x_0) = \boldsymbol{\gamma}$, then (3-99) will hold.

The basic existence theorem for linear differential equations (Theorem AIII-2 of Appendix III) guarantees that we can generate such a solution.

There is a unique continuous solution with $\mathbf{s}(x_0) = \boldsymbol{\gamma}$ over the interval x_0 to x^*, x^* being the first corner of $\mathbf{z}(x)$. Let $\mathbf{s}^*$ be the value of $\mathbf{s}$ at x^*. Then there is a unique solution with $\mathbf{s}(x^*) = \mathbf{s}^*$ over the interval x^* to x^{**}, x^{**} being the next corner of $\mathbf{z}(x)$, and so on. Thus for any λ_0 and $\boldsymbol{\gamma}$ there is a unique continuous $\mathbf{s}(x)$ which satisfies (3-99), and hence a unique $\boldsymbol{\lambda}(x)$ which is continuous, except possibly at the corners of $\mathbf{z}(x)$, and which satisfies (3-94). (That $\boldsymbol{\lambda}(x)$ may be discontinuous at the corners of $\mathbf{z}(x)$ follows from the fact that $\mathbf{Q}(x)$ and/or $\mathbf{r}(x)$ in (3-96) may have discontinuous components.) Both $\mathbf{Q}(x)$ and $\mathbf{r}(x)$, and hence $\boldsymbol{\lambda}(x)$, have right and left side limits at corners $\mathbf{z}(x)$. This proves the lemma.

We can also observe, from the existence theorem for linear differential equations, that if there is any x, say x_v, for which $\mathbf{s}(x_v) = \mathbf{0}$ and $\lambda_0 = 0$ then $\mathbf{s}(x) \equiv \mathbf{0}$ and there is no x for which $(\lambda_0, \mathbf{s}(x)) = \mathbf{0}$ unless $(\lambda_0, \mathbf{s}(x)) \equiv \mathbf{0}$. From (3-95) we see that then there can be no x for which $(\lambda_0, \boldsymbol{\lambda}(x)) = \mathbf{0}$ unless $\boldsymbol{\lambda}(x) \equiv \mathbf{0}$, $\lambda_0 = 0$.

3.9. The comparison functions

We are now ready to derive rigorously and in detail the necessary conditions. The approach will be that introduced by McShane [26] in 1940. We wish to establish not only the multiplier rule but also the Weierstrass and Legendre conditions. For this purpose we make use of a class of comparison functions rather similar to those introduced in Section 2.15. If we were interested only in deriving the multiplier rule, the argument could be considerably simplified (as we ask the reader to show in the problems). To obtain also the Weierstrass and Legendre conditions complicates matters considerably.

In the previous section we constructed a set of solutions $\mathbf{y}(x; \boldsymbol{\xi})$ to $G^i = 0$, $i = 1, \ldots, r$ using a specified set of admissible variations $\boldsymbol{\eta}_k(x)$, $k = 1, \ldots, \sigma$. These functions will be used in the present section to construct a more complicated set of solutions to the differential equation constraints. Let X be any value of x which is not an end point or corner of $\mathbf{z}(x)$. We now construct a new set of solutions to $G^i = 0$, $i = 1, \ldots, r$ over a short interval $X - d$ to X, $d \geq 0$. We first select an arbitrary vector $\mathbf{p}'$ which is different from $\mathbf{z}'(X)$ and which has the properties that: (1) $(X, \mathbf{z}(X), \mathbf{p}') \in \mathscr{R}$, so that the rank of the $r \times n$ matrix $\|\partial G^i/\partial y_j'\|$ at $(X, \mathbf{z}(X), \mathbf{p}')$ is r and (2) $G^i(X, \mathbf{z}(X), \mathbf{p}') = 0$, $i = 1, \ldots, r$. (It will be recalled that $\mathscr{R}$ is the manifold formed by the intersection of the r hypersurfaces (3-24).) Next we add to the functions G^i, $n - r$ linear functions $\bar{G}^i(\mathbf{y}')$ chosen so that the rank of the Jacobian matrix of the G^i and $\bar{G}^i$ with respect to $\mathbf{y}'$ is n at $(X, \mathbf{z}(X), \mathbf{p}')$.

Let $\delta_i = \bar{G}^i(\mathbf{p}')$, $i = r + 1, \ldots, n$. Consider now the set of equations

$$\begin{aligned} G^i(x, \mathbf{y}, \mathbf{y}') &= 0, \quad i = 1, \ldots, r \\ \bar{G}^i(\mathbf{y}') - \delta_i &= 0, \quad i = r + 1, \ldots, n \end{aligned} \tag{3-101}$$

in the variables $(x, \mathbf{y}, \mathbf{y}')$. Then $(X, \mathbf{z}(X), \mathbf{p}')$ is a solution to (3-101); and, from the rank condition given above and the first implicit function theorem of Appendix II we know that there exists a unique function

$$\mathbf{y}' = \mathbf{\Theta}(x, \mathbf{y}) \tag{3-102}$$

which is defined in a neighborhood of $(X, \mathbf{z}(X), \mathbf{p}')$, which is continuous and the components of which have continuous first partial derivatives with respect to $(x, \mathbf{y})$. Equation (3-102) can be viewed as a system of first order differential equations in normal form. From the basic existence theorem (Theorem AIII-1 of Appendix III) we know that for any initial point $(x_-, \mathbf{y}_-)$ which is sufficiently close to $(X, \mathbf{z}(X))$ but otherwise arbitrary there exists a solution defined over some finite (perhaps very short) interval. Let us choose as the initial point $(X, \mathbf{y}(X; \xi))$, where $\mathbf{y}(x; \xi)$ is one of the solutions constructed in the previous section. When $|\xi|$ is sufficiently close to 0, this point will be in the required neighborhood. We denote the resulting solution by $\mathbf{Y}(x; \xi)$. There exists such a solution for each ξ, and if d is chosen small enough it will exist on the interval $X - d \leq x \leq X$. Furthermore, $\mathbf{Y}(X; \xi) = \mathbf{y}(X; \xi)$ so that there is no discontinuity between these solutions at X.

We can accept $\mathbf{y}(x; \xi)$ as a solution in the interval $X \leq x \leq x_1(\xi)$ and $\mathbf{Y}(x; \xi)$ in the interval $X - d \leq x \leq X$. We now construct a third solution, which will be denoted by $\bar{\mathbf{y}}(x; \xi)$ and which has as domain the interval $x_0(\xi) \leq x \leq X - d$. Consider the $n - r$ new functions G^i introduced in the previous section, and let $\delta_i(x, \xi) = G^i(x, \mathbf{y}(x; \xi), \mathbf{y}'(x; \xi))$, $\mathbf{y}(x; \xi)$ again referring to the solutions constructed in the previous section. The system of equations

$$\begin{aligned} G^i(x, \mathbf{y}, \mathbf{y}') &= 0, & i &= 1, \ldots, r \\ G^i(x, \mathbf{y}, \mathbf{y}') &= \delta_i(x, \xi), & i &= r + 1, \ldots, n \end{aligned} \tag{3-103}$$

has the solution $\mathbf{y}(x; \xi)$. Consequently, applying the second implicit function theorem and the existence theorem AIII-3, it is possible to obtain a solution $\bar{\mathbf{y}}(x; \xi, d)$ to (3-103) (and hence to $G^i = 0$, $i = 1, \ldots, r$), defined for $x_0(\xi) \leq x \leq x_1(\xi)$ and with the property that $\bar{\mathbf{y}}(X - d; \xi, d) = \mathbf{Y}(X - d; \xi)$. This can be done for all ξ, $|\xi|$ sufficiently small.

Consider now the set of solutions

$$\mathbf{y}(x;\xi,d) = \begin{cases} \bar{\mathbf{y}}(x;\xi,d), & x_0(\xi) \le x \le X - d \\ \mathbf{Y}(x;\xi), & X - d \le x \le X \\ \mathbf{y}(x;\xi), & X \le x \le x_1(\xi) \end{cases} \tag{3-104}$$

to $G^i = 0$, $i = 1, \ldots, r$. It is characteristic of these solutions that in the interval $X - d \le x \le X$ the slopes of the components of $\mathbf{y}(x;\xi,d)$ can be quite different from the slopes of the corresponding components of $\mathbf{z}(x)$. This fact is not needed in the development of the multiplier rule, but it is required in the derivation of the Weierstrass condition. The situation is illustrated graphically by Figure 3.4. We note that by the same procedure

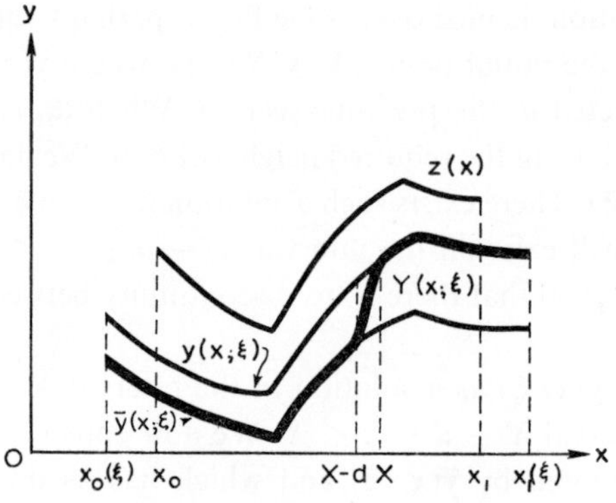

Fig. 3.4.

one can insert an arbitrary number of special intervals $X_l - d_l \le x \le X_l$. One simply starts with the largest X_l and then progressively works towards smaller values of x. The solutions $\mathbf{y}(x;\xi,\mathbf{d})$ so obtained must be continuous and possess continuous first partial derivatives with respect to $(\xi, \mathbf{d})$ in a neighborhood of $\mathbf{0}$, $\mathbf{d}$ being restricted to non-negative components.

Let us denote $J[\mathbf{y}(x;\xi,\mathbf{d})]$ by $\Phi(\xi,\mathbf{d})$ and define $\boldsymbol{\eta}_l(x) = \mathbf{y}_{d_l+}(x;\mathbf{0},\mathbf{0})$, the latter expression being a right side derivative. Then $\mathbf{y}'_{d_l+}(x;\mathbf{0},\mathbf{0}) = \boldsymbol{\eta}'_l(x)$. Now suppose that we set equal to zero both ξ and all components of $\mathbf{d}$ except d_l. Then

$$\Phi(\mathbf{0}, d_l\mathbf{e}_l) = \int_{x_0}^{X_l - d_l} F(x, \bar{\mathbf{y}}, \bar{\mathbf{y}}')\mathrm{d}x + \int_{X_l - d_l}^{X_l} F(x, \mathbf{Y}, \mathbf{Y}')\mathrm{d}x$$

$$+ \int_{X_l}^{x_1} F(x, \mathbf{y}, \mathbf{y}')\mathrm{d}x. \tag{3-105}$$

For small positive d_l, Φ possesses a partial derivative with respect to d_l; and, at $d_l = 0$, Φ possesses a right side derivative. Moreover the third integral in (3-105) does not involve d_l, and the integrand of the second integral is independent of d_l. Hence, applying (2-175),

$$\frac{\partial}{\partial d_l +} \Phi(\mathbf{0}, \mathbf{0}) = - F(X_l, \mathbf{z}(X_l), \mathbf{z}'(X_l))$$

$$+ \int_{x_0}^{X_l} [\mathbf{F}_{\mathbf{y}}(x, \mathbf{z}, \mathbf{z}') \cdot \boldsymbol{\eta}_l(x) + \mathbf{F}_{\mathbf{y}'}(x, \mathbf{z}, \mathbf{z}') \cdot \boldsymbol{\eta}_l'(x)]\mathrm{d}x$$

$$+ F(X_l, \mathbf{z}(X_l), \mathbf{p}'). \tag{3-106}$$

The appearance of $\mathbf{p}'$ in the last term of (3-106) may need explanation. For a specific positive value of d_l, the derivative of the second term in (3-105) is $F(X_l - d_l, \mathbf{Y}, \mathbf{Y}')$. In the limit, as $d_l \to 0+$, $\mathbf{Y} \to \mathbf{z}$. However $\mathbf{Y}'$ approaches $\mathbf{Y}'_-(X_l; \mathbf{0}, \mathbf{0})$, which is not equal to $\mathbf{z}'$. On the other hand, $(X_l, \mathbf{z}, \mathbf{Y}'_-)$ must be a solution to (3-101); and we know that $(X_l, \mathbf{z}, \mathbf{p}')$ is a solution to that system of equations; hence, by the implicit function theorem, the only solution, given X_l and $\mathbf{z}$, is one with $\mathbf{Y}' = \mathbf{p}'$. Thus $\mathbf{Y}_-(X_l, \mathbf{0}, \mathbf{0}) = \mathbf{p}'$.

We next determine those equations, similar to (3-84), which must be satisfied by the $\boldsymbol{\eta}_l(x)$ over the interval $x_0 \leq x \leq X_l$. The required equations are obtained from (3-84) by setting $\zeta_{il}(x) \equiv 0$ since $\bar{\mathbf{y}}$ satisfies all equations in (3-103) for all d_l sufficiently small. Let us recall now that in the preceding section we have shown that, for arbitrary λ_0 and γ_u, the n equations (3-94) determine a unique set of functions $\lambda_i(x)$ which are continuous except possibly at corners of $\mathbf{z}(x)$. Let us now multiply equation i of (3-84) by $\lambda_i(x)$ and sum over i, then add the result to λ_0 times (3-106). After integration by parts, using the right hand side of (3-94) as a primitive function for the left hand side, we obtain

$$\lambda_0 \frac{\partial}{\partial d_l +} \Phi(\mathbf{0}, \mathbf{0}) = - \lambda_0 F(X_l, \mathbf{z}(X_l), \mathbf{z}'(X_l))$$

$$+ \mathbf{H}^*_{\mathbf{y}'}(X_l, \mathbf{z}(X_l), \mathbf{z}'(X_l)) \cdot \boldsymbol{\eta}_l(x) - \boldsymbol{\gamma} \cdot \boldsymbol{\eta}_l(x_1)$$

$$+ \lambda_0 F(X_l, \mathbf{z}(X_l), \mathbf{p}'). \tag{3-107}$$

Let us next multiply the ith equation of (3-101) by $\lambda_i(x)$ and add over i; then add the result to (3-107). This changes the last term in (3-107) to $H^* - \Sigma_{i=r+1}^{n}\lambda_i(x)\delta_i$. Similarly, let us multiply equation i of (3-103) by $\lambda_i(x)$ and add over i; then add the result to (3-107). This changes the first term to $H^* - \Sigma_{i=r+1}^{n}\lambda_i(x)\delta_i(x;\,\boldsymbol{\xi})$. Thus (3-107) becomes

$$-\,H^*(X_l, \mathbf{z}(X_l), \mathbf{z}'(X_l)) + H^*(X_l, \mathbf{z}(X_l), \mathbf{p}')$$
$$+\,\mathbf{H}^*_{\mathbf{y}'}(X_l, \mathbf{z}(X_l), \mathbf{z}'(X_l)) \cdot \boldsymbol{\eta}_l(x) - \boldsymbol{\gamma} \cdot \boldsymbol{\eta}_l(x_1) + \boldsymbol{\lambda}_T \cdot (\boldsymbol{\delta} - \boldsymbol{\delta}(x;\,\boldsymbol{\xi})) \quad (3\text{-}108)$$

where $\boldsymbol{\lambda}_T$ contains the last $n - r$ components of $\boldsymbol{\lambda}$.

Let us next examine $\boldsymbol{\eta}_l(x) = \bar{\mathbf{y}}_{d_l+}(x;\,\mathbf{0},\,\mathbf{0})$. We recall that $\bar{\mathbf{y}}(X_l - d_l;\,\boldsymbol{\xi},\,d_l) = \mathbf{Y}(X_l - d_l;\,\boldsymbol{\xi})$ for all $d_l \geq 0$. On differentiating with respect to d_l and taking the limit as $d_l \to 0+$, we have

$$-\,\bar{\mathbf{y}}'(X_l;\,\mathbf{0},\,\mathbf{0}) + \boldsymbol{\eta}_l(X_l) = -\,\mathbf{Y}'(X_l;\,\mathbf{0}) \quad (3\text{-}109)$$

or

$$-\,\mathbf{z}'(X_l) + \boldsymbol{\eta}_l(X_l) = -\,\mathbf{p}'. \quad (3\text{-}110)$$

If (3-110) is applied to (3-108), we obtain

$$\lambda_0 \frac{\partial}{\partial d_l+}\,\Phi(\mathbf{0},\,\mathbf{0}) = E^*(X_l, \mathbf{z}(X_l), \mathbf{z}'(X_l), \mathbf{p}') - \boldsymbol{\gamma} \cdot \boldsymbol{\eta}_l(x_1)$$
$$+\,\boldsymbol{\lambda}_T \cdot (\boldsymbol{\delta} - \boldsymbol{\delta}(x;\,\boldsymbol{\xi})) \quad (3\text{-}111)$$

where E^* is the Weierstrass E function (2-169) for H^*.

3.10. The convex polyhedral cone $\mathscr{K}$

Before continuing it will be convenient to introduce a more symmetric notation by writing $d_l = \xi_l$, $l = 1, \ldots, \Theta$. Thus henceforth all variables ($\sigma + \Theta$ of them) will be called ξ variables; and $\mathbf{y}(x;\,\boldsymbol{\xi})$ will take the place of $\mathbf{y}(x;\,\boldsymbol{\xi},\,\mathbf{d})$. In Section 3.8, we indicated that we would seek complete generality by allowing both end points to be variable. Suppose then that the left hand end point must lie in a smooth manifold generated by $S^u(x, \mathbf{y}) = 0$, $u = 1, \ldots, s_1$ and that the right hand end point must lie in a smooth manifold generated by $S^u(x, \mathbf{y}) = 0$, $u = s_1 + 1, \ldots, s_1 + s_2$. Let $s = s_1 + s_2$. Next we define the functions

$$\Omega^0(\boldsymbol{\xi}) = \Phi(\boldsymbol{\xi}) - \Phi(\mathbf{0})$$
$$\Omega^u(\boldsymbol{\xi}) = S^u(x_1(\boldsymbol{\xi}), \mathbf{y}(x_1(\boldsymbol{\xi});\,\boldsymbol{\xi})), \quad u = 1, \ldots, s_1 \quad (3\text{-}112)$$
$$\Omega^u(\boldsymbol{\xi}) = S^u(x_0(\boldsymbol{\xi}), \mathbf{y}(x_0(\boldsymbol{\xi});\,\boldsymbol{\xi})), \quad u = s_1 + 1, \ldots, s.$$

The S^u are defined and possess continuous partial derivatives for all $\boldsymbol{\xi}$, $|\boldsymbol{\xi}|$ sufficiently small, with the last Θ components non-negative. We write

$$\mathbf{a}_u = \boldsymbol{\Omega}^u_{\xi}(\mathbf{0}), \quad u = 0, \ldots, s \tag{3-113}$$

the last Θ components being one sided derivatives, and define $\mathbf{A}$ as the matrix with the $\mathbf{a}_u$ as rows (not columns).

Next we let $\mathscr{K}$ be the convex polyhedral cone generated by the columns of $\mathbf{A}$, that is, $\mathscr{K}$ is the set of points $\mathbf{v} = \mathbf{A}\boldsymbol{\mu}$, $\boldsymbol{\mu} \geq \mathbf{0}$. (See Hadley [16], pp. 219–227, for a discussion of convex cones.) Consider the Euclidean space in which $\mathscr{K}$ lies and write $\mathbf{v} = (v_0, v_1, \ldots, v_s)$. Now $v_0 = \boldsymbol{\Omega}^0_{\xi}(\mathbf{0}) \cdot \boldsymbol{\mu}$. The components of $\boldsymbol{\Omega}^0_{\xi}$ are $\partial\Phi/\partial\xi_j$. Since $\mathbf{z}(x)$ maximizes $J[\mathbf{y}]$, we should expect that a condition similar to $\partial\Phi/\partial\xi_j = 0$, which would hold in the absence of constraints, would also apply here. The precise form of the condition is described in the following lemma.

Lemma. No interior point $\mathbf{v}$ *of* $\mathscr{K}$ *has the form* $(v_0, \mathbf{0})$ *with* $v_0 > 0$.

This lemma will be proved by contradiction. Suppose that $\bar{\mathbf{v}} = (\bar{v}_0, \mathbf{0})$ is an interior point of $\mathscr{K}$ and that $\bar{v}_0 > 0$. However, $\bar{\mathbf{v}} = \mathbf{A}\bar{\boldsymbol{\mu}}$, $\bar{\boldsymbol{\mu}} \geq \mathbf{0}$. Since $\bar{\mathbf{v}}$ is an interior point, there exists an ε-neighborhood of $\bar{\mathbf{v}}$ containing only points of $\mathscr{K}$. Let $\mathbf{1}$ be the vector each component of which is 1, and τ a positive number. If $\mathbf{v}_1 = \mathbf{A}(\bar{\boldsymbol{\mu}} + \tau\mathbf{1}) = \bar{\mathbf{v}} + \tau\mathbf{A1}$ then $|\mathbf{v}_1 - \bar{\mathbf{v}}| = \tau|\mathbf{A1}|$; and if $\tau < \varepsilon/|\mathbf{A1}|$ then $\mathbf{v}_1$ lies in an ε-neighborhood of $\bar{\mathbf{v}}$ and is in $\mathscr{K}$. This condition is satisfied if $|\mathbf{A1}| \neq 0$, that is, if $\mathbf{A} \neq \mathbf{0}$. We shall see that this must be the case. Then $\mathbf{v}_2 = 2\bar{\mathbf{v}} - \mathbf{v}_1$ also lies in an ε-neighborhood of $\bar{\mathbf{v}}$ and in $\mathscr{K}$. However,

$$\bar{\mathbf{v}} = \tfrac{1}{2}\mathbf{v}_1 + \tfrac{1}{2}\mathbf{v}_2 = \tfrac{1}{2}\mathbf{A}(\boldsymbol{\mu}_1 + \boldsymbol{\mu}_2)$$

and $\boldsymbol{\mu}_1 = \bar{\boldsymbol{\mu}} + \tau\mathbf{1}$, with each component of $\boldsymbol{\mu}_1$ positive. Since each component of $\boldsymbol{\mu}_2$ is non-negative and $\bar{\boldsymbol{\mu}} = (\boldsymbol{\mu}_1 + \boldsymbol{\mu}_2)/2$, each component of $\bar{\boldsymbol{\mu}}$ must be strictly positive.

Consider next the rows of $\mathbf{A}$. Recall that in our earlier discussion of transversality we used one more function $\boldsymbol{\eta}_k$ than there were equations $S^u = 0$. Let us assume now that there are at least $s + 1$ functions $\boldsymbol{\eta}_k$ in total. Denote by m the number of columns in $\mathbf{A}$. Thus $\mathbf{A}$ has at least as many columns as rows. We shall show that the $s + 1$ rows of $\mathbf{A}$ are linearly independent.

Suppose that the rows are linearly dependent. Then there exist numbers v_i not all zero such that $\Sigma v_i\mathbf{a}_i = \mathbf{0}$, i.e., $\mathbf{vA} = \mathbf{0}$, $\mathbf{v} \neq \mathbf{0}$. Consider any point $\mathbf{v} = \mathbf{A}\boldsymbol{\mu}$ in $\mathscr{K}$. If we take the scalar product of $\mathbf{v}$ and $\mathbf{v} = \mathbf{A}\boldsymbol{\mu}$ we obtain $\mathbf{v} \cdot \mathbf{v} = \mathbf{v} \cdot \mathbf{A}\boldsymbol{\mu} = (\mathbf{vA}) \cdot \boldsymbol{\mu} = \mathbf{0}$; thus every point in $\mathscr{K}$ lies on a hyperplane through the origin and is a boundary point. Hence $\mathscr{K}$ cannot have interior points, which contradicts our assumption that there exists at least one interior point. Hence, the rows of $\mathbf{A}$ cannot be linearly dependent and thus the rank of $\mathbf{A}$ is $s + 1$. $\mathbf{A}$ has m columns; hence it is possible to annex $m - s - 1$ additional rows $\mathbf{a}_u$ such that the square matrix so formed has rank m. (The additional rows can be unit vectors if desired–see Hadley [16].) Corresponding to these additional rows we can add Θ linear functions $\mathbf{\Omega}^u(\boldsymbol{\xi}) = \mathbf{a}_u \cdot \boldsymbol{\xi}$, $u = s + 2, \ldots, m$ to (3-112). Evidently the new matrix, say $\mathbf{A}^*$, is non-singular.

We next study the system of (in general nonlinear) equations

$$\mathbf{v} - \mathbf{\Omega}(\boldsymbol{\xi}) = \mathbf{0}, \qquad \mathbf{\Omega} = (\Omega^0, \ldots, \Omega^m) \tag{3-114}$$

where $\mathbf{v}$ and $\mathbf{\Omega}$ now have m components. This system possesses a solution $\boldsymbol{\xi} = \mathbf{0}$, $\mathbf{v} = \mathbf{0}$. Furthermore the Jacobian of $\mathbf{\Omega}(\boldsymbol{\xi})$ at $\boldsymbol{\xi} = \mathbf{0}$ is $\mathbf{A}^*$, which is nonsingular. Thus, by the first implicit function theorem, there exist functions $\boldsymbol{\xi} = \mathbf{\Upsilon}(\mathbf{v})$ which are continuous and have continuous first partial derivatives in a neighborhood of $\mathbf{v} = \mathbf{0}$, which represent solutions to (3-114), and which are such that $\mathbf{\Upsilon}(\mathbf{0}) = \mathbf{0}$.

Let us now return to the point $\bar{\mathbf{v}}$. An additional Θ components may be annexed to $\bar{\mathbf{v}}$ by writing $\bar{v}_u = \mathbf{a}_u \cdot \bar{\boldsymbol{\mu}}$, $u = s + 2, \ldots, m$. Then, from the derivation of $\mathbf{\Upsilon}$, for τ sufficiently small

$$\tau\bar{\mathbf{v}} \equiv \mathbf{\Omega}[\mathbf{\Upsilon}(\tau\bar{\mathbf{v}})]. \tag{3-115}$$

On differentiating with respect to τ and setting $\tau = 0$, we obtain

$$\bar{\mathbf{v}} = \mathbf{A}^* \frac{\mathrm{d}}{\mathrm{d}\tau} \boldsymbol{\xi}(\mathbf{0}). \tag{3-116}$$

However, $\mathbf{A}^*$ is nonsingular and $\bar{\mathbf{v}} = \mathbf{A}^*\bar{\boldsymbol{\mu}}$; hence $\mathrm{d}\boldsymbol{\xi}(\mathbf{0})/\mathrm{d}\tau = \bar{\boldsymbol{\mu}}$ and each component of $\mathrm{d}\boldsymbol{\xi}(\mathbf{0})/\mathrm{d}\tau$ is positive. By continuity, $\mathrm{d}\boldsymbol{\xi}/\mathrm{d}\tau$ has positive components for all arguments $\tau\bar{\mathbf{v}}$, if τ is sufficiently small; and, by Taylor's theorem, $\boldsymbol{\xi}(\tau\bar{\mathbf{v}}) = \tau\mathrm{d}\boldsymbol{\xi}(\theta\tau\bar{\mathbf{v}})/\mathrm{d}\tau > \mathbf{0}$ when $\tau > 0$ and sufficiently close to 0. Thus all components of $\boldsymbol{\xi}(\tau\bar{\mathbf{v}})$ are positive for $\tau > 0$ and sufficiently close to 0. Furthermore, by making τ sufficiently close to 0, $\mathbf{y}(x; \boldsymbol{\xi})$ can be made arbitrarily close to $\mathbf{z}(x)$.

We now recall that $\bar{\mathbf{v}} = v_0\mathbf{e}_1$, where $v_0 > 0$ and $\mathbf{e}_1 = (1, 0, \ldots, 0)$. Thus (3-115) reduces to

$$\begin{aligned} \tau v_0 &= \Omega^0[\boldsymbol{\xi}(\tau\bar{\mathbf{v}})] \\ 0 &= \Omega^u[\boldsymbol{\xi}(\tau\bar{\mathbf{v}})], \quad u = 1, \ldots, m. \end{aligned} \tag{3-117}$$

We recall also that the functions $\mathbf{y}(x; \boldsymbol{\xi})$ were constructed to satisfy the differential equation constraints. Thus when τ is sufficiently close to 0, $\mathbf{y}(x; \boldsymbol{\xi}(\tau\bar{\mathbf{v}}))$ satisfies $G^i = 0$, $i = 1, \ldots, s$. Referring back to (3-112) and to the definition of the $\boldsymbol{\Omega}^u$, however, we see that (3-117) implies that $\mathbf{y}(x; \boldsymbol{\xi}(\tau, \bar{\mathbf{v}}))$ also satisfies the end point conditions and hence is admissible. Furthermore, from the first member of (3-117), bearing in mind that $\tau v_0 > 0$, $\Phi[\boldsymbol{\xi}(\tau\bar{\mathbf{v}})] > \Phi(\mathbf{0})$. However, this is a contradiction, for $\mathbf{z}(x)$ maximizes $J[\mathbf{y}]$ subject to the constraints.

We have restricted our attention thus far to the case where the number of columns m of $\mathbf{A}$ is at least equal to the number of rows. If $m < s + 1$, $r(\mathbf{A}) < s + 1$ and the above proof shows that $\mathscr{K}$ must lie on a hyperplane and cannot have an interior point. Thus the lemma is proved for all values of m.

3.11. The convex cone $\mathscr{K}^*$

The cone $\mathscr{K}$ considered in the previous section was generated for specific functions $\boldsymbol{\eta}_k(x)$ and for specific values of X_l and $\mathbf{p}'_l$. If any or all of these are changed, in general the cone $\mathscr{K}$ will change. Consider now the union of all cones $\mathscr{K}$ which can be generated by all possible choices of the functions $\boldsymbol{\eta}_k$ and all possible choices of X_l and $\mathbf{p}'_l$, and denote by $\mathscr{K}^*$ the closure of this union, that is, the union plus its boundary points. We shall prove the following lemma.

Lemma. The set $\mathscr{K}^*$ is convex.

From the definition of $\mathscr{K}^*$, if $\boldsymbol{\alpha} \in \mathscr{K}^*$ then either $\boldsymbol{\alpha}$ is a member of some cone $\mathscr{K}$ or $\boldsymbol{\alpha}$ is a boundary point of $\mathscr{K}^*$ and every ε-neighborhood of $\boldsymbol{\alpha}$ contains a point $\mathbf{v}$ such that $\mathbf{v}$ is a member of some cone $\mathscr{K}$. Suppose then that $\boldsymbol{\alpha}_1$ and $\boldsymbol{\alpha}_2$ are any two points in $\mathscr{K}^*$. Then there exist points $\mathbf{v}_1$ and $\mathbf{v}_2$ which lie in ε-neighborhoods of $\boldsymbol{\alpha}_1$ and $\boldsymbol{\alpha}_2$ respectively and which are elements of cones $\mathscr{K}_1$ and $\mathscr{K}_2$ respectively. (Note that it is possible that $\boldsymbol{\alpha}_1 = \mathbf{v}_1$ and/or $\boldsymbol{\alpha}_2 = \mathbf{v}_2$.) Let $\boldsymbol{\eta}_{k1}, \boldsymbol{\Delta}_{01}, \boldsymbol{\Delta}_{11}, X_{l1}, \mathbf{p}'_{l1}$ define $\mathscr{K}_1$ and $\boldsymbol{\eta}_{k2}, \boldsymbol{\Delta}_{02}, \boldsymbol{\Delta}_{12}, X_{l2}, \mathbf{p}'_{l1}$ define $\mathscr{K}_2$.

Without loss of generality we may assume that the numbers X_{l1} are different from the numbers X_{l2}. For if two or more were the same we could change by an arbitrarily small amount the corresponding values with subscript 1. Since the $\boldsymbol{\Omega}^u_\xi$ are continuous functions of the X_l, it is possible to make an arbitrarily small change in the components of $\mathbf{A}_1$. Hence if $\mathbf{A}^0_1$ is the new $\mathbf{A}_1$ and if $\mathbf{v}_1 = \mathbf{A}_1\boldsymbol{\mu}_1$, then $\mathbf{v}^0_1 = \mathbf{A}^0_1\boldsymbol{\mu}_1$ lies in an ε-neighborhood of $\boldsymbol{\alpha}_1$ and can be used in place of $\mathbf{v}_1$.

Consider next the cone $\mathscr{K}_3$ defined by $\boldsymbol{\eta}_{k1}, \boldsymbol{\eta}_{k2}, \boldsymbol{\Delta}_{01}, \boldsymbol{\Delta}_{02}, \boldsymbol{\Delta}_{11}, \boldsymbol{\Delta}_{12}, X_{l1}, X_{l2}, \mathbf{p}'_{l_1}$ and $\mathbf{p}'_{l_2}$. The matrix $\mathbf{A}_3$ which generates this cone can be written $\mathbf{A}_3 = (\mathbf{A}_1, \mathbf{A}_2)$ and contains the columns of both $\mathbf{A}_1$ and $\mathbf{A}_2$. Thus $\mathscr{K}_1$ and $\mathscr{K}_2$ are subsets of $\mathscr{K}_3$; hence $\mathbf{v}_1 \in \mathscr{K}_3$ and $\mathbf{v}_2 \in \mathscr{K}_3$. However, $\mathscr{K}_3$ is convex; hence the line segment joining $\mathbf{v}_1$ and $\mathbf{v}_2$ lies in $\mathscr{K}_3$ and $\mathscr{K}^*$.

Let us next examine the line segment joining $\boldsymbol{\alpha}_1$ and $\boldsymbol{\alpha}_2$. Any point $\boldsymbol{\alpha}$ on this line segment can be written $\boldsymbol{\alpha} = \lambda\boldsymbol{\alpha}_2 + (1 - \lambda)\boldsymbol{\alpha}_1, 0 \le \lambda \le 1$, while any point $\mathbf{v}$ on the line segment joining $\mathbf{v}_1$ and $\mathbf{v}_2$ can be written $\mathbf{v} = \lambda\mathbf{v}_2 + (1 - \lambda)\mathbf{v}_1$. For the same value of λ, $|\boldsymbol{\alpha} - \mathbf{v}| = |\lambda(\boldsymbol{\alpha}_2 - \mathbf{v}_2) + (1 - \lambda)(\boldsymbol{\alpha}_1 - \mathbf{v}_1)| \le \varepsilon$; and ε can be made arbitrarily small. It then follows that every point on the line segment joining $\boldsymbol{\alpha}_1$ and $\boldsymbol{\alpha}_2$ lies in $\mathscr{K}^*$. To see this, suppose that $\boldsymbol{\alpha}^*$ is on the line segment but not in $\mathscr{K}^*$. However, from what we have just shown, every ε-neighborhood of $\boldsymbol{\alpha}^*$ contains a point in $\mathscr{K}^*$. This implies that $\boldsymbol{\alpha}^*$ is either an interior or boundary point of $\mathscr{K}^*$. Since $\mathscr{K}^*$ is closed, either conclusion leads to a contradiction. Thus the line segment joining $\boldsymbol{\alpha}_1$ and $\boldsymbol{\alpha}_2$ lies in $\mathscr{K}^*$ and $\mathscr{K}^*$ is convex.

We shall next prove the following lemma.

Lemma. $\mathscr{K}^*$ *contains no interior point of the form* $\mathbf{v} = v_0\mathbf{e}_1, v_0 > 0$.

The proof is by contradiction. Suppose that there is such a point $\bar{\mathbf{v}}$. Since $\bar{\mathbf{v}}$ is an interior point, there is an ε-neighborhood of $\bar{\mathbf{v}}$ in $\mathscr{E}^{s+1}$ which contains only points in $\mathscr{K}^*$. Consider now any simplex (see Hadley [16], p. 209) lying entirely within the ε-neighborhood of $\bar{\mathbf{v}}$ and such that $\mathbf{b}$ is an interior point of the simplex. Let us denote by $\boldsymbol{\alpha}_u$, $u = 1, \ldots, s + 2$, the $s + 2$ extreme points of the simplex. Then arbitrarily close to each $\boldsymbol{\alpha}_u$ is a point $\mathbf{v}_u$ which lies in a cone $\mathscr{K}_u$ generated by the quantities $\boldsymbol{\eta}_{ku}$ etc. The $\mathbf{v}_u$ can be chosen sufficiently close to the $\boldsymbol{\alpha}_u$ that the $\mathbf{v}_u$ generate a simplex containing $\bar{\mathbf{v}}$ in its interior. Let us next consider the cone $\mathscr{K}_+$ generated by all the $\boldsymbol{\eta}_{ku}$ etc. combined. Then each $\mathscr{K}_u \subset \mathscr{K}_+$; hence the convex cone $\mathscr{K}_+$ contains each $\mathbf{v}_u$ and hence the convex hull of these points, i.e. the simplex generated by the $\mathbf{v}_u$. Thus $\bar{\mathbf{v}}$ is an interior point of $\mathscr{K}_+$. This, however, contradicts the lemma of the previous section. Therefore we have proved the lemma under consideration.

The lemma shows that there are points in $\mathscr{E}^{s+1}$ not in $\mathscr{K}^*$. Thus $\mathscr{K}^*$ contains at least one boundary point. Let $\mathbf{v}_b$ be any boundary point of $\mathscr{K}^*$. Then $\mathscr{K}^*$ has a supporting hyperplane (see Hadley [16], p. 212) at $\mathbf{v}_b$. If $\mathbf{c} \cdot \mathbf{v} = \beta$ is the equation of this hyperplane, $\mathbf{c}$ can be chosen so that $\mathbf{c} \cdot \mathbf{v} \ge \beta$ for $\mathbf{v} \in \mathscr{K}^*$. Also, of course, $\mathbf{c} \cdot \mathbf{v}_b = \beta$. We can now show that $\beta = 0$, so that this supporting hyperplane passes through the origin. This follows at once if $\mathbf{v}_b = \mathbf{0}$. Suppose that $\mathbf{v}_b \neq \mathbf{0}$. Clearly $\mathbf{0} \in \mathscr{K}^*$ since $\mathbf{0}$ is in each $\mathscr{K}$. We now show that $2\mathbf{v}_b \in \mathscr{K}^*$. To this end, we note that every neighborhood of $\mathbf{v}_b$ contains a point $\mathbf{v}$ which lies in a cone $\mathscr{K}$. Since $\mathscr{K}$ is a cone, $2\mathbf{v} \in \mathscr{K}$ and hence in $\mathscr{K}^*$. Also, $|2\mathbf{v}_b - 2\mathbf{v}| = 2|\mathbf{v}_b - \mathbf{v}|$, so that $2\mathbf{v}$ lies in an ε-neighborhood of $2\mathbf{v}_b$ if $\mathbf{v}$ lies in an $(\varepsilon/2)$-neighborhood of $\mathbf{v}_b$. Thus every ε-neighborhood of $2\mathbf{v}_b$ contains points in $\mathscr{K}^*$; and $2\mathbf{v}_b$ is either an interior or boundary point of $\mathscr{K}^*$, and hence is in $\mathscr{K}^*$. (We note in passing that the same argument shows that if $\mathbf{v}_\alpha \in \mathscr{K}^*$ then so is $\tau\mathbf{v}_\alpha$, $\tau \geq 0$, and this in turn shows that $\mathscr{K}^*$ is a cone.) Since both $\mathbf{0}$ and $2\mathbf{v}_a$ are in $\mathscr{K}^*$, we have $\mathbf{c} \cdot \mathbf{0} = 0 \geq \beta$. Also $2\mathbf{c} \cdot \mathbf{v}_b \geq \beta$ and $\mathbf{c} \cdot \mathbf{v}_b = \beta$, so that $2\beta \geq \beta$ or $\beta \geq 0$. Since we know already that $\beta \leq 0$, we may conclude that $\beta = 0$.

Let us denote the first component of $\mathbf{c}$ by λ_0. We next prove that it is possible to choose $\mathbf{c}$, a normal vector for the supporting hyperplane, so that $\lambda_0 \geq 0$. This is accomplished by choosing an appropriate boundary point of $\mathscr{K}^*$. If $\mathbf{e}_1$ is a boundary point of $\mathscr{K}^*$, we use the supporting hyperplane at $\mathbf{e}_1$. Then $\mathbf{c} \cdot \mathbf{e}_1 = \lambda_0 = 0$. Suppose that $\mathbf{e}_1$ is not a boundary point of $\mathscr{K}^*$. From the above lemma, $\mathbf{e}_1$ is not an element of $\mathscr{K}^*$. Hence, from the theorem of the separating hyperplane (see Hadley [16], p. 212), there exists a supporting hyperplane $\mathbf{c} \cdot \mathbf{v} = \beta$ at some boundary point of $\mathscr{K}^*$ (that closest to $\mathbf{e}_1$) such that $\mathbf{c} \cdot \mathbf{v} \leq \beta$ for every $\mathbf{v} \in \mathscr{K}^*$ and $\mathbf{c} \cdot \mathbf{e}_1 > \beta$ for the point $\mathbf{e}_1$. The above analysis shows that $\beta = 0$ and hence that $\lambda_0 > 0$. Without loss of generality, λ_0 can be chosen to be 1 in this case. (If $\mathbf{c}$ is a normal to the hyperplane then so is $\tau\mathbf{c}$, $\tau > 0$.) Note also that $\mathbf{c} \neq \mathbf{0}$ (from the definition of a normal to a hyperplane). Furthermore if $\mathbf{v} = \mathbf{A}\boldsymbol{\mu}$, $\boldsymbol{\mu} \geq \mathbf{0}$, then $\mathbf{v} \in \mathscr{K}^*$ and $(\mathbf{cA}) \cdot \boldsymbol{\mu} \leq 0$. Thus we have proved the following theorem.

Theorem 3.11.1. There exists a non-null vector $\mathbf{c}$ *with its first component* λ_0 *non-negative and such that, for every finite set of values* X_l, $\mathbf{p}_l'$ *with* $(X_l, \mathbf{z}(X_l), \mathbf{p}_l') \in \mathscr{R}$ *and* X_l *not a corner or end point of* $\mathbf{z}(x)$, *and for every finite set of admissible variations* $\boldsymbol{\eta}_k$ *(and for arbitrarily chosen* Δ_0, Δ_1*),* $(\mathbf{cA}) \cdot \boldsymbol{\mu} \leq 0$ *whenever* $\boldsymbol{\mu} \geq \mathbf{0}$, *the* u*th row of* $\mathbf{A}$ *being* $\boldsymbol{\Omega}_\xi^u(\mathbf{0})$.

3.12. The multiplier rule and the Weierstrass and Legendre necessary conditions

We are at last in a position to prove the results which we originally set out to prove. Suppose first of all that there are no special intervals $X_l - d_l$ to X_l. Suppose also that there is only one admissible variation $\boldsymbol{\eta}(x)$ and an arbitrarily specified pair of numbers Δ_0 and Δ_1. Then $\mathbf{A}$ has just one column and, if $\mathbf{c} = (\lambda_0, \boldsymbol{\rho})$, $(\mathbf{cA}) \cdot \boldsymbol{\mu} \leq 0$ becomes

$$\lambda_0 \Phi_\xi(0) + \sum_{u=1}^{s} \rho_u \Omega_\xi^u(0) \leq 0 \tag{3-118}$$

since $\boldsymbol{\mu}$ is here a non-negative scalar. Now $-\boldsymbol{\eta}(x)$ is admissible and $-\Delta_0$ and $-\Delta_1$ can be used in place of Δ_0 and Δ_1. Thus we obtain a matrix $\mathbf{A}$ which is the negative of the above matrix; therefore (3-118) must also hold with the sign reversed. Consequently,

$$\lambda_0 \Phi_\xi(0) + \sum_{u=1}^{s} \rho_u \Omega_\xi^u(0) = 0. \tag{3-119}$$

We now introduce certain transformations which will ease the derivation of the multiplier rule. We recall that $\boldsymbol{\eta}(x)$ satisfies (3-84); and that for an arbitrary $\boldsymbol{\gamma}$ it is possible, using the λ_0 determined above, to determine uniquely n functions $\lambda_u(x)$ which satisfy (3-94). Let us multiply equation u of (3-84) by the $\lambda_u(x)$ so determined, add the equations, and integrate from x_0 to x_1. The value of the integral is 0; hence it may be added to $\lambda_0 \Phi_\xi(0)$ without changing the value of that expression. Thus

$$\lambda_0 \Phi_\xi(0) = \int_{x_0}^{x_1} \left[\mathbf{H}^*_{\mathbf{y}'} \cdot \boldsymbol{\eta}' + \mathbf{H}^*_{\mathbf{y}} \cdot \boldsymbol{\eta} - \sum_{u=r+1}^{n} \lambda_u \zeta_u \right] dx$$
$$+ \lambda_0 F(x_1, \mathbf{z}(x_1), \mathbf{z}'(x_1))\Delta_1 - \lambda_0 F(x_0, \mathbf{z}(x_0), \mathbf{z}'(x_0))\Delta_0. \tag{3-120}$$

We now integrate by parts, apply the Euler equations and corner conditions implied by (3-94), and note that since $G^i = 0$, $i = 1, \ldots, r$ at x_0 and x_1 it follows that $\lambda_0 F = H$ (not H^*). We obtain

$$\lambda_0 \Phi'(0) = - \int_{x_0}^{x_1} \sum_{u=r+1}^{n} \lambda_u \zeta_u dx + \mathbf{H}^*_{\mathbf{y}'}(x_1, \mathbf{z}(x_1), \mathbf{z}'(x_1)) \cdot \boldsymbol{\eta}(x_1)$$
$$- \boldsymbol{\gamma} \cdot \boldsymbol{\eta}(x_0) + H(x_1, \mathbf{z}(x_1), \mathbf{z}'(x_1))\Delta_1 - H(x_0, \mathbf{z}(x_0), \mathbf{z}'(x_0))\Delta_0 \tag{3-121}$$

where at x_1, the right hand side of (3-94) is taken to be $\mathbf{H}^*_{y'}$ while at x_0 it is taken to be $\boldsymbol{\gamma}$ (not $\mathbf{H}^*_{y'}$).

We recall next that $\Omega_\xi^u(0)$ is given by (3-54), evaluated at x_1 for $u = 1, \ldots, s_1$ and at x_0 for $u = s_1 + 1, \ldots, s$. If then we apply (3-121) and (3-54) to (3-119), we obtain

$$-\int_{x_0}^{x_1} \sum_{u=r+1}^{n} \lambda_u \zeta_u dx + \left[\mathbf{H}^*_{\mathbf{y}'}(x_1, \mathbf{z}(x_1), \mathbf{z}'(x_1) + \sum_{u=1}^{s_1} \rho_u \mathbf{S}^u_{\mathbf{y}}(x_1, \mathbf{z}(x_1))\right] \cdot \boldsymbol{\eta}(x_1)$$

$$+ \left[-\boldsymbol{\gamma} + \sum_{u=s_1+1}^{s} \rho_u \mathbf{S}^u_{\mathbf{y}}(x_0, \mathbf{z}(x_0))\right] \cdot \boldsymbol{\eta}(x_0)$$

$$+ \left[H(x_1, \mathbf{z}(x_1), \mathbf{z}'(x_1)) + \sum_{u=1}^{s_1} \rho_u (S^u_x + \mathbf{S}^u_{\mathbf{y}} \cdot \mathbf{z}')\right] \Delta_1$$

$$+ \left[-H(x_0, \mathbf{z}(x_0), \mathbf{z}'(x_0)) + \sum_{u=s_1+1}^{s} \rho_u (S^u_x + \mathbf{S}^u_{\mathbf{y}} \cdot \mathbf{z}')\right] \Delta_0 = 0. \tag{3-122}$$

Until now the vector $\boldsymbol{\gamma}$ has been arbitrary. We now choose $\boldsymbol{\gamma}$ so that the vector coefficient of $\boldsymbol{\eta}(x_0)$ is $\mathbf{0}$. Thus

$$\boldsymbol{\gamma} = \sum_{u=s_1+1}^{s} \rho_u \mathbf{S}^u_{\mathbf{y}}(x_0, \mathbf{z}(x_0)). \tag{3-123}$$

However, $\boldsymbol{\gamma} = \mathbf{H}_{\mathbf{y}'}(x_0, \mathbf{z}(x_0), \mathbf{z}'(x_0))$; (3-123) implies therefore that

$$\mathbf{H}^*_{\mathbf{y}'}(x_0, \mathbf{z}(x_0), \mathbf{z}'(x_0)) = \sum_{u=s_1+1}^{s} \rho_u \mathbf{S}^u_{\mathbf{y}}(x_0, \mathbf{z}(x_0)). \tag{3-124}$$

We pause at this point to make an observation that will be useful later. If the left hand end point is fixed, the $S^u = 0$ become $t - t_1 = 0$, $\mathbf{y} - \mathbf{y}_0 = \mathbf{0}$ and the $\mathbf{S}^u_{\mathbf{y}}$ are $\mathbf{0}, \mathbf{e}_1, \ldots, \mathbf{e}_n$. Thus (3-123) reduces to $\boldsymbol{\gamma} = \Sigma^n_{u=1} \rho_u \mathbf{e}_u$, which merely tells us that $\boldsymbol{\gamma}$ is an element of $\mathscr{E}^n$ and places no other restriction on $\boldsymbol{\gamma}$. When the left hand end point is fixed, therefore, $\boldsymbol{\gamma}$ remains arbitrary in spite of (3-123). Let us now return to the problem at hand.

We next observe that since Δ_0 is arbitrary its coefficient must vanish. It follows that

$$-H(x_0, \mathbf{z}(x_0), \mathbf{z}'(x_0) + \sum_{u=s_1+1}^{s} \rho_u (S^u_x + \mathbf{S}^u_{\mathbf{y}} \cdot \mathbf{z}') = 0 \tag{3-125}$$

which, on applying (3-124), becomes

$$-H + \mathbf{H}^*_{\mathbf{y}'} \cdot \mathbf{z}' + \sum_{u=s_1+1}^{s} \rho_u S^u_x = 0. \tag{3-126}$$

Equations (3-124) and (3-126), taken together, imply that at x_0 the vector

$$(H - \mathbf{H}^*_{\mathbf{y}'} \cdot \mathbf{z}', \mathbf{H}^*_{\mathbf{y}'}) \tag{3-127}$$

is a linear combination of $\boldsymbol{\nabla} S^u$, $u = 1, \ldots, s_1$.

The admissible variation $\boldsymbol{\eta}(x)$ can be chosen so that at x_1 its components have arbitrarily selected values; hence the coefficient of $\boldsymbol{\eta}(x_1)$ must vanish. Similarly, Δ_1 is arbitrary and its coefficient must vanish. When these results are combined, we see that the vector (3-127) evaluated at x_1 must be a linear combination of ∇S^u, $u = s_1 + 1, \ldots, s$.

Finally, let us examine

$$\int_{x_0}^{x_1} \left(\sum_{u=r+1}^{n} \lambda_u \zeta_u \right) dx.$$

Originally we thought of the ζ_u as determined by $\boldsymbol{\eta}(x)$. However, if the ζ_u are specified arbitrarily then there exists a solution to (3-84) which passes through an arbitrary point at x_1. Thus the ζ_u are completely arbitrary and, therefore, $\lambda_u(x) \equiv 0$, $u = r + 1, \ldots, n$. The last $n - r$ multipliers are identically 0; hence $H^* = H$ always and, in (3-127) and (3-94), H^* can be replaced by H.

We can now show that the multipliers cannot all be 0 for any value of x. To see this, recall from the last paragraph of Section 3.8 that, if $\boldsymbol{\lambda}(x) = \mathbf{0}$ for any x, then $\boldsymbol{\lambda}(x) \equiv \mathbf{0}$. However, if $\boldsymbol{\lambda}(x) \equiv \mathbf{0}$, $H \equiv 0$ and the transversality conditions yield $\rho_u = 0$, $u = 1, \ldots, s$. This, together with $\lambda_0 = 0$, contradicts the fact that $\mathbf{c} \neq \mathbf{0}$. For each x, therefore, $(\lambda_0, \boldsymbol{\lambda}(x)) \neq \mathbf{0}$. This then completes the proof of Theorem 3.3.1.

We can now easily obtain the Weierstrass necessary condition with the aid of (3-111). We have shown that $\boldsymbol{\lambda}_T \equiv \mathbf{0}$ and $E^* = E$. Let us now use one X_l and no $\boldsymbol{\eta}_k$ or (Δ_0, Δ_1). However there will be an $\boldsymbol{\eta}_l(x)$. Notice that $\boldsymbol{\eta}_l(x)$ influences only the right hand end point. Once again $\mathbf{A}$ has only one column and the condition $(\mathbf{cA}) \cdot \boldsymbol{\mu} \leq 0$ becomes

$$\lambda_0 \frac{\partial}{\partial d+} \Phi(0) + \sum_{u=s_1+1}^{s} \rho_u \frac{\partial}{\partial d+} \Omega^u(0) \leq 0 \tag{3-128}$$

or

$$E - \mathbf{H}_{\mathbf{y}'} + \sum_{u=s_1+1}^{s} \rho_u \frac{\partial}{\partial d+} \Omega^u(0) \leq 0 \tag{3-129}$$

which, in view of the transversality condition at x_0, reduces to $E \leq 0$ for H along $\mathbf{z}(x)$ at all points which are not corners or end points of $\mathbf{z}(x)$. However by continuity and using one sided limits, $E \leq 0$ for each x, $x_0 \leq x \leq x_1$. Thus we have proved the following theorem.

Theorem 3.12.1. Weierstrass Necessary Condition. Suppose that $\mathbf{z}(x)$ *is an optimal solution to the problem of Lagrange. Then there exists a set of multi-*

pliers which satisfy the conditions of Theorem 3.3.1 and which are such that if E is the Weierstrass E function for the Hamiltonian function generated by the multipliers, then for each x, $x_0 \le x \le x_1$,

$$E(x, \mathbf{z}(x), \mathbf{z}'(x), \mathbf{p}') \le 0$$

whenever $(x, \mathbf{z}(x), \mathbf{p}') \in \mathscr{R}$.

That the Legendre or Clebsch necessary condition also must hold follows in exactly the same way as in Section 2.15. Thus we have

Theorem 3.12.2. Legendre Necessary Condition. Under the conditions of Theorem 3.12.1, it is necessary that the matrix $\mathbf{H}_{\mathbf{y}'\mathbf{y}'}(x, \mathbf{z}, \mathbf{z}')$ *be negative semidefinite at each point along* $\mathbf{z}(x)$.

In later applications of the theory relating to the problem of Lagrange we shall find a use both for the Weierstrass and for the Legendre condition. The following necessary condition also will be useful. If a parametric representation is introduced, the condition may be obtained quite easily from the necessary conditions of Theorem 3.3.1.

Theorem 3.12.3. Let $\mathbf{z}(x)$ *be an optimal solution to the Lagrange problem which satisfies the necessary conditions of Theorem 3.3.1 and let* H *be the Hamiltonian function introduced there. Then it is necessary that there exist a constant* γ_0 *such that for each* x, $x_0 \le x \le x_1$,

$$H - \mathbf{H}_{\mathbf{y}'} \cdot \mathbf{z}' = \int_{x_0}^{x} H_x dx + \gamma_0 \tag{3-130}$$

when H, $\mathbf{H}_{\mathbf{y}'}$ *and* H_x *are evaluated along* $\mathbf{z}(x)$.

Let us write $\mathbf{z}(x)$ in parametric form as $x = \tau$, $\mathbf{z}(\tau)$. Then $\dot{x} = 1$, which is positive along the entire curve. Consider now a P_ε neighborhood in $\mathscr{E}^{2n+3}$ of the curve $(\tau, x(\tau), \mathbf{z}(\tau)) = (\tau, \tau, \mathbf{z}(\tau))$, and any piecewise smooth curve $x = X(\tau)$ and $\mathbf{y} = \mathbf{Y}(\tau)$ lying in this neighborhood. Then if ε is small $\dot{X} > 0$ and $x = X(\tau)$ has an inverse $\tau = g(x)$; hence the curve can be represented in nonparametric form as $\mathbf{Y}(g(x))$. If $X(\tau)$, $\mathbf{Y}(\tau)$ satisfies

$$G^i\left(X(\tau), \mathbf{Y}(\tau), \frac{\dot{\mathbf{Y}}}{\dot{X}}\right) = 0, \quad i = 1, \ldots, r \tag{3-131}$$

then $\mathbf{Y}(g(x))$ satisfies the constraints $G^i = 0$ in nonparametric form.

Let τ_0 be the initial value of τ and τ_1 the final value. If

$$\begin{aligned} S^u(X(\tau_1), \mathbf{Y}(\tau_1)) &= 0, \quad u = 1, \ldots, s_1 \\ S^u(X(\tau_0), \mathbf{Y}(\tau_0)) &= 0, \quad u = s_1 + 1, \ldots, s \end{aligned} \tag{3-132}$$

then $\mathbf{Y}(g(x))$ also satisfies the end point conditions and thus is admissible. Hence for any $X(\tau)$, $\mathbf{Y}(\tau)$ with $\dot{X} > 0$ which satisfies (3-131) and (3-132) it is possible to construct an admissible solution to the original Lagrange problem. Furthermore the value of $J[\mathbf{y}]$ for such a solution is

$$J[X, \mathbf{Y}] = \int_{\tau_0}^{\tau_1} F\left(X(\tau), \mathbf{Y}(\tau), \frac{\dot{\mathbf{Y}}(\tau)}{\dot{X}(\tau)}\right) \dot{X}(\tau) d\tau. \qquad 3\text{-}133)$$

Now $x = \tau$, $\mathbf{z}(\tau)$ satisfies (3-131) and (3-132) and is a maximizing solution to the original problem. It must also yield a relative maximum of (3-133) subject to (3-131) and (3-132). For suppose that there were another solution to the new problem, lying in a P_ε neighborhood of $(\tau, \tau, \mathbf{z}(\tau))$ and yielding a larger value of (3-133). Then it would be possible to find an admissible solution to the original problem which yields a larger value of $J[\mathbf{y}]$.

We observe next that any X, $\mathbf{Y}$ with $\dot{X} > 0$ which satisfies (3-131) also satisfies

$$G^i\left(X, \mathbf{Y}, \frac{\dot{\mathbf{Y}}}{\dot{X}}\right) \dot{X} = 0, \quad i = 1, \ldots, r. \tag{3-134}$$

Thus $x = \tau$, $\mathbf{z}(\tau)$ must yield a relative maximum of (3-133) subject to (3-134) and (3-132). The new problem is another Lagrange problem, and the matrix with columns $(G^i_{\dot{X}}, \mathbf{G}^i_{\dot{\mathbf{Y}}})$ has rank r at each point where $||G^i_{\dot{Y}_j}||$ has rank r; hence $x = \tau$, $\mathbf{z}(\tau)$ must satisfy the necessary conditions for the new problem. In particular, the DuBois-Reymond equations must hold. Those for $\mathbf{H}_{\dot{\mathbf{Y}}}$ show that the same set of λ's are determined for $x = \tau$, $\mathbf{z}(\tau)$ as for $\mathbf{z}(x)$ in the original problem. The DuBois-Reymond equation for the variable X becomes

$$H_{\dot{X}} = \int_{\tau_0}^{\tau} H_X d\tau + \gamma_0. \tag{3-135}$$

However, when $x = \tau$ and $\dot{x} = 1$

$$H_{\dot{X}} = H - \mathbf{H}_{\mathbf{y}'} \cdot \mathbf{z}'. \tag{3-136}$$

Also $H_X = H_x$. Noting that $x_0 = \tau_0$ and $x = \tau$, we obtain (3-130), as desired.

We have not considered the necessary conditions of Jacobi, which we derived earlier when considering problems without constraints. It has not been found possible to derive the Jacobi condition for the problem of Lagrange without imposing conditions additional to those which sufficed for the Weierstrass and Legendre conditions. These additional restrictions involve the concept of normality. This concept will be briefly considered in a later section, but in a different context.

3.13. Unbounded intervals of integration

We shall conclude our study of the necessary conditions for the problem of Lagrange by considering briefly the case in which the interval of integration is unbounded.

If $\mathbf{z}(x)$ optimizes $J[\mathbf{y}]$ over the infinite interval $x \geq x_0$ then it also optimizes $J[\mathbf{y}]$ over any finite interval $x_0 \leq x \leq x_1$ if we specify that at x_1, $\mathbf{y}(x_1) = \mathbf{z}(x_1)$. If this were not true, $\mathbf{z}(x)$ could be replaced by another function $\mathbf{z}^*(x)$ over the interval $x_0 \leq x \leq x_1$ and $J[\mathbf{y}]$ could be made larger. Suppose then that the right hand end point is fixed at $\mathbf{y}(x_1) = \mathbf{z}(x_1)$. We know that $\mathbf{z}(x)$ must satisfy the necessary conditions of Theorem 3.3.1 over this interval. Furthermore, $\boldsymbol{\lambda}(x)$ does not change as x_1 is changed, because $\boldsymbol{\gamma}$ is determined by conditions at x_0. Hence the necessary conditions of Theorem 3.3.1 must be satisfied over the entire interval and a $\boldsymbol{\lambda}(x)$ can be determined.

It remains to examine the conditions which must be satisfied as $x \to \infty$. Suppose that the left hand end point is fixed and that $\mathbf{z}(x)$ has only a finite number of corners. Suppose further that it is possible to determine a one parameter family of admissible solutions $\mathbf{y}(x; \xi)$ with $\mathbf{y}(x; 0) = \mathbf{z}(x)$. Let $\boldsymbol{\eta}(x) = \mathbf{y}_\xi(x; 0)$. There is, of course, no guarantee that such a family can be found. However, we shall only study cases in which this is possible. Then, assuming that the appropriate differentiations of the integral can be carried out, $\Phi'(0) = 0$ and $\boldsymbol{\eta}(x)$ satisfies (3-30). On multiplying the ith equation of (3-30) by $\lambda_i(x)$, adding over i and integrating from x_0 to ∞, we obtain 0. If this is added to $\Phi'(0)$ and then an integration by parts is carried out with the aid of the Euler equations and the corner conditions, we obtain

$$\Phi'(0) = \lim_{x \to \infty} \mathbf{H}_{\mathbf{y}'}(x, \mathbf{z}(x), \mathbf{z}'(x)) \cdot \boldsymbol{\eta}(x) = 0. \tag{3-137}$$

Thus when all relevant integrations can be performed it is necessary that (3-137) hold.

If it is required that $\lim_{x \to \infty}[\mathbf{y}(x) - \mathbf{g}(x)] = \mathbf{0}$, where $\mathbf{g}(x)$ is specified, then $\lim_{x\to\infty}\mathbf{\eta}(x) = \mathbf{0}$ and (3-137) places on the limit of $\mathbf{H}_{\mathbf{y}'}$ only the weak restriction that it be bounded.

Suppose next that there is a free boundary for each component of $\mathbf{y}(x)$ as $x \to \infty$. (The analysis may be extended without difficulty to cover mixed cases in which some components are assigned free boundaries while others must satisfy $\lim [y_j(x) - g_j(x)] = 0$. However we shall not study that case in detail.) We cannot immediately conclude that $\mathbf{H}_{\mathbf{y}'}$ must approach $\mathbf{0}$, as we did for $\mathbf{F}_{\mathbf{y}'}$ in the case of no constraints. The reason is that in general $\mathbf{\eta}(x)$ cannot be chosen arbitrarily. However, if the left hand end point is fixed and if it is possible to find n different sets of admissible solutions with the characteristics that $\lim_{x\to\infty}\mathbf{\eta}_j(x) = \mathbf{a}_j$ and the $\mathbf{a}_j$ are linearly independent, then $\lim_{x\to\infty}\mathbf{H}_{\mathbf{y}'} \cdot \mathbf{a}_j = 0$, $j = 1, \ldots, n$ and we shall show that this implies that $\lim_{x\to\infty}\mathbf{H}_{\mathbf{y}'} = \mathbf{0}$. Thus if we multiply the jth equation by an arbitrary δ_j and sum over j, $\lim_{x\to\infty}\mathbf{H}_{\mathbf{y}'} \cdot [\Sigma_{j=1}^{n}\delta_j\mathbf{a}_j] = 0$. If the δ_j are selected so that $\Sigma_j\delta_j\mathbf{a}_j = \mathbf{e}_k$ then $\lim_{x\to\infty}H_{y_k'} = 0$, and this is true for each $k = 1, \ldots, n$.

Consider finally the case in which it is required that $\lim_{x\to\infty}\mathbf{y}(x) = \mathbf{b}$ but $\mathbf{b}$ is not specified, the only requirement being that $\mathbf{b}$ lie in the smooth manifold $\mathscr{M}$ defined by $S^u(\mathbf{y}) = 0$, $u = 1, \ldots, s$. We shall assume that $\mathscr{M}$ is bounded and that $\lim_{x\to\infty}\mathbf{z}'(x)$ exists. Then $\lim_{x\to\infty}\mathbf{H}_{\mathbf{y}'}$ exists when evaluated along $\mathbf{z}(x)$. Suppose now that for $x_0 \le x$ there can be found $s + 1$ solutions $\mathbf{\eta}_k$ to (3-30) which are bounded for all x, which approach definite limits as $x \to \infty$, and which are such that for $x \ge x_0$ there can be constructed a family of solutions $\mathbf{y}(x; \boldsymbol{\xi})$ to $G^i = 0$ with $\mathbf{y}(x; \mathbf{0}) = \mathbf{z}(x)$ and $\mathbf{y}_{\xi_k}(x; \mathbf{0}) = \mathbf{\eta}_k$. If the interval of integration is finite we can be sure that it is possible to construct the s parameter family $\mathbf{y}(x; \boldsymbol{\xi})$; but if the interval of integration is infinite our earlier proof does not apply. However, if it were possible to construct such a family, then (provided the integrals were differentiable) we could carry out precisely the same analysis as above and conclude that it is necessary that $\lim_{x\to\infty}\mathbf{H}_{\mathbf{y}'}$ be orthogonal to $\mathscr{M}$ at the terminal point $\mathbf{b}$.

We have noted earlier that, when the left hand end point is fixed, the γ of the DuBois-Reymond equations is unrestricted. We are therefore free to assign to it any convenient value. Let us choose γ so that the resulting multipliers yield an $\mathbf{H}_{\mathbf{y}'}$ which, when evaluated at the terminal point of $\mathbf{z}(x)$, is orthogonal to $\mathscr{M}$ at that point. Then we may be sure that, if the type of construction referred to above can be carried out, the necessary conditions will be satisfied. We shall not consider any other possible boundary conditions. The results we have obtained are summarized in the following theorem.

Theorem 3.13.1. Unbounded Interval of Integration. Suppose that $\mathbf{z}(x)$ *yields an optimal solution to the Lagrange problem when the interval of integration is infinite and the left hand end point is fixed; and suppose that* $\mathbf{z}(x)$ *has only a finite number of corners. Then* $\mathbf{z}(x)$ *must satisfy the necessary conditions of Theorem 3.3.1 except for the transversality condition at the right hand end point. Furthermore, if there exists a one parameter family of admissible solutions* $\mathbf{y}(x;\,\xi)$ *with* $\mathbf{y}(x;\,0) = \mathbf{z}(x)$ *and* $\mathbf{y}_\xi(x;\,0) = \boldsymbol{\eta}(x)$, *then it is necessary that*

$$\lim_{x\to\infty} \mathbf{H}_{\mathbf{y}'}(x, \mathbf{z}(x), \mathbf{z}'(x)) \cdot \boldsymbol{\eta}(x) = 0. \tag{3-138}$$

If it is required that $\lim_{x\to\infty}[\mathbf{y}(x) - \mathbf{g}(x)] = \mathbf{0}$, *where* $\mathbf{g}(x)$ *is specified, so that* $\lim_{x\to\infty}\boldsymbol{\eta}(x) = 0$, *then (3-138) does not place any special restrictions on* $\mathbf{H}_{\mathbf{y}'}$ *other than the requirement that (3-138) must hold. In the case of a free boundary it cannot be immediately concluded from (3-138) that* $\lim_{x\to\infty} \mathbf{H}_{\mathbf{y}'} = \mathbf{0}$; *this follows, however, if there exist n different one parameter families with* $\lim_{x\to\infty}\boldsymbol{\eta}_j(x) = \mathbf{a}_j$ *and the* $\mathbf{a}_j$ *are linearly independent. Finally, if the system is autonomous and it is required that* $\lim_{x\to\infty}\mathbf{y}(x) = \mathbf{b}$, *where* $\mathbf{b}$ *is not specified but is required only to lie in a bounded manifold* $\mathscr{M}$, *then if* $\lim_{x\to\infty} \mathbf{z}'(x)$ *exists so does* $\lim_{x\to\infty}\mathbf{H}_{\mathbf{y}'}(\mathbf{z}, \mathbf{z}')$. *In this case it is possible to define* $\boldsymbol{\lambda}(x)$ *so that* $\mathbf{H}_{\mathbf{y}'}$ *is orthogonal to* $\mathscr{M}$ *at the terminal point, and if this is done the necessary conditions which may apply will be satisfied.*

3.14. Normality

In developing the multiplier rule we noted that, for arbitrarily specified λ_0 and $\boldsymbol{\gamma}$, $\lambda_1(x), \ldots, \lambda_r(x)$ are uniquely determined. This does not imply, however, that the multipliers $\boldsymbol{\lambda}(x)$ appearing in the multiplier rule are always uniquely determined up to a scale factor. For it may be possible to determine a set of multipliers both for the case in which $\lambda_0 = 0$ and for the case in which $\lambda_0 > 0$ (that is, $\lambda_0 = 1$). Furthermore, $\boldsymbol{\gamma}$ may not be uniquely determined by the requirements imposed earlier; for each of the different values of $\boldsymbol{\gamma}$ which might be used, it may be possible to generate a set of linearly independent functions $\boldsymbol{\lambda}(x)$. Thus there may be many different sets of multipliers $\boldsymbol{\lambda}(x)$ for which the multiplier rule and the transversality conditions are satisfied. There may even be more than one set for which the Weierstrass necessary condition is satisfied.

For present purposes it should be borne in mind that the necessary conditions are satisfied even if $\mathbf{z}(x)$ is the only function satisfying the constraints and the end point conditions. In such cases $\lambda_0 = 0$ and the influence of F disappears. It seems natural to describe as abnormal problems for which there exists a set of multipliers with $\lambda_0 = 0$ and which are such that the necessary conditions are satisfied. Many different kinds of abnormal behavior are possible (the situation is much more complex than for ordinary maxima and minima). The following definition provides one way of classifying abnormalities.

Abnormality of Order q. The function $\mathbf{z}(x)$ *is said to have an abnormality of order q if q is the maximum number of linearly independent functions* $\boldsymbol{\lambda}(x)$ *with* $\lambda_0 = 0$ *for which* $\mathbf{z}(x)$ *satisfies both the multiplier rule and the transversality conditions. (If* $q = 0$ *there are no multipliers with* $\lambda_0 = 0$ *other than* $\boldsymbol{\lambda}(x) \equiv \mathbf{0}$.)

Normality. The function $\mathbf{z}(x)$ *is said to be normal if it has an abnormality of order* 0, *that is, if every function* $\boldsymbol{\lambda}(x)$ *for which* $\mathbf{z}(x)$ *satisfies the multiplier rule has* $\lambda_0 > 0$.

If $\mathbf{z}(x)$ is normal then the multiplier function $\boldsymbol{\lambda}(x)$ is unique if λ_0 is chosen to be 1. To see that this is so, suppose that there are two linearly independent multiplier functions $\boldsymbol{\lambda}_1(x)$ and $\boldsymbol{\lambda}_2(x)$, each with $\lambda_0 = 1$. Then $\boldsymbol{\lambda}_3(x) \equiv \boldsymbol{\lambda}_1(x) - \boldsymbol{\lambda}_2(x)$ is a solution to $\dot{\boldsymbol{\lambda}} = -\mathbf{H}_\mathbf{y}$ if $\lambda_0 = 0$. Moreover, $\boldsymbol{\lambda}_3(x)$ is never $\mathbf{0}$, for this would imply that $\boldsymbol{\lambda}_3 \equiv \mathbf{0}$, in contradiction of the fact that $\boldsymbol{\lambda}_1 \not\equiv \boldsymbol{\lambda}_2$. Finally, $\boldsymbol{\lambda}_3(x)$ satisfies the transversality conditions. Thus $(0, \boldsymbol{\lambda}_3)$ is a set of multipliers which satisfies the necessary conditions. Hence $\mathbf{z}(x)$ is abnormal, which is a contradiction.

Suppose that $\mathbf{z}(x)$ satisfies both the constraints and the end point conditions. In general there is no guarantee that there exist other functions with these properties. If $\mathbf{z}(x)$ is normal, however, there do exist other admissible functions, so that the variational problem is not trivial. We shall prove the following theorem.

Theorem 3.14.1. If $\mathbf{z}(x)$ *is normal, there exists a one parameter family of functions* $\mathbf{y}(x; \xi)$ *which satisfy* $G^i = 0$, $i = 1, \ldots, r$ *and the end points of which lie in* $\mathcal{M}_1$ *and* $\mathcal{M}_2$ *respectively.*

Suppose that $\mathcal{M}_1$ is formed by the intersection of s_1 hypersurfaces and $\mathcal{M}_2$ by the intersection of s_2 hypersurfaces, and let $s = s_1 + s_2$. From the fundamental imbedding lemma of Section 3.8 we know that there exists an $(s + 1)$-parameter family of functions $\mathbf{y}(x; \boldsymbol{\xi})$ which satisfy $G^i = 0$, $i = 1, \ldots, r$ in the interval $x_0(\boldsymbol{\xi}) \leq x \leq x_1(\boldsymbol{\xi})$ and for which $\mathbf{z}(x) = \mathbf{y}(x; \mathbf{0})$. Consider now the matrix the rows of which are $\boldsymbol{\Phi}_{\boldsymbol{\xi}}(\mathbf{0})$, $\boldsymbol{\Omega}^u_{\boldsymbol{\xi}}(\mathbf{0})$, $u = 1, \ldots, s$.

The argument developed on p. 194 shows that this matrix must have rank s; and in fact a submatrix from the last s rows, $\mathbf{\Omega}^u_{\xi}(\mathbf{0})$, $u = 1, \ldots, s$, has rank s. Otherwise, there would exist a set of numbers $\lambda_0 = 0, \rho_u, u = 1, \ldots, s$, not all 0, which satisfy (3-51). This is a contradiction, however, since $\lambda_0 \neq 0$.

To be specific, we assume that the components of $\boldsymbol{\xi}$ are named so that the submatrix of order s found from the first s columns of $||\mathbf{\Omega}^u_{\xi}(\mathbf{0})||$ has rank s. The equations $\Omega^u(\boldsymbol{\xi}) = 0$, $u = 1, \ldots, s$ then have a solution $\boldsymbol{\xi} = \mathbf{0}$, and by the first implicit function theorem of Appendix II there exists a function $\boldsymbol{\xi}^* = \mathbf{\Lambda}(\xi_{s+1})$, $\boldsymbol{\xi}^* = (\xi_1, \ldots, \xi_s)$ which is continuous and has continuous partial derivatives and which yields a solution to $\Omega^u = 0$ for each ξ_{s+1} sufficiently close to 0. For simplicity, we write $\xi = \xi_{s+1}$. Then the functions $\mathbf{y}^*(x; \xi)$, which are obtained from $\mathbf{y}(x; \boldsymbol{\xi}^*, \xi)$ by replacing $\boldsymbol{\xi}^*$ with $\mathbf{\Lambda}(\xi)$, satisfy both $G^i = 0$, $i = 1, \ldots, r$ and the end point conditions and thus are admissible.

It remains only to demonstrate that the set $\mathbf{y}^*(x; \xi)$ does in fact contain functions different from $\mathbf{z}(x)$. Recall that from the manner in which $\mathbf{y}(x; \boldsymbol{\xi})$ was constructed $\mathbf{y}_{\xi_k}(x; \mathbf{0}) = \boldsymbol{\eta}_k(x)$. Thus

$$\begin{aligned} \mathbf{y}^*_{\xi}(x; 0) &= \sum_{k=1}^{s} \mathbf{y}_{\xi_k}(x; \mathbf{0})\Lambda'_k(0) + \mathbf{y}_{\xi_{s+1}}(x; \mathbf{0}) \\ &= \sum_{k=1}^{s} \Lambda'_k(0)\boldsymbol{\eta}_k(x) + \boldsymbol{\eta}_{s+1}(x). \end{aligned} \tag{3-139}$$

By Taylor's theorem $\mathbf{y}^*(x; \xi) = \mathbf{z}(x) + \xi\mathbf{y}^*_{\xi}(x; \theta\xi)$ and unless the right hand side of (3-139) is identically $\mathbf{0}$, $\mathbf{y}^*(x; \xi)$ must differ from $\mathbf{z}(x)$ when $\xi \neq 0$. We now note that it is always possible to choose the $\boldsymbol{\eta}_k$ so that the right hand side of (3-132) is not identically $\mathbf{0}$. Suppose that the $\boldsymbol{\eta}_k(x)$, $k = 1, \ldots, s$ are so chosen that $||\Omega^u_{\xi_k}(\mathbf{0})||$ has rank s. This determines the $\zeta_{ik}(x)$ in (3-84). Suppose now that $\boldsymbol{\zeta}(x)$ is any continuous function which is linearly independent of the $\boldsymbol{\zeta}_i(x)$. Then we determine $\boldsymbol{\eta}(x) = \boldsymbol{\eta}_{s+1}(x)$ as the solution to (3-84) for $\boldsymbol{\zeta}(x)$. The function $\boldsymbol{\eta}(x)$ is linearly independent of the $\boldsymbol{\eta}_k(x)$ (why?); hence (3-132) cannot vanish identically. That completes the proof.

The following corollary can be easily proved.

Corollary 3.14.1. Suppose that $\boldsymbol{\eta}(x)$ *is admissible and that* Δ_0 *and* Δ_1 *are arbitrary numbers. If* $\mathbf{z}(x)$ *is normal and if* $\boldsymbol{\eta}(x)$, Δ_0 *and* Δ_1 *satisfy* $\Omega^u_{\xi}(0) = 0$, $u = 1, \ldots, s$, *then there exists a one parameter family of admissible functions* $\mathbf{y}(x; \xi)$ *with* $\mathbf{y}_{\xi}(x; 0) = \boldsymbol{\eta}(x)$.

The one parameter family of Theorem 3.14.1 has the characteristics described in the corollary if $\boldsymbol{\eta}(x)$, Δ_0, Δ_1 satisfy $\Omega_\xi(0) = 0$, $u = 1, \ldots, s$ and if $\boldsymbol{\Lambda}'(0) = \mathbf{0}$, for then the admissible family $\mathbf{y}^*(x; \xi)$ constructed there satisfies $\mathbf{y}^*_\xi(x; 0) = \boldsymbol{\eta}(x)$. The fact that $\boldsymbol{\Lambda}'(0) = \mathbf{0}$ in this case follows immediately from the implicit function theorem; for if $\mathbf{A}$ contains the first s columns of $||\Omega^u_{\xi_k}(\mathbf{0})||$ then $\boldsymbol{\Lambda}'(0)$ must satisfy the system of linear equations $\mathbf{A}\boldsymbol{\Lambda}'(0) + \boldsymbol{\Omega}_{\xi_{s+1}}(\mathbf{0}) = \mathbf{0}$. However, $\boldsymbol{\Omega}_{\xi_{s+1}}(\mathbf{0}) = \boldsymbol{\Omega}'(0) = \mathbf{0}$ and $\mathbf{A}$ is non-singular. Thus $\boldsymbol{\Lambda}'(0) = \mathbf{0}$ and the corollary is proved.

Theorem 3.14.2. For $\mathbf{z}(x)$ to be normal it is necessary and sufficient that the rank of $||\Omega^k_{\xi_k}(\mathbf{0})||$ be s when all possible admissible $\boldsymbol{\eta}_k(x)$ functions and arbitrary $\boldsymbol{\Delta}_0$ and $\boldsymbol{\Delta}_1$ are considered.

We have already noted that if $\mathbf{z}(x)$ is normal then the indicated matrix has rank s. We now prove sufficiency. If the rank is p, the only solution to (3-51) with $\lambda_0 = 0$ is $c_u = 0$, $u = 1, \ldots, s$. This would require that $\mathbf{H}_{\mathbf{y}'}(x_0) = \mathbf{0}$, which in turn implies that $\boldsymbol{\lambda}(x_0) = \mathbf{0}$ and hence $\boldsymbol{\lambda}(x) \equiv \mathbf{0}$. Such a $\boldsymbol{\lambda}(x)$ does not satisfy the necessary conditions. Thus there are no functions $\boldsymbol{\lambda}(x)$ which satisfy the necessary conditions and for which $\lambda_0 = 0$. Hence $\mathbf{z}(x)$ is normal, and the theorem is proved.

Unfortunately, this theorem usually is awkward to apply and therefore not very helpful when the normality of a problem is under consideration.

3.15. Sufficiency based on the concavity of H

The type of sufficiency conditions introduced in Section 2.17 can be easily extended to the problem of Lagrange with fixed end points. The following theorem provides a suitable generalization.

Theorem 3.15.1. Sufficiency Conditions for Fixed End Point Lagrange Problem. Suppose that $\mathbf{z}(x)$ satisfies the necessary conditions of Theorem 3.3.1 for the fixed end point problem of Lagrange with $\mathbf{y}(x_0) = \mathbf{y}_0$ and $\mathbf{y}(x_1) = \mathbf{y}_1$. Let $\boldsymbol{\lambda}(x)$ be the set of multipliers obtained from the necessary conditions and suppose that $\lambda_0 = 1$. Let $H(x, \mathbf{y}, \mathbf{y}')$ be the Hamiltonian formed by this specific set of multipliers. Then if $H(x, \mathbf{y}, \mathbf{y}')$ is a concave function of $(\mathbf{y}, \mathbf{y}')$ over some open convex set containing the set of points $(x, \mathbf{y}, \mathbf{y}')$ satisfying $G^i = 0$, $i = 1, \ldots, r$, $\mathbf{z}(x)$ yields the absolute maximum of $J[\mathbf{y}]$ subject to the constraints. If H is a convex function under the same conditions then $\mathbf{z}(x)$ yields the absolute minimum of $J[\mathbf{y}]$.

The method of proof is essentially the same as that used in Section 2.17. Let $\mathbf{y}(x)$ be *any* other admissible function (in $\mathscr{R}$) and let $\boldsymbol{\eta}(x) = \mathbf{y}(x) - \mathbf{z}(x)$. Then $\boldsymbol{\eta}(x_0) = \boldsymbol{\eta}(x_1) = \mathbf{0}$. By Theorem 2.17.1

$$H(x, \mathbf{y}, \mathbf{y}') \leq H(x, \mathbf{z}, \mathbf{z}') + \mathbf{H}_{\mathbf{y}'}(x, \mathbf{z}, \mathbf{z}') \cdot \boldsymbol{\eta}' + \mathbf{H}_{\mathbf{y}}(x, \mathbf{z}, \mathbf{z}') \cdot \boldsymbol{\eta}. \quad (3\text{-}140)$$

However, since $\mathbf{y}(x)$ and $\mathbf{z}(x)$ satisfy the constraints $G^i = 0$, $i = 1, \ldots, r$, $H(x, \mathbf{y}, \mathbf{y}') = F(x, \mathbf{y}, \mathbf{y}')$ and $H(x, \mathbf{z}, \mathbf{z}') = F(x, \mathbf{z}, \mathbf{z}')$. Thus

$$J[\mathbf{y}] \leq J[\mathbf{z}] + \int_{x_0}^{x_1} [\mathbf{H}_{\mathbf{y}'} \cdot \boldsymbol{\eta}' + \mathbf{H}_{\mathbf{y}} \cdot \boldsymbol{\eta}] dx. \quad (3\text{-}141)$$

Integrating by parts, applying the Euler equations and corner conditions, and recalling that $\boldsymbol{\eta}(x_0) = \boldsymbol{\eta}(x_1) = \mathbf{0}$, we find that $J[\mathbf{y}] \leq J[\mathbf{z}]$, which is what we wished to prove.

When the interval of integration is unbounded, the above integration by parts yields the term $\lim_{x\to\infty} \mathbf{H}_{\mathbf{y}'} \cdot \boldsymbol{\eta}$. If it can be shown that this limit is non-positive for *every* admissible $\mathbf{y}(x)$ then it again follows that $\mathbf{z}(x)$ yields the global optimum. This establishes the following corollary.

Corollary 3.15.1. Sufficiency for an Unbounded Interval of Integration. Suppose that the left hand end point is fixed and that the interval of integration is unbounded. Then if H is concave or convex as described in Theorem 3.15.1, if the integral has the proper convergence properties and if, in addition, it can be shown that $\lim_{x\to\infty} \mathbf{H}_{\mathbf{y}'}(x, \mathbf{z}, \mathbf{z}') \cdot \boldsymbol{\eta}$ *is non-positive for every admissible* $\mathbf{y}(x)$, *it follows that* $\mathbf{z}(x)$ *yields the global optimal (over* $\mathscr{R}$*) for the problem.*

We note that, if it is required that $\lim_{x\to\infty} \mathbf{y}(x) = \mathbf{b}$, then $\lim_{x\to\infty} \boldsymbol{\eta}(x) = \mathbf{0}$. It follows immediately that if $\mathbf{H}_{\mathbf{y}'}$ has bounded components then $\lim_{x\to\infty} \mathbf{H}_{\mathbf{y}'}(x, \mathbf{z}, \mathbf{z}') \cdot \boldsymbol{\eta} = 0$.

No attempt will be made to discuss the classical sufficiency conditions; these are quite complex and not especially useful in economic problems.

Example. Consider Example 1 of Section 3.7. For this problem $F = U(C)$, a concave function of C and, therefore, of C, $\dot{K}$ and K; and $G = C + \dot{K} - \Psi(K)$. Since $\Psi(K)$ is a concave function of K, G is a *convex* function of C, $\dot{K}$ and K. The solution to the problem allows us to set $\lambda_0 = 1$ and hence $\lambda_1 = -U'$. Thus $\lambda_1 \leq 0$ when C is less than or equal to the bliss value C^* (but not if $C > C^*$ and it is the utility function which saturates). Therefore H is a concave function of C, $\dot{K}$ and K in the region $C \leq C^*$; hence any $K(t)$ and $C(t)$ which satisfy the necessary conditions of Theorem 3.3.1 and for which $C \leq C^*$ yield the global optimum when the interval of integration is finite (it would never be optimal to have $C > C^*$ in such a case).

If we had written the differential equation constraint as $\Psi(K) - \dot{K} - C = 0$, G would have been a concave function and λ_1 would have been equal to $U' \geq 0$ if $C \leq C^*$. H would have emerged again as a concave function, showing that nothing essential depends on the manner in which the constraints are expressed. The signs of the multipliers, however, do depend on the precise way in which the constraints are written.

3.16. The problem of Bolza

The most general problem studied in the classical theory of the calculus of variations is referred to as the problem of Bolza. The problem is to determine the piecewise smooth function $\mathbf{y}(x)$ which satisfies the differential equations

$$G^i(x, \mathbf{y}, \mathbf{y}') = 0, \quad i = 1, \ldots, r, \; r < n \tag{3-142}$$

satisfies the end point conditions

$$S^u(x_1, \mathbf{y}_1) = 0, \quad u = 1, \ldots, s_1; \qquad S^u(x_0, \mathbf{y}_0) = 0, \quad u = s_1 + 1, \ldots, s \tag{3-143}$$

with $s \leq 2n + 2$, and maximizes the integral

$$J[\mathbf{y}] = g_0(x_0, \mathbf{y}_0) + g_1(x_1, \mathbf{y}_1) + \int_{x_0}^{x_1} F(x, \mathbf{y}, \mathbf{y}')dx. \tag{3-144}$$

The conditions imposed on the G^i and S^u are the same as in the problem of Lagrange. It is assumed also that $g_0 \in C''$ and $g_1 \in C''$. The problem as we have formulated it is said to have separated end points. In a slightly more general form of the problem, (3-143) is replaced by $S^u(x_0, \mathbf{y}_0, x_1, \mathbf{y}_1) = 0$, $u = 1, \ldots, s$ and in (3-144) $g_0 + g_1$ is replaced by $g(x_0, \mathbf{y}_0, x_1, \mathbf{y}_1)$. The problem of Bolza is the problem of Lagrange except for the appearance of $g_0(x_0, \mathbf{y}_0) + g_1(x_1, \mathbf{y}_1)$ in the functional to be optimized. Notice that g_0 depends only on the *end point* $(x_0, \mathbf{y}_0)$ while $g_1(x_0, \mathbf{y}_1)$ depends only on the end point $(x_1, \mathbf{y}_1)$.

When $F \equiv 0$ the problem of Bolza is referred to as the problem of Mayer.

In essentials, the problem of Bolza is no more general than the problem of Lagrange. Indeed it can be very simply reduced to the problem of Lagrange, as we shall now show. Let us introduce two new variables y_{n+1} and y_{n+2}, two additional differential equations $y'_{n+1} = 0$ and $y'_{n+2} = 0$, two new constraints

$$y_{n+1}(x_0)(x_1 - x_0) - g_0(x_0, \mathbf{y}_0) = 0 \tag{3-145}$$

$$y_{n+2}(x_1)(x_1 - x_0) - g_1(x_1, \mathbf{y}_1) = 0 \tag{3-146}$$

and seek to optimize the functional

$$J[\mathbf{y}] = \int_{x_0}^{x_1} [F + y_{n+1} + y_{n+2}]dx$$

$$= y_{n+1}(x_1 - x_0) + y_{n+2}(x_1 - x_0) + \int_{x_0}^{x_1} Fdx$$

$$= g_1 + g_2 + \int_{x_0}^{x_1} Fdx.$$

This is not quite a standard problem of Lagrange, for the new constraints (3-145) and (3-146) are of a mixed type. To overcome this difficulty we introduce two more new variables, y_{n+3} and y_{n+4}. Let $y'_{n+3} = 1$ and $y_{n+3}(x_0) = 0$, so that $y_{n+3}(x_1) = x_1 - x_0$; and let $y'_{n+4} = -1$ and $y_{n+4}(x_1) = 0$, so that $y_{n+4}(x_0) = x_1 - x_0$. Then (3-145), (3-146) become $y_{n+1}(x_0)$ $y_{n+4}(x_0) - g_0 = 0$ and $y_{n+2}(x_1)y_{n+3}(x_1) - g_1 = 0$. The latter are in the separated form of the Lagrange problem.

The problem of Bolza is therefore equivalent to the problem of Lagrange and may be rephrased as the problem of finding the piecewise smooth function $[\mathbf{y}(x), y_{n+1}(x), y_{n+2}(x), y_{n+3}(x), y_{n+4}(x)]$ which satisfies the differential equations

$$\begin{aligned} &G^i(x, \mathbf{y}, \mathbf{y}') = 0, \quad i = 1, \ldots, r \\ &y'_{n+1} = 0, \qquad y'_{n+2} = 0, \qquad y'_{n+3} = 1, \qquad y'_{n+4} = -1 \end{aligned} \tag{3-147}$$

the right hand and left hand end points of which lie, respectively, in the smooth manifold $\mathscr{M}$, described by

$$\begin{aligned} &S^u(x, \mathbf{y}) = 0, \quad u = 1, \ldots, s_1 \\ &y_{n+2}y_{n+3} - g_1(x, \mathbf{y}) = 0 \\ &y_{n+4} = 0 \end{aligned} \tag{3-148}$$

and in the smooth manifold $\mathcal{M}_0$ described by

$$\begin{aligned} &S^u(x, \mathbf{y}) = 0, \quad u = s_1 + 1, \ldots, s \\ &y_{n+1}y_{n+4} - g_1(x, \mathbf{y}) = 0 \\ &y_{n+3} = 0 \end{aligned} \tag{3-149}$$

and which maximizes the functional

$$J[\mathbf{y}] = \int_{x_0}^{x_1} [F(x, \mathbf{y}, \mathbf{y}') + y_{n+1} + y_{n+2}]\mathrm{d}x. \tag{3-150}$$

Problems

Section 3.2

1. Find the extremals for the functional

$$J[y] = \int_1^2 [(y')^2 + x^2]dx$$

subject to

$$\int_1^2 y^2 dx = 5$$

and $y(1) = 0$, $y(2) = 0$.

2. Find the extremals for the functional

$$J[y] = \int_0^1 [(y_1')^2 + (y_2')^2 - 4xy_2' - 4y_2]dx$$

subject to

$$\int_0^1 [(y_1')^2 - xy_1' - (y_2')^2]dx = 3$$

and

$$y_1(0) = y_2(0) = 0; \qquad y_1(1) = y_2(1) = 1.$$

3. Consider some closed curve in the plane which is represented parametrically by $x(\tau)$, $y(\tau)$, $\tau_0 \leq \tau \leq \tau_1$, where $x(\tau)$ and $y(\tau)$ are piecewise smooth. Show that the area enclosed by the curve is

$$A = \tfrac{1}{2}\int_{\tau_0}^{\tau_1} (x\dot{y} - y\dot{x})d\tau.$$

Hint: First show that

$$A = -\int_{\tau_0}^{\tau_1} y\dot{x}d\tau.$$

Then integrate by parts and average the results obtained.

4. Use the result of Problem 3 to formulate the isoperimetric problem. Attempt to solve the problem using the formulation obtained.

5. Consider all curves in the xy-plane which are represented by piecewise smooth functions $y(x)$ joining the point (0, 1) to a point on the x-axis and such that the area between the curve and the x-axis is a specified value A. Determine the particular curve from this set which when rotated about the x-axis yields a surface of revolution with the smallest possible area. *Ans.* A straight line.

6. Suppose that it is of interest to maximize $z = f(\mathbf{x})$ subject to the constraints $g_u(\mathbf{x}) = 0$, $u = 1, \ldots, r$, $r < n$, where n is the number of components in $\mathbf{x}$. This is an ordinary constrained maximization problem. Suppose that $f \in C'$ and that each $g_u \in C'$. Consider the $(r + 1) \times n$ matrix $\mathbf{G}$ the rows of which are $\nabla f(\mathbf{x}_0)$, $\nabla g_u(\mathbf{x}_0)$. Use the first implicit function theorem of Appendix II to show that if the rank of $\mathbf{G}$ at x_0 is $r + 1$, then $f(\mathbf{x})$ cannot have either a relative maximum or minimum at $\mathbf{x}_0$ subject to the constraints. Thus conclude that if $f(\mathbf{x})$ has a relative maximum or minimum at $\mathbf{x}_0$ it is necessary that there exist numbers $\lambda_0, \lambda_1, \ldots, \lambda_r$, not all zero, such that

$$\lambda_0 \nabla f(\mathbf{x}_0) + \sum_{u=1}^{r} \lambda_u \nabla g_u(\mathbf{x}_0) = \mathbf{0}.$$

This is the general form of the Lagrange multiplier rule. Under what conditions is $\lambda_0 \neq 0$? Show that if $\lambda_0 \neq 0$, one can without loss of generality take $\lambda_0 = 1$. Under what conditions are the Lagrange multipliers uniquely determined?

7. Can the multiplier rule for the isoperimetric problem be proved merely by noting that $\Phi(\boldsymbol{\xi})$ must have a relative maximum at $\mathbf{0}$ subject to the constraints $\Omega^u(\boldsymbol{\xi}) = 0$; and then applying the theory of Lagrange multipliers? Here $\Phi(\boldsymbol{\xi})$ is $J[\mathbf{y}]$ for $\mathbf{y}$ given by (3-13).

8. An optimal solution $\mathbf{z}(x)$ to the isoperimetric problem is said to be

normal if and only if there exist r functions $\boldsymbol{\eta}_u$ such that $||\boldsymbol{\Omega}^u_{\boldsymbol{\xi}}(0)||$ is nonsingular. Show that when $\mathbf{z}(x)$ is normal it is possible to select $\lambda_0 = 1$ and that then the remaining λ's are uniquely determined. Show that in this case there exist no multipliers which satisfy the necessary conditions and which include $\lambda_0 = 0$.

9. Suppose that $\mathbf{z}(x)$ is normal as defined in Problem 8. Prove that if $\boldsymbol{\eta}(x)$ is any piecewise smooth function satisfying the system of equations

$$\int_{x_0}^{x_1} (\mathbf{G}^i_{\mathbf{y}'} \cdot \boldsymbol{\eta}' + \mathbf{G}^i_{\mathbf{y}} \cdot \boldsymbol{\eta})dx = 0, \quad i = 1, \ldots, r,$$

then there exists a one parameter family $\mathbf{y}(x;\ \xi)$ which satisfies the constraints for all ξ sufficiently close to 0 and for which $\mathbf{y}_\xi(x;\ 0) = \boldsymbol{\eta}(x)$, $\mathbf{y}'_\xi(x;\ 0) = \boldsymbol{\eta}'(x)$. Hint: There exist functions $\boldsymbol{\eta}_k$, $k = 1, \ldots, r$ with the properties stated in Problem 8. Consider the functions $\mathbf{y}(x;\ \boldsymbol{\xi}, \xi_{r+1}) = \mathbf{z}(x) + \Sigma^r_{k=1}\xi_k\boldsymbol{\eta}_k + \xi_{r+1}\boldsymbol{\eta}$ and the corresponding equations $\Omega_u(\boldsymbol{\xi}, \xi_{r+1}) = 0$. Apply the first implicit function theorem.

10. Prove that if $\mathbf{z}(x)$ optimizes a problem with isoperimetric constraints and $\mathbf{z}(x)$ is normal as defined in Problem 8, then $\mathbf{z}(x)$ satisfies the Weierstrass and Legendre necessary conditions for the function H. Hint: Let x^* be a value of x not a corner or an end point of $\mathbf{z}(x)$. Let $\boldsymbol{\eta}(x;\varepsilon) = 0, x_0 \leq x \leq x^*$, $\boldsymbol{\eta}(x;\varepsilon) = (\mathbf{u} - \mathbf{z}'(x^*))(x - x^*)$, $x^* \leq x \leq x^* + \varepsilon$, $\boldsymbol{\eta}(x;\varepsilon) = (x_1 - x^* - \varepsilon)^{-1}\varepsilon(\mathbf{u} - \mathbf{z}'(x^*))(x_1 - x)$, $x^* + \varepsilon \leq x \leq x_1$. Also let $\boldsymbol{\eta}_k$, $k = 1, \ldots, r$ be defined as in Problem 8. Apply the methods used in solving Problem 9 to show that $\mathbf{y}(x;\varepsilon) = \mathbf{z}(x) + \Sigma^r_{k=1}\xi_k(\varepsilon)\boldsymbol{\eta}_k(x) + \boldsymbol{\eta}(x;\varepsilon)$ is a one parâmeter family of admissible solutions for $\varepsilon > 0$ and sufficiently close to 0. Denote by $\Phi(\varepsilon)$ the value of $J[\mathbf{y}]$ for this set. Since $\varepsilon \geq 0$, and $\Phi(0) = J[\mathbf{z}]$, it must be true that $\Phi'_+(0) \leq 0$ for a maximum.

11. Give a parametric formulation of a problem involving isoperimetric constraints.

12. Derive the formula for the area of the segment of a circle and verify the result stated in the example.

13. A heavy, flexible rope of length L is hung from two pegs (not necessarily lying on a horizontal line). The mass per unit length of the rope is ρ. Derive the equation of the curve determined by the rope when hanging freely under the action of gravity. Hint: Minimize the potential energy. (The potential energy is minimized when the center of mass is made as low as possible.)

14. Consider the following pair of isoperimetric problems.

(a) $$\max_{\mathbf{y}(x)} J[\mathbf{y}] = \max_{\mathbf{y}(x)} \int_{x_0}^{x_1} F(x, \mathbf{y}(x), \mathbf{y}'(x))\mathrm{d}x$$

$$\text{subject to} \int_{x_0}^{x_1} G(x, \mathbf{y}(x), \mathbf{y}'(x))\mathrm{d}x = \gamma = \text{constant}$$

$$\text{and } \mathbf{y}(x_0) = \mathbf{y}_0, \ \mathbf{y}(x_1) = \mathbf{y}_1$$

(b) $$\min_{\mathbf{y}(x)} \gamma[\mathbf{y}] = \min_{\mathbf{y}(x)} \int_{x_0}^{x_1} G(x, \mathbf{y}(x), \mathbf{y}'(x))\mathrm{d}x$$

$$\text{subject to} \int_{x_0}^{x_1} F(x, \mathbf{y}(x), \mathbf{y}'(x))\mathrm{d}x = J = \text{constant}$$

$$\text{and } \mathbf{y}(x_0) = \mathbf{y}_0, \ \mathbf{y}(x_1) = \mathbf{y}_1.$$

What relationship can you establish between the two optimal paths?

Sections 3.3 through 3.7

1. Consider the problem of finding that piecewise smooth curve which lies on a given sphere and joins two specified points on the sphere and which has the shortest length. Set up the problem as one in the calculus of variations with a holonomic constraint. Solve the problem.

2. Solve completely Example 1 of Section 2.11 treating it as a Lagrange problem. Show that $\lambda_0 > 0$ and hence can be taken to be 1. Determine the precise time behavior of $\lambda_1(t)$. Construct a diagram showing how λ_1 is related to K.

3. Re-solve Problem 2 using Example 2 of Section 2.11.

4. Re-solve Problem 2 using Example 5 of Section 2.11.

5. Re-solve Problem 2 using Example 6 of Section 2.11.

6. Show how the Samuelson-Solow n-sector model can be treated as a Lagrange problem.

7. Can the analysis associated with (3-51) be employed to provide a rigorous development of the multiplier rule for isoperimetric problems when use is made of the suggestion made in Problem 7 for Section 3.2?

8. Provide the detailed derivation of the transversality conditions in the case of holonomic constraints.

9. For the case of holonomic constraints discussed in the text, show that

if $\boldsymbol{\eta}(x)$ satisfies (3-43) then there exists a one parameter family of solutions $\mathbf{y}(x;\ \xi)$ to $G^i = 0$, with the property of $\mathbf{y}_\xi(x;\ 0) = \boldsymbol{\eta}(x)$. This implies that $\mathbf{y}(x;\ \xi) = \mathbf{z}(x) + \xi\boldsymbol{\eta}(x) + \mathbf{o}(\xi)$ where $\lim_{\xi\to 0}\mathbf{o}(\xi)/\xi = 0$. Hint: Use the appropriate implicit function theorem and the appropriate result concerning derivatives.

10. Prove that a problem with isoperimetric constraints can be converted to a Lagrange problem. Show that the set of necessary conditions obtained in this way is the same as those obtained in Section 3.2. Hint: Introduce new variables y_{n+i} by means of the equations $\dot{y}_{n+i} = G^i$.

11. Obtain the transversality conditions for problems with holonomic constraints.

12. Modify the treatment of the Ramsey model in Example 1 of Section 3.7 by introducing a piecewise smooth variable M to replace C. Show that the same necessary conditions are obtained. Hint: M has a free boundary.

Sections 3.8 through 3.16

1. Develop a simplified rigorous proof of the multiplier rule which does not involve showing that the Weierstrass necessary condition is also satisfied.

2. Show that $\mathbf{y}(x;\ \boldsymbol{\xi}, \mathbf{d})$ has continuous partial derivatives with respect to $(\boldsymbol{\xi}, \mathbf{d})$. Is this also true of $\mathbf{y}'$? Do we make any use in the proof of the derivatives of $\mathbf{y}'$ with respect to $(\boldsymbol{\xi}, \mathbf{d})$?

4

Optimal control theory

4.1. Introduction

In Chapters 2 and 3 we have studied the classical theory of the calculus of variations. This chapter and the next will be devoted to the modern theory of the calculus of variations, often referred to as *optimal control theory*. The modern theory grew out of attempts to control optimally the behavior through time of some system such as a rocket or space vehicle. However the theory has a very wide field of applicability, including much of economic theory.

The new theory allows for inequalities in the constraints; and, technically, this is the most important advance beyond the classical theory. Moreover, the new theory is based on a new way of viewing and formulating variational problems; it enables us therefore to see even 'classical' problems in quite a new light.

The theory of optimal control was developed by the well known Russian mathematician L. S. Pontryagin and his co-workers in the late 1950's and became easily accessible in English speaking countries with the publication in 1962 of *The Mathematical Theory of Optimal Processes*, an English translation of an earlier Russian publication by Pontryagin *et al.* Like most pioneers, Pontryagin had his precursors. Variational analysis dealing with inequalities goes back to the paper by Valentine [40], which until recently remained largely unknown. Hestenes in 1949 wrote a report for the RAND Corporation [20] based on an approach somewhat similar to that of the Russian school. Work by Bellman and others in dynamic programming is also related to the subject of optimal control. But it was the work of Pontryagin and his associates which was chiefly responsible for a radically new approach to the calculus of variations and for a dramatic revitalizing of interest in the subject.

4.2. The basic control problem

We shall in this section describe in general terms the type of problem that we shall be studying throughout the chapter. The focus of our study will be some real or hypothetical *system*. The system might be a space vehicle, a nuclear reactor, a temperature control device or a multisectoral economy. The problem of interest is that of optimizing, in some specified sense, the behavior of the system through time. It will be assumed that the manner in which the system changes through time can be described by specifying the time behavior of a finite collection of variables, say $y_1(t), \ldots, y_n(t)$, which will be referred to as *state variables*. The y_j are assumed to be piecewise smooth functions of time with not more than a finite number of corners. For an economic system, the state variables might be the capital stocks of the several goods.

It will be assumed also that there exists a set of *control variables* $v_1, \ldots, v_m$ such that if the time paths of the control variables are specified then the time variation of the state variables, and therefore the evolution of the system through time, is determined. A *control* is a vector valued function of time whose components are the control variables. The control variables may undergo jump changes and are restricted only to be piecewise continuous. In Ramsey's model, for example, C or $\dot{K}$ (or both) might be treated as control variables.

It will be assumed that every variable of interest can be classified as a state variable or as a control variable.

In view of the restrictions placed on the two classes of variables, one may think of the control variables as governing not the values of the state variables but their rates of change. More specifically, it will be assumed that the dependence of the state variables on the control variables can be described by a set of first order differential equations

$$\dot{\mathbf{y}} = \mathbf{f}(t, \mathbf{y}, \mathbf{v}) \tag{4-1}$$

or, in component form,

$$\frac{dy_j}{dt} = f^j(t, y_1, \ldots, y_n, v_1, \ldots, v_m), \qquad j = 1, \ldots, n. \tag{4-2}$$

We shall assume that each $f^j \in C'$ over some open subset $\mathscr{R}$ of points $(t, \mathbf{y}, \mathbf{v})$ in $\mathscr{E}^{m+n+1}$ which contains all points that will be of interest.

The control variables will not be allowed to take on arbitrary values. It will be assumed that, for each t, $\mathbf{v}(t) \in \mathscr{V}$ where $\mathscr{V}$ is some arbitrary, fixed, prespecified subset of $\mathscr{E}^m$. $\mathscr{V}$ is called the *control region*. $\mathscr{V}$ may be open or closed and is not restricted in any special way. It is important to observe, however, that in the formulation of Pontryagin *et al.*, $\mathscr{V}$ *is independent of time and of the values of the state variables.* In the next chapter we shall introduce a somewhat different formulation in which the set $\mathscr{V}$ can depend both on the values of the state variables and on time. This is a useful generalization. In the present chapter, however, $\mathscr{V}$ will be fixed, and at each point in time the control variables must be chosen so that $\mathbf{v}(t)$ is in $\mathscr{V}$. Any piecewise continuous control $\mathbf{v}(t)$, $\mathbf{v}(t) \in \mathscr{V}$, will be called *admissible.*

To complete our statement of the problem of optimal control we must define a measure of the effectiveness of a control. Such a measure is provided by

$$J[\mathbf{y}, \mathbf{v}] = \int_{t_0}^{t_1} F(t, \mathbf{y}(t), \mathbf{v}(t))dt \tag{4-3}$$

where it is assumed that $F \in C'$ over $\mathscr{R}$ also. The control problem then is that of selecting a control $\mathbf{v}(t)$ such that $\mathbf{v}(t) \in \mathscr{V}$ for each t and such that, when $\mathbf{y}(t)$ is determined from (4-1) and an initial condition $\mathbf{y}(t_0) = \mathbf{y}_0$ is given, the functional (4-3) is maximized or minimized. A control which satisfies these conditions will be called an *optimal control.*

We are by now accustomed to thinking of any $\mathbf{y}(t)$ as a curve in $\mathscr{E}^{n+1}$. Normally we shall think of $\mathbf{y}(t)$ as starting from a fixed point. As in the classical theory, however, a variety of conditions may be imposed at the right hand end point. When the time interval is finite, each of these conditions can be interpreted as requiring that the terminal point lie on a smooth manifold. We shall also allow for the possibility that there is no right hand end point and that the system operates for all future time.

We have described in general terms the type of problem which was considered by Pontryagin and his associates and which will be studied in the present chapter. It will be noted that in the problem as formulated there are no restrictions on the values which may be assumed by the state variables. Problems involving restricted state variables (or, in the jargon of the control literature, restricted phase coordinates) were also considered by Pontryagin and will be studied in the next chapter. In the present chapter, however, *it will be assumed that there are no constraints on the state variables.*

To illustrate how a variational problem can be formulated as a control problem, let us consider again the familiar Ramsey model. As we shall see, it may be necessary to consider several alternative formulations before one is found with the desired structure.

At first sight it might seem reasonable to choose the investment rate $\dot{K}$

as the sole control variable. Then the integrand would be

$$F = U[\Psi(K) - \dot{K}] \tag{4-4}$$

and (4-1) would take the special form

$$\dot{K} = v. \tag{4-5}$$

However, it is necessary that $\dot{K} \leq \Psi(K)$, that is,

$$v \leq \Psi(K). \tag{4-6}$$

But then $\mathscr{V}$ is not independent of the state variables. Hence the formulation must be abandoned.

Alternatively, we might choose C as the control variable. It would then be necessary to give up (4-4), for the F of (4-3) does not involve derivatives of the state variables. Instead we should have

$$F = U(C) \tag{4-7}$$

and, as the special case of (4-1),

$$\dot{K} = \Psi(K) - C. \tag{4-8}$$

The only restriction on C is

$$C \geq 0. \tag{4-9}$$

The set of admissible values of C is completely fixed and independent both of time and of the state variable. Thus we have succeeded in formulating Ramsey's problem as a control problem of the type studied by Pontryagin.

4.3. Necessary conditions–the maximum principle

In this section we shall set down the necessary conditions which must be satisfied by an optimal solution to the control problem formulated in Section 4.2.

The necessary conditions for the control problem are in many ways similar to those for the problem of Lagrange. We introduce a vector $(\lambda_0, \boldsymbol{\lambda}(t))$ of multipliers or conjugate variables, the first component of which is a constant; and a Hamiltonian function, now of the form $H = \lambda_0 F + \Sigma_{j=1}^n \lambda_j(t) f^j$. There can then be given a set of differential equations which must be satisfied by an optimal solution; however, instead of n second order differential equations, there are $2n$ first order differential equations (just as in the Hamiltonian formulation of the simplest problem in the calculus of variations – see Problem 6 of Section 2.13). There can be given also a set of transversality conditions for the end points. Thus far there is nothing strikingly new in the necessary conditions. The new feature is the manner in which the control variables are determined at each point in time. It will be shown that, at each point t, $\mathbf{v}$ should be chosen to maximize H for the specified value of $\mathbf{y}$ at that t and for $\mathbf{v} \in \mathscr{V}$. This rule is usually called the maximum principle. (Sometimes, inappropriately, the whole set of necessary conditions is referred to as Pontryagin's maximum principle. In fact, the maximum principle is only one part of the complete set of necessary conditions.)

Before stating the necessary conditions it will be useful to say a little more about smooth manifolds. For in considering the end point conditions we shall find it necessary to place an additional restriction on the type of manifolds admitted. Recall that we have defined a smooth manifold $\mathscr{M}$ in $\mathscr{E}^{n+1}$ as the intersection of one or more smooth hypersurfaces $S^u(t, \mathbf{y}) = 0$ (we now use t instead of x), and that we have assumed that at each point in the manifold the matrix with columns ∇S^u has rank equal to the number of equations $S^u = 0$ involved.

Consider the manifold $\mathscr{M}$ generated by the equations $S^u(t, \mathbf{y}) = 0$. The equation $t - t_1 = 0$ may or may not be included in this set of equations. Denote by $\mathscr{M}_f$ the manifold generated by $t - t_1 = 0$ (this manifold is, of course, a hyperplane). Let $\mathscr{M}_1$ be the manifold generated by all equations in the set which generate $\mathscr{M}$ except $t - t_1 = 0$. If $t - t_1 = 0$ is the only equation, set $\mathscr{M}_1 = \mathscr{E}^{n+1}$. Then if the set generating $\mathscr{M}$ contains $t - t_1 = 0$, $\mathscr{M} = \mathscr{M}_1 \cap \mathscr{M}_f$, while if $t - t_1 = 0$ is absent $\mathscr{M} = \mathscr{M}_1$. In the case where $\mathscr{M}_1 \neq \mathscr{E}^{n+1}$, we shall find it desirable to place the following restriction on the equations which generate $\mathscr{M}_1$:

Restriction on $\mathscr{M}_1$. Let $\mathscr{M}_1$ be the intersection of s, $s \geq 1$, smooth hypersurfaces $S^u(t, \mathbf{y}) = 0$. Then the $s \times n$ matrix $\|\partial S^u/\partial y_j\|$ has rank s at each point in $\mathscr{M}_1$.

Notice that the restriction relates to derivatives with respect to the variables $\mathbf{y}$ only, not derivatives with respect to t. Thus $\mathbf{y}$ must appear non-trivially in each constraint. Furthermore, $\mathscr{M}_1$ must be defined by not more than n equations (otherwise, the rank condition could not be satisfied); hence $\mathscr{M}_1$ has dimension at least 1 in $\mathscr{E}^{n+1}$ in all cases.

Now in formulating the necessary conditions, we shall make use not of $\mathscr{M}$ but of $\mathscr{M}_1$ only. Indeed, we shall not make direct use even of $\mathscr{M}_1$; instead we shall work with a family of manifolds $\mathscr{M}_1(t_1)$ in $\mathscr{E}^n$, which can be obtained from $\mathscr{M}_1$ in $\mathscr{E}^{n+1}$. We now describe in detail the manifold $\mathscr{M}_1(t_1)$.

Suppose that $S^u(t, \mathbf{y}) = 0$, $u = 1, \ldots, s$ serve to define the manifold $\mathscr{M}_1$. Now we set $t = t_1$ and consider the set of points $\mathbf{y}$ satisfying $S^u(t_1, \mathbf{y}) = 0$, $u = 1, \ldots, s$. (Possibly not all S^u involve t, but that does not matter.) In view of the restriction placed on $\mathscr{M}_1$, this set of points generates a smooth manifold in $\mathscr{E}^n$ of dimension $n - s$; this manifold will be denoted by $\mathscr{M}_1(t_1)$. For each t_1 in some set we can obtain a manifold $\mathscr{M}_1(t_1)$; hence by varying t_1 we can generate a one parameter family of manifolds in $\mathscr{E}^n$. We note also that the set of points $(t_1, \mathbf{y})$, $\mathbf{y} \in \mathscr{M}_1(t_1)$ represents the intersection of the manifold $\mathscr{M}_1$ with the hyperplane $t = t_1$. For example, suppose that, in $\mathscr{E}^3$, $\mathscr{M}_1$ is the hypersurface $2y_1 + 3y_2 - t = 0$. Then $\mathscr{M}_1(t_1)$ is the line $2y_1 + 3y_2 = t_1$ in $\mathscr{E}^2$ (alternatively, $\mathscr{M}_1(t_1)$ is a line in $\mathscr{E}^3$ lying in the plane $t = t_1$); and the one parameter family of manifolds $\mathscr{M}_1(t_1)$ is a family of parallel lines in the plane. Notice, finally, that if there are no S^u and $\mathscr{M}_1 = \mathscr{E}^{n+1}$ then $\mathscr{M}_1(t_1) = \mathscr{E}^n$.

We can now state the following basic theorem.

Theorem 4.3.1. Necessary Conditions for the Control Problem. Suppose that $\mathbf{w}(t)$ *is an admissible control and let* $\mathbf{z}(t)$, $\mathbf{z}(t_0) = \mathbf{y}_0$ *be the corresponding solution to (4-1). Then if* $(\mathbf{z}(t), \mathbf{w}(t))$ *yields the absolute maximum of* $J[\mathbf{y}, \mathbf{v}]$, *when the curve representing* $\mathbf{z}(t)$ *must end on the smooth manifold* $\mathscr{M}$, *it is necessary that there exist a number* $\lambda_0 \geq 0$ *(which without loss of generality may be taken to be* 0 *or* 1*) and a vector-valued function* $\boldsymbol{\lambda}(t) = (\lambda_1(t), \ldots, \lambda_n(t))$, *the components of which are continuous functions of time with the characteristic that* $(\lambda_0, \boldsymbol{\lambda}(t)) \neq \mathbf{0}$ *for any t and such that if*

$$H(t, \mathbf{y}, \mathbf{v}, \boldsymbol{\lambda}) = \lambda_0 F(t, \mathbf{y}, \mathbf{v}) + \sum_{j=1}^{n} \lambda_j(t) f^j(t, \mathbf{y}, \mathbf{v}) \tag{4-10}$$

then

$$\dot{\mathbf{z}} = \mathbf{H}_\lambda(t, \mathbf{z}, \mathbf{w}, \boldsymbol{\lambda}) = \mathbf{f}(t, \mathbf{z}, \mathbf{w}) \tag{4-11}$$

and

$$\dot{\boldsymbol{\lambda}} = -\mathbf{H}_\mathbf{y}(t, \mathbf{z}, \mathbf{w}, \boldsymbol{\lambda}). \tag{4-12}$$

Furthermore, if

$$M(t, \mathbf{z}, \boldsymbol{\lambda}) = \sup_{\mathbf{v} \in \mathscr{V}} H(t, \mathbf{z}, \mathbf{v}, \boldsymbol{\lambda}) \tag{4-13}$$

then

$$H(t, \mathbf{z}, \mathbf{w}, \boldsymbol{\lambda}) = M(t, \mathbf{z}, \boldsymbol{\lambda}), \tag{4-14}$$

that is, for each t, H attains at $\mathbf{w}(t)$ *its maximum with respect to* $\mathbf{v}$*, for* $\mathbf{v} \in \mathscr{V}$ *and* $(t, \mathbf{z}, \boldsymbol{\lambda})$ *fixed. Finally, as a transversality condition, if* $\mathbf{z}(t)$ *ends at the point* $(t_1, \mathbf{z}(t_1)) \in \mathscr{M}$ *then the vector* $\boldsymbol{\lambda}(t_1)$*, i.e.* $\boldsymbol{\lambda}(t)$ *evaluated at the terminal time, must be orthogonal to* $\mathscr{M}_1(t_1)$ *(not* $\mathscr{M}$*) at* $\mathbf{z}(t_1)$*. If* $\mathbf{z}(t)$*,* $\mathbf{w}(t)$ *minimizes* $J[\mathbf{y}, \mathbf{v}]$*, all of the above conditions carry over except that in (4-13)* sup *must be replaced by* inf.

If the curve must both begin and end on a smooth manifold, the transversality condition must be satisfied at each end point. The differential equations (4-11) and (4-12), together with the initial and terminal conditions are sometimes referred to as the *canonical equations.*

This rather long theorem provides us with conditions which must be satisfied by an optimal solution to the control problem. We now offer some observations concerning the theorem. Notice first that the multipliers or conjugate variables $\boldsymbol{\lambda}(t)$ here are continuous for all t; in our analysis of the problem of Lagrange, on the other hand, the multipliers could be discontinuous at corners of $\mathbf{z}(x)$. The equations of motion for the system, that is, the equations which determine its time behavior, are the $2n$ first order ordinary differential equations (4-11) and (4-12). These are called Hamilton's equations because of their similarity in form to Hamilton's equations in classical mechanics. Equations (4-11) simply relate the rate of change of the state variables to the control variables. Equations (4-12) describe the behavior of the conjugate variables over time. Written out in detail,

$$\dot{\lambda}_i(t) = -\lambda_0 F_{z_i}(t, \mathbf{z}, \mathbf{w}) + \sum_{j=1}^{n} \lambda_j(t) f^j_{z_i}(t, \mathbf{z}, \mathbf{w}). \tag{4-15}$$

Equations (4-13) and (4-14) tell us that at each instant of time $\mathbf{w}$ is chosen to maximize H.

In principle, the control problem can be solved in the following way. First determine a function $\mathbf{v} = \boldsymbol{\Upsilon}(t, \mathbf{y}, \boldsymbol{\lambda})$, which expresses the control variables as a function of t, $\mathbf{y}$ and $\boldsymbol{\lambda}$, by maximizing H with respect to $\mathbf{v} \in \mathscr{V}$. Then substitute this function into Hamilton's equations to obtain

$$\dot{\mathbf{y}} = \mathbf{f}(t, \mathbf{y}, \boldsymbol{\Upsilon}(t, \mathbf{y}, \boldsymbol{\lambda})) \tag{4-16}$$

$$\dot{\boldsymbol{\lambda}} = -\mathbf{H}_{\mathbf{y}}(t, \mathbf{y}, \boldsymbol{\Upsilon}(t, \mathbf{y}, \boldsymbol{\lambda}), \boldsymbol{\lambda}). \tag{4-17}$$

These $2n$ equations can be solved for $\mathbf{y}(t)$ and $\boldsymbol{\lambda}(t)$, and the constants of integration can be determined from the initial conditions $\mathbf{y}(t_0) = \mathbf{y}_0$ and the necessary condition that $\boldsymbol{\lambda}(t)$ be orthogonal to $\mathscr{M}_1(t_1)$ at the terminal point.

While we shall not be concerned with problems of numerical computation, we note that in practice the solution procedure usually is not nearly as straightforward as this outline might suggest. The principal difficulty lies in determining $\boldsymbol{\Upsilon}(t, \mathbf{y}, \boldsymbol{\lambda})$ and in expressing it in a convenient form. It is a further unfortunate feature of the problem that the constants of integration depend on both the initial and terminal conditions. This rules out any simple computational procedure which works progressively from the initial conditions to the terminal point, optimizing at each step with respect to $\mathbf{v}$.

We now examine several special cases which are of considerable practical importance and for which the necessary conditions allow of some simplification.

When the right hand end point is fixed and it is required that $\mathbf{y}(t_1) = \mathbf{y}_1$, the manifold $\mathscr{M}$ is defined by $\mathbf{y} - \mathbf{y}_1 = \mathbf{0}$, $t - t_1 = 0$. The manifold $\mathscr{M}_1(t_1)$ then has dimension 0 and every vector in $\mathscr{E}^n$ is normal to $\mathscr{M}_1(t_1)$. Thus the transversality condition places no restriction on $\boldsymbol{\lambda}(t_1)$. Thus we have the following corollary.

Corollary 1. Fixed End Points. If both end points are fixed, Theorem 4.3.1 applies. However, the transversality condition places no restriction on $\boldsymbol{\lambda}(t_1)$.

In the other special case of interest there is a free boundary at the right hand end point. The manifold $\mathscr{M}$ in this case is simply $t - t_1 = 0$ and $\mathscr{M}_1(t_1) = \mathscr{E}^n$. The only vector which is orthogonal to every vector $\mathbf{a} \in \mathscr{E}^n$ is $\mathbf{0}$. Thus $\boldsymbol{\lambda}(t_1) = \mathbf{0}$. Since $(\lambda_0, \boldsymbol{\lambda}(t)) \neq \mathbf{0}$ for any t, it cannot be true that $\lambda_0 = 0$; hence we can set $\lambda_0 = 1$ and we have the following corollary.

Corollary 2. Free Boundary. If there is a free boundary at the right hand end point t_1, *Theorem 4.3.1 applies. However, the transversality condition now requires that* $\boldsymbol{\lambda}(t_1) = \mathbf{0}$ *so that without loss of generality* $\lambda_0 = 1$.

We have yet to consider the modifications which must be introduced when the interval of integration is unbounded, that is, when the system is supposed to move along some trajectory for all future time. For this case we can state the following theorem.

Theorem 4.3.2. Unbounded Planning Horizon. If the interval over which the time behavior of the system is to be optimized is unbounded then, except for the transversality condition at the right hand end point, the necessary conditions of Theorem 4.3.1 must still be satisfied. The transversality condition must be modified. Suppose that $\mathbf{z}(t)$ *has only a finite number of corners. If it is required that*

$$\lim_{t\to\infty} [\mathbf{y}(t) - \mathbf{g}(t)] = \mathbf{0}$$

where $\mathbf{g}(t)$ *is a specified function, then no condition is imposed on* $\boldsymbol{\lambda}(t)$ *as* $t \to \infty$. *If for each component of* $\mathbf{y}(t)$ *there is a free boundary at infinity, so that the set of admissible trajectories may include some which differ from* $\mathbf{z}(t)$ *for all t sufficiently large, then, for any one parameter family of admissible trajectories* $\mathbf{y}(t; \xi)$ *with* $\mathbf{y}(t; 0) = \mathbf{z}(t)$ *which can be constructed, it is necessary that*

$$\lim_{t\to\infty} \boldsymbol{\lambda}(t) \cdot \boldsymbol{\eta}(t) = 0 \tag{4-18}$$

where $\boldsymbol{\eta}(t) = \mathbf{y}_{\xi}(t; 0)$. *If it is required that* $\lim_{t\to\infty}\mathbf{y}(t) = \mathbf{b}$, *where* $\mathbf{b}$ *is not specified but is merely required to lie in a bounded manifold* $\mathscr{M}_1$ *in* $\mathscr{E}^n$, *and if* $\lim_{t\to\infty}\mathbf{z}'(t)$ *exists, then it is possible to choose the multipliers so that* $\lim_{t\to\infty}\boldsymbol{\lambda}(t)$ *is orthogonal to* $\mathscr{M}$ *at the terminal point; and, when this is done, any necessary conditions at the terminal point of the trajectory will be satisfied.*

When there is a free boundary it is sometimes possible to infer from (4-18) that $\lim_{t\to\infty}\boldsymbol{\lambda}(t) = \mathbf{0}$. The inference is not generally valid, however; one must be prepared to examine carefully each problem to ascertain whether the inference is warranted.

We shall not give the detailed proof of Theorem 4.3.1 developed by Pontryagin and his co-workers. The complete proof is quite long and would occupy more than sixty pages of text. Instead, we shall in the next chapter provide a rigorous derivation of the necessary conditions for a more general control problem. Theorem 4.3.1. will emerge as a special case. We shall be able to offer a rather short and simple proof which is based on the analysis of the problem of Lagrange provided in Chapter 3. It is not worth going through Pontryagin's proof in detail; however, his approach is an interesting one and can be described in general terms without difficulty. In Section 4.5, therefore, we shall provide a heuristic version of Pontryagin's proof.

4.4. The conversion of a nonautonomous system into an autonomous system

A control problem will be called *autonomous* if t does not appear explicitly in F or $\mathbf{f}$ and $\mathscr{M}$ does not involve t. Otherwise, it will be called *nonautonomous*. (We have used this terminology earlier.) We shall prove that it is always possible to convert a nonautonomous system into an autonomous one. It therefore suffices to prove the necessary conditions for autonomous systems.

Consider the problem of optimizing (4-3), where (4-1) relates the time rate of change of the state variables to the control variables and where the curve representing $\mathbf{y}(t)$ must terminate on the smooth manifold $\mathscr{M}$ described by $S^u(t, \mathbf{y}) = 0$, $u = 1, \ldots, s$.

To convert the problem into the autonomous form we introduce a new variable y_{n+1} by means of the differential equation

$$\dot{y}_{n+1} = 1, \qquad y_{n+1}(t_0) = t_0. \tag{4-19}$$

It is clear that $y_{n+1} = t$. Consider now the problem of determining the control $\mathbf{v}(t)$, $\mathbf{v}(t) \in \mathscr{V}$, which optimizes

$$J[\mathbf{y}, y_{n+1}, \mathbf{v}] = \int_{t_0}^{t_1} F(y_{n+1}, \mathbf{y}, \mathbf{v}) dt \tag{4-20}$$

where

$$\dot{\mathbf{y}} = \mathbf{f}(y_{n+1}, \mathbf{y}, \mathbf{v}), \qquad \dot{y}_{n+1} = 1 \tag{4-21}$$

and where $\mathbf{y}(t_0) = \mathbf{y}_0$, $y_{n+1}(t_0) = t_0$ and $[\mathbf{y}(t), y_{n+1}(t)]$ must end on the smooth manifold described by $S^u(y_{n+1}, \mathbf{y}) = \mathbf{0}$, $u = 1, \ldots, s$. This problem is autonomous; moreover, it is equivalent to the original problem in the sense that if $\mathbf{v}$ is an optimal control for the original problem it is also an optimal control for the new problem, and vice versa.

Suppose now that we have proved the necessary conditions for autonomous systems. These are just the conditions given in Theorem 4.3.1 except that t does not appear explicitly in any of the arguments. We now show how one can use the procedure for converting a nonautonomous system into an autonomous system, described in the preceding paragraph, to translate the necessary conditions for an autonomous system into the necessary conditions for the corresponding nonautonomous system.

If $\mathbf{z}(t)$, $z_{n+1}(t)$, $\mathbf{w}(t)$ provide an optimal solution then, from Theorem 4.3.1, there exists a vector-valued function $(\lambda_0, \boldsymbol{\lambda}(t), \lambda_{n+1}(t))$ which is never $\mathbf{0}$ and of which the first component λ_0 is a non-negative constant and the remaining components are continuous functions of time. Furthermore, if

$$H^* = \lambda_0 F + \sum_{j=1}^{n} \lambda_j f^j + \lambda_{n+1} = H + \lambda_{n+1} \tag{4-22}$$

then (4-21) holds and

$$\dot{\boldsymbol{\lambda}} = -\mathbf{H}_{\mathbf{y}}^* = -\mathbf{H}_{\mathbf{y}}; \qquad \dot{\lambda}_{n+1} = -H_{y_{n+1}}^* = -H_t. \tag{4-23}$$

Also, $(\boldsymbol{\lambda}(t_1), \lambda_{n+1}(t_1))$ must be orthogonal to the manifold $\mathscr{M}$ ($\mathscr{M}$ is $\mathscr{M}_1$ when t is absent) at the terminal point of the trajectory $(t_1, \mathbf{z}(t_1), z_{n+1}(t_1))$.

We now examine the form of the transversality condition in several special cases. To obtain the condition of Theorem 4.3.1 for the nonautonomous case it is necessary to eliminate λ_{n+1} and to replace H^* with H. We already know from (4-23) that H can be substituted for H^*. The equation for $\dot{\lambda}_{n+1}$ merely tells us something about the behavior of H through time and is of no concern at the moment. The elimination of λ_{n+1} from the transversality conditions is a much more complicated problem.

Consider first the case in which the original $S^u(t, \mathbf{y})$ do not involve t explicitly. Then the $S^u(\mathbf{y}, y_{n+1})$ do not involve y_{n+1} explicitly and can be written $S^u(\mathbf{y}) = 0$, $u = 1, \ldots, s$. Thus ∇S^u, viewed as an $(n + 1)$-component vector, has 0 in the last place, corresponding to $S^u_{y_{n+1}}$, and $\nabla S^u = (\mathbf{S}^u_{\mathbf{y}}, 0)$. Since $(\boldsymbol{\lambda}(t_1), \lambda_{n+1}(t_1))$ must be a linear combination of these vectors it then follows that $\lambda_{n+1}(t_1) = 0$. Hence the condition that $(\boldsymbol{\lambda}(t_1), \lambda_{n+1}(t_1))$ be orthogonal to $\mathscr{M}$, viewed as a manifold in $\mathscr{E}^{n+1}$, reduces to the condition that $\boldsymbol{\lambda}(t_1)$ be a linear combination of the $\mathbf{S}^u_{\mathbf{y}}$ $(t_1,\mathbf{z}(t_1))$. Thus $\boldsymbol{\lambda}(t_1)$ must be orthogonal to $\mathscr{M}_1(t_1)$.

Consider next the case in which the $S^u(t, \mathbf{y})$ involve t but the rank of $||\partial S^u/\partial y_j||$ is s, so that each S^u must involve $\mathbf{y}$. We can write $\nabla S^u = (\mathbf{S}^u_{\mathbf{y}}, \mathbf{S}^u_{y_{n+1}})$. Since $(\boldsymbol{\lambda}(t_1), \lambda_{n+1}(t_1))$ must be a linear combination of these vectors, $\boldsymbol{\lambda}(t_1)$ must be a linear combination of the $\mathbf{S}^u_{\mathbf{y}}$. Thus $\boldsymbol{\lambda}(t_1)$ must be orthogonal to $\mathscr{M}_1(t_1)$. Also, because of the above rank condition, if $\boldsymbol{\lambda}(t_1) = \Sigma_{u=1}^s \rho_u \mathbf{S}^u_{\mathbf{y}}$, then

$$\lambda_{n+1}(t_1) = \sum_{u=1}^{s} \rho_u S^u_{y_{n+1}} = \sum_{u=1}^{s} \rho_u S^u_t. \tag{4-24}$$

We examine next the case in which $\mathscr{M}$ is represented by the single hypersurface $S = t - t_1 = 0$ or $y_{n+1} - y^*_{n+1} = 0$. Here $\nabla S = (\mathbf{0}, 1)$; since $(\boldsymbol{\lambda}(t_1), \lambda_{n+1}(t_1))$ must be a linear combination of this vector, $\boldsymbol{\lambda}(t_1) = \mathbf{0}$ but nothing can be said about $\lambda_{n+1}(t_1)$. In this case, the constraint $t - t^* = 0$ places no restriction on $\mathbf{y}$; hence $\mathscr{M}_1(t_1) = \mathscr{E}^n$. Thus again $\boldsymbol{\lambda}(t_1)$ must be orthogonal to $\mathscr{M}_1(t_1)$.

We consider finally the case in which there is a set of constraints $S^u(t, \mathbf{y}) = 0$, $u = 1, \ldots, s$, each of which involves $\mathbf{y}$ and for which $||\partial S^u/\partial y_j||$ has rank s. These serve to define $\mathscr{M}_1$. In addition, there is the constraint $t - t_1 = 0$. The normal vectors for $\mathscr{M} = \mathscr{M}_1 \cap \mathscr{M}_f$ are $(\mathbf{S}^u_{\mathbf{y}}, \mathbf{S}^u_{y_{n+1}})$, $u = 1, \ldots, s$, and $(\mathbf{0}, 1)$. Since $(\boldsymbol{\lambda}(t_1), \lambda_{n+1}(t_1))$ must be a linear combination of these vectors, $\boldsymbol{\lambda}(t_1)$ is a linear combination of the $\mathbf{S}^u_{\mathbf{y}}$ and hence is orthogonal to $\mathscr{M}_1(t_1)$. In this case also, nothing can be said about $\lambda_{n+1}(t_1)$.

Looking back over the four cases considered, we see that in every case $\boldsymbol{\lambda}(t_1)$ must be orthogonal to $\mathcal{M}_1(t_1)$. Furthermore, $\dot{\boldsymbol{\lambda}} = -\mathbf{H}_\mathbf{y}$ and $\dot{\mathbf{y}} = \mathbf{H}_\lambda$. Finally, since $H^* = H + \lambda_{n+1}$, the requirement that $\mathbf{w}$ maximize H^* reduces to the requirement that $\mathbf{w}$ maximize H. We have therefore completely eliminated λ_{n+1} from the necessary conditions and shown that the resulting necessary conditions for the problem involving time are those of Theorem 4.3.1. Thus we have shown that if Theorem 4.3.1 holds for an autonomous system then it must hold for a nonautonomous system also. It therefore suffices to prove Theorem 4.3.1 for an autonomous system. (This is the procedure of Pontryagin also.)

In the course of the above analysis, we also obtained in certain cases some information about $\lambda_{n+1}(t_1)$. This information can be used in these cases to develop formulas for the time behavior of H. We shall say more about this in the next section, although we shall only rarely need to refer to such formulas in our later analysis.

4.5. An heuristic derivation of the necessary conditions

Suppose that $\mathbf{w}(t)$ is an optimal (maximizing) control for the autonomous version of the control problem we have been studying, and let $\mathbf{z}(t)$ represent the time behavior of the state variables under this control when $\mathbf{z}(t_0) = \mathbf{y}_0$. Then if $\mathbf{v}(t)$ is any other admissible control and if $\mathbf{y}(t)$ is the corresponding time behavior of the state variables we can be sure that $J[\mathbf{y}, \mathbf{v}] \leq J[\mathbf{z}, \mathbf{w}]$. As with the classical theory, the essential step in the derivation of the necessary conditions is the construction of a suitable collection of admissible controls $\mathbf{v}(t)$ for comparison with $\mathbf{w}(t)$.

The control problem differs from the classical problem in two important respects. In the first place, the $\mathbf{y}$ variables cannot be varied independently of the $\mathbf{v}$ variables. In fact, once a control $\mathbf{v}(t)$ is selected, the time behavior of the state variables is completely determined. In the second place, the control variables need not be continuous. They can have jump discontinuities. Thus an admissible control $\mathbf{v}(t)$ can be equal to $\mathbf{w}(t)$ everywhere except over a short interval, and at the end points of this interval the components of $\mathbf{v}(t)$ can change discontinuously from the corresponding values of $\mathbf{w}(t)$. Figure 4.1 displays a $\mathbf{v}(t)$ of this type. Such $\mathbf{v}(t)$ will be said to differ from $\mathbf{w}(t)$ by a *pulse*, and the $\mathbf{v}(t)$ themselves will be called pulse variations. To obtain the necessary conditions one need consider only variations of this kind.

Let us now consider an admissible control $\mathbf{v}(t)$ which differs from $\mathbf{w}(t)$ only by a pulse over the interval $t_c - \varepsilon$ to t_c. We seek to compute $\mathbf{y}(t)$, the

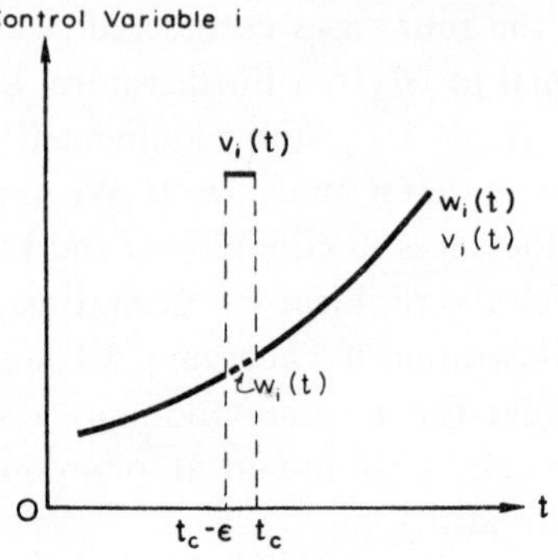

Fig. 4.1.

time behavior of the state variables corresponding to $\mathbf{v}(t)$. Up to $t_c - \varepsilon$, $\mathbf{y}(t) = \mathbf{z}(t)$ since $\mathbf{v}(t) = \mathbf{w}(t)$. However, at $t_c - \varepsilon$ and for a very short period thereafter, $\mathbf{v}(t)$ deviates from $\mathbf{w}(t)$. This means that for a very short period $\mathbf{y}'$ differs from $\mathbf{z}'$. For $t > t_c$, we again have $\mathbf{v}(t) = \mathbf{w}(t)$. Generally speaking, this brief deviation of $\mathbf{v}(t)$ from $\mathbf{w}(t)$ will cause $\mathbf{y}(t)$ to deviate slightly from $\mathbf{z}(t)$ for all $t > t_c - \varepsilon$. (Figure 4.2 depicts the behavior of the jth component of $\mathbf{y}$.) However, this deviation can be made as small as desired by making ε sufficiently small.

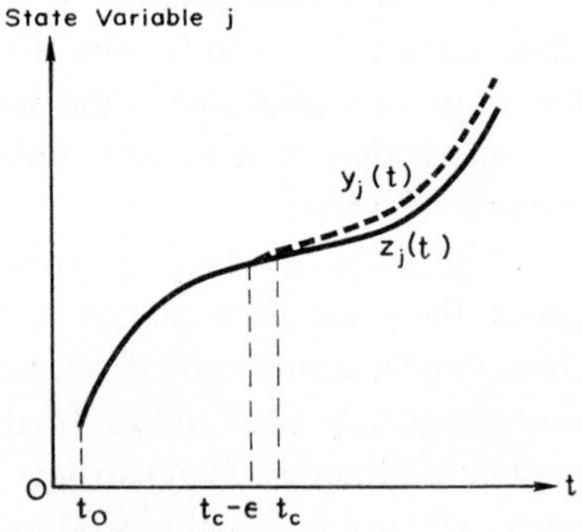

Fig. 4.2.

Let us now try to determine $\mathbf{y}(t)$ in more detail for $t > t_c$. We recall from the existence theorems for differential equations that, for all $\mathbf{y}^*$ in a neighborhood of $\mathbf{z}(t_c)$, there will be a solution to $\dot{\mathbf{y}} = \mathbf{f}$ beginning at $\mathbf{y}^*$. Now the value of $\mathbf{y}(t)$ at t_c is a function of ε and will lie in such a neighborhood when ε is sufficiently small. To remind us of this dependence, we write $\mathbf{y}(t; \varepsilon)$. The existence theorem indicates also that the solution is differentiable with respect to the initial values; hence $\mathbf{y}(t;\,\varepsilon)$ is differentiable with respect to ε. Let us write $\zeta(t) = \mathbf{y}_\varepsilon(t;\,0)$. Then $\mathbf{y}(t;\,\varepsilon) = \mathbf{z}(t) + \varepsilon\zeta(t) + \mathbf{o}(t;\,\varepsilon)$ since $\mathbf{y}(t;\,0) = \mathbf{z}(t)$.

We now obtain a system of linear differential equations with solution $\zeta(t)$. For all ε we must have

$$\dot{\mathbf{y}}(t;\,\varepsilon) = \mathbf{f}(\mathbf{y}(t;\,\varepsilon), \mathbf{v}). \tag{4-25}$$

If we now differentiate with respect to ε and set $\varepsilon = 0$, we obtain the required system of equations

$$\dot{\zeta}_j = \mathbf{f}^j_{\mathbf{y}}(\mathbf{z}, \mathbf{v}) \cdot \zeta, \quad j = 1, \ldots, n. \tag{4-26}$$

Thus if its value at t_c were specified $\zeta(t)$ could be determined by solving (4-26).

We can determine $\zeta(t_c)$ in the following way. Notice that

$$\frac{1}{\varepsilon}[\mathbf{y}(t;\,\varepsilon) - \mathbf{z}(t)] = \zeta(t) + \frac{1}{\varepsilon}\mathbf{o}(t;\,\varepsilon). \tag{4-27}$$

Taking the limit as $\varepsilon \to 0+$, we obtain $\zeta(t)$ on the right. However,

$$\frac{1}{\varepsilon}[\mathbf{y}(t;\,\varepsilon) - \mathbf{z}(t)] = \frac{1}{\varepsilon}\int_{t_c-\varepsilon}^{t_c}(\dot{\mathbf{y}} - \dot{\mathbf{z}})\mathrm{d}t = \frac{1}{\varepsilon}\int_{t_c-\varepsilon}^{t_c}[\mathbf{f}(\mathbf{y}, \mathbf{v}) - \mathbf{f}(\mathbf{z}, \mathbf{w})]\mathrm{d}t \tag{4-28}$$

since $\mathbf{y}(t;\,\varepsilon)$ and $\mathbf{z}(t)$ are equal at $t_c - \varepsilon$. Taking the limit as $\varepsilon \to 0+$, we obtain

$$\zeta(t_c) = \mathbf{f}(\mathbf{z}, \mathbf{v}) - \mathbf{f}(\mathbf{z}, \mathbf{w}) \tag{4-29}$$

the right hand side of (4-28) being evaluated at t_c+.

We now notice that the same procedure can be used to determine the change in $J[\mathbf{y}, \mathbf{v}]$ when $\mathbf{w}$ changes to $\mathbf{v}$. Let $\mathbf{y}_0(t;\,\varepsilon)$ be defined by $\dot{\mathbf{y}}_0(t;\,\varepsilon) = \mathbf{F}(\mathbf{y}(t;\,\varepsilon), \mathbf{v})$ and let $\zeta_0(t) = \mathrm{d}y_0(t;\,0)/\mathrm{d}\varepsilon$. Then

$$\dot{\zeta}_0 = \mathbf{F}_{\mathbf{y}}(\mathbf{z}, \mathbf{w}) \cdot \zeta. \tag{4-30}$$

Also

$$\zeta_0(t_c) = F(\mathbf{z}, \mathbf{v}) - F(\mathbf{z}, \mathbf{w}). \tag{4-31}$$

Let us now restrict our attention to cases in which there is a free boundary or a fixed right hand end point, so that the terminal time, call it t_1, is fixed. Cases in which the terminal time is variable are not so easy to discuss at the heuristic level of this section. Given $\zeta(t)$, (4-30) and (4-31) can be used to determine $\zeta_0(t)$ and $J[\mathbf{y}, \mathbf{v}] = J[\mathbf{z}, \mathbf{w}] + \varepsilon\zeta_0(t_1) + o(t_1; \varepsilon)$. (Notice that this could not be written if t_1 were not fixed.)

To proceed, we notice that, since $\mathbf{w}(t)$ is an optimal control, $\zeta_0(t_1) \leq 0$ if $\mathbf{y}(t; \varepsilon)$ is admissible. We now translate this requirement into a more useful form. Let us select a vector $(\lambda_0, \boldsymbol{\lambda}(t_1))$ such that, if $\mathbf{y}(t; \varepsilon)$ is admissible or if $\mathbf{y}(t; \varepsilon)$ is not admissible but $\zeta_0(t_1) = 0$ then

$$\lambda_0\zeta_0(t_1) + \boldsymbol{\lambda}(t_1) \cdot \boldsymbol{\zeta}(t_1) = \zeta_0(t_1). \tag{4-32}$$

In the free boundary case, any $\mathbf{y}(t; \varepsilon)$ is admissible, as is any $\zeta_0(t_1)$ computed for such a $\mathbf{y}(t; \varepsilon)$. Hence $\lambda_0 = 1$ and we may set $\boldsymbol{\lambda}(t_1) = \mathbf{0}$. For the fixed end points case, $\mathbf{y}(t_1; \varepsilon) = \mathbf{y}_1$ and $\boldsymbol{\zeta}(t_1) = \mathbf{0}$, so no restriction is placed on $\boldsymbol{\lambda}(t_1)$. Again $\lambda_0 = 1$ if $\mathbf{y}(t; \varepsilon)$ is admissible. However, in the fixed end points case, there may not exist any trajectory other than $\mathbf{z}(t)$ which satisfies the end point conditions; hence there may be no admissible control other than $\mathbf{w}(t)$. To take care of such cases we introduce λ_0, which is then 0 since there is no variation in J; thus we arrange things so that the right hand side of (4-32) is 0. We shall assume that, if $\lambda_0 = 0$, $\boldsymbol{\lambda}(t_1)$ is chosen to be different from $\mathbf{0}$. To continue, let us next explore whether it is possible to find a vector function $(\lambda_0(t), \boldsymbol{\lambda}(t))$ such that, for every t, $t_0 \leq t \leq t_1$,

$$\lambda_0(t)\zeta_0(t) + \boldsymbol{\lambda}(t) \cdot \boldsymbol{\zeta}(t) = \zeta_0(t_1). \tag{4-33}$$

Notice first that the right hand side of (4-33) is a constant. Thus if (4-33) is differentiated with respect to t we obtain

$$\lambda_0\dot{\zeta}_0 + \dot{\lambda}_0\zeta_0 + \boldsymbol{\lambda}(t) \cdot \dot{\boldsymbol{\zeta}}(t) + \dot{\boldsymbol{\lambda}}(t) \cdot \boldsymbol{\zeta}(t) = 0. \tag{4-34}$$

Applying (4-27) and (4-29), this becomes

$$\lambda_0\mathbf{F}_{\mathbf{y}}(\mathbf{z}, \mathbf{w}) \cdot \boldsymbol{\zeta} + \dot{\lambda}_0\zeta_0 + \sum_{j=1}^{n} \lambda_j(t)\mathbf{f}^j_{\mathbf{y}}(\mathbf{z}, \mathbf{w}) \cdot \boldsymbol{\zeta} + \dot{\boldsymbol{\lambda}}(t) \cdot \boldsymbol{\zeta}(t) = 0 \tag{4-35}$$

which can be rearranged as

$$\dot{\lambda}_0\zeta_0 + \sum_{u=1}^{n} \left[\dot{\lambda}_u + \lambda_0 F_{y_u}(\mathbf{z}, \mathbf{w}) + \sum_{j=1}^{n} \lambda_j(t) f^j_{y_u}(\mathbf{z}, \mathbf{w})\right] \zeta_u(t) = 0. \tag{4-36}$$

If we choose $(\lambda_0(t), \boldsymbol{\lambda}(t))$ to be a solution to the system of linear differential equations

$$\begin{aligned} \dot{\lambda}_0 &= 0 \\ \dot{\lambda}_u &= -\lambda_0 F_{y_u}(\mathbf{z}, \mathbf{w}) - \sum_{j=1}^{n} \lambda_j(t) f^j_{y_u}(\mathbf{z}, \mathbf{w}) \end{aligned} \tag{4-37}$$

then (4-36) will indeed hold and the left hand side of (4-33) will be a constant.

With $(\lambda_0(t_1), \boldsymbol{\lambda}(t_1))$ selected in this way, the constant is $\zeta_0(t_1)$; hence (4-33) must hold for all t. There always exist continuous solutions to (4-37); hence the λ's can indeed be determined. Notice that λ_0 is a constant. Notice also that $\boldsymbol{\lambda}(t)$ in no way depends on $\mathbf{v}(t)$; it depends only on $\mathbf{z}(t)$ and $\mathbf{w}(t)$.

We can now suppose that λ_0 and $\boldsymbol{\lambda}(t)$ have been chosen so that (4-33) holds for all t. In particular, it holds for $t = t_c$. However, at t_c, $\zeta_0(t_c)$ is given by (4-30) and $\boldsymbol{\zeta}(t_c)$ is given by (4-28). We recall also that $\zeta_0(t_1) \leq 0$. Thus, at t_c, (4-33) reduces to

$$\lambda_0[F(\mathbf{z}, \mathbf{v}) - F(\mathbf{z}, \mathbf{w})] + \boldsymbol{\lambda}(t_c)[\mathbf{f}(\mathbf{z}, \mathbf{v}) - f(\mathbf{z}, \mathbf{w})] \leq 0. \tag{4-38}$$

If we now introduce the Hamiltonian function, (4-38) becomes

$$H(t_c, \mathbf{z}, \mathbf{v}) \leq H(t_c, \mathbf{z}, \mathbf{w}) \tag{4-39}$$

and it is necessary that $\mathbf{w}$ maximize $H(t_c, \mathbf{z}, \mathbf{v})$ with respect to $\mathbf{v}$. However, the pulse in $\mathbf{w}(t)$ can be introduced at any time t_c; and, from the linearity of (4-27) and (4-29), two or more pulses at different times make additive contributions to $\zeta_0(t_1)$. Thus at every t_c, $t_0 \leq t_c \leq t_1$, (4-39) must hold; and that is the maximum principle.

That almost completes our 'derivation' of the necessary conditions for an autonomous system with a free boundary or a fixed end point on the right. It remains only to show that $(\lambda_0, \boldsymbol{\lambda}(t))$ is never $\mathbf{0}$. However this follows from the existence theorems for differential equations. If $(\lambda_0, \boldsymbol{\lambda}(t)) = \mathbf{0}$ for any t, it must be identically $\mathbf{0}$.

Consider next the case in which the interval of integration is infinite. If it is required that $\lim_{t\to\infty}[\mathbf{y}(t) - \mathbf{g}(t)] = \mathbf{0}$, where $\mathbf{g}(t)$ is specified, then, if $\mathbf{y}(t;\, \varepsilon)$ is admissible, $\lim_{t\to\infty}\boldsymbol{\zeta}(t) = \mathbf{0}$ and no restriction is placed on $\boldsymbol{\lambda}(t)$ as $t \to \infty$. If there is a free boundary, it is necessary that $\lim_{t\to\infty}\boldsymbol{\lambda}(t) \cdot \boldsymbol{\zeta}(t) = 0$; and, normally, this implies that $\lim_{t\to\infty}\boldsymbol{\lambda}(t) = \mathbf{0}$.

One additional piece of information, not contained in the necessary conditions, is sometimes useful. Let us consider $\mathrm{d}H/\mathrm{d}t$. We have

$$\frac{\mathrm{d}}{\mathrm{d}t} H(\mathbf{z}(t), \mathbf{w}(t), \boldsymbol{\lambda}(t)) = \lambda_0 \frac{\mathrm{d}F}{\mathrm{d}t} + \boldsymbol{\lambda} \cdot \frac{\mathrm{d}\mathbf{f}}{\mathrm{d}t} + \dot{\boldsymbol{\lambda}} \cdot \mathbf{f}$$

$$= \lambda_0 \mathbf{F}_{\mathbf{y}} \cdot \dot{\mathbf{z}} + \lambda_0 \mathbf{F}_{\mathbf{w}} \cdot \dot{\mathbf{w}} + \sum_{j=1}^{n} \lambda_j \mathbf{f}_{\mathbf{y}}^j \cdot \dot{\mathbf{z}} + \sum_{j=1}^{n} \lambda_j \mathbf{f}_{\mathbf{v}}^j \cdot \dot{\mathbf{w}} + \dot{\boldsymbol{\lambda}}\mathbf{f} \tag{4-40}$$

$$= \mathbf{H}_{\mathbf{y}} \cdot \dot{\mathbf{z}} + \mathbf{H}_{\mathbf{v}} \cdot \dot{\mathbf{w}} + \dot{\boldsymbol{\lambda}} \cdot \mathbf{f}.$$

Now $\dot{\mathbf{z}} = \mathbf{f}$ and $\dot{\boldsymbol{\lambda}} = -\mathbf{H}_{\mathbf{y}}$. Hence

$$\frac{\mathrm{d}H}{\mathrm{d}t} = \mathbf{H}_{\mathbf{v}} \cdot \dot{\mathbf{w}}. \tag{4-41}$$

Now if $\mathbf{w}$ lies in the interior of $\mathscr{V}$ then, by the maximum principle, $\mathbf{H}_v = \mathbf{0}$. Suppose alternatively that $\mathbf{w}$ is on the boundary of $\mathscr{V}$, and consider a value of t for which dH/dt and $\dot{\mathbf{w}}$ exist. If it is possible to move in the direction defined by $\dot{\mathbf{w}}$, the vector $\mathbf{H}_v$ must be orthogonal to $\dot{\mathbf{w}}$; for if $\mathbf{H}_v \cdot \dot{\mathbf{w}} > 0$, $\mathbf{w}$ could not maximize $\mathbf{H}_v$ at t, and if $\mathbf{H}_v \cdot \dot{\mathbf{w}} < 0$, the movement would be away from a value of $\mathbf{w}$ which maximizes $\mathbf{H}_v$. Thus $\mathbf{H}_v \cdot \dot{\mathbf{w}} = 0$ always. By continuity, the same conclusion holds for jump points of $\mathbf{w}(t)$. Hence $dH/dt = 0$ whenever the derivative exists. We also note that $H(t, \mathbf{z}, \mathbf{w})$ must be a continuous function of t. To prove this, we need only show that H is continuous across a jump in $\mathbf{w}(t)$. At a point t^* where a jump occurs, $\mathbf{w}_-(t^*)$ and $\mathbf{w}_+(t^*)$ provide alternative optimal solutions; hence H has the same value for both and is therefore continuous across a jump in $\mathbf{w}(t)$. If this were not true, either $\mathbf{w}_-(t)$ or $\mathbf{w}_+(t)$ could be extended to yield a larger value of H, which is a contradiction. Since when it exists $dH/dt = 0$, and since H is continuous, the Hamiltonian for an autonomous system must be constant along the optimal path. If we now go back to (4-22) and (4-24), we see that, since H^* is a constant, $\lambda_{n+1} = -dH/dt = -H_t$. Hence

$$\frac{dH}{dt} = H_t = -\dot{\lambda}_{n+1}$$

and for nonautonomous systems

$$H(t, \mathbf{z}(t), \mathbf{w}(t)) = -H(t_1, \mathbf{z}(t_1), \mathbf{w}(t_1)) - \int_{t_1}^{t} H_t dt. \tag{4-42}$$

Thus we have obtained the following additional result.

Theorem 4.5.1. Time Variation of H. For an autonomous system, H is a constant along an optimal trajectory. For a nonautonomous system, H need not be a constant; but $\dot{H} = H_t$ so that the time variation of H is given by (4-42).

This theorem is often useful, as later examples will illustrate.

The developments of this section are not rigorous. However, they do provide a good intuitive idea of what is involved in obtaining the necessary conditions. They also indicate the kind of approach followed by Pontryagin and his associates in their proofs. As indicated earlier, we shall in the next chapter provide a rigorous derivation of the necessary conditions; but we shall adopt a rather different approach. We shall also provide a complete proof of Theorem 4.5.1. for a somewhat more general type of problem.

4.6. The Ramsey model: finite planning horizon

Before going on to give a complete proof of the necessary conditions, we shall provide several examples which illustrate how control theory may be applied. In particular, we shall see how it serves to resolve those special cases of the Ramsey model with which the classical theory could not cope.

Let us first reconsider the general Ramsey problem with a finite planning horizon as a special type of control problem. We have already formulated the problem as a control problem and have noted that the consumption rate C must be used as the control variable. Thus we wish to maximize

$$J[K, C] = \int_0^T U(C)\mathrm{d}t \tag{4-43}$$

where

$$\dot{K} = \Psi(K) - C \tag{4-44}$$

and where $C \geq 0$ and $K(0) = K_0$, $K(T) = K_1$.

Here

$$H = \lambda_0 U(C) + \lambda_1(t)[\Psi(K) - C] \tag{4-45}$$

so that

$$\dot{\lambda}_1 = -H_K = -\lambda_1 \Psi'. \tag{4-46}$$

If C yields an interior maximum of H, then

$$H_C = 0 = \lambda_0 U' - \lambda_1. \tag{4-47}$$

The system is autonomous; from Theorem 4.5.1, therefore, H is a constant along any optimal path. Thus

$$\lambda_0 U(C) + \lambda_1(t)[\Psi(K) - C] = \lambda, \quad \lambda \text{ a constant.} \tag{4-48}$$

Let us examine first the case in which $C > 0$ maximizes H so that (4-47) holds. In this interior case $\lambda_0 \neq 0$; for if $\lambda_0 = 0$, $\lambda_1 = 0$ also, and the necessary conditions would be violated. Hence we can set $\lambda_0 = 1$ and $\lambda_1 = U'$. In view of (4-44), (4-48) reduces to

$$U + U'\dot{K} = \lambda \tag{4-49}$$

which is the familiar result obtained from the classical theory.

In the only remaining case, the C which maximizes H lies on the boundary, that is, $C = 0$. In this case

$$\dot{K} = \Psi(K) \tag{4-50}$$

and the behavior through time of K can be determined. Thus we may conclude that there are only two possibilities. Either $K(t)$ satisfies the differential equation (4-49) or it satisfies the differential equation (4-50).

We can now see what the nature of the solution must be in all cases. If K_0 is such that $C > 0$ initially then, from our earlier discussion, C never decreases and the system remains always on the trajectory determined by (4-49), that is, the trajectory yielded by the classical approach. If initially K_0 is so small that $C = 0$ maximizes H, the system moves along the boundary with $\dot{K} = \Psi(K)$ until K increases to a point at which a change occurs; then the system switches from the trajectory determined by $\dot{K} = \Psi(K)$ to the trajectory determined by (4-49).

The interesting problem is that of determining the exact point at which a change occurs. Now if $U(C)$ is strictly concave there can be no discontinuous changes in C and hence no discontinuities in $\dot{K}$. To see this, suppose that at t_e there occurs a discontinuous change in C from 0 to some positive value $C+$. Now λ_1 and K are continuous. Hence both 0 and $C+$ must maximize H at t_e, so that the maximum is not unique. However, H is a concave function of C, and if $U(C)$ is strictly concave so is H. As we ask the reader to show in the problems, the point which maximizes a strictly concave function is unique; there cannot be two different values of C which maximize H. Hence C and $\dot{K}$ must be continuous. At the transition time t_e, therefore, λ, K and $\dot{K}$ must be continuous.

In general, it is not easy to determine precisely the transition point, but we can now see what is involved. It will be helpful to consider, as an example, the $K\dot{K}$-phase diagram of Figure 2.22. Recall that it is desired to reach K_1 at time T. Imagine now that in Figure 2.22 each solid curve which intersects the dotted boundary curve is labeled with the time required to move from the point of intersection to K_1. When $C = 0$, the economy moves along the dotted boundary curve. As it moves from K_0 along the boundary curve, time goes by. Suppose that we continually note the remaining time needed to reach K_1. The switch should be made at the point where the remaining time is precisely the time label on the solid curve that is being crossed at that moment. If such a curve is never met, the system stays on the boundary until K_1 is reached. Notice that in this account we have required that $\dot{K}$ be continuous.

When the planning horizon is infinite the problem is much easier. For then there is only one solid curve in Figure 2.22, and this corresponds to the solution to the Euler equation. Thus the system moves along the boundary until this curve is reached. In other words, if $\dot{K}_e$ is the value of $\dot{K}$ at the intersection of $\dot{K} = \Psi(K)$ with $U + U'\dot{K} = 0$, the system moves along the boundary until $\dot{K} = \dot{K}_e$. Then the system switches over to the trajectory defined by $U + U'\dot{K} = 0$. Observe that in this account K and $\dot{K}$ have been taken to be continuous.

We have noted above that, for any solution in which ultimately $C > 0$, λ_0 must be equal to 1. When the solution lies entirely on the boundary, we need not be concerned about the value of λ_0; for the time behavior of K can be determined without knowing λ_0. Furthermore, λ_1 can be determined without knowledge of λ_0 except for the constant of integration. For a boundary solution it is necessary that λ_1 be positive, but suitable values for λ_1 can be found, both when $\lambda_0 = 1$ and when $\lambda_0 = 0$.

Since the system is autonomous, H is constant along any optimal path. When the planning horizon is infinite, $U \to 0$ and $U'\dot{K} \to 0$; hence $H \to 0$. It follows that H must be equal to 0 along the entire path.

4.7. A phase diagram using conjugate variables

At a very early stage we introduced the notion of a phase diagram which, for a variable y, shows the relationship between y' and y. We indicated then that there is another diagram, also called a phase diagram, which displays the relationship between a variable and its conjugate. We can now offer a more detailed description of the second kind of phase diagram, as well as a specific example. Let us recall that the variables λ_j which appear in the solutions to control problems are called conjugate variables as well as multipliers. In particular λ_j is called the variable conjugate to y_j. A graph which shows the relationship, along a path satisfying the necessary conditions, of a state variable y_j to its multiplier or conjugate variable λ_j will also be referred to as a phase diagram. As we noted in Chapter 2, there is in mechanics no essential difference between the two kinds of phase diagram, for λ_j is proportional to y_j'. In other areas, however, this need not be the case. Phase diagrams involving conjugate variables are used quite frequently in economics, especially in the recent literature dealing with optimal growth. We now illustrate with a specific example just how such a diagram may be constructed.

Consider again the example of Section 2.10, and the accompanying Figure 2.22. In that example $U = -\alpha(C - C^*)^2$ and $\Psi = \beta K$. We recall also that

$$\dot{K}^2 - (\beta K - C^*)^2 = \gamma \tag{4-51}$$

when the Euler equation is satisfied and $C > 0$.

Now for the Ramsey model we have shown that when $C > 0$, $\lambda_1 = U'$. From the above expression for U, therefore,

$$\lambda_1 = -2\alpha(C - C^*) = 2\alpha(C^* - C). \tag{4-52}$$

However, $C = \Psi(K) - \dot{K}$; hence

$$\lambda_1 = 2\alpha(C^* - \beta K + \dot{K})$$

and, when $C > 0$,

$$\dot{K} = \beta K - C^* + \frac{\lambda_1}{2\alpha}. \tag{4-53}$$

If this is substituted into (4-51) we obtain, for $C > 0$,

$$\left(\beta K - C^* + \frac{\lambda_1}{2\alpha}\right)^2 - (\beta K - C^*)^2 = \gamma \tag{4-54}$$

or

$$\lambda_1 = 2\alpha[-(\beta K - C^*) \pm \sqrt{\gamma + (\beta K - C^*)^2}]. \tag{4-55}$$

It follows that

$$\frac{d\lambda_1}{dK} = -2\alpha\beta \pm 2\alpha\beta \frac{\beta K - C^*}{\sqrt{\gamma + (\beta K - C^*)^2}} \tag{4-56}$$

We know from Section 2.10 that γ can be positive, negative or zero. Consider first the case in which $\gamma = 0$. Then (4-55) yields the two lines

$$\lambda_1 = 0 \quad \text{and} \quad \lambda_1 = -4\alpha(\beta K - C^*). \tag{4-57}$$

Each of these lines passes through the point $(K^*, 0)$, $K^* = C^*/\beta$. The two lines are displayed in Figure 4.3, the heavy line representing the second of the two equations (4-57).

Consider next the case in which $\gamma > 0$ and the plus sign appears in (4-55) and (4-56). For $K = 0$,

$$\lambda_1 = 2\alpha[-C^* + \sqrt{\gamma + (C^*)^2}] > 0 \tag{4-58}$$

and λ_1 increases as γ increases. As $K \to \infty$, λ_1 approaches 0 asymptotically. Furthermore $d\lambda_1/dK$ is always negative and approaches 0 asymptotically as $K \to \infty$. Thus the trajectories for this case are like those drawn in Figure 4.3 above the two lines defined by (4-57).

Suppose now that $\gamma > 0$ and the negative sign holds in (4-55) and (4-56).

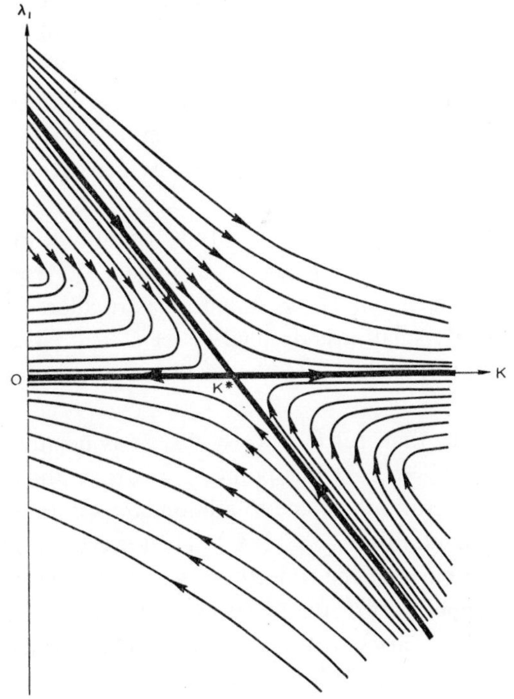

Fig. 4.3.

Then, for $K = 0$,

$$\lambda_1 = -\, 2\alpha[C^* + \sqrt{\gamma + (C^*)^2}] < 0 \tag{4-59}$$

and λ_1 decreases as γ increases. Furthermore, $\mathrm{d}\lambda_1/\mathrm{d}K$ is always negative and approaches $-4\alpha\beta$ as $K \to \infty$. Thus the trajectories for this case look like those drawn in Figure 4.3 below the two lines defined by (4-57).

Suppose, finally, that $\gamma < 0$. In this case it is more convenient to solve for K in terms of λ_1 than to work with (4-55). From (4-54),

$$\left(\frac{\lambda_1}{2\alpha}\right)^2 + 2(\beta K - C^*)\left(\frac{\lambda_1}{2\alpha}\right) = \gamma \tag{4-60}$$

so that

$$K = K^* - \frac{\alpha}{\beta\lambda_1}\left[|\gamma| + \left(\frac{\lambda_1}{2\alpha}\right)^2\right], \quad \alpha < 0. \tag{4-61}$$

Note that $K \to -\infty$ as $\lambda_1 \to 0+$ and that $K \to \infty$ as $\lambda_1 \to 0-$. To any particular value of K, there may correspond 0, 1 or 2 values of λ_1; the number depends on the value of γ. The trajectories in this case lie between the two lines defined by (4-57). To determine the direction of motion along the trajectories we examine the equations $\dot{\lambda}_1 = -\lambda_1 \Psi' = -\beta\lambda_1$. Thus, when $\lambda_1 > 0$, λ_1 is decreasing; and, when $\lambda_1 < 0$, λ_1 is increasing. On the line $\lambda_1 = 0$, $U' = 0$ and $C = C^*$; the motion on this line must therefore be away from the point $(K^*, 0)$, since $\dot{K}$ must be negative if $K < K^*$ and positive if $K > K^*$.

Thus if there were no boundary $C = 0$ to worry about, Figure 4.3 would be the phase plane diagram for K and its conjugate λ_1. However, we must allow for the requirement that $C \geq 0$ and, in particular, for the fact that when K_0 is sufficiently small it is optimal to set $C = 0$, at least for a time. How must we modify Figure 4.3 so that it includes trajectories along part of which $C = 0$?

From (4-52) we see that, for $0 < C < C^*$, λ_1 is positive and increases as C decreases until $C = 0$. At this point $\lambda_1 = 2\alpha C^*$, and this defines the point at which the transition is made to a boundary solution. Let us add to Figure 4.3 the horizontal line $\lambda_1 = 2\alpha C^*$. Then everything below the line is correct. On those parts of the trajectories which lie above the line, however, $C < 0$; the upper part of the figure must therefore be revised. Let us now determine how λ_1 varies with K on the boundary, where $C = 0$. It is always true that $\dot{\lambda}_1 = -\beta\lambda_1$. When $C = 0$, $\dot{K} = \beta K$. Hence

$$\frac{d\lambda_1}{dK} = \frac{\dot{\lambda}_1}{\dot{K}} = -\frac{\lambda_1}{K} \tag{4-62}$$

and

$$\lambda_1 K = \delta \tag{4-63}$$

where δ is chosen so that the curve in the $\lambda_1 K$-plane is continuous. These curves will be continuous since both λ_1 and K are continuous functions of time. They are in fact rectangular hyperbolas with a vertical asymptote at $K = 0$.

We can now complete the revision of Figure 4.3. Consider the line defined by the second equation (4-57); it cuts the λ_1 axis at $4\alpha C^*$. On this line $\gamma = 0$; hence, from (4-57), if $\lambda_1 = 2\alpha C^*$ then $K = K^*/2$. If $K_0 < K^*/2$, part of the optimal trajectory must lie on the boundary; then, from (4-63), $\delta = 2\alpha C^* K^*/2 = \alpha C^* K^* = \alpha\beta(K^*)^2$. The continuation of the line above $\lambda_1 = 2\alpha C^*$, where $C = 0$, is therefore defined by $\lambda_1 K = \alpha\beta(K^*)^2$. The slope of this hyperbola at the junction point where $K = K^*/2$ is $d\lambda_1/dK = -4\alpha\beta$ which is precisely the slope of the line to which the hyperbola is joined. This must be true in all cases; $\dot{\lambda}_1 = \beta\lambda_1$ and λ_1 is continuous, hence

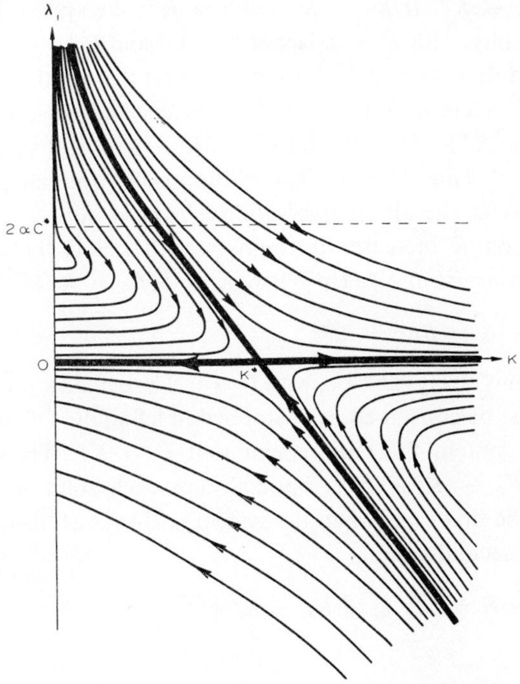

Fig. 4.4.

$\dot{\lambda}_1$ is continuous. Hence the complete phase diagram, showing the relationship between λ_1 and K in all cases, is given by Figure 4.4. Notice that the behavior of the two most important variables in the problem has been represented on a single diagram, and that this has been accomplished without solving the differential equations explicitly.

4.8. The Ramsey model: infinite planning horizon

Let us take the above example a step further by solving it in detail under the assumptions that the planning horizon is infinite and that the initial stock of capital K_0 is arbitrary. We know that, when C does not lie on the boundary, $\gamma = 0$ and the trajectory is represented by the heavy curve which passes through the point $(K^*, 0)$ in Figure 4.4. In arriving at the solution we shall obtain in a slightly different way some of the results of Example 2.

From (2-98) we know that when $C > 0$ the solution is

$$K(t) = K^* + \rho e^{-\beta t} \quad \text{or} \quad K(t) = K^* + \rho e^{\beta t} \tag{4-64}$$

where $\rho = K_0 - K^*$. If $K_0 = K^*$, $K(t) = K^*$; the system begins at bliss and remains at bliss with $\dot{K} = 0$. Hence $C = C^*$ and $U' = 0$, so that $\lambda_1 = 0$.

Suppose next that $K_0 > K^*$, and consider first the solution $K(t) = K^* + (K_0 - K^*)e^{-\beta t}$. Here K decreases and approaches K^* asymptotically. Also, $\dot{K} = -\beta(K_0 - K^*)e^{-\beta t} < 0$; and $C = \beta K - \dot{K} > C^*$ since $K > K^* = C^*/\beta$ and $\dot{K} < 0$. Thus $U < 0$. This solution is *not* optimal. To see this we need only consider the alternative solution $K(t) = K^* + (K_0 - K^*)e^{\beta t}$. For this solution K increases unendingly with t and the system moves further and further from K^*. However, $\dot{K} = \beta(K_0 - K^*)e^{-\beta t}$, so that

$$C = \beta K - \dot{K} = \beta K^* = C^*. \tag{4-65}$$

Thus the system is always at bliss, with $U = 0$. The evil day, on which surplus production must be consumed, is postponed indefinitely. Of course one may impose on the system the requirement that $K \to K^*$. Then the solution $K = K^* + (K_0 - K^*)e^{-\beta t}$ *is* optimal. For each solution λ_1 is easy to determine. In the first case, when the system is always at bliss, $\lambda_1 = 0$ since $U' = 0$. In the second case,

$$C = \beta K - \dot{K} = C^* + 2\beta(K_0 - K^*)e^{-\beta t} \tag{4-66}$$

so that

$$\lambda_1 = U' = 2\alpha(C^* - C) = -4\alpha\beta(K_0 - K^*)e^{-\beta t}. \tag{4-67}$$

Finally, substituting from (4-67) into the second solution, we obtain $K = K^* - (\lambda_1/4\alpha\beta)$, as in Example 2.

Let us consider finally the case in which $K_0 < K^*$. Here it is clear that the solution $K = K^* - (K^* - K_0)e^{\beta t}$ is not optimal, for the stock of capital is eventually used up and the integral diverges. In the alternative solution $K \to K^*$ as $t \to \infty$; also, $\dot{K} = \beta(K^* - K_0)e^{-\beta t}$ and

$$C = \beta K - \dot{K} = C^* - 2\beta(K^* - K_0)e^{-\beta t}. \tag{4-68}$$

When $t = 0$, $C = C^* - 2C^* + 2\beta K_0$ or $C = 2\beta K_0 - C^*$. If $K_0 < C^*/2\beta$, $C(0) < 0$, which is impossible. Thus this solution applies only for $K_0 \geq C^*/2\beta = K^*/2$. This is the criterion obtained in a different way in Example 2. For the case in which $K_0 \geq K^*/2$,

$$\lambda_1 = U' = 2\alpha(C^* - C) = 4\alpha\beta(K^* - K^0)e^{-\beta t} > 0 \tag{4-69}$$

and $K = K^* - (\lambda_1/4\alpha\beta)$, as when $K_0 > K^*$.

It remains to examine the case in which $K_0 < K^*/2$. Then $C = 0$ initially and $\dot{K} = \Psi(K) = \beta K$, so that

$$K = K_0 e^{\beta t}. \tag{4-70}$$

Moreover, $\dot{\lambda}_1 = -\beta\lambda_1$, so that

$$\lambda_1 = \gamma e^{-\beta t} \tag{4-71}$$

where γ must be determined so that λ_1 is continuous. From (4-70) and (4-71) we obtain $\lambda_1 K = K_0$, a conclusion already reached in a slightly different way in Example 2.

We consider now the problem of deciding when to make the transition from a boundary to an interior solution. On the boundary the solution is

$$K = K_0 e^{\beta t} \quad \text{and} \quad \lambda_1 = \gamma e^{-\beta t} \tag{4-72}$$

while in the interior

$$K = K^* + \rho e^{-\beta t}; \qquad \lambda_1 = -\,4\alpha\beta\rho e^{-\beta t}. \tag{4-73}$$

At time t_e a change from (4-72) to (4-73) will be made, and both K and λ_1 will be continuous. By equating the values of λ_1 at t_e we find that $\gamma = -4\alpha\beta\rho$. On equating the values of K at t_e we obtain

$$K_0 e^{\beta t_e} = K^* + \rho e^{-\beta t_e}. \tag{4-74}$$

In the case we are considering, $U(C)$ is a strictly concave function of C; hence there can be no jumps in C. From Example 1, therefore, $\dot{K}$ also is continuous at t_e. Thus by equating the two values of $\dot{K}$ we may obtain the additional restriction

$$\beta K_0 e^{\beta t_e} = -\,\beta\rho e^{-\beta t_e} \tag{4-75a}$$

or

$$\rho = -\,K_0 e^{2\beta t_e}. \tag{4-75b}$$

Applying (4-75a) to (4-74),

$$e^{\beta t_e} = \frac{K^*}{2K_0} \quad \text{or} \quad t_e = \frac{1}{\beta}\log\frac{K^*}{2K_0} \tag{4-76}$$

so that

$$\rho = -\,\frac{(K^*)^2}{4K_0} \tag{4-77}$$

$$K = K^*\left[1 - \frac{K^*}{4K_0}\,e^{-\beta t}\right], \quad t \geq t_e \tag{4-78}$$

and

$$\lambda_1 = -\,4\alpha\beta\rho e^{-\beta t} = \frac{\alpha C^* K^*}{K_0}\,e^{-\beta t}, \quad \text{all } t. \tag{4-79}$$

From (4-78) or (4-72), $K = K^*/2$ when $t = t_e$. Thus the transition from the boundary occurs at $K = K^*/2$, which is independent of K_0, at a time t_e, which depends on K_0. These conclusions are in agreement with those reached by a different route in Example 2.

We can now summarize the complete solution for the case in which the planning horizon is infinite and K_0 is arbitrary:

$$\left.\begin{aligned} &\frac{K^*}{2} \le K_0 \le K^* \\ &K(t) = K^* - (K^* - K_0)e^{-\beta t}; \qquad \lambda_1(t) = 4\alpha\beta(K^* - K_0)e^{-\beta t} \end{aligned}\right\} \tag{4-80}$$

$$\left.\begin{aligned} &0 < K_0 < \frac{K^*}{2} \\ &K(t) = \begin{cases} K_0 e^{\beta t}, & t \le t_e \\ K^*\left[1 - \dfrac{K^*}{4K_0} e^{-\beta t}\right], & t \ge t_e \end{cases}; \quad \lambda_1(t) = \frac{\alpha C^* K^*}{K_0} e^{-\beta t} \end{aligned}\right\} \tag{4-81}$$

where t_e, the optimal changeover time, is given by (4-76). When $K_0 > K^*$, the optimal solution depends on the condition placed on K as $t \to \infty$. If it is required that $K \to K^*$ then (4-80) is optimal. If no restriction is placed on K, it is optimal to increase K unendingly, with bliss maintained throughout.

4.9. A situation in which it may be optimal to reach bliss in a finite time

In Section 1.20 we proved that if F is a strictly concave function of K and $\dot{K}$ then bliss will not be reached in a finite time along an optimal trajectory, even though only a finite amount of capital is needed to achieve bliss. We now provide an example in which the planning period is infinite but it is optimal to reach bliss in a finite time. In this example F is concave, but not strictly concave. In particular,

$$U(C) = \alpha(C - C^*); \qquad \Psi(K) = C^* - \beta(K - K^*)^2. \tag{4-82}$$

From the classical theory, or from Section 4.6, we know that, for an interior solution with $C > 0$,

$$U + U'\dot{K} = 0 \quad \text{or} \quad \alpha C + \alpha\dot{K} = \alpha C^*. \tag{4-83}$$

However, $C = \Psi(K) - \dot{K}$ so that (4-83) reduces to $\Psi(K) = C^*$ or $K = K^*$. This is the only interior solution. For $K_0 \neq K^*$, the solution must lie on the boundary. We shall confine our attention to the case in which $K_0 < K^*$.

In terms of the theory of control, we have

$$H = \lambda_0(\alpha C - U^*) + \lambda_1[C^* - \beta(K - K^*)^2 - C] \tag{4-84}$$

$$\dot{K} = C^* - \beta(K - K^*)^2 - C \tag{4-85}$$

and

$$\dot{\lambda}_1 = -H_K = \lambda_1 \beta(K - K^*). \tag{4-86}$$

If $C > 0$ maximizes H, then $H_C = 0$ at that point. However

$$H_C = \lambda_0 \alpha - \lambda_1 = 0 \quad \text{so} \quad \lambda_1 = \alpha \lambda_0. \tag{4-87}$$

Thus $\lambda_0 \neq 0$; for if λ_0 vanishes so does λ_1. Hence $\lambda_1 = \alpha$ for an interior maximum. Thus H is independent of C and any value of C can be considered to maximize H–in particular, C^*. From Example 1 we know that $H = 0$ along the entire path. On setting $H = 0$, and noting that $\lambda_0 = 1$, $\lambda_1 = \alpha$, we find that

$$-\alpha\beta(K - K^*)^2 = 0$$

or $K = K^*$. Hence $\dot{K} = 0$ and, from (4-85), $C = C^*$. Thus the only interior solution is $C = C^*$, $K = K^*$, $\lambda_1 = \alpha$, which is, of course, the conclusion reached using the classical theory.

It follows that if the initial stock of capital is $K_0 < K^*$, $C = 0$ and $\dot{K} = \Psi(K)$ until K^* is reached. Then C jumps discontinuously to C^* and $\dot{K}$ drops discontinuously to 0. (Mathematically, the existence of discontinuous changes in optimal C is related to the fact that the C which maximizes H is not unique.) Until that point is reached, $K = K_0 e^{-\beta t}$ and $\dot{\lambda}_1 = -\beta\lambda_1$, so that $\lambda_1 = \rho e^{-\beta t}$. The time required to increase the stock of capital from K_0 to K^* is

$$t_e = \int_{K_0}^{K^*} \frac{dK}{K} = \frac{1}{\beta} \log \frac{K^*}{K_0}. \tag{4-88}$$

At t_e, λ_1 must have the value α. Hence

$$\rho e^{\log K^*/K_0} = \alpha$$

or

$$\rho = \frac{\alpha K_0}{K^*}. \tag{4-89}$$

Thus the complete solution for $K_0 < K^*$ is

$$K(t) = \begin{cases} K_0 e^{-\beta t}, & t \leq t_e \\ K^*, & t \geq t_e \end{cases} ; \quad \lambda_1(t) = \begin{cases} \dfrac{\alpha K_0}{K^*} e^{-\beta t}, & t \leq t_e \\ \alpha, & t \geq t_e. \end{cases} \tag{4-90}$$

The above analysis can now be easily extended to cover the case of a finite planning horizon with a prescribed terminal capital stock. Suppose first that $K(T) = K_1 > K^*$ and let τ be the time required to move from K^* to K_1 with $C = 0$ and $\dot{K} = \Psi(K)$. Then at time $T - \tau$ the system will switch from an interior trajectory to the boundary, and thereafter move along the boundary to K_1.

Suppose next that $K_0 < K_1 < K^*$. If $T < t_e$, the system will move from K_0 to K_1 with $C = 0$ throughout. If $T > t_e$, the system will stay at bliss for a time, then drop back to K_1, using up capital along the way. So far, we have placed no lower bound on $\dot{K}$; it can be made arbitrarily small. Thus the system could at the very last moment jump discontinuously from bliss to K_1. Suppose then that we place a lower limit $-\sigma$ on $\dot{K}$. Let τ_1 be the length of time required to reduce the stock of capital from K^* to K_1 when $\dot{K} = -\sigma$. Then if by time $T - \tau_1$ the system has reached bliss, it is optimal to set $\dot{K} = -\sigma$ thereafter. If by time $T - \tau_1$ the system has not reached bliss then, at a calculable time before bliss is reached, the system will switch from $\dot{K} = \Psi(K)$ to $\dot{K} = -\sigma$, so that K_1 is reached at time T.

If $K_1 < K_0$ then, depending on T, K may increase and then decrease, or steadily decrease. If K_1 is too small in relation to T, it may not be possible to reach K_1 in time T. Several possible trajectories are displayed in Figure 4.5.

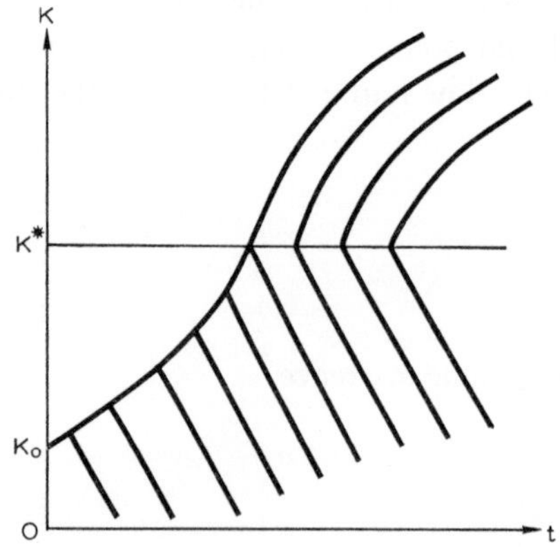

Fig. 4.5.

4.10. The Ramsey model with discounting

In the next example we show how the Ramsey model may be modified by the introduction of discounting. In particular, we illustrate some of the pitfalls associated with discounting. Suppose then that the functional to be maximized is

$$J[K, C] = \int_0^\infty e^{-\delta t} U(C(t))dt, \quad \delta > 0 \tag{4-91}$$

where δ is the constant rate of discount. Intuitively, we should expect that discounting would bias the time profile of consumption towards the present (and the profile of capital accumulation towards the future). This expectation is basically correct, as we shall see.

Now

$$H = \lambda_0 e^{-\delta t} U + \lambda_1 [\Psi(K) - C] \tag{4-92}$$

and

$$\dot{K} = \Psi(K) - C \tag{4-93}$$

$$\dot{\lambda}_1 = -\lambda_1 \Psi'. \tag{4-94}$$

Equations (4-93) and (4-94) do not contain δ and are precisely the same as in the absence of discounting. When $C > 0$ maximizes H,

$$H_C = \lambda_0 e^{-\delta t} U' - \lambda_1 = 0.$$

Moreover

$$\lambda_1 = e^{-\delta t} U' \tag{4-95}$$

because, as in Example 1, λ_0 is non-zero and hence can be set equal to 1. The only difference between the current model and the one without discounting is the appearance of $e^{-\delta t}$ in (4-95).

Let us now turn to a specific example. We retain the model of Sections 4.7 and 4.8, with $U = -\alpha(C - C^*)^2$ and $\Psi = \beta K$. Then $\dot{\lambda}_1 = -\beta\lambda_1$ and $\lambda_1 = \rho e^{-\beta t}$; and $U' = 2\alpha(C^* - C)$. If these results are applied to (4-95) we see that, for an interior maximum,

$$\rho e^{-\beta t} = 2\alpha e^{-\delta t}(C^* - C) \tag{4-96}$$

or

$$C = C^* - \frac{\rho}{2\alpha} e^{(\delta - \beta)t}. \tag{4-97}$$

If this is substituted into (4-93), we obtain

$$\dot{K} - \beta K = \frac{\rho}{2\alpha} e^{(\delta-\beta)t} - C^*. \tag{4-98}$$

Let us try a solution of the form

$$K = \gamma e^{(\delta-\beta)t} - \varepsilon. \tag{4-99}$$

Substituting into (4-98) we see that it is indeed a solution if

$$\gamma = -\frac{\rho}{2\alpha(2\beta - \delta)}; \qquad \varepsilon = K^* \tag{4-100}$$

and if $2\beta - \delta \neq 0$. Thus

$$K = K^* - \frac{\rho}{2\alpha(2\beta - \delta)} e^{(\delta-\beta)t}, \qquad 2\beta - \delta \neq 0. \tag{4-101}$$

If $K(0) = K_0$, we find that

$$\rho = (K^* - K_0)(2\alpha)(2\beta - \delta) \tag{4-102}$$

so that

$$K = K^* - (K^* - K_0)e^{(\delta-\beta)t}; \qquad \lambda_1 = (K^* - K_0)(2\alpha)(2\beta - \delta)e^{-\beta t}. \tag{4-103}$$

Thus the behavior of the system through time varies according as $\beta \gtreqless \delta$. As we shall see, it also depends on whether $2\beta \leq \delta$ or $2\beta > \delta > \beta$. Let us examine first the possibility that $\beta > \delta$. Then, as $t \to \infty$, $K \to K^*$ and $C \to C^*$, i.e. the system approaches bliss. This solution differs from that obtained in Example 3 in that the exponential is now $e^{-(\beta-\delta)t}$ rather than $e^{-\beta t}$; thus K grows more slowly under the influence of discounting. The initial value of C is

$$C(0) = \beta K_0 - \dot{K}(0) = \beta K_0 + (\beta - \delta)(K_0 - K^*) =$$
$$(2\beta - \delta) K_0 - (\beta - \delta)K^*. \tag{4-104}$$

Thus $C(0) \geq 0$ if

$$K_0 \geq \left(\frac{\beta - \delta}{2\beta - \delta}\right) K^* = K_e. \tag{4-105}$$

If $K_0 < K_e$, the solution will lie on the boundary for a time, with $C = 0$. We shall not consider the details of the boundary solution; the manner in which it can be obtained has been described in Example 2. If $\delta = 0$, $K_e =$

$K^*/2$, as in Example 2. For $\delta > 0$, $K_e > K^*/2$; and as δ increases to β, K_e decreases to 0, at which point no part of the optimal trajectory can lie on the boundary.

We next consider the case in which $\delta = \beta$. Then, from (4-103), $K = K_0$ and, from (4-97), $C = C^* - (\rho/2\alpha)$; moreover, $\rho/2\alpha = C^* - \beta K_0$. Thus $C = \beta K_0$ for all time, and $\dot{K} = 0$. In this case, then, there is no accumulation of capital at all; and the economy never approaches bliss. Instead, the consumption rate is fixed at the maximum level maintainable with the initial stock of capital.

It remains to consider the possibility that $\delta > \beta$. Let us restrict our attention for the time being to the case in which $2\beta > \delta > \beta$. Then ρ, given by (4-102), is positive. In this case $\dot{K} < 0$, K decreases to 0, and C, starting at a value greater than βK_0, decreases as t increases. The point of time t_f at which K reaches 0 is, from (4-103),

$$t_f = \frac{1}{\delta - \beta} \log \frac{K^*}{K^* - K_0} \tag{4-106}$$

and the value of C at t_f is, from (4-97),

$$\begin{aligned} C(t_f) &= C^* - (K^* - K_0)(2\beta - \delta)K^*(K^* - K_0)^{-1} \\ &= \delta K^* - C^* > 0. \end{aligned} \tag{4-107}$$

Also, $C(t_f) < C^*$.

When δ increases to 2β, ρ becomes 0. Then, from (4-97), $C = C^*$. When $\rho = 0$, equation (4-101) does not apply; from (4-98), however, $\dot{K} - \beta K = C^*$, with solution $K = K^* - (K^* - K_0)e^{\beta t}$, where $K(0) = K_0$.

Suppose, finally, that $\delta > 2\beta$. Then, if $\rho \neq 0$, (4-102) must hold and $\rho < 0$, which implies that $C > C^*$ and $K > K^*$. This, clearly, is not possible.

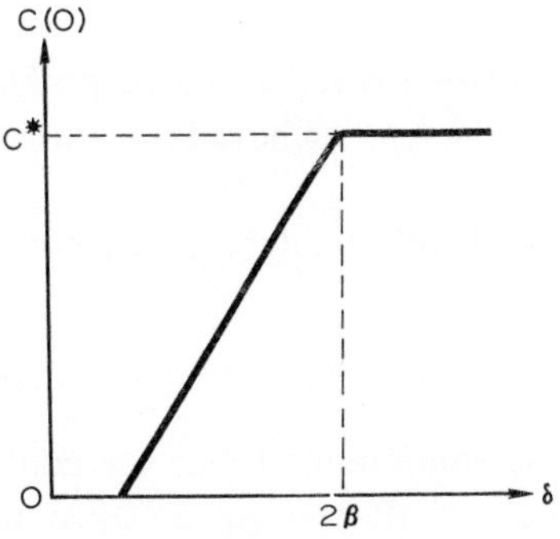

Fig. 4.6.

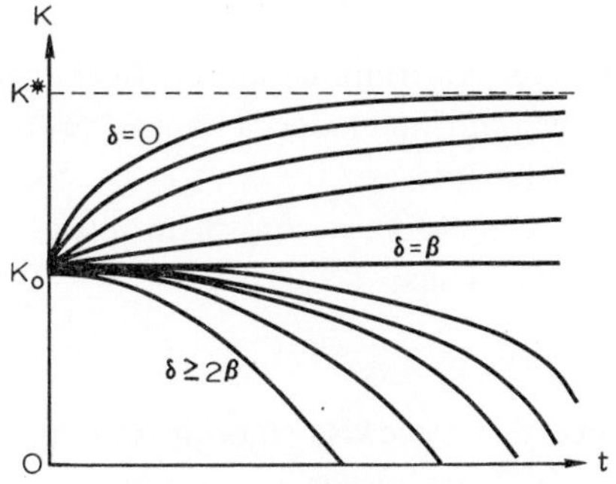

Fig. 4.7.

Hence, for all $\delta \geq 2\beta$, $\rho = 0$ and it is optimal to set $C = C^*$ and use up the initial stock of capital.

In Figure 4.6 we have shown how the initial consumption rate $C(0)$ varies as a function of δ for a typical K_0. In Figure 4.7 is shown the time path of $K(t)$ for various values of δ.

This example is interesting because it shows that for a sufficiently large discount factor it is not optimal to accumulate capital at any time.

4.11. Optimal transfer from K_0 to K_1 with $\dot{K} \to 0$ as $K \to K_1$

Continuing with our study of the Ramsey model, let us next examine the problem of optimally changing the stock of capital from K_0 to K_1 subject to the requirement that $\dot{K}$ approach 0 as K_1 is approached. The time required to reach K_1 is not specified.

It will be convenient to refer again to Figure 2.21. Notice that for any $K_0 < K_1 < K^*$ there is only one path which crosses the K-axis at K_1, that is, for which $\dot{K} = 0$ at K_1. This is the required path. (If K_0 is sufficiently small, the system must move along the boundary for a time, until this path is reached.) If $K_0 > K_1 > K^*$ there is again a unique path with the required features. In all other cases (for example, $K_0 < K^* < K_1$) there is no solution with the desired characteristics.

4.12. The conversion of classical problems into control problems

Let us consider again the problem (already studied in Chapter 2) of finding the curve which joins $(x_0, \mathbf{y}_0)$ to $(x_1, \mathbf{y}_1)$ and which maximizes

$$J[\mathbf{y}] = \int_{x_0}^{x_1} F(x, \mathbf{y}, \mathbf{y}')dx.$$

Provided a certain condition (to be stated below) is satisfied, this problem can be reformulated as a control problem of the type we have been studying in this chapter.

To convert to a control problem, we need only treat $\mathbf{y}'$ as the control variable. Thus

$$\mathbf{y}' = \mathbf{v}. \tag{4-108}$$

Since $\mathbf{y}$ is piecewise smooth, $\mathbf{y}'$ is piecewise continuous; hence the control variables are piecewise continuous, as required. Earlier we assumed that there is a set $\mathscr{R}$ in extended phase space such that the graph of $\mathbf{y}(x)$ must lie in $\mathscr{R}$. Let us denote by $\mathscr{V}$ the set of $\mathbf{v}$ for which $(x, \mathbf{y}, \mathbf{v}) \in \mathscr{R}$ for a given $(x, \mathbf{y})$. In general $\mathscr{V}$ may depend on $(x, \mathbf{y})$. However, if $\mathscr{V}$ does not depend on $(x, \mathbf{y})$ and is independent of the $(x, \mathbf{y})$ chosen, then the control problem is of the type we have been studying. The problem therefore is to find a control $\mathbf{v}(x)$ such that $\mathbf{v} \in \mathscr{V}$ for each x and such that, when $\mathbf{y}$ is determined from (4-108) and $\mathbf{y}(x_0) = \mathbf{y}_0$, then $\mathbf{y}(x_1) = \mathbf{y}_1$ and $J[\mathbf{y}, \mathbf{v}]$ is maximized. The case in which $\mathscr{V}$ is not independent of $(x, \mathbf{y})$ can normally be handled by an alternative formulation of the control problem to be given in the next chapter.

Given the control formulation we no longer need restrict our attention to interior maxima. If, however, $\mathbf{v}$ never lies on the boundaries of $\mathscr{V}$, we can derive both the Euler equations and the corner conditions from the necessary conditions for the control problem. Suppose that $\mathbf{w}(t)$, $\mathbf{z}(t)$ represent an optimal interior solution to the control problem. Then

$$H = \lambda_0 F + \boldsymbol{\lambda}\mathbf{v} \tag{4-109}$$

and it is necessary that

$$\mathbf{z}' = \mathbf{w} \tag{4-110}$$

and that there exists a $\boldsymbol{\lambda}(x)$ such that

$$\boldsymbol{\lambda}' = -\mathbf{H}_{\mathbf{y}} = -\lambda_0 \mathbf{F}_{\mathbf{y}}. \tag{4-111}$$

For an interior maximum

$$\mathbf{H}_{\mathbf{v}} = \lambda_0 \mathbf{F}_{\mathbf{y}'} + \boldsymbol{\lambda} = \mathbf{0} \tag{4-112}$$

Hence $\lambda_0 \neq 0$ and we can set $\lambda_0 = 1$. Thus $\boldsymbol{\lambda} = -\mathbf{F}_{\mathbf{y}'}$, and, since $\boldsymbol{\lambda}$ is continuous, so is $\mathbf{F}_{\mathbf{y}'}$. This gives us the corner conditions. Points of discontinuity of $\boldsymbol{\lambda}'$ can occur only where jumps in $\mathbf{w}(t)$ occur, that is, at corners of $\mathbf{z}(x)$. Between corners of $\mathbf{z}(x)$, $\boldsymbol{\lambda}$ is differentiable; hence, from (4-111), it is necessary that $\mathbf{z}(x)$ and $\mathbf{w}(x)$ satisfy

$$\frac{d}{dx}\mathbf{F}_{\mathbf{y}'} - \mathbf{F}_{\mathbf{y}} = \mathbf{0} \tag{4-113}$$

and these are the familiar Euler equations.

4.13. The synthesis problem

We have formulated the control problem as that of determining the optimal values of the control variables as functions of time, that is, of finding an optimal control $\mathbf{w}(t)$. Let us now pause for a moment to examine some of the practical problems encountered in applying this function. The system to be controlled might be a space vehicle or an economy. Suppose that a computer is controlling the system. It would be possible to install in the computer a very accurate electronic clock and to program the computer so that it adjusts the values of the control variables at each point in time in accordance with the function $\mathbf{w}(t)$.

Such a procedure would not work properly in practice, either for controlling a space vehicle or an economy. Why? The difficulty is that if an error is made by the control mechanism (because the valves of a rocket motor function imperfectly, for example) and for some period of time a control variable does not have precisely the value it should have, then the system will deviate from the optimal path and the computer will be quite ignorant of the fact. As a result, the system may follow a path which leads to catastrophe. In practice it is impossible to construct control devices, either for space vehicles or for economies, which function perfectly and never introduce error. Thus a control system which never attempts to determine what the actual state of the system is, but merely attempts to set the control variables according to some prespecified time program, cannot be expected to function in a satisfactory manner.

It is desirable that a control system be able to observe, at least occasionally the actual state of the system and, if the system has deviated from the initially determined optimal path, to determine a new path appropriate to the current state of the system. The process of observing and correcting is called *feedback*.

Feedback can be introduced quite straightforwardly by requiring the computer to periodically determine the state of the system and, after each observation, to calculate a completely new trajectory. Such a procedure can be and in fact is applied to certain types of systems. It has the disadvantage, however, that serious errors may develop before a check on the state of the system is made. Furthermore, to determine a new trajectory may be an extremely complicated and time-consuming task, even for a large computer; and in certain types of control situations it simply may not be feasible to wait while a new trajectory is being calculated.

It now seems clear that we really need not a function which gives optimal values of the control variables at each point in time but instead a function which gives optimal values of the control variables for each possible state $\mathbf{y}$ of the system, that is, a function $\mathbf{w}(\mathbf{y})$. This function is called a *synthesizing function* and the problem of determining such a function is referred to as the problem of synthesizing an optimal control (or as the problem of converting an optimal open loop control into an optimal closed loop control). One could allow the synthesizing function to depend not only on the state variables but also on time. However such a function would introduce great complications; its usefulness depends on the existence of a clock with which to measure time, but there is no way of checking on the accuracy of the clock.

Suppose that a synthesizing function were available. With the aid of a suitable set of *sensors* the computer might then continuously monitor the state of the system **y** and, in the light of its reading, continuously adjust the control variables to their optimal values. Time does not directly enter the synthesizing functions; and the computer is concerned not with time elapsed or the history of the system but only with the current state of the system.

Unfortunately, the general problem of synthesizing an optimal control is unsolved. However the problem can be easily solved in certain special cases. Let us consider again Example 3, which is concerned with a special case of the Ramsey model with an infinite planning horizon. In that case the synthesizing function relates the control C to the state of the system K. Suppose that at some point in the evolution of the system $K = K_0$; how K happened to reach that particular value is of no interest to us. We want to move the system from K_0 to bliss along an optimal path. This requires that we determine $C(K_0)$. Now in Example 3 we have determined the optimal path for every $K_0 < K^*$. The C that we are looking for is simply $C(0)$, the consumption rate at $t = 0$. This is 0 for $K_0 < K^*/2$. For $K_0 \geq K^*/2$, $C(0)$ can be found by setting $t = 0$ in (4-68), i.e., $C = 2\beta K_0 - C^*$. Thus the synthesizing function for Example 3 is

$$C = \begin{cases} 0, & K_0 \leq K^*/2 \\ 2\beta K_0 - C^*, & K^*/2 \leq K_0 \leq K^*. \end{cases} \tag{4-114}$$

4.14. The model of Samuelson and Solow again

In Sections 2.16 and 2.24 we studied special cases of the Samuelson-Solow model. We were unable with the classical theory to obtain complete solutions for those cases. We shall in this section show how the examples can be reformulated and solved completely with the aid of control theory. We shall consider first the example of Section 2.16. (It may be helpful for the reader to now review that example.) We recall that

$$U(C_1, C_2) = -\alpha_1(C_1 - C_1^*)^2 - \alpha_2(C_2 - C_2^*)^2 \tag{4-115}$$

and

$$C_1 + \dot{K}_1 = \gamma - \beta_1(K_1 - K_1^*)^2 - \beta_2(K_2 - K_2^*)^2 - C_2 - \dot{K}_2. \tag{4-116}$$

Moreover, in Section 2.16 we confined ourselves to the case in which $\gamma = C_1^* + C_2^*$, so that the value of K at which the production function saturates also produces bliss. We have solved the problem for those cases in which $K_1^0 \geq K_1^*$ and $K_2^0 \geq K_2^*$ or in which (K_1^0, K_2^0) lies on the critical line (2-199). We now seek to determine the solutions for the remaining initial points (K_1^0, K_2^0). Non-negativity constraints, which were not binding in the cases examined in Section 2.16, must now be acknowledged:

$$C_1 \geq 0, \qquad C_2 \geq 0, \qquad \dot{K}_1 + C_1 \geq 0, \qquad \dot{K}_2 + C_2 \geq 0. \tag{4-117}$$

Let us treat C_1, C_2 and $v = \dot{K}_2$ as control variables. Then the problem becomes that of maximizing

$$J[\mathbf{K}, \mathbf{v}] = \int_0^\infty U(C_1, C_2)\mathrm{d}t \tag{4-118}$$

where

$$\begin{aligned} \dot{K}_1 &= \gamma - \beta_1(K_1 - K_1^*)^2 - \beta_2(K_2 - K_2^*)^2 - C_1 - C_2 - v \\ \dot{K}_2 &= v \end{aligned} \tag{4-119}$$

and where (C_1, C_2, v) must satisfy

$$C_1 \geq 0, \qquad C_2 \geq 0, \qquad C_2 + v \geq 0. \tag{4-120}$$

There is one possible difficulty in this formulation. It is asymmetric. Since $\dot{K}_1$ is not a control variable, expression cannot be given to the constraint $C_1 + \dot{K}_1 \geq 0$. Hence the present formulation may be adopted only for regions for which it is clear that the constraint is not active. The values of (K_1^0, K_2^0) to be considered here do fall in such regions; we shall therefore work with the formulation (4-118) to (4-120). (Alternatively, $\dot{K}_1$ might have been substituted for $\dot{K}_2$ as a control; but then it would have been impossible to express the constraint $C_2 + \dot{K}_2 \geq 0$. Or both $\dot{K}_1$ and $\dot{K}_2$ might have been treated as controls; but this symmetric formulation would require the introduction of a further constraint which depends on the state variables, and this is not allowed for in our present formulation of the control problem (although, as we shall see, it is allowed in the more general formulation to be given in Chapter 5).)

In the present case

$$\begin{aligned} H = \lambda_0 U + \lambda_1[\gamma - \beta_1(K_1 - K_1^*)^2 - \beta_2(K_2 - K_2^*)^2 \\ - C_1 - C_2 - v] + \lambda_2 v \end{aligned} \tag{4-121}$$

and

$$\dot{\lambda}_1 = -H_{K_1} = 2\lambda_1\beta_1(K_1 - K_1^*) \tag{4-122}$$

$$\dot{\lambda}_2 = -H_{K_2} = 2\lambda_1\beta_2(K_2 - K_2^*). \tag{4-123}$$

For an interior maximum

$$H_{C_1} = -2\lambda_0\alpha_1(C_1 - C_1^*) - \lambda_1 = 0 \tag{4-124}$$

$$H_{C_2} = -2\lambda_0\alpha_2(C_2 - C_2^*) - \lambda_1 = 0 \tag{4-125}$$

$$H_v = -\lambda_1 + \lambda_2 = 0 \tag{4-126}$$

so that $\lambda_0 \neq 0$ and, hence, $\lambda_0 = 1$. Also, $\lambda_1 = \lambda_2$ and

$$\alpha_1(C_1 - C^*) = \alpha_2(C_2 - C_2^*). \tag{4-127}$$

Furthermore, since $\lambda_1 = \lambda_2$, $\dot{\lambda}_1 = \dot{\lambda}_2$; and, if $C_1 \neq C_1^*$, $\lambda_1 \neq 0$. Hence, from (4-122) and (4-123),

$$\beta_1(K_1 - K_1^*) = \beta_2(K_2 - K_2^*). \tag{4-128}$$

In this case, therefore, (K_1, K_2) must lie on the critical line. This is precisely the result obtained in Section 2.16. To resolve the remaining cases we must investigate the boundary solutions.

We note first that H is a concave function of (C_1, C_2, v) and a strictly concave function of (C_1, C_2). Since H is strictly concave in (C_1, C_2), there cannot be two points (C_1^+, C_2^+, v^+) and (C_1^-, C_2^-, v^-) which maximize H and for which $C_1^+ \neq C_2^-$ and/or $C_2^+ \neq C_2^-$. Consequently, the variables C_1 and C_2 must be continuous. However, H is not strictly concave in the control variable v; hence v need not be continuous. There may exist two points (C_1, C_2, v^+) and (C_1, C_2, v^-) both of which maximize H.

Given the continuity of C_1 and C_2 we may obtain a reasonably clear picture of the behavior of the boundary solutions. In general, neither C_1 nor C_2 can always remain at zero. For the boundary solution must either intersect the critical line and become an interior solution or approach bliss directly. But conversion to an interior solution implies a discontinuous change in the value of $\mathbf{C}$, which is not possible. Similarly, if bliss is approached directly neither C_1 nor C_2 can always remain 0. Thus both C_1 and C_2 will ultimately be positive in any boundary solution. On the other hand, not all of C_1, C_2 and v can be positive, for this would yield an interior optimum with the system on the critical line. The only other possibility is that the constraint $C_2 + v \geq 0$ is active, so that

$$v = -C_2 \tag{4-129}$$

and $v = \dot{K}_2$ is negative. Clearly this cannot occur if the initial point lies below the critical line. Thus our present formulation applies only when the initial point lies above the critical line. For points lying below the critical line, $\dot{K}_1$ is negative on the boundary and should be treated as the control variable.

We can now see what happens if (K_1^0, K_2^0) lies above the critical line and $K_1^0 < K_1^*$, $K_2^0 < K_2^*$. Initially, K_2 decreases while $C_2 = -\dot{K}_2$ is positive; simultaneously, K_1 increases while C_1 is positive; and

$$\dot{K}_1 + C_1 = \gamma - \beta_1(K_1 - K_1^*)^2 - \beta_2(K_2 - K_2^*)^2 \tag{4-130}$$

is satisfied. After a certain time the curve representing the time behavior of K_1 and K_2 in the K_1K_2-plane intersects the critical line. The path must be such that at the point of intersection C_1 and C_2 remain continuous. There will, however, be a discontinuous change in $\dot{K}_1$ and $\dot{K}_2$; $\dot{K}_1$ will decrease and $\dot{K}_2$ will change from negative to positive.

We now develop the differential equations which determine the time behavior of C_1, C_2, K_1 and K_2 on the boundary where $v = \dot{K}_2 = -C_2$. Given that $v = -C_2$, C_1 and C_2 must both be chosen to maximize H, and if these are positive they will yield an interior maximum for H when v in H is replaced by $-C_2$. Hence

$$H_{C_1} = -2\lambda_0\alpha_1(C_1 - C_1^*) - \lambda_1 = 0 \tag{4-131}$$

$$H_{C_2} = -2\lambda_0\alpha_2(C_2 - C_2^*) - \lambda_1 - \lambda_2 = 0 \tag{4-132}$$

Again $\lambda_0 \neq 0$, so we can set $\lambda_0 = 1$. From (4-122) and (4-123), we see that $\dot{\lambda}_1$ and $\dot{\lambda}_2$ exist everywhere; hence, on differentiating (4-131) and (4-132) with respect to time, we find that

$$\dot{\lambda}_1 = -2\alpha_1\dot{C}_1 \tag{4-133}$$

$$\dot{\lambda}_2 = 2\alpha_1\dot{C}_1 - 2\alpha_2\dot{C}_2. \tag{4-134}$$

If we now substitute the values for λ_1, λ_2, $\dot{\lambda}_1$ and $\dot{\lambda}_2$ into (4-122) and (4-123) we find that

$$\dot{C}_1 = 2\beta_1(C_1 - C_1^*)(K_1 - K_1^*) \tag{4-135}$$

$$2\alpha_1\dot{C}_1 - 2\alpha_2\dot{C}_2 = -4\alpha_1\beta_2(C_1 - C_1^*)(K_2 - K_2^*) \tag{4-136}$$

or

$$\dot{C}_2 = 2\frac{\alpha_1}{\alpha_2}(C_1 - C_1^*)[\beta_2(K_2 - K_2^*) + \beta_1(K_1 - K_1^*)]. \tag{4-137}$$

In addition we have two equations for $\dot{K}_1$ and $\dot{K}_2$. After applying $v = -C_2$, the four equations are

$$\dot{K}_1 = \gamma - \beta_1(K_1 - K_1^*)^2 - \beta_2(K_2 - K_2^*)^2 - C_1 \tag{4-138}$$

$$\dot{K}_2 = -C_2 \tag{4-139}$$

$$\dot{C}_1 = 2\beta_1(C_1 - C_1^*)(K_1 - K_1^*) \tag{4-140}$$

$$\dot{C}_2 = 2\frac{\alpha_1}{\alpha_2}(C_1 - C_1^*)[\beta_2(K_2 - K_2^*) + \beta_1(K_1 - K_1^*)]. \tag{4-141}$$

Here we have a system of four first order differential equations in standard form to solve for C_1, C_2, K_1 and K_2. We have also the conditions that $K_1(0) = K_1^0$, $K_2(0) = K_2^0$; and, at the point where the critical line is intersected, the values of C_1 and C_2 must be those appropriate to the critical line at that point. Thus we have four conditions to pin down the four constants of integration. Thus it should be possible to determine a unique path from (K_1^0, K_2^0) to the critical line and with the property that, when the system changes over to an interior optimum on reaching the critical line, C_1 and C_2 are continuous.

Unfortunately, equations (4-138) to (4-141) are quite complicated and it is not possible to derive the complete solutions in convenient form. We therefore shall not consider the solutions in detail; instead, we shall be content to determine the slope of the curve representing the time behavior of K_1 and K_2 in the K_1K_2-plane at the point at which it crosses the critical line. Let $\dot{K}_1^-$ and $\dot{K}_2^-$ be the values we wish to determine at the point of intersection and let $\dot{K}_1^+$ and $\dot{K}_2^+$ be the corresponding values on the critical line immediately after the transition has been made. Now on the curve under consideration, just as it reaches the critical line, output is $\dot{K}_1^- + C_1$; and, immediately after, output is $\dot{K}_1^+ + \dot{K}_2^+ + C_1 + C_2$. Also, $C_2 = -\dot{K}_2^-$. Thus

$$\dot{K}_1^- + C_1 = \dot{K}_1^+ + \dot{K}_2^+ + C_1 + C_2 = \dot{K}_1^+ + \dot{K}_2^+ + C_1 - \dot{K}_2^-$$

or

$$\dot{K}_1^- + \dot{K}_2^- = \dot{K}_1^+ + \dot{K}_2^+. \tag{4-142}$$

From (2-200) and (2-205), with $a = \beta_1$, we see that

$$\dot{K}_1^+ = \beta_1(K_1^* - K_1)^2; \qquad \dot{K}_2^+ = \frac{\beta_1^2}{\beta_2}(K_1^* - K_1)^2. \tag{4-143}$$

Thus

$$\dot{K}_1^- + \dot{K}_2^- = \beta_1\left[1 + \frac{\beta_1}{\beta_2}\right](K_1^* - K_1)^2. \tag{4-144}$$

The value of C_2 on the critical line at the point of intersection is given by

$$C_2 = C_2^* - \left(\frac{\beta_1 + \beta_2}{\alpha_1 + \alpha_2}\right)\left(\frac{\alpha_1\beta_1}{\beta_2}\right)(K_1 - K_1^*)^2 = -\dot{K}_2^- \tag{4-145}$$

as may be seen by combining (2-206) and (2-208) and evaluating explicitly $\Delta + \beta_1\omega$. Then $\dot{K}_1^-$ can be obtained immediately from (4-144). Thus

$$\left(\frac{dK_2}{dK_1}\right)_- = \frac{\dot{K}_2^-}{\dot{K}_1^-} = \frac{\sigma(K_1 - K_1^*)^2 - C_2^*}{\left[\beta_1\left(1 + \frac{\beta_1}{\beta_2}\right) - \sigma\right](K_1 - K_1^*)^2 + C_2^*} \tag{4-146}$$

where σ is the coefficient of $(K_1 - K_1^*)^2$ in (4-145). Thus as the value of K_1 at the point of intersection approaches K_1^* the slope approaches -1, and as K_1 approaches 0 the slope approaches a number greater than 1 in magnitude. The curves must then look rather like those shown in Figure 4.8. By symmetry, we can also fill in the curves for points lying below the critical line. And we have already discussed the behavior of the system in the shaded region.

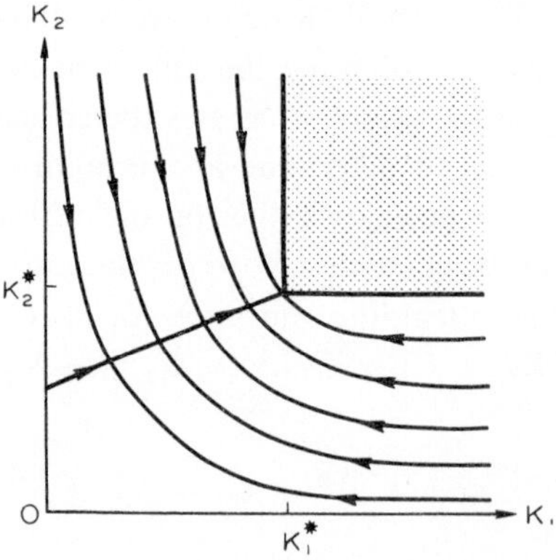

Fig. 4.8.

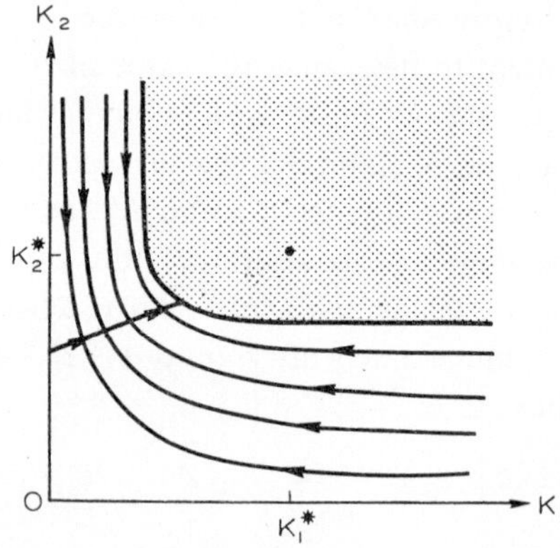

Fig. 4.9.

The general form of an optimal solution for an initial point not on the critical line, say a point lying above the critical line with $K_1^0 < K_1^*$ and $K_2^0 < K_2^*$, is as follows. Initially, $\dot{K}_2$ is negative and $C_2 = -\dot{K}_2$. Typically, C_2 increases with time. Simultaneously $\dot{K}_1$ (and typically C_1) increase. After a finite time, the curve so generated reaches the critical line. At this point

$\dot{K}_1$ and $\dot{K}_2$ change discontinuously and $\dot{K}_2$ becomes positive. The system then moves up the critical line to bliss. No discontinuous changes in C_1 or C_2 occur. Because of the mathematical difficulties involved, we have not provided a complete analysis, determining the function in detail. Nor have we attempted to ascertain whether, when K_1^0 and/or K_2^0 is small enough, the constraints $C_1 \geq 0$ and/or $C_2 \geq 0$ may become active also, so that the consumption rates may be 0 for a time.

Precisely the same sort of behavior emerges for that version of the Samuelson-Solow model given in Section 2.24, and we can sketch the general form of the curves for initial points not on the critical line (as in Figure 4.9). We have discussed earlier the behavior of the system when the initial point lies in the shaded region.

Problems

Section 4.2

1. A particle of unit mass moves along the x-axis under the action of a force which can be varied between -1 and 1 as desired, the value being changeable with time. At time 0, the particle is at x_0, moving with speed v_0. It is desired to bring the particle to the origin as quickly as possible. Formulate the problem as a control problem.

Section 4.3

1. Consider the manifold $\mathscr{M}_1$ introduced in the text. Assume that it has dimension $n + 1 - s$. Consider also $\mathscr{M}_1(t_1)$. What is the dimension of this manifold? Show that every vector $\mathbf{a}$ which is tangent to $\mathscr{M}_1(t_1)$ at $\mathbf{z}(t_1)$ has the property that $(0, \mathbf{a})$ is tangent to $\mathscr{M}_1$ at $(t_1, \mathbf{z}(t_1))$. How many linearly independent vectors of this sort are there? Thus prove that there exists a vector $(1, \mathbf{b})$ which is tangent to $\mathscr{M}_1$ at $(t_1, \mathbf{z}(t_1))$.

2. Set down the necessary conditions for Problem 3 of Section 4.2.

Section 4.5

1. Attempt to provide a heuristic derivation of the necessary conditions when the right hand end point must lie on a smooth manifold $\mathscr{M}_1$. What problems are encountered?

Sections 4.6 to 4.13

1. Reformulate the Ramsey model with the saving ratio (i.e. the fraction of income saved) as the control variable.

2. Rewrite the example of Section 4.6 to allow for an exponentially growing labor force.

3. Revise the analysis of Section 4.7 to suit the model represented in Figure 2.25.

4. Attempt to revise the analysis of Section 4.8 to suit the model of Figure 2.25.

5. Construct a $K\lambda_1$-phase diagram for the example of Section 4.9.

6. Is $H = 0$ always along the optimal paths in the example of Section 4.9? Verify this directly if possible.

7. When discounting is applied, is it necessary to assume that either the utility or production function must saturate? Can you construct an example in which there exists an optimal solution and in which neither function saturates?

8. Refer back to the example of Section 4.10 and consider cases in which K goes to 0. What happens after the point in time at which K reaches 0?

9. Attempt a detailed solution for the example of Section 4.11 using the model represented in Figure 2.21.

10. Attempt to derive the necessary conditions for a Lagrange problem with $G^i = y_i - f^i = 0$ from the necessary conditions for a control problem.

11. Prove that a strictly concave function cannot attain its global maximum at two or more different points.

Section 4.14

1. Reformulate the Samuelson-Solow model in terms of the piecewise smooth variables M_j instead of the C_j and obtain the same sort of necessary conditions.

2. Is $H = 0$ along the critical line in the Samuelson-Solow example?

3. In the Samuelson-Solow example, are there boundaries on which $C_1 = C_2 = 0$?

5

Connections with the classical theory

5.1 Introduction

In Chapter 4 we discussed the formulation of control problems introduced by Pontryagin and his associates. We also indicated, in Section 4.5, the general nature of Pontryagin's derivation of the necessary conditions. Because the control variables need not be continuous, Pontryagin's derivation took a form rather different from that of the earlier classical derivations. These differences might lead the reader to believe that control problems differ so radically from classical problems that the former cannot be transformed into the format of the latter. Such a belief would be mistaken, however. In the present chapter it will be shown that any control problem of the Pontryagin type can be expressed as a problem of Lagrange and that therefore it is possible to deduce the necessary conditions for the control problem (including the maximum principle) from those for the problem of Lagrange obtained in Chapter 3. Indeed this is the procedure we shall follow to develop a rigorous proof of the necessary conditions for control problems.

We shall in this chapter consider a type of control problem which in one important respect is more general than that studied in Chapter 4. It was assumed there that the set $\mathscr{V}$ in which $\mathbf{v}(t)$ must lie for each t depends neither on the state variables nor on time. We now allow $\mathscr{V}$ to depend on both $\mathbf{y}$ and t. In Chapter 3, $\mathscr{V}$ could be specified in any way desired. We shall here assume that there exists a set of h constraints

$$R^u(t, \mathbf{y}, \mathbf{v}) \leq 0, \quad u = 1, \ldots, h \tag{5-1}$$

which must be satisfied, and take $\mathscr{V}$ to be the set of points $\mathbf{v}$ which satisfy (5-1) for a specified $(t, \mathbf{y})$. Thus in general $\mathscr{V}$ will change with $(t, \mathbf{y})$ although we can admit the special case in which the R^u are independent of $(t, \mathbf{y})$. Equation (5-1) can be written in vector form as

$$\mathbf{R}(t, \mathbf{y}, \mathbf{v}) \leq \mathbf{0} \tag{5-2}$$

and this can be interpreted as requiring that the vector-valued function $\mathbf{R}(t, \mathbf{y}, \mathbf{v})$ is never positive.

Associated with the above gain in generality there is a slight loss in generality, for now $\mathscr{V}$ must be specified in a particular way. This is not of great significance, however, for in practice $\mathscr{V}$ is nearly always specified in terms of inequalities.

The problem we shall consider is then that of determining a piecewise continuous control $\mathbf{v}(t)$ (and a corresponding trajectory $\mathbf{y}(t)$ for the state variables) which optimizes the functional

$$J[\mathbf{y}, \mathbf{v}] = \int_{t_0}^{t_1} F(t, \mathbf{y}, \mathbf{v})dt \tag{5-3}$$

when

$$\dot{\mathbf{y}} = \mathbf{f}(t, \mathbf{y}, \mathbf{v}) \tag{5-4}$$

and when at each instant of time $\mathbf{v}(t)$ satisfies

$$\mathbf{R}(t, \mathbf{y}, \mathbf{v}) \leq \mathbf{0}, \tag{5-5}$$

Furthermore, the trajectory $\mathbf{y}(t)$ must begin at $(t_0, \mathbf{y}_0)$ and end on the smooth manifold $\mathscr{M}$ described by $\mathbf{S}(t, \mathbf{y}) = \mathbf{0}$. We shall assume that $\mathbf{y}$ has n components, that $\mathbf{v}$ has m components, $\mathbf{R}$ a total of h components, and $\mathbf{S}$ a total of s components. We shall require also that $R^q \in C''$ and $f^j \in C''$ over an open set in $\mathscr{E}^{n+m+1}$ containing the set of solutions to (5-5). Notice that we are now requiring that $f^j \in C''$ whereas in Chapter 4 we required only that $f^j \in C'$. Thus we are being somewhat more restrictive at this point; but in practice the difference is of little consequence.

We must also place certain restrictions on $\mathbf{R}$. These will be called the control variable constraint qualifications.

Control Variable Constraint Qualifications. (a) If h, the number of constraints R^u, is greater than m, the number of control variables, then there does not exist any point $(t, \mathbf{y}, \mathbf{v})$ which satisfies (5-5) and for which more than m of the constraints are active, that is, hold as strict equalities. (b) Let $(t, \mathbf{y}, \mathbf{v})$ be any solution to (5-5). If exactly k of the constraints (5-5) are active, then the $m \times k$ matrix $\|\partial R^q/\partial v_i\|$, the columns of which are the $\mathbf{R}^q_{\mathbf{v}}$ from the active constraints, has rank k.

Notice that (b) rules out the possibility that a constraint R^q can be active and yet involve only t and $\mathbf{y}$ (and not $\mathbf{v}$). At least one control variable must appear explicitly in each of the constraints. Thus we shall not discuss at this stage problems in which there appear constraints on the state variables only. Such problems will be studied later in the chapter.

The procedure which we shall use for reducing a control problem to a problem of Lagrange will in its essentials be that of Berkovitz [2], who in turn based his approach on earlier work of Valentine [40] and Hestenes [20].

5.2. Valentine's procedure

In a paper [40] which until recently received little attention F. A. Valentine suggested an ingenious procedure for converting a differential inequality such as $R(t, \mathbf{y}, \mathbf{y}') \le 0$ into a differential equation of the type allowed for in the formulation of the Lagrange problem. Roughly speaking, the procedure is similar to the introduction of slack and surplus variables in linear programming.

Let us consider any piecewise smooth function $\mathbf{y}(t)$ such that $R(t, \mathbf{y}, \mathbf{y}') \le 0$ for $t_0 \le t \le t_1$; and let

$$\phi(t) = -\ R(t, \mathbf{y}(t), \mathbf{y}'(t)). \tag{5-6}$$

Thus $\phi(t)$ is piecewise continuous and $\phi(t) \ge 0$. Next consider the function $\theta(t) = \sqrt{\phi(t)}$. Then $\theta(t)$ is piecewise continuous also and has discontinuities only at the corners of $\mathbf{y}(x)$. Next, let

$$\gamma(t) = \int_{t_0}^{t} \theta(\tau)d\tau. \tag{5-7}$$

$\gamma(t)$ is piecewise smooth and $\dot{\gamma}(t) = \theta(t)$ at all points where $\theta(t)$ exists. Furthermore,

$$R(t, \mathbf{y}, \mathbf{y}') + \dot{\gamma}^2 = 0. \tag{5-8}$$

We have then proved that for every piecewise smooth function $\mathbf{y}(t)$ which satisfies $R'' \le 0$, there exists a piecewise smooth function $\gamma(t)$ with $\gamma(t_0) = 0$ such that $(\mathbf{y}, \gamma)$ satisfy the differential equation (5-8). Consequently, it is possible to convert a differential inequality into a differential equation by adding a new variable γ defined by means of (5-8), and we know that (5-8) has a solution whenever the inequality has a solution. This then is the method used by Valentine to convert differential inequalities into differential equations.

5.3. The conversion of a control problem into a problem of Lagrange

We now show that the control problem (5-3) to (5-5) can be converted into a problem of Lagrange. It will be recalled that the classical theory deals only with variables which are piecewise smooth. The first step then must be to eliminate the control variables, which are only piecewise continuous. In doing so we rely again on the fact that the integral of a piecewise continuous variable is piecewise smooth. (Cf. p. 284.) In particular, we shall introduce a new set of variables the derivatives of which are the control variables. Let us write $\dot{\mathbf{V}} = \mathbf{v}$ and then in (5-3) to (5-5) replace $\mathbf{v}$ with $\dot{\mathbf{V}}$. Following Valentine's procedure, we now introduce new variables $\boldsymbol{\gamma}$ to convert the differential inequalities into differential equations. This done, our problem is that of finding the piecewise smooth functions $\mathbf{y}(t)$, $\mathbf{V}(t)$, and $\boldsymbol{\gamma}(t)$ which maximize the functional

$$J[\mathbf{y}, \mathbf{V}] = \int_{t_0}^{t_1} F(t, \mathbf{y}, \dot{\mathbf{V}})dt \tag{5-9}$$

and satisfy the differential equation constraints

$$-\dot{\mathbf{y}} + \mathbf{f}(t, \mathbf{y}, \dot{\mathbf{V}}) = \mathbf{0} \tag{5-10}$$

$$\mathbf{R}(t, \mathbf{y}, \dot{\mathbf{V}}) + \dot{\boldsymbol{\gamma}}^2 = \mathbf{0}. \tag{5-11}$$

Furthermore, at t_0, $\mathbf{y}(t_0) = \mathbf{y}_0$ while $\dot{\mathbf{V}}$ and $\boldsymbol{\gamma}$ can be imagined to have free boundaries. At t_1, $\mathbf{y}(t_1)$ must lie in the manifold $\mathscr{M}$ while again $\mathbf{V}$ and $\boldsymbol{\gamma}$ can be treated as having free boundaries. The problem just formulated has the form of a Lagrange problem. In addition, there is a one to one correspondence between the admissible functions for the control problem and those for the Lagrange problem; that is, given an admissible function for one problem one can immediately obtain a corresponding admissible function for the others. Finally, if a given admissible function optimizes one problem the corresponding function for the other problem must also be optimal. Thus the problems are equivalent.

Consider any point $(t, \mathbf{y}, \dot{\mathbf{V}}, \dot{\boldsymbol{\gamma}})$ which is a solution to (5-10) and (5-11). Let $\mathbf{A}$ be the $m \times n$ matrix the columns of which are $\mathbf{f}^j_{\dot{\mathbf{V}}}$ evaluated at that point, and let $\mathbf{B}$ be the $m \times h$ matrix the columns of which are $\mathbf{R}^u_{\dot{\mathbf{V}}}$ evaluated at that point. Also let $\mathbf{D} = ||2\dot{\gamma}_u \delta_{ui}||$, δ_{ui} being the Kronecker delta. Consider now the $(n + m + h) \times (n + h)$ matrix

$$\mathbf{P} = \begin{bmatrix} -\mathbf{I} & \mathbf{0} \\ \mathbf{A} & \mathbf{B} \\ \mathbf{0} & \mathbf{D} \end{bmatrix} \tag{5-12}$$

If we write the constraints (5-10) and (5-11) as

$$G^i(t, \mathbf{Y}, \dot{\mathbf{Y}}) = 0, \quad i = 1, \ldots, n + h \tag{5-13}$$

where $\mathbf{Y} = (\mathbf{y}, \mathbf{V}, \gamma)$, then $\mathbf{P}$ is exactly the matrix the columns of which are $\mathbf{G}^i_{\dot{\mathbf{Y}}}$ evaluated at the point under consideration.

We next show that $\mathbf{P}$ has rank $n + h$ at every point which represents a solution to (5-10) and (5-11). To this end we construct a nonsingular submatrix $\mathbf{J}$ of order $n + h$. The first n rows of $\mathbf{J}$ are the first n rows of $\mathbf{P}$. For the point under consideration we shall assume that α constraints from (5-11) are active, so that for these constraints $\dot{\gamma}_u = 0$. The constraints can be numbered so that they are the first α constraints. Now, from the control variable constraint qualification, in the first α columns of $\mathbf{B}$ there is a submatrix with rank α. For rows $n + 1$ to $n + \alpha$ of $\mathbf{J}$ we choose those rows of $\mathbf{P}$ which contain the rows of the submatrix just referred to. And for the final $h - \alpha$ rows of $\mathbf{J}$ we take the last $h - \alpha$ rows from $\mathbf{P}$. Thus $\mathbf{J}$ has the form

$$\mathbf{J} = \begin{bmatrix} -\mathbf{I} & \mathbf{0} & \mathbf{0} \\ \mathbf{A}_1 & \mathbf{B}_1 & \mathbf{B}_2 \\ \mathbf{0} & \mathbf{0} & \mathbf{D}_2 \end{bmatrix} \tag{5-14}$$

where the α columns of $\mathbf{B}_1$ are linearly independent and $\mathbf{D}_2$ is a nonsingular diagonal matrix since $\dot{\gamma}_u \neq 0$ for these constraints. It can be seen that the columns $\mathbf{j}_u$ of $\mathbf{J}$ are linearly independent. For suppose the contrary, that $\mathbf{J}\boldsymbol{\rho} = \mathbf{0}$. Then the first n equations imply that the first n components of $\boldsymbol{\rho}$ are $\mathbf{0}$; the last $h - \alpha$ equations imply that components $n + \alpha + 1$ to $n + h$ of $\boldsymbol{\rho}$ are $\mathbf{0}$; and, since $\mathbf{B}_1$ is nonsingular, equations $n + 1$ to $n + \alpha$ imply that components $n + 1$ to $n + \alpha$ of $\boldsymbol{\rho}$ are $\mathbf{0}$.

We are now ready for our main task, that of stating the necessary conditions for the Lagrange problems and then translating them into necessary conditions for the control problem.

5.4. Necessary conditions

Suppose that $\mathbf{y}(t) = \mathbf{z}(t)$, $\mathbf{V}(t) = \mathbf{W}(t)$ and $\gamma(t) = \boldsymbol{\phi}(t)$ is an admissible solution to the problem of Lagrange defined by (5-9) to (5-11) and maximizes the functional (5-9); that, in other words,

$$\mathbf{Z}(t) = (\mathbf{z}(t), \mathbf{W}(t), \boldsymbol{\phi}(t)) \tag{5-15}$$

provides an admissible and optimal solution to the problem of Lagrange when the constraints are written in the form (5-13). From Section 5.3 we know that the matrix $||G^u_{\dot{\gamma}_j}||$ has rank $n + h$ over $\mathscr{R}$ and hence along $\mathbf{Z}(t)$. Consequently, $\mathbf{Z}(t)$ must satisfy the necessary conditions developed for the problem of Lagrange in Chapter 3.

What are those conditions? First of all, there must exist a set of $n + h + 1$ multipliers, which we shall write as $(\lambda_0, \boldsymbol{\lambda}(t), \boldsymbol{\mu}(t))$, $\lambda_0 \geq 0$, which do not all vanish simultaneously, which are continuous except possibly at corners of $\mathbf{Z}(t)$, and which are such that if we form the Hamiltonian function

$$\begin{aligned} H^* &= \lambda_0 F + \sum_{j=1}^{n} \lambda_j(t) G^j + \sum_{q=1}^{h} \mu_q(t) G^q \\ &= \lambda_0 F + \sum_{j=1}^{n} \lambda_j(t)[f^j - \dot{y}_j] + \sum_{q=1}^{h} \mu_q(t)[R^q + \dot{\gamma}_u^2] \end{aligned} \tag{5-16}$$

then, between corners of $\mathbf{Z}(t)$, $\mathbf{Z}(t)$ satisfies the Euler equations

$$\frac{\mathrm{d}}{\mathrm{d}t}\mathbf{H}^*_{\dot{\mathbf{Z}}} - \mathbf{H}^*_{\mathbf{Z}} = \mathbf{0} \tag{5-17}$$

and the corner conditions (that $\mathbf{H}^*_{\dot{\mathbf{Z}}}$ is continuous across any corner).

Let us now rewrite the Euler equations explicitly in terms of the functions which appear in the statement of the control problem. Let us observe first that

$$\mathbf{H}^*_{\mathbf{y}} = \lambda_0 \mathbf{F}_{\mathbf{y}} + \sum_{j=1}^{n} \lambda_j(t)\mathbf{f}^j_{\mathbf{y}} + \sum_{q=1}^{h} \mu_q(t)\mathbf{R}^q_{\mathbf{y}}. \tag{5-18}$$

Now let us re-introduce the Hamiltonian H defined in Chapter 3 for the control problem, that is,

$$H = \lambda_0 F + \sum_{j=1}^{n} \lambda_j(t) f^j. \tag{5-19}$$

Then

$$\mathbf{H}^*_{\mathbf{y}} = \mathbf{H}_{\mathbf{y}} + \sum_{q=1}^{h} \mu_q(t)\mathbf{R}^q_{\mathbf{y}}. \tag{5-20}$$

Also,

$$\mathbf{H}^*_{\mathbf{v}} = \mathbf{0}; \qquad \mathbf{H}^*_{\boldsymbol{\gamma}} = \mathbf{0}. \tag{5-21}$$

Furthermore,

$$\mathbf{H}^*_{\mathbf{y}'} = -\,\boldsymbol{\lambda}(t) \tag{5-22}$$

$$\mathbf{H}^*_{\dot{\mathbf{v}}} = \mathbf{H}_{\mathbf{v}} + \sum_{q=1}^{h} \mu_q(t)\mathbf{R}^q_{\mathbf{v}} \tag{5-23}$$

$$H^*_{\dot\gamma_q} = 2\mu_q(t)\dot\gamma_q. \tag{5-24}$$

That part of the Euler equations (5-17) corresponding to **y** yields, after the application of (5-20) and (5-22),

$$\dot{\boldsymbol\lambda} = -\mathbf{H}_{\mathbf{y}} - \sum_{q=1}^{h} \mu_q \mathbf{R}^q_{\mathbf{y}}. \tag{5-25}$$

Furthermore, from the fact that $\mathbf{H}^*_{\mathbf{y}'} = -\boldsymbol\lambda(t)$ is continuous across corners it follows that $\boldsymbol\lambda(t)$ must be continuous. Here then we have the equivalent of $\dot{\boldsymbol\lambda} = -\mathbf{H}_{\mathbf{y}}$ for the control problem studied in Chapter 4. From (5-21) and (5-23) we see that those components of (5-17) corresponding to **V** reduce to

$$\mathbf{H}^*_{\dot{\mathbf{V}}} = \mathbf{H}_{\mathbf{v}} + \sum_{q=1}^{h} \mu_q(t)\mathbf{R}^q_{\mathbf{v}} = \text{constant vector.} \tag{5-26}$$

Similarly,

$$H^*_{\dot\gamma_q} = \mu_q(t)\dot\gamma_q = \text{constant.} \tag{5-27}$$

Let us turn now to the transversality conditions. Since $(\mathbf{V}, \boldsymbol\gamma)$ has a free boundary at both end points, it must be true that $\mathbf{H}^*_{\dot{\mathbf{V}}} = \mathbf{0}$ at the end points; and, in view of (5-26), $\mathbf{H}^*_{\dot{\mathbf{V}}} = \mathbf{0}$ along the entire path, i.e.

$$\mathbf{H}_{\mathbf{v}} + \sum_{q=1}^{h} \mu_q \mathbf{R}^q_{\mathbf{v}} = \mathbf{0}. \tag{5-28}$$

Similarly $\mathbf{H}^*_{\dot{\boldsymbol\gamma}} = \mathbf{0}$ at the end points and therefore, from (5-27), everywhere. Thus

$$\mu_q\dot\gamma_q = 0, \quad q = 1, \ldots, h. \tag{5-29}$$

If we multiply component u of (5-11) by μ_u and apply (5-29), we see immediately that

$$\mu_q R^q = 0 \quad \text{or} \quad \boldsymbol\mu \cdot \mathbf{R} = 0. \tag{5-30}$$

It remains to consider the transversality conditions for the **y** components. These state that $\mathbf{H}^*_{\dot{\mathbf{y}}}$ or $-\boldsymbol\lambda(t_1)$ must be a linear combination of the $\mathbf{S}^u_{\mathbf{y}}$ at the terminal point. Suppose that one constraint is $t - t_1 = 0$. For that constraint $\mathbf{S}^u_{\mathbf{y}} = \mathbf{0}$; hence the only relevant S^u are those other than $t - t_1 = 0$, that is, those which form what we called $\mathscr{M}_1$ in Chapter 4. Furthermore, the $\mathbf{S}^u_{\mathbf{y}}$ evaluated at t_1 are the normal vectors for $\mathscr{M}_1(t_1)$; thus the transversality conditions require that $\boldsymbol\lambda$ be orthogonal to $\mathscr{M}_1(t_1)$ at the terminal point.

Before leaving the transversality conditions we note that the first of these simply tells us something about the value of H at t_1. We have $\mathbf{H}^*_{\dot{\mathbf{y}}} \cdot \dot{\mathbf{y}} = -\boldsymbol{\lambda} \cdot \dot{\mathbf{y}}$; also $R^q - \dot{\gamma}_q^2 = 0$ along any admissible path. Consequently,

$$H^* - \mathbf{H}^*_{\dot{\mathbf{Y}}} \cdot \dot{\mathbf{Z}} = H^* - \mathbf{H}^*_{\dot{\mathbf{y}}} \cdot \dot{\mathbf{y}} = H. \tag{5-31}$$

Thus H at t_1 must be a linear combination of the S_t^u evaluated at t_1. This does not provide much useful information if $t - t_1 = 0$ appears. However, if it does not appear, and if $\boldsymbol{\lambda}(t_1) = \Sigma_{u=1}^s \rho_u \mathbf{S}_{\mathbf{y}}^u$, then $H = \Sigma_{u=1}^s \rho_u S_t^u$. In particular, if the S^u are independent of t, then $H = 0$ at t_1; and, for an autonomous system, this then implies that $H = 0$ along the entire path for, as we have shown heuristically and will prove later, for such systems H must be a constant.

We have now extracted from the Euler equations and corner conditions everything of use to us. However, we have not obtained anything corresponding to the maximum principle. Where does it come from? The answer must lie in the fact that we have not brought into the picture *all* of the classical necessary conditions. In particular, we have not made use of the Weierstrass necessary condition, that E^*, the Weierstrass E function for H^*, satisfy $E^* \leq 0$ along $\mathbf{Z}(t)$. Let us now see where this necessary condition leads us. Here

$$E^*(t, \mathbf{Z}, \dot{\mathbf{Z}}, \dot{\mathbf{Y}}) = H^*(t, \mathbf{Z}, \dot{\mathbf{Y}}) - H^*(t, \mathbf{Z}, \dot{\mathbf{Z}}) - \mathbf{H}^*_{\dot{\mathbf{Y}}} \cdot (\dot{\mathbf{Y}} - \dot{\mathbf{Z}}) \tag{5-32}$$

and, for all $(t, \mathbf{Z}, \dot{\mathbf{Y}})$ satisfying $G^u = 0$, i.e. (5-10) and (5-11), $E^* \leq 0$. Let us select $\dot{\mathbf{Y}}$ so that $\dot{\mathbf{y}} = \dot{\mathbf{z}}$ and $\dot{\boldsymbol{\gamma}} = \boldsymbol{\phi}$; thus we allow only $\dot{\mathbf{V}} = \mathbf{v}$ to differ from $\dot{\mathbf{W}} = \mathbf{w}$. What does E^* reduce to in this case? Then

$$\mathbf{H}^*_{\dot{\mathbf{Y}}} \cdot (\dot{\mathbf{Y}} - \dot{\mathbf{Z}}) = \mathbf{H}^*_{\dot{\mathbf{V}}} \cdot (\mathbf{v} - \mathbf{w}) = 0 \tag{5-33}$$

for, as we have noted, $\mathbf{H}^*_{\dot{\mathbf{V}}} = \mathbf{0}$ along $\mathbf{Z}(t)$. However, $(t, \mathbf{Z}, \dot{\mathbf{Y}})$ satisfies the constraints; thus (5-11) holds for $(t, \mathbf{Z}, \dot{\mathbf{Y}})$ and for $(t, \mathbf{Z}, \dot{\mathbf{Z}})$. Hence $H^* = H$ in both cases and

$$E^* = H(t, \mathbf{z}, \mathbf{v}, \boldsymbol{\lambda}) - H(t, \mathbf{z}, \mathbf{w}, \boldsymbol{\lambda}). \tag{5-34}$$

Thus the requirement that $E^* \leq 0$ for all admissible $\mathbf{v}$ implies that

$$H(t, \mathbf{z}, \mathbf{v}, \boldsymbol{\lambda}) \leq H(t, \mathbf{z}, \mathbf{w}, \boldsymbol{\lambda}) \tag{5-35}$$

or $\mathbf{w}$ maximizes $H(t, \mathbf{z}, \mathbf{v}, \boldsymbol{\lambda})$. Here then we have the maximum principle. It follows from the Weierstrass necessary condition. It is interesting that the Weierstrass condition, of which we made almost no use in our study of the classical theory, should play such an important role in control theory.

So far we have made no use of the Legendre necessary condition. We now show that it can be made to yield one additional piece of useful information. The Legendre condition states that the quadratic form $\mathbf{d} \cdot \mathbf{H}^*_{\dot{\mathbf{Y}}\dot{\mathbf{Y}}}\mathbf{d}$ must be negative semidefinite along $\mathbf{Z}(t)$. If we choose $\mathbf{d} = (\mathbf{0}, \mathbf{0}, \mathbf{e})$, so that only those components which correspond to the $\dot{\gamma}$ components of $\dot{\mathbf{Y}}$ are different from zero, and then apply (5-24), we see that

$$\mathbf{H}_{\dot{\gamma}\dot{\gamma}} = \|2\mu_q\delta_{qi}\| \tag{5-36}$$

and, hence, that

$$2\sum_{q=0}^{h} \mu_q e_q^2 \leq 0 \quad \text{or} \quad \sum_{q=1}^{h} \mu_q e_q^2 \leq 0 \tag{5-37}$$

for all e_q. Thus, for all t, each $\mu_q(t) \leq 0$; that is, the $\mu_q(t)$ are nonpositive on the trajectory.

We show finally that $(\lambda_0, \boldsymbol{\lambda}(t))$ is never $\mathbf{0}$. We already know that $(\lambda_0, \boldsymbol{\lambda}(t), \boldsymbol{\mu}(t))$ is never $\mathbf{0}$. Suppose now that for some t, say t_c, $(\lambda_0, \boldsymbol{\lambda}(t_c)) = \mathbf{0}$. Then, from (5-28),

$$\sum_{u=1}^{h} \mu_u \mathbf{R}^u_{\mathbf{v}} = \mathbf{0}. \tag{5-38}$$

Suppose that α of the constraints R^u are active. Then $\mu_u = 0$ for the $h - \alpha$ inactive constraints. However, corresponding to the active constraints there is in $\|R^u_{v_i}\|$ a submatrix of rank α; in view of (5-38), therefore, $\mu_u = 0$ for these also. Thus, if $(\lambda_0, \boldsymbol{\lambda}(t_c)) = \mathbf{0}$, $(\lambda_0, \boldsymbol{\lambda}(t_c), \boldsymbol{\mu}(t_c)) = \mathbf{0}$, which is a contradiction.

We have now derived, for one version of the control problem, the equivalent of the necessary conditions stated in Chapter 4. We summarize the results obtained in Theorem 5.4.1. First, however, we restate for convenience the equations for the control problem to which it applies. The problem is that of maximizing or minimizing the functional

$$J[\mathbf{y}, \mathbf{v}] = \int_{t_0}^{t_1} F(t, \mathbf{y}, \mathbf{v})dt \tag{5-39}$$

subject to the constraints

$$\dot{\mathbf{y}} = \mathbf{f}(t, \mathbf{y}, \mathbf{v}) \tag{5-40}$$

and

$$\mathbf{R}(t, \mathbf{y}, \mathbf{v}) \leq \mathbf{0} \tag{5-41}$$

with $\mathbf{y}(t_0) = \mathbf{y}_0$ and $\mathbf{y}(t)$ ending on the smooth manifold $\mathscr{M}$. It is also assumed that the constraint qualification is satisfied.

Theorem 5.4.1. Necessary Conditions for Control Problem. Suppose that $\mathbf{w}(t)$ *is an admissible control for the control problem (5-39) through (5-41) and let* $\mathbf{z}(t)$, $\mathbf{z}(t_0) = \mathbf{y}_0$, *be the corresponding trajectory for the state variables which ends on the smooth manifold* $\mathscr{M}$. *Then if* $(\mathbf{z}(t), \mathbf{w}(t))$ *maximizes* $J[\mathbf{y}, \mathbf{v}]$ *it is necessary that there exist a constant* $\lambda_0 \geq 0$ *(which without loss in generality can be taken to be* 0 *or* 1*) and a continuous vector-valued function* $\boldsymbol{\lambda}(t)$ *such that* $(\lambda_0, \boldsymbol{\lambda}(t)) \neq \mathbf{0}$ *for any* t, *as well as a vector-valued function* $\boldsymbol{\mu}(t) \leq \mathbf{0}$ *which is continuous except possibly at corners of* $\mathbf{z}(x)$, *with the properties that if*

$$H = \lambda_0 F + \sum_{j=1}^{n} \lambda_j f^j \tag{5-42}$$

then

$$\dot{\mathbf{z}} = \mathbf{f}(t, \mathbf{z}, \mathbf{w}) = \mathbf{H}_{\boldsymbol{\lambda}} \tag{5-43}$$

and

$$\dot{\boldsymbol{\lambda}} = -\mathbf{H}_{\mathbf{y}}(t, \mathbf{z}, \mathbf{w}, \boldsymbol{\lambda}) - \sum_{u=1}^{h} \mu_u \mathbf{R}_{\mathbf{y}}^u(t, \mathbf{z}, \mathbf{w}) \tag{5-44}$$

and

$$\mathbf{H}_{\mathbf{v}}(t, \mathbf{z}, \mathbf{w}, \boldsymbol{\lambda}) + \sum_{u=1}^{h} \mu_u(t)\mathbf{R}_{\mathbf{v}}^u(t, \mathbf{z}, \mathbf{w}) \equiv \mathbf{0} \tag{5-45}$$

Also $\mu_q(t) = 0$ *if* $R^q(t, \mathbf{z}, \mathbf{w}) < 0$, *that is,*

$$\mu_q(t)R^q(t, \mathbf{z}, \mathbf{w}) = 0. \tag{5-46}$$

Furthermore, if $\mathscr{V}(t, \mathbf{y})$ *is the set of* $\mathbf{v}$ *satisfying (5-41) and if*

$$M(t, \mathbf{z}, \boldsymbol{\lambda}) = \sup_{\mathbf{v} \in \mathscr{V}(t,\mathbf{y})} H(t, \mathbf{z}, \mathbf{v}, \boldsymbol{\lambda}) \tag{5-47}$$

then for each t *along the path*

$$H(t, \mathbf{z}, \mathbf{w}, \boldsymbol{\lambda}) = M(t, \mathbf{z}, \boldsymbol{\lambda}). \tag{5-48}$$

Finally, if $\mathbf{z}(t)$ *intersects* $\mathscr{M}$ *at time* t_1 *then* $\boldsymbol{\lambda}(t_1)$ *must be orthogonal to* $\mathscr{M}_1(t_1)$.

It will be noted that the statement of the necessary conditions here is not exactly the same as in Theorem 4.3.1. The reason is that we are now allowing $\mathscr{V}$ to depend on t and $\mathbf{y}$, which was not the case in Chapter 4. This puts additional terms in the equation for $\dot{\boldsymbol{\lambda}}$; and to determine the new multipliers $\boldsymbol{\mu}$ we need additional conditions, which are given by (5-45). If the R^q do not depend on $\mathbf{y}$ then the additional terms in the equation for $\boldsymbol{\lambda}$ disappear and we can forget about the $\boldsymbol{\mu}(t)$; equations (5-45) and (5-46) specify their values, but they are no longer needed in the analysis.

Let us now suppose that the interval of integration is infinite and seek the counterpart to Theorem 4.3.2 by applying Theorem 3.13.1. From the proof of Theorem 5.4.1 it will be clear that, with one exception, all conditions of that theorem carry over. The exception is the transversality condition at the right hand end point. That condition must be modified in the following way. We note first that, on applying (5-22), (5-23), (5-24), (5-26), (5-28) and (5-29), $\mathbf{H}_{\dot{\mathbf{z}}} = (\mathbf{H}_{\dot{\mathbf{y}}}, \mathbf{H}_{\dot{\mathbf{v}}}, \mathbf{H}_{\dot{\boldsymbol{\gamma}}})$ becomes

$$\mathbf{H}_{\dot{\mathbf{z}}} = (-\boldsymbol{\lambda}, \mathbf{0}, \mathbf{0}) \tag{5-49}$$

In the case in which $\lim_{t\to\infty}[\mathbf{y}(t) - \mathbf{g}(t)] = \mathbf{0}$, no restriction is placed on $\mathbf{H}_{\dot{\mathbf{z}}}$ as $t \to \infty$; hence none is placed on $\boldsymbol{\lambda}(t)$. In this case, then, the conditions of Theorem 5.4.1 must be satisfied except that no restriction is placed on $\boldsymbol{\lambda}(t)$ as $t \to \infty$.

Consider next the case in which there is a free boundary for each component of $\mathbf{y}(t)$ as $t \to \infty$, so that $\mathbf{Y}(t)$ also has a free boundary at ∞. Then for every admissible one parameter family $\mathbf{y}(t; \xi)$ with $\mathbf{y}(t; 0) = \mathbf{z}(t)$ which can be constructed, it is necessary that $\mathbf{H}_{\dot{\mathbf{z}}}\boldsymbol{\eta}^*$ approach 0, i.e. $\lim_{t\to\infty}\boldsymbol{\lambda}(t) \cdot \boldsymbol{\eta}(t) = 0$, $\boldsymbol{\eta}(t) = \mathbf{y}_\xi(t; 0)$. This does not by itself imply that $\lim_{t\to\infty}\boldsymbol{\lambda}(t) = \mathbf{0}$. However, if it is possible to find n different admissible solutions $\mathbf{y}_k(x; \xi)$ such that $\lim_{t\to\infty}\boldsymbol{\eta}_k = \mathbf{a}_k$, where the $\mathbf{a}_k$ are linearly independent, then it must be true that $\lim_{t\to\infty}\boldsymbol{\lambda}(t) = \mathbf{0}$.

Consider finally the case in which it is required that $\lim_{t\to\infty}\mathbf{y}(t) = \mathbf{b}$, with $\mathbf{b}$ not specified explicitly but required only to lie in a bounded manifold $\mathscr{M}_1$. Suppose also that the system is autonomous and that $\lim_{t\to\infty}\mathbf{z}'(t)$ exists. Then $\lim_{t\to\infty}\mathbf{H}_{\dot{\mathbf{z}}}$ must exist since $\lim_{t\to\infty}\mathbf{y}(t)$ exists. Thus $\lim_{t\to\infty}\boldsymbol{\lambda}(t)$ exists. Furthermore, since the multipliers can be chosen so that the limit of $\mathbf{H}_{\dot{\mathbf{z}}}$ is orthogonal to the terminal manifold, it is possible for $\lim_{t\to\infty}\boldsymbol{\lambda}(t)$ to be orthogonal to $\mathscr{M}_1$, and then any necessary conditions will be satisfied. This completes the proof of Theorem 4.3.2. We have not considered every conceivable condition which might be imposed as $t \to \infty$, but we have considered those most frequently encountered.

5.5. The time variation of H

In Section 4.5 we provided a heuristic 'proof' that $H(t, \mathbf{z}(t), \mathbf{w}(t), \boldsymbol{\lambda}(t))$ is a continuous function of time and that $\dot{H} = H_t$ at all points where H possesses a derivative. Thus for an autonomous system H is a constant. In the present section we shall prove a generalization of this result appropriate to the control problem now being studied. This will be done by applying Theorem 3.12.3 to the Lagrange version of the control problem. Theorem 3.12.3 tells us that, if the present problem has a solution, there must exist a constant γ_0 such that

$$H^* - \mathbf{H}^*_{\dot{\mathbf{Y}}} \cdot \dot{\mathbf{Z}} = \int_{t_0}^{t} H^*_t dt + \gamma_0. \tag{5-50}$$

From (5-31)

$$H^* - \mathbf{H}^*_{\dot{\mathbf{Y}}} \cdot \dot{\mathbf{Z}} = H. \tag{5-51}$$

Also, from (5-16),

$$H^*_t = H_t + \sum_{q=1}^{h} \mu_q R^q_t. \tag{5-52}$$

Hence

$$H = \int_{t_0}^{t} \left[H_t + \sum_{q=1}^{h} \mu_q R^q_t \right] dt. \tag{5-53}$$

Thus H is continuous across jumps in $\mathbf{w}(t)$; and, between corners of H,

$$\dot{H} = H_t + \sum_{q=1}^{h} \mu_q R^q_t. \tag{5-54}$$

This gives us the required generalization of Theorem 4.5.1.

Theorem 5.5.1. Time Variation of H. Let $\mathbf{z}(t)$, $\mathbf{w}(t)$ yield an optimal solution to the control problem (5-39) to (5-41). Then there exists a constant γ_0 such that for each t, $t_0 \leq t \leq t_1$,

$$H(t, \mathbf{z}(t), \mathbf{w}(t), \boldsymbol{\lambda}(t)) = \int_{t_0}^{t} [H_t(\tau, \mathbf{z}(\tau), \mathbf{w}(\tau), \boldsymbol{\lambda}(\tau))$$

$$+ \sum_{q=1}^{h} \mu_q(\tau) R^q_t(t, \mathbf{z}(\tau), \mathbf{w}(\tau))] d\tau + \gamma_0. \tag{5-55}$$

Thus H is a continuous function of t; and, between corners of H, (5-54) holds. If the system is autonomous, $\dot{H} = 0$ and H is a constant along the trajectory.

The above theorem still holds, of course, if the interval of integration is infinite.

We can now apply some results obtained in the previous section for finite time horizons to eliminate the unspecified constant γ_0 in (5-55). Suppose first that the S^u do not involve t explicitly. We know that in this case $H = 0$ at t_1 (see p. 289). Moreover, integrating from t_1 to t we obtain

$$H(t) = \int_{t_1}^{t} \left[H_t + \sum_{q=1}^{h} \mu_q R_t^q \right] d\tau. \tag{5-56}$$

Hence, for an autonomous system $H = 0$ along the entire trajectory in this case.

Suppose that the S^u involve t, but $t - t_1 = 0$ is not a constraint; suppose also that the matrix with columns $\mathbf{S}_{\mathbf{y}}^u(t_1, \mathbf{y})$ has rank s. Then, if $-\boldsymbol{\lambda}(t_1) = \sum_{u=1}^{s} \rho_u \mathbf{S}_{\mathbf{y}}^u(t_1, \mathbf{z}(t_1))$, $H = \sum_{u=1}^{s} \rho_u S_t^u(t_1, \mathbf{z}(t_1))$ at time t_1, as we have shown in the previous section; hence for any time t

$$H(t) = \sum_{u=1}^{s} \rho_u S_t^u(t_1, \mathbf{z}(t_1)) + \int_{t_1}^{t} \left[H_t + \sum_{q=1}^{h} \mu_q R_t^q \right] d\tau. \tag{5-57}$$

We cannot determine γ_0 when $t - t_1 = 0$ is one of the hypersurfaces which define $\mathscr{M}$.

5.6. Examples

1. Consider once again the Ramsey model; the planning horizon may be either finite or infinite. In Chapter 4 it was not possible to treat $\dot{K}$ as the control variable; for this would have required the introduction of the constraint $\dot{K} \leq \Psi(K)$, which depends on the state variable K. In the present chapter, however, we have allowed for constraints on the control variables which involve both time and the state variables. Thus we can now formulate the problem with $\dot{K}$ as the control variable. The problem is to find a control $v(t)$ which maximizes

$$J[K, v] = \int_{0}^{T} U[\Psi(K) - v] dt \tag{5-58}$$

where

$$\dot{K} = v \tag{5-59}$$

and v must satisfy

$$v - \Psi(K) \leq 0. \tag{5-60}$$

Now

$$H = \lambda_0 U[\Psi(K) - v] + \lambda_1 v \tag{5-61}$$

and $R = v - \Psi(K)$. The equation (5-44) for $\dot{\lambda}_1$ then becomes

$$\dot{\lambda}_1 = - \lambda_0 U'\Psi' + \mu\Psi' \tag{5-62}$$

and (5-45) becomes

$$- \lambda_0 U' + \lambda_1 + \mu = 0 \tag{5-63}$$

while (5-46) reduces to $\mu R = 0$.

If the value of v which maximizes H does not lie on the boundary then $\mu = 0$ and

$$H_v = - \lambda_0 U' + \lambda_1 = 0. \tag{5-64}$$

Then, as in Chapter 4, we can immediately conclude that $\lambda_0 \neq 0$, so that we can set $\lambda_0 = 1$; thus $\lambda_1 = U'$ as before. Then also $\dot{\lambda}_1 = -U'\Psi' = -\lambda_1\Psi'$. Furthermore, since the system is autonomous, $\dot{H} = 0$ or $H = \lambda$; hence $U + \lambda_1 v = \lambda$ or $U + U'\dot{K} = \lambda$, which is the familiar integrated form of the Euler equation.

Suppose alternatively that the value of v which maximizes H lies on the boundary, so that $v = \Psi(K)$. Then $\dot{K} = \Psi(K)$ and $\mu = \lambda_0 U' - \lambda_1$ so that (5-62) becomes

$$\dot{\lambda}_1 = - \lambda_0 U'\Psi' + \lambda_0 U'\Psi' - \lambda_1\Psi' = - \lambda_1\Psi'. \tag{5-65}$$

Not unexpectedly, these are precisely the conditions obtained in Example 1 of Section 4.6.

If $U(C)$ is a strictly concave function then H is a strictly concave function of v; thus the v which maximizes H is unique. Consequently, there cannot be any jumps in v and $v = \dot{K}$ must be continuous. This again precisely matches the conclusion reached in Example 1 of Section 4.6.

2. In our discussion of the Ramsey model we have always allowed $\dot{K}$ to take negative values, implying that capital could be consumed. We can now see how to handle problems in which this possibility is denied, so that $\dot{K} \geq 0$ always. We need only annex to the formulation of Example 1 the additional constraint

$$v \geq 0 \tag{5-66}$$

on the control variable. Notice that we could not handle this case with the theory of Chapter 4 because we could not treat $\dot{K}$ as a control variable.

We now require that $0 \leq v \leq \Psi(K)$; thus the solution will lie on the boundary either if $v = 0$ or if $v = \Psi(K)$. If $U(C)$ is strictly concave then there are no jumps in v, that is, $\dot{K}$ is continuous; and this enables us to determine how transitions are made between boundary and interior solutions.

Suppose that it is desired to increase the initial stock of capital from K_0 to K_1 at time T, with $K_0 < K_1 < K^*$. From the catenary turnpike theorem, we know that if T is large enough then, in the absence of the constraint $v \geq 0$, K would rise above K_1 and then finally drop back to K_1 with $v < 0$. Such a time pattern is impossible when it is required that $v \geq 0$; for sufficiently large T, therefore, the constraint $v = 0$ must be active. Along the optimal path K must increase to K_1 at some time $T_f < T$ and then remain at K_1 from T_f to T. Let us now study in more detail the nature of the solution.

If $v = 0$ from, say, T_f to T, then $\dot{K} = 0$ during that period. However, $\dot{K}$ must be continuous; hence the trajectory which transfers the system from K_0 to K_1 at time T_f must have the property that $\dot{K}$ approaches 0 as K_1 is approached. This is all we need to know in order to solve the problem in complete detail. It will be helpful to refer to Figure 2.22. Notice that there is only one curve with the characteristic that at K_1, $\dot{K} = 0$. Thus the system must move along this curve when T is large enough. Let K_e be the value of K at the point of intersection between this curve and the boundary curve $\dot{K} = \Psi(K)$. If $K_0 < K_e$ the system moves along the boundary with $\dot{K} = \Psi(K)$ until K_e is reached. Then a transition is made to the curve which takes the system to K_1 in such a way that $\dot{K} = 0$ when K_1 is reached. When K_1 is reached (at time T_f), the system makes a transition to the boundary solution $v = 0$, and remains at K_1 until time T. If $T < T_f$, the boundary $v = 0$ is not active at any stage and the problem is solved in the manner described in Example 1 of Section 4.6.

3. In Section 4.7 we explained how the Samuelson-Solow model could be formulated as a control problem. It was there necessary to adopt an asymmetric formulation which required advance knowledge of the constraints which might be active. This caused no problems, because it was fairly obvious which constraints would be active in any particular case. Now, however, we can allow $\mathscr{V}$ to depend on the state variables; thus the way is clear to the adoption of a completely symmetric formulation. Let us choose $v_1 = \dot{K}_1$, $v_2 = \dot{K}_2$, C_1 and C_2 as control variables. The control variables must satisfy

$$-C_1 \leq 0, \qquad -C_2 \leq 0, \qquad -v_1 - C_1 \leq 0, \qquad -v_2 - C_2 \leq 0, \quad (5\text{-}67)$$

and

$$C_1 + C_2 + v_1 + v_2 - \beta_1(K_1 - K_1^*)^2 - \beta_2(K_2 - K_2^*)^2 \leq 0. \tag{5-68}$$

In fact the constraint (5-68) must hold as a strict inequality, but this emerges as part of the solution.

Here

$$H = -\lambda_0\alpha_1(C_1 - C_1^*)^2 - \lambda_0\alpha_2(C_2 - C_2^*)^2 + \lambda_1 v_1 + \lambda_2 v_2. \tag{5-69}$$

The necessary conditions are

$$\dot{K}_1 = v_1; \qquad \dot{K}_2 = v_2 \tag{5-70}$$

$$\dot{\lambda}_1 = \mu_5\beta_1(K_1 - K_1^*); \qquad \dot{\lambda}_2 = \mu_5\beta_2(K_2 - K_2^*) \tag{5-71}$$

and, from (5-45),

$$\begin{aligned} &-\mu_1 - \mu_3 + \mu_5 = 0; \qquad -\mu_2 - \mu_4 + \mu_5 = 0 \\ &\lambda_1 - \mu_3 + \mu_5 = 0; \qquad \lambda_2 - \mu_4 + \mu_5 = 0. \end{aligned} \tag{5-72}$$

Also, $\mu_q = 0$ unless constraint q is active. Finally, (C_1, C_2, v_1, v_2) must be chosen to maximize H.

This, then, is the symmetric formulation of the problem. It is easy to reduce it to the asymmetric version studied in Chapter 4. For example, if $v_1 + C_1 > 0$ then $\mu_3 = 0$ and $\lambda_1 = -\mu_5$. Then (5-71) becomes (4-126) and (4-127). Furthermore, to maximize H, (5-68) must always be active; and, if this equation is used to solve for v_2 and the result is substituted into $\dot{K}_2 = v_2$ and H, the remaining parts of the asymmetric formulation are obtained.

5.7. Sufficiency

In Section 3.15 we proved a sufficiency theorem for the problem of Lagrange with fixed end points or free boundaries. From that theorem we can now derive a sufficiency theorem for control problems of the type we have been studying. The theorem to be proved is in terms of the concavity properties of the functions and is therefore especially useful in economic analysis. Let us suppose that either there is a free boundary at the right hand end point or the right hand end point is fixed, and that we have found a function $\mathbf{Z}(t)$ defined by (5-15) and satisfying the necessary conditions for the Lagrange form of the control problem. From Theorem 3.15.1 we know that if for each t H^* given by (5-16) is a concave function of $(\mathbf{Z}, \mathbf{Z}')$ for the multipliers λ_0, $\boldsymbol{\lambda}(t)$, $\boldsymbol{\mu}(t)$ determined in the solution then the solution yields the absolute maximum of $J[\mathbf{Z}]$.

Let us now see what this reduces to when we convert back to the control formulation. We recall that $\boldsymbol{\mu}(t) \leq \mathbf{0}$, so that $\boldsymbol{\mu} \cdot \dot{\boldsymbol{\gamma}}^2$ is a concave function of $\dot{\boldsymbol{\gamma}}^2$. Furthermore, if each R^q is a *convex* function of $(\mathbf{y}, \mathbf{v})$ then $\boldsymbol{\mu} \cdot \mathbf{R}$ will be a *concave* function of $(\mathbf{y}, \mathbf{v})$. The requirement that each R^q be a convex function of $(\mathbf{y}, \mathbf{v})$ implies that, for each t, the set of points $(\mathbf{y}, \mathbf{v})$ satisfying $\mathbf{R}(t, \mathbf{y}, \mathbf{v}) \leq \mathbf{0}$ is a convex set. Let us assume that this is the case. Notice also that $-\boldsymbol{\lambda} \cdot \dot{\mathbf{y}}$ is a concave function of $\dot{\mathbf{y}}$ regardless of the signs of the components of $\boldsymbol{\lambda}$. Now

$$H^* = H - \boldsymbol{\lambda} \cdot \dot{\mathbf{y}} + \boldsymbol{\mu} \cdot \mathbf{R} - \boldsymbol{\mu} \cdot \dot{\boldsymbol{\gamma}}^2 \tag{5-73}$$

where H, the Hamiltonian for the control problem, is given by (5-19). In view of what we have just shown, if H is a concave function of $(\mathbf{y}, \mathbf{v})$ for each t, and if the R^q are convex, H^* will be a concave function of $(\mathbf{Z}, \mathbf{Z}')$ for each t; and this is what is required for the control problem. Thus we have proved the following sufficiency theorem for the control problem.

Theorem 5.7.1. Sufficiency Conditions for Problems with Fixed End Points or Free Boundaries. Let $\mathbf{w}(t)$ *be an admissible control for the control problem (5-39) to (5-41) with fixed end points or free boundaries, and let* $\mathbf{z}(t)$ *be the function which describes the corresponding time behavior of the state variables. Suppose that* $\mathbf{w}(t)$ *and* $\mathbf{z}(t)$ *satisfy the necessary conditions of Theorem 5.4.1 when the multipliers are* $(\lambda_0, \boldsymbol{\lambda}(t), \boldsymbol{\mu}(t))$, *and let* $H(t, \mathbf{y}, \mathbf{w})$ *be the Hamiltonian function which corresponds to the multipliers* $(\lambda_0, \boldsymbol{\lambda}(t))$ *just described. Then if the* R^q, $q = 1, \ldots, h$ *are convex functions of* $(\mathbf{y}, \mathbf{v})$ *for each t and if* $H(t, \mathbf{y}, \mathbf{v})$ *is a concave function of* $(\mathbf{y}, \mathbf{v})$ *for each t and for* $(\mathbf{y}, \mathbf{v})$ *in the convex set defined by* $R^q \leq 0$, $q = 1, \ldots, h$, $\mathbf{w}(t)$ *is an optimal control and* $\mathbf{z}(t)$, $\mathbf{w}(t)$ *yields the absolute maximum of* $J[\mathbf{z}, \mathbf{w}]$. *If H is a convex function under the same conditions,* $\mathbf{z}(t)$, $\mathbf{w}(t)$ *yield the absolute minimum of* $J[\mathbf{z}, \mathbf{w}]$.

Consider next the case in which the time horizon is infinite. Then, from Theorem 3.15.2, we can obtain a corresponding sufficient condition for the control problem. Suppose that $\mathbf{w}(t)$ is an admissible control which satisfies the necessary conditions of Theorem 5.4.1, and let $\mathbf{Z}(t) = (\mathbf{z}(t), \mathbf{W}(t), \boldsymbol{\phi}(t))$ be the corresponding solution to the problem of Lagrange. Given the concavity assumptions relating to H^*, we know that if it can be shown that

$$\lim_{t \to \infty} \mathbf{H}^*_{\mathbf{Y}'}(t, \mathbf{Z}(t), \mathbf{Z}'(t)) \cdot \boldsymbol{\eta}^*(t) \tag{5-74}$$

is non-positive for any other admissible solution $\mathbf{Y}(t)$, $\boldsymbol{\eta}^*(t) = \mathbf{Y}(t) - \mathbf{Z}(t)$, then the solution under consideration yields a global maximum. From (5-49) it then follows that, if $\boldsymbol{\eta}(t) = \mathbf{y}(t) - \mathbf{z}(t)$, the condition that (5-74) be non-positive reduces to the condition that $\lim_{t\to\infty}\boldsymbol{\lambda}(t)\cdot\boldsymbol{\eta}(t)$ is non-negative. Thus we have proved the following theorem.

Theorem 5.7.2. Sufficiency when the Time Interval is Unbounded. Consider a control problem in which the time interval is unbounded. Let $\mathbf{w}(t)$ *be an admissible control and* $\mathbf{z}(t)$ *the corresponding function which describes the time behavior of the state variables. Suppose that there is a vector-valued function* $(\lambda_0, \boldsymbol{\lambda}(t), \boldsymbol{\mu}(t))$ *such that* $\mathbf{z}(t)$ *and* $\mathbf{w}(t)$*, together with* $(\lambda_0, \boldsymbol{\lambda}(t), \boldsymbol{\mu}(t))$*, satisfy the necessary conditions (5-42) through (5-48) of Theorem 5.4.1. Suppose also that the* R^q *are convex functions of* $(\mathbf{y}, \mathbf{v})$ *for each* t*. Suppose finally that the Hamiltonian* $H(t, \mathbf{y}, \mathbf{v})$ *formed with* $(\lambda_0, \boldsymbol{\lambda})$ *is a concave function of* $(\mathbf{y}, \mathbf{v})$ *for all* t *such that* $(t, \mathbf{y}, \mathbf{v})$ *satisfies* $R^q \le 0$, $q = 1, \ldots, n$*. Then if for every other admissible control* $\mathbf{v}(t)$

$$\lim_{t\to\infty} \boldsymbol{\lambda}(t)\cdot\boldsymbol{\eta}(t)$$

is non-negative, where $\boldsymbol{\eta}(t) = \mathbf{y}(t) - \mathbf{z}(t)$ *and* $\mathbf{y}(z)$ *describes the time behavior of the state variables corresponding to* $\mathbf{v}(t)$*, the control* $\mathbf{w}(t)$ *is such that* $(\mathbf{z}(t), \mathbf{w}(t))$ *yields the absolute maximum of* $J[\mathbf{y}, \mathbf{v}]$.

We shall not attempt to state sufficiency conditions for cases other than those in which the end points are fixed or the boundaries free.

5.8. Linear control problems

A control problem is said to be *linear* if the functions F, $\mathbf{f}$ and $\mathbf{R}$ are linear functions of the variables $(\mathbf{y}, \mathbf{v})$. Such a problem can be written

$$J[\mathbf{y}, \mathbf{v}] = \int_{t_0}^{t_1} [\mathbf{c}(t)\cdot\mathbf{y} + \mathbf{e}(t)\cdot\mathbf{v}]dt \tag{5-75}$$

where

$$\dot{\mathbf{y}} = \mathbf{A}(t)\mathbf{y} + \mathbf{B}(t)\mathbf{v} + \mathbf{g}(t) \tag{5-76}$$

and the control variables must satisfy the constraints

$$\mathbf{D}(t)\mathbf{y} + \mathbf{R}(t)\mathbf{v} \le \mathbf{m}(t) \tag{5-77}$$

Here the upper case bold face letters stand for matrices the elements of which are functions of time and the lower case bold face letters stand for vectors the elements of which are functions of time. As usual we can require that $\mathbf{y}(t_0) = \mathbf{y}_0$ and that the trajectory $\mathbf{y}(t)$ ends on a smooth manifold $\mathscr{M}$.

Now the Hamiltonian is

$$H = \lambda_0 \mathbf{c}(t) \cdot \mathbf{y} + \lambda_0 \mathbf{e}(t) \cdot \mathbf{v} + \boldsymbol{\lambda} \cdot \mathbf{A}(t)\mathbf{y} + \boldsymbol{\lambda} \cdot \mathbf{B}(t)\mathbf{v} + \boldsymbol{\lambda} \cdot \mathbf{g}(t) \tag{5-78}$$

and the necessary conditions become

$$\dot{\boldsymbol{\lambda}} = -\lambda_0 \mathbf{c}(t) - \mathbf{A}^T(t)\boldsymbol{\lambda} - \mathbf{D}^T(t)\boldsymbol{\mu} \tag{5-79}$$

and

$$\lambda_0 \mathbf{e}(t) + \mathbf{B}^T(t)\boldsymbol{\lambda} + \mathbf{R}^T\boldsymbol{\mu} = \mathbf{0}. \tag{5-80}$$

Furthermore,

$$\boldsymbol{\mu} \cdot [\mathbf{D}(t)\mathbf{y} + \mathbf{R}(t)\mathbf{v} - \mathbf{m}(t)] = 0 \tag{5-81}$$

and $\boldsymbol{\mu} \leq \mathbf{0}$. Note that all of the expressions are linear in the variables involved.

Let us now study in more detail the special case in which the system is autonomous, with t not appearing explicitly in any of the coefficients. For specified values of λ_0, $\boldsymbol{\lambda}$ and $\mathbf{y}$, H can be written

$$H = \mathbf{h} \cdot \mathbf{v} + \Phi \tag{5-82}$$

and (5-77) becomes

$$\mathbf{R}\mathbf{v} \leq \boldsymbol{\theta}. \tag{5-83}$$

The problem of maximizing H with respect to $\mathbf{v}$ subject to (5-83) is a linear programming problem. Let us suppose that the set of $\mathbf{v}$ satisfying (5-83) is a convex polyhedron. Then H has a maximum and we know from the theory of linear programming that at least one of the extreme points of the convex polyhedron is optimal.

The convex polyhedron has only a finite number of extreme points, say $\mathbf{v}_1, \ldots, \mathbf{v}_s$, and at least one of these vectors maximizes H. For any extreme point $\mathbf{v}_i$, those of the constraints (5-83) which are active may be determined; hence the set of μ^q which must be 0 also may be determined. With the aid of (5-80), those μ^q which are not necessarily 0 may be expressed in terms of $(\lambda_0, \boldsymbol{\lambda})$; thus $\boldsymbol{\mu}$ can be eliminated from (5-79) to yield a system of first order linear homogeneous equations in $(\lambda_0, \boldsymbol{\lambda})$:

$$\begin{aligned} \dot{\lambda}_0 &= 0 \\ \dot{\boldsymbol{\lambda}} &= \mathbf{p}\lambda_0 + \mathbf{P}\boldsymbol{\lambda}. \end{aligned} \tag{5-84}$$

From the general theory of homogeneous linear differential equations with constant coefficients we know that it is possible to construct $n + 1$ linearly independent solutions to (5-84) and that every other solution must be a linear combination of these. Hence, in principle, it is possible to find the general solution to (5-84) for each extreme point. Similarly, for each extreme point, the general solution to (5-76) can be found. We note next that over a certain time interval the control variables are constant, with $\mathbf{w} = \mathbf{v}_i$; then a jump is made to another (normally adjacent) extreme point, with the control variables again constant for a time with $\mathbf{w} = \mathbf{v}_q$; and so on. Thus the general form of the solutions to (5-76) and (5-79) is known. There remains the problem of joining together the several pieces of the solution so that it satisfies the necessary conditions. This can be a very difficult problem, and there are no procedural rules of general applicability.

Suppose, however, that the constraints (5-77) are independent of $\mathbf{y}$ as well as t. Then the $\boldsymbol{\mu}$ variables do not appear in (5-79); hence there is only one set of equations (5-79). These equations do not change as the control variables change value. This can lead to a great simplification. Suppose, for example, that there is a free boundary at t_1, so that $\lambda_0 = 1$ and $\boldsymbol{\lambda}(t_1) = \mathbf{0}$. Then there is determined a unique solution $\boldsymbol{\lambda}(t)$ to (5-79), and this is the only $\boldsymbol{\lambda}(t)$ which satisfies the necessary conditions. This $\boldsymbol{\lambda}(t)$ can be substituted into H; then, using a parametric programming approach, we can determine for each t an optimal extreme point $\mathbf{w}(t)$. Thus $\mathbf{w}(t)$ is an optimal control. Given $\mathbf{w}(t)$, the trajectory $\mathbf{z}(t)$ for the state variables can be calculated from (5-76). In this case, then, the complete optimal solution can be determined without difficulty, in spite of the fact that there may be several discontinuous changes in the control variables.

We conclude this section by describing an interesting connection between linear autonomous control problems and those of mathematical programming. (See G. B. Dantzig in [11].) Consider the equations (5-76), and suppose that any admissible control $\mathbf{v}(t)$ is selected. Let

$$\dot{y}_0 = \mathbf{c}(t) \cdot \mathbf{y} + \mathbf{e}(t) \cdot \mathbf{v}, \qquad y_0(0) = 0 \tag{5-85}$$

so that $y_0(t)$ is the value of (5-75) when the upper limit is t. And let

$$\mathbf{Q} = \begin{bmatrix} 0 & \mathbf{c} \\ \mathbf{0} & \mathbf{A} \end{bmatrix} \quad \text{and} \quad \mathbf{Y} = (y_0, \mathbf{y}). \tag{5-86}$$

We now show how to write down the general solution to (5-76).

Consider the homogeneous system $\dot{\mathbf{Y}} = \mathbf{QY}$ and let $\mathbf{Y}_0(t), \ldots, \mathbf{Y}_n(t)$ be a fundamental set of solutions, i.e. a set of linearly independent solutions with the characteristic that $\mathbf{Y}_j(0) = \mathbf{e}_j$. Also, let $\mathbf{M}$ be the matrix the columns of which are the $\mathbf{Y}_j(t)$. Then

$$\dot{\mathbf{M}} = \mathbf{QM} \quad \text{and} \quad \mathbf{M}(0) = \mathbf{I}. \tag{5-87}$$

We shall denote the matrix $\mathbf{M}$ by $\mathbf{e}^{\mathbf{Q}t}$ (by analogy with the definition of the exponential function as the solution to the one-variable version of (5-87)). Then $\mathrm{d}\mathbf{e}^{\mathbf{Q}t}/\mathrm{d}t = \mathbf{Q}\mathbf{e}^{\mathbf{Q}t}$. The matrix $\mathbf{M}$ is nonsingular. Its inverse $\mathbf{M}^{-1}$ will be denoted by $\mathbf{e}^{-\mathbf{Q}t}$. Notice that it is *not* true that $\mathrm{d}\mathbf{e}^{-\mathbf{Q}t}/\mathrm{d}t = -\mathbf{Q}\mathbf{e}^{-\mathbf{Q}t}$. Let us determine the appropriate result. Since $\mathbf{M}^{-1}\mathbf{M} = \mathbf{I}$, $\dot{\mathbf{M}}^{-1}\mathbf{M} + \mathbf{M}^{-1}\dot{\mathbf{M}} = \mathbf{0}$ or $(\dot{\mathbf{M}}^{-1} + \mathbf{M}^{-1}\mathbf{Q})\mathbf{M} = \mathbf{0}$; hence $\dot{\mathbf{M}}^{-1} = -\dot{\mathbf{M}}^{-1}\mathbf{Q}$. It follows that $\mathrm{d}\mathbf{e}^{-\mathbf{Q}t}/\mathrm{d}t = -\mathbf{e}^{-\mathbf{Q}t}\mathbf{Q}$.

We now notice that

$$\frac{\mathrm{d}}{\mathrm{d}t}(\mathbf{e}^{-\mathbf{Q}t}\mathbf{Y}) = \mathbf{e}^{-\mathbf{Q}t}\dot{\mathbf{Y}} - \mathbf{e}^{-\mathbf{Q}t}\mathbf{QY}. \tag{5-88}$$

Hence if we multiply the system (5-87) and (5-76) by $\mathbf{e}^{-\mathbf{Q}t}$ we obtain

$$\frac{\mathrm{d}}{\mathrm{d}t}(\mathbf{e}^{-\mathbf{Q}t}\mathbf{Y}) = \mathbf{e}^{-\mathbf{Q}t}[\mathbf{Tv}(t) + \mathbf{g}_1] \tag{5-89}$$

or

$$\mathbf{Y}_n(t) = \mathbf{e}^{\mathbf{Q}t}Y_0 + \mathbf{e}^{\mathbf{Q}t}\int_0^t \mathbf{e}^{-\mathbf{Q}\tau}[\mathbf{Tv}(\tau) + \mathbf{g}_1]\mathrm{d}\tau \tag{5-90}$$

where

$$\mathbf{T} = \begin{bmatrix} \mathbf{e} \\ \\ \mathbf{B} \end{bmatrix}; \qquad \mathbf{g}_1 = \begin{bmatrix} 0 \\ \\ \mathbf{g} \end{bmatrix}. \tag{5-91}$$

Thus we have obtained an explicit expression for $\mathbf{Y}(t)$. Notice that we have made use of $t_0 = 0$. Equation (5-90) can be used to compute $\mathbf{Y}(t)$ for any specified control $\mathbf{v}(t)$.

Suppose that the right hand end point is specified, so that $\mathbf{y}(t_1) = \mathbf{y}_1$. And let us write $\mathbf{Y}(t_1) = y_0\mathbf{e}_1 + (0, \mathbf{y}_1) = y_0\mathbf{e}_1 + \mathbf{Y}_1$, and

$$\mathbf{b} = \mathbf{Y}_1 - \mathbf{e}^{\mathbf{Q}t_1}\mathbf{Y}_0; \qquad \mathbf{X} = \mathbf{e}^{\mathbf{Q}t_1}\int_0^{t_1} \mathbf{e}^{-\mathbf{Q}\tau}[\mathbf{Tv}(\tau) + \mathbf{g}_1]\mathrm{d}\tau. \tag{5-92}$$

Then (5-90) becomes

$$-y_0\mathbf{e}_1 + \mathbf{X} = \mathbf{b} \tag{5-93}$$

where $\mathbf{b}$ is fixed and $\mathbf{X}$ and y_0 vary with the control $\mathbf{v}(t)$.

We shall now suppose that the set $\mathscr{V}$ is a closed, bounded convex set. Let us examine the nature of the set $\mathscr{X}$ of all vectors $\mathbf{X}$ which can be generated by an admissible control. Since $\mathscr{V}$ is bounded so is $\mathscr{X}$; furthermore $\mathscr{X}$ is convex. To see that $\mathscr{X}$ is convex, let $\mathbf{X}_1$ and $\mathbf{X}_2$ be in $\mathscr{X}$ and suppose that the controls $\mathbf{v}_1(t)$ and $\mathbf{v}_2(t)$ generate $\mathbf{X}_1$ and $\mathbf{X}_2$ respectively. Consider now the point $\mathbf{X}_3 = \lambda\mathbf{X}_2 + (1 - \lambda)\mathbf{X}_1$, $0 \leq \lambda \leq 1$. This point can be generated by the control $\lambda\mathbf{v}_2(t) + (1 - \lambda)\mathbf{v}_1(t)$, which is admissible since $\mathscr{V}$ is a convex set; hence $\mathbf{X}_3$ lies in $\mathscr{X}$.

The problem then reduces to that of finding the point $\mathbf{X} \in \mathscr{X}$ which yields the largest value of y_0 and satisfies (5-93). We notice that this is a very simple type of generalized linear programming problem. In a generalized linear programming problem, it is required to determine that $\mathbf{x}$ which maximizes z and satisfies $\mathbf{x} \geq \mathbf{0}$ and

$$- z + \mathbf{c}\mathbf{x} = \alpha \tag{5-94}$$

$$\mathbf{A}\mathbf{x} = \mathbf{b}$$

where α is a constant usually taken to be 0. (See Hadley [17], pp. 183–186). The problem described thus far is an ordinary linear programming problem if it is assumed that the vectors $(c_j, \mathbf{a}_j)$ are given. It becomes a generalized linear programming problem if these vectors are not specified, but instead each vector $(c_j, \mathbf{a}_j)$ can be freely chosen from a convex set $\mathscr{A}_j$. Thus if we write (5-93) as

$$\begin{aligned} - y_0 e_1 + \mathbf{X}x &= \mathbf{b} \\ x &= 1 \end{aligned} \tag{5-95}$$

we have a generalized linear programming problem in which $\mathbf{A}$ has only one column and the variable x must always be 1.

Generalized linear programming problems may be solved by means of the decomposition principle. (See Hadley [17], pp. 400–411.) We suppose that $\mathbf{X}$ is expressed as a convex combination of extreme points of $\mathscr{X}$, say $\mathbf{X} = \Sigma\delta_i\mathbf{X}_i^*$, $\Sigma\delta_i = 1$, $\delta_i \geq 0$, where the $\mathbf{X}_i^*$ are extreme points of $\mathscr{X}$. (We do not require that $\mathscr{X}$ have a finite number of extreme points.) Then (5-93) becomes

$$\begin{aligned} - y_0\mathbf{e}_1 + \sum_i \delta_i\mathbf{X}_i^* &= \mathbf{b} \\ \sum \delta_i &= 1 \end{aligned} \tag{5-96}$$

with $\delta_i \geq 0$. The problem then is to determine a set of extreme points $\mathbf{X}_i^*$ and values of the δ_i so that y_0 is maximized. From the theory of linear programming we know that no more than $n + 1$ extreme points need be included at a positive level, for a basis here (excluding the objective function) must be of order $n + 1$. At each iteration of the simplex method one column (extreme point) is removed and another inserted. When applying the decomposition principle, the smalled $z_j - c_j$ is found by solving a set of linear programming subproblems. In the present case there is just one subproblem. Let us now see what it is. The constraints for **X** are not of the usual form; they tell us that **X** can be computed according to (5-93). The decomposition process generates a vector $\boldsymbol{\sigma}$ such that the objective function to be minimized is $\boldsymbol{\sigma} \cdot \mathbf{X}$. The minimum value of this function is the smallest $z_j - c_j$ and the solution so generated is the next extreme point to enter the basis.

It remains to see what minimizing $\boldsymbol{\sigma} \cdot \mathbf{X}$ involves. We can write

$$\mathbf{X} = \int_0^{t_1} \mathbf{e}^{-\mathbf{Q}(\tau - t_1)}[\mathbf{T}\mathbf{v}(\tau) + g_1]d\tau \tag{5-97}$$

and if we define the row vector

$$\boldsymbol{\beta}(\tau) = \boldsymbol{\sigma}\mathbf{e}^{-\mathbf{Q}(\tau - t_1)}\mathbf{T} \tag{5-98}$$

then

$$\boldsymbol{\sigma} \cdot \mathbf{X} = \int_0^{t_1} \boldsymbol{\beta}(\tau) \cdot \mathbf{v}(\tau)d\tau + v \tag{5-99}$$

where v is a constant. For each t, the control $\mathbf{v}$ generating the extreme point which minimizes $\boldsymbol{\sigma} \cdot \mathbf{X}$ should be chosen to minimize $\boldsymbol{\beta}(t) \cdot \mathbf{v}$. If the minimum value of $\boldsymbol{\sigma} \cdot \mathbf{X}$ is non-negative then an optimal solution has been obtained. Otherwise, the extreme point generated is the next column to enter the basis. Notice that the process of actually determining the extreme point does not follow from linear programming. The point must be found by integration after $\mathbf{v}(t)$ has been determined. Suppose that $\boldsymbol{\sigma}^*$ is the $\boldsymbol{\sigma}$ associated with the optimal solution, and let $\boldsymbol{\beta}^*(t)$ be the corresponding $\boldsymbol{\beta}(t)$. Then the optimal control $\mathbf{w}(t)$ must minimize $\boldsymbol{\beta}^*(t) \cdot \mathbf{v}$ for each t. This is simply the maximum principle. When the control system is linear and continuous, the principle can be derived by means of the theory of linear programming.

5.9. Constrained state variables – introduction

We have not yet shown how to accommodate constraints of the form $T(t, \mathbf{y}) = 0$ or $T(t, \mathbf{y}) \leq 0$, involving the state variables but not the control variables. We now proceed to show how this can be done. It will be shown that constraints $T = 0$ or $T \leq 0$ can be converted into differential equation constraints so that, once again, it is possible first to convert the control problem into a problem of Lagrange and then to convert the necessary conditions for the Lagrange problem into necessary conditions for the control problem.

Let us begin by showing how the new constraints can be converted into differential equations. Consider first a constraint of the form $T(t, \mathbf{y}) = 0$. For any given $\mathbf{y}(t)$, T becomes a function $\phi(t)$ of t only. If $\mathbf{y}(t)$ satisfies the constraint for all t, then $\dot{\phi}(t) \equiv 0$, i.e.

$$\dot{\phi}(t) = T_t + \mathbf{T}_\mathbf{y} \cdot \dot{\mathbf{y}} \equiv 0. \tag{5-100}$$

Suppose now that we have found a function $\mathbf{y}(t)$ which satisfies (5-100). Then $\dot{\phi} \equiv 0$ and ϕ = constant, i.e. T = constant. If we add the additional requirement that

$$T(t_0, \mathbf{y}(t_0)) = 0 \tag{5-101}$$

then any function $\mathbf{y}(t)$ which satisfies (5-100) and (5-101) will have the property that $T(t, \mathbf{y}(t)) \equiv 0$ and the constraint will be satisfied. Thus if the appropriate derivatives of T exist the constraint $T = 0$ is equivalent to (5-100) and (5-101).

Consider next a constraint of the form $T(t, \mathbf{y}) \leq 0$. The essential step is the introduction of a carefully chosen slack variable; then the above procedure may be followed again. We could write $\mathscr{T}(t, \mathbf{y}, \theta) = T(t, \mathbf{y}) + \theta = 0$, where $\theta \geq 0$. However, we have no way of ensuring that $\theta \geq 0$. To avoid this difficulty we could redefine $\mathscr{T}$ as

$$\mathscr{T}(t, \mathbf{y}, \theta) = \begin{cases} T(t, \mathbf{y}) + \theta, & \theta \geq 0 \\ T(t, y), & \theta \leq 0. \end{cases} \tag{5-102}$$

Then, if $\mathscr{T} = 0$, $T \leq 0$. However this definition poses other difficulties. It will be recalled that the functions G^i in the problem of Lagrange must have continuous derivatives of the second order. Now G^i itself involves the first derivatives of $\mathscr{T}$, as in (5-100). Thus $\mathscr{T}$ should possess continuous derivatives of the third order. This is not true at $\theta = 0$ if the above definition is adopted. We need a higher power of θ, say θ^n. It is necessary that the third derivative of θ^n involve θ. Hence n must be at least 4. We shall let $n = 4$, and write

$$\mathscr{T}(t, \mathbf{y}, \theta) = \begin{cases} T(t, \mathbf{y}) + \theta^4, & \theta \geq 0 \\ T(t, y) & \theta \leq 0. \end{cases} \tag{5-103}$$

Then when $T \in C''$ it is also true that $\mathcal{T} \in C'''$. Observe that, for any $(t, \mathbf{y})$ such that $T(t, \mathbf{y}) \leq 0$, there exists a θ (not unique if $T = 0$) such that $\mathcal{T}(t, \mathbf{y}, \theta) = 0$. Furthermore, for any $(t, \mathbf{y}, \theta)$ such that $\mathcal{T}(t, \mathbf{y}, \theta) = 0$, $T(x, \mathbf{y}) \leq 0$. Thus the constraint $T(x, \mathbf{y}) \leq 0$ is equivalent to the constraint $\mathcal{T}(t, \mathbf{y}, \theta) = 0$. However, we can represent this constraint by the differential equation

$$\mathcal{T}_t + \mathcal{T}_{\mathbf{y}} \cdot \dot{\mathbf{y}} + \mathcal{T}_\theta \dot{\theta} = 0 \quad \text{or} \quad T_t + \mathbf{T}_{\mathbf{y}} \cdot \dot{\mathbf{y}} + \mathcal{T}_\theta \dot{\theta} = 0 \tag{5-104}$$

together with

$$\mathcal{T}(t_0, \mathbf{y}(t_0), \theta(t_0)) = 0. \tag{5-105}$$

With this background, we can now convert a control problem involving constraints on the state variables into a problem of Lagrange.

5.10. The control problem and the equivalent problem of Lagrange

We shall consider a control problem of the form (5-39) to (5-41) with, in addition, constraints on the state variables of the form

$$\begin{aligned} T^l(t, \mathbf{y}) &= 0, \quad l \in \mathcal{L}_1 \\ T^l(t, \mathbf{y}) &\leq 0, \quad l \in \mathcal{L}_2. \end{aligned} \tag{5-106}$$

Either, but not both, of the sets $\mathcal{L}_1$ and $\mathcal{L}_2$ may be empty. Suppose that there are α constraints in $\mathcal{L}_1$ and β in $\mathcal{L}_2$, and that $\alpha \leq m$, $\alpha \leq n$.

We now introduce a constraint qualification which is a generalization of that given on p.

Control and State Variable Constraint Qualifications. (a) If h (the number of R^q constraints) plus β (the number of constraints in $\mathcal{L}_2$) is greater than or equal to m (the number of control variables), not more than $m - \alpha$ of these constraints can be active at any particular point (α being the number of constraints in $\mathcal{L}_1$). (b) Let $(t, \mathbf{y}, \mathbf{v})$ be any solution to $R^q \leq 0$, $T^l = 0$, $l \in \mathcal{L}_1$, $T^l \leq 0$, $l \in \mathcal{L}_2$, and suppose that exactly k of the constraints $R^q \leq 0$, $T^l \leq 0$ are active. Consider now the $m \times (k + \alpha)$ matrix $\mathbf{P}$ the columns of which consist of the $\mathbf{R}^q_{\mathbf{v}}$ from the active R^q and the vectors $\mathbf{A}\mathbf{T}^l_{\mathbf{y}}$ for those $l \in \mathcal{L}_2$ for which $T^l \leq 0$ is active and for all $l \in \mathcal{L}_1$. Here $\mathbf{A}$ is the $m \times n$ matrix the jth column of which is $\mathbf{f}^j_{\mathbf{v}}$. Notice that the vectors $\mathbf{T}^l_{\mathbf{y}}$ are not used directly; instead, the vectors $\mathbf{A}\mathbf{T}^l_{\mathbf{y}}$ appear. We shall see below why this form is used. Notice also that there is a column for each constraint $T^l = 0$ which must always be active.

The requirement we shall impose is that at every point where k of the constraints are active **P** *has rank* $k + \alpha$.

The purpose of the constraint qualification is to guarantee that we can apply the theory of Chapter 3 to that problem of Lagrange which is equivalent to the control problem now being studied.

Let us now convert the control problem formulated in this section into a problem of Lagrange. We use the method of Valentine to convert the constraints $R^q \leq 0$ into differential equations and then follow the procedure introduced in the preceding section to convert the constraints (5-106) into differential equations. The problem then becomes that of determining a piecewise smooth function $\mathbf{Y}(t) = (\mathbf{y}(t), \mathbf{V}(t), \boldsymbol{\gamma}(t), \boldsymbol{\theta}(t))$ which maximizes

$$J[\mathbf{Y}] = \int_{t_0}^{t_1} F(t, \mathbf{y}, \dot{\mathbf{V}})dt \tag{5-107}$$

subject to the differential equation constraints

$$-\dot{\mathbf{y}} + \mathbf{f}(t, \mathbf{y}, \dot{\mathbf{V}}) = \mathbf{0} \tag{5-108}$$

$$\mathbf{R}(t, \mathbf{y}, \dot{\mathbf{V}}) + \dot{\boldsymbol{\gamma}}^2 = \mathbf{0} \tag{5-109}$$

$$T_t^l(t, \mathbf{y}) + \mathbf{T}_{\mathbf{y}}^l(t, \mathbf{y}) \cdot \dot{\mathbf{y}} = 0, \quad l \in \mathscr{L}_1 \tag{5-110}$$

$$T_t^l(t, \mathbf{y}) + \mathbf{T}_{\mathbf{y}}^l(t, \mathbf{y}) \cdot \dot{\mathbf{y}} + \mathscr{T}_{\theta_l}\dot{\theta}_l = 0, \quad l \in \mathscr{L}_2. \tag{5-111}$$

The end point conditions are the following. At t_0:

$\mathbf{y}(t_0) = \mathbf{y}_0$; $\boldsymbol{\gamma}(t_0)$ has a free boundary; $\mathbf{V}(t_0)$ has a free boundary;

$$\mathscr{T}^l(t_0, \mathbf{y}_0, \boldsymbol{\theta}(t_0)) = 0, \quad l \in \mathscr{L}_2.$$

We assume that $(t_0, \mathbf{y}_0)$ satisfies $T^l = 0$, $l \in \mathscr{L}_1$, for otherwise there is no solution.

At t_1:

$(t_1, \mathbf{y}(t_1)) \in \mathscr{M}$; $\boldsymbol{\gamma}(t_1)$ has a free boundary; $\mathbf{V}(t_1)$ has a free boundary;

$$\mathscr{T}^l(t_1, \mathbf{y}(t_1), \boldsymbol{\theta}(t_1)) = 0, \quad l \in \mathscr{L}_2.$$

Here then we have a problem of Lagrange. By studying the conditions which must be satisfied by an optimal solution to this problem we shall obtain the corresponding necessary conditions for the control problem.

5.11. Necessary conditions for the problem of Lagrange

Suppose that the admissible function

$$\mathbf{Z}(t) = (\mathbf{z}(t), \mathbf{w}(t), \boldsymbol{\phi}(t), \boldsymbol{\kappa}(t)) \tag{5-112}$$

provides an optimal solution to the problem of Lagrange formulated in the previous section. We shall prove that if the constraint qualification is satisfied then the matrix $||G^i_{\dot{Y}_k}||$ is nonsingular at every solution $(t, \mathbf{Y}, \dot{\mathbf{Y}})$ to the constraints $G^i = 0$. Hence $\mathbf{Z}(t)$ must satisfy the necessary conditions for the problem of Lagrange developed in Chapter 3. The G^i are given by (5-108) to (5-111) and $\dot{\mathbf{Y}} = (\dot{\mathbf{y}}, \mathbf{v}, \dot{\boldsymbol{\gamma}}, \dot{\boldsymbol{\theta}})$. Therefore

$$||G^i_{\dot{Y}_k}|| = \begin{bmatrix} -\mathbf{I} & \mathbf{0} & \mathbf{T}_1 & \mathbf{T}_2 \\ \mathbf{A} & \mathbf{B} & \mathbf{0} & \mathbf{0} \\ \mathbf{0} & \mathbf{D} & \mathbf{0} & \mathbf{0} \\ \mathbf{0} & \mathbf{0} & \mathbf{0} & \mathbf{M} \end{bmatrix}. \tag{5-113}$$

The rows here refer to variables and the columns to the constraints $G^i = 0$. $\mathbf{T}_1$ is the matrix the columns of which are $\mathbf{T}^l_{\mathbf{y}}$, $l \in \mathscr{L}_1$ and $\mathbf{T}_2$ is the matrix the columns of which are $\mathbf{T}^l_{\mathbf{y}}$, $l \in \mathscr{L}_2$. $\mathbf{A}$ is the matrix the columns of which are $\mathbf{f}^j_{\mathbf{v}}$ and $\mathbf{B}$ is the matrix the columns of which are $\mathbf{R}^q_{\mathbf{v}}$. The matrix $\mathbf{D}$ is the diagonal matrix $||2\dot{\gamma}_q\delta_{qi}||$ and $\mathbf{M}$ is the diagonal matrix $||\mathscr{T}_{\theta_l}\delta_{li}||$. The matrix (5-113) has $n + m + h + \beta$ rows and $n + h + \alpha + \beta$ columns. The number of columns must be less than or equal to the number of rows, that is, the number of differential equation constraints cannot be greater than the number of variables in $\dot{\mathbf{Y}}$. Thus it is necessary that $\alpha \leq m$, as we assumed earlier.

Suppose now that the matrix (5-113) is evaluated at some specific point $(t, \mathbf{Y}, \dot{\mathbf{Y}})$ which satisfies $G^i = 0$. We shall show that the matrix has rank $n + h + \alpha + \beta$ at any such point. Let us begin by recalling that the rank of a matrix is not changed if we add to column i a linear combination of any collection of columns different from i. Consider now the matrix $[-\mathbf{T}_1, \mathbf{AT}_1, \mathbf{0}, \mathbf{0}]$. Each column is a linear combination of the first n columns of (5-113). Thus we can add this matrix to the third (block) column of (5-113) without changing the rank. Similarly, if $\mathbf{T}_1$ is replaced by $\mathbf{T}_2$ we can add the resulting matrix to the last (block) column of (5-113) without changing the rank. Thus the rank of (5-113) is the same as the rank of

$$\begin{bmatrix} -\mathbf{I} & \mathbf{0} & \mathbf{0} & \mathbf{0} \\ \mathbf{A} & \mathbf{B} & \mathbf{AT}_1 & \mathbf{AT}_2 \\ \mathbf{0} & \mathbf{D} & \mathbf{0} & \mathbf{0} \\ \mathbf{0} & \mathbf{0} & \mathbf{0} & \mathbf{M} \end{bmatrix} \tag{5-114}$$

We now select a nonsingular submatrix $\mathbf{J}$ of order $n + h + \alpha + \beta$ from (5-114) and thus demonstrate that the matrix has rank $n + h + \alpha + \beta$. As the first n rows of $\mathbf{J}$ we choose the first n rows of (5-114). Next, we take those columns of $(\mathbf{B}, \mathbf{AT}_1, \mathbf{AT}_2)$ corresponding to the constraints R^q and T^l which are active at the point under consideration. This yields the submatrix $(\mathbf{B}_1, \mathbf{AT}_1, \mathbf{AT}_{2a})$. From the constraint qualification, this matrix has at least as many rows as columns; moreover, again from the constraint qualification, if $k + \alpha$ constraints are active the matrix has rank $k + \alpha$ and $(\mathbf{B}_1, \mathbf{AT}_1, \mathbf{AT}_{2a})$ contains a nonsingular submatrix of order $k + \alpha$. As the next $k + \alpha$ rows of $\mathbf{J}$ we choose those rows of $(\mathbf{B}_1, \mathbf{AT}_1, \mathbf{AT}_{2a})$ which contain the nonsingular submatrix.

For those columns for which R^q is active $\dot{\gamma}_q = 0$ and a 0 entry appears in $\mathbf{D}$, whereas for those columns for which R^q is inactive $\dot{\gamma}_q > 0$ and a positive entry appears in $\mathbf{D}$. Let us choose as the next set of rows in $\mathbf{J}$ those for which a positive entry appears in $\mathbf{D}$. Finally, if T^l, $l \in \mathscr{L}_2$, is active $\mathscr{T}_\theta = 0$ and a 0 entry appears in $\mathbf{M}$, whereas if T^l, $l \in \mathscr{L}_2$, is not active, $\mathscr{T}_\theta > 0$ and a positive entry appears in $\mathbf{M}$. As the final set of rows in $\mathbf{J}$ we select those for which a positive entry appears in $\mathbf{M}$. At the last two steps, $h + \beta - k$ rows are selected, giving $n + h + \alpha + \beta$ in all. The resulting matrix has the form

$$\mathbf{J} = \begin{bmatrix} -\mathbf{I} & \mathbf{0} & \mathbf{0} \\ \mathbf{A} & \mathbf{Q} & \mathbf{P} \\ \mathbf{0} & \mathbf{0} & \mathbf{D}_1 \end{bmatrix}. \tag{5-115}$$

Here we have permuted the columns so that the last columns correspond to the inactive constraints. $\mathbf{Q}$ is the nonsingular submatrix from $(\mathbf{B}_1, \mathbf{AT}_1, \mathbf{AT}_{2a})$ and $\mathbf{D}_1$ is a diagonal matrix containing the nonzero elements from $\mathbf{D}$ and $\mathbf{M}$.

The columns of $\mathbf{J}$ are linearly independent. To see this, consider the set of equations $\mathbf{J}\boldsymbol{\rho} = \mathbf{0}$. From the first n equations we see that the first n components of $\boldsymbol{\rho}$ must be zero; the last $h + \beta - k$ equations show that the last $h + \beta - k$ components of $\boldsymbol{\rho}$ are zero; and from the nonsingularity of $\mathbf{Q}$ we deduce that the remaining components of $\boldsymbol{\rho}$ are zero. Thus $||G^i_{\dot{Y}_k}||$ has rank $n + h + \alpha + \beta$ at each point in $\mathscr{R}$ and the necessary conditions of Chapter 3 must be satisfied by $\mathbf{Z}(t)$.

Before setting out the necessary conditions, it will be convenient to rewrite the differential equation constraints. Using $\dot{\mathbf{y}} = \mathbf{f}$ to eliminate $\dot{\mathbf{y}}$ in (5-110) and (5-111), the constraints become

$$\begin{aligned} &T^l_t(t, \mathbf{y}) + \mathbf{T}^l_{\mathbf{y}}(t, \mathbf{y}) \cdot \mathbf{f}(t, \mathbf{y}, \dot{\mathbf{V}}) = 0, \quad l \in \mathscr{L}_1 \\ &T^l_t(t, \mathbf{y}) + \mathbf{T}^l_{\mathbf{y}}(t, \mathbf{y}) \cdot \mathbf{f}(t, \mathbf{y}, \dot{\mathbf{V}}) + \mathscr{T}_{\theta_l}\dot{\theta}_l = 0, \quad l \in \mathscr{L}_2. \end{aligned} \tag{5-116}$$

Given this new formulation, the matrix $||G^i_{\dot{Y}_k}||$ has rank $n + h + \alpha + \beta$; indeed, the matrix is simply (5-114).

We now proceed to state the necessary conditions for the problem of Lagrange and to translate them into conditions for the control problem. There must exist a $\lambda_0 \geq 0$ and multipliers $\boldsymbol{\lambda}_f(t)$, $\boldsymbol{\mu}(t)$, $\boldsymbol{\sigma}(t)$ and $\boldsymbol{\delta}(t)$ which are continuous, except possibly at corners of $\mathbf{Z}(t)$, for which $(\lambda_0, \boldsymbol{\lambda}_f, \boldsymbol{\mu}, \boldsymbol{\sigma}, \boldsymbol{\delta}) \neq \mathbf{0}$ for any t, and which are such that if

$$\begin{aligned} H^* = \lambda_0 F + \boldsymbol{\lambda}_f \cdot (\mathbf{f} - \dot{\mathbf{y}}) + \boldsymbol{\mu} \cdot (\mathbf{R} + \dot{\gamma}^2) + \sum_{l \in \mathscr{L}_1} \sigma_l(T^l_t + \mathbf{T}^l_{\mathbf{y}} \cdot \mathbf{f}) \\ + \sum_{l \in \mathscr{L}_2} \delta_l(T^l_t + \mathbf{T}^l_{\mathbf{y}} \cdot \mathbf{f} + \mathscr{T}^l_{\theta_l}\dot{\theta}_l) \end{aligned} \tag{5-117}$$

then $\mathbf{Z}(t)$ satisfies the Euler equations and corner conditions for H^*. The reason for using $\boldsymbol{\lambda}_f$ rather than $\boldsymbol{\lambda}$ will appear below. For convenience we shall write

$$Q^l(t, \mathbf{y}, \mathbf{v}) = T^l_t(t, \mathbf{y}) + \mathbf{T}^l_{\mathbf{y}}(t, \mathbf{y}) \cdot \mathbf{f}(t, \mathbf{y}, \mathbf{v}). \tag{5-118}$$

Here

$$\mathbf{H}^*_{\mathbf{y}} = \lambda_0 \mathbf{F}_{\mathbf{y}} + \sum_{j=1}^{n} \lambda_{fj}\mathbf{f}^j_{\mathbf{y}} + \sum_{q=1}^{h} \mu_q \mathbf{R}^q_{\mathbf{y}} + \sum_{l \in \mathscr{L}_1} \sigma_l \mathbf{Q}^l_{\mathbf{y}} + \sum_{l \in \mathscr{L}_2} \delta_l \mathbf{Q}^l_{\mathbf{y}} \tag{5-119}$$

$$\mathbf{H}^*_{\mathbf{V}} = \mathbf{0}; \qquad \mathbf{H}^*_{\boldsymbol{\gamma}} = \mathbf{0} \tag{5-120}$$

$$H^*_{\theta_l} = \delta_l \mathscr{T}^l_{\theta_l\theta_l}\dot{\theta}_l, \quad l \in \mathscr{L}_2. \tag{5-121}$$

Also

$$\mathbf{H}^*_{\dot{\mathbf{y}}} = -\boldsymbol{\lambda}_f \tag{5-122}$$

$$\mathbf{H}^*_{\dot{\mathbf{V}}} = \mathbf{H}^*_{\mathbf{v}} = \lambda_0 \mathbf{F}_{\mathbf{v}} + \sum_{j=1}^{n} \lambda_{fj}\mathbf{f}^j_{\mathbf{v}} + \sum_{q=1}^{h} \mu_q \mathbf{R}^q_{\mathbf{v}} + \sum_{l \in \mathscr{L}_1} \sigma_l \mathbf{Q}^l_{\mathbf{v}} + \sum_{l \in \mathscr{L}_2} \delta_l \mathbf{Q}^l_{\mathbf{v}} \tag{5-123}$$

$$H^*_{\dot{\gamma}_q} = 2\mu_q\dot{\gamma}_q; \qquad H^*_{\dot{\theta}_l} = \delta_l \mathscr{T}^l_{\theta_l}, \quad l \in \mathscr{L}_2. \tag{5-124}$$

From the Euler equations we then obtain

$$\dot{\boldsymbol{\lambda}}_f = -\mathbf{H}^*_{\mathbf{y}}. \tag{5-125}$$

From the continuity of $\mathbf{H}^*_{\dot{\mathbf{y}}}$ it follows that $\boldsymbol{\lambda}_f(t)$ is continuous. Next

$$\mathbf{H}^*_{\mathbf{v}} = \text{constant}; \qquad H^*_{\dot{\gamma}_q} = \text{constant}. \tag{5-126}$$

Since $\mathbf{V}$ and $\boldsymbol{\gamma}$ have free boundaries, we may conclude immediately that the constants in (5-126) are zero, so that

$$\lambda_0 \mathbf{F}_{\mathbf{v}} + \sum_{j=1}^{n} \lambda_{fj} \mathbf{f}^j_{\mathbf{v}} + \sum_{q=1}^{h} \mu_q \mathbf{R}^q_{\mathbf{v}} + \sum_{l \in \mathscr{L}_1} \sigma_l \mathbf{Q}^l_{\mathbf{v}} + \sum_{l \in \mathscr{L}_2} \delta_l \mathbf{Q}^l_{\mathbf{v}} = \mathbf{0} \tag{5-127}$$

$$\mu_q \dot{\gamma}_q = 0 \quad \text{or} \quad \mu_q R^q = 0. \tag{5-128}$$

Let us now examine $\mathrm{d}H^*_{\dot{\theta}_l}/\mathrm{d}t = H^*_{\theta_l}$. From (5-124)

$$\frac{\mathrm{d}}{\mathrm{d}t} H^*_{\dot{\theta}_l} = \dot{\delta}_l \mathscr{T}^l_{\theta_l} + \delta_l \mathscr{T}^l_{\theta_l \theta_l} \dot{\theta}_l \tag{5-129}$$

and, on applying (5-121), the Euler equation reduces to

$$\dot{\delta}_l \mathscr{T}^l_{\theta_l} = 0. \tag{5-130}$$

We also observe that since $H^*_{\dot{\theta}_l}$ is continuous, so also is $\delta_l \mathscr{T}^l_{\theta_l}$.

We next turn to the Legendre and Weierstrass conditions. As in Section 5.4, we may deduce from the Legendre condition that $\boldsymbol{\mu} \leq \mathbf{0}$ for each t. Consider then the Weierstrass E function for the present problem. Here

$$E = H^*(t, \mathbf{Z}, \dot{\mathbf{Y}}) - H^*(t, \mathbf{Z}, \dot{\mathbf{Z}}) - \mathbf{H}^*_{\dot{\mathbf{Z}}} \cdot (\dot{\mathbf{Y}} - \dot{\mathbf{Z}}). \tag{5-131}$$

Let us apply the results obtained above to evaluate more explicitly the last term in (5-131). Since $\mathbf{H}^*_{\dot{\mathbf{y}}} = -\boldsymbol{\lambda}_f$,

$$\mathbf{H}^*_{\dot{\mathbf{y}}} \cdot (\dot{\mathbf{y}} - \dot{\mathbf{z}}) = \boldsymbol{\lambda}_f \cdot \dot{\mathbf{z}} - \boldsymbol{\lambda}_f \cdot \dot{\mathbf{y}}. \tag{5-132}$$

And, since $\mathbf{H}_{\dot{\mathbf{V}}} = \mathbf{0}$,

$$\mathbf{H}^*_{\dot{\mathbf{V}}} \cdot (\dot{\mathbf{V}} - \mathbf{W}) = 0. \tag{5-133}$$

Furthermore, since $\mathbf{H}_{\dot{\boldsymbol{\gamma}}} = \mathbf{0}$,

$$\mathbf{H}^*_{\dot{\boldsymbol{\gamma}}} \cdot (\dot{\boldsymbol{\gamma}} - \dot{\boldsymbol{\phi}}) = 0. \tag{5-134}$$

Finally,

$$H_{\dot{\theta}_l}(\dot{\theta}_l - \dot{\kappa}_l) = \delta_l \mathscr{T}^l_{\theta_l} \dot{\theta}_l - \delta_l \mathscr{T}^l_{\theta_l} \dot{\kappa}_l. \tag{5-135}$$

Notice that if constraint l, $l \in \mathscr{L}_2$, is active then $\mathscr{T}^l_{\theta_l} = 0$ and $H^*_{\dot{\theta}_l}(\dot{\theta}_l - \dot{\kappa}_l) = 0$. If constraint l is not active then, from (5-104) and $\dot{\mathbf{y}} = \mathbf{f}$,

$$\mathscr{T}^{l}_{\theta_l}\dot{\theta}_l = -\ T^l_t(t, \mathbf{z}(t)) - \mathbf{T}^l_{\mathbf{y}}(t, \mathbf{z}(t)) \cdot \mathbf{f}(t, \mathbf{z}, \mathbf{v}) \tag{5-136}$$

$$\mathscr{T}^{l}_{\theta_l}\dot{\kappa}_l = -\ T^l_t(t, \mathbf{z}(t)) - \mathbf{T}^l_{\mathbf{y}}(t, \mathbf{z}(t)) \cdot \mathbf{f}(t, \mathbf{z}, \mathbf{w}). \tag{5-137}$$

Thus

$$H^*_{\dot{\theta}_l}(\dot{\theta}_l - \dot{\kappa}_l) = \delta_l \mathbf{T}^l_{\mathbf{y}}(t, \mathbf{z}(t)) \cdot \mathbf{f}(t, \mathbf{z}, \mathbf{w}) - \delta_l \mathbf{T}^l_{\mathbf{y}}(t, \mathbf{z}(t)) \cdot \mathbf{f}(t, \mathbf{z}, \mathbf{v}). \tag{5-138}$$

To proceed from this point, it will be necessary to study individual cases. This will be our task in the remaining sections.

5.12. An interior segment

Let us now consider a case in which $\mathscr{L}_1$ is empty. We denote by $\mathscr{S}$ the set of points $(t, \mathbf{y})$ which satisfy $T^l(t, \mathbf{y}) \leq 0$, $l \in \mathscr{L}_2$; that is, $\mathscr{S}$ is the set of solutions to the inequalities. We shall call a solution $(t, \mathbf{y})$ an *interior point* if none of the constraints is active at that point; the solution $(t, \mathbf{y})$ will be called a *boundary point* if at least one of the constraints is active. The boundary $\mathscr{S}^*$ of $\mathscr{S}$ is the set of all solutions for which at least one constraint is active. Then during certain intervals of time the function $\mathbf{z}(t)$ which describes the time behavior of the state variables under an optimal control may lie in the interior of $\mathscr{S}$; and during other intervals of time $\mathbf{z}(t)$ may lie on the boundary of $\mathscr{S}$. Suppose, for example, that $n = 2$ and the constraints

$$y_1 + y_2 \leq 6; \qquad y_1 + 2y_2 \leq 10; \qquad y_1 \geq 0; \qquad y_2 \geq 0.$$

Then $\mathscr{S}$ is the shaded region of Figure 5.1. An optimal trajectory might then take the form shown, starting in the interior of $\mathscr{S}$, then moving along

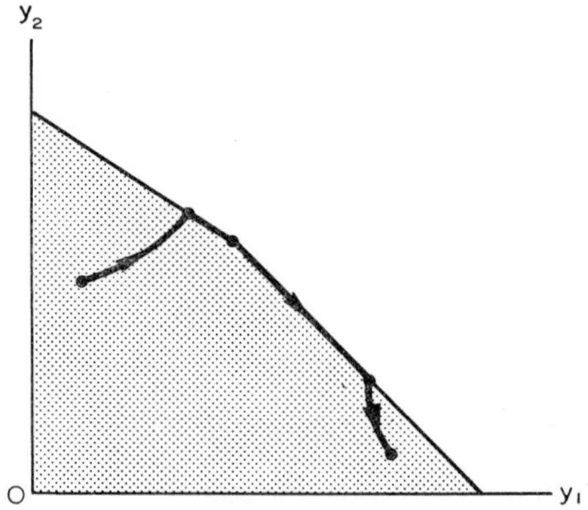

Fig. 5.1.

the boundary defined by $y_1 + 2y_2 \le 10$, next switching to the boundary defined by $y_1 + y_2 \le 6$, and finally returning to the interior of $\mathscr{S}$.

In this section we shall consider the necessary conditions which must be satisfied at each point along a segment $\mathscr{P}$ of $\mathbf{z}(t)$ which lies entirely in the interior of $\mathscr{S}$ (except perhaps for the end points of the segment, which may lie on the boundaries).

At each point in $\mathscr{P}$ which is not an end point, none of the constraints is active. Let us then determine E, relying on (5-136) and (5-137) for $\mathscr{T}^l_{\theta_l}\dot{\theta}_l$ and $\mathscr{T}^l_{\theta_l}\dot{\kappa}_l$, respectively. Thus

$$E = \lambda_0 F(t, \mathbf{z}, \mathbf{v}) + \left[\boldsymbol{\lambda}_f(t) + \sum_{l \in \mathscr{L}_2} \delta_l(t)\mathbf{T}^l_{\mathbf{y}}(t, \mathbf{z}(t))\right] \cdot \mathbf{f}(t, \mathbf{z}, \mathbf{v})$$

$$- \lambda_0 F(t, \mathbf{z}, \mathbf{w}) + \left[\boldsymbol{\lambda}_f(t) + \sum_{l \in \mathscr{L}_2} \delta_l(t)\mathbf{T}^l_{\mathbf{y}}(t, \mathbf{z}(t))\right] \cdot \mathbf{f}(t, \mathbf{z}, \mathbf{w}) \qquad (5\text{-}139)$$

and it is necessary that $E \le 0$. We now define

$$\boldsymbol{\lambda}(t) = \boldsymbol{\lambda}_f(t) + \sum_{l \in \mathscr{L}_2} \delta_l(t)\mathbf{T}^l_{\mathbf{y}}(t, \mathbf{z}(t)). \qquad (5\text{-}140)$$

Notice that $\boldsymbol{\lambda}(t)$ is a function of t only and is independent of the control variables. The Hamiltonian is defined in terms of $\boldsymbol{\lambda}$ as

$$H = \lambda_0 F + \boldsymbol{\lambda} \cdot \mathbf{f}. \qquad (5\text{-}141)$$

Then $E \le 0$ becomes

$$H(t, \mathbf{z}, \mathbf{v}) \le H(t, \mathbf{z}, \mathbf{w}) \qquad (5\text{-}142)$$

and we have the familiar maximum principle that, given $(t, \mathbf{z})$, $\mathbf{w}$ maximizes the Hamiltonian.

Let us now return to (5-125) and convert it into a form involving $\boldsymbol{\lambda}$ instead of $\boldsymbol{\lambda}_f$. Notice that

$$\sum_{j=1}^{n} \lambda_{fj}\mathbf{f}^j_{\mathbf{y}} = \sum_{j=1}^{n} \lambda_j \mathbf{f}^j_{\mathbf{y}} - \sum_{j=1}^{n} \sum_{l \in \mathscr{L}_2} \delta_l T^l_{y_j}\mathbf{f}^j_{\mathbf{y}} \qquad (5\text{-}143)$$

and

$$\dot{\boldsymbol{\lambda}}_f = \dot{\boldsymbol{\lambda}} - \sum_{l \in \mathscr{L}_2} \dot{\delta}_l \mathbf{T}^l_{\mathbf{y}} - \sum_{l \in \mathscr{L}_2} \delta_l[\mathbf{T}^l_{t\mathbf{y}} + \mathbf{T}^l_{\mathbf{yy}}\dot{\mathbf{z}}]. \qquad (5\text{-}144)$$

Since the constraints are not active $\mathscr{T}^l_{\theta_l} \ne 0$, and, from (5-130), $\dot{\delta}_l = 0$. Thus $\dot{\delta}_l \mathbf{T}^l_{\mathbf{y}} = \mathbf{0}$ and these terms disappear. Substitution of (5-143) and (5-144) into (5-131) yields

$$\dot{\boldsymbol{\lambda}} = -\mathbf{H}_{\mathbf{y}} - \sum_{q=1}^{h} \mu_q \mathbf{R}_{\mathbf{v}}^q \tag{5-145}$$

and the terms in δ_l cancel out (the terms in σ_l do not appear, since $\mathscr{L}_1$ is empty). If (5-140) is applied to (5-127), we obtain

$$\mathbf{H}_{\mathbf{v}} + \sum_{q=1}^{h} \mu_q \mathbf{R}_{\mathbf{v}}^q = \mathbf{0} \tag{5-146}$$

since again the terms in δ_l cancel.

It will be observed that (5-142), (5-145), (5-146), $\boldsymbol{\mu} \leq \mathbf{0}$, and (5-128) express the essence of the necessary conditions given in Theorem 5.4.1 for the case in which there are no constraints on the state variables. This is not surprising; over an interval where the constraints are inactive we should expect that with the exception of the end point conditions the necessary conditions would be the same as when there are no constraints.

There are still a couple of points to be cleared up. We must show that $\boldsymbol{\lambda}(t)$ is continuous. To do this we note that, when the constraints are inactive, $\dot{\delta}_l = 0$ between corners, so that δ_l is a constant between corners. Now $\mathscr{T}_{\theta_l}^l$ involves only θ_l, which is continuous. Hence the continuity of $H_{\dot{\theta}_l}^*$ and (5-124) guarantee the continuity of δ_l. Thus δ_l is a constant over $\mathscr{P}$. Furthermore, $\mathbf{T}_{\mathbf{y}}(t, \mathbf{y})$ is continuous; hence $\boldsymbol{\lambda}(t)$ is continuous. We shall not for the present require that $(\lambda_0, \boldsymbol{\lambda}(t)) \neq 0$ for every t. (The earlier arguments on which this was based involved the end points.) We note, however, that if $(\lambda_0, \boldsymbol{\lambda}(t)) = \mathbf{0}$ for any t, then both $\boldsymbol{\lambda}(t) \equiv \mathbf{0}$ and $\boldsymbol{\mu}(t) \equiv \mathbf{0}$ over the entire interval. Thus we can solve (5-146) for $\boldsymbol{\mu}$ in terms of $(\lambda_0, \boldsymbol{\lambda})$, then substitute into (5-145); together with $\dot{\lambda}_0 = 0$ this yields a system of homogeneous linear differential equations in $(\lambda_0, \boldsymbol{\lambda})$. One solution is $(\lambda_0, \boldsymbol{\lambda}(t)) \equiv \mathbf{0}$, and any solution which vanishes at some point must be this solution. We shall return later to the possibility that $(\lambda_0, \boldsymbol{\lambda})$ vanishes at some point.

Thus we have proved the following theorem.

Theorem 5.12.1. Necessary Conditions for an Interior Segment. If $\mathbf{w}(t)$ *is an optimal control for the control problem with constrained state variables and if* $\mathbf{z}(t)$ *represents the corresponding trajectory for the state variables then over any segment* $\mathscr{P}$ *of* $\mathbf{z}(t)$ *which lies in the interior of* $\mathscr{S}$ *the necessary conditions of Theorem 5.4.1 (which deals with the case in which there are no constraints on the state variables) still apply, with the exception of the end point conditions and the requirement that* $(\lambda_0, \boldsymbol{\lambda})$ *does not vanish at any point.*

It remains to examine the transversality conditions which must be satisfied when the trajectory $\mathbf{z}(t)$ ends at an interior point of $\mathscr{S}$, so that the final segment lies in the interior. We shall suppose that $\mathbf{z}(t)$ must end on the smooth manifold $\mathscr{M}$ described by $S^u(t, \mathbf{y}) = 0$, $u = 1, \ldots, s$. In addition, $\mathbf{z}(t)$ must end on the manifold defined by $\mathscr{T}^l(t, \mathbf{y}, \theta_l) = 0$, $l \in \mathscr{L}_2$. Thus, at the terminal time t_1, $(t_1, \mathbf{Z}(t_1))$ must lie in the manifold $\mathscr{M}^* = \mathscr{M} \cap \mathscr{M}_c$. It follows from the general transversality condition of Chapter 3 that there exist ρ_u and ρ_l such that

$$\mathbf{H}_{\dot{\mathbf{y}}} = -\boldsymbol{\lambda}_f = \sum_{u=1}^{s} \rho_u \mathbf{S}^u_{\mathbf{y}} + \sum_{l \in \mathscr{L}_2} \rho_l \mathbf{T}^l_{\mathbf{y}} \tag{5-147}$$

$$H_{\dot{\theta}_l} = \delta_l \mathscr{T}^l_{\theta_l} = \rho_l \mathscr{T}^l_{\theta_l}. \tag{5-148}$$

Since $\mathscr{T}^l_{\theta_l} \neq 0$ here, $\delta_l = \rho_l$; also, $\boldsymbol{\lambda}$ is related to $\boldsymbol{\lambda}_f$ by (5-140). Hence

$$-\boldsymbol{\lambda} = \sum_{u=1}^{s} \rho_u \mathbf{S}^u_{\mathbf{y}} \tag{5-149}$$

and $\boldsymbol{\lambda}$ must be orthogonal to the manifold $\mathscr{M}(t_1)$, as might have been expected.

Corollary. If the trajectory $\mathbf{z}(t)$ terminates at an interior point of $\mathscr{S}$ at time t_1 then $\boldsymbol{\lambda}(t_1)$ must be orthogonal to $\mathscr{M}(t_1)$ at the point $(t_1, \mathbf{z}(t_1))$.

It immediately follows that if the interval of integration is infinite and $\mathbf{z}(t)$ lies in the interior of $\mathscr{S}$ for all t sufficiently large then the conditions of Theorem 4.3.2 must be satisfied.

5.13. A boundary segment

Let us next turn our attention to those parts of the trajectory $\mathbf{z}(t)$ which lie on the boundary of $\mathscr{S}$. We now allow $\mathscr{L}_1$ to be nonempty. If $\mathscr{L}_1$ is nonempty, the entire trajectory $\mathbf{z}(t)$ lies on the boundary of $\mathscr{S}$; as Figure 5.1 illustrates, however, the subset of constraints from $\mathscr{L}_2$ which are active can change as the trajectory is traversed. We shall in this section study a segment $\mathscr{P}$ of $\mathbf{z}(t)$ with the characteristic that along this segment the set of active constraints does not change. To make this more precise we define what Pontryagin *et al.* have called a junction point.

Junction Point. A boundary point $(t^*, \mathbf{z}^*)$ of $\mathscr{S}$ will be called a junction point of the trajectory $\mathbf{z}(t)$ if $\mathbf{z}(t^*) = \mathbf{z}^*$ and if either (a) there exists an $\varepsilon > 0$ such that the set of constraints which are active in the interval $t^* - \varepsilon < t < t^*$

is not the same as the set of constraints which are active in the interval $t^* < t < t^* + \varepsilon$, *or (b) when* $\mathscr{L}_1$ *is empty, if all constraints in* $\mathscr{L}_2$ *are inactive, both in the interval* $t^* - \varepsilon < t < t^*$ *and in the interval* $t^* < t < t^* + \varepsilon$.

Note that if (b) holds then $\mathbf{z}(t)$ is in the interior of $\mathscr{S}$, both for $t < t^*$ and for $t > t^*$, but is on the boundary at $t = t^*$. We shall assume that there is only a finite number of junction points, so that the set of constraints which is active changes only a finite number of times.

Consider two adjacent junction points $(t_1^*, \mathbf{z}_1^*)$ and $(t_2^*, \mathbf{z}_2^*)$. For present purposes we may broaden the concept of a junction point to include an end point of the trajectory if the end point lies on the boundary. Thus we include cases in which the initial or final segment lies on the boundary.

Let us denote by $\mathscr{P}$ that segment of the trajectory $\mathbf{z}(t)$ which begins at $(t_1^*, \mathbf{z}_1^*)$ and ends at $(t_2^*, \mathbf{z}_2^*)$. Let $\mathscr{L}_{2+}$ be a subset of $\mathscr{L}_2$, containing constraints which are active along $\mathscr{P}$; and let $\mathscr{L}_{2-}$ be a subset of $\mathscr{L}_2$, containing constraints which are not active along $\mathscr{P}$. It may be true that $\mathscr{L}_{2+} = \mathscr{L}_2$ or $\mathscr{L}_{2+} = \emptyset$. Let us now return to the material of Section 5.11 to see what it reduces to in the case under consideration.

For $l \in \mathscr{L}_1 \cap \mathscr{L}_{2+}$, $\mathscr{T}^l_{\theta_l} = 0$ and $H^*_{\dot{\theta}_l}(\dot{\theta}_l - \dot{\kappa}_l) = 0$. For $l \in \mathscr{L}_{2-}$, $\mathscr{T}^l_{\theta_l} \neq 0$; thus for such l we can apply the transformations (5-136) and (5-137) to obtain (5-138). If we now define

$$\boldsymbol{\lambda}(t) = \boldsymbol{\lambda}_f(t) + \sum_{l \in \mathscr{L}_{2-}} \delta_l(t) \mathbf{T}^l_{\mathbf{y}}(t, \mathbf{z}(t)) \tag{5-150}$$

and define the Hamiltonian as in (5-141), then (5-142) follows; thus, given these definitions, the maximum principle must apply. Notice that in (5-150) we sum over only those constraints which are not active. Consequently, the analysis of Section 5.12 shows that $\boldsymbol{\lambda}(t)$ must be continuous.

If (5-150) is applied to (5-125) we obtain

$$\dot{\boldsymbol{\lambda}} = -\mathbf{H}_{\mathbf{y}} - \sum_{q=1}^{h} \mu_q \mathbf{R}^q_{\mathbf{y}} - \sum_{l \in \mathscr{L}_1} \sigma_l \mathbf{Q}^l_{\mathbf{y}} - \sum_{l \in \mathscr{L}_{2+}} \delta_l \mathbf{Q}^l_{\mathbf{y}}. \tag{5-151}$$

Notice that the terms in δ_l for $l \in \mathscr{L}_{2-}$ cancel, just as similar terms cancelled in Section 5.12. Furthermore, (5-127) now becomes

$$\mathbf{H}_{\mathbf{v}} + \sum_{q=1}^{h} \mu_q \mathbf{R}^q_{\mathbf{v}} + \sum_{l \in \mathscr{L}_1} \sigma_l \mathbf{Q}^l_{\mathbf{v}} + \sum_{l \in \mathscr{L}_{2+}} \delta_l \mathbf{Q}^l_{\mathbf{v}} = \mathbf{0}. \tag{5-152}$$

In view of the constraint qualification, this system of equations can be solved uniquely for the μ_q, σ_l and δ_l, $l \in \mathscr{L}_{2+}$, in terms of the λ's at each point in time. Thus we have obtained a set of necessary conditions which must be satisfied along $\mathscr{P}$. These are summarized in the following theorem.

Theorem 5.13.1. Necessary Conditions for a Boundary Segment. If $\mathbf{w}(t)$ *is an optimal control for the control problem with constrained state variables, and if* $\mathbf{z}(t)$ *represents the corresponding trajectory for the state variables, then over any segment* $\mathscr{P}$ *of* $\mathbf{z}(t)$ *which lies on the boundary of* $\mathscr{S}$ *and joins two adjacent junction points, and along which the constraints* $l \in \mathscr{L}_{2+}$ *are active, it is necessary that there exist a* $\lambda_0 \geq 0$ *(which can be taken to be 0 or 1 without loss of generality), a continuous vector-valued function* $\boldsymbol{\lambda}(t)$*, a piecewise continuous vector-valued function* $\boldsymbol{\mu}(t)$, $\boldsymbol{\mu}(t) \leq \mathbf{0}$, *of which the only possible points of discontinuity are at corners of* $\mathbf{z}(t)$*, and a set of piecewise continuous functions* $\sigma_l(t)$, $l \in \mathscr{L}_1$, *and* $\delta_l(t)$, $l \in \mathscr{L}_{2+}$, *of which the only possible points of discontinuity are the corners of* $\mathbf{z}(t)$*, such that if*

$$H = \lambda_0 F + \boldsymbol{\lambda} \cdot \mathbf{f} \tag{5-153}$$

then the functions $\mathbf{w}(t)$, $\mathbf{z}(t)$, $\boldsymbol{\lambda}(t)$, $\boldsymbol{\mu}(t)$, $\boldsymbol{\sigma}(t)$ *and* $\delta_l(t)$ *satisfy*

$$\dot{\mathbf{y}} = \mathbf{H}_{\boldsymbol{\lambda}} = \mathbf{f} \tag{5-154}$$

$$\dot{\boldsymbol{\lambda}} = -\mathbf{H}_{\mathbf{y}} - \sum_{q=1}^{h} \mu_q \mathbf{R}_{\mathbf{y}}^q - \sum_{l \in \mathscr{L}_1} \sigma_l \mathbf{Q}_{\mathbf{y}}^l - \sum_{l \in \mathscr{L}_{2+}} \delta_l \mathbf{Q}_{\mathbf{y}}^l \tag{5-155}$$

$$\mu_q R^q = 0 \tag{5-156}$$

$$\mathbf{H}_{\mathbf{v}} + \sum_{q=1}^{h} \mu_q \mathbf{R}_{\mathbf{v}}^q + \sum_{l \in \mathscr{L}_1} \sigma_l \mathbf{Q}_{\mathbf{v}}^l + \sum_{l \in \mathscr{L}_{2+}} \delta_l \mathbf{Q}_{\mathbf{v}}^l = \mathbf{0}. \tag{5-157}$$

Furthermore, if

$$M(t, \mathbf{y}, \boldsymbol{\lambda}) = \sup_{\mathbf{v}} H(t, \mathbf{y}, \mathbf{v}, \boldsymbol{\lambda}) \tag{5-158}$$

then

$$H(t, \mathbf{y}, \mathbf{w}, \boldsymbol{\lambda}) = M(t, \mathbf{y}, \boldsymbol{\lambda}). \tag{5-159}$$

We can easily determine the end point condition which must be satisfied if the trajectory $\mathbf{z}(t)$ ends at a point $(t_1, \mathbf{z}(t_1))$ on the boundary of $\mathscr{S}$. We shall assume that $\mathbf{z}(t)$ must end on the smooth manifold $\mathscr{M}$ described by $S^u(t, \mathbf{y}) = 0$. We shall assume also that $(t_1, \mathbf{z}(t_1))$ satisfies $T^l(t, \mathbf{y}) = 0$, $l \in \mathscr{L}_1$, where the equations are assumed to generate a smooth manifold $\mathscr{M}_a$. Finally, the equations $\mathscr{T}^l(t, \mathbf{y}, \theta_l) = 0$, $l \in \mathscr{L}_2$, must be satisfied, and these generate a smooth manifold $\mathscr{M}^*$. Thus $(t_1, \mathbf{z}(t_1))$ must lie in $\mathscr{M} \cap \mathscr{M}_a \cap \mathscr{M}^*$. Then, as in (5-147) and (5-148),

$$\mathbf{H}_{\dot{\mathbf{y}}} = -\boldsymbol{\lambda}_f = \sum_{u=1}^{s} \rho_u \mathbf{S}_{\mathbf{y}}^u + \sum_{l \in \mathscr{L}_1} \rho_l \mathbf{T}_{\mathbf{y}}^l + \sum_{l \in \mathscr{L}_2} \rho_l \mathbf{T}_{\mathbf{y}}^l \tag{5-160}$$

$$H_{\dot{\theta}_l} = \delta_l \mathscr{T}^l_{\theta_l} = \rho_l \mathscr{T}^l_{\theta_l}, \quad l \in \mathscr{L}_2. \tag{5-161}$$

Since $\mathscr{T}^l_{\theta_l} \neq 0$, $l \in \mathscr{L}_{2-}$, $\delta_l = \rho_l$, $l \in \mathscr{L}_{2-}$. For $l \in \mathscr{L}_{2+}$, $\mathscr{T}^l_{\theta_l} = 0$ and (5-161) is satisfied for any δ_l and ρ_l. Thus, using (5-150) to replace $\boldsymbol{\lambda}_f$ with $\boldsymbol{\lambda}$,

$$-\boldsymbol{\lambda} = \sum_{u=1}^{s} \rho_u \mathbf{S}^u_{\mathbf{y}} + \sum_{l \in \mathscr{L}_1 \cap \mathscr{L}_{2+}} \rho^l \mathbf{T}^l_{\mathbf{y}}. \tag{5-162}$$

Let $\mathscr{M}_+(t_1)$ be the manifold formed by $\mathscr{T}^l(t_1, \mathbf{y}) = 0$, $l \in \mathscr{L}_1 \cap \mathscr{L}_{2+}$. Then $\boldsymbol{\lambda}$ must be orthogonal to $\mathscr{M}(t_1) \cap \mathscr{M}_+(t_1)$.

Corollary. If the final segment of the trajectory $\mathbf{z}(t)$ *lies on the boundary of* $\mathscr{S}$ *where the constraints for* $l \in \mathscr{L}_{2+}$ *are active then, if* $(t_1, \mathbf{z}(t_1))$ *is the terminal point,* $\boldsymbol{\lambda}(t_1)$ *must be orthogonal to* $\mathscr{M}(t_1) \cap \mathscr{M}_+(t_1)$.

Consider finally the case in which the interval of integration is infinite and in which, for all t sufficiently large, $\mathbf{z}(t)$ lies on the boundary of $\mathscr{S}$ and the constraints for $l \in \mathscr{L}_{2+}$ are active. If we have a one parameter family of admissible solutions $\mathbf{Y}(t; \xi)$ to the Lagrange problem with $\mathbf{Y}(t; 0) = \mathbf{Z}(t)$ and $\mathbf{Y}_\xi(t; 0) = \boldsymbol{\eta}^*$, then $\lim_{t\to\infty} \mathbf{H}^*_{\dot{\mathbf{Y}}} \cdot \boldsymbol{\eta}^* = 0$, where $\mathbf{H}^*_{\dot{\mathbf{Y}}}$ is evaluated along $\mathbf{Z}(t)$. Now $\mathbf{H}^*_{\dot{\mathbf{Y}}}$ evaluated along $\mathbf{Z}(t)$ has the form $(-\boldsymbol{\lambda}_f, 0, 0, \delta_l \mathscr{T}^l_{\theta_l})$; moreover, $\mathscr{T}^l_{\theta_l} = 0$ for active constraints. Hence

$$\mathbf{H}^*_{\dot{\mathbf{Y}}} \cdot \boldsymbol{\eta}^* = -\boldsymbol{\lambda}_f \cdot \boldsymbol{\eta} + \sum_{l \in \mathscr{L}_2} \delta_l \mathscr{T}^l_{\theta_l} \eta_l = -\boldsymbol{\lambda}_f \cdot \boldsymbol{\eta} + \sum_{l \in \mathscr{L}_{2-}} \delta_l \mathscr{T}^l_{\theta_l} \eta_l. \tag{5-163}$$

Here $\boldsymbol{\eta} = \mathbf{y}_\xi(t; 0)$ and η_l is the corresponding variation for $\theta_l(t; \xi)$. However, $\mathscr{T}^l(t, \mathbf{y}(t; \xi), \theta_l(t; \xi)) = 0$; hence, differentiating with respect to ξ and setting $\xi = 0$, we obtain

$$\mathbf{T}_{\mathbf{y}} \cdot \boldsymbol{\eta} = -\mathscr{T}^l_{\theta_l} \eta_l. \tag{5-164}$$

Thus

$$\mathbf{H}^*_{\dot{\mathbf{Y}}} \cdot \boldsymbol{\eta}^* = -\boldsymbol{\lambda}(t) \cdot \boldsymbol{\eta}(t) \tag{5-165}$$

and we conclude that it is necessary that $\lim_{t\to\infty} \boldsymbol{\lambda}(t) \cdot \boldsymbol{\eta}(t) = 0$, as usual. If it is required that $\lim_{t\to\infty} [\mathbf{y}(t) - \mathbf{g}(t)] = \mathbf{0}$, so that $\lim_{t\to\infty} \boldsymbol{\eta}(t) = \mathbf{0}$, no special restrictions are placed on $\boldsymbol{\lambda}(t)$ as $t \to \infty$. If the system is autonomous and it is required that $\lim_{t\to\infty} \mathbf{y}(t) = \mathbf{b}$, where $\mathbf{b} \in \mathscr{M} \cap \mathscr{M}_+$ and $\mathscr{M} \cap \mathscr{M}_+$ is bounded, then the above analysis shows that $\lim_{t\to\infty} \boldsymbol{\lambda}(t)$ must be orthogonal to $\mathscr{M} \cap \mathscr{M}_+$.

5.14. Transition conditions

We have obtained the necessary conditions which must be satisfied along an interior segment of the trajectory and along a boundary segment between two adjacent junction points. It remains to consider what changes take place across a junction point. Of course $\mathbf{z}(t)$ must be continuous. However, jumps can occur in $\mathbf{w}(t)$, $\boldsymbol{\mu}(t)$, $\boldsymbol{\sigma}(t)$ and the $\delta_l(t)$. The question of greatest interest concerns the behavior of $\boldsymbol{\lambda}(t)$, which we know to be continuous along an interior segment and along a boundary segment between two adjacent jump points.

Consider a junction point $(t^*, \mathbf{z}^*)$ and denote by $\boldsymbol{\lambda}_-(t^*)$ the $\lim_{t \to t-*}\boldsymbol{\lambda}(t)$ and by $\boldsymbol{\lambda}_+(t^*)$ the $\lim_{t \to t+*}\boldsymbol{\lambda}(t)$. Let us now recall that $\boldsymbol{\lambda}_f$ is continuous across all corners, so that $\boldsymbol{\lambda}_{f-} = \boldsymbol{\lambda}_{f+}$; and let us denote by $\mathscr{L}_{2-}^-$ the set of constraints which are inactive to the left of t^* and by $\mathscr{L}_{2-}^+$ the set of constraints which are inactive to the right of t^*. Then, from (5-150) and the continuity of $\boldsymbol{\lambda}_f$,

$$\boldsymbol{\lambda}_- - \sum_{l \in \mathscr{L}_{2-}{}^-} \delta_{l-} T_{\mathbf{y}}^l = \boldsymbol{\lambda}_+ - \sum_{l \in \mathscr{L}_{2-}{}^+} \delta_{l+} \mathbf{T}_{\mathbf{y}}^l. \tag{5-166}$$

This is the required condition, connecting the values of $\boldsymbol{\lambda}$ across a junction point; it is sometimes referred to as the *jump condition.*

Let us examine this condition in more detail. We recall that, as long as a constraint remains inactive, δ_l is continuous, so that $\delta_l^- = \delta_l^+$. Hence, if $l \in \mathscr{L}_{2-}^- \cap \mathscr{L}_{2-}^+$, the corresponding terms in (5-166) cancel. Let us denote by $\mathscr{L}^-$ those indices in $\mathscr{L}_{2-}^-$ but not in $\mathscr{L}_{2-}^- \cap \mathscr{L}_{2-}^+$, and by $\mathscr{L}^+$ the set of indices in $\mathscr{L}_{2-}^+$ but not in $\mathscr{L}_{2-}^- \cap \mathscr{L}_{2+}^+$. Thus $\mathscr{L}^-$ is the set of constraints which are inactive to the left of t^* but become active on passing through t^*, while $\mathscr{L}^+$ is the set of constraints which are active to the left of t^* but become inactive on passing through t^*. Thus

$$\boldsymbol{\lambda}_- - \sum_{l \in \mathscr{L}^-} \delta_l^- \mathbf{T}_{\mathbf{y}}^l = \boldsymbol{\lambda}_+ - \sum_{l \in \mathscr{L}^+} \delta_l^+ \mathbf{T}_{\mathbf{y}}^l. \tag{5-167}$$

Notice that the δ_l^- in (5-167) correspond to inactive constraints for their intervals. The conditions we have derived earlier do serve to determine the δ_l for inactive constraints. Thus the δ_l's for such constraints could be chosen arbitrarily and all earlier results would still hold. It is (5-167) which finally serves to place restrictions on the δ_l for inactive constraints; the δ_l^- must be chosen so that (5-167) is satisfied.

Consider the singular case in which $\mathscr{L}_1$ is empty and all constraints in $\mathscr{L}_2$ are inactive both to the right and to the left of t^*, so that the trajectory moves through the interior to strike the boundary at t^* and is then deflected back into the interior. Then (5-167) reduces to $\boldsymbol{\lambda}_- = \boldsymbol{\lambda}_+$ and $\boldsymbol{\lambda}$ is continuous. In general, however, it may be necessary for $\boldsymbol{\lambda}$ to be discontinuous to ensure that (5-167) is satisfied.

Continuing our investigation of the behavior of the system at a junction point, we now return to the case, studied in the previous section, in which a segment of $\mathbf{z}(t)$ lies on the boundary of $\mathscr{S}$ and the constraints $l \in \mathscr{L}_1 \cap \mathscr{L}_{2+}$ are active. Let us form the matrix $\mathbf{T}(t)$ the columns of which are $\mathbf{T}_\mathbf{y}^l(t, \mathbf{z}(t))$ for $l \in \mathscr{L}_1 \cap \mathscr{L}_{2+}$, that is, for the active constraints. Notice that if we choose multipliers $\lambda_0 = 0$, $\boldsymbol{\lambda} = \mathbf{A}(t)\boldsymbol{\zeta}$ where $\boldsymbol{\zeta}$ is an arbitrary vector, $\boldsymbol{\mu} = \mathbf{0}$, $\sigma_l = \zeta_l$, $\delta_l = \zeta_l$, $l \in \mathscr{L}_{2+}$, then the necessary conditions of Theorem 5.13.1 are satisfied. In fact (5-151) and (5-152) become identities and $H \equiv 0$. Such a set of multipliers will be called a *trivial set*, since with this set of multipliers any control $\mathbf{v}(t)$ and the corresponding $\mathbf{y}(t)$ determined from $\dot{\mathbf{y}} = \mathbf{f}$ satisfy the necessary conditions; the latter provide no information. This observation points to another. If we have a set of multipliers λ_0, $\boldsymbol{\lambda}$, $\boldsymbol{\mu}$, $\boldsymbol{\sigma}$, δ_l, $l \in \mathscr{L}_{2+}$ which satisfy the necessary conditions for $\mathbf{w}(t)$ and $\mathbf{z}(t)$, and if we then form a new set of multipliers $\lambda_0^* = \lambda_0$, $\boldsymbol{\lambda}^* = \boldsymbol{\lambda} + \mathbf{A}(t)\boldsymbol{\zeta}$, $\boldsymbol{\mu}^* = \boldsymbol{\mu}$, $\sigma_l^* = \sigma_l + \zeta_l$, $\delta_l^* = \delta_l + \zeta_l$, $l \in \mathscr{L}_2$, this new set will also satisfy the necessary conditions for $\mathbf{w}(t)$ and $\mathbf{z}(t)$.

Unfortunately, the jump condition (5-167) can yield multipliers which, over some segment, form a trivial set. Of course, this can occur only if $\lambda_0 = 0$. Such a case cannot be ruled out in practice, and it is instructive to examine how it can emerge. Suppose that $\mathbf{A}(t)$ contains as columns the $\mathbf{T}_\mathbf{y}^l$ for those constraints which are active to the right of t^*. If the vector

$$\boldsymbol{\lambda}_- + \sum_{l \in \mathscr{L}^+} \delta_{l+}\mathbf{T}_\mathbf{y}^l$$

is a linear combination of the columns in $\mathbf{A}(t^*)$, say $\mathbf{A}(t^*)\boldsymbol{\zeta}_1$, then

$$\boldsymbol{\lambda}_+ = \mathbf{A}(t^*)\boldsymbol{\zeta}_1 - \sum_{l \in \mathscr{L}^-} \delta_{l-}\mathbf{T}_\mathbf{y}^l. \tag{5-168}$$

It follows that $\boldsymbol{\lambda}_+$ is a linear combination of the columns of $\mathbf{A}(t^*)$ no matter what values are assigned to the δ_{l-}, for the $\mathbf{T}_\mathbf{y}^l$, $l \in \mathscr{L}^-$, are themselves columns of $\mathbf{A}(t)$. When $\lambda_0 = 0$ we then obtain a trivial set of multipliers along the entire segment beginning at t^*.

It is always possible to determine for each segment a set of multipliers such that $(\lambda_0, \boldsymbol{\lambda}(t)) \neq \mathbf{0}$ at any point and the multipliers do not represent a trivial set. To accomplish this, however, it is necessary to abandon the multipliers for the originally formulated problem of Lagrange and to instead determine as needed multipliers for individual segments. When this is done for any segment, the jump condition need not be satisfied at the end points.

Suppose that the jump condition (5-167) would yield a trivial set of multipliers to the right of t^*. Consider the segment $\mathscr{P}$ of $\mathbf{z}(t)$ beginning at $(t^*, \mathbf{z}^*)$ and continuing until the next junction point, say $(t^{**}, \mathbf{z}^{**})$. If the control $\mathbf{w}(t)$ is optimal, then that part of it in the interval $t^* < t < t^{**}$ must yield an optimal solution over the interval when it is specified that $\mathbf{z}(t^*) = \mathbf{z}^*$ and $z(t^{**}) = \mathbf{z}^{**}$. Here we have a problem with fixed end points, which can be converted into a problem of Lagrange. Examination of the proof given in Chapter 3 shows that, for a problem with fixed end points, $\boldsymbol{\lambda}_f(t^{**})$ can be chosen freely; in particular, it can be so chosen that it is not a linear combination of the $\mathbf{T}_{\mathbf{y}}^l$ for the active constraints. Thus $\boldsymbol{\lambda}(t^{**}) \neq \mathbf{0}$ and hence does not vanish anywhere on the interval. The necessary conditions, omitting the end point conditions, are satisfied for this set of multipliers. Consequently, it is always possible to determine a set of multipliers with $(\lambda_0, \boldsymbol{\lambda}(t)) \neq \mathbf{0}$ such that Theorems 5.12.1 and 5.13.1 hold, for those theorems say nothing about end point conditions. However, the multipliers obtained in this way will not in general be those which satisfy the necessary conditions for the problem of Lagrange with which we began, for the jump conditions will not be satisfied. Thus we have proved the following theorem.

Theorem 5.14.1. Jump Conditions. For a problem with $\lambda_0 = 1$ (which is the usual case), the jump condition (5-167) must be satisfied at each junction point. If $\lambda_0 = 0$, the jump condition must be satisfied at each junction point except where it leads to a trivial set of multipliers over some interval. If the jump condition leads to a trivial set of multipliers along some segment of $\mathbf{z}(t)$, a new set of multipliers with $(\lambda_0, \boldsymbol{\lambda}(t)) \neq \mathbf{0}$ can be determined by treating the problem as one with fixed end points and noting that the necessary conditions of Theorems 5.12.1 and 5.13.1 must be satisfied. However, these multipliers do not in general satisfy end point conditions such as the jump condition.

Problems

Section 5.2

1. Consider the differential inequality $\dot{y} + y \leq 0$. Determine the set of solutions to this inequality. Show how Valentine's procedure can be used to convert the inequality into a differential equation; and for each solution $y(t)$ to the inequality find a $\gamma(t)$ such that $(y(t), \gamma(t))$ satisfies the differential equation.

Section 5.3

1. Convert the general Ramsey model into a problem of Lagrange.

Section 5.4

1. Make use of the fact that $(H - \mathbf{H}_{\dot{\mathbf{Y}}} \cdot \dot{\mathbf{Z}}, \mathbf{H}_{\dot{\mathbf{Y}}})$ must be orthogonal to the terminal manifold to derive in detail all of the transversality conditions given piecemeal in the text. Interpret the first component of the orthogonality equation.

2. What information, if any, can be obtained from the Legendre condition in addition to $\boldsymbol{\mu} \leq \mathbf{0}$?

3. Show that if the R^u do not involve t or $\mathbf{y}$ then the necessary conditions of Theorem 5.4.1 become the same as the Pontryagin necessary conditions given in the previous chapter.

4. Develop a set of necessary conditions for control problems in which there are no state variables, only control variables.

Section 5.6

1. For the specific system represented in Figure 2.22, discuss the difficulties

involved in actually determining the trajectory which transfers a system from an initial capital stock of K_0 to a final capital stock of K_1 with $\dot{K} \geq 0$.

2. Study the special case of the Ramsey model given in Section 4.10, but with discounting and the restriction $\dot{K} \geq 0$ added.

3. Analyze the formulation of the Samuelson-Solow model given in Example 3 and obtain the same conclusions as in Section 4.14.

Section 5.7

1. Discuss the applicability of the sufficiency conditions considered in this section to the Samuelson-Solow example we have studied.

2. Discuss the applicability of the sufficiency conditions considered in this section to the Ramsey model when the solution lies partly on the boundary.

Section 5.9

1. Express $y_1^2 + y_2^2 = 7t$ as a differential equation constraint. Express $y_1^2 + y_2^2 \leq 7t$ as a differential equation constraint.

2. Follow the procedure introduced in this section to convert the problem of optimizing

$$J[\mathbf{y}] = \int_{x_0}^{x_1} F(x, \mathbf{y}, \mathbf{y}')dx$$

subject to the holonomic constraints $T^i(x, \mathbf{y}) = 0, i = 1, \ldots, m, m < n$, into a Lagrange problem. Obtain the necessary conditions for the Lagrange problem. How can these necessary conditions be reconciled with those obtained in Section 3.4?

Section 5.11

1. Illustrate the conversion from (5-113) to (5-114) when there is only one constraint in $\mathscr{L}_1$ and one in $\mathscr{L}_2$.

Section 5.12

1. Are there any conditions which determine the values of the δ_l along an interior segment?

Section 5.13

1. What would happen if $\lambda(t)$ were here defined as in Section 5.12? Is there any reason why $\lambda(t)$ should not be defined in this way? Investigate the matter in detail.

Section 5.14

1. Suppose that $\mathscr{L}_1$ is empty and there is only one constraint in $\mathscr{L}_2$. Show that if λ is properly defined the jump condition can be interpreted as saying that λ is continuous across junction points.

2. Suppose that it is required that the control variables be continuous. Show how the theory should be modified to handle this case. Hint: Treat control variables as state variables and use their derivatives as control variables.

3. Suppose that in a control problem $F = e^{-\delta t}G(\mathbf{y}, \mathbf{v})$ and that t appears only in the discount factor $e^{-\delta t}$. Let J^* be the optimal value of the functional to be optimized. Denote by $H(t)$ the value of the Hamiltonian at time t on an optimal trajectory. Then prove that $J^* = \delta^{-1}[H(t^*) - H(t_0)]$. In particular, if $H(t^*) = 0$, $J^* = -\delta^{-1}H(t_0)$. Show that this holds even when the planning horizon is infinite if $\lim_{t\to\infty}H(t) = 0$.

4. Check the result obtained in Problem 3 by applying it to several of the Ramsey examples given in Chapter 2.

5. An interesting potential application of optimal control theory lies in the area of optimal development of reservoirs of crude petroleum. Petroleum occurs in the pores of rocks at some distance beneath the surface of the earth (typically, several thousand feet). The oil occurs in more or less well defined reservoirs, the boundaries of which may be determined in a variety of ways; for example, by impermeable faults or aquifers (water boundaries). The crude is produced by drilling wells into the reservoir rock. The petroleum then flows through the pores of the rock into the wells. The driving force may be the expansion of the oil itself, expansion of dissolved gas, expansion of an aquifer or expansion of a gas cap above the oil. Sometimes, especially after the natural driving forces are nearly exhausted by the removal of large quantities of oil, an artificial driving force may be introduced by pumping water or a detergent mixture into certain wells to drive the oil into other wells. The oil does not always occur in just a single layer. It may occur in two or more layers at different depths, separated by layers of rock which contain no oil. A well may be drilled to produce from only one layer or from two or more layers simultaneously. Also it may be used initially for one layer and then later for another.

The length of time over which production takes place from a reservoir can be varied between rather wide limits depending on the number of wells drilled, the rate at which they are drilled, and the production rate which is set for each well (this can be varied from 0 up to some maximum value). It is of interest to control the production from the reservoir in such a way as to maximize discounted profits. Due to the nature of taxes and royalties, this is not necessarily achieved by producing all the petroleum as quickly as possible. For example, in the United States, the depletion allowance introduces a nonlinear factor into the tax computations.

In this problem we shall consider only a very simple situation. We shall imagine that all the wells for a given reservoir have been drilled and that no oil has been taken from any of the wells. Production is now ready to begin and it is desired to so control the production rate r from the entire reservoir that discounted profit over the life t^* of the field is maximized. Assume that the rate at which taxes and royalties are paid is ar^2, that π is the selling price per barrel and that c is the production and transportation cost per barrel, so that the profit rate is $(\pi - c)r - ar^2$. Let L be the total quantity of oil in the reservoir initially and R the total amount withdrawn up to time t. Then the production rate must satisfy $0 \le r \le \beta(L - R)$. How should the production rate be controlled if discounted profit is to be maximized? Is it optimal to completely deplete the reservoir in finite time?

6. Modify Problem 5 to take account of the possibility that there is a minimum rate d of production costs. In particular, consider that production and transportation costs are incurred at the rate $cr + d$.

6

Two-sector models of optimal economic growth

6.1. Introduction

In a series of exercises scattered through Chapters 2–5 we have provided a fairly comprehensive treatment of Ramsey's model of optimal economic growth. The model is of simple mathematical structure yet displays in a clear light some of the fundamental and inescapable economic issues associated with economy-wide planning. For purposes of illustration, therefore, it has been almost ideal. Nevertheless, the model is based on several assumptions which to an economist seem highly restrictive. Given these assumptions, some important issues cannot be posed and others can be stated only in an incomplete or distorted form. In particular, it has been assumed that the population and the state of the arts are constant; that the economy produces just one multi-purpose commodity which, new or old, can serve both as consumption-good and as capital-good; and that plans once implemented are never reviewed.

In this final chapter, with the development of mathematical technique behind us, we explore the implications of relaxing some of these assumptions. Specifically, we drop the assumption that the economy produces only one commodity and suppose instead that it produces two commodities, a specialized consumption good and a specialized capital good, by processes which are distinguishable one from the other in the sense that, whatever the factor rentals, the cost-minimizing capital : labor ratio differs from industry to industry. It will be assumed also that both the population and the labor force are growing autonomously and exponentially at rate γ. (This assumption, and the way in which production functions are handled, distinguishes the model from that of Samuelson and Solow.) On the other hand, we introduce the simplifying assumption that the capital good is immortal, not subject to decay or depreciation. As an alternative to this assumption we might have assumed that depreciation is proportional to the stock of capital ('radio-active' depreciation); but this would have complicated the notation without changing the analysis or conclusions in any essential.

Brief remarks on the possibility of accommodating systematically recurring technical improvements and on the questions raised by the periodical or continual review of a plan are contained in the final section of the chapter.

A minor purpose of this chapter is to confirm the reader in his grasp of mathematical technique. A much more important purpose is to provide him with practice in formulating complex economic problems of a variational kind and in bringing to bear on those problems the appropriate mathematical tools. Accordingly there is in this chapter much less attention given to the computation of solutions in specific cases and more emphasis on general economic analysis.

6.2. The capital good freely transferable between industries

For the time being it will be assumed that the capital good is freely transferable, without cost or delay, from one industry to the other. The conditions of optimal growth under this simplifying assumption were first studied by Srinivasan [36] and Uzawa [39].

Before immersing ourselves in detailed calculations we stand off and consider in general terms how Ramsey's problem is changed by the admission of two specialized goods. Most obviously, consumption is now restricted to the current output of the consumption good and cannot be supplemented from the stock of capital.

Next we notice that at each point of time there is a problem of factor allocation. In the uncomplicated world of Ramsey both labor and capital are fully employed in producing a single commodity. In a world of two commodities, however, it is necessary to decide how much of each factor shall be used in each industry; and this decision must be taken for each t. One might imagine that each of the four factor allocations is directly controlled by the Planning Authority and then seek the optimal time paths of each allocation. Or, alternatively, one might imagine that the detail of factor allocation is left to the managers of competitive firms who seek to maximize profits in the light of product prices and factor rentals which, directly or indirectly, are set by the Authority. Even if the Authority is blessed with perfect knowledge it is not always true that the same results can be achieved by either method. Throughout this section we shall assume that the Authority controls the allocation of factors indirectly by setting the commodity price ratio. Managers of individual firms take both this price and the competitively determined factor rentals as data to which they adjust.

(In Section 6.3 it will be assumed that planning takes a more direct form.)

Once the allocation of factors is determined so is the output of each industry and hence the rate of capital accumulation. Given the time path of prices and the community's initial endowment of factors, therefore, we may trace the future course of the whole economy. Of course it is necessary also that the Planning Authority be able to regulate the demand for each product, and the reader may imagine that this is done by means of taxes and subsidies; but the method of regulation need not concern us here since it does not figure explicitly in the analysis.

In Ramsey's formulation, total population was held constant. It was therefore merely a question of mathematical form whether the argument of the 'instantaneous utility function' U was taken to be average or total consumption, or whether both arguments were employed. When population is changing over time, however, the question is one of substance. Throughout this chapter it will be assumed that utility depends on average consumption only, implying that in itself population size is of no welfare significance. (Cf. Sections 1.2 and 2.12.)

The problem facing the Planning Authority then is that of finding the path of commodity prices which maximizes

$$\int_0^\infty U(c(t))\mathrm{d}t,$$

where $c(t)$ is to be read as average consumption at time t.

We must now describe the constraints subject to which maximization takes place or, equivalently, the economic mechanism through which commodity prices influence the path of average consumption. We begin by setting out the basic production relationships. Two commodities are produced, at rates (physical quantities per unit of time) Y_1 and Y_2 with the aid of two homogeneous factors of production, labor and capital, in total quantities L and K, respectively. K_j is the amount of capital employed in the jth industry, L_j is the amount of labor employed in the jth industry. The jth production relationship is written

$$Y_j = \Psi_j(K_j, L_j) \quad j = 1, 2$$

where Ψ_j is assumed to be a concave and differentiable function. It is assumed also that both factors are indispensable, in the sense that

$$\Psi_j(0, L_j) = \Psi_j(K_j, 0) = 0 \; j = 1, 2. \tag{6-1}$$

It is assumed further that Ψ_j is homogeneous of the first degree in K_j and

L_j ('constant returns'), so that the average product of labor depends only on the capital:labor ratio, $k_j \equiv K_j/L_j$, and total output may be expressed as the product of a scale factor L_j and a function ψ_j of k_j:

$$Y_j = L_j \Psi_j \left(\frac{K_j}{L_j}, 1\right) \equiv L_j \psi_j(k_j) \quad j = 1, 2. \tag{6-2a}$$

Writing $y_j \equiv Y_j/L$ for the per capita output of the jth commodity and $l_j \equiv L_j/L$ for the proportion of the labor force employed by the jth industry, we therefore have

$$y_j = l_j \psi_j(k_j) \quad j = 1, 2. \tag{6-2b}$$

The marginal product of capital in terms of the jth commodity is then

$$\psi_j'(k_j) \equiv \frac{d\psi_j}{dk_j} \equiv \frac{\partial}{\partial K_j} \Psi_j(K_j, L_j) \quad j = 1, 2 \tag{6-3a}$$

and the corresponding marginal product of labor is

$$\psi_j(k_j) - k_j \psi_j'(k_j) \equiv \frac{\partial}{\partial L_j} \Psi_j(K_j, L_j) \quad j = 1, 2. \tag{6-3b}$$

Note that the marginal products also depend on factor proportions only. All marginal products are assumed to be positive if something of each factor is employed; and all positive marginal products are assumed to be diminishing. Thus

$$\left.\begin{aligned} &\psi_j'(k_j) > 0 \\ &\psi_j''(k_j) < 0. \end{aligned}\right\} \quad \text{if} \quad k_j > 0 \tag{6-4}$$

From (6-1) and the assumption of differentiability,

$$\lim_{k_j \to 0} \psi_j(k_j) = 0. \tag{6-5a}$$

To this, the first of Inada's 'derivative conditions' [22], we add

$$\lim_{k_j \to \infty} \psi_j(k_j) = \infty \tag{6-5b}$$

$$\lim_{k_j \to 0} \psi_j'(k_j) = \infty \tag{6-5c}$$

$$\lim_{k_j \to \infty} \psi_j'(k_j) = 0. \tag{6-5d}$$

Then the graph of $\psi_j(k_j)$ is as depicted in Figure 6.1.

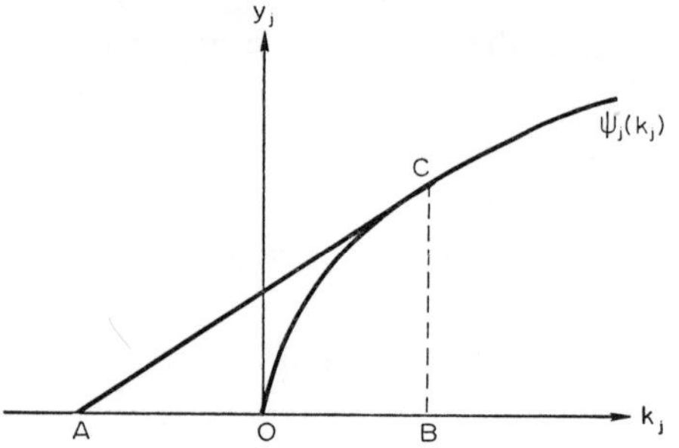

Fig. 6.1.

Under competitive conditions with something of each commodity produced, the value of the marginal product of a factor must be equal to the reward of that factor and therefore the same in each industry. If we denote by p_j the price of the jth commodity, by r the rental of a unit of capital, and by w the wage rate, each in terms of some arbitrary unit of account, the required equalities may be expressed as

$$\begin{aligned} r &= p_j\psi'_j \\ w &= p_j(\psi_j - k_j\psi'_j). \end{aligned} \tag{6-6}$$

It follows that the ratio of factor rewards is equal to

$$\omega \equiv \frac{w}{r} = \frac{\psi_j}{\psi'_j} - k_j \quad j = 1, 2. \tag{6-7}$$

Suppose that $k_j = OB$ in Figure 6.1. Then

$$\omega = \frac{BC}{BC/AB} - AO.$$

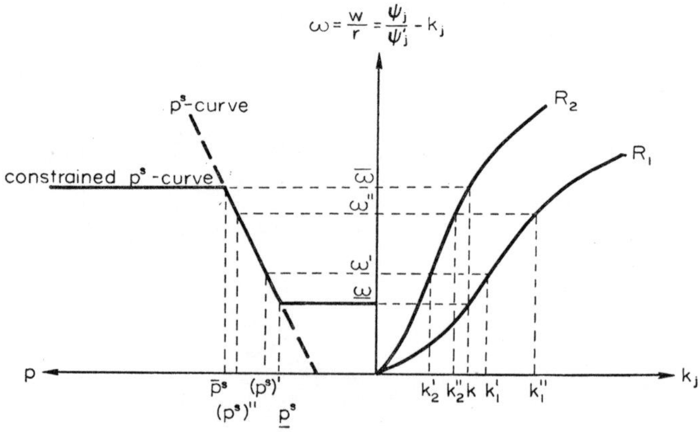

Fig. 6.2(a).

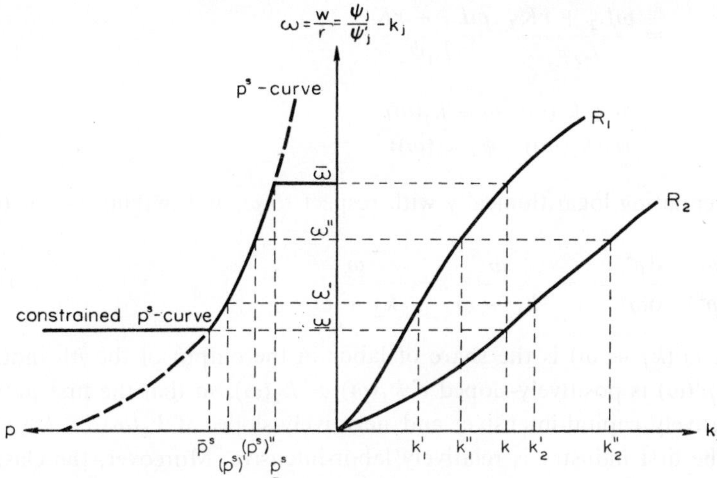

Fig. 6.2(b).

In view of the restrictions placed on $\psi_j(k_j)$, (6-7) determines k_j uniquely in terms of ω, with

$$\frac{dk_j}{d\omega} = -\frac{(\psi_j')^2}{\psi_j\psi_j''} > 0. \tag{6-8}$$

The relationship between k_j and ω is illustrated by Figure 6.2. The $k_j(\omega)$-curve shows, for the jth industry, the relationship between the factor ratio in that industry and the ratio of factor rewards (which in turn is equal to the ratio of marginal products); it slopes upwards from left to right in keeping with (6-8) and emerges from the origin in accordance with (6-5). To any assigned ratio of factor rewards, say ω', there corresponds a pair of cost-minimizing factor ratios, k_2' and k_2'. If the ratio of factor rewards is raised, say to ω'', both industries are induced to economize in the employment of labor and a new pair of cost-minimizing factor ratios, k_2'' and k_2'', is established, with $k_j'' > k_j'$. Given ω, and therefore k_j, one can calculate the relative unit costs or supply prices of the two commodities. Thus if we denote by p^s the relative supply price of the second commodity in terms of the first, we have, in easy steps,

$$p^s(\omega) = \frac{\text{average cost of producing the second commodity}}{\text{average cost of producing the first commodity}}$$

$$= \frac{\omega L_2 + rK_2}{L_2\psi_2} \bigg/ \frac{\omega L_1 + rK_1}{L_1\psi_1}$$

$$= \frac{\omega + k_2(\omega)}{\psi_2(k_2(\omega))} \bigg/ \frac{\omega + k_1(\omega)}{\psi_1(k_1(\omega))}. \tag{6-9}$$

Differentiating logarithmically with respect to ω, and making use of (6-7),

$$\frac{\omega}{p^s} \cdot \frac{\mathrm{d}p^s}{\mathrm{d}\omega} = -\frac{\omega}{k_1 + \omega} + \frac{\omega}{k_2 + \omega} \tag{6-10}$$

where $\omega/(k_j + \omega)$ is the share of labor in the output of the jth industry. Thus $p^s(\omega)$ is positively-sloped if $k_1(\omega) > k_2(\omega)$, so that the first industry is relatively capital-intensive, and negatively-sloped if $k_2(\omega) > k_1(\omega)$, so that the first industry is relatively labor-intensive. Moreover, the elasticity of the p^s-curve is always less than one in magnitude. On the other hand, the behavior of p^s as ω goes to zero cannot be pinned down without assumptions about the production functions more restrictive than those so far made. If $k_1(\omega) > k_2(\omega)$, p^s may go either to zero or to some finite positive number; and, if $k_1(\omega) < k_2(\omega)$, p^s may go either to infinity or to some positive finite number. For example if $\psi_i(k_i) = A_i k_i^{\alpha_i}$, with $1 > \alpha_1 > \alpha_2 > 0$, then $p^s(\omega)$ goes to zero as ω goes to zero; but if $\psi_1(k_1) = A_1 k_1^{\alpha_1}$ and $\psi_2(k_2) = A_2 k_1^{\alpha_2(k_2)}$, with $1 > \alpha_1 \geq \alpha_2 > 0$ and $\alpha_2(k_2)$ approaching α_1 from below as ω goes to zero, then as ω goes to zero $p^s(\omega)$ approaches a positive constant which depends on A_1 and A_2. In Figures 6.2(a) and 6.2(b), $p^s(\omega)$ is depicted as approaching a finite positive number as ω goes to zero. [The behavior of $\alpha_2(k_2)$ has been specified only in the limit, as k_2 goes to zero; and, for present purposes, that is all that is needed. We note however that, without additional restrictions on $\alpha_2(k_2)$, $\psi_2(k_2) = A_2 k_2^{\alpha_2(k_2)}$ does not qualify as a production function. In particular, without additional restrictions, one cannot be sure that for all $k > 0$ both marginal products are positive. The function $\psi_2(k_2) = A_2 k_2^{\alpha_1/1+k_2}$, for example, is acceptable only for sufficiently small k_2; for k_2 such that $(1 + k_2)/k_2 < \log k_2$ the derivative is negative.]

The relative supply price is defined for all observable values of ω. However, not all positive values of ω are observable. To show this, we note that under competitive conditions, with production functions of the type depicted in Figure 6.1, both factors of production must be fully employed; that is,

$$L_1 + L_2 = L$$

$$K_1 + K_2 = K$$

or, equivalently,

$$\begin{aligned} l_1 + l_2 &= 1 \\ k_1 l_1 + k_2 l_2 &= k. \end{aligned} \tag{6-11}$$

For arbitrary ω [and $k_j(\omega)$], however, we cannot be sure that (6-11) will yield non-negative l_1 and l_2. The point may be illustrated in terms of Figure 6.2. Let

$$\begin{aligned} \bar{\omega} &= \max\{\omega_1, \omega_2\} \\ \underline{\omega} &= \min\{\omega_1, \omega_2\} \end{aligned} \tag{6-12}$$

where ω_j is defined by $k = k_j(\omega)$. Thus $\underline{\omega}$ and $\bar{\omega}$ are found successively by reading up from k until the two $k_j(\omega)$-curves are encountered. Then any ω greater than $\bar{\omega}$ or less than $\underline{\omega}$ will induce the two industries to adopt factor ratios both lying on the same side of k and therefore incompatible with the full employment of both factors. Under competitive conditions, therefore, one would observe only those ω lying between $\underline{\omega}$ and $\bar{\omega}$:

$$\underline{\omega} \leqq \omega \leqq \bar{\omega}.$$

It follows that the *constrained* p^s-curve (the heavy curve in the left hand quadrant of Figure 6.2) becomes perfectly elastic at $\underline{\omega}$ and $\bar{\omega}$. Let us now define

$$\underline{p}^s = \min\{p^s(\underline{\omega}), p^s(\bar{\omega})\} \tag{6-13a}$$

and

$$\bar{p}^s = \max\{p^s(\underline{\omega}), p^s(\bar{\omega})\} \tag{6-13b}$$

and suppose that the market price ratio $p \equiv p_2/p_1$ lies at or below $\underline{p}^s$. Clearly the country must be completely specialized in the production of the first commodity, with $\omega = \underline{\omega}$ or $\omega = \bar{\omega}$ according as, respectively, the first or second industry is relatively capital-intensive. Similarly, if $p > \bar{p}^s$ the country must be completely specialized in the production of the second commodity, with $\omega = \underline{\omega}$ or $\omega = \bar{\omega}$ according as, respectively, the first or second industry is relatively labor-intensive. In whichever industry is idle both marginal products are zero. To accommodate the possibility of complete specialization in production, it is necessary to write (6-6) less restrictively as

$$\begin{aligned} r &\geqq p_j \psi'_j \\ \omega &\geqq p_j(\psi_j - k_j \psi'_j) \end{aligned} \tag{6-14}$$

with strict equality for $j = 1$ and/or $j = 2$.

That completes the description of the static constraints of our problem. Equivalently, we have now accumulated enough relationships between the variables, and enough restrictions on the form of those relationships, to permit us in principle, at any point of time t and given only the capital : labor ratio $k(t)$, to regulate production, factor allocations and factor rewards by means of a single control, the commodity price ratio. It will be convenient to have these constraints collected in one place:

$$y_j = l_j\psi_j(k_j) \quad j = 1, 2 \tag{6-15}$$

$$l_1 + l_2 = 1 \tag{6-16a}$$

$$l_1k_1 + l_2k_2 = k \tag{6-16b}$$

$$r \geqq p_j\psi_j'(k_j) \quad K_j[r - p_j\psi_j'(k_j)] = 0 \tag{6-17a}$$

$$\omega \geqq p_j(\psi_j - k_j\psi_j'(k_j)) \quad l_j[\omega - p_j(\psi_j - k_j\psi_j'(k_j))] = 0 \tag{6-17b}$$

$$\omega = \frac{\psi_j(k_j)}{\psi_j'(k_j)} - k_j \quad j = 1 \text{ and/or } 2 \tag{6-17c}$$

$$l_j \geqq 0 \quad \text{with} \begin{cases} l_1 = 0 & \text{if} \quad p > \bar{p}^s \\ l_2 = 0 & \text{if} \quad p < \underline{p}^s \end{cases} \tag{6-18}$$

$$\omega_j \equiv \frac{\psi_j(k)}{\psi_j'(k)} - k \quad j = 1, 2 \tag{6-19}$$

$$\bar{\omega} = \max\{\omega_1, \omega_2\} \tag{6-20a}$$

$$\underline{\omega} = \min\{\omega_1, \omega_2\} \tag{6-20b}$$

$$\begin{aligned} \bar{p}^s &= \max\{p^s(\underline{\omega}), p^s(\bar{\omega})\} \\ &= \max\left\{\frac{\psi_1'(k_1(\underline{\omega}))}{\psi_2'(k_2(\underline{\omega}))}, \frac{\psi_1'(k_1(\bar{\omega}))}{\psi_2'(k_2(\bar{\omega}))}\right\} \end{aligned} \tag{6-21a}$$

$$\begin{aligned} \underline{p}^s &= \min\{p^s(\underline{\omega}), p^s(\bar{\omega})\} \\ &= \min\left\{\frac{\psi_1'(k_1(\underline{\omega}))}{\psi_2'(k_2(\underline{\omega}))}, \frac{\psi_1'(k_1(\bar{\omega}))}{\psi_2'(k_2(\bar{\omega}))}\right\}. \end{aligned} \tag{6-21b}$$

Only (6-17) and (6-19)–(6-21) merit comment: in (6-17) we have given formal expression to the fact that for each industry the weak marginal inequalities hold as equalities if something is produced; (6-19)–(6-21) serve to define recursively $\underline{p}^s$ and $\bar{p}^s$. As already noted, given p and k the system

(6-15)–(6-21) may be solved uniquely for the remaining variables. Thus we may write, for example,

$$y_j = y_j(p, k) \quad j = 1, 2. \tag{6-22}$$

To these static constraints we must add a description of the process by which the two factors of production change through time. It is assumed that the population and labor force grow at the same exponential rate γ:

$$L(t) = L(0)e^{\gamma t} \quad \gamma > 0.$$

The process of capital accumulation, on the other hand, is described by $\dot{K}(t) = Y_2(t)$, whence

$$\begin{aligned} \dot{k}(t) &\equiv \frac{\mathrm{d}}{\mathrm{d}t} K(t)/L(t) \\ &= \frac{\dot{K}(t)L(t) - \dot{L}(t)K(t)}{[L(t)]^2} \\ &= y_2(p(t), k(t)) - \gamma k(t). \end{aligned} \tag{6-23}$$

When (6-23) is added to the static constraints listed above we are able in principle, given only the value of k at some point of time, say

$$k(0) = k_0 \tag{6-24}$$

to control the complete time paths of production, factor allocations and factor rewards by means of the single control, the price ratio.

Before we can describe the problem of optimal control in detail it remains only to specify more closely the 'instantaneous utility' function U. Suppose that the first industry produces the consumption good and the second industry the capital good. Then we may write $U = U(y_1)$. It is desirable that we build into our statement of the maximum problem the requirement that at every point of time average consumption be not 'too low'. This might be done by insisting that $y_1(t)$ be not less than some constant or variable 'subsistence' level. However this assumption is mathematically inconvenient since optimal consumption may for some of the time lie on the boundary so defined. Accordingly we adopt the alternative assumption, due to Koopmans [25]:

$$\lim_{y_1 \to 0} U(y_1) = -\infty. \tag{6-25}$$

This assumption ensures that it will never be optimal to consume nothing.

The restrictions we have imposed on U and ψ_j do not ensure that the integral

$$\int_0^{\infty} U(y_1(t))\mathrm{d}t$$

converges. The problem of non-convergence is a familiar one. In earlier chapters the problem was disposed of by suitably restricting the utility function and/or the single production function. A similar device is adopted in this chapter. However, it is here assumed that the population and work force are growing exponentially; and it was shown in Section 2.12 that this makes it possible to relax somewhat the restrictions imposed on the utility and production functions. In particular, it is no longer necessary to assume that one of the functions saturates. It suffices to assume that there exists a value of k, say k^*, such that $\phi(k) \equiv \psi(k) - \gamma k$ reaches a maximum at k^* and such that $U^* \equiv U(\phi(k^*)) = 0$ with $U(\phi)$ monotonic increasing. Similarly, in the present two-sector model we choose our instantaneous utility function so that $U^* \equiv U(c^*) = 0$, $U'(c) > 0$, where c^* is the highest level of per capita consumption consistent with the steady balanced growth of the economy, that is, with outputs and factor allocations growing at the same exponential rate γ and all prices constant. Of course, it is necessary that k^* exist; and this implies some additional restrictions on the production functions. Thus for both outputs to grow exponentially it is necessary that the stock of capital should grow at the same rate γ as the labor force, so that k is a constant. This in turn implies that

$$y_2(p, k) = \gamma k \tag{6-26}$$

as we see from (6-23). Now p must be chosen so that average consumption $y_1(p, k)$ is a maximum subject to (6-26). Differentiating y_1 totally with respect to p, and equating to zero, we obtain

$$\frac{\partial}{\partial p} y_1(p, k) + \frac{\partial}{\partial k} y_1(p, k) \cdot \frac{\mathrm{d}k}{\mathrm{d}p} = 0.$$

From (6-26), however,

$$\frac{\mathrm{d}k}{\mathrm{d}p} = \frac{\partial y_2(p, k)/\partial p}{\gamma - \partial y_2(p, k)/\partial k}.$$

Moreover, under competitive conditions

$$\frac{\partial}{\partial p} y_1(p, k) + p \frac{\partial}{\partial p} y_2(p, k) = 0. \tag{6-27}$$

Hence

$$\frac{1}{p} \cdot \frac{\partial}{\partial k} y_1(p, k) + \frac{\partial}{\partial k} y_2(p, k) = \gamma.$$

The left hand side however is the rate at which per capita output (in terms of the second commodity) changes when the total stock of capital changes. It is therefore equal to the marginal product of capital in terms of itself:

$$\psi_2'(k_2) = \gamma. \tag{6-28}$$

(6-26) and (6-28) are necessary conditions of golden age growth. The existence of a $k(p)$ such that (6-26) holds is ensured by our earlier restrictions (6-5) on the production function ψ_2. However, (6-5) does *not* by itself imply the existence of an ω and a $k_2(\omega)$ such that (6-28) is satisfied. The existence of such values is an additional assumption which we now introduce.

Having guaranteed the existence of k^*, the problem of optimal economic growth may be described as that of finding the control $p(t)$ such that

$$\int_0^\infty U(y_1(p(t), k(t))\mathrm{d}t \tag{6-29}$$

is a maximum subject to (6-15)–(6-21) and (6-23)–(6-25), and with all variables constrained to be non-negative.

The problem can be solved by applying Theorems 5.11.1 and 5.12.1 and their respective corollaries, together with Theorem 5.7.2. Consider the Hamiltonian expression

$$H(k, \lambda, p) = U(y_1(p, k)) + \lambda[y_2(p, k) - \gamma k] \tag{6-30}$$

where for convenience the time dependence of all variables is suppressed. The multiplier λ may be interpreted as the utility per unit of investment per capita, that is, as the community's demand price, in terms of utility, of capital goods. It follows that H itself may be interpreted as the utility of total output per capita. Bearing in mind that p need never be zero, even when it is optimal to devote all resources to the production of consumption goods, and that p is unbounded upwards, we have as a first necessary condition of optimality,

$$\begin{aligned} 0 &= \frac{\partial}{\partial p} H(p, k) \\ &= U'(y_1(p, k)) \cdot \frac{\partial}{\partial p} y_1(p, k) + \lambda \frac{\partial}{\partial p} y_2(p, k) \end{aligned}$$

or, in view of (6-27),

$$0 = \left[U'(y_1(p, k)) - \frac{\lambda}{p} \right] \frac{\partial}{\partial p} y_1(p, k). \tag{6-31}$$

As a second necessary condition we have

$$\dot{\lambda} = -\frac{\partial}{\partial k} H(p, k)$$

$$= -\left[U'(y_1(p, k)) \frac{\partial}{\partial k} y_1(p, k) + \lambda \frac{\partial}{\partial k} y_2(p, k) \right] + \lambda \gamma. \tag{6-32}$$

In economic terms, the social demand price of capital goods must change through time in conformity with the imputed net marginal product of capital (that is, net after allowing for the equipment of the addition to population).

The differential equations (6-23) and (6-32), together with the optimum condition (6-31) and the constraints (6-15)–(6-21) and (6-23)–(6-25), determine the time paths of λ, p and k. We now seek to determine some of the general characteristics of those paths. To that end we construct a phase diagram for λ and k. Evidently the structure of the two differential equations depends on whether the second good is produced (we know from (6-25) that the first good must be produced).

We therefore begin by marking out on the non-negative quadrant the boundary between those values of k and λ for which the economy is completely specialized in producing the first or consumer good and those values for which it produces both commodities. This boundary is defined by (k, λ)-pairs which satisfy

$$\underline{\lambda}(k) \equiv \underline{p}^s(k) \cdot U'(\psi_1(k)). \tag{6-33}$$

To confirm that this is so, we note first that, when the economy is specialized in producing the first commodity but is on the verge of producing both, the right hand derivative $\partial y_1(p, k)/\partial p+$ is negative so that, from (6-31),

$$pU'(y_1(p, k)) - \lambda = 0. \tag{6-34}$$

We note further that, under the same conditions,

$$y_1 = \psi_1. \tag{6-35}$$

(6-33) follows from (6-34) and (6-35), and our assertion follows from the definition of $\underline{p}^s(k)$. To pin down the shape of the boundary we must treat separately the two cases in which, respectively, the first or second industry is relatively capital-intensive.

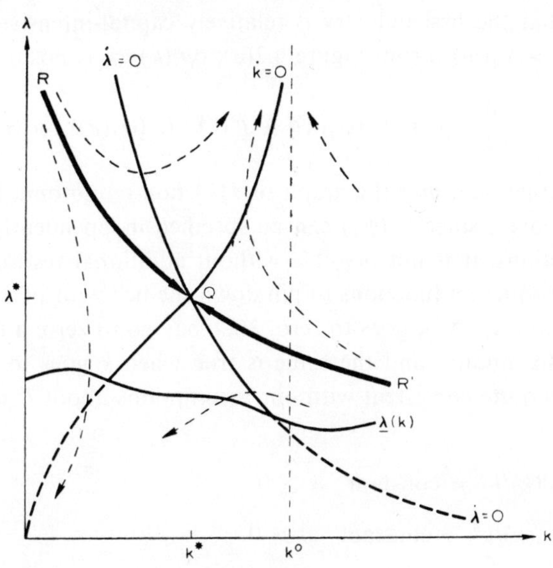

Fig. 6.3(a).

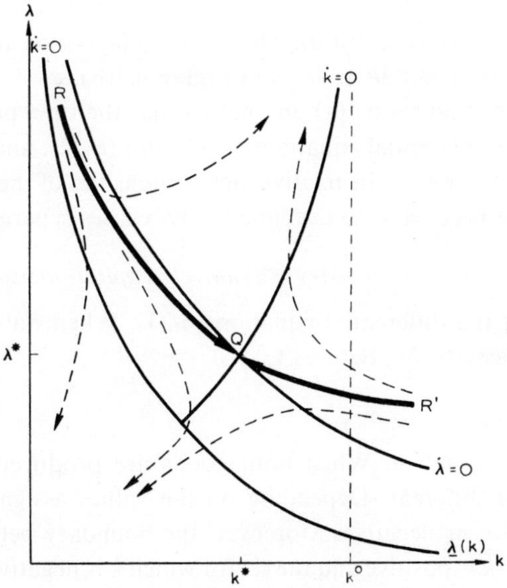

Fig. 6.3(b).

Suppose that the first industry is relatively capital-intensive so that, for all ω, $k_1(\omega) > k_2(\omega)$. From Figure 6.2(a), $\mathrm{d}\underline{p}^s(k)/\mathrm{d}k$ is positive; hence

$$\frac{\mathrm{d}}{\mathrm{d}k}\underline{\lambda}(k) = \frac{\mathrm{d}}{\mathrm{d}k}\underline{p}^s(k) \cdot U'(\psi_1(k)) + \underline{p}^s(k) \cdot U''(\psi_1(k)) \cdot \psi_1'(k) \qquad (6\text{-}36)$$

may be of either sign and the graph of $\underline{\lambda}(k)$ non-monotonic (as in Figure 6.3(a)). Moreover, since $U'(\psi_1)$ can be specified independently of the production functions, it is not possible without additional restrictions on the utility and production functions to pin down the behavior of $\underline{\lambda}(k)$ as k goes to zero and infinity. As k goes to zero, $\underline{\lambda}(k)$ may go to zero, a finite positive number, or to infinity; and the same is true when k goes to infinity. For example, it is quite consistent with our assumptions about U and the ψ_i to suppose that

$$\lim_{k\to 0} \underline{p}^s(k)/k^\alpha = \text{constant} \quad \alpha \geq 0$$

$$\lim_{k\to 0} \psi_1(k)/k^\beta = \text{constant} \quad \beta > 0$$

$$\lim_{\psi_1\to 0} U'(\psi_1)/\psi_1^\gamma = \text{constant} \quad \gamma \leq 0.$$

But then $\lim_{k\to 0}\underline{p}^s(k)U'(\psi_1(k))/k^{\alpha+\gamma\beta} = \text{constant}$, so that $\lim_{k\to 0}\underline{p}^s(k) \cdot U'(\psi_1(k)) = 0$, a positive constant or ∞ according as $\gamma > -\alpha/\beta$, $\gamma = -\alpha/\beta$, $\gamma < -\alpha/\beta$, respectively. In Figure 6.3(a) the graph of $\underline{\lambda}(k)$ is shown beginning at a positive finite value of λ.

Suppose alternatively that the second industry is relatively capital-intensive so that, for all ω, $k_1(\omega) < k_2(\omega)$. Then $\lim_{k\to 0}\underline{\lambda}(k) = \infty$ and, from (6-36) and Figure 6.2(b), $\mathrm{d}\underline{\lambda}(k)/\mathrm{d}k < 0$, as in Figure 6.3(b).

It is clear from Figures 6.3(a) and 6.3(b) that the time paths of λ and k generated by the differential equations (6-23) and (6-32), and the associated phase diagram, depend on the relative factor intensities of the two industries. It is tedious, but necessary, to examine the two cases separately.

The case in which the first industry is relatively capital-intensive

Consider first the differential equation (6-23). When only the first commodity is produced (6-23) reduces to

$$\dot{k} = -\gamma k$$

which is always negative. When both goods are produced, however, the situation is very different. Depending on the values assigned to k and λ, $\dot{k}$ may be positive or negative. Moreover, the boundary between the set of points for which $\dot{k}$ is positive and the set for which $\dot{k}$ is negative is a positively-sloped curve which begins at the origin and approaches a finite vertical asymptote at the maximum value of k which the economy can maintain; for points in this curve, $\dot{k} = 0$. To show this, we note first, with the aid of (6-23), that for each p there exists a k such that $\dot{k} = 0$, that to $p = 0$ there corresponds $k = 0$, and that an increase in p generates an increase in the critical k. Figure 6.4(a) provides an illustration. From the restrictions placed on the production function in the second industry, however, there exists a k, say k^0, such that, for all finite p, $y_2(p, k^0) < \gamma k^0$ and such that

$$\lim_{p \to \infty} y_2(p, k^0) = \gamma k^0.$$

In the non-negative (k, p)-quadrant, therefore, we can draw a positively-sloped curve which begins at the origin and is asymptotic to $k = k^0$. For points which lie off the curve in the k-direction, $\dot{k} < 0$; and for points which lie off the curve in the p-direction, $\dot{k} > 0$. Figure 6.4(b) illustrates. From (6-31), on the other hand, we infer that for every λ there exists between

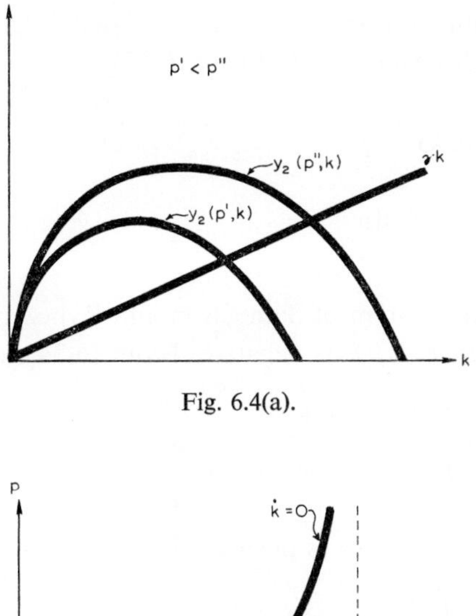

Fig. 6.4(a).

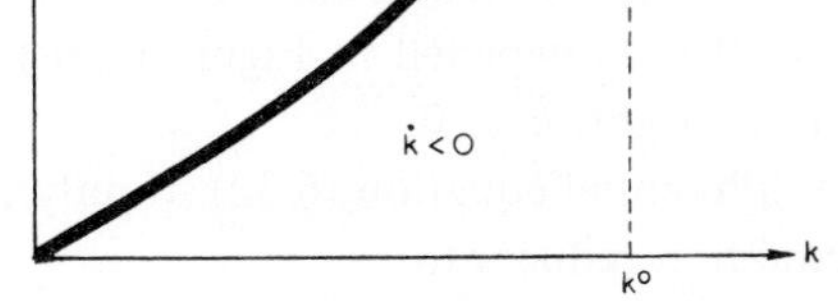

Fig. 6.4(b).

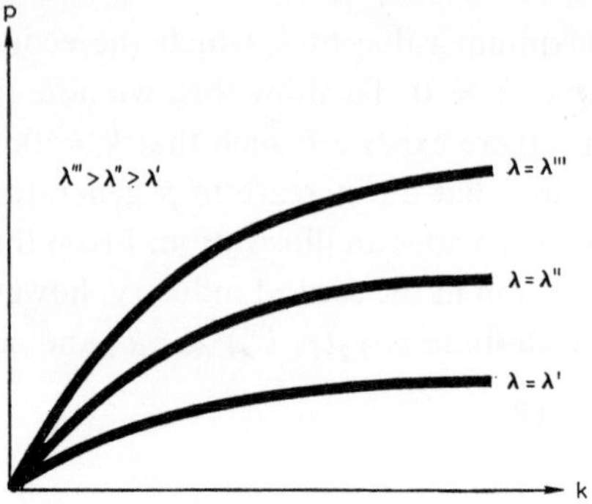

Fig. 6.4(c).

p and k a monotonic relationship which begins at the origin and shifts up with increases in λ, as in Figure 6.4(c). From Figures 6.4(b) and 6.4(c) we now see that for every sufficiently small k there exists a p, and therefore a λ, such that $\dot{k} = 0$, and that the critical λ goes to zero as k goes to zero. To complete our demonstration, we must show that higher values of λ are associated with higher values of k. From (6-23)

$$\frac{\partial \dot{k}}{\partial k} = \frac{\partial}{\partial k} y_2(p, k) - \gamma$$

$$\frac{\partial \dot{k}}{\partial \lambda} = \frac{\partial}{\partial p} y_2(p, k) \cdot \frac{\mathrm{d}p}{\mathrm{d}\lambda}.$$

From a well-known theorem of Samuelson and Rybczynski, $\partial y_2/\partial k < 0$ if $k_1(\omega) > k_2(\omega)$; hence $\partial \dot{k}/\partial k$ is negative. From (6-34), on the other hand,

$$\frac{\mathrm{d}p}{\mathrm{d}\lambda} = \frac{1}{U'(y_1(p, k)) + pU''(y_1(p, k)) \dfrac{\partial}{\partial p} y_1(p, k)} \tag{6-37}$$

which is positive; hence $\partial \dot{k}/\partial \lambda$ is positive. Thus

$$\left.\frac{\mathrm{d}\lambda}{\mathrm{d}k}\right|_{\dot{k}=0} = -\frac{\partial \dot{k}}{\partial k}\bigg/\frac{\partial \dot{k}}{\partial \lambda} > 0$$

and the required boundary between (k, λ)-values for which $\dot{k} > 0$ and values for which $\dot{k} < 0$ is as depicted in Figure 6.3(a). To the left of the boundary, $\dot{k} > 0$; to the right, $\dot{k} < 0$.

Consider now the differential equation (6-32). If only consumption goods are produced, the equation reduces to

$$\dot{\lambda} = -U'(\psi_1(k))\psi_1'(k) + \gamma\lambda.$$

It is clear that, for any λ consistent with complete specialization, $\dot{\lambda} > 0$ for sufficiently large k and $\dot{\lambda} < 0$ for sufficiently small k; thus for any permissible λ there exists a k such that $\dot{k} = 0$. Moreover, the critical k increases as λ decreases. Thus

$$\frac{\partial \dot{\lambda}}{\partial k} = - U''(\psi_1(k))(\psi_2'(k))^2 - U'(\psi_1(k))\psi_1''(k) > 0$$

and

$$\frac{\partial \dot{\lambda}}{\partial \lambda} = \gamma > 0$$

whence

$$\left.\frac{d\lambda}{dk}\right|_{\dot{\lambda}=0} = - \frac{\partial \dot{\lambda}}{\partial k} \Big/ \frac{\partial \dot{\lambda}}{\partial \lambda} < 0.$$

Finally, we notice that as λ goes to zero the critical k goes to infinity. Suppose alternatively that something is produced of both goods. With the aid of (6-34) we may reduce (6-32) to

$$\begin{aligned}\dot{\lambda} &= - \lambda\left\{\left[\frac{1}{p}\frac{\partial}{\partial k}\, y_1(p, k) + \frac{\partial}{\partial k}\, y_2(p, k)\right] - \gamma\right\}\\ &= - \lambda\{ f_2'(k_2) - \gamma\}.\end{aligned}$$

For $\lambda \neq 0$, therefore, $\dot{\lambda} = 0$ implies that k_2 is constant. But k_2 is constant only if ω and p are constant. From (6-34), constant p implies that k and λ are negatively associated:

$$\frac{d\lambda}{dk} = p \cdot U''(y_1(p, k)) \cdot \frac{\partial}{\partial k}\, y_1(p, k) < 0.$$

Moreover, from (6-34), as k approaches from above that critical value at which, given p, specialization in the production of capital goods is complete, λ goes to infinity. The complete curve $\dot{\lambda} = 0$ is displayed in Figure 6.3(a). Above the curve, $\dot{\lambda} > 0$; below the curve $\dot{\lambda} < 0$.

The two curves $\dot{k} = 0$ and $\dot{\lambda} = 0$ intersect at the point (k^*, λ^*). It is easily verified, by applying (6-34) to (6-23) and (6-32), that the point (k^*, λ^*) satisfies the 'golden rule' conditions (6-26) and (6-28).

A glance at Figure 6.3(a) suggests that most trajectories veer away from the point (k^*, λ^*) but that there may exist two paths which do approach (k^*, λ^*), one from the left ($k(0) < k^*$) and one from the right ($k(0) > k^*$). That this is so may be verified by applying a theorem from the theory of differential equations. First let us linearize the two differential equations, (6-23) and (6-32), at the point (k^*, λ^*) and examine the characteristic roots of the resulting coefficient matrix:

$$\begin{pmatrix} \partial\dot{k}/\partial k & \partial\dot{k}/\partial\lambda \\ \partial\dot{\lambda}/\partial k & \partial\dot{\lambda}/\partial\lambda \end{pmatrix}.$$

The roots are

$$\tfrac{1}{2}\left\{\left(\frac{\partial\dot{k}}{\partial k} + \frac{\partial\dot{\lambda}}{\partial\lambda}\right) \pm \left(\left(\frac{\partial\dot{k}}{\partial k} + \frac{\partial\dot{\lambda}}{\partial\lambda}\right)^2 - 4\Delta\right)^{\frac{1}{2}}\right\}$$

where Δ is the determinant of the coefficient matrix. From earlier calculations we know that the coefficient matrix has the sign pattern:

$$\begin{pmatrix} - & + \\ + & + \end{pmatrix}$$

Hence $\Delta < 0$ and the roots are real; moreover, since

$$\left(\left(\frac{\partial\dot{k}}{\partial k} + \frac{\partial\dot{\lambda}}{\partial\lambda}\right) - 4\Delta\right)^{\frac{1}{2}} > \left(\frac{\partial\dot{k}}{\partial k} + \frac{\partial\dot{\lambda}}{\partial\lambda}\right)$$

the roots are of opposite sign. Hence, by definition, (k^*, λ^*) is a saddlepoint in the set of pairs of functions $(k(t), \lambda(t))$ which satisfy the necessary conditions and we may be sure that there exist two trajectories which tend asymptotically to the point (k^*, λ^*) as $t \to \infty$. These trajectories are called stable branches of the saddle. In Figure 6.3(a) they are labelled RQ and $R'Q$. (For the relevant mathematical theorem, see Pontryagin [28], p. 246.)

Thus we have established that for each $k(0)$ there is a unique trajectory which converges on the golden rule path. It remains to show that for this path the integral (6-29) converges, that for every other path satisfying Pontryagin's necessary conditions the integral diverges to $-\infty$, and that therefore one of the stable branches of the saddle is the unique optimal time path.

That for all other paths the integral diverges to $-\infty$ is easy to show. If $k(t) \to 0$ as $t \to \infty$ this is obvious, for then both per capita outputs go to zero and, from (6-25), $U(y_1(t)) \to -\infty$; and if $k(t) \to k^0$ as $t \to \infty$ then $y_1(t) \to 0$, with the same outcome for U.

The case in which the second industry is relatively capital-intensive

Let us again begin with the differential equation (6-23). When only the first commodity is produced $\dot{k} = -\gamma k$ and is always negative. When both commodities are produced, however, $\dot{k}$ may be positive or negative, depending on the values of k and λ. As in our analysis of the case in which the first industry is relatively capital-intensive, we seek the boundary locus of points for which $\dot{k} = 0$. This is an intricate construction requiring not a little patience. We begin by considering p_ε, defined as the infimum of those values of p such that for arbitrarily small positive k something is produced of the second commodity. For all $p > p_\varepsilon$ there exists a unique k such that $\dot{k} = 0$; and the larger is p the larger is the associated value of k; moreover, as p goes to infinity, the associated value of k goes to k^0, the maximum permanently sustainable value of k. Figure 6.5(a) provides an illustration. For each $p < p_\varepsilon$ and sufficiently large, there exists a pair of k-values such that $\dot{k} = 0$; and, finally, there exists a critical p, which we call p_δ, such that the two associated k-values coincide and below which $k(p)$ is not defined. Figure 6.5(b) illustrates. Putting together Figures 6.5(a) and 6.5(b) we obtain the locus of (k, p)-pairs for which $\dot{k} = 0$. This locus is displayed in Figure 6.5(c); the arrows indicate the direction in which k moves for values of k and p off the locus.

That completes the first step of the construction. We next try to derive from the curve $\dot{k} = 0$ of Figure 6.5(c) its counterpart in the (k, λ)-plane. With this end in mind, we return to (6-31) or, since $\partial y_1/\partial p \neq 0$ when specialization is incomplete, to (6-34). From (6-34), bearing in mind (6-25), we infer that for every λ there exists a monotonic decreasing relationship

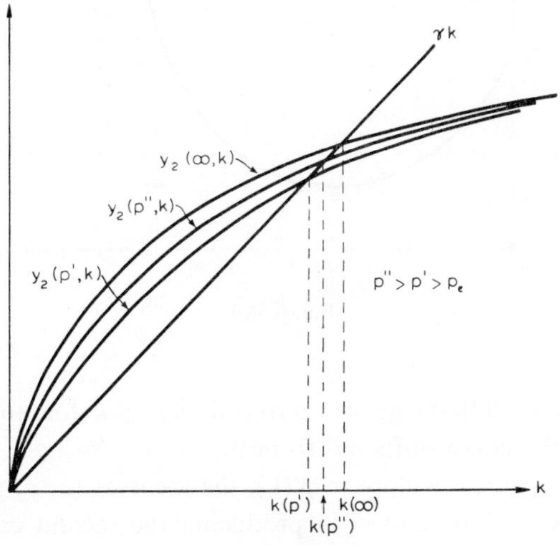

Fig. 6.5(a).

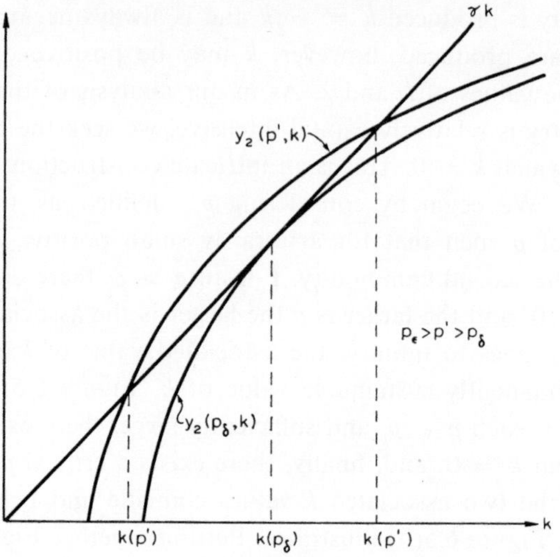

Fig. 6.5(b).

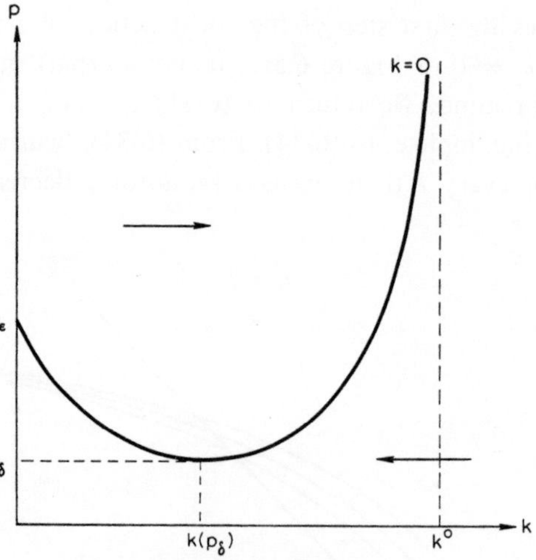

Fig. 6.5(c).

between k and p such that p goes to zero (infinity) as k goes to infinity (zero). As λ increases the curve shifts out from the origin. As λ goes to infinity the curve becomes arbitrarily close to $\bar{p}^s(k)$, the locus of (k, p)-pairs for which the economy is just specialized in producing the second commodity; and as λ approaches $\underline{\lambda}(k)$ the curve becomes arbitrarily close to $\underline{p}^s(k)$, the locus

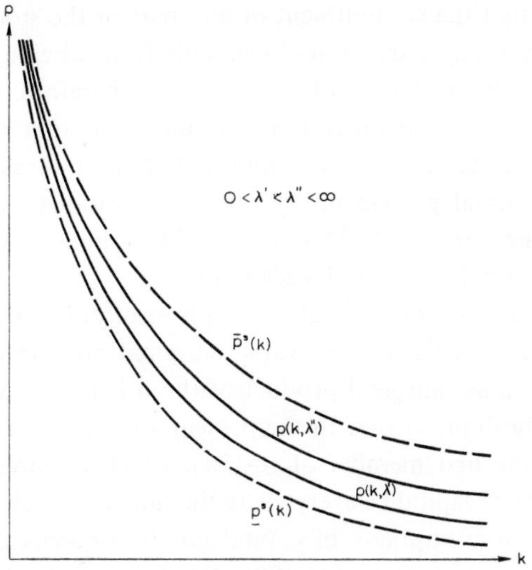

Fig. 6.5(d).

of (k, p)-pairs for which the economy is just specialized in producing the first commodity. Figure 6.5(d) provides an illustration. Next we superimpose Figure 6.5(d) on Figure 6.5(c) and note that the slope of the curve $\dot{k} = 0$ is algebraically greater than the slope of the curves $p(k, \lambda)$. We see that for every permissible λ (that is, every λ for which incomplete specialization is possible) there exists a k such that $\dot{k} = 0$, and that the relationship between λ and k is monotonic increasing.

Putting together this information with what we already know about the behavior of $\dot{k}$ when the economy is completely specialized, we obtain at last the locus $\dot{k} = 0$ of Figure 6.3(b). (The negatively-sloped segment is borrowed from the curve $\underline{\lambda}(k)$.) When we add the curve $\dot{\lambda} = 0$, which is the same as in Figure 6.3(a), we have all of the ingredients for the construction of the phase diagram. Again the two curves $\dot{k} = 0$ and $\dot{\lambda} = 0$ intersect at the golden rule point (k^*, λ^*); and that point is, again, a saddlepoint in the set of pairs of functions which satisfy the necessary conditions of an optimum. Again there is for each $k(0)$ a unique trajectory which converges on the golden rule path.

6.3. The capital good immobile between industries

Throughout Section 6.2 it was assumed that the stock of capital could be moved from one sector to the other without cost and without delay; that is, it was assumed that the commitment of any part of the stock to a sector is tentative only and may later be undone. This is an obviously extreme and unrealistic assumption. To restore perspective, therefore, we shall in the present section adopt the other polar assumption, that equipment once committed to a sector is forever committed. Earlier investigations of the conditions of optimal growth under this assumption have been made by Bose [6], Chakravarty [9], Dasgupta [12], Johansen [23] and, most recently and most helpfully, by Ryder [31].

In effect there are now *two* capital goods, physically identical but committed to different industries. Clearly the value marginal product of one need not be equal to the value marginal product of the other, even when something is produced by both industries. In the present section, therefore, there is no counterpart to the first member of (6-17a), which requires that the value marginal product of capital be everywhere the same. A much more important implication of the multiplicity of capital goods concerns the feasibility of controlling the economy by means of commodity prices only. Thus suppose that, as in Section 6.2, the Planning Authority is attempting to control a market economy by regulating the commodity price ratio, that the prevailing price ratio and distribution of capital between industries happen to be such that the two value marginal products are equal, and that investors are short-sightedly guided solely by the current value marginal productivity of capital in the two industries. Then it is a matter of indifference to individual investors where their newly formed equipment takes root. Thus the competitive allocation of new capital is indeterminate and the economy cannot be kept on an optimal course merely by exercising control over commodity prices. Nor can the difficulty be overcome by endowing investors with some degree of foresight. Suppose, for example, that investors base their decisions both on the two current value marginal products of capital and on the (accurately foreseen) rates at which the prices of the two types of capital change. Then it is easy to describe circumstances in which the same indeterminacy occurs.

The indeterminacy can be avoided in either of two ways. One might introduce suitably restrictive assumptions concerning private investment decisions. In Problem 3 the reader is asked to examine in detail the implications of one set of assumptions. In the present section, on the other hand, we suppose that the Planning Authority takes under its direct control each of the four relevant factor allocations – the allocation of labor and newly produced equipment to each of the two industries – and seeks the optimal time path of each. The allocation of labor determines the rate at which the aggregate stock of capital grows; the flow of newly formed equipment must then be channeled to the two industries.

Having changed our assumptions, we must slightly modify and extend our notation. In Section 6.2 we found it convenient to merge the separate identities of K_j and L_j and to work with the industrial factor ratio $k_j \equiv K_j/L_j$. Under our new assumptions, however, the numerator and the denominator of that expression play quite dissimilar roles: at any moment of time K_j is given, beyond the Authority's control; but this is not true of L_j. If we are to avoid confusion we must adopt a notation which allows us to follow the separate histories of the two variables. To this end we define

$$m_j \equiv K_j/L \tag{6-38}$$

and write the production relationships as

$$y_j = l_j \psi_j(m_j/l_j). \tag{6-39}$$

It will be convenient, however, to submerge the l_j's and write

$$l = L_2/L. \tag{6-40}$$

Similarly, we denote by

$$v = \dot{K}_2/Y_2$$

the proportion of newly formed equipment flowing to the second industry. The proportion of newly formed equipment flowing to the first industry is then $1 - v$, and the proportion of the labor force engaged by the first industry is $1 - l$. In terms of this new notation we have

$$\begin{aligned}\dot{m}_1 &= \frac{\mathrm{d}}{\mathrm{d}t}(K_1/L)\\ &= (1 - v)l\psi_2(m_2/l) - \gamma m_1\end{aligned}$$

and

$$\begin{aligned}\dot{m}_2 &= \frac{\mathrm{d}}{\mathrm{d}t}(K_2/L)\\ &= vl\psi_2(m_2/l) - \gamma m_2.\end{aligned}$$

We now notice a further important implication of our new assumptions: that it can never be optimal to specialize completely in producing consumption goods. [(6-25) still ensures that it can never be optimal to specialize completely in producing capital goods.] Suppose the contrary, that at some point of time it is optimal to specialize completely. Then from the restrictions (6-5) placed on the production functions the marginal product of labor in the second industry is infinite. Hence the indirect marginal product of labor in producing capital goods *times* the marginal product of capital in producing consumption goods, is infinite. From the continuity of the utility function it then follows that the utility integral must increase if a sufficiently small amount of labor is transferred from the first to the second industry. The same argument holds for all points in the planning interval. Hence we may restrict l to lie in the open interval (0, 1).

Our problem may now be stated as that of finding

$$\max_{v,l} \int_0^\infty U((1 - l)\psi_1(m_1/(1 - l)))\mathrm{d}t \tag{6-41}$$

subject to the constraints

$$\dot{m}_1 = (1 - v)l\psi_2(m_2/l) - \gamma m_1 \tag{6-42}$$

$$\dot{m}_2 = vl\psi_2(m_2/l) - \gamma m_2 \tag{6-43}$$

$$m_j(0) = m_j^0 \tag{6-44}$$

$$0 \leq v \leq 1 \tag{6-45}$$

$$0 < l < 1 \tag{6-46}$$

Since $\mathscr{V}$ does not depend on t or the state variables m_j, our problem lies within the scope of Theorems 4.3.1 and 4.3.2. Consider the Hamiltonian expression

$$\begin{aligned} H(m_1, m_2, \lambda_1, \lambda_2, l, v) \equiv\ & U((1 - l)\psi_1(m_1/(1 - l))) \\ & + \lambda_1[(1 - v)l\psi_2(m_2/l) - \gamma m_1] \\ & + \lambda_2[vl\psi_2(m_2/l) - \gamma m_2] \end{aligned} \tag{6-47}$$

and the associated

$$M(m_1, m_2, \lambda_1, \lambda_2) = \sup_{\substack{0 \leqslant v \leqslant 1 \\ 0 < l < 1}} H(m_1, m_2, \lambda_1, \lambda_2, l, v). \tag{6-48}$$

The multipliers λ_j may be interpreted as the utility per unit of investment per capita in the jth industry, that is, as the community's demand price, in terms of utility, of equipment installed in the jth industry. It follows that H itself may be interpreted as the utility of total output per capita. As our 'instantaneous' condition of optimality we have

$$M(m_1, m_2, \lambda_1, \lambda_2) = H(m_1, m_2, \lambda_1, \lambda_2, l, v). \tag{6-49}$$

From (6-45) and (6-49) we deduce that

$$\textit{if}\ \frac{\partial H}{\partial v} \equiv (\lambda_2 - \lambda_1) l\psi_2(m_2/l)\ \textit{is} \begin{Bmatrix} > & 0 \\ = & 0 \\ < & 0 \end{Bmatrix}\ \textit{then} \begin{Bmatrix} v = 1 \\ 0 \leq v \leq 1 \\ v = 0 \end{Bmatrix}. \tag{6-49a}$$

And from (6-46) and (6-49) we deduce that

$$\frac{\partial H}{\partial l} \equiv -U' \cdot [\psi_1 - (m_1/(1-l))\psi_1'] + [\lambda_1(1-v) + \lambda_2 v][\psi_2 - (m_2/l)\psi_2'] = 0. \tag{6-49b}$$

To (6-49) must be added the further necessary conditions

$$\dot{m}_1 = \frac{\partial H}{\partial \lambda_1} = (1-v) l\psi_2(m_2/l) - \gamma m_1 \tag{6-50}$$

$$\dot{m}_2 = \frac{\partial H}{\partial \lambda_2} = v l\psi_2(m_2/l) - \gamma m_2 \tag{6-51}$$

$$\dot{\lambda}_1 = -\frac{\partial H}{\partial m_1} = -U'\psi_1' + \lambda_1\gamma \tag{6-52}$$

$$\dot{\lambda}_2 = -\frac{\partial H}{\partial m_2} = -\lambda_1(1-v)\psi_2' - \lambda_2(v\psi_2' - \gamma) \tag{6-53}$$

$$m_j(0) = m_j^0 \tag{6-54}$$

$$0 \leq v \leq 1 \tag{6-55}$$

$$0 < l < 1 \tag{6-56}$$

$$\lim_{t\to\infty} \lambda_j(t) = 0. \tag{6-57}$$

The conditions of Theorem 5.7.2 are satisfied; hence any control $(l(t), v(t))$ and the associated $m_j(t)$ and $\lambda_j(t)$ which satisfy the necessary conditions (6-49) to (6-57) and yield a relative maximum of $\int U dt$ also yield an absolute maximum.

We have three cases to consider according as $\lambda_1 \gtreqless \lambda_2$. In each case the dynamic behavior of the system has its characteristic pattern. In the *first case* $\lambda_1 > \lambda_2$. From (6-49a),

$$v = 0. \tag{6-58}$$

Hence, from (6-49b),

$$U' \cdot [\psi_1 - (m_1/(1 - l))\psi_1'] = \lambda_1[\psi_2 - (m_2/l)\psi_2'] \tag{6-59}$$

and

$$\lambda_1 > 0. \tag{6-60}$$

Conditions (6-50) to (6-53) then take the special forms

$$\dot{m}_1 = l\psi_2 - \gamma m_1 \tag{6-61}$$

$$\dot{m}_2 = -\gamma m_2 \tag{6-62}$$

$$\dot{\lambda}_1 = -U'\psi_1' + \lambda_1\gamma \tag{6-63}$$

and

$$\dot{\lambda}_2 = -\lambda_1\psi_2' + \lambda_2\gamma \tag{6-64}$$

respectively.

In the *second case* $\lambda_1 < \lambda_2$. From (6-49a)

$$v = 1. \tag{6-65}$$

Hence, from (6-49b),

$$U' \cdot [\psi_1 - (m_1/(1 - l))\psi_1'] = \lambda_2[\psi_2 - (m_2/l)\psi_2'] \tag{6-66}$$

and

$$\lambda_2 > 0. \tag{6-67}$$

Conditions (6-50) to (6-53) then take the special forms

$$\dot{m}_1 = -\gamma m_1 \tag{6-68}$$

$$\dot{m}_2 = l\psi_2 - \gamma m_2 \tag{6-69}$$

$$\dot{\lambda}_1 = -U'\psi_1' + \lambda_1\gamma \tag{6-70}$$

and

$$\dot{\lambda}_2 = -\lambda_2(\psi_2' - \gamma) \tag{6-71}$$

respectively.

In the *third case* $\lambda_1 = \lambda_2$. Hence, from (6-49a) and (6-49b),

$$0 \leq v \leq 1 \tag{6-72}$$

$$U' \cdot [\psi_1 - (m_1/(1 - l))\psi_1'] = \lambda_j[\psi_2 - (m_2/l)\psi_2'] \tag{6-73}$$

and

$$\lambda_1 = \lambda_2 > 0. \tag{6-74}$$

Moreover, conditions (6-50) to (6-53) take the special forms

$$\dot{m}_1 = (1 - v)l\psi_2 - \gamma m_1 \tag{6-75}$$

$$\dot{m}_2 = vl\psi_2 - \gamma m_2 \tag{6-76}$$

$$\dot{\lambda}_1 = - U'\psi'_1 + \lambda_j\gamma \tag{6-77}$$

and

$$\dot{\lambda}_2 = - \lambda_j(\psi'_2 - \gamma) \tag{6-78}$$

respectively.

We examine the three cases in turn.

Case 1: Consider equations (6-61) and (6-62). Clearly $m_2(t)$ goes monotonically to zero. $m_1(t)$, on the other hand, may increase initially; indeed for any $m_1(0)$ there always exists a sufficiently large initial value of m_2 such that $\dot{m}_1$ must be positive. But $\dot{m}_1$ cannot remain positive indefinitely. Suppose the contrary. Then K_1 must grow faster than L indefinitely; and this is impossible. In the long run, indeed, K_1 cannot even grow as fast as L. Thus eventually $m_1(t)$ must decline and approach zero. Possible trajectories are displayed in Figure 6.6. Notice that all paths converge on $m_1 = 0$,

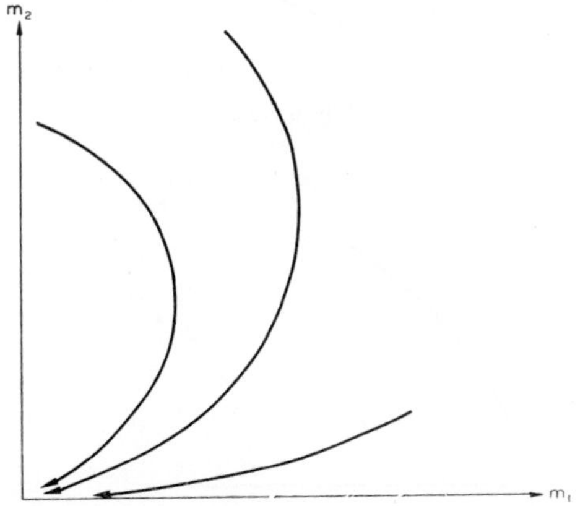

Fig. 6.6.

implying that consumption per capita goes to zero and 'instantaneous' utility to minus infinity. It is clear therefore that the optimal path cannot be forever of the type displayed in Figure 6.6. We shall see, however, that it may be of this type during one or more finite time intervals.

Case 2: Consider equations (6-68) and (6-69). Clearly $m_1(t)$ goes asymptotically to zero. The possible trajectories of $m_2(t)$ are a little more difficult to chart. If $l = 0$, $\dot{m}_2 = -\gamma m_2$ and the paths of $m_1(t)$ and $m_2(t)$ are as displayed in Figure 6.7(a). If, at the other extreme, $l = 1$, $\dot{m}_2 = \psi_2(m_2) - \gamma m_2$ and m_2 rises or falls according as it falls short of or exceeds its permanently maintainable level m_2^0, where m_2^0 is defined by $\psi_2(m_2^0) = \gamma m_2^0$. The possible paths of $m_1(t)$ and $m_2(t)$ are displayed in Figure 6.7(b). Suppose, finally, that $l = \bar{l}$ where $0 < \bar{l} < 1$. Then from (6-69) we see that

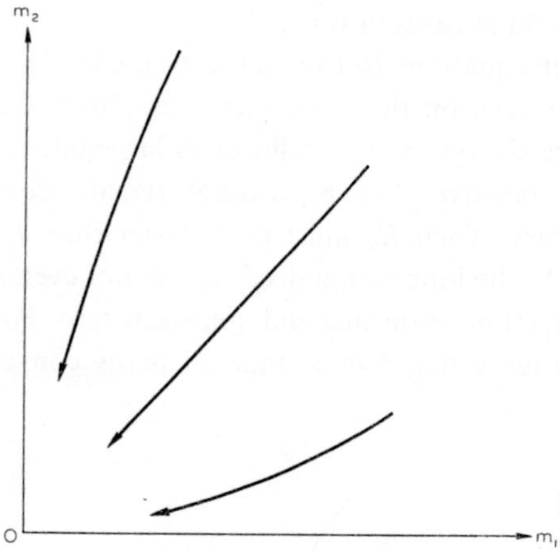

Fig. 6.7(a).

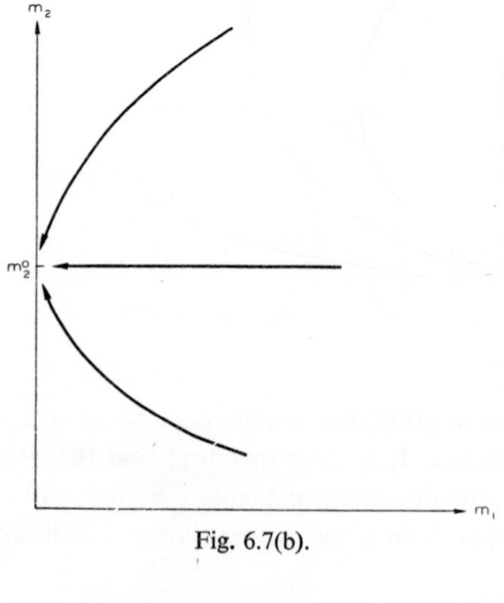

Fig. 6.7(b).

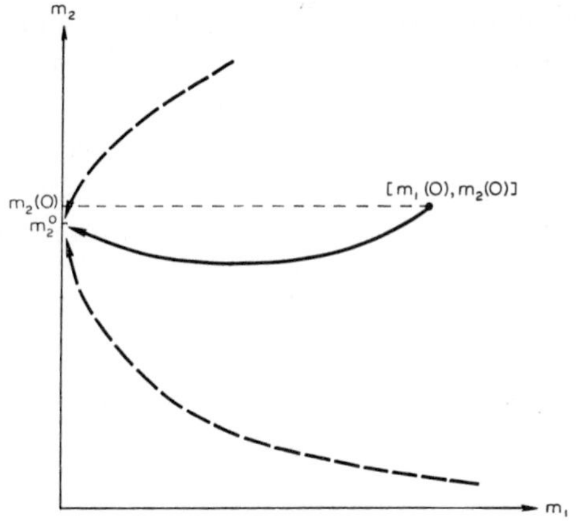

Fig. 6.7(c).

there exists some critical value of m_2, say $0 < \overline{m}_2 < m_2^0$, defined by $\overline{l}\psi_2(\overline{m}_2/\overline{l}) = \gamma\overline{m}_2$, such that $\dot{m}_2 \gtreqless 0$ as $m_2 \lesseqgtr \overline{m}_2$. Figure 6.8 illustrates. (As $\overline{l} \to 0$, $\overline{m}_2 \to 0$; as $\overline{l} \to 1$, $\overline{m}_2 \to m_2^0$.) If l were held at $\overline{l}$, $m_2(t)$ would approach $\overline{m}_2$ monotonically. But $l(t)$ is not constant. From (6-66) and the fact that $\lim_{t\to\infty} m_1(t) = 0$ we see that, provided U'/λ_2 does not go to infinity as $t \to \infty$, $\lim_{t\to\infty} l(t) = 1$. Thus $m_2(t)$ is chasing a moving target; and while the target variable approaches m_2^0 monotonically, the same is not necessarily true of m_2 itself. Suppose that $m_2(0) > m_2^0$; then in particular it is possible for $m_2(t)$ to at first decline, to overshoot m_2^0, and to later approach m_2^0 from below. The heavy line in Figure 6.7(c) illustrates this possibility; the dotted

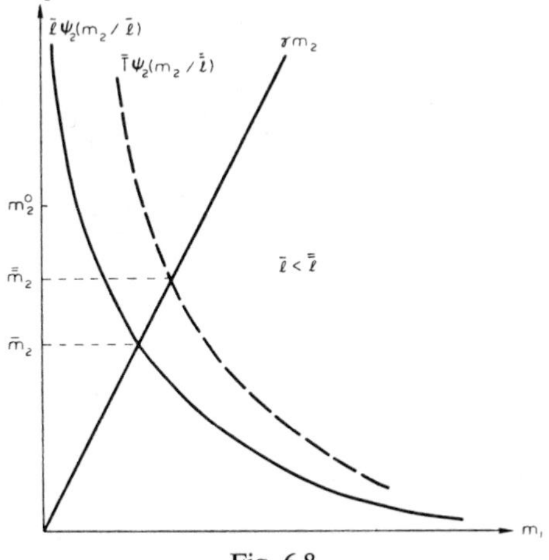

Fig. 6.8.

curves indicate trajectories associated with alternative initial values of the m_j. Now we know already that along an optimal trajectory $0 < l < 1$. To the extent that Case 2 is relevant at all, therefore, the optimal trajectory must be described by a curve from Figure 6.7(c), not by a curve from Figure 6.7(a) or Figure 6.7(b). On the other hand, in Figure 6.7(c) all paths converge on $m_1 = 0$, implying that the optimal path cannot be forever of this type.

Case 3: From (6-74), (6-77) and (6-78)

$$U'\psi_1' = \lambda_2\psi_2'. \tag{6-79}$$

And, from (6-73) and (6-79), the marginal rate of substitution between labor and capital is the same everywhere:

$$\omega = \frac{\psi_1 - \dfrac{m_1}{1-l}\psi_1'}{\psi_1'} = \frac{\psi_2 - \dfrac{m_2}{l}\psi_2'}{\psi_2'}. \tag{6-80}$$

The economy therefore behaves just as though equipment were freely transferable from one industry to the other; the restriction on capital transfer is inoperative. In suitably modified form, the analysis of Section 6.2 carries over to this case. In particular we are assured that there exists a stationary saddlepoint with $0 \leq v \leq 1$. The phase diagrams displayed in Section 6.2, however, are in terms of $\lambda(t)$ and $k(t)$ and therefore do not conform to Figures 6.6 and 6.7. We seek now to construct a phase diagram in terms of

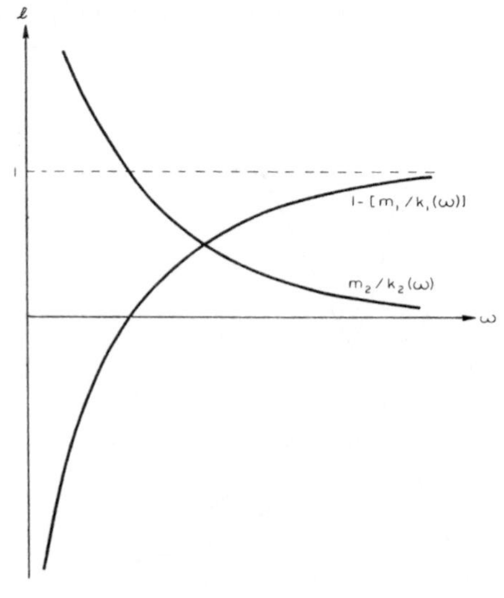

Fig. 6.9.

$m_1(t)$ and $m_2(t)$, fortified in the prior knowledge that a stationary point exists and is a saddlepoint.

The construction is an intricate one. We begin by noting that equations (6-80) can be solved uniquely for ω and l in terms of m_1 and m_2. Thus we know that (6-7) can be solved uniquely for k_1 and k_2 in terms of ω. (See, for example, Figure 6.2.) We know also that

$$k_j'(\omega) = -(\psi_j')^2/\psi_j\psi_j'' > 0. \tag{6-8}$$

But $k_1 \equiv m_1/(1 - l)$ and $k_2 \equiv m_2/l$, yielding two monotonic relations between l and ω, with asymptotic properties which ensure the existence of a solution. Figure 6.9 illustrates. From the identity

$$(m_1/k_1) + (m_2/k_2) = 1 \tag{6-81}$$

we then calculate that

$$\frac{\partial}{\partial m_j}\omega(m_1, m_2) = 1/k_j\left[\frac{m_1k_1'(\omega)}{k_1^2} + \frac{m_2k_2'(\omega)}{k_2^2}\right] > 0. \tag{6-82}$$

This inequality also emerges from Figure 6.9.

As our next step we construct the locus of (m_1, m_2)-values for which $\dot{\lambda}_1 = \dot{\lambda}_2 = 0$. From (6-78) we see that on this locus

$$\frac{\dot{\lambda}_j}{\lambda_j} = \gamma - \psi_2'(k_2(\omega)). \tag{6-83}$$

Thus $\dot{\lambda}_j = 0$ if and only if $\omega = \omega^*$, the stationary-state value of ω. If now we substitute the stationary-state values of k_1 and k_2 into (6-81) we obtain the required locus of (m_1, m_2)-values. It is of course a straight line. From (6-82), (6-75) and (6-76)

$$\begin{aligned}\dot{\omega} &= [(\dot{m}_1/k_1) + (\dot{m}_2/k_2)]\Big/\left[\frac{m_1k_1'(\omega)}{k_1^2} + \frac{m_2k_2'(\omega)}{k_2^2}\right] \\ &= k_1k_2\left\{\frac{[v(k_1 - k_2) + k_2]l\psi_2 - \gamma(k_2m_1 + k_1m_2)}{m_1k_2^2k_1'(\omega) + m_2k_1^2k_2'(\omega)}\right\}.\end{aligned} \tag{6-84}$$

Thus, when $\dot{\lambda}_j = 0$,

$$v = \frac{\gamma(k_2m_1 + k_1m_2) - kl\psi_2}{(k_1 - k_2)l\psi_2}$$

or, more conveniently,

$$v = \frac{\gamma k_2}{\psi_2} - \frac{k_2}{k_1 - k_2} + \frac{\gamma k_2^2}{(k_1 - k_2)\psi_2}\left(\frac{m_1 + m_2}{m_2}\right) \tag{6-85}$$

where along the locus $\dot{\lambda}_j = 0$ the first and second terms on the right are constants. Suppose now that m_2 increases along the locus $\dot{\lambda}_j = 0$, beginning at m_2^* where $v = \gamma m_2/l\psi_2$ and $\dot{m}_2 = 0$. From (6-85) the new value of v is greater or less than $\gamma m_2/l\psi_2$ as $k_1 \gtrless k_2$; hence, from (6-76),

$$\textit{if} \quad k_1 \gtrless k_2 \quad \textit{then} \quad \dot{m}_2 \gtrless 0. \tag{6-86}$$

Next we construct the locus of (m_1, m_2)-values for which

$$\dot{m}_1 + \dot{m}_2 = l\psi_2 - \gamma(m_1 + m_2) = 0. \tag{6-87}$$

The locus obviously begins at the origin. Rewriting (6-87) as

$$\frac{\psi_2(k_2) - \gamma k_2}{\gamma k_2} = \frac{1 - l}{l} \cdot \frac{k_1}{k_2} \tag{6-88}$$

we see that there exists a $k_2 > 0$ and therefore an associated $\omega > 0$, say k_2^0 and ω^0, such that the left hand side vanishes. The pair $(k_1, k_2) = (0, k_2^0)$ therefore satisfies (6-88), and the point $(m_1, m_2) = (0, k_2^0)$ lies on the locus. (Recall that at that point $l = 1$.) Beginning at the origin the locus is at first positively sloped and then negatively sloped, as in Figures 6.10(a) and 6.10(b). To the right of the locus $\dot{m}_1 + \dot{m}_2 < 0$, to the left of the locus $\dot{m}_1 + \dot{m}_2 > 0$:

$$\frac{\partial}{\partial m_1}(\dot{m}_1 + \dot{m}_2) < 0. \tag{6-89}$$

The two loci intersect at the stationary point (m_1^*, m_2^*) and divide the positive quadrant into four regions, each with its characteristic motion of

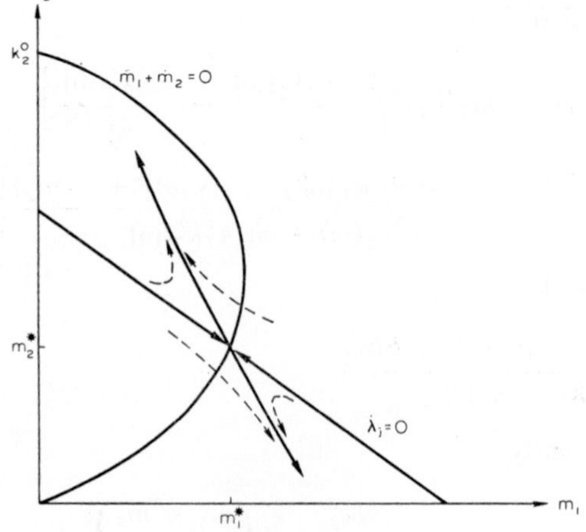

Fig. 6.10(a).

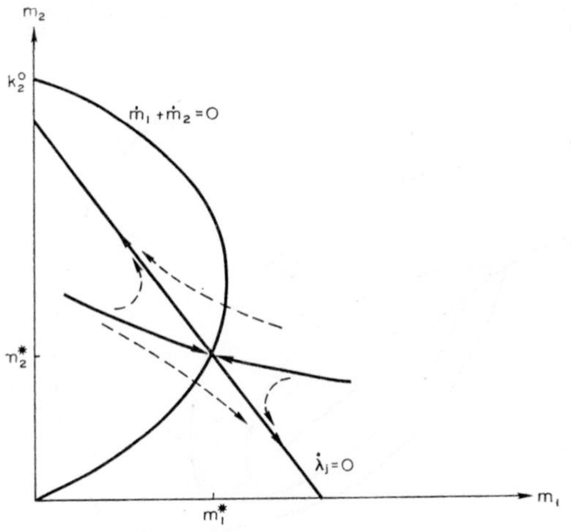

Fig. 6.10(b).

$m_1(t)$ and $m_2(t)$. The information contained in (6-86) and (6-89) is sufficient to determine the motion of $m_1(t)$ and $m_2(t)$ in each region. Figures 6.10(a) and 6.10(b) illustrate.

That concludes our discussion of Case 3.

We have at hand the materials from which to piece together the optimal path. We know that the optimal path cannot be forever of Type 1 (Figure 6.6) or of Type 2 (Figure 6.7(c)). Nor can it be of Types 1 and 2 for a non-converging infinite sum of finite intervals. Nor, as will become clear presently, can it be of Types 1 and 2 for a converging infinite sum of finite intervals. The optimal path must eventually be of Type 3 and converge on (m_1^*, m_2^*) along one or other of the stable arms of the saddle. It is even possible for the optimal path to begin on, and never depart from, one of those arms. For this outcome, however, it is necessary both that $m_1(0)$ and $m_2(0)$ be in exactly the right ratio one to the other and also that they be sufficiently close to the stationary values m_1^* and m_2^*. If either condition is violated, part of the optimal trajectory must be of Type 1 and/or Type 2. Suppose, for example, that the first industry is relatively capital-intensive and that $(m_1(0), m_2(0))$ lies in the locus $\dot{\lambda}_j = 0$ of Figure 6.10(a). Then, from (6-85), for sufficiently small m_1, $v < 0$ and, for sufficiently small m_2, $v > 1$. A similar proof can be constructed for the case in which the first industry is relatively labor-intensive.

Drawing upon these observations we see that, when the first industry is relatively capital-intensive, the motion of $(m_1(t), m_2(t))$ must be as depicted in Figure 6.11(a). From the initial point $(m_1(0), m_2(0))$, for example, we

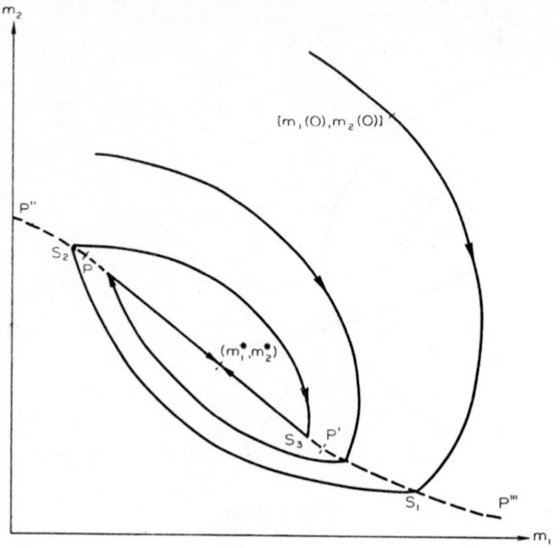

Fig. 6.11(a).

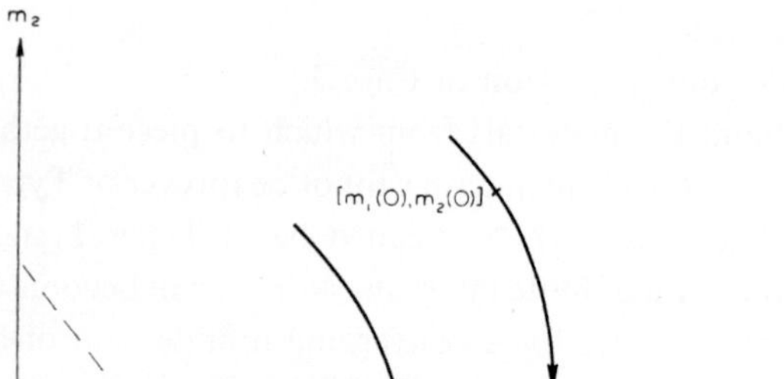

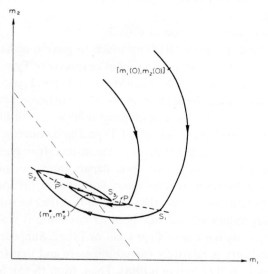

Fig. 6.11(b).

travel optimally by a path of Type 1 until we reach the switching point S_1. We then journey along a path of Type 2 until a second switching point S_2 is reached. We next travel by another path of Type 1 until S_3 is reached. The journey is completed along the lower of the two arms of the saddle. The straight line PP' is that part of the locus $\dot{p} = 0$ of Figure 6.10(a) for which $0 \leqq v(m_1, m_2) \leqq 1$. The switching points all lie on PP' or on the dotted extensions of PP', PP'' and $P'P'''$. That these extensions must veer away from the locus $\dot{\lambda}_j = 0$ in the manner shown can be seen by reflecting that, as m_1 (or m_2) decreases along the locus $\dot{\lambda}_j = 0$, $v(m_1, m_2)$ eventually reaches zero (or one), implying that we are on the boundary of a region in which the optimal motion is of Type 1 (or Type 2). Finally, we confirm an earlier statement by noticing that PP' is not degenerate and that therefore endless switching back and forth between paths of Type 1 and paths of Type 2 must occupy endless or infinite time.

The phase diagram for the case in which the first industry is relatively labor-intensive is quite similar. See Figure 6.11(b). Notice, however, that this time the curve PP' does not form part of the locus $\dot{\lambda}_j = 0$ and therefore is not necessarily a straight-line segment. The locus $\dot{\lambda}_j = 0$ of Figure 6-10(b) is reproduced as the dashed straight line of Figure 6-11(b).

6.4. Final remarks

In this final section we provide some references and a few brief and fairly obvious remarks concerning the possibility of relaxing the assumption that the state of the arts is constant and concerning the implications of plan review. Technical improvements of a purely labor-augmenting kind can be easily accommodated provided they accrue exponentially and are not biased towards particular industries or particular 'vintages' of equipment; in many respects, indeed, such improvements are equivalent to a once-over increase in the rate of population growth. Other kinds of steady improvements may also be handled, but only at the cost of added complexity. For detail the interested reader may refer to Brock and Gale [7].

It is not difficult to see that when the utility functional is of the form

$$\int_0^\infty e^{-\delta t} U(c(t)) \mathrm{d}t,$$

$\delta \geq 0$, the review of a plan can never result in regret concerning its past implementation or in the revision of its unexpired part. If at time $t = 0$ it was optimal to plan to move along one of the stable branches of a saddle point, that is still so; the only change is in the initial condition imposed on k. Nor are matters different if the utility functional has the form

$$\int_0^T e^{-\delta t} U(c(t)) \mathrm{d}t,$$

$\delta \geq 0$, *provided T is given once and for all.* Suppose, however, that T is fixed not in relation to the calendar but in relation to the point in time at which the plan is reviewed. Then regret and revision are inevitable. Each 'generation' is concerned with a planning interval which only partly overlaps that of its predecessor. It views any particular point in time in the light of its own peculiar set of initial conditions and has to plan for points which did not concern its predecessor. The interesting questions then concern the actual regret- and revision-ridden time path of the economy. On these questions the reader may consult Strotz [37], Goldman [14] and [15], and Pollak [29].

Problems

1. Suppose that, for all ω, $k_1(\omega) = k_2(\omega)$. Is it still possible to guide the economy by means of $p(t)$?

2. Generalize the analysis of these sections by introducing labor-augmenting technical progress and exponential (or 'radio-active') depreciation.

3. Suppose that capital is not transferable between industries and, following Inada [23], let us introduce an investment function

$$v = V(K_1, K_2, \psi'_1, p\psi'_2)$$

where v is the proportion of newly formed capital allocated to the second industry (so that $1 - v$ is the proportion allocated to the second industry) and where ψ'_1 and $p\psi'_2$ are, respectively, the marginal productivity of capital in the first and second industries, in terms of the first or consumption good. Suppose that V is a continuous function of its arguments and that, when $\psi'_1 \lesseqqgtr p\psi'_2$, $V \gtreqqless K_2/(K_1 + K_2)$. Show that, when $v = V$, the economy can be controlled by means of the ratio of commodity prices only. Derive the necessary conditions for an optimal time path $p(t)$ and describe the properties of the path in terms of a suitable phase diagram. Is the optimal path equivalent to that described in Section 6.3?

Appendix I

Uniqueness of the utility functional and the utility function

In Chapter 2 we introduced the notion of a utility functional $\mathscr{U}[C(t)]$, which is a real-valued functional defined on some function space of consumption functions. This functional provides a numerical measure of merit or desirability for a specified consumption pattern $C(t)$ over a given time interval $\mathscr{T}$, $\mathscr{T} = \{t | t_1 \leq t \leq t_2 \text{ (or } \infty)\}$, or over the union of several such intervals. The utility functionals used were always of the form

$$\mathscr{U}[C] = \int_{t_1}^{t_2} U(C(t))\mathrm{d}t \tag{AI-1}$$

where $U(C)$ is a real-valued function called an instantaneous utility function or utility rate. A utility functional defined in this way was said to be time additive. We now provide a general definition of time additivity for utility functionals.

Let $C_1(t)$ be a consumption function the domain of which is the time interval $\mathscr{T}_1$, and let $C_2(t)$ be a consumption function the domain of which is the time interval $\mathscr{T}_2$. Suppose that the time intervals do not overlap, so that $\mathscr{T}_1 \cap \mathscr{T}_2 = \emptyset$. Let us next define a consumption function $C_3(t)$ on the set of time values $\mathscr{T}_1 \cup \mathscr{T}_2$ as

$$C_3(t) = \begin{cases} C_1(t), & t \in \mathscr{T}_1 \\ C_2(t), & t \in \mathscr{T}_2. \end{cases} \tag{AI-2}$$

Then the utility functional $\mathscr{U}$ is time additive if

$$\mathscr{U}[C_3] = \mathscr{U}[C_1] + \mathscr{U}[C_2] \tag{AI-3}$$

for all $\mathscr{T}_1$ and $\mathscr{T}_2$ and all $C_1(t)$ and $C_2(t)$. Time additivity implies that contributions to the utility measure from consumption in different time intervals are additive. The particular type of utility functional defined by (AI-1) is additive since

$$\mathscr{U}[C_3] = \int_{\mathscr{T}_1 \cup \mathscr{T}_2} U(C_3)dt = \int_{\mathscr{T}_1} U(C_1)dt + \int_{\mathscr{T}_2} U(C_2)dt$$

$$= \mathscr{U}[C_1] + \mathscr{U}[C_2]. \quad \text{(AI-4)}$$

Suppose that we have a specified time additive utility functional $\mathscr{U}[C]$. Let us now define a new utility functional $\mathscr{U}^*[C]$ by the transformation

$$\mathscr{U}^*[C] = h(\mathscr{U}[C]) \quad \text{(AI-5)}$$

where h is a real-valued differentiable function of a real variable. *We shall prove that if $\mathscr{U}^*$ is also a legitimate time additive utility functional then $\mathscr{U}^*$ is obtained from $\mathscr{U}$ by a positive affine transformation, that is,*

$$\mathscr{U}^* = a\mathscr{U} + b, \quad a > 0. \quad \text{(AI-6)}$$

Furthermore any functional $\mathscr{U}^*$ given by (AI-6) is time additive if $\mathscr{U}$ is time additive and is a legitimate utility functional if $\mathscr{U}$ is legitimate. In other words, a time additive $\mathscr{U}$ is uniquely determined to the same extent that a thermometer scale is determined–only the zero point and unit of measure can be chosen arbitrarily.

The proof is not difficult. Let $C_1(t)$ be any consumption function not identically 0 and defined over $\mathscr{T}_1$, and let $C_2(t)$ be any consumption function not identically 0 and defined over $\mathscr{T}_2$, $\mathscr{T}_1 \cap \mathscr{T}_2 = \emptyset$. Consider next the consumption functions $C_1^* = \xi_1 C_1$, $\xi_1 > 0$, $C_2^* = \xi_2 C_2$, $\xi_2 > 0$; and let C_3^* be defined as in (AI-2). Then $\mathscr{U}[C_1^*]$ is a function $\Lambda_1(\xi_1)$ and $\mathscr{U}[C_2^*]$ is a function $\Lambda_2(\xi_2)$. If $\mathscr{U}$ is time additive then $\mathscr{U}[C_3^*]$ is a function $\Omega(\xi_1, \xi_2) = \Lambda_1(\xi_1) + \Lambda_2(\xi_2)$. We shall assume (as in the calculus of variations) that Λ_1 and Λ_2 are differentiable with respect to ξ_1 and ξ_2. Similarly, $\mathscr{U}^*[C_3^*]$ is a function $\Upsilon(\xi_1, \xi_2) = \Delta_1(\xi_1) + \Delta_2(\xi_2)$ if $\mathscr{U}^*$ is time additive. Thus by (AI-5)

$$\Upsilon(\xi_1, \xi_2) = h[\Omega(\xi_1, \xi_2)] = \Delta_1(\xi_1) + \Delta_2(\xi_2). \quad \text{(AI-7)}$$

On taking partial derivatives, we see immediately that

$$\frac{\partial^2 \Upsilon}{\partial \xi_1 \partial \xi_2} = h'' \Lambda_1' \Lambda_2' \equiv 0. \quad \text{(AI-8)}$$

Furthermore, $\Lambda_1' \neq 0$ and $\Lambda_2' \neq 0$. This holds for every C_1 and C_2. Thus $h'' \equiv 0$ over the range of $\mathscr{U}$, so that $h(x) = ax + b$. Therefore, $\mathscr{U}^* = a\mathscr{U} + b$ if $\mathscr{U}$ and $\mathscr{U}^*$ are time additive. Furthermore, if $\mathscr{U}^*$ is a legitimate utility functional then when $\mathscr{U}[C_\alpha] > \mathscr{U}[C_\beta]$ it must also be true that $\mathscr{U}^*[C_\alpha] > \mathscr{U}^*[C_\beta]$; hence $a > 0$. Thus (AI-6) holds.

Suppose now that $\mathscr{U}^* = a\mathscr{U} + b$, $a > 0$. Then $\mathscr{U}^*$ is time additive if $\mathscr{U}$ is time additive, and the same ordering of consumption paths is provided by $\mathscr{U}$ and $\mathscr{U}^*$. Thus $\mathscr{U}$ and $\mathscr{U}^*$ serve equally well as a utility functional. That completes the proof.

Suppose, finally, that two legitimate utility functionals $\mathscr{U}$ and $\mathscr{U}^*$ are both of the form (AI-1). Then

$$\int_{t_1}^{t_2} U^*(C)dt = \mathscr{U}^*[C] = a\mathscr{U}[C] + b$$

$$= a\int_{t_1}^{t_2} U(C)dt + b, \quad a > 0$$

and $\mathscr{U}^* = aU$, $a > 0$. Thus U is unique up to a positive scalar multiple, that is, to the unit of measure adopted.

Appendix II

Implicit function theorems

In this appendix we state without proof two implicit function theories which were relied on in the text. Theorem AII-1 is the better known and the proof can be found in many texts. Theorem AII-2 is less well known and the proof is not so easy to find. Proofs of both theorems are given in Bliss [5] and Hestenes [21].

Theorem AII-1. Consider the system of equations $h^u(\mathbf{r}, \mathbf{s}) = 0$, $u = 1, \ldots, m$, *where* $\mathbf{r}$ *is an m-component vector and* $\mathbf{s}$ *an n-component vector. Suppose that the point* $(\mathbf{r}_0, \mathbf{s}_0) \in \mathscr{E}^{m+n}$ *is a solution to the system of equations, so that* $h^u(\mathbf{r}_0, \mathbf{s}_0) = 0$, $u = 1, \ldots, m$; *that each* $h^u \in C^k$, $k \geq 1$, *in a* δ*-neighborhood of* $(\mathbf{r}_0, \mathbf{s}_0)$; *and that the Jacobian matrix* $\|\partial h^u/\partial r_i\|$ *of order m is nonsingular at* $(\mathbf{r}_0, \mathbf{s}_0)$. *Then there exists a vector-valued function* $\mathbf{\Lambda}(\mathbf{s}) = (\Lambda^1(\mathbf{s}), \ldots, \Lambda^m(\mathbf{s}))$ *and an* ε*-neighborhood* $\mathscr{D}$ *of* $\mathbf{s}_0$ *in* $\mathscr{E}^n$ *such that for each* $\mathbf{s}$ *in* $\mathscr{D}$, *the point* $(\mathbf{\Lambda}(\mathbf{s}), \mathbf{s})$ *is a solution to the system of equation* $h^u = 0$. *Also* $\mathbf{r}_0 = \mathbf{\Lambda}(\mathbf{s}_0)$. *Furthermore, over* $\mathscr{D}$, *the* Λ^q *have the same differentiability properties as the* h^u, *that is,* $\Lambda^q \in C^k$, $q = 1, \ldots, m$. *Finally, there exists a* $\theta > 0$, *such that, when* $\mathbf{s} \in \mathscr{D}$, $(\mathbf{\Lambda}(\mathbf{s}), \mathbf{s})$ *is the only solution to the equations* $h^u = 0$ *for this* $\mathbf{s}$ *with* $|\mathbf{r} - \mathbf{\Lambda}(\mathbf{s})| < \theta$.

There are several points concerning Theorem AII-1 that are worth bearing in mind. The theorem tells us something about the conditions under which it is possible to solve the equation $h^u = 0$ explicitly for the variables $\mathbf{r}$ in terms of the variables $\mathbf{s}$. It guarantees that under certain conditions a function $\mathbf{r} = \mathbf{\Lambda}(\mathbf{s})$ exists. It does not indicate how $\mathbf{\Lambda}$ may be determined. In general, the determination of $\mathbf{\Lambda}$ is difficult; it is only in very special cases that $\mathbf{\Lambda}$ can be expressed in terms of familiar functions. Furthermore, no indication is given as to how large the domain of $\mathbf{\Lambda}$ is. It is guaranteed that the domain of $\mathbf{\Lambda}$ includes an ε-neighborhood of $\mathbf{s}_0$, but ε may be extremely small. If the equations are linear, however, we know that the domain of $\mathbf{\Lambda}$ is all of $\mathscr{E}^n$.

Thus the theorem says nothing about the magnitude of ε, and gives no indication of how ε can be computed.

The second implicit function theorem is really a generalization of the first and includes it as a special case. Before stating Theorem AII-2 we shall define what is meant by an ε-neighborhood of a set. This is a generalization of the notion of an ε-neighborhood of a point. Let $\mathscr{A}$ be any non-null set in $\mathscr{E}^n$. An ε-neighborhood $\mathscr{N}$ of $\mathscr{A}$ is the set of all points in $\mathscr{E}^n$ with the

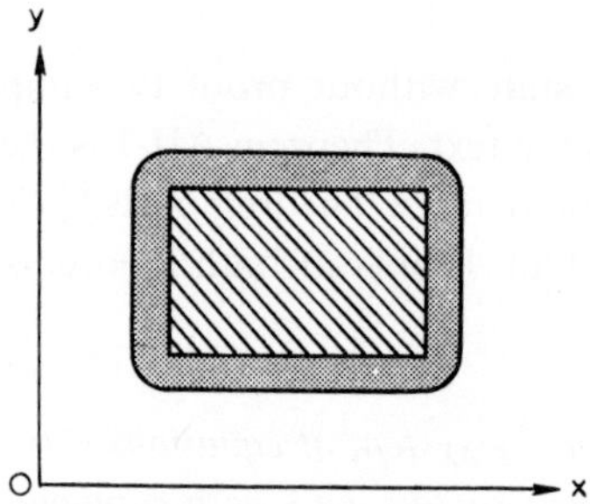

Fig. AII.1.

characteristic that if $\mathbf{x} \in \mathscr{N}$, then there is a point $\mathbf{y} \in \mathscr{A}$ such that $|\mathbf{x} - \mathbf{y}| < \varepsilon$, so that $\mathscr{N}$ contains all points the distance of which from at least one point in $\mathscr{A}$ is less than ε. Note that $\mathscr{A} \subset \mathscr{N}$. If in Figure AII.1 $\mathscr{A}$ is the cross-hatched rectangle then an ε-neighborhood of $\mathscr{A}$ consists of the rectangle plus the shaded band. A special case, of interest to us in the text, is that in

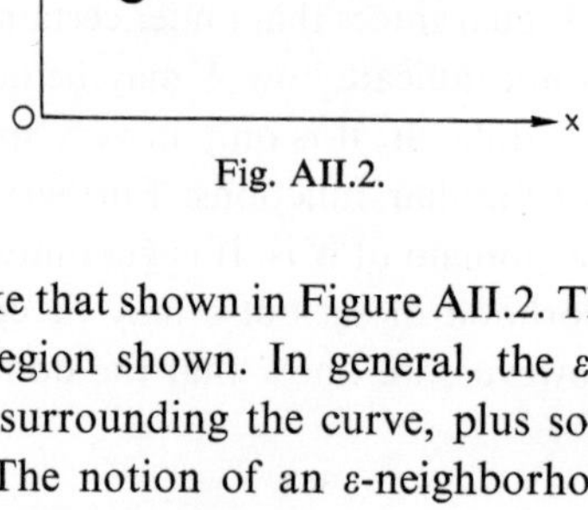

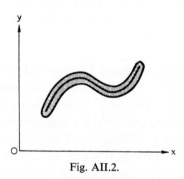

Fig. AII.2.

which $\mathscr{A}$ is a curve, like that shown in Figure AII.2. Then an ε-neighborhood of $\mathscr{A}$ is the shaded region shown. In general, the ε-neighborhood can be thought of as a tube surrounding the curve, plus some overlap at the end points of the curve. The notion of an ε-neighborhood of a set is used in

Theorem AII-2. The notion of continuity employed in the theorem is that introduced in Problem 19 for Section 2.3.

Theorem AII-2. Let $\mathscr{S}$ be a closed and bounded set in $\mathscr{E}^n$. Suppose that there exists a vector-valued function $\mathbf{\Omega}(\mathbf{s})$ *which has $\mathscr{S}$ as a domain, the m components of which are continuous over $\mathscr{S}$, and which has the characteristic that, for each* $\mathbf{s} \in \mathscr{S}$, *the point* $(\mathbf{\Omega}(\mathbf{s}), \mathbf{s})$ *is a solution to the equations* $h^u(\mathbf{r}, \mathbf{s}) = 0, u = 1, \ldots, m$. *Let us denote by $\mathscr{P}$ the set of points* $(\mathbf{\Omega}(\mathbf{s}), \mathbf{s})$, $\mathbf{s} \in \mathscr{S}$, *and suppose that there exists a δ-neighborhood of $\mathscr{P}$ such that each* $h^u \in C^k$, $k \geq 1$, *over this neighborhood, and that the Jacobian matrix* $\|\partial h^u/\partial r_i\|$ *is nonsingular at each point in $\mathscr{P}$. Then there exists a vector-valued function* $\mathbf{\Lambda}(\mathbf{s})$ *the domain of which is an ε-neighborhood $\mathscr{D}$ of $\mathscr{S}$, such that for each* $\mathbf{s} \in \mathscr{D}$, $(\mathbf{\Lambda}(\mathbf{s}), \mathbf{s})$ *is a solution to the system of equations* $h^u = 0$. *Furthermore, if* $\mathbf{s} \in \mathscr{S}$, $\mathbf{\Lambda}(\mathbf{s}) = \mathbf{\Omega}(\mathbf{s})$. *Also, the components Λ^i of* $\mathbf{\Lambda}$ *satisfy* $\Lambda^i \in C^k$ *over $\mathscr{D}$. Finally, there exists a* $\theta > 0$ *such that, when* $\mathbf{s} \in \mathscr{D}$, $(\mathbf{\Lambda}(\mathbf{s}), \mathbf{s})$ *is the only solution to the equations* $h^u = 0$ *for this* $\mathbf{s}$ *with* $|\mathbf{r} - \mathbf{\Lambda}(\mathbf{s})| < \theta$.

Appendix III

Existence theorems for systems of ordinary differential equations

In some of the proofs of the text it was necessary to make use of certain of the basic existence theorems for ordinary differential equations. We shall state these theorems here without proof. A good reference for ordinary differential equations, which includes clear and complete proofs of these existence theorems, is Pontryagin [28]. The existence theorems are always stated for a system of first order differential equations which can be written in the form

$$\mathbf{y}' = \mathbf{f}(x, \mathbf{y}). \tag{AIII-1}$$

We shall suppose that (AIII-1) represents a system of n, in general non-linear, first order differential equations. It will be assumed that the compo-ponents of $\mathbf{f}$ are continuous and have continuous first partial derivatives with respect to the variables $\mathbf{y}$ over some open convex set $\mathscr{R}$ in $\mathscr{E}^{n+1}$. By a solution to (AIII-1) over a specified interval we mean a vector-valued function $\mathbf{y}(x)$ which has continuous components, for which $\mathbf{y}'(x)$ exists with continuous components, and which satisfies the differential equation for each x in the interval.

Theorem AIII-1. Existence of a Solution Through a Given Initial Point. Let $(x_0, \mathbf{y}_0)$ *be any point in* $\mathscr{R}$. *Then there exists a unique solution to (AIII-1) passing through* $(x_0, \mathbf{y}_0)$. *This solution will be defined over an interval* $|x-x_0| < \varepsilon$ *for some* $\varepsilon > 0$.

When it is stated that there is a unique solution $\mathbf{y}(x)$ passing through $(x_0, \mathbf{y}_0)$, it is meant that there exists one and only one solution with $\mathbf{y}_0 = \mathbf{y}(x_0)$. Note that the above existence theorem says nothing about the length of the interval over which the solution is defined except that it is positive. The interval may be very short. When the system of equations is linear, however, much more precise statements are possible.

Theorem AIII-2. Existence Theorem for Linear Differential Equations. Suppose that the system of differential equations (AIII-1) is linear and

$$\mathbf{y}' = \mathbf{A}(x)\mathbf{y} + \mathbf{B}(x). \tag{AIII-2}$$

Suppose also that the elements of the matrices $\mathbf{A}(x)$ *and* $\mathbf{B}(x)$ *are all continuous over the interval* $\alpha \leq x \leq \beta$. *Then through each point* $(x_0, \mathbf{y}_0)$ *with* $\alpha \leq x_0 \leq \beta$, *there exists a unique solution to (AIII-2) which is defined over the entire interval* $\alpha \leq x \leq \beta$. *In the event that the elements of* $\mathbf{A}(x)$ *and* $\mathbf{B}(x)$ *are constants, then through each point in* $\mathscr{E}^{n+1}$ *there passes a unique solution which is defined for all x, i.e. for* $-\infty < x < \infty$.

In the statement of Theorem AIII-1 there are no assumptions about the existence of solutions to the system (AIII-1). Suppose now that we are told that there exists a solution $\mathbf{y}(x)$ to (AIII-1) defined over the interval $x_0 \leq x \leq x_1$. Theorem (AIII-1) guarantees that through each point in $\mathscr{R}$ there passes a unique solution which is defined over some, perhaps very short, interval. Now, however, for points close to the curve $\mathbf{y}(x)$ we can say more. In this case we can be sure that there is a unique solution which passes through the point and which is defined over an interval $x_0 - \varepsilon \leq x \leq x_1 + \varepsilon$. This result is given precise expression in Theorem AIII-3, which is usually called the imbedding theorem. In stating Theorem AIII-3 we refer to an ε-neighborhood of the curve $\mathbf{y}(x)$. An ε-neighborhood of a curve is used in the sense of an ε-neighborhood of a set, a concept introduced in Appendix II. It is equivalent to an N_ε-neighborhood plus some overhang at the end points.

Theorem AIII-3. The Imbedding Theorem. Suppose that $\mathbf{y}(x)$ *is a solution to (AIII-1) which is defined on the interval* $x_0 \leq x \leq x_1$ *of finite length. Then there exists an* ε*-neighborhood of* $\mathbf{y}(x)$, *call it* $\mathscr{N}$, *which is contained in* $\mathscr{R}$, *such that for each point* $(\alpha, \mathbf{a}) \in \mathscr{N}$ *there exists a unique solution to (AIII-1), denoted by* $\mathbf{Y}(x; \alpha, \mathbf{a})$, *which passes through* $(\alpha, \mathbf{a})$ *and is defined on the interval* $x_0 - \varepsilon \leq x \leq x_1 + \varepsilon$. *Furthermore* $\mathbf{Y}(x; \alpha, \mathbf{a})$ *is a continuous function of* $(\alpha, \mathbf{a})$ *and if* $\mathbf{y}(x)$ *passes through* $(x_0, \mathbf{y}_0)$ *then* $\mathbf{Y}(x; x_0, \mathbf{y}_0) = \mathbf{y}(x)$, $x_0 \leq x \leq x_1$.

We can think of the functions $\mathbf{Y}(x; \alpha, \mathbf{a})$ as an $(n + 1)$-parameter family of solutions to $\mathbf{y}' = \mathbf{f}(x, \mathbf{y})$. The following theorem states the conditions under which there exist partial derivatives with respect to α and the components of $\mathbf{a}$.

Theorem AIII-4. Differentiation with Respect to Initial Values $(\alpha, \mathbf{a})$. *If the components of* **f** *possess continuous partial derivatives of all orders up to and including r with respect to the variables* **y** *over* $\mathscr{R}$, *then the functions* $\mathbf{Y}(x; \alpha, \mathbf{a})$ *and also* $\mathbf{Y}'(x; \alpha, \mathbf{a})$ *of Theorem AIII-3 have continuous partial derivatives of all orders up to and including r with respect to the variables* **a** *for each x*, $x_0 - \varepsilon \leq x \leq x_1 + \varepsilon$ *and for* $(\alpha, \mathbf{a}) \in \mathscr{N}$. *Furthermore, if the components of* **f** *have continuous partial derivatives of all orders up to and including r with respect to the variables* $(x, \mathbf{y})$ *over* $\mathscr{R}$, *then* $\mathbf{Y}(x; \alpha, \mathbf{a})$ *and* $\mathbf{Y}'(x; \alpha, \mathbf{a})$ *have continuous partial derivatives of all orders up to and including r with respect to the variables* $(\alpha, \mathbf{a})$ *and x for* $x_0 - \varepsilon \leq x \leq x_1 + \varepsilon$ *and* $(\alpha, \mathbf{a}) \in \mathscr{N}$.

On occasion it is necessary to deal with a system of equations of the form $\mathbf{y}' = f(x, \mathbf{y}, \boldsymbol{\lambda})$, where the components of $\boldsymbol{\lambda}$ are parameters. This system is equivalent to the one obtained above if we write $\mathbf{y}' = f(x; \mathbf{y}, \boldsymbol{\lambda})$, $\boldsymbol{\lambda}' = \mathbf{0}$, i.e. $\mathbf{z}' = \mathbf{F}(x, \mathbf{z})$, $\mathbf{z} = (\mathbf{y}, \boldsymbol{\lambda})$, $\mathbf{F} = (\mathbf{f}, \mathbf{0})$. The preceding theorems can then be applied to obtain corresponding theorems for the case in which **f** involves some parameters. In particular, we can obtain immediately the following theorem.

Theorem AIII-5. Parameters in **f**. *Suppose that the system of equations* $\mathbf{y}' = \mathbf{f}(x, \mathbf{y}, \boldsymbol{\lambda})$ *has a solution* $\mathbf{y}(x)$ *defined over the interval* $x_0 \leq x \leq x_1$ *when* $\boldsymbol{\lambda} = \boldsymbol{\lambda}_0$. *Suppose also that the components of* **f** *are continuous and have continuous first partial derivatives with respect to the variables* $(\mathbf{y}, \boldsymbol{\lambda})$ *in a neighborhood* $\mathscr{R}^*$ *of the set of points* $\mathscr{D}$ *of the form* $(x, \mathbf{y}(x), \boldsymbol{\lambda}_0)$, $x_0 \leq x \leq x_1$, *in* $\mathscr{E}^{n+m+1}$ *(*$\boldsymbol{\lambda}$ *having m components). Then there exists an* ε*-neighborhood* $\mathscr{N}^*$ *of* $\mathscr{D}$ *such that if* $(\alpha, \mathbf{a}, \boldsymbol{\lambda}) \in \mathscr{N}^*$, *there exists a solution* $\mathbf{Y}(x; \alpha, \mathbf{a}, \boldsymbol{\lambda})$ *to* $\mathbf{y}' = \mathbf{f}(x, \mathbf{y}, \boldsymbol{\lambda})$ *which passes through* $(\alpha, \mathbf{a})$ *and is defined on the interval* $x_0 - \varepsilon \leq x \leq x_1 + \varepsilon$. *Furthermore, if the components of* **f** *have continuous partial derivatives of all orders up to and including r with respect to the variables* $(\mathbf{y}, \boldsymbol{\lambda})$ *over* $\mathscr{R}^*$ *then the functions* **Y** *and* $\mathbf{Y}'$ *have continuous partial derivatives of all orders up to and including r with respect to the variables* $(\mathbf{a}, \boldsymbol{\lambda})$ *over* $\mathscr{N}^*$. *Finally, if the components of* **f** *have continuous derivatives of all orders up to and including r with respect to the variables* $(x, \mathbf{y}, \boldsymbol{\lambda})$ *over* $\mathscr{R}^*$, *then the functions* **Y** *and* $\mathbf{Y}'$ *have continuous partial derivatives of all orders up to and including r with respect to the variables* $(x, \alpha, \mathbf{a}, \boldsymbol{\lambda})$ *over* $\mathscr{N}^*$.

The final theorem we shall state concerns a system of linear differential equations.

Theorem AIII-6. Let $\mathbf{y}' = \mathbf{A}(x)\mathbf{y} + \mathbf{B}(x)$ *be a system of n linear differential equations. Then there exists a set of n linearly independent solutions* $\mathbf{y}_1(x), \ldots,$

$\mathbf{y}_j(x)$ *to this system of equations, and every other solution* $\mathbf{y}(x)$ *can be written as a linear combination of these n linearly independent solutions, i.e.* $\mathbf{y}(x) = \sum_{j=1}^{n} \lambda_j \mathbf{y}_j(x)$ *for some numbers* λ_j.

References

[1] Apostol, T. M., *Mathematical Analysis. A Modern Approach to Advanced Calculus* (Reading, Mass.: Addison-Wesley Publishing Company, Inc., 1957).

[2] Berkovitz, L. D., 'Variational Methods in Problems of Control and Programming', *Journal of Mathematical Analysis and Applications*, 3 (1960), 145–169.

[3] Berkovitz, L. D., 'On Control Problems with Bounded State Variables', *Journal of Mathematical Analysis and Applications*, 5 (1962), 488–498.

[4] Bliss, G. A., 'The Problem of Mayer with Variable End Points', *Transactions of the American Mathematical Society*, XIX (1918), 305–314.

[5] Bliss, G. A., *Lectures on the Calculus of Variations* (Chicago: University of Chicago Press, 1946).

[6] Bose, S., 'Optimal Growth and Investment Allocation', *Review of Economic Studies*, XXXV (4), No. 104 (October 1968), 465–480.

[7] Brock, W. A. and D. Gale, 'Optimal Growth under Factor Augmenting Progress', *Journal of Economic Theory*, I, No. 3 (October 1969), 229–243.

[8] Cass, D., 'Optimal Growth in an Aggregative Model of Capital Accumulation', *Review of Economic Studies*, XXXII (3), No. 3 (July 1965), 233–240.

[9] Chakravarty, S., *Capital and Development Planning* (Cambridge, Mass.: The M.I.T. Press, 1969).

[10] Chakravarty, S. and A. S. Manne, 'Optimal Growth when the Instantaneous Utility Function Depends upon the Rate of Change in Consumption', *American Economic Review*, LVIII, No. 5, Pt. 1 (December 1968), 1351–1354.

[11] Dantzig, G. B., 'Linear Control Processes and Mathematical Programming', *Journal SIAM Control*, 4, No. 1 (1966), 56–60.

[12] Dasgupta, P. S., 'Optimum Growth when Capital is Non-transferable', *Review of Economic Studies*, XXXVI (1), No. 105 (January 1969), 77–88.

[13] Farrell, M. J. and F. H. Hahn (eds.), *Infinite Programmes in Economics* (Edinburgh: Oliver and Boyd, 1967).

[14] Goldman, S. M., 'Optimal Growth and Continual Planning Revision', *Review of Economic Studies*, XXXV (2), No. 102 (April 1968), 145–154.

[15] Goldman, S. M., 'Sequential Planning and Continual Planning Revision', *Journal of Political Economy*, LXXVII, No. 4, Part II (July/August 1969), 653–664.

[16] Hadley, G., *Linear Algebra* (Reading, Mass.: Addison-Wesley Publishing Company, Inc., 1961).

[17] Hadley, G., *Linear Programming* (Reading, Mass.: Addison-Wesley Publishing Company, Inc., 1962).

[18] Hadley, G., *Nonlinear and Dynamic Programming* (Reading, Mass.: Addison-Wesley Publishing Company, Inc., 1964).

[19] Herberg, H. and M. C. Kemp, 'Some Implications of Variable Returns to Scale', *Canadian Journal of Economics*, II, No. 3 (August 1969), 403–415.

[20] Hestenes, M. R., 'A General Problem in the Calculus of Variations with Applications to Paths of Least Time', RAND Corporation RM-100 (1950), ASTIA Document No. AD-112382.

[21] Hestenes, M. R., *Calculus of Variations and Optimal Control Theory* (New York: John Wiley and Sons, Inc., 1966).

[22] Inada, K., 'On a Two-Sector Model of Economic Growth: Comment and a Generalization', *Review of Economic Studies*, XXX (2), No. 83 (June 1963), 119–127.

[23] Inada, K., 'Investment in Fixed Capital and the Stability of Growth Equilibrium', *Review of Economic Studies*, XXXIII (1), No. 93 (January 1966), 19–30.

[24] Johansen, L., 'Some Theoretical Properties of a Two-Sector Model of Optimal Growth', *Review of Economic Studies*, XXXIV (1), No. 97 (January 1967), 125–141.

[25] Koopmans, T. C., 'On the Concept of Optimal Economic Growth', in *Semaine d'Étude sur le rôle de l'analyse économétrique dans la formulation de plans de développement*, 225–300, Pontificiae Academiae Scientiarum Scripta Varia No. 28, 1965.

[26] McShane, E. J., 'On Multipliers for Lagrange Problems', *American Journal oj Mathematics*, 61 (1939), 809–819.

[27] Pollak, R. A., 'Consistent Planning', *Review of Economic Studies*, XXXV (2), No. 102 (April 1968), 201–208.

[28] Pontryagin, L. S., *Ordinary Differential Equations* (Reading, Mass.: Addison-Wesley Publishing Company, Inc., 1962).

[29] Pontryagin, L. S., V. G. Boltyanskii, R. V. Gramkrelidze and E. F. Mischenko, *The Mathematical Theory of Optimal Processes* (New York: Interscience Publishers, Inc., 1962).

[30] Ramsey, F. P., 'A Mathematical Theory of Saving', *Economic Journal*, XXXVIII, No. 152 (December 1928), 543–549.

[31] Ryder, H. E., 'Optimal Accumulation in a Two-Sector Neoclassical Economy with Non-Shiftable Capital', *Journal of Political Economy*, 77, No. 4, Part II (July-August 1969), 665–683.

[32] Samuelson, P. A., 'A Catenary Turnpike Theorem Involving Consumption and the Golden Rule', *American Economic Review*, 55, No. 3 (June 1965), 486–496.

[33] Samuelson, P. A. and R. M. Solow, 'A Complete Capital Model Involving Heterogeneous Capital Goods', *Quarterly Journal of Economics*, LXX, No. 4 (November 1956), 537–562.

[34] Shell, K. (ed.), *Essays on the Theory of Optimal Economic Growth* (Cambridge, Mass.: The M.I.T. Press, 1967).

[35] Solow, R. M., 'A Contribution to the Theory of Economic Growth', *Quarterly Journal of Economics*, LXX, No. 1 (February 1956), 65–94.

[36] Srinivasan, T. N., 'Optimal Savings in a Two-Sector Model of Growth', *Econometrica*, XXXII, No. 3 (July 1964), 358–373.

[37] Strotz, R. H., 'Myopia and Inconsistency in Dynamic Utility Maximization', *Review of Economic Studies*, XXIII (3), No. 62 (1955–56), 165–180.

[38] Swan, T. W., 'Economic Growth and Capital Accumulation', *Economic Record*, XXXII, No. 63 (November 1956), 334–361.

[39] UZAWA, H., 'Optimal Growth in a Two-Sector Model of Capital Accumulation', *Review of Economic Studies*, XXXI (1), No. 85 (January 1964), 1–24.

[40] VALENTINE, F. A. 'The Problem of Lagrange with Differential Inequalities as Added Side Conditions', in *Contributions to the Calculus of Variations 1933–37*, Department of Mathematics, University of Chicago (Chicago: University of Chicago Press, 1937), 407–448.

Index